DATE DUE

AG 5 04			

DEMCO 38-296

The Spectre of Comparisons

Nationalism, Southeast Asia, and the World

BENEDICT ANDERSON

V

VERSO

London • New York

First published by Verso 1998
© Benedict Anderson 1998
All rights reserved

Verso
UK: 6 Meard Street, London W1V 3HR
USA: 180 Varick Street, New York NY 10014–4606

Verso is the imprint of New Left Books

ISBN 1–85984–813–3
ISBN 1–85984–184–8 (pbk)

British Library Cataloguing in Publication Data
A catalogue record for this book is available from the British Library

Library of Congress Cataloging-in-Publication Data
Anderson, Benedict R. O'G. (Benedict Richard O'Gorman), 1936–
The spectre of comparisons : nationalism, Southeast Asia,
and the world / Benedict Anderson.
          p.   cm.
Includes index.
ISBN 1–85984–813–3 (hc.). — ISBN 1–85984–184–8 (pbk.)
1. Asia, Southeastern—Politics and government.
2. Nationalism—Asia, Southeastern.   3. Nationalism.   I. Title.
DS685.A737   1998
320.959—dc21   98–35495
                                                          CIP

Typeset by M Rules
Printed by Biddles Ltd, Guildford and King's Lynn

For my teacher: George Kahin
For my family: Rory, Melanie and Louisa
For my comrades: Ben Abel, Pipit and Komang;
    Charnvit, Kasian and Thanet; Ambeth and Doreen
For my young ones: Benny, Ade and Yudi; Ali;
    Tuy and Teuy; Henry, Badick and the other demonitos.

Svetit vsegda,
Svetit vezde,
Do dnei poslednikh dontsa,
Svetit—
I nikakikh gvozdei!
Vot lozung moi—
I solntsa!

Shine always,
Shine everywhere,
To the depths of the last days,
Shine—
And to hell with everything else!
That's my motto—
And the sun's!

V. Mayakovsky, "Neobychainoe Priklyuchenie, Byvshee s Vladimirom
Mayakovskim Letom na Dache" (An Extraordinary
Adventure which Befell Vladimir Mayakovsky
in a Summer Cottage), 1920

Contents

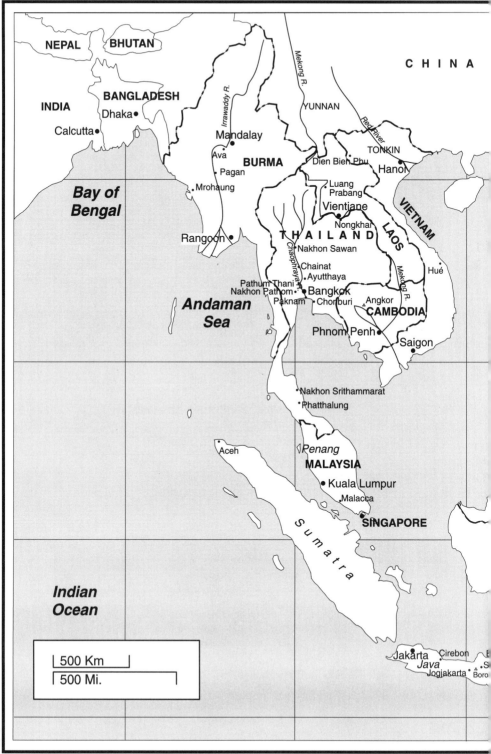

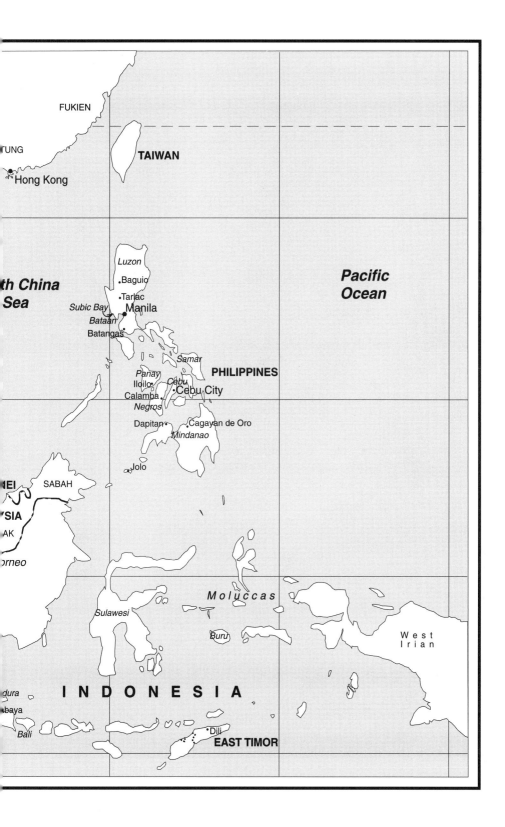

Author's Note

On May 21, 1998, as the proofs for this book were being corrected, Suharto abruptly resigned as President of Indonesia after over thirty-two years in power. The immediate cause of his decision was an ultimatum from the armed forces' leadership that he would be impeached if he did not step down immediately. The military in turn were responding to the massive rioting in Jakarta earlier in the week, precipitated by the murder of six unarmed and peaceful student demonstrators at Trisakti University. The riots themselves were the culmination of weeks of nation-wide protests at the economic catastrophe that destroyed the value of the Indonesian currency, ruined the country's financial institutions, and produced vast unemployment and steeply rising prices for basic commodities. To that catastrophe, the cronyism, nepotism, repression, and cynical political manipulations of the kleptocratic dictatorship made central contributions. When Sukarno, the man whom Suharto drove from power over three decades ago, died under house arrest, millions wept at his departure. There will be only dry eyes when the old tyrant finally meets his Maker.

Suharto's successor, the Buginese aeronautical engineer, Vice-President B.J. Habibie, is Suharto's own creation, and should not be expected to survive for long. The forces unleashed in the collapse of the dictatorship can not be satisfied without a complete overhaul of Indonesia's economy and political system. The first crucial step to be taken will be Indonesia's first free national elections since 1955, which, with luck, will take place by the end of this year.

Acknowledgements

I am grateful to the publishers of the following books and journals for their kind permission to reproduce the texts listed below.

"Nationalism, Identity, and the Logic of Seriality" is closely based on a text of the same title in *Cosmopolitics*, edited by Bruce Robbins and Pheng Cheah (University of Minnesota Press, 1998).

"Replica, Aura, and Late Nationalist Imaginings" is adapted from an article that first appeared in *Qui Parle*, 7: 1 (Fall/Winter 1993).

"Long-Distance Nationalism" is a hybrid of two texts. The first appeared as "Exodus" in *Critical Inquiry*, 20 (Winter 1994), and the second, "Long-Distance Nationalism: World Capitalism and the Rise of Identity Politics," was issued by the University of Amsterdam Centre for Asian Studies.

"A Time of Darkness and a Time of Light" originally appeared in *Perceptions of the Past in Southeast Asia*, edited by Anthony Reid and David Marr (Hong Kong: Heinemann, 1979); it was reprinted with permission in my *Language and Power: Exploring Political Cultures in Indonesia* (Ithaca, NY: Cornell University Press, 1990).

"Professional Dreams" is based on a paper presented in 1984 to the Southeast Asian Summer Studies Institute and first published in my *Language and Power: Exploring Political Cultures in Indonesia* (Ithaca, NY: Cornell University Press, 1990).

"Gravel in Jakarta's Shoes," "The First Filipino," and "Sauve Qui Peut" first appeared in *London Review of Books*, 17: 21 (Nov. 2, 1995), 19: 20 (Oct. 16, 1997), and 20: 8 (April 16, 1998), respectively.

"Withdrawal Symptoms" was first published in the *Bulletin of Concerned Asian Scholars*, 9: 3 (July–Sept. 1977).

"Murder and Progress in Modern Siam," "Cacique Democracy in the

Philippines," and "Radicalism after Communism" were first published in *New Left Review*, nos. 181 (May–June 1990), 169 (May–June 1988), and 202 (Nov.–Dec. 1993), respectively.

"Elections in Southeast Asia" first appeared in *The Politics of Elections in Southeast Asia*, edited by Robert Taylor, published jointly by the Woodrow Wilson Center Press and Cambridge University Press, 1996.

"Majorities and Minorities" is a version of my introduction to *Southeast Asian Tribal Groups and Ethnic Minorities*, edited by Jason Clay (Cambridge, Mass.: Cultural Survival, 1987).

"The Goodness of Nations" is a version of an essay that will appear in *Religion and Nationalism*, edited by Peter van der Veer (Princeton: Princeton University Press, 1998).

Introduction

THE SPECTRE OF COMPARISONS

On February 2, 1963, about a year after my initial encounter with what I had been trained to imagine as "Southeast Asia," I had a strange experience to which at that time I could not give a name. The then President of Indonesia, Sukarno, was to receive an honorary degree from the University of Indonesia, and he had invited the *corps diplomatique* to join the students and faculty for the occasion. Somehow I ended up as whispering interpreter for an elderly European diplomat. Sukarno was speaking about two of his favourite topics: nationalism and leadership. All went pleasantly until, out of the blue, he began to talk about Adolf Hitler, and in a strange manner—not as mass murderer, not even as a fascist and anti-Semite, but as a nationalist. Still more strangely for the two of us, the President, surely suspecting that few of the students had ever heard of Hitler, attempted to give the distant spectre of the *Führer* some local life by ventriloquizing in his own inimitable style of public speaking:[1]

> Take Hitler, for example—wah, Hitler was extraordinarily clever really—perhaps he wanted to say that happiness isn't possible on a material basis alone, and thus he pronounced another ideal, the ideal he called the Dritte Reich, the Third Kingdom. This Third Reich would really and truly bring happiness to the people of Germany. The First Kingdom was that of der alte Fritz, a kingdom led by Old

---

1. The official printed version of this speech is Soekarno [Sukarno], *Ilmu Pengetahuan Sekadar Alat Mentjapai Sesuatu* [Scientific Knowledge as an Instrument for Achieving Something] (Jakarta: Departemen Penerangan Republik Indonesia, Penerbitan Chusus no. 253, 1963). Further quotations from the speech, some analysis of its themes, and a comparison with the rhetoric of Charles de Gaulle, are given in chapter 2 ("Further Adventures of Charisma") of my *Language and Power: Exploring Political Cultures in Indonesia* (Ithaca, NY: Cornell University Press, 1990).

Fritz; the Second Kingdom was what existed just before the World War, and now this kingdom had been destroyed in the World War. "Come, let us build a Third Kingdom, a Dritte Reich, and in this Third Reich, hey, sisters, you will live happily; hey, brothers, you will live happily; hey, kids, you will live happily; hey, you German patriots, you will see Germany sitting enthroned above all peoples in this world." How clever Hitler was, brothers and sisters, in depicting these ideals!

As I whispered along, the elderly diplomat became increasingly agitated and incredulous. "Are you sure that's really what he's saying?" he asked me over and over. I had often heard Sukarno speak in this ventriloquizing style about Sun Yat-sen, Kemal Atatürk, Gandhi, De Valera, and Ho Chi Minh when he wanted to remind his fellow-countrymen that nationalism was a universal, and inseparable from internationalism. I tried, without success, to explain this to the diplomat, who stormed back to his embassy surer than ever that Sukarno was a demented and dangerous mountebank.

For myself, I felt a kind of vertigo. For the first time in my young life I had been invited to see my Europe as through an inverted telescope. Sukarno regarded himself as a man of the Left, and he was perfectly aware of the horrors of Hitler's rule. But he seemed to regard these horrors with the kind of calm with which a devout Christian contemplates the centuries of massacres and tortures committed in His Name—or perhaps with the brisk distance from which my schoolteachers had spoken of Genghiz Khan, the Inquisition, Nero, or Pizarro. It was going to be difficult from now on to think of "my" Hitler in the old way.

I did not find a good name for this experience till almost a quarter of a century later, when I was in the Philippines and teaching myself to read Spanish by stumbling through José Rizal's extraordinary nationalist novel *Noli Me Tangere*. There is a dizzying moment early in the narrative when the young mestizo hero, recently returned to the colonial Manila of the 1880s from a long sojourn in Europe, looks out of his carriage window at the municipal botanical gardens, and finds that he too is, so to speak, at the end of an inverted telescope. These gardens are shadowed automatically—Rizal says *maquinalmente*—and inescapably by images of their sister gardens in Europe. He can no longer matter-of-factly experience them, but sees them simultaneously close up and from afar. The novelist arrestingly names the agent of this incurable doubled vision *el demonio de las comparaciones*.[2] So that's what it was in 1963, I said to myself: the spectre of comparisons.

---

2. This moment occurs in chapter 8 ("Recuerdos"). See José Rizal, *Noli Me Tangere* (Manila: Instituto Nacional de Historia, 1978; offset from the original Berlin edition of 1887), p. 43. A fairly good new English translation of the novel, under the same title, came out from the University of Hawaii Press in 1997.

THE ORIGINS OF "SOUTHEAST ASIA"

For me, "Southeast Asia" has been an exceptionally good *locus* from which to try to get accustomed to this kind of haunting. As a meaningful imaginary, it has had a very short life, shorter than my own. Not surprisingly, its naming came from outside, and even today very few among the almost 500 million souls inhabiting its roughly 1,750,000 square miles of land (to say nothing of water), ever think of themselves as "Southeast Asians." The older Chinese concept *nan-yang* referred vaguely to a "southern" region to be reached by sea.[3] Its later Japanese derivation, *nampō,* stretched out broadly and elastically into what the Americans would call the Southwest Pacific. Southeast Asia, as such, emerged as a significant *political* term only in the summer of 1943 with the creation of Louis Mountbatten's South-East Asia Command, an offshoot of the more traditional India Command. But this command was based in Kandy, and its territorial responsibilities included both Ceylon and the Raj's Northeast Frontier (neither in "Southeast Asia" today) and excluded the Netherlands Indies (till July 1945), as well as the Philippines. Yet the naming clearly was a response to the fact that for the first time in history a single power—that of Hirohito's armies—effectively controlled the entire stretch between British Burma and the Hispano-American Philippines.[4]

It was at almost exactly the same time that academics began to use the term seriously, above all those from the two Anglo-Saxon maritime imperial states.[5]

---

3. The term literally means "southern foreign" and is an antonym to *pei-yang,* or "northern foreign." But the word *yang* includes a radical for water, so that both terms were used for places Peking associated with the sea. It is a matter of curiosity that *pei-yang* was used to denote, not merely the Liao-ning and Shantung peninsulas but even Chih-li, the coastal province in which the imperial capital was itself located. (Hence in the 1920s, the warlords operating out of Peking were called the Peiyang Clique.) The vast areas to the north of the Great Wall were never referred to in this way. Similarly, *nan-yang* was used both for the coastal provinces of southeast China, especially Kwangtung and Fukien, and for the Malay archipelago (today's Malaysia, Indonesia, and the Philippines), but not for land-accessible Burma or Laos. (My thanks to Vivienne Shue for illumination on this point.)

4. British Burma, Malaya, and Singapore, the American Philippines, and the Dutch Indies all fell to direct military assault. Because Vichy was an ally of the Axis powers, the Japanese did not get rid of the French till March 1945. But they maintained a dominating presence, as an "ally," before that, and the colonial Vichy regime had to do their bidding. In Siam, the shrewd military dictator Phibunsongkhram, to avoid the worst, had allied himself with Tokyo early on, but he still had to permit Japanese armies to march through his country, and to submit to their demands in other ways.

5. The formidable exception is perhaps the *magnum opus* of the French colonial-era scholar Georges Coedès, *Les États hindouisés d'Indochine et d'Indonésie* (Paris: E. de Boccard, 1948). In this grand comparative study of the Sanskritized states in pre-fifteenth-century "Southeast Asia," "Indochine" and "Indonésie" are merely shorthand geographical denotations—but enough to indicate that Burma and the Philippines are not within its purview. When this book was finally published in English translation twenty years later, American Cold War anachronizing had turned the title into *The Indianized States of Southeast Asia.*

The new wave can be said to have begun in 1941, when the great Burma scholar and former British colonial civil servant John Furnivall published—in New York—his *Welfare and Progress in South-East Asia,* followed two years later—again in New York—by his *Educational Progress in Southeast Asia.* In 1942 the American political scientist Rupert Emerson, with his colleagues Lennox Mills and Virginia Thompson, issued *Government and Nationalism in Southeast Asia.* The left-wing American Bruno Lasker published *Peoples of Southeast Asia* in 1944 and the splendid *Human Bondage in Southeast Asia* in 1950. British colonial civil servant Victor Purcell produced in 1951 a nervous *The Chinese in Southeast Asia.* The following year, the British historian Quaritch Wales anachronized "Southeast Asia" centuries into the pre-European past in his *Ancient South-East Asian Warfare.* With the appearance of former British colonial civil servant D.G.E. Hall's magisterial *A History of South-East Asia* in 1955, the concept was grandly normalized (though Hall did not include the Philippines in the first edition of the work, this absence was partly made up for in successive later editions).

Why so late? And why the final rush? To begin with, there was the absence of a historic hegemonic power like the Ottomans for the Near or Middle East, the Habsburgs and Bourbons for "Latin" America, the Mughals for "India," and the successive dynasts of Peking who made "China" a plausible bounded mirage. Next was the extraordinary religious heterogeneity of the region once Islam (from the thirteenth century) and Christianity (from the sixteenth) broke up a Hindu-Buddhist syncretic civilization whose residues are still among the world's wonders—Angkor in Cambodia, Borobudur in Java, Ayutthaya in Siam, and Pagan and Mrohaung in Burma.[6] Today, Burma, Siam, Laos, and Cambodia are variously Buddhist, Malaysia, Indonesia, and Brunei predominantly Muslim, and the Philippines mainly Catholic, while Vietnam has inherited chiefly from Confucianism, Taoism, and Mahayana Buddhism. But there is no doubt that the central factor was the strange history of mottled imperialism in the region.[7] Only the Belgians and Italians were missing. The British in Burma, Malaya, Singapore, and northern Borneo, the Dutch in the Indies, Portugal in eastern Timor, the Spaniards and Americans in the Philippines, and the French in Laos,

---

6. To avoid misunderstanding: Hinduism and tantric Mahayana Buddhism came to some parts of Southeast Asia very early in the Christian era, and were the bases of court cults at least from the fourth century. But one can be certain that for many centuries most of the populations were animist. Hindu and Buddhist cults could compete or intermix without intractable conflicts. Major change did not come till the end of the twelfth century, when a more austere form of Buddhism (Hinayana or Theravada), brought from Ceylon, pushed its predecessors more and more aside.

7. Mottled—"marked by an irregular arrangement of patches of colour"—seems more visually precise and less morally dubious than either "white" or "Caucasian."

Cambodia, and Vietnam: plus the buffer-state of quasi-independent Siam, surviving on sufferance between the colonies of rival London and Paris. Furthermore, mottled imperialism came not in a late nineteenth-century rush, as happened to most of Africa, but stretched across the centuries: the Portuguese and Spaniards arrived in the late feudal sixteenth century, the Dutch in the mercantilist seventeenth, the British in the enlightened eighteenth, the French in the industrial nineteenth, and the Americans in the motorized twentieth. Each imperial power, jealous of, and rivalrous with, its competitors, worked to close off its possessions from the rest, so that at the beginning of this century young educated people in Batavia (Jakarta) knew more about Amsterdam than they did about a Cambodia with which their ultimate ancestors had once had close ties, while their cousins in Manila knew more about Madrid and New York than about the Vietnamese littoral a short step across the South China Sea. Furthermore, these colonies were, even in the age of the aeroplane, the telegraph, and the telephone, the most remote of all. Vietnam was farther from Paris, the Philippines from either Madrid or Washington, East Timor from Lisbon, and Malaya from London (with the exception of mottled Australia and New Zealand) than any other of their domains. Remote, heterogeneous, and, so to speak, imperially segmented, it is not so very surprising that the region was late in its unitary naming.

Yet by the beginning of this century the terrain was becoming bordered for the first time, not least thanks to the heritage of Mercator.[8] What is today's Burma was, between 1885 and 1937, an integral part of colonial India—its only Buddhist province. But in that time it was given continuous, mapped borders which it largely retains to this day. Paris marked clearly out where China ended and Franco-Vietnamese Tonkin began, erasing centuries of osmotic interconnections, not to speak of a millennium of incorporation of parts of today's Vietnam into the Middle Kingdom.[9] At the beginning of this century the half of New Guinea lying west of longitude 141 was included in the Netherlands Indies and is today part of Southeast Asia. The eastern half, however, is not. The northern half of this half was, between 1885 and the Great War, Kaiser Wilhelmland and attached to the no less ludicrously named Bismarck Archipelago as a German colony. The southern half was British. After 1920 both passed by stages into a fragile unit controlled by

---

8. Already the *locus classicus* on the cartographic revolution is Thongchai Winichakul, *Siam Mapped: A History of the Geo-Body of a Nation* (Honolulu: University of Hawaii Press, 1994).

9. From the second half of the first century AD until the middle of the tenth. The standard work is Keith Welker Taylor, *The Birth of Vietnam* (Berkeley: University of California Press, 1983).

Australian secondary imperialism. One can see the real importance of the map if one considers not only Papua-New Guinea's exclusion from Southeast Asia, but also the quite recent decision of the Association of Southeast Asian Nations (ASEAN) to reject the application of Ceylon/Sri Lanka for admission. Ceylon has cultural, mercantile, and even political associations with Southeast Asia going back a millennium, and it shares Theravada Buddhism with Burma, Siam, Cambodia, and Laos (two-way pilgrimages continue today across the Bay of Bengal as they have for centuries). Its agriculture, climate, food, and culture have strong resemblances to those in significant parts of Southeast Asia. But it has ended up, uncomfortably perhaps, in "South Asia."

The rush came from the Pacific War, rapid postwar decolonization, the onset of the Cold War, and a sustained American attempt to replace the Japanese as the single regional hegemon. The abrupt and humiliating collapse of all the mottled imperialisms in the region between early 1942 and 1945, the arming and military training of "natives" by an increasingly desperate Japan from 1943, the rise of anti-Japanese guerrilla groups sometimes assisted by the Allies from afar, and the traumatic battles fought between Japanese and Allies in Burma and the Philippines, all meant that after Japan's capitulation in August 1945, the Europeans could not make an effective comeback. Nothing like this happened anywhere else in the colonized zones of Asia and Africa. It also meant that Southeast Asia was the one colonized region—after Spanish America 140 or so years earlier—where armed struggle for independence—and more—was commonplace. Curiously enough, the process had started in 1896 in that westernmost part of Latin America, the Philippines, when an early (for Asia) and late (for Latin America) uprising led by Andrés Bonifacio, Emilio Aguinaldo, and Apolinario Mabini created a free Philippine Republic in 1898—though it was soon crushed by the United States. Burma, Laos, Cambodia, Vietnam, Indonesia, even in a certain way Malaya, actually fought, mostly with bitter success, for their independence—and were increasingly aware of each other doing so. Already in early 1947 the progressive civilian Prime Minister of Siam, Pridi Phanomyong, in the brief period before he was overthrown by the military, launched an abortive Southeast Asian League, to build regional networks of mutual help against imperialism.[10]

It was, however, the opening of the Cold War in Asia that really began the long process of making Southeast Asia the kind of imagined reality it is

---

10. But there was no sense of a bloc. All groups sought alliances with progressive groups in the imperial metropoles. Indonesian revolutionaries built effective ties to Australia, Egypt, and Nehru's newly independent India. All the radically Left organizations hooked up to various degrees with the Soviet Union and (after 1949) the CPR.

today. Seen from the United States, the major states of Big Asia had a more or less settled position. Japan had been occupied by the Americans, and was firmly subordinated to Washington's military and economic machinery. India, after the crisis of Partition, appeared stably quasi-British under the uncontested hegemony of Nehru and the Congress Party. China, alas, after 1949, was "lost" to communism, but it was too huge to warrant more than hit-and-run, semi-clandestine interventions. The new states of the zone between India–Pakistan and China were another matter. In almost all of them, indigenously created, and typically armed, communist-led movements contested the legitimacy of the postwar order that the Allies had attempted to create. In Burma, in 1949, a year after formal independence was achieved, two competing communist parties, along with assorted ethnic rebel groups, left U Nu's government in control of little more than Rangoon. In the French colonies to the east, the First Indochina War had broken out late in 1946, a year after Ho Chi Minh had declared Vietnam's independence. As this war lurched towards its end at Dien Bien Phu, communist movements spread across the hill country of Laos, and, a good bit later, into Sihanouk's Cambodia. In the Philippines, the American reimposition of a corrupt cacique order to lead the country after the formalization of independence (on, of course, the Fourth of July, 1946), led to a major communist insurrection (1948 to about 1954) based on the Hukbalahap anti-Japanese guerrilla forces of the war years. In Indonesia, it initially appeared that the indigenous Left had been crushed in 1948 by forces loyal to revolutionary President Sukarno and Vice-President Hatta, but after the transfer of sovereignty, the Communist Party made an extraordinary (and legal) comeback, and within little more than a decade had become the largest communist party outside the communist bloc. In Malaya, which did not become formally independent till 1957, London found, after the spring of 1948, the longest and fiercest resistance it ever faced in the history of its modern empire—from a Malayan communist party which grew out of the Malayan People's Anti-Japanese Army. Only in Siam did "normality" appear to prevail; armed communism only began to emerge in the mid-1960s.

No other region of the world—not Latin America, not the Near East, not Africa, and not South Asia—had this kind of alarming profile. The new hegemon was determined that it not be "lost" like China. Out of this, in 1954, came SEATO (the Southeast Asia Treaty Organization), formed in American Manila, and later headquartered in Bangkok, which was designed to save the whole postcolonial region from the communist spectre.[11] In the following

---

11. A certain instability in Southeast Asia was still evident in SEATO's membership. Of the local states only Siam and the Philippines joined—their colleagues included the United States, Ukania, France, New Zealand, Pakistan, and Australia.

decade, two different attempts were made by local governments in Southeast Asia to create a regional organization less wholly dominated by outsiders; both proved abortive. ASA (Association of Southeast Asia), created in 1961 by Siam, the Philippines, and what was still Malaya, proved incapable of solving the growing quarrel created by Manila's claim to North Borneo (Sabah).[12] Maphilindo, a 1963 inspiration of Indonesia's radical-populist president Sukarno—meant to include the "Malay" nations of Indonesia, Malaysia and the Philippines—quickly foundered when Whitehall cobbled together "Malaysia" out of Malaya, Singapore, North Borneo, and the once-fabled Sarawak of the White Rajahs.[13] Only in 1967, after Sukarno had been driven from power in an orgy of mass murder, was a more permanent institution created: that Association of Southeast Asian Nations which recently—after a thirty-year interval—admitted Vietnam, Burma, and Laos, and will probably incorporate Hun Sen's Cambodia and Xanana Gusmão's East Timor one day.[14]

SOUTHEAST ASIAN STUDIES, SOUTHEAST ASIANS, SOUTHEAST ASIANISTS

In a quite different sphere from that of diplomats, generals, intelligence services, and heads of state, Southeast Asia was becoming, earlier and with more success, a kind of reality. Just as heterogeneous colonialisms had produced substantial bodies of scholarship framed by each colony for itself—in the English language for Burma and Malaya, in American for the Philippines, in Dutch for the Indies/Indonesia, and in French for Vietnam, Cambodia, and Laos, so postwar American anticommunist hegemony created the initial bases for the new field of Southeast Asian studies. The first academic programme to pursue such studies was set up at Yale University in 1947, followed shortly thereafter by a sister programme at my own university, Cornell. In the condition of alarm created by the launching of Sputnik in October 1957, and with the onset of the Second Indochina War, comparable programmes multiplied across the United States. Subsequently, the format spread, with differing emphases, to Australia, Japan, Ukania, France, Canada, Germany, Scandinavia, and so forth.

---

12. This remote and sparsely populated terrain was run by the North Borneo Company from the end of the nineteenth century until the Japanese military swept its commercial regime away. Whitehall took it over after the Pacific War ended.

13. Sukarno's fury at this move from London led eventually to a semi-armed confrontation between his government and Harold Wilson's residual empire in the East. Most of what fighting there was took place in Borneo, where Gurkha mercenaries performed perhaps their final combat mission.

14. In the interim—i.e. between the founding of SEATO and the creation of ASEAN—Siam had become the military, economic, and political hub of massive American interventions across the mainland states.

There was, from the start, a key difference between Southeast Asian studies, as pioneered in the United States, and the colonial-era scholarship that preceded it.[15] Virtually all the great names of the colonial era—say, John Furnivall and Gordon Luce (Burma); Henri Maspéro and Paul Mus (Indochina); Richard Winstedt and R.J. Wilkinson (Malaya); Theodoor Pigeaud and Bertram Schrieke (the Netherlands Indies); Roy Barton and Ralston Hayden (the Philippines)—were, or had been, colonial civil servants. They lived long periods of their lives in the colonies and knew them pretty well. The condition for this immersion, however, was that, even if they privately doubted the colonial enterprise, they could not say so publicly.[16] In the postwar, postcolonial era, this kind of figure disappeared. Southeast Asia, or at least the non-communist parts of it, encountered hordes of American officials—dealing with everything from military and intelligence matters to education and capitalist development—but they were busy people who rarely understood local vernaculars, had little time or inclination for the leisured research that the colonial calm had made possible, and were rotated too rapidly to understand anything very deeply.

As a result, Southeast Asian studies came to be the province of a metropolitan professoriat, who were financial beneficiaries not primarily of the American national state, but rather of private and state universities as well as private foundations (in particular the Ford and Rockefeller foundations). Since the framing of their work—Southeast Asia—was the consequence of decolonization and the attempted American Cold War hegemony in the region, their studies were heavily concentrated in disciplinary fields quite different from those of their colonial-era predecessors: political science above all, but also modern history and anthropology, as opposed to archaeology, ancient history, and classical literatures. This transformation meant that its leaders were not civil-servant-minded or bureaucratically beholden (a good many had active, public sympathies with non-communist anticolonial nationalism, and not a few were publicly critical of Washington's policies).[17]

---

15. This theme is substantially elaborated in my "The Changing Ecology of Southeast Asian Studies in the United States, 1950–1990," in Charles Hirschman, Charles F. Keyes, and Karl Hutterer, eds., *Southeast Asian Studies in the Balance: Reflections from America* (Ann Arbor: The Association for Asian Studies, 1992), pp. 25–40.

16. Furnivall was a partial exception. He started to publish biting critiques of British colonialism in Burma as early as the 1930s, but only after he had resigned from the colonial civil service.

17. It should, however, be noted that many of the first generation of "Southeast Asianists" served in the American armed forces or were drawn from pre-war university circles into the Office of Strategic Services and the Office of Naval Intelligence during the Pacific War. A number stayed on as a progressive, anticolonial nucleus in the Department of State for a few years after the war, till the rise of McCarthyism drove them out. (The OSS, ancestor of the CIA, was founded in 1942 and disbanded in October 1945, whereupon its functions and functionaries were absorbed by the Departments of State and War. The CIA proper was not established until 1947.)

The creation of an institutionalized field of research called Southeast Asian studies, in the heart of a continental power with immense financial resources and huge political ambitions had, for present purposes, two critical consequences. First, professors and graduate students were clustered together, across disciplines, not by particular country interests but by region. The former gave, the latter took, classes in "Southeast Asian history," "Southeast Asian politics," "The economies of Southeast Asia," "Myth and symbol in Southeast Asia," and so forth.[18] Such classes had the real advantage of forcing all students to think more or less comparatively across an extremely diverse "region," and to bring students together, cheek by jowl, even if one was interested in ancient Vietnam, another in Philippine public administration, and still another in Javanese mystical cults. (It also had the disadvantage of frequently segmenting these students from professors and students studying Korea, Sri Lanka, the Middle East, China, etc.) Intense student classroom and personal relationships eventually lengthened out into academic careers which were deeply bound up with and committed to Southeast Asia as a real place. This commitment also transcended immediate Cold War divisions in that, in principle, communist, neutralist, and pro-American countries were to be studied side by side within a single frame.[19] In this sense, Southeast Asia was more real, in the 1950s and 1960s, to people in American universities than to anyone else. Second, America had in those days the resources to create "Southeast Asian" libraries which had no parallels anywhere in the world;[20] it also had the scholarship monies to bring over interested students from many different countries, of whom far

---

18. The format of such courses demanded the demonstration of unifying factors prior to the Cold War, and of a "deeper" kind than the political conflicts of those years. It was no means plain sailing: it is symptomatic that the standard (collective) history textbook for the region (originally published in 1971, in Kuala Lumpur, by Oxford University Press) is still, in its updated, revised form, plaintively called *In Search of Southeast Asia.* The most interesting "unifier" is certainly the wide prevalence of bilateral kinship-systems and uxorilocal residence patterns, both of which tend to give women a relatively good social position. There is here an obvious contrast with the patrilineal, virilocal systems predominant in China, Japan, and India, which strongly subordinate women. A less serious common element is the use along the littorals of Southeast Asia, but not to the north and west, of condiments made from fermented fish and molluscs – which give the local cuisines a distinctive, kindred, flavour.

19. Compare the much harder line dividing the study of "Western" and "Eastern" Europe in the same Cold War period.

20. The most extraordinary example is the Echols Collection on Southeast Asia at Cornell University, which currently contains close to half a million printed volumes, microfilms, and microfiches in western languages and local vernaculars, as well as 23,000 serials—half as large again as the Library of Congress's holdings. In the same era, cash-strapped universities in European imperial centres tended, even where they nominally adopted a Southeast Asian format, to focus on their countries' former colonies and on the use of their already existing and voluminous colonial archives.

the most important were students from the accessible countries of Southeast Asia itself. The long years of student life, with their shared studies, cross-national friendships, love affairs and sometimes marriages, began already in the 1950s to create young people who could imagine themselves as Southeast Asians, as well as Indonesians or Filipinos or Siamese.[21] When they returned home, often to important positions in national universities, national educational bureaucracies, and the higher-quality mass media, they often kept these personal connections alive for decades. Furthermore, a significant number of these students were enabled by study in America to publish their research (in the United States and elsewhere) in a single common language. For people of this kind, English became, without this being at all emphasized, the real lingua franca of Southeast Asia—in a way also a guarantor of its reality—long before this was true of diplomats, politicians, generals, and even technocrats.

In the second half of the 1960s, the deepening of the Vietnam War into the Second Indochina War, had as one side effect the further crystallization of Southeast Asia, in university communities and beyond. For the American mass media, Vietnam was almost invariably located in Southeast Asia—though given its centuries of irritable intimacy with China and its communist government in Hanoi, it should have been possible to see it as part of a Sinitic sphere of influence. As conscription started to bite, college enrolments in courses on Southeast Asia shot up; books on Southeast Asia were more and more available. What is more striking in retrospect is the number of professors and students who, without deep specialization on Vietnam or knowledge of the Vietnamese language, thought themselves morally bound, and intellectually able, to speak publicly about the country, and the war, with the authority of Southeast Asian studies.[22] Still more interesting, the politicization and polarization of campus life caused by the war (which in fact deeply split the Southeast Asianists) had its effects on Southeast Asian students studying in America, and elsewhere outside their

---

21. Although most students coming from Southeast Asia quite naturally did their master's degree and doctoral research on their own countries, already in the late 1960s and early 1970s a few were working on other countries in the region—something virtually unthinkable before that era.

22. How surprisingly real this odd authority was struck me first when I realized that no one ever asked angrily what my citizenship (actually Irish) was, though my accent was distinctly un-American. A decade later, when I was summoned by a subcommittee of the US House of Representatives to testify on the subject of East Timor under Indonesian occupation, I experienced the same mild astonishment. I had never been to East Timor, I knew none of its languages, and had the haziest ideas about its history and politics: but that did not stop a veteran Southeast Asianist from feeling entitled to weigh in—nor did it stop the subcommittee from asking for my testimony in the first place!

own countries. It was possible to find Thai and Filipino students, whose governments were deeply complicit with the American war machine, protesting and marching against the war, and in solidarity with the peoples of Indochina.[23] Such students had, of course, their own national-political, as well as radical and humanitarian reasons for marching, but the crucial thing was that they recognized each other as fellow marchers, along with the American, European, Australian, and Canadian Southeast Asianist students who protested with them. Some of these students in the following decades became among the most serious and well-informed spokespersons for a genuinely democratized and inclusive ASEAN. They are the sort of people who in Bangkok urge the Thai government to give public support to Aung San Suu Kyi, and in Manila and Kuala Lumpur resist the Philippine and Malaysian governments' odious eagerness to appease the Suharto regime by suppressing conferences demanding the freedom of East Timor. Without much success, of course.

THE "CHINESE" AS SOUTHEAST ASIAN LABOURERS AND CAPITALISTS

When historians began—not so long ago—to imagine Southeast Asia as an ancient, pre-Cold War, precolonial reality, one key place for disinterring and viewing this reality was the enormous, centuries-old archive of the Middle Kingdom. From this kingdom, Buddhist pilgrims passed through littoral Southeast Asia on their way to and from holy shrines in today's South Asia, and some left detailed travel accounts. Until the Europeans put a stop to the practice, many of the more significant kingdoms in Southeast Asia were accustomed to sending missions to the incumbent Son of Heaven, for purposes of trade, intelligence, and political legitimacy; the imperial courts, which liked to think of these missions as "tributary," nonetheless used them to gather information on their "barbarous" southern periphery. (There are ironical parallels here between ancient Peking and contemporary Washington.) It is thus not by chance that the most distinguished contemporary historian of "ancient Southeast Asia," O.W. Wolters—whose *oeuvre* moves majestically across the terrain today occupied by Indonesia, Malaysia, Vietnam, Thailand, and Cambodia—started out as a young Sinologist

---

23. This identification is not accidental. After the coup of March 1962, the Burmese military dictatorship effectively barred students from studying abroad. The war-torn countries of Indochina were burning up their youths on the battlefield. Indonesians were traumatized by the horrors of 1965–66. Malaysia, still Ukania-oriented in those days, sent few students to the US.

working for the absurdly misnamed "Chinese Protectorate" division of the colonial civil service in Malaya.[24]

Typically evading the often ferocious imperial prohibitions against such movements, males from Fukien and Kwangtung, two southeast littoral provinces of today's China, emigrated to Southeast Asia from early times, marrying into local families, and working as artisans, traders, harbourmasters, and, in some cases, as powerful courtiers. Occasionally even higher: the current dynasty in Siam is, so to speak, 50 per cent of "Chinese" ancestry, and the Norodoms of Cambodia not much less. Most, on arrival, had no means, in an alien environment, to rear their mixed progeny as they themselves were reared. Barring unexpected external interventions, their descendants became absorbed into the local populations. This absorption was all the easier since the original migrants had no idea that they were "Chinese." They were overwhelmingly illiterate, and mostly spoke such mutually unintelligible languages as Hokkien and Cantonese; hence they identified themselves by occupation, clan, and home locality, not by a nationality which would emerge only centuries later.

Three fundamental forces worked to change this condition of gradual seepage and osmosis. The first was the arrival of the Europeans, who, understanding none of these languages, with their eyes glued on physiognomies, costumes, and occupations, and their ambitions set on controlling trade in the region, decided that all such people were "Chinese," and proceeded to act on the basis of this decision.[25] (Massacres of "Chinese" in Southeast Asia were initiated in the eighteenth century by the region's first racists: Dutchmen in Batavia/Jakarta and Spaniards in Manila.) Second was the great Tai-p'ing insurrection of the mid-nineteenth century which caused enormous devastation in southeast China, and cost the Ch'ing dynasty practically all control over its southern maritime borders. The near-simultaneous

---

24. There are paradoxes here. Wolters remains a deep admirer of Gerald Templar, the military proconsul who, with great difficulty, and at enormous cost to the resident "Chinese" communities—a quarter of a million of whom were forcibly sequestered in "New Villages"—broke the back of the communist insurgency in postwar Malaya. But since he became a scholar, he has resolutely, eupeptically, confined his work to a Southeast Asia still uncontaminated by Europeans. A masterly, short demonstration of his views and his learning is his *History, Culture and Religion in Southeast Asian Perspectives* (Singapore: Institute for Southeast Asian Studies, 1982).

25. Not at all exactly in the same vein. As I have noted elsewhere, the (barely Dutch) United East India Company used every means—sumptuary codes, residential sequestrations, imposed inheritance regulations, as well as collaborationist business elites—to insist on the Chineseness of people who spoke no "Chinese" language of any kind. In Las Islas Filipinas, such people were legally designated as "mestizos," with their own distinct tax obligations, residential possibilities, and so on. "Mestizo" always signalled, indirectly, alien. (See my "Recensement et politique en Asie du Sud-est," *Genèses*, 26 [April 1997], pp. 55–76.) "Chinese" should be read in the same syntax as today's "Asians." People in western countries believe in the massive existence of "Asians," but very few people in "Asia" share this curious idea.

appearance of the steamship, and a vast labour-hungry market in capitalist-colonial Southeast Asia, made possible mass migrations of young males from different language groups on a completely unprecedented scale.[26] Third was the appearance at the end of the century of Chinese nationalisms, not only in urban China itself, but also, and sometimes even earlier, in the Nanyang.[27] In the zone of today's Indonesia, Malaysia, and Singapore, in particular, these nationalisms accompanied an increase in literacy, in both Chinese and Roman orthographies, the arrival of the newspaper, and normalized sex ratios among the immigrants leading to more settled families. By contrast, in Siam and the Philippines, where, for different reasons, assimilation had proceeded rather rapidly and smoothly, the tendency was much less strong, and the identification with Siamese and Filipino nationalism much greater.

With the fall of the Ch'ing in 1911, and the unsteady emergence of a national Chinese republic, the question of nationality and citizenship for people in Southeast Asia who either identified themselves in some ways as Chinese and/or were regarded as such by local populations and colonial governments, began to become pressing. The question became even more urgent in the postcolonial era, for local, regional, and international reasons. Locally (at least in the capitalist states) the removal of the Europeans from political-economic control opened the way for a rapid increase in the economic power of burgeoning Chinese entrepreneurs, while at the same time exposing them more deeply to extortion by indigenous elites and to resentment on the part of the national masses.[28] Regionally, Chinese business

---

26. Mary Somers Heidhues offers a vivid synopsis of the variations. Hokkienese were dominant in the Philippines, Java, and the commercial enclaves of Malacca, Penang, Singapore, and Cholon-Saigon; Cantonese dominated in rural Malaya, and, until World War II, in Cambodia; Teochiu in Siam, Sumatra, and postwar Cambodia; Hakka in northern and western Borneo; while the late arriving Hainanese mostly settled in southern Vietnam and Siam. In Burma a substantial number of emigrants came overland from Yunnan. Density of settlement also varied greatly. Colonial Malaya lay at one extreme; on the eve of World War II, there were actually more "Chinese" in the peninsula than there were "Malays." By contrast, in the Netherlands Indies, Burma, and Laos, the "Chinese" percentage was probably never higher than 5. See her *Southeast Asia's Chinese Minorities* (Hawthorn, Victoria: Longmans Australia, 1974), pp. 2–6.

27. See Liren Zheng, "Overseas Chinese Nationalism in British Malaya, 1894–1941" (Ph.D. thesis, Cornell University, 1997).

28. All three of the national languages of Southeast Asia with which I am familiar have derogatory words for "Chinese," but only Suharto's Indonesia has insisted on the official use of such a word. Hence the rather melancholy situation in which young people of Chinese origin describe themselves in advice columns and elsewhere as, using the English word, "Chinese." (*Saya seorang Chinese* [I am a Chinese], rather than the self-degrading *Saya seorang Cina* [I am a Chink].) While popular resentment of the Chinese is commonplace everywhere in the region, neither Siam nor the Philippines have experienced an anti-Chinese pogrom or race riot in this century; by contrast, there has been a continuing history of such violence in Indonesia from the onset of modern politics in the 1910s.

interests spread across national frontiers, as capitalists sought to diversify their risks and opportunities. At the same time, the rival Chinas, based in then left-wing Peking and right-wing Taipei, attempted, each in its own way, to win friends among local nation-state elites, local oppositions, and the émigré Chinese. There was, in due course, also the anomaly of the municipality of Singapore: formally multi-ethnic or multi-racial, but in effect a third Chinese national possibility,[29] under the interminable regime of Lee Kwan-yew and his henchmen.[30]

In the postcolonial period, it was not unusual for those (typically outside observers) who believed in the singular reality of the Chinese, to view them as the unique and necessary transregional basis for a truly Southeast Asian economy in the making. As the Cold War in Asia abated, as electronic communications developed, and as the long boom of the 1970s and 1980s deepened, the belief that the Chinese would do for Southeast Asia economically what the diplomats of ASEAN were trying to do for it politically and strategically became more widespread. Whether this vision corresponds to reality is, however, rather doubtful. In the first place, the economies of the region's nation-states are (with the exception of Singapore) essentially competitive rather than complementary. It is a striking fact that in the pre-Crash era of the early 1990s, intraregional trade was still of minor significance. In 1992, for example, intra-ASEAN exports amounted to a mere 17.4 per cent of total exports.[31] Even this 17.4 per cent is deceptive since goods going into the entrepôt of Singapore were substantially not for local consumption, but for transshipment outside the region.[32] The figures for the Philippines (5.9 per

---

29. I experienced the poignancy of this conundrum when teaching a graduate class at Yale University in the autumn of 1996. Among the students was one, American-born, with a completely American style of speech, who insisted that he was "absolutely" Chinese. A second student, born to an elite Kuomintang mainland family, informed me that he considered himself Taiwanese and had come to Yale partly to learn to be fluent in Taiwanese. A third expressed his fury at constantly being picked out as Chinese in America. "I am not Chinese," he said, with the most determinedly winning of smiles. "I am Singaporean."

30. Lee first became Chief Minister in 1957, thanks to the support of the then powerful organized Left. Once in power, he collaborated with the British in trying to crush these allies. London's concern to keep Singapore out of left-wing hands, especially in view of the radical-talking Indonesian government next door, led it to dream up the idea of Malaysia, into which uncertain Singapore would be absorbed. Conservative Malay leaders, initially balking at the prospect of so many Chinese entering their polity, were persuaded to agree by having putatively "indigenous" Sabah and Sarawak turned over to them at the same time. The union lasted only two years (1963–65), mainly because Lee had ambitions greater than being a mayor. By that time he had achieved such absolute control of Singapore that he could decide to make the town a putative nation.

31. See Gerald Tan, *ASEAN: Economic Development and Cooperation* (Singapore: Times Academic Press, 1996), pp. 188–90.

32. Good "Singaporean" and "ASEAN-ist" that he is, Tan is careful not to mention this inconvenient matter.

cent), Siam (12.7 per cent), and Indonesia (11.6 per cent) are particularly unimpressive. The data on intra-ASEAN imports are virtually identical.[33] Nor, again with the exception of Singapore, were the countries of Southeast Asia investing substantially in one another's development. After the Crash, and with the rapidly increasing economic might of both China and Taiwan, it is quite likely that even these low percentages will diminish. Few observers have failed to notice that when hard times arrived, the ASEAN states and their capitalists could do little to help one another, and indeed tended to act on the ancient and sensible principle of *sauve qui peut.*

SOUTHEAST ASIA AS A POLITICAL BLOC?

It is a striking fact that when ASEAN was formed, in 1967, invitations to join it were issued to all the existing states in Southeast Asia (and to none outside it); these included not merely Singapore (which had only just become an independent state), but the two Vietnams, Cambodia, Laos, Burma, and even the oil sheikdom of Brunei (which only became officially independent of London seventeen years later). Although none of these latter invitations was then accepted, this invitation list, drawn up a few months away from the Tet offensive, was in principle a break with the conventions of the Cold War, and can be seen today as the first step towards creating a regional diplomatic bloc along the lines of the existing arrangements in Africa, the Americas, and Western Europe. The core idea was to create institutional arrangements for resolving intraregional quarrels without Great Power interventions, and for creating a joint "world presence" of which none of the countries on their own was capable.

The degree to which these objectives have actually been achieved is limited and equivocal. Confrontation came to an end not because of ASEAN but because General Suharto overthrew Sukarno, its architect. Marcos decided not to pursue Filipino claims to Sabah when he discovered that Malaysian politicians were capable of damaging retaliation by helping the Muslim (Bangsa Moro) secessionist rebellion that broke out in the southern Philippines in 1972—at the onset of his dictatorship. But the withdrawal of British troops from Southeast Asia at the end of the 1960s, and the collapse of the American position in Indochina in 1975, provided ASEAN with a more favourable environment for flexing its local muscles.[34] The focus, not surprisingly, was Indochina. Led principally by Siam, Malaysia, and

---

33. See Tan, *ASEAN,* p. 12.
34. This was really the only possibility. None of the member states had armed forces capable of interstate conventional warfare. In any case these forces were mostly busy oppressing their own nationals and propping up the existing authoritarian regimes.

Singapore, a vociferous campaign was launched to prevent ASEAN countries from being forced to take in the bulk of the refugees fleeing by boat and overland from the victorious communist governments in Hanoi, Vientiane, and Phnom Penh. Following the overwhelming success of the Vietnamese armies in Cambodia in 1978–79, ASEAN collaborated closely with Peking and Washington to prevent the Heng Samrin government created by Hanoi from assuming Cambodia's seat at the United Nations, and to provide support of various kinds for the forces of Pol Pot and other groups resisting the Vietnam-imposed *fait accompli*. In this way, during the late 1970s and 1980s, ASEAN functioned less as an anticommunist than as an anti-Vietnam bloc. This condition did not come to an end through ASEAN efforts, but rather because of the co-ordinated intervention of the major world powers through the United Nations, and because Hanoi had decided that its objectives in Cambodia had essentially been achieved.

ASEAN was also lame because of the authoritarian nature of most of its governments. Few of these regimes tolerated serious domestic criticism, and their co-operation from the start depended on the principle of "non-interference" in each other's self-defined affairs.[35] Hence ASEAN has been impotent to do anything substantial about the Bangsa Moro problem in the Philippines or Jakarta's self-defeating imperialism in East Timor. The recent inclusion of the dictatorships of Vietnam, Laos, and Burma within ASEAN is unlikely to diminish this impotence. ASEAN's humiliating ditherings over what to do about Hun Sen's Cambodia—to say nothing of Burma's and Vietnam's refusal to accept the quite recent ASEAN principle of visa-less movement of its peoples across national borders—simply confirm this impression. At the same time, it is clear that over the past decade ASEAN has more and more managed to have itself taken seriously in international diplomacy, and a generational change in the political leaderships of the region, long overdue, may open the way to democratization and less unprincipled coalitions.[36]

---

35. It is perhaps worth offering a word or two about the only ideological formula proffered to justify this tactical principle: "Asian values." First, and most noticeably, they are—mercifully—*not* "Southeast Asian values." For good reason: the largely Christian Philippines got rid of its dictatorship in 1986; and monarchical Buddhist Siam has been "democratizing" by fits and starts since the end of the 1970s. Neither has shown any substantial interest in "Asian values." Nor, however, has inward-looking, deeply divided Indonesia, despite the decades-old Suharto dictatorship. The noise has come principally from the Singaporean dictatorship, and to a lesser extent from the permanent Malay government in Kuala Lumpur, each for its own reasons eager to justify its behaviour on non-religious grounds ("Asian" is meant above all, in a postcommunist age, to conceal/supersede religious differences) and to build profitable bridges with the "Confucian" world to the north and east.

36. As of present writing, the heads of state of the Philippines, Indonesia, Malaysia, Vietnam, Siam, and Laos are in their seventies. "Elder statesman" Ne Win in Burma is even older. Curiously enough, only Cambodia has a young "strongman."

PERSONAL VECTORS

I came to study at Cornell University in January 1958 for the most superficial of reasons: curiosity. Indonesia was then on the front pages of the newspapers because it had a huge and legal communist party, and because a CIA-fostered civil war was on the verge of breaking out. It so happened that George Kahin, the scholar who had written *the* pathbreaking book about the modern politics of a country which, in those days, most Americans and Europeans would have had difficulty locating on a world map, was teaching at Cornell.[37] He was also, however, an enormously creative Executive Director of the United States's second Southeast Asia programme, who assembled a remarkable array of professorial talents around him, and sought energetically to recruit students interested in every one of the emerging Southeast Asian nation-states on the assumption that they had every reason to study together and learn from each other. (For me, it was therefore institutionally impossible to study Indonesia on its own; it could only be done in a regional context.) One last decisive aspect of Kahin's formative influence was his patriotism. Precisely because he wanted to be proud, not ashamed, of his country, his scholarly career was, indeed still is, shaped by his political activism. He had been deprived of a passport in the early 1950s for his sharp criticisms of American foreign policy. Later, as the American intervention in Indochina deepened, he would switch his main focus of concern there, rather than to his first love, Indonesia.[38] Looking back, it seems to me that Kahin was the logical-historical antithesis

---

37. This is the classic *Nationalism and Revolution in Indonesia* (Ithaca, NY: Cornell University Press, 1952). A striking feature of this book which, alas, disappeared in the writings of his students, was its assumption of Indonesia's utter modernity. It says nothing about "Java Man," ancient kingdoms and chronicles, even early colonialism. It assumes that Indonesia came into existence with its nationalist movement.

38. The centrality of Kahin in forming the best traditions of Southeast Asian studies cannot be understated. He had begun his Asian connections in the earliest days of the Pacific War when he had helped a Quaker campaign to compel the debtors of Japanese Americans interned on the West Coast to honour their obligations. He later joined the Army, and was trained in the Malay (Indonesian) language for eventual parachuting behind Japanese lines in Java or Sumatra. The military being what it was, he ended up actually serving in Italy. In 1948 he left, as a student at the Johns Hopkins University, to do fieldwork in Indonesia while the revolutionary war against the returning Dutch was going on. He became an intimate of many of the Indonesian leaders, and, on his return to the United States, actively lobbied in Washington for their cause. *Nationalism and Revolution in Indonesia* exerted a powerful scholarly and ethical-political hold on my generation of Southeast Asianists. In the 1960s and 1970s he was the earliest and most prominent Southeast Asianist critic of American intervention in Indochina. Out of this engagement came *The United States in Vietnam* (New York: Bell, 1967), written in collaboration with John F. Lewis, and the masterly *Intervention: How America became Involved in Vietnam* (New York: Knopf, 1986). In the 1990s, he returned to the study of Indonesia, from which came *Subversion as Foreign Policy: The Secret Eisenhower and Dulles Debacle in Indonesia* (New York: New Press, 1995), written together with Audrey Kahin.

of the postwar American hegemonic project for Southeast Asia. His students learned from him the inseparability of politics and scholarship.

Indonesia was certainly a special place to study in the late 1950s and 1960s, by comparison with the other countries of Southeast Asia. Kahin had recruited the courtly linguist and lexicographer John Echols, who published the first good postcolonial dictionary of a national Southeast Asian language, and who by his teaching made young "Indonesianists" the first sizeable group of Southeast Asianists to be fluent in the national vernacular.[39] He had also recruited the Riga-born, Jewish-Russian dancer, archaeologist, and art historian Claire Holt, who had lived and studied in the Netherlands Indies for much of the 1930s, and returned to independent Indonesia in the 1950s to continue and extend her earlier work.[40] A few hours' car drive away at Yale was the Jewish-Czech historian Harry Benda, who had worked for an Austrian company in the Indies during the late 1930s and had been interned by the Japanese. Both these teachers brought students a sceptical European attitude towards the imperial aspects of American Southeast Asian studies, and both brought to students a vivid sense of the continuities and discontinuities between the colonial era and the era of independence. Finally, there was the accident—as he himself later recorded—that one of the most influential American anthropologists of the 1960s and 1970s, Clifford Geertz, did his most important fieldwork in Java and Bali.

Special in some ways Indonesia might be in those days, but it was always thought about and studied in a Southeast Asian frame. This frame was only reinforced by the experience of the Vietnam War years, which, to various extents, forced scholars and students studying very different countries and problems to take stands, for or against the war, as Southeast Asianists. And not merely for intellectual or political reasons. No matter what our particular scholarly research interests, we had grown up together, studied together, and read and criticized each other's work; in a certain way, we were chained together by a Southeast Asia to which, in one sense, we had helped give a certain reality.

Such were the institutional circumstances which made it possible for me, after being banned from Indonesia in April 1972, to think nothing of shifting over to the study of Siam (in 1974–75), and, a decade later, of moving on to the Philippines (though for a short time I seriously considered the unheard-of: venturing outside Southeast Asia, to Sri Lanka). Siam and the

---

39. Thai specialists followed soon after. But it was not until the 1980s that knowledge of Vietnamese, Burmese, and Filipino came to be regarded as *de rigueur* for specialists on these countries.

40. She had worked in the State Department during and after the war, till she resigned in protest against the ravages of McCarthyism.

Philippines appeared as the "natural" comparisons with Indonesia, and Cornell had all the resources to make the shifts and comparisons possible: excellent language teaching, an outstanding faculty, and, thanks to the then power of the dollar, and the selfless endeavours of John Echols, the best library in the world on Southeast Asia. It was also from a Southeast Asia incorporating the *ci-devant* revolutionary states of former Indochina that it was possible for me later to stray still farther afield. The initial impetus for writing *Imagined Communities* in 1982–83 came from the triangular Third Indochina War that broke out in 1978–79 between China, Vietnam, and Cambodia (if this anthropomorphism is permissible). But I could also not forget the telescopic view of Hitler from Jakarta, which had made it forever impossible to take Europe for granted.

A few years later, the collapse of the Soviet Union brought the Cold War and actually existing communism to an end, and conjured up new spectres to the western official imagination: most notably, (bad) nationalism. Under these circumstances, and at a time in my life when the possibilities of serious and immersed fieldwork in Southeast Asia were, for all kinds of reasons, diminishing, I was gradually led to wider, and more pretentiously theoretical-universal, considerations and framings. Yet these recent studies remain rooted, with whatever solidity they have, in Southeast Asia. So that even if, in the pages that follow, I have wandered as far as Peru, to which I have come no closer than a few days in Rio de Janeiro, my steps were turned in that direction from the Philippines, which, in a certain stage-lighting, can seem to have floated away to the distant west from the littoral of the Hispanic Andes.

THE SHAPE OF THE BOOK

It remains only to append some words about the rather strange shape of this book, which is intended to show the relationship between country studies, area studies in the strict sense of the word, and "theory," as well as their collective embedment in our portion of homogeneous, empty time.

At its core are a few texts on each of the three countries of Southeast Asia where I have done extended fieldwork, and of whose languages I have some knowledge: Indonesia, Siam, and the Philippines. Following these country studies is a group of essays which try to draw thematic comparisons between these countries in a Southeast Asian framework. Encasing these texts, fore and aft, are five theoretical pieces devoted almost entirely to various aspects of nationalism. The idea is to invite the reader to reflect first on some theoretical considerations, then move downwards to the empirical studies out of which they grew, and finally to return to the initial more rarefied atmosphere.

It is now more than twenty-five years since I was banned from General

Suharto's Indonesia, but the country continues to exercise a powerful hold on my affection and imagination. As I have described elsewhere, "exile" meant that after 1972 much of my work on Indonesia was based on documents rather than on direct experience of a living society.[41] This, however, had the advantage of pushing my inquiries back into the nineteenth century, and from everyday politics to the transformations of consciousness that made presently existing Indonesia thinkable. "A Time of Darkness and a Time of Light," first published in 1979, is a study of the extraordinary autobiography—but is it really that?—of the Javanese Dr. Soetomo, one of Indonesia's earliest and most attractive nationalist leaders. Looking back on it today, I see clearly now that in it the seeds of *Imagined Communities* were already sown. For the autobiography was about the two most salient signs that haunt the imagination of nationalism—death and light. The second piece, "Professional Dreams," I finished writing a decade later. It is a study of parts of two long and, to contemporary Indonesian eyes, scandalous poems written in Javanese, one dating from the beginning of the nineteenth century and the other from the 1860s, perhaps the darkest era in Java's colonial history—and only a generation before Soetomo's birth. The essay was written at a time when I was considering how to revise and correct *Imagined Communities*, in particular how to explain why, after about 1810, utterly new nationalisms began to figure themselves as ancient. Considering the epistemic abyss between these poems and nationalist Soetomo's memoirs helped ground my theoretical conclusion that the rise of nationalism meant a change of consciousness so thoroughgoing that a prenationalist consciousness had become inaccessible and thus had to be substituted for by History and Tradition.

These two studies have perhaps an antiquarian aura to them, and do not properly convey my continuing engagement with contemporary Indonesia. At about the time that "A Time of Light and a Time of Darkness" was first published, I had the, for me, unusual experience of being summoned to give professional testimony before two subcommittees of the American Congress which were considering what, if anything, should and could be done about the horrendous human-rights abuses committed by the Suharto regime inside Indonesia, and its brutal invasion (Pearl Harbor Day, 1975) and occupation of the former Portuguese colony of East Timor. As I have mentioned earlier, I had never been to East Timor, and understood none of the languages used there, but at least I had become an expert on the imperialist aggressor. Furthermore, I had the inestimable advantage of being banned from Indonesia, so that I was no longer haunted by the fear—which kept

---

41. In the introduction to *Language and Power: Exploring Political Cultures in Indonesia* (Ithaca, NY: Cornell University Press, 1990).

most of my Indonesia-specialist colleagues circumspectly silent—of being denied access to the country as punishment for speaking out. Curiously enough, the experience of preparing testimony, and giving it, brought back the flavour of the Vietnam War era. It was as if the "enemy" had never changed—the same equivocal State Department spokesmen, the same deceitful ambassadors, the same Cold Warrior military and intelligence officers. From that time on, I came increasingly in touch with East Timorese patriots in exile overseas, and with a growing international network of supporters of the East Timorese cause. A recent outcome of this engagement is "Gravel in Jakarta's Shoes," which attempts to explain why after twenty years of occupation the Suharto regime has failed to turn East Timorese into Indonesians, why East Timorese nationalism is spread far more widely and deeply than it was at the moment of Jakarta's invasion, more than twenty years ago, and what costs Indonesians have paid for their rulers' savage folly.

I spent a year (1974–75) in Siam, studying its dominant language, reading about its history, and following its politics. It was a wonderful time to be there, because in October 1973 a massive popular and unarmed uprising in Bangkok had created the conditions for the collapse of the long-standing American-backed, -armed, and -financed military regime of Sarit Thanarat and his lieutenants Thanom Kittikajon and Praphat Jarusathien. In 1974 and most of 1975, Siam was an extraordinarily free and exhilarating place, full of student demonstrations, workers' strikes, peasant mobilizations, and the sharpest political debates. In the spring of 1975 the country's first-ever genuinely free election took place, and for the first—and last—time a substantial number of left-wing people were elected to parliament. A better contrast to Indonesia under Suharto could hardly be imagined. At almost the same moment as this election, however, the American position in Indochina abruptly crumbled to dust, creating panic in conservative circles in next-door Siam. The year 1976 was marked by an intensifying campaign of terroristic violence against people seen as on the Left, culminating in the coup of October 6, 1976, which was accompanied by gruesome murders of students in downtown Bangkok itself. In the wake of this violence hundreds of the most intelligent and dedicated left-wing youngsters fled to the maquis where they were initially welcomed by the Communist Party of Thailand (CPT).

"Withdrawal Symptoms" was written a few months after the coup and the murders, and was my first venture in publishing about Siam. Composed at a moment when nobody could have predicted that within two years Vietnam would successfully invade Cambodia, that China would unsuccessfully invade Vietnam, and that the three-cornered war would quickly lead to the collapse of the CPT, it read the domestic polarization of 1976–77 as the irreversible outcome of the Cold War and the domineering, transforming American presence over the previous quarter of a century.[42] Thus while the analysis of the October 6, 1976 coup and its background seem to me still correct, the predictions with which it ended soon proved illusory. "Murder and Progress in Modern Siam," published more than ten years later, when a corrupt, conservative civilian regime seemed to have stabilized in the country after the elimination of any organized Left, is a sort of melancholy correction to "Withdrawal Symptoms," as well as the beginning of some work on "bourgeois democracy" in Southeast Asia, a topic addressed more fully in the chapter "Elections in Southeast Asia."

I had briefly visited the Philippines in early 1972, mainly to see friends, and had the presentiment that Ferdinand Marcos was close to proclaiming a dictatorship. This presentiment was confirmed by the arch-cacique's declaration of martial law that September. I did not return to Manila until after February 1986, when the ill and ageing tyrant, along with his laughable wife and her gimcrack valuables, were whisked off to Hawaii by the Americans. It was another good time—like Siam in 1974–75. A substantial number of my students poured into Cory Aquino's Philippines, and I found myself swept along in their wake. From my adolescence I had always wanted to learn Spanish, and now there was a good reason to get started, for in the heroic era of modern Philippine history—the 1880s to the 1900s, when the country pioneered the rise of nationalism in Asia—virtually all the documents were written in that language. Using dictionaries, my residual French and Latin, and a dissembling crib—I taught myself the language in the most enjoyable way imaginable: by reading in the original José Rizal's great incendiary novels *Noli Me Tangere* and *El Filibusterismo*. But it was not Rizal alone who caught my imagination—there was also the courage of the original insurrectionary, Andrés Bonifacio, the formidable intellect and exemplary character of Apolinario Mabini, architect of the Revolutionary Republic of 1898, the military genius of Antonio Luna, and the lucidity and organizing ability of Marcelo del Pilar. All were dead by 1903, when the Americans had largely consolidated their rule.[43] Living in Manila in 1988–89, watching the shaky

---

42. The entirety of the "American era"—beginning with American backing for the coup-makers of November 1947 and ending with the final withdrawal of American troops and the closing of American military installations in Siam in 1975–76—is considered through the lens of Thai literature in my *In the Mirror: Literature and Politics in Siam in the American Era* (Bangkok: Duang Kamon, 1985).

43. Rizal was executed by the Spanish at the very end of 1896. Del Pilar had died in poverty in Barcelona six months earlier. Bonifacio was murdered by followers of his usurper Emilio Aguinaldo in May 1897. Luna was also assassinated by Aguinaldo's men—in June 1899. After the conquest, Mabini, who was paralysed from the waist down, refused to take the oath of allegiance to the new colonial regime, and was exiled to another recent American acquisition, the Spanish Marianas. He died of cholera in 1903, a few months after returning to Manila.

Aquino regime buffeted by repeated weird coup attempts by right-wing colonels,[44] it was impossible not to reflect on the question of why figures of comparable eminence had never again appeared, and why the colony of the most powerful of the capitalist states had become visibly the most immiserated of the independent countries of the region outside the communist bloc.

"Cacique Democracy" was written in 1988, not long before "Murder and Progress in Modern Siam," and it has the same tonality, although its schematic scope is the entire modern history of the Philippines. It was also the occasion for a more distanced reflection on American imperialism (whose effects I had run into earlier, in different ways, in Indonesia, Indochina, and Siam), since American domination in Manila had preceded the Cold War by almost half a century. Furthermore, Rizal and his comrades of the 1880s and 1890s were so extraordinarily unlike anyone I could think of in other parts of Southeast Asia, and indeed their "time" was so out of sync with Southeast Asian time, that it was necessary to consider them outside a standard Southeast Asian framing. One might think of the problem on the pivot of 1887—the year in which *Noli Me Tangere* was published in Berlin. Dr. Soetomo had not yet been born. Britain had completed its conquest of Burma only two years earlier, while the French initiated their Union of Indochina only as Rizal was finishing his manuscript. To the south, London's sovereignty over the Malay peninsula had been formalized only in 1874.

The obvious context for contemplating the late nineteenth-century Philippines was, first, the paradoxically creaky but enlightened Spanish Empire which had started to fall apart in South America three-quarters of a century earlier; and, from there, the larger comparative framework of mottled colonialism. "The First Filipino," written very recently, tries to situate Rizal in these contexts, while at the same time tampering with the hardening shell of Southeast Asian studies. It would have been impossible for me to have written it a decade earlier, though in principle the world-framing of *Imagined Communities,* and especially the chapter on creole pioneers, should have prodded my thinking in this direction. "Hard to Imagine," drafted in the early 1990s, considers the strange fate of *Noli Me Tangere* in the age of official nationalism and postindependence cacique democracy.

---

44. Here I cannot resist an exemplary anecdote. At the height of the last and most serious of these attempted coups, I found myself seeking safety from likely tank and helicopter fire by crouching along the wall of the capital's Mormon Tabernacle. Next to me was a rebel junior officer shouting imprecations at the Americans, whom he understood to be helping the Aquino regime. My fear that his anger would be vented on me as a probable American was only allayed when the officer fixed on a fellow croucher—a large and corpulent man with two cameras, who announced himself nervously as a German. To my complete astonishment, the young rebel gave the stout fellow a Heil Hitler salute and enquired eagerly about the health of Field Marshal Rommel. This was a perfect moment to slink further away behind the sheltering Tabernacle.

The group of essays that follow are, as mentioned above, attempts to make formal comparisons within the frame of Southeast Asia. The first two, written in the early 1990s, are, though very different in style, closely connected. "Elections in Southeast Asia" considers the paradoxical character of "free elections" as they cropped up in the Cold War and post-Cold War trajectories of Siam, Indonesia, and the Philippines. At the spectral extremes: why dozens of "free elections" have made little difference to the misery of the Philippines, while the absence of "free elections" has been catastrophic for Indonesia. "Radicalism after Communism" compares the contrasting fates of the communist movements in Siam and Indonesia, and the residues of refusal left behind for what was, in those now distant days, dubbed the end of history. It was also an occasion to pay personal tribute to a few Siamese and Indonesians who commanded my unstinting admiration. Today, in the midst of the collapse of the Asian bubble economies, its tone may seem unduly melancholy.

"Sauve Qui Peut" was forced on me by the accident of this book's date of publication—more or less a year after this financial collapse. So unexpected was this collapse, so painful its immediate local effects, and so uncertain its longer-term consequences for the world economy, that it could not reasonably be ignored in a book with the subtitle "Nationalism, Southeast Asia, and the World." Rather than focusing on the immediate causes of the crisis, which are now well known, I have tried to ask these less often posed questions. What were the conditions of possibility for the (Southeast) Asian "miracle" of the last twenty-five years? How far have these conditions now disappeared? What connections can reasonably be claimed between the variable severity of financial collapse and the character of the political regimes in contemporary Southeast Asia? It is no more than a preliminary sketch, however, for which I ask the reader's indulgence.

"Majorities and Minorities" arose out of a 1987 meeting, mainly of anthropologists, arranged by David Maybury-Lewis's Cultural Survival organization, to consider together the fates and prospects of "tribal minorities" trapped and variously oppressed in the postcolonial nation-states of Southeast Asia. The sessions in Cambridge, Massachusetts, were salutory for me in two ways. First of all, they forced me, by the sheer wealth and variety of the grim material at hand, to look for a useful, steady frame in which their juxtaposition could be made intelligible. I found this frame through reflection on the means through which the very idea of "minorities" had come into being, and then been materialized in Southeast Asia: to wit, through the transfer into the colonial world, from the end of the nineteenth century, of the metropolitan institution of the census, the administrative practices that were built around the census, and the "scientific" anthropology whose truth was mortgaged to it. From that time on, my theoretical interest in censuses as narratives of power developed steadily, leading a few years later to one major addition to the original *Imagined Communities*—the chapter entitled "Census, Map, Museum." Second, my long attachment to, and interest in, anticolonial nationalism had occluded from my vision its menacing potentialities once it got married to the state. A new recognition of this menace was the start of a process which has, more than a decade later, led to the essay in this volume (chapter 16) devoted to Mario Vargas Llosa's *El Hablador*—an extraordinary, aporetic, nationalist novel about modern Peru and its Amazonian "tribal minorities." Picked up originally for a casual read, it worked on me like a madeleine, bringing back, powerfully and unexpectedly, remembrances of Southeast Asia's past.

The fore-and-aft framing studies consist initially of three "theoretical" essays which try to probe more deeply than I had managed hitherto into the origin, nature, and prospects of nationalism in general. They had their messy origins in the Carpenter Lectures which I was invited to give at the University of Chicago in April 1993. They consider in turn the underlying grammar of nationalism, the peculiarity of nationalist images as replicas without originals, and the growing disjunction between nation-states and national identity as a consequence of contemporary mass migrations and revolutions in communications and transportation. In each case, I started out with the big end of my telescope in "Southeast Asia": the sugar belt of colonial Java, the monument to Rizal in downtown contemporary Manila, and the airport in Bangkok, where frail migrants set off every day to all quarters of their unseen employers' world.

At the end of the book come the reflections on the implications of Vargas Llosa's *El Hablador*, mentioned above, and "The Goodness of Nations," which briefly considers why it is both possible and necessary, against, one might say, the evidence, to think well of nationalism around the time of its two-hundredth birthday.

PART I

THE LONG ARC OF NATIONALISM

1

Nationalism, Identity, and the Logic of Seriality

Wenn die Tiger trinkend sich im Wasser erblicken werden
sie oft gefährlich.

Bertolt Brecht

The purposes of this essay are essentially three. The first, and most important, is to reframe the problem of the formation of collective subjectivities in the modern world by consideration of the material, institutional, and discursive bases that necessarily generate two profoundly contrasting types of seriality, which I will call *unbound* and *bound*. Unbound seriality, which has its origins in the print market, especially in newspapers, and in the representations of popular performance, is exemplified by such open-to-the-world plurals as nationalists, anarchists, bureaucrats, and workers. It is, for example, the seriality that makes the United Nations a normal, wholly unparadoxical institution. Bound seriality, which has its origins in governmentality, especially in such institutions as the census and elections, is exemplified by finite series like Asian-Americans, *beurs*, and Tutsis. It is the seriality that makes a United Ethnicities or a United Identities unthinkable. The second purpose is to draw as clear an analytic line as feasible between nationalism and ethnicity, and, in related, indirect fashion, between universality and "cosmopolitan" hybridity. The third is to dispose of such bogeys as "derivative discourses," and "imitation" in understanding the remarkable planetary spread, not merely of nationalism, but of a profoundly standardized conception of politics, in part by reflecting on the everyday practices, rooted in industrial material civilization, that have displaced the cosmos to make way for the world. I will draw a good deal of my illustrative material from the *ci-devant* Third World, where the speed and scale of change experienced over the past century has been so rapid as to throw the rise of the two serialities into the highest relief.

SERIALITY UNBOUND

On February 29, 1920, in the little Central Java town of Delanggu, surrounded on all sides by gigantic colonial and local royal sugar plantations, the
first-ever open-air public rally in the region took place. Among the speakers
who addressed the probably bewildered but excited assembly of peasants and
sugar-factory workers, none seems today, and perhaps was even then, more
strangely striking than Haji Misbach, pious returned pilgrim from Mecca and
ardent communist, with his dark face positioned between a gleaming-white
pith helmet and a smartly tailored, Dutch-style white jacket. In the course of
his speech, he bellowed the following[1]:

> The present age can rightly be called the *djaman balik boeono* [an ancient Javanese
> folk-expression meaning "age of the world-turned-upside-down"]—for what used
> to be above is now certainly under. It is said that in the country of Oostenrijk
> [Dutch for "Austro-Hungary"], which used to be headed by a Radja [Indonesian
> for "monarch"], there has now been a *balik boeono*. It is now headed by a Republic,
> and many *ambtenaar* [Dutch for "government official"] have been killed by the
> Republic. A former *ambtenaar* has only to show his nose for his throat to be cut.
> So, Brothers, remember! The land belongs to no one other than ourselves.

Indeed, Charles VII *had* renounced his imperial-dynastic rights in
November 1918. A *balik boeono* of sorts *had* followed in both Vienna and
Budapest. Béla Kun's Hungarian Communist Party *had* taken power on
March 21, 1919, and, in the four months before this regime collapsed in the
face of Czech and Romanian invasions, it *did* summarily execute a substantial
number of class enemies. But by November 25, the Allies had helped put into
power Admiral Miklós Horthy, who proceeded to launch a terror of his own.
Misbach was seven months (but only seven!) sadly out of date, whether he
was aware of it or not.

Nonetheless, his words were in many ways as new to colonial Central Java
as the rally that he was addressing, for he spoke to his audience with the
fullest confidence in the existence of the country of Oostenrijk—for which his
own language had as yet no name, and which he himself had never seen with
his own eyes—on the other side of the "world." Furthermore, the revolutionary events he described were depicted as simultaneous with events in
Java, and thus, so to speak, co-ordinated within a single frame of time—the
age of the world-turned-upside-down. This co-ordination allowed him to
expect that what had just happened to *radja* and *ambtenaar* in Oostenrijk

---

1. Takashi Shiraishi, *An Age in Motion, Popular Radicalism in Java, 1912–1926* (Ithaca, NY:
Cornell University Press, 1990), p. 193.

would imminently happen to their counterparts in the Netherlands Indies. What is still more startling, however, is Misbach's use of the little word "a." "A" *radja*, "a" *balik boeono*, "a" Republic, "a" former *ambtenaar*—in each case "a" shows that what follows will be a component of a single category-series which spans visible Java and invisible Oostenrijk. That the names of the categories could indifferently be Dutch-European, Indonesian Malay, or Javanese also indicates an understanding of life then very new: that languages are transparent to each other, interpenetrate each other, map each other's domains—at an equal remove from, or proximity to, the material world. For this equality to be possible—and it was not possible during the youth of Misbach's father—Dutch had to descend from its status as the language of colonial power, and Javanese from its position as the language of ancestral truth. Finally, one notes a deep, surely unconscious shift in the semantic load of *boeono*. Its prior meaning was something close to "cosmos," a natural, vertical universe arranged hierarchically from the Deity, or deities, down through kings, aristocrats, and peasants, to fauna and flora and the landscapes in which they were embedded. It was a meaning that explains why petty Javanese princes called themselves by such grandiloquent titles as Paku Buwono (Nail of the Cosmos) and Hamengku Buwono (Upholder of the Cosmos) without finding the terminology at all ridiculous. But Misbach was clearly using *boeono* in the quite new sense of "world," a horizontal universe of visible and invisible human beings from which volcanoes, demons, water buffalo, and divinities had vanished.

One can see vividly the abrupt character of the change involved by considering another Javanese/Netherlands Indies comparison. In *Imagined Communities*, I discussed an exemplary newspaper article of 1913 composed by Soewardi Soerjaningrat, Misbach's aristocratic contemporary and anti-colonial comrade-in-arms.[2] It was entitled "Als ik eens Nederlander was," which can best be translated as "If I were, for the nonce, *a* Dutchman." The purpose of the article was to point out the incongruity of Dutch colonials celebrating the Netherlands' independence from Napoleonic subjugation while forcing the natives they themselves held in subjugation to contribute to the cost of the festivities.[3] But we can also see that Soewardi's sarcastic rhetoric

---

2. *Imagined Communities: Reflections on the Origin and Spread of Nationalism*, rev. edn. (London: Verso, 1991), p. 117.

3. Curiously enough, Soewardi failed to notice the comic and reactionary character of this commemoration. Instead of reminding Dutch men and women of their ancestors' genuinely heroic declaration of independence from Felipe II's empire in 1581, or Madrid's final acceptance of that independence in 1648, after decades of bitter fighting, it celebrated the Holy Alliance's defeat of Napoléon, the Congress of Vienna's imposition of a mediocre monarchy on a people with a long republican tradition, and the forcible inclusion into the new kingdom of what is today's Belgium.

took nonchalantly for granted this anonymous series: Dutchmen. By contrast, if one looks at the memoirs composed in imprisoned exile by his not-too-distant ancestral kinsman, Prince Diponegoro, who led so lengthy a military struggle against Dutch colonialism between 1825 and 1830 that he is today independent Indonesia's premier historical hero, "the Dutch" as such never appear.[4] His successful enemies are recorded, in feudal, manuscript style, by personal name and rank. And if these enemies are not part of the series "Dutchmen," neither is he himself "a" Prince, or "a" Javanese.

There is another word absent from Diponegoro's melancholy reflections, and that is anything that we could honestly translate as "politics." This absence is not in the least idiosyncratic. In almost all of Asia and Africa, neologisms have had to be coined for this concept during the past hundred years, and the birthdate of each coinage is typically close to that of nationalism. For "politics" to become thinkable, as a distinctly demarcated domain of life, two things had to happen. (1) Specialized institutions and social practices had to be visible, and of a kind that could not heedlessly be glossed in the old vocabularies of cosmologically and religiously sustained kingship: to wit, general elections, presidents, censors, parties, trade unions, rallies, police, leaders, legislatures, boycotts, and the like—nations too. (2) The world had to be understood as one, so that no matter how many different social and political systems, languages, cultures, religions, and economies it contained, there was a common activity—"politics"—that was self-evidently going on *everywhere*.

Unlike, say, "industrialism," or "militarism," which, we know, were coined in Europe decades after the phenomena they attempted to denote were in motion, the vocabularies of "politics" almost always preceded their institutional realization in Asia and Africa. They were read about, then modelled from—hence so often the earliest indigenous mini-dictionaries were "how-to" glossaries to politics.

Newspapers

That such glossaries were typically circulated through early newspapers and periodicals allows one to consider the special character of the modelling process, and, as it were, the grammar that underlay it. This modelling worked more basically by serialization than by copying in any simple manner. In my 1983 discussion of the newspaper in the genesis of that apprehension of time required for the imagining of nations, I emphasized, one-sidedly I am now

---

4. A substantial part of the text of these verse memoirs appears in Ann Kumar, "Dipanegara (1787?–1855)," *Indonesia*, 13 (April 1972), pp. 69–118.

sure, the significance of the calendrical simultaneity of apparently random occurrences that each daily edition proffers to its readers.[5] I completely missed two other interconnected principles of coherence. The first is that newspapers everywhere take "this world of mankind" as their domain no matter how partially they read it.[6] It would be *contra naturam* for a newspaper to confine its reports to events within the political realm in which it is published. Rwandan horrors in Tokyo's newspapers, the eruption of Mount Pinatubo in Stockholm's, the European Football Cup final in those of Rangoon, all seem absolutely natural in exactly the same way. The second is that this natural universality has been profoundly reinforced—everywhere— by an unself-conscious standardization of vocabulary which radically overrides any formal division in the newspaper between local and foreign news. This is not a recent development. In Misbach's era, Peru, Austro-Hungary, Japan, the Ottoman Empire—no matter how vast the real differences between the populations, languages, beliefs, and conditions of life within them—were reported on in a profoundly homogenized manner. Tennô there might be inside Japan, but he would appear in newspapers everywhere else as (an) Emperor. Gandhi might be the Mahatma in Bombay, but elsewhere he would be described as "a" nationalist, "an" agitator, "a" [Hindu] leader. St. Petersburg, Caracas, and Addis Ababa—all capitals. Jamaica, Cambodia, Angola—all colonies.

This is not to say that real comparabilities did not exist, as everyday institutional modelling was going on furiously around the planet during the nineteenth and twentieth centuries. Rather, it was the case that the very format of the newspaper precluded anything else from being imagined, by the very randomness of its ceaselessly changing contents. One might even go so far as to say that the periodical appearance of the Lion of Judah and the Son of Heaven—physically invisible to more than two tiny groups of utterly separated courtiers and officials—to the simultaneous imaginations of millions of people around the world demanded their location in a single categorical series: monarchs. Series of this kind were quotidian universals that seeped through and across all print-languages, by no means necessarily in a unidirectional flow. To give only one example, when in the 1950s young Thai Marxists seized the term *sakdina*, which from medieval times had denoted, on bended knee, the traditional monarch-centred status-system in Siam, and then critically inverted its meaning, it seemed to them quite normal to use the same term in a universal sense, and thus write of the *sakdina* social system of

---

5. *Imagined Communities*, pp. 22–36.
6. The English translation of *Bumi Manusia*, the title of the first of the great Indonesian writer Pramoedya Ananta Toer's tetralogy of novels on the origins of Indonesian nationalism.

medieval Europe.[7] *Sakdina* and "feudal" stood in, as it were, for one another (just as, one can see, did *balik boeono* and "revolution"). This does not mean that they meant exactly the same thing, but rather that from Bangkok and Birmingham two parallel series were stretching out across, and seamlessly mapping, a singular world. This example is also emblematic of the way in which from the start the new serial thinking could be operated diachronically up and down homogeneous, empty time, as well as synchronically, on the newspaper page.

It was from within this logic of the series that a new grammar of representation came into being, which was also a precondition for imagining the nation. The late colonial environment is an especially apt site for appreciating this development because one can there see how the logic was working in the same way, if in separate institutional milieux, among both white rulers and coloured ruled. To illustrate this process, let us continue for the moment with the late nineteenth-century and early twentieth-century Netherlands Indies.

Market performance

Up until this epoch all forms of popular indigenous theatre, including the well-known, traditional shadow-play, were grounded in a logic that one might call iconographic. The stories, presented by live actors or by puppets voiced over by puppeteers, were drawn from local legends or from episodes in the Mahabharata and Ramayana epics, which over the centuries had become so indigenized that only a tiny literate minority was aware of their Indic provenance. Not only were the stories thoroughly familiar to audiences, their presentation was iconographically fixed. Playbills were unimaginable because the characters were all meticulously differentiated by standardized body types, coiffures, costumes, speech styles, and gestural repertoires. There was only one Indra or Rama or Arjuna, who was recognizable the very second he came into stage view. Since there was no question of *interpreting* such figures, who were often understood as quite real beings outside the performance, the identities of actors, indeed often their genders, were a matter of indifference. Paradoxically enough, the iconographic rules governing what Rama could conceivably say were so strict that scripts were never thought of, and easy improvisation was the normal order of the day.

But towards the very end of the nineteenth century a new form of theatre crystallized in newspaper towns, which in its own idiosyncratic way drew on the vaudeville and operetta performances of travelling Eurasian and

---

7. See the sophisticated discussion in Craig J. Reynolds, *Thai Radical Discourse: The Real Face of Thai Feudalism Today* (Ithaca, NY: Cornell University, Southeast Asia Program, 1987).

European troupes. When indigenous players began to stage, for saleable tickets, vernacular versions of *The Merchant of Venice*, the draw was precisely the
easy mystery of the exotic title (Venice? Where was it? But one could find it on
any printed map of the "world"—which had no insets for Heaven or Hell).[8]
Shylock, like most of the characters in such dramas, could not be presented
iconographically. There was as yet no convention as to how he should look,
dress, talk, and move his body. No Jews had ever figured in traditional
drama—no money-lenders either. Hence there was no way of playing Shylock
except, quasi-sociologically, as a *social type* or combination of types. The
actor (by now gender mattered) could no longer improvise, but required the
help of script and rehearsal to be able to present a plausible Jewish usurer;
and this plausibility depended on persuading audiences of the social verisimilitude of Shylock, in other words, his placeability, replaceability too, within
such intersecting universal series as cruel money-lenders, doting fathers, and
obsessive misers. Yet his representativenesses were not only grounded in experienced colonial life—to be sure, everyone knew money-lenders, misers, and
doting fathers personally, yet in the Indies Jews were few and almost
invisible—they were also based in the kingdom of representation itself, the
world of print. There fictive Shylocks, Hamlets, and Genevièves aligned themselves "grammatically" not only with real, serial capital cities, strikes,
elections, and football matches, but also with pictorial advertisements, which
are always unintelligible except as beguiling synecdoches for serial cornu-
copias of desirable commodities.

SERIALITY BOUND

Meanwhile, on high, serialization was advancing from a rather different direction. In 1920, just as Haji Misbach was campaigning for revolution in the
sugar belt of Central Java, the colonial regime executed the first "scientific
census" in its domain.[9] Doubtless this came a bit late in world time, but not
terribly late. The newly independent United States of America had been,

---

8. See A. Th. Manusama, *Komedie Stamboel of de Oost-Indische Opera* (Batavia [Jakarta]:
n.p., 1922) for a splendid account. Manusama offers a provisional repertoire of forty-three
shows that, in a nice illustration of my argument above, are thoroughly cosmopolitan-local in
thematic character: 9 drawn from *The Arabian Nights*, 9 from local tales and legends, 6 from
Persia, 6 from India [Hindustan], 3 from China, and 10 from Europe (pp. 24–27). In this last
group we find not only *The Merchant of Venice* and *Hamlet*, but also *Geneveva* [Geneviève of
Brabant], *Somnambule* [*La Somnambula*], *Robertson de duiker* [probably Robert de Duivel,
Robert the Devil], and so on.

9. Peter Boomgaard, *Population Trends, 1795–1942* (Amsterdam: Royal Tropical Institute,
1991), gives a good account of this endeavour, and the contrast it forms with previous enumerations for tax and corvée purposes.

with its rough-and-ready *national* population count of 1790, the first state to undertake proto-scientific and public-census activity—preceding France, the Netherlands, and the United Kingdom by a decade.[10] But until 1850, the unit of enumeration was the household, and only the name of the household's head was recorded. Not until 1880 was a central Census Office set up in Washington, and not till 1902 was this office, renamed a bureau, made a permanent, full-time agency of the state. In a broader frame, one observes that it was only in 1853, in the immediate aftermath of the European nationalist upheavals of 1848, that the First International Statistical Congress, held in Brussels, adopted a resolution establishing the basic "scientific" requirements for achieving international comparability of census data and the standardization of census content and techniques.[11]

That such a resolution had to be voted over and over at the Paris Congress in 1855, the London Congress in 1860, and the Florence Congress in 1867, indicates that all was not plain sailing with the statisticians' political campaign to modernize and transnationalize the processing of population counts. We should probably not be surprised that it was only in the infancy of the League of Nations that the campaign more or less reached fruition,[12] still less that this coincided with the very abrupt and rapid spread of suffrage for women.

As many observers have noted, not only is the taking of a census an elaborate, expensive, and thoroughly public affair, but, with some nonetheless quite predictable exceptions, census results are highly visible public texts. In principle, then, they should be open to the same kind of "grammatical" scrutiny that we have summarily applied to the newspaper and the popular theatre. In this light, I am inclined to focus on three peculiar aspects of the census's conventions.

The first of these conventions is the impermissibility of fractions, or, to put it the other way round, a mirage-like integrity of the body. For example, if a simple, hypothetical classificatory system proposes to sort a population into, say, Blacks and Whites, and then runs into the messy reality that a substantial group is of ancestries mixed in varying proportions, one logical option would be to assign halves, quarters, eighths, and sixteenths to the Black and the White columns. But since the convention forbids this possibility, the practical choices are either arbitrary assignment to Black or White, or the

---

10. The reasons for the early start of the United States will be considered below.

11. The 1820s and the 1830s have been described as an era of "statistical enthusiasm," in which statistical societies were formed for the first time in the United Kingdom and the United States. See Paul Starr, "The Sociology of Official Statistics," in William Alonso and Paul Starr, eds., *The Politics of Numbers* (New York: Russell Sage Foundation, 1986), pp. 24 and 15.

12. Much of the above material I owe to Marc Ventresca of Stanford University.

proliferation of categories and subcategories—as it were, mulattoes, quadroons, and octoroons—in which mixedness, or fractionality, can resume integral status.[13] Naturally, this does not at all mean that each countee does not anonymously reappear in dozens of other classificatory enumerations within the same census, in each instance as an integer, but it does mean that this complex fractionality is inscribed in invisible ink. In one lighting, every countee is an indivisible whole; in another, merely the site of a maze of intersecting series.

The second convention is anonymity. One might say that the names fully recorded in individual census forms are the highly classified sections of these documents that the state keeps jealously to itself. It is a matter for some amusement that in the United States this top secret classification lasts for seventy-two years. (Furthermore, one can be punished for "secretly" lying to the state on one's schedule.)[14] The convention of namelessness has two related reality effects, as Roland Barthes used to say. On the one hand, it shores up the census's truth, in the sense that it becomes nigh impossible for anyone to match the census up with his or her world of personal knowledge and community acquaintance. On the other hand, through the equivalency of integers, it maps a stable (ten-year) social field, sealed by the imposing page-by-page row of identical totals. This nameless, tabularly crisscrossed field, is, say, Denmark, imagined serially, synchronically, and as a self-portrait.

The third convention, totality, contrasts vividly with the effervescent boundlessness of newspapers' serial imaginings. Totality (nicely inflated to "universe" in the argot of social science) is in fact required for most secondary statistical computations. But it has a political ancestry of its own, which it may be useful briefly to recall. Up along one family line is William Petty (1623–87), Hobbes's acolyte and Adam Smith's John the Baptist, who won a certain posthumous immortality in 1691 with the publication of his *Political Arithmetic*, of which the comparable analytic units were then-existing political states.[15] Up along another line was a seventeenth- and eighteenth-century "German" cameralist tradition of *comparative* study of *Staaten*, which eventually permitted Göttingen professor Gottfried Achenwall (1719–72) to coin, by derivation, the very term *Statistik*. New-minted, the term speedily crossed

---

13. For example, between 1840 and 1910, the major category "Negroes" in the US census contained within it four subcategories: mulatto, quadroon, octoroon, and black. See William Petersen, "Politics and the Measurement of Ethnicity," in Alonso and Starr, eds., *The Politics of Numbers*, p. 208.

14. Information kindly provided, over the telephone, by the New York City office of the Bureau of the Census.

15. As a ruthless young *esprit fort*, he had in 1654 been sent to Ireland by the Lord Protector to make a count of persons and property that could serve as the basis for systematic colonial exploitation and oppression.

the Channel and entered English with John Sinclair's 21-volume *Statistical Account of Scotland*, published—of course serially—between 1791 and 1799.[16] In effect, before it was settled by the internal logic of statistics itself, the politically moated state of the age of enlightened absolutism had given "totality" its primal shape: just in time for the age of nationalism.

Statistical logic and politics, married in the census, sheared off every series at the same temporal edges (in the twentieth-century American census, the westward press of "females," "Blacks," and "medical practitioners" all end isomorphically on the coastline of the Pacific and the Bering Sea). But at the same time, by their mutual interaction, they created something that newspapers were ill-equipped to engender: serial, aggregable, counterposed majorities and minorities, which, starting as formal entities, were positioned in due course to assume political reality. (Here is the matrix from which, exactly in the 1830s when statistical associations were being formed in the anglophone states on both sides of the Atlantic, Alexis de Tocqueville commenced feverishly to imagine tyrannies that were ultimately census-grounded.[17])

The linking bridge was, of course, the suffrage. The reason that the infant United States could so get the start of the majestic world was simply its novel republican and federal character. In the absence of monarchy and estates, it seemed that sovereignty could be manifested only in the will of the citizenry expressed through electoral processes. The national counting of 1790, and all later decennial countings up until the age of Haji Misbach, were designed primarily to ensure, arithmetically, the fair apportionment of electoral representation in the two houses of the national legislature. It was not that the numbers of voters in any obvious way matched the census count, but suffrageless females and male minors were assumed to be distributed evenly across the states, and thus the household head (whose name, as I have noted, was the only one the census recorded until 1850) could, in a statistical-apportionment sense, represent them. Slaves, however, were not distributed evenly. Property they might be, but Southern slave-owners were not eager to surrender the chance to count them, once every ten years, as persons. Hence the bizarre compromise arrangement—showing that William Petty's political arithmetic had come fully into its own—whereby each unfree American recorded through the census was fractionally counted as three-fifths of a person for purposes of congressional reapportionment.

---

16. See, *inter alia*, Starr, "The Sociology of Official Statistics," pp. 13–15, and the sources therein cited.

17. See the celebrated chapter XII in *De la Démocratie en Amérique* (Paris: Pagnerre, 1850), pp. 226–34, especially at p. 230. "*De nos temps*, la liberté d'association *est devenue* une garantie nécessaire contre la tyrannie de la majorité" (emphasis added). Was a majority, let alone a tyrannical majority, seriously conceivable under the *ancien régime*?

Fanning out from the United States, electoralism exerted an ever-increasing influence on the style of census-taking, as notions of popular sovereignty spread, as the state acquired a welfare-and-development mission, and as the suffrage widened. It was not long before voters began to influence the very categories through which the machinery of enumerations whirred.[18] There were, under the new conditions, for the first time good reasons to wish to be counted, if in a certain style, rather than to hope to be overlooked by the taxman who was the census-taker's early shadow. By the beginning of the century the "electoral" mode of population enumeration had assumed such normalcy in the metropoles that it penetrated silently even into the colonial autocracies, where it could only have long-term subversive effects.

The Philippines affords a vivid example of this process. The first serious enumeration was undertaken in 1818.[19] Its category roster included such strange, unelectoral bedfellows as: *difuntos* (the dead), *negros infieles* (infidel blacks), *tributos* (tribute-payers), *mestizos españoles* (persons of mixed Spanish descent), *morenos* (the brown-skinned), and *individuos contribuyentes* (individual taxpayers). Its devisers were clearly thinking, from on high, in primarily ecclesiastical and financial terms. The word *almas* (souls) and the primary opposition between *infieles* and *convertidos* (infidels and converted) showed up for the last, and first, time. Cross-category totals, the necessary basis for majority–minority groupings, were scarce. There was no trace of territorialism, nor of the dozens of ethnolinguistic groups dotted across the islands.[20] The next census, that of 1877, was completely secular and the shadow of the tax-collector had disappeared. The three simple axes on which the count was based marked the presence/absence of residents, their character as *españoles* or *extranjeros* (foreigners), and their skin colour: *blancos, pardos,* and *morenos*.[21] Everything here breathed a backward, but definitely nineteenth-century, autocracy. The 1903 census, however, taken by the

---

18. This is probably the right place to remind the reader that, all the same, the census includes two contrasting types of series—the categorical and the scalar. The modal case of the first is gender, for which only two exclusive lifetime possibilities are open; the modal case of the second is income distribution, which proceeds by a long series of graded steps with fuzzy endings so that billionaires and paupers are made invisible. The scalar format offers every possibility for people to move up and down these steps in the course of their lives. From this rises the agreeable utopian idea of a census in which gender becomes scalar, with several graded steps, and income binary-categorical: as it were, divided simply between haves and have-nots.

19. It was sponsored, however, not by the colonial government but by the Ayuntamiento of Manila, and relied on the apparatus of the Church rather than the State for its implementation.

20. There was no real attempt to count the substantial Muslim and hill-tribe pagan populations residing within what on paper was the Spanish Philippines.

21. In the meantime, first Manila, then other ports, had been thrown open to international trade, so that foreigners were now appearing there for the first time. Furthermore, the arrival of the steamship made the presence/absence of residents a real question.

Americans within months of the official termination of their brutal war of conquest, was already structured proto-electorally in the peculiar American manner, categorizing (in alphabetic order!) twenty-five so-determined "wild" or "civilized" native ethnolinguistic groups, five skin-colour tones from white through black, as well as a skein of birthplaces and, where relevant, citizenships.[22] In the publicized pages of *this* census, the words Tagalog and Ilocano had, for the first time, numbers attached to them, which were perfectly available for Tagalog- and Ilocano-speakers to read. And the reality effect of the official census, its claim that what was being counted was, socially speaking, profoundly "there," gave these figures a kind of calm monumentality. More striking still, with a category structure of this kind, the Americans in the Philippines, who could not imagine *not* counting themselves, since they so pre-eminently counted, appeared as a visible, sealed-in, numbered *minority*. Exactly the same thing happened in the 1921 census of the Netherlands Indies, and more generally in the twentieth-century colonial world. From a certain angle, one can see each of these censuses as smoking entrails from which the impending collapse of a particular colonialism lay ready to be deciphered.

PRACTICE

From the contrast between two styles of serialization—one, figured by the newspaper, unbound and unenumerated, the other, figured by the census, bound and numerated—the lineaments of two kinds of politicization and political practice emerge, both of which, however, show how basic to the modern imagining of collectivity seriality always is.

One can get a vivid sense of the dynamic of the first from the following passage, which I have translated from *Dia Jang Menjerah* ("She Who Gave Up"), a mesmerizing tale originally published in 1952 by the most celebrated of Indonesian writers, Pramoedya Ananta Toer. It describes how Is, teenage elder sister of the tale's heroine, comes to join the radical organization Pesindo (Socialist Youth of Indonesia) in the revolutionary upsurge that followed immediately after the end of the brutal Japanese occupation of Indonesia (1942–45):

> In such times too the rage for politics roared along like a tidal wave, out of control. Each person felt as though she, he could not be truly alive without being political,

---

22. The most elaborate discussion of Philippine population counts, and the politics thereof, is in the appendix to the first volume of Onofre Corpuz, *The Roots of the Filipino Nation* (Quezon City: Aklahi Foundation, 1989), pp. 515–70.

without debating political questions. In truth, it was as though they could stay alive even without rice. Even schoolteachers, who had all along lived "neutrally," were infected by the epidemic rage for politics—and, so far as they were able, they influenced their pupils with the politics to which they had attached themselves. Each struggled to claim new members for his party. And schools proved to be fertile battlefields for their struggles. Politics! Politics! No different from rice under the Japanese Occupation. Soon enough courses followed. And those who had only just obtained an understanding of capitalism–socialism–communism competed to give lectures at food-stalls, on street corners, and in the buildings that snarled in each of their skulls. And Pesindo too sprang up in the barren, limestone soil of our village. By now, Is knew the society she was entering. She had found a circle of acquaintances far wider than the circle of her brothers, sisters and parents. She now occupied a defined position in that society: as a woman, as a typist in a government office, as a free individual. She had become a new human being, with new understanding, new tales to tell, new perspectives, new attitudes, new interests— newnesses that she had managed to pluck and assemble from her acquaintance. And all of this proceeded, untouched, amid the suffering of day-to-day existence.[23]

The circle of Is's brothers, sisters, and parents is without series. But at the revolutionary moment, to which she makes her small contribution, she imagines herself, for the first time in her tender life, serially: as "a" woman, "a" typist, "a" free individual, "a" new human being. This serialization so transforms her consciousness that everything to her now glows new. But these series, in their plasticity and universality, can never appear in a census, and not merely because they cannot be enumerated and totalled.[24] Furthermore, it is clear that she sees these series as of a kind, so that being a woman, a typist, and a new human being fulfil rather than counteract her commitment to the struggle for her country's freedom. We understand, too, that the series mentioned are at any moment available for kaleidoscopic transformation, enlargement, and contraction. Nothing is fixed in fated stone. Tomorrow, she may become "a" revolutionary, "a" prisoner, "a" youth, "a" spy, indeed "a" nationalist in that boundless, but grounded, universal series that included, in 1946, Clement Attlee and Jawaharlal Nehru, but only and always on a provisional basis. And if Is understands herself now as a part of the world-in-motion, so to speak summoned by quotidian universals to battle, we too read her under the same signs. We may not share her young womanhood, her typing skills, her native language, her religion, or her culture, but

---

23. This story can be found in his collection *Tjerita dari Blora* [Tales of Blora] (Jakarta: Balai Pustaka, 1952), p. 279.
24. One might think that "a" typist in "a" government office should be occupationally censusable. But the whole passage shows that here "typist" is a planetary series.

she speaks to us not, ethnographically, as an informant, but as a member of series that are open to us if we wish to act on them.

It is crucial to note that most of the series into which she sees herself entering require, as their entrance fee, that she act, in both senses of that word. She will have to learn how to "do" a revolutionary member of Pesindo, as others had had to learn how to "do" Hamlet, or strike-organizer, or nationalist. But she understands all this as emancipation, and the last thing on her mind is her identity or her roots. (We can from the start sense that she will sweep herself away towards subsequent tragedy.)

The logic of the modern census series appears to move in the opposite direction. One might initially pursue this logic by considering the primal act that censuses appear quietly to elicit: namely, voting. Under optimal conditions, this act requires joining a one-day queue of people, each taking his or her turn to go into an enclosed space as strangely private as a public toilet, and for which the drawn curtains seem to serve as decent clothing. Once inside, these people pull the same levers or write standardized words or signs on identical pieces of paper. At exactly that point they cease, whether they like it or not, to "be" voters, except in an ascriptive sense, until the next moveable feast comes around.

The extraordinary minimality and periodicity of the act of voting reminds us of how far the ballot is isomorphic with the census schedule in its refusal of fractions, its studied, aggregable anonymity, and its ensconcement, in due course, in strictly bounded totals. But this also shows us the basis of its real and symbolic political efficacy. This basis is *entitlement* (with all the ironic, antique overtones of its etymology). Before one can "do" voting, one must be entitled to do it, through an act of law of which one is never the singular beneficiary. And one is not simply "entitled" to vote; the very act of voting "entitles" *someone else* to act, on one's behalf. This someone else, however, operates not by power of attorney, but as the representative of a bounded series. The finite numerology of such series in turn works within overlapping, stratified, majoritarian/minoritarian matrices. It is this that makes possible, for example, the quite normal situation that the minute elections are over, no one but political professionals ascribes any importance to the exact numbers by which a winning candidate defeats her or his opponent, and even voters who voted against the winner feel completely entitled to make claims upon that winner on the morrow of her victory. Encapsulating each level of electoral majority is always a higher whole. Voters have always the totality— the "n" of entitled voters—in their minds.

Out of this framing have emerged, over the last half-century in particular, two signal consequences for the development of collective subjectivities. Both point in the same direction, if for somewhat different reasons.

The first is proportional entitlement, on the ground of "n." As the twentieth-century electorally based service state multiplied its functions, and enlarged its welfare capabilities, the census, ever more elaborate, increasingly became the integrated data base from which every type of planning and budgetary allocation departed. Consequently, the census itself became the object of a more visible politicization. Take, for one extreme example, Nigeria, where for years a census was politically out of the question, precisely because of fears as to what it would show about the "true" numbers of the country's self-imagined ethnic groups, and thus imply for the distribution of political power and economic benefits. For another, more agreeable case, note how voter pressure in the turbulent "long" 1960s led to the abolition of the census (the last was held in 1971) in the Netherlands, which to this day remains the one country in the world to have repudiated this powerful instrument of governmentality.[25] The turmoil over the United States census of 1980 is still more indicative of the degree to which census definitions of categories have hardened into essentialized political realities through their role in organizing the allocation of economic and other benefits and the expectations of such benefits.[26] Of such categories none has proven more important than the ethnic, originally devised a century ago, in a pre-welfare age, to monitor disdainfully the flows of immigrants from different parts of Europe. After the shutting off of large new immigrations in the 1920s, however, these categories became, thanks to the revolution in communications, the bases for electoral mobilizations even at the national level. The powerful interlocking effects of census categorization and entitlement politics can be seen from the political emergence of such recent American imaginings as the Hispanic vote, and the Asian-American constituency, perhaps even in the electoral elision of race into ethnicity in the case of "Blacks."

This kind of late twentieth-century political identification, in which the census and its young cousin the random-sample survey replace the neighbourhood and the home town, is not only of growing political importance, but enables us to see more clearly that fragile but sharp line between ethnicity and nationalism. Ethnic politics are played out on the basis of people's prior *national* entitlement as voters, and are justified on the basis of proportionality within the framing of the existing census. When, or better if, a *soi-disant* ethnic group remagines itself as a nation (as, for example, has been happening with the Québecois), and seeks to acquire an independent state, then it

---

25. See J.J. Woltjer, *Recent Verleden* (Amsterdam: Balans, 1992), p. 414.

26. See the excellent chapters "The 1980 Census in Historical Perspective," by Margo A. Conk, and "Politics and the Measurement of Ethnicity," by William Petersen, in Alonso and Starr, eds., *The Politics of Numbers*. Petersen's mordant pages on "The Creation of the 'Hispanics,'" is particularly telling.

discards this census in the name of a new one of its own figuring. It is exactly at the moment of independence, however, that the logic of proportionality re-emerges, within a new "n."

The second consequence is reinforcement for identitarian politics. I noted earlier the essentialist implications of the bounded, numbered series that cen-suses best exemplify. But I suspect that the series operates in the same direction at another level. Consider it this way. Identity is logically a function of duality: it exists at the moment when "b" encounters "=b." This is a dry, algebraic way to gloss Woyle Soyinka's biting dismissal of Léopold Sénghor's series *négritude*: the Tiger has no need of Tigritude. In other words, Tigritude appears necessary only at the point where two uncertain beasts mirror them-selves in each other's exiled eyes.

The word *exile* is not employed here idly. We are all only too aware of how incessantly people speak, not merely of "seeking" "roots," but of "exploring," "finding," and, alas, "coming close to losing" their "identities." But these searches, which rhetorically move inward towards the site that once housed the soul, in fact proceed outward towards real and imagined censuses, where, thanks to capitalism, state machineries, and mathematics, integral bodies become identical, and thus serially aggregable as phantom communities.

In our time, moreover, such communities are no longer confined to the interiors of already-existing nation-states. As I have argued at greater length elsewhere, the revolutions in communications and transportation of the post-World War II era have combined with postindustrial world capitalism to produce cross-national migrations on an historically unprecedented scale.[27]

The same forces have worked to create "diasporic" collective subjectivities which are imagined, census-fashion, as bounded series. Few texts give one a more emblematic view of this transformation than the well-meaning *Penguin Atlas of Diasporas*.[28] Opening with more than seventy pages devoted to a Jewish diaspora that begins in the eighth century before Christ, it proceeds through Armenians, Gypsies, Blacks, Chinese, Indians, Irish, Greeks, Lebanese, and Palestinians to end with Vietnamese and Koreans. In each case, the remarkable thing is the authors' insistence on providing numerical totals and subtotals—so to speak Total world-Armenians and Total Armenians in France, in Georgia, in Australia, or in Argentina. No less instructively, these totals are calmly, if implausibly, rounded off: 42,000 "Indians" in Kenya in 1920, 40,000 "Jews" in Portugal in 1250. Is it necessary

---

27. See "Exodus," *Critical Inquiry*, 20 (Winter 1994), pp. 314–27.
28. Gérard Chaliand and Jean-Pierre Rageau, *The Penguin Atlas of Diasporas* (Harmondsworth: Viking, 1995). The French original, *Atlas des Diasporas*, was published in 1991 by Éditions Odile Jacob.

to underline that these countings were made by imperial state machineries for their own reasons and by their own peculiar logics, that it is quite uncertain how many of the 42,000 "Indians" in fact imagined themselves as such, and that there was every sort of ambiguity and arbitrariness involved in deciding who was a Jew in thirteenth-century Portugal? The truth is that an ersatz-historical atlas of this kind, far from depicting historical subjectivities, actually represents a certain contemporary vision of cosmopolitanism based on a quasi-planetary dispersion of bounded identities. Wherever the "Chinese" happen to end up—Jamaica, Hungary, or South Africa—they remain countable Chinese, and it matters very little if they also happen to be citizens of those nation-states. It would occasion no surprise if a book of this kind finds today a warm reception in circles whose members are attracted by the idea of finding themselves "in exile," entitled to belong to ancient bounded communities which nonetheless stretch impressively across the planet in the age of globalization.

Whether any of this represents a meaningful cosmopolitanism seems to me very doubtful, since it is at bottom simply an extension of a census-style, identitarian conception of ethnicity, and lacks any universal grounding. Nothing offers a greater contrast with the young Javanese girl who imagined herself a "new human being," not a member of a Javanese diaspora, and who enrolled herself, like Haji Misbach, as a firmly local member of the unbounded series of the world-in-motion.

2

Replica, Aura, and Late Nationalist Imaginings

"There is nothing in this world as invisible as a monument," wrote Robert Musil in his *Nachlass zu Lebzeiten*, elegantly Anglicized as *Posthumous Papers of a Living Author*.

> They are no doubt erected to be seen—indeed to attract attention. But at the same time they are impregnated with something that repels attention, causing the glance to roll right off, like water droplets off an oilcloth, without even pausing for a moment. You can walk down the same street for months, know every address, every show window, every policeman along the way, and you won't even miss a coin that someone dropped on the sidewalk; but you are very surprised when, one day, staring up at a pretty chambermaid on the first floor of a building, you notice a not-at-all tiny metal plaque on which, engraved in indelible letters, you read that from eighteen hundred and such and such to eighteen hundred and a little more the unforgettable So-and-so lived and created here. Many people have the same experience even with larger-than-life-sized statues . . . You never look at them, and do not generally have the slightest notion of whom they are supposed to represent, except that maybe you know if it's a man or a woman.

Musil continued sardonically as follows:

> If we mean well by monuments, we must inevitably come to the conclusion that they make demands on us that run contrary to our nature, and for the fulfilment of which very particular preparations are required . . . Monuments ought really to try a little harder, as we must all do nowadays . . . Why doesn't our bronze-cast hero at least resort to the gimmick, long since outdated elsewhere, of tapping with his finger on a pane of glass? Why don't the figures in a marble group turn, as those better-made figures in show windows do, or at least blink their eyes open and shut? The very minimum we ought to ask of monuments, to make them attract

attention, would be tried and true logos, like "Goethe's Faust is the Best!" or "The dramatic ideas of the famous poet X are the cheapest!" Unfortunately our sculptors won't have any of this. They do not, it seems, comprehend our age of noise and movement.[1]

The Living Author was probably right in general, but his slyly nonchalant remarks strike one as peculiarly true of the commemorational difficulties of late official nationalism—all those nationalisms which, by the late twentieth century, have got married to states.[2] In this essay, an attempt is made to explore the underlying nature of these particular national difficulties, and the imaginative impasse of this kind of nationalism, by reflecting on the distinctive fates of certain public memorials to the national dead. Most of the material in it refers to the United States and to its half-forgotten former colony, the Philippines, both because the imaginings of the latter have been profoundly shaped by the former, and because, at the same time, the latter offers instructive examples of how late official nationalism is politically resisted. Europe, which invented official nationalism, necessarily shows its face here and there.

The Lincoln Memorial in Washington, DC was unveiled in 1922, well into the age of radio, the Model-T, and the airplane, but Railsplitter does not, as Musil sardonically proposes, rotate slowly on his pedestal; his eyes do not open and shut, his toes do not tap, and there is no simple logo, such as "Lincoln, Number One President," emblazoned below him. On the other hand, the bureaucrat in charge of the project carefully recorded that along with Railsplitter's image—

125 Mazda electric lamps, equipped with X-ray reflectors, [have been] placed in the attic space . . . In addition, there are 24 powerful electric floodlights placed about 20 inches above 12 glass panels, each about 30 by 47 inches in size, in the ceiling of the central Memorial Hall, that are intended to reverse the unnatural shadows cast upon the statue by the daylight entering through the entrance portal.[3]

---

1. Translated by Peter Wortsman (Hygiene, Col.: Eridanos Press, 1987), pp. 61–3.
2. The term "official nationalism" was coined by Hugh Seton-Watson in his splendid *Nations and States: An Enquiry into the Origins of Nations and the Politics of Nationalism* (Boulder, Col.: Westview, 1977). I adapted and enlarged upon it in my *Imagined Communities: Reflections on the Origin and Spread of Nationalism* (London: Verso, 1983; revised, enlarged edn., 1991), esp. chapter 6. In its nineteenth-century origins, this was the Machiavellian "policy nationalism," by which dynastic states and archaic nobilities attempted to exploit, for their own survival, elements of the existing models ("creole-republican" and "ethnolinguistic") of popular nationalism. The huge proliferation of nation-states that began after 1918 has encouraged almost everywhere the utilization by these states of the dynasts' policy instruments.
3. Edward F. Concklin, *The Lincoln Memorial* (Washington, DC: Government Printing Office, 1927), p. 45.

Furthermore, on the wall behind the statue's head, there *is* a logo, which reads: In this temple/as in the hearts of the people/for whom he saved the union/the memory of Abraham Lincoln/is enshrined forever."[4]

Something peculiarly late-nationalist is here at work. Railsplitter's image is placed within a "temple," mimicked by architect Henry Bacon from the religious edifices of a safely pagan Greece. Inside, a cunningly engineered mimicry of the penumbral interior of a medieval church is achieved by summoning the Mazda Corporation to ward off unnatural, indifferent sunlight. (If one envisaged history as a relay race, this would be the point where the nation seizes the baton from religion's exhausted hand.)

The logo operates by a parallel logic. We are first reassured that the edifice we have entered is *a* temple, and a "real" one, something we might not have guessed from a façade not too stylistically different from those of many banks, fraternity houses, insurance companies, and courts of law. In addition, this temple is part of the series "enshrinement sites" to which the "hearts of the people" also belong; or perhaps the "hearts of the people" actually are simply serial temples. What is enshrined is not the singular skeleton of Lincoln himself—as if he were a latterday saint—but something both ghostly and indefinitely replicable: his "memory." The enshrinement, moreover, is "forever"—a "forever" which is visibly coterminous with "the people," this nation, rather than pointing towards Judgment Day.

There is no doubt that the ingenious stagecraft sketched out above creates, especially after dark, a certain *son et lumière* presence—which, however, would disappear at once if the image were removed to Hearst Castle and the temple to Dartmouth College. At the same time, the Lincoln Memorial shares something interesting with the monuments of which Musil makes fun: the ever-present possibility of vanishing from attention. One understands this from its inability to give one directions. Kneel? Take off one's shoes? Circle it seven times widdershins? Sing? Pray? Beg for a blessing? Bow? Ask for advice? Offer something? Stare fixedly for twenty minutes? None of these seem especially plausible.[5] For almost everyone understands that the statue and its setting are replicas, and peculiar replicas at that, *because there is no original.*[6]

---

4. Ibid., p. 44.

5. This implausibility is amusingly shown in the section of *The Simpsons* episode entitled Mr. Lisa Goes to Washington where Bart Simpson's little sister Lisa seeks advice from the statue of Railsplitter. Her voice is drowned by a hubbub of adult visitor requests: "I can't get my little boy to brush properly," "Is this a good time to buy a house?" "What can I do to make this a better country?" "Would I look good with a moustache?" Railsplitter's immobile silence upsets no one. A brilliantly witty analysis of this *Simpsons* episode can be found in Lauren Berlant, "The Theory of Infantile Citizenship," *Public Culture*, vol. 5 (Spring 1993), pp. 1–16 (reprinted in Geoff Eley and Ronald Gregor Suny, eds., *Becoming National: A Reader* [New York and Oxford: Oxford University Press, 1996], pp. 495–508).

6. The ultimate model here is every country's national flag.

(This is probably why many people, who would like to feel reverential, decide that the right thing to do is to take photographs, of Lincoln alone, or of Lincoln with themselves, their families, friends, or lovers—between whatever hours the Memorial's authorities permit them so to do.)

But at the same time, the Lincoln Memorial's replica is immediately associated with the nearby replica of Thomas Jefferson. It is here that one starts to realize the singularity of late official nationalism's human images, which is that they can never, as such, be singular. Hardly has one noticed Mazzini, than one is jostled by Machiavelli, Cavour, Dante, and D'Annunzio, who stand in for each other, without hesitation, as national heroes, because the series itself requires this of them. Exactly the nonchalant substitutability of effigies one observes at Mount Rushmore. This means that heroic national monuments do not have auras, such as one senses in the *originality* of: *Las Meninas*—under any, even unnatural lighting[7]—the Wailing Wall, or Angkor Wat. In their presence, one is never surprised to find oneself forbidden to take photographs, and this taboo is usually gratifying: one knows one is in the presence of the sacred when it is beyond the reach of one's lens. For the moment, one has ceased to be a tourist and become a pilgrim. On the other hand, the fact that national hero monuments are auraless also means that they circulate extremely easily through different media—stamps, t-shirts, postcards, wallpapers, posters, videotapes, place mats, and so on—without anyone feeling profaned. Most exemplary, perhaps, is American money. It is not simply that five replicas of George Washington will get you a good cigar, and five Andrew Jacksons a middling one-night hotel room. But the descending rank order in prestige—Washington, Lincoln, Jefferson, Jackson—inverts the descending rank order of purchasing power (thus Washington is worth one-twentieth of Jackson, Lincoln half of Jefferson) and no one minds one bit, or even thinks about it.

One can understand this condition still more clearly if one considers what happens when aura unexpectedly makes its presence felt within the replicatory series. On December 30, 1896, the great novelist, poet, and moralist, José Rizal, was publicly executed in downtown Manila by a Spanish-officered, native-manned firing squad. On the first anniversary of his death, Emilio Aguinaldo's revolutionary government issued a proclamation urging patriots to commemorate his martyrdom in whatever way they thought suitable. The first "Rizal monument" went up while the revolution was still very much in progress. It was not, however, a statue of Rizal, but a Masonic-tinged

---

7. This aura is partly that of "great works of art" measured by the astronomical difference between their market prices and the prices of even the most skilful replicas. But *Las Meninas* has its own special glow. In the Prado, as I remember, it is the one painting with a penumbral room all to itself.

abstraction on which only the titles of his two electrifying novels were inscribed—as if to say, Read Them! Then Fight for Your Country's Liberty!

Quite soon after the revolutionary Philippine Republic had been crushed by American imperialism, statues began suddenly to proliferate across the pacified plazas of the territory, where previously they had been strictly confined to the interiors and façades of churches. Almost all were set up by local *hacendados* or other notables, who had their names inscribed on the pedestals, and a very high percentage were replicas of Rizal. Thus started Rizal's serialization, not only by his own mechanical reduplication, but also by his appearance alongside other statued, heroic dead. He began to be referred to by the new English-educated elite as the "First Filipino," soon after the Americans started census-counts of "Filipinos." Finally, the colonial regime permitted the erection of a Rizal monument, crowned by a statue of the martyr, on the reputed site of his execution, which eventually became the focal point of today's well-laid out Luneta Park. Since 1946, when America granted the Philippines its second independence, it has become customary for the cabinet to show up at this monument at the dawn hour of the martyr's death for a brief formal ceremony, while warships in Manila's harbour strangely, given the occasion, fire off a many-gunned salute. Something quite similar, if on a smaller scale, will take place some months later at the Manila monument to the Second Filipino, the revolutionary Andrés Bonifacio, who, alas, was executed at Aguinaldo's orders. So far, so typical.

But if one waits at Luneta till later in the morning, one will observe, streaming in from all sides, a wide array of pilgrims, many of them dressed in white, or in the colours of the original flag of the Revolution of 1896. They know exactly what to do: they chant, they sing, they pray, they kneel, they close their eyes in meditation, they march in rows, they hold hands, they weep, they ask for blessings, according to their respective protocols. People speak of them loosely as Rizalistas, meaning that some of them believe that Rizal was Christ Recrucified, or the Filipino Christ, and Luneta thus is Golgotha; others believe that he never died, but, on some sacred mountaintop, awaits the hour when he will return to Redeem his suffering people;[8] still others believe his powerful spirit is accessible by esoteric methods especially at certain holy sites and times—which include, *inter alia*, the Luneta monument and what the state calls Rizal Day. In a word, he is still here. Such people trust in mediums, rather than in the media. These pilgrims the government studiously ignores,[9] not only because it does not relish the idea that the First

---

8. See, e.g., Reynaldo Clemeña Ileto, *Pasyón and Revolution: Popular Movements in the Philippines, 1840—1910* (Manila: Ateneo de Manila Press, 1979), pp. 77 and 206–7.

9. The pilgrims come faithfully each Rizal Day, but no officials greet or speak to them, and no police are mobilized to drive them away.

Filipino might return in judgement, but primarily because its own protocol depends on Rizal's substitutability. But for the pilgrims themselves, Rizal is The One—irreplaceable, untradable, unserialized—and his magnetic aura arises exactly from his *Las Meninas* singularity.

If we now turn from replicas of the national dead to the official sites where their remains are variously interred, it is not hard to find parallels between the contrasting fates of Railsplitter and Rizal.

The United States seems to have pioneered the National Cemetery—but one should not be surprised that it did so almost a century after the War of Independence. In the immediate aftermath of the battle of Gettysburg, the Congress voted funds to create a special burial place for the recent fallen— soldiers of the Union, soldiers of the Confederacy, and soldiers no one recognized—on the battlefield itself. The body of each dead voter, or voter-to-be, was given its own separate grave and marker.[10] But Gettysburg had a hasty and experimental character, and the dead of no other of the great bloody battles of the Civil War were handled in this political manner. It was, as we know, during, and immediately after, World War I that the prototype went, so to speak, into general production. As might be expected, the most successful manufacturer was the most experienced industrial capitalist state, that Great Britain which still, but only just, incorporated Ireland.

As Thomas Laqueur so well describes it, in March 1915, on the eve of Rupert Brooke's death in Skyros, an official Graves Registration Commission for the fallen and future fallen was created, followed by negotiations with Paris for the development of permanent cemeteries for Britons in France.[11] By March 1916, the "corners" of "some [200] foreign fields" has been settled on by London, with plans for an additional 300 to 3,000 cemeteries depending on the extent of future fighting. Thus began a process that only ended in 1938, by which time 1,850 such graveyards had been organized, most in France and Belgium. From Gettysburg, the British government took over the idea that the dead should have their own individual and marked graves, but tidily grouped together, as far as possible, around the battlesites where they

---

10. By the 1860s, American governments had been, for more than a generation, elected by near-universal white male adult suffrage, and American armies were, in time of war, recruited by voter–citizen compulsory conscription. Thus politicians were intensely aware that the dead had been voters, or, if still teenagers, were provisionally destined to become voters; and that their male survivors were continuing to vote. The contrast with the situation during the War for (National) Independence scarcely needs underlining. Does this not suggest why the dead at Valley Forge were left unmarked?

11. The following section borrows heavily from Thomas W. Laqueur, "Memory and Naming in the Great War," in John R. Gillis, ed., *Commemorations: The Politics of National Identity* (Princeton, NJ: Princeton University Press, 1994), pp. 150–67.

had died. By 1930, some 557,520 soldiers of the Empire, four-fifths of them from the UK, had been identified and buried in separate, named graves. A further 180,861 unidentified bodies were also put in separate graves. For the enumerated 336,912 whose bodies had vanished, blown to pieces or ground into the deep mud, all that could be done was to have their names recorded on stelae set up as near as possible to the places where they were last remembered alive. More than a million in all.

The real British innovation lay in keeping these cemeteries going. How this was managed is exceptionally instructive. The crucial step was nationalization—in every sense of the word. In the first place, the state took monopoly control of all bodies, all monuments, and all cemeteries. Families of the fallen were legally prohibited from moving the remains of their loved ones back home across the Channel. In other words—and this would have startled Rupert Brooke—it was the British government that made sure that so many corners of foreign fields would "remain forever England." In the second place, it did everything in its power to make, and keep, the dead national (perhaps in the spirit of George von Sachsen-Coburg-Gotha [aka George V], who, on July 17, 1917, issued a royal proclamation that he, along with all other male descendants of his grandmother Victoria, provided they were British subjects, would adopt the national surname "Windsor"). The most important means to achieve this goal was to insist, often against strong domestic opposition, that the graves and their markers be as uniform as possible, and that they be laid out in minutely regulated spatial grids. There was to be nothing that visibly marked off middle-class from working men, officers from NCOs and privates, English from Scots, Welsh, and Irish. Families were permitted to propose no more than a 66-character inscription of any sort, which had to meet with the Graves Commission's approval,[12] and for which a per-letter fee was exacted. Thus, seen from even a short distance, no grave-marker would stand out from the rest. The visitor would perhaps get the impression that, in each vast cemetery, the dead were, so to speak, still at attention, even if horizontally. She would also be encouraged to start tallying those substitutable symbolic integers which, so often placed over the remains of fractioned soldiers, show us how central to late official nationalism are body counts, and not merely for the census, or on election days.

---

12. There were two impulses here at work, ruling-class arrogance and official nationalism. Wrote the permanent secretary of the Ministry of Works, "We must make every effort to make these cemeteries as attractive as possible, and prevent them from becoming eyesores on the countryside of France through the hideous effigies relatives often have a tendency to erect" (ibid., p. 155). But the compulsory absence of vulgarian "relatives" also ensured that the bodies remained uniformly "national property."

Paris and Washington were signally less successful than London, and it is instructive to see why. In France, the state did not have the Channel to help maintain its monopoly claims. "Relatives" quickly took to bodysnatching, which became bolder as time passed. The powerful Catholic Church made plain its dislike of cemeteries which, so visibly separated from traditional places of religious worship, seemed tainted by the miasma of Third Republic anticlericalism. It proved impossible not to differentiate the dead by faith— a cross for Christians (whether Protestant or Catholic), a Star of David for Jews, and a mosque-ish dome for Muslims (many from that Algeria which had already been made a part of metropolitan France). In the case of the United States, a historically weak federal state, poised over a strong civil society, had no chance of emulating Whitehall's official-nationalist nationalizations. Despite the energetic efforts of some influential politicians to keep the American dead in "American" cemeteries on French, Belgian, and English soil, where they could stand in for the recent and perhaps future military glory of the United States in Europe, nothing systematic was achieved.[13] Only 30 per cent of the dead failed to make the trans-Atlantic journey home, and it was the relatives of the other 70 per cent, not the state, who decided whether they would be buried privately or in state or national cemeteries. Doubtless among the reasons for this democratic victory against Leviathan was the fact that the Republic's most recent wars had taken place in Cuba and the Philippines, barbarous climes in which no American could conceivably wish to be interred. A tradition was in place which would later ensure the long journey home of so many Americans who died at war in Korea and Vietnam. More curiously, in due course the Congress felt obliged to finance the round-trip tickets and other expenses of all mothers (not wives) who wished to visit their Europe-interred sons. Yet there was a characteristic American difference. White mothers travelled cabin-class on luxury ocean liners, and stayed at first-class hotels; black mothers had to be content with commercial steamers, and lodging in quarters which were never five-star.

If such was the commemorative fate of the obscure masses of the nation's war dead, how did official nationalism attempt to deal with the exemplary famous, most of whom died in their beds? France offers a peculiarly instructive example.

In 1764, at the orders of Louis Quinze, the architect Soufflot started the construction of a church dedicated to the patron saint of Paris, Sainte Geneviève, but designed in a "classical" style borrowed from St. Paul's Cathedral in London. Perhaps this style was what ensured that during the

---

13. Much of this paragraph is drawn from G. Kurt Piehler, "The War Dead and the Gold Star: American Commemoration of the First World War," in Gillis, ed., *Commemorations*, pp. 168–85.

Revolution it could be recommissioned as the Panthéon for the reinterment of such national divinities as Voltaire and Rousseau.[14] The change of ownership from dynast to nation-state was signalled by this blaring advertisement added to its façade: *Aux Grands Hommes La Patrie Reconnaissante.* It reverted briefly to religious status between 1828 and 1830, and then again between 1851 and 1870 under Napoléon's mountebank great-nephew. Not till the 1880s did La Patrie Reconnaissante win a stable legal victory over Sainte Geneviève. But aura has always eluded the Panthéon, even though it is a reliable tourist attraction. If one wonders why, part of the explanation should come from reflecting on the comparison with the Mount Rushmore *National* Park and on the logic of substitutability in the *grands hommes* national series. Neither Washington, Jefferson, T. Roosevelt, nor Lincoln are buried at Mount Rushmore, but it would make no difference if they were. The visitor stands at the railing by the edge of a huge parking lot, gazes up at the representations of "our greatest presidents," whose stature is guaranteed by each other's presence, and then drives off east or west. It is the same in the Panthéon: the visitor looks at the names of "great Frenchmen," in a bounded series where Voltaire and Rousseau stand in for one another, before moving on.[15] The bodies are actually there, prisoners of official nationalism, but this is of no moment in a shrine of this type, because the visiting eyes are fixed everywhere but on the ground.

As is so often the case, "unsuccessful" tombs are especially revealing of the mechanisms behind their rivals' successes. Early in the 1910s, in Norte, a brand-new municipal cemetery planned by an American urban designer, a small pantheon was constructed for the interment of Filipino national heroes, and indeed the remains of a certain number of such accredited heroes were lodged there in the American era. Today, hardly anyone in the Philippines is aware of this dilapidated pantheon's existence. From the outside it is still recognizable as such, but the interior has become an apartment for the caretaker and his family, and the niches along the walls are now mainly filled with toys, cassette

---

14. For a good history of the Panthéon, see Valérie-Noëlle Jouffre, *Le Panthéon* (Paris: Éditions Ouest-France, 1994). The change took place in April 1791, following Mirabeau's death. The Constituent Assembly voted to place his remains in a site worthy of his heroic contributions to the Revolution. (Alas, he was summarily "depantheonized" in November 1793 when compromising documents about his political past were discovered.) Voltaire arrived in July 1791 and Rousseau two years later. Marat's remains lasted only from September 1794 to February 1795, when they shared Mirabeau's fate.

15. Jouffre provides a list of seventy-one personages who have a tomb or urn in the Panthéon. Given the building's chequered history, it is not surprising that most of these flourished in the revolutionary and Napoleonic eras, and are today quite obscure. The revival of the Panthéon as a grand patriotic site came only with the Third Republic, especially by the interment of Victor Hugo in 1885. Later there followed, among others, Émile Zola, Jean Jaurès, Jean Moulin, and, most recently, Jean Monnet.

tapes, canned goods, and kitchenware. What has happened is that the Filipino Voltaire and Rousseau have managed to escape, summoning devoted, often familial, bodysnatchers, to convey them to home-town shrines where they may be attended to in a spirit of ancestral reverence, and perhaps, vanished from official-national view, acquire the magic aura of the singular. Meantime, Norte leads a magnificent life of its own, culminating each year on La Víspera de Todos los Santos, All Saints' Eve, when families in their thousands pour in, each to its own graves, and spend a cheerful day with the visiting dead, flying kites, playing cards or mahjongg, smoking cigarettes or marijuana, drinking, praying, gambling, making offerings, and smacking children.

There is something exhilarating here that one rarely sees in national celebrations, maybe because the structure of the ceremonial is not serial, but entirely cellular. Each family may be doing more or less the same thing, but the *abuelos* of each are absolutely unsubstitutable, and are of no interest to anyone else. Most of the Philippines' presidents are at rest here, in pompous tombs along the cemetery's main avenue, but no one pays attention to them, even in the spirit of Mount Rushmore; and only their separate descendants come to attend them.

Somewhere between the replica-effigy and the dead lie those two strange creations of official nationalism, the Tomb of the Unknown Soldier and the Cenotaph. But as will become evident below, their initial huge success was full of contradictions, and depended on a certain aura of singularity, which was doomed by their creators' underlying project.

The British government, which seems to have pioneered these memorials in the immediate aftermath of World War I, was seriously worried, from the start, about the possibility that the Unknown Soldier might escape or be body-snatched, in the Norte sense, if his identity could be tracked down. Curzon, for example, insisted vehemently that the Unknown Soldier "remain unknown."[16] The search for the right remains was thus limited to those who had been killed in the first months of the war, so that, maximally decayed, they would be as much like dust and as little like bodies as possible. Four such remains were picked out by military officials, and one was chosen, by lot, to be the sole exception to the total ban on dead subjects of His Majesty George V coming home. In fact, what was transported across the Channel by a Navy destroyer, was sixteen barrels containing fifty bags of French soil. Yet the burial in Westminster Abbey drew an astonishing outpouring of attachment. Over a million and a quarter people filed slowly past the open grave in the days after November 11, 1920. The Cenotaph unveiled by the monarch on the same day had a comparable effect. Thousands of mourners placed wreaths around it.

---

16. See Laqueur, "Memory and Naming," p. 163.

For the ruling class's view of these events, we can do no better than turn to the London *Times*, which commented:

> Never before has there been such a proclamation, gladly made, that we are all equal, all members of one body, or rather one soul . . . All of us were members of one orchestra . . . there was one forgetfulness of self in that quiet ritual, one desire that prophecy be fulfilled . . . that we may, indeed, all become members of one body politic and of one immortal soul.[17]

The tell-tale phrase "gladly made," inserted between "a proclamation" and "that we are all equal," shows us that it is a hypocritical official nationalism pattering. But the interesting question is why these novel ceremonies actually then "worked" for ordinary people. The better explanations probably arise at two different levels. One is certainly the unplanned consequence of the state's nationalization of the fallen, and their forcible sequestration outside Great Britain. None of the millions of bereaved were permitted to bury their dead in the cellular manner of Norte. In their complementary ways, the emptiness of the Cenotaph and the solitary plenitude of the grave of the Unknown Soldier made possible the insertion of private memory and grief. The beauty of the slow file-past was that each mourner had the momentary opportunity to make that insertion, and yet to be aware of those before and behind her making insertions of their own, to which, of course she could not be privy. All Hallow's Eve? The other answer is simply the novelty of the rituals themselves. People did not attend them with the thought that they would be repeated annually into the indefinite future, and in hundreds of different places—in other words the rites were still outside the grip of seriality and the logic of the originless replica. They had, in 1920, the aura of the singular.[18] But such successes, at the contingent juncture of late official nationalism and private grief, were always running on a timer. The logical of serialization and replication quickly came into play. Arlington now has four Unknown US Soldiers, one each for World War I, World War II, the Korean War, and the Vietnam War, as well as an Unknown Confederate. Memorial Day oscillates between Friday and Monday to ensure—in the unending series of calendar years—a leisurely late-spring holiday.

Here, at the moment when the real dead are simultaneously forgotten, replicated, sequestered, serialized, and unknowned, one returns to the paradoxical question of the origins of what one can only call originlessness. In the last

---

17. *Times Armistice Day Supplement I*, Nov. 20, 1920, p. 1, as cited in ibid., p. 158.

18. So, in our time, has the black-granite, name-scarred "Vietnam Wall" in Washington, DC, before which people still cellularly weep.

chapter of *Imagined Communities*, I suggested that the ruptures of the later eighteenth century—themselves the vectoral conjuncture of long-standing transformations—generated, quite suddenly, a new consciousness. This consciousness, embedded in homogeneous, empty time, created amnesias and estrangements exactly parallel to the forgetting of childhood brought on by puberty. An abyss had opened up which required, and also enabled, Jules Michelet to make the unprecedented claim to speak *for* generation after generation of dead "French" men and women who did not know themselves to be such. At just this juncture emerged the narrative of the nation, with its strange antigenealogical teleology, moving "up time . . . [towards] wherever the lamp of archaeology casts its fitful gleam."[19]

In Michelet's impassioned, pioneering, and personal claim to "rescue" the dumb dead, there was as yet no real awareness of himself as transient Originator. But once he was there for all to read, a model was in place for anyone to pirate. Ironically enough, no people, no institutions were better positioned for such piracy than those which hoped to claim legitimacy by descent from the past—nobilities, postcolonial elites, and so forth. The putative descendants of the Norman-French speaking barons who compelled John to sign the Latin Magna Carta in this way emerge, via Michelet's reversal of teleologies, as the rightful bearers of English nationalism's banners.

---

19. This reverse teleology is what transformed the Great War into World War I, and made the state of Israel the ancestor of the Warsaw uprising. Hence there is no Originator of the nation, or rather the Originator is a ceaselessly changing, here-and-now, "Us."

Long-Distance Nationalism

In a celebrated essay written in the 1860s, the eminent, liberal–Catholic, Neapolitan–English, politician–historian Lord Acton warned presciently that three powerful and subversive ideas were threatening "presently existing civilisation." These three ideas were egalitarianism, aimed at the principle of aristocracy; communism (he was thinking of Baboeuf rather than Marx), aimed at the principle of property; and nationalism, or nationality, aimed at the principle of legitimacy. Of the third he wrote that it was "the most recent in its appearance, the most attractive at the present time, and the richest in promise of future power."[1] If we look at the world around us, 130 years later, it looks very much as if Acton was right. Aristocracy has been eliminated as a serious political idea, and adult suffrage has become almost everywhere a present fact or an ineluctable, imminent future.[2] Communism in all its forms seems headed for the historical scrap-heap. But legitimacy has also almost everywhere been overthrown, such that the current membership of the United Nations is four times that of the originary League of Nations of seven decades ago. One after another the great polyglot empires constructed over hundreds of years have disintegrated—those vast realms once ruled from London, Istanbul, Moscow, Madrid, Lisbon, The Hague, Vienna, Paris, even Addis Ababa. Only the residues of the Celestial Empire more or less stand, and who will bet any large sum that one day Tibet and Taiwan, perhaps Inner

---

1. John Dahlberg-Acton, *Essays in the Liberal Interpretation of History* (Chicago and London: University of Chicago Press, 1967), chapter v, p. 134.

2. This does not mean that fraudulent elections are not widespread; but such frauds would not be necessary if elections had not become signs of modernity and civilization, even in societies such as Islamic Iran, where much ado is made of rejecting "western" political values. Even Saudi Arabia and Kuwait are headed down the electoral road.

Mongolia and Sinkiang, will not find a seat at the UN? It is also quite easy to envisage an independent East Timor, Puerto Rico, Kurdistan, or Kosovo up ahead.

Yet at the same time as this enormous process of disintegration, which is also a process of liberation, the world has become ever more tightly integrated into a single capitalist economy—one in which, in our epoch, billions of dollars can be sped almost instantaneously around the globe at the pressing of a computer key. How is this paradoxical double movement of integration and disintegration to be grasped? Are these forces in contradiction or merely obverse faces of a single historical process? Furthermore, is capitalism, in its eternal restlessness, producing new forms of nationalism?

A good starting point for exploring these questions is a pair of further passages in Acton's essay. The first is actually an excerpt from a sermon of the great seventeenth-century clerical orator Jacques Bénigne Bossuet, which our historian mentions with approbation:

> Ainsi la société humaine demande qu'on aime la terre où l'on habite ensemble; on la regarde comme une mère et une nourrice commune . . . Les hommes en effet se sentent liés par quelque chose de fort, lorsqu'ils songent, que la même terre qui les a portés et nourris étant vivants, les recevra dans son sein quand ils seront morts.

The second is Acton's own aphorism that "exile is the nursery of nationality."[3]

Acton was attempting to draw a contrast between two types of political loyalty, one fully compatible with legitimacy, the other profoundly inimical to it. For Bossuet did not speak of France (let alone of the French), but rather of a general social condition in which human beings feel themselves powerfully connected together by whatever mother-terrain has nourished them, and in whose bosom—so they dream—they will attain their final rest. It seemed to him absolutely normal that people would dream of dying exactly where they were born and raised. This immobility, contained at the limit by the involuntary, fatal moments of birth and death, aligned itself with the social axioms of feudal society: that it was built as a God-given, unchangeable hierarchy. Combined with a profound attachment to local soil, this made possible the sedate and stately agglomeration of hundreds of such communities into the huge, ramshackle imperia of legitimacy, and where necessary, their detachment to other imperia through dynastic marriages, diplomacy,

---

3. Acton, *Essays,* pp. 154 and 146. The Bossuet quotation Acton uses is given here in the original French. "Politique tirée de l'Écriture Sainte," in *Oeuvres de Bossuet* (Paris: Firmin Didot Frères, 1870), vol. 1, p. 304.

and war.[4] Bossuet's focus was thus on *Heimat*, or perhaps better *patria*, the wonderful Iberian word that can gently stretch from "home-village," through "home-town" and "home-region," on to "home-country."

By contrast, Acton believed, "nationality" arose from exile, when men could no longer easily dream of returning to the nourishing bosom that had given them birth. It is quite likely that what the liberal historian had mainly in mind were the great nationalist leaders of his own era—Mazzini, Garibaldi, Kossuth, and so on—many of whom, for obvious political reasons, lived for long periods outside their *Heimat* and sometimes died there. But Acton's exile had really begun much earlier. Bossuet was already an anachronism, for he was born in 1627, seven years after the Puritan Pilgrim Fathers had landed at Plymouth Rock, and over a century after the Catholic Hernán Cortés had stormed the fabled capital of Moctezuma. From the later sixteenth century on, millions of at least nominally free Europeans, and millions more enslaved Africans, went "into exile," as it were, across the Atlantic. These migrations, which had no historical precedent in their scale and distance, made necessary the inventions in Lisbon, Madrid, and London of the strange neologisms *crioulo, criollo,* and "the colonial," to denote a new type of displaced person and culture. Nothing offers a more vivid picture of this emerging consciousness of displacement than the naive recollections of Mary Rowlandson, a newly married nineteen-year-old Massachusetts woman, who in February 1675 was briefly abducted by a band of local Algonquin and Narragansett warriors. She pitifully wrote:

> I saw a place where English Cattle had been: that was a comfort to me, such as it was: quickly after that we came to an English Path, which so took with me, that I thought I could have freely lyen down and dyed. That day, a little after noon, we came to Squaukheag, where the Indians quickly spread themselves over the deserted English Fields.[5]

One observes the strange, thoroughly creole crosscurrents in her words. On the one hand, she feels no need to explain to her readers where Squaukheag is located, let alone how to pronounce this strikingly un-European toponym. Her familiarity is not surprising, Squaukheag is, so to speak, that place down

---

4. Note the famous passage in *King Richard II*, Act 2, Scene 1, which is so often quoted to claim an early nationalism for Shakespeare: "This royal seat of Kings, this sceptred isle / This earth of majesty, this seat of Mars / This other-Eden, demi-paradise . . . This blessed plot, this earth, this realm, this England." Yet, aside from Mars and some kings, this demi-paradise has no visible inhabitants, certainly not a jumble of Scots, Welsh, English, and Cornish, many of whom could not have understood each other's speech.

5. Mary Rowlandson, "A Narrative of the Captivity and Restauration of Mrs. Mary Rowlandson, 1682," in Charles H. Lincoln, ed., *Narratives of the Indian Wars, 1675–99* (New York: Barnes & Noble, 1952), p. 132. Squaukheag is today Squakeag, near Bear's Plain, Northfield, Massachusetts.

the road, since she had been born and spent all her young life in the no less un-European Massachusetts. On the other hand, she sees before her "English Cattle," an "English Path," and "deserted English Fields," though she has never been within three thousand miles of England. These are not pluckings from the Cotswolds or the Downs—real places, as it were—but acts of imagination that would never have occurred to a young minister's wife in seventeenth-century Gloucestershire or Surrey. They are, in a way, getting ready to be "English" exactly because they are in Massachusetts, not in England, and are so because they bear for Mary the traces of her "English" people's agricultural labours. But we can also guess that up till the point of her abduction she had thought matter-of-factly about cattle as cattle and fields as fields. Her "nationalizing" moment comes when, in the power of the Algonquins and Narragansetts, she is torn out of the quotidian and—right in the very midst of her native Massachusetts—finds herself in fearful exile. She struggles along a path that becomes English at the exact juncture where she is sure she may not lie down and die upon it. When she is finally ransomed and returns to her community of origin, her "nationalist" frisson vanishes. For she has managed, more or less, to come home. But this home is Lancaster; it is not yet America.[6] The paradox here is that we today can without much trouble read Mary Rowlandson *as* American precisely because, in captivity, she saw English fields before her.

On the other side of the Atlantic, Mary Rowlandson's narrative was published within a year of the Massachusetts first edition and proved very popular, accumulating thirty editions over the eighteenth century.[7] A rapidly growing reading public in the recently united kingdom—Mary was captured two decades before Scotland—was becoming aware of anomalous English-writing women who had never been to England but who could be dragged through English fields by "savages." What were they? Were they really English? The photographic negative of "the colonial," the non-English Englishwoman, was coming into view.

Because the Spanish conquests in the Caribbean and southern Americas had begun a century before permanent English settlements in the north, non-Spanish Spaniards began to loom up very early. Already in 1612, the *madrileño* Dominican theologian Juan de la Puente was writing that "the heavens of America induce inconstancy, lasciviousness and lies: vices

---

6. It is striking that even a hundred years later, the Proclamation of Independence did not speak in the name of "Americans," and, after the splendid, much quoted opening paragraphs, ended with a whinging list of grievances inflicted by George III on his trans-Atlantic "English subjects."

7. See Nancy Armstrong and Leonard Tennenhouse, *The Imaginary Puritan: Literature, Intellectual Labor, and the Origins of Personal Life* (Berkeley: University of California Press, 1992), p. 204 and the references there cited.

characteristic of the Indians and which the constellations make characteristic of the Spaniards who are born and bred there."[8] The creole was being invented figuratively, later to be realized culturally and politically.[9] We can see here—especially if we recall the century-long rage at de la Puente made possible by the quiet two-way hiss of print across the Atlantic—the real historical origins of the "native," a persona that persists under sometimes other names well into our own times, in Europe as much as anywhere else.

For the native is, like colonial and creole, a white-on-black negative. The nativeness of natives is always unmoored, its real significance hybrid and oxymoronic. It appears when Moors, heathens, Mohammedans, savages, Hindoos, and so forth are becoming obsolete, that is, not only when, in the proximity of real print-encounters, substantial numbers of Vietnamese read, write, and perhaps speak French but also when Czechs do the same with German and Jews with Hungarian. Nationalism's purities (and thus also cleansings) are set to emerge from exactly this hybridity.

What set all these engines in motion? To put it a bit differently, what made Mary Rowlandson's—and in due course London's—unstable Englishness possible? The simple answer is capitalism, the institutions of which enabled the transportation, from the mid-sixteenth century on, of millions of free, indentured, and enslaved bodies across thousands of miles of water. But the materialities of this transportation—ships, firearms, and navigational equipment—were guided by the mathematically inspired Mercatorian map and the vast, accumulating knowledge stored and disseminated in print. It was also through print moving back and forth across the ocean that the unstable, imagined worlds of Englishnesses and Spanishnesses were created.

The essential nexus of long-distance transportation and print-capitalist communications prepared the grounds on which, by the end of the eighteenth century, the first nationalist movements flowered. It is striking that this flowering took place first in North America and later in the Catholic, Iberian colonies to the south, the economies of which were all *pre*-industrial. Nothing underlines this process better than the fact that in the second half of the eighteenth century there were more presses in colonial North America than in the metropole. So it was that by 1765, in the words of Michael Warner, "Print had come to be seen as indispensable to political life, and could appear to such men as Adams to be the primary agent of world emancipation. What makes this transformation of the press particularly remarkable is that, unlike

8. Quoted in D.A. Brading, *The First America: The Spanish Monarchy, Creole Patriots, and the Liberal State, 1492–1867* (Cambridge: Cambridge University Press, 1991), p. 200.

9. Brading also notes that already in the sixteenth century some *criollo* intellectuals were starting to seek ancestors among Incan royalty as well as among the conquistadors. Ibid., chapter 14.

the press explosion of the nineteenth century, it involved virtually no techno-logical improvements in the trade."[10]

Meanwhile, across the Atlantic, and subsequently all over the world, a newly industrial capitalism was starting to create more local forms of exile. In his bizarre 1847 novel, *Tancred, or The New Crusade,* Benjamin Disraeli observed that "London is a modern Babylon."[11] In this oxymoron, the echoes of a captivity narrative are as loud as those of a proverbial trope for luxury and corruption. It sprang quite logically from the celebrated subtitle of *Sybil, or The Two Nations,* which Disraeli had published two years earlier. Deepening industrial capitalism had by then created within a single, very small territorial state—smaller, if we exclude Ireland, than Pennsylvania and New York combined—"two nations," that, however, in no way corresponded to any putative ethnic or religious communities. When Friedrich Engels arrived in Manchester in 1842 and began his studies of the condition of the working class, George Stephenson had preceded him. The world's textile cap-ital already had a railway station. The locomotive had begun its world-historical mission of transporting millions of rural villagers into urban slums, a mission scarcely less epochal than that which the transatlantic sail-ing ship had performed over the preceding three centuries.[12] Only a minority

---

10. Michael Warner, *The Letters of the Republic: Publication and the Public Sphere in Eighteenth-Century America* (Cambridge, Mass.: Harvard University Press, 1990), p. 32. This evi-dence strongly suggests the untenability of Ernest Gellner's argument that industrialism was the historical source of nationalism's emergence. (See his *Nations and Nationalism* [Ithaca, NY: Cornell University Press, 1983], *passim.*) One could add that most of the zones where early nineteenth-century European nationalisms were most visible—say, Ireland, Greece, Poland, and Bohemia—were almost entirely innocent of industrial progress.

11. Benjamin Disraeli, *Tancred, or The New Crusade* (1847; London: Longmans, Green & Co., 1882), p. 378. Regarding his England and his Europe as mortally threatened by Enlightenment rationalism, bourgeois commercialism, and the heritage of the French Revolution, the young Lord Montacute sets off in his yacht for the Holy Land, seeking spiritual revival in "the only por-tion of the world which the Creator of that world has deigned to visit" (p. 421). This quest leads him into proto-T.E. Lawrence political adventures in Palestine and Lebanon, in which he is guided by wise, courageous Hebrews and from which he has to be rescued by Mum and Dad, the Duchess and Duke of Bellamont. What is especially striking about the novel is the manner in which the Jewish Disraeli, Anglicized at his father's orders by baptism into the Church of England at the age of thirteen, discovers his "ethnicity" in Babylonian exile. Montacute, immensely rich, aristocratic, un-English, but, as it were, spiritually Jewish—Disraeli repeatedly insists that Christ and the Apostles were all Jews—is a hilariously snobbish self-projection of the future Conservative prime minister of the United Kingdom.

12. How quickly this profane mission was understood is entertainingly shown by the con-versation in *Tancred* (p. 162) in which the hero suggests to Lady Bertie and Bellair that she and her husband join him on a pilgrimage to Jerusalem:

"That can never be," said Lady Bertie; "Augustus will never hear of it; he never could be absent more than six weeks from London, he misses his clubs so. If Jerusalem were only a place one could get at, something might be done; if there were a railroad to it for example."

"A railroad!" exclaimed Tancred, with a look of horror. "A railroad to Jerusalem!"

"No, I suppose there can never be one," continued Lady Bertie in a musing tone. "There is no traffic."

would return to end their days in those narrow cells where the rude fore-fathers of the hamlet lay. How the novel experience of industrial life radically transformed these people's lives and how this transformation made them, as it were, available for nationalism is splendidly described by Gellner, but his description should be read under the sign of exile. It was beginning to become possible to see "English fields" in England—from the window of a railway carriage. Meanwhile, exile of another sort was emerging from the very wealth that industrial capitalism was producing for European states. For this wealth was making possible the spread of a centralized, standardized, steeply hier-archical system of public education. Eric Hobsbawm reminds us that at the time of *Tancred*'s publication, on the eve of the upheavals of 1848, there were only 48,000 or so university students in all of Europe, a number substantially lower than the current enrolment at Ohio State University.[13] But in the second half of the century, ministries of education sprang up like mushrooms every-where—Sweden in 1852, England in 1870, and France in 1882—and children began to be compelled to migrate to schools.[14]

When the elderly Filipino Pedro Calosa was interviewed in the mid-1960s and asked to compare the conditions of that time with those of the uprising of 1931 that he had led against American colonialism, he observed with nos-talgic satisfaction that "there were no teenagers" then.[15] For this new human type—nomad between childhood and working adulthood—was then only beginning to emerge from the imperialists' novel apparatus for mass educa-tion. More generally, however, the teenager was, from the second half of the nineteenth century, the site on which the state imposed its standardized ver-nacular. Whether this vernacular was a socially valorized dialect of a language widely understood among the state's subjects (say, the King's English), or a vernacular determined from among a multiplicity of vernacu-lars (say, German in Austria-Hungary), the effect was typically to restratify and rationalize the social and political hierarchy of vernaculars and dialects; all the more so in that the new education was increasingly linked to employ-ment possibilities and opportunities for social mobility. Small wonder that people were becoming ever more self-conscious about their linguistic prac-tices and the consequences of those practices. Quite often the effect was a kind of exile. The more a standardized vernacular ceased to be merely the internal language of officials and became the official language of a

---

13. See E.J. Hobsbawm, *The Age of Revolution, 1789–1848* (New York: Mentor, 1962), pp. 166–7.

14. A characteristic industrial side to the process was the official invention of adult educa-tion in this era.

15. "An interview with Pedro Calosa," in David Sturtevant, *Popular Uprisings in the Philippines, 1840–1940* (Ithaca, NY: Cornell University Press, 1976), p. 276.

propagandizing state, the more likely became the emergence in Old Europe of something reminiscent of the creole or native: the not-really-German German, the not-quite-Italian Italian, the non-Spanish Spaniard. As in the Americas, a kind of unstable negativity appeared. Nothing, therefore, is less surprising than that the nationalist movements which transformed the map of Europe by 1919 were so often led by young bilinguals, a pattern to be followed after 1919 in Asia and Africa. How could a boy who learned Czech from his mother and German from his schooling unlearn a Czech that had left no contaminating traces on his German-speaking classmates? How could he not see his Czech as though in exile, through the inverted telescope of his German?

From the perspective sketched out so far, one might be inclined to view the rise of nationalist movements and their variable culminations in successful nation-states as a project for coming home from exile, for the resolution of hybridity, for a positive printed from a negative in the darkroom of political struggle. Czechs would finally be born, and eventually buried, in Czechoslovakia, Poles in their very own Poland. Cultural life and political allegiance would be finally and stably aligned—so to speak—*à la* Bossuet. In the colonial domains outside Europe the same logic was—consciously or unconsciously, unwillingly or with enthusiasm—pursued. Modern, bounded state-terrains had been Mercatorianly mapped, and more or less effectively policed, as it were only awaiting appropriate inhabitants. Here, seen from a certain perspective, colonialism seemed like a stutterer haunted by a nightmare. Stutterer because by its very nature it could not name such inhabitants. No better example is afforded than the Philippines, which by the end of Spanish rule had been imagined for already 350 years as—qua *terre nourrice*—Las Filipinas. But Filipino? Simply the scornful metropolitan name for the tiny stratum of local creoles: in Las Filipinas, yes, but alongside far more numerous *peninsulares, mestizos, chinos,* and *indios.* Not the general name for the whole people of the patria, until the revolutionaries of the 1890s, who eventually included members of all the above categories, self-willed themselves into a common Filipinoness. Colonialism was also nightmare-haunted, because one can plausibly argue, on the evidence, that it dreamed of incipient nationalisms before nationalists themselves came into historical existence.[16] From this point on, as the old republican-American model had originally implied, mapped Mali would have to find its Malians, mapped Ceylon its Ceylonese, mapped Papua-New Guinea its Papua-New Guineans. Not by any means always with total success.

---

16. This theme is elaborated on in chapter 10 of my *Imagined Communities*, rev. edn. (London: Verso, 1991).

One can thus see why nation-statehood was so central to the nineteenth- and twentieth-century nationalist projects that destroyed the huge, polyglot imperial dynastic realms inherited from the age of absolutism, and the even larger colonial-imperialist conglomerations that survived them. For it was felt to represent, with its characteristically republican institutions, a new-found alignment of imagined home and imagined home-owners, and to guarantee the stabilization of that alignment through the organized deployment of its political powers and economic resources. Hence the plausibility of the Listian dream of the self-supplying "national economy," guarded, moatlike, by the tariff.

Ironically, however, just as this classical nation-state project was coming fully into its own with the formation of the League of Nations in 1919, advancing capitalism was beginning to sap its foundations. As in an earlier age, the most visible transformations took place in the areas of transportation and communications. On land, motor vehicles increasingly displaced the locomotive, while the vast proliferation of macadamized road surfaces on which they sped were never gauge-calibrated to national frontiers. In the air, commercial aviation was, with the exception of a few very large and rich nations like the United States, primarily transnational from its earliest days. One flew to leave or to return to one's nation-state rather than to move about within it, and "national airspace" had only a short plausible life before the advent of the satellite made it obsolete. The pace and thrust of these changes is vividly demonstrated by the statistics on the admission of non-immigrant aliens into historically immigrant America[17]:

1931–40	1,574,071
1941–50	2,461,359
1951–60	7,113,023
1961–70	24,107,224
1971–79	61,640,389
1981–91	142,076,530

(The 1930s were the first decade in which non-immigrants outnumbered immigrants, and they already did so by a ratio of three to one.)

Radio brought even illiterate populations within the purview of the mass media, and its reception was never effectively limited to nation-state audiences. No newspaper could ever hope to command the range of planetary acolytes that became available to the BBC or the Voice of America.

---

17. *Information Please Almanac, Atlas, and Yearbook, 1987* (Boston: McGraw-Hill, 1987), p. 787, and *Information Please Almanac, Atlas, and Yearbook, 1993* (Boston: McGraw-Hill, 1993), p. 830. These tables lack figures for 1980, which probably were somewhere between eight and nine million.

Subsequently, the telephone and telex, film, television, cassettes, video recorders, and the personal computer accelerated and enormously magnified nearly everything that radio had initiated.

These developments have had and will continue to have vast consequences precisely because they are integral components of the transnationalization of advanced capitalism and of the steepening economic stratification of the global economy. As things now stand, less than 25 per cent of the world's population appropriates 85 per cent of world income, and the gap between rich and poor is steadily widening. In the 1980s, over 800 million people—more than the population of the United States, the European Community, and Japan combined—"became yet more grindingly poor, and one out of three children went hungry."[18] Yet, thanks to the airplane, the bus, the truck, and even the old locomotive, this inequality and misery is in all senses closer to privilege and wealth than ever before. Hence migration has moved not, as in earlier centuries, outwards to peripheries in the New World or the Antipodes but inwards towards the metropolitan cores.

Between 1840 and 1930, about 37,500,000 immigrants, overwhelmingly from Europe, came to the United States; approximately 416,000 per annum on average. In the 1970s, the annual figure was almost 500,000 and in the 1980s almost 740,000; 80 per cent of the newcomers from the "Third World."[19] Paul Kennedy notes that some demographers currently believe that as many as 15 million immigrants will enter America in each of the next three decades, that is, at an annual average rate of 1.5 million, double that of the 1980s.[20]

These estimates are already proving to be only somewhat exaggerated. Early in 1997, the US Immigration and Naturalization Service announced that in the previous four years no less than 5 million *illegal* (to say nothing of legal) immigrants had penetrated America—an average rate of 1,250,000 a year.[21] Western Europe absorbed over 20 million immigrants in the three decades between the end of World War II and the oil crisis of the early 1970s. (The figure would have been much higher had it not been for the helpfulness of Stalin's iron curtain.) But in the latter part of the 1980s the numbers have swelled and will probably do so through the 1990s. Of Germany's 79 million

---

18. Perry Anderson, *A Zone of Engagement* (London: Verso, 1992), p. 353. See as well the sources there cited.

19. "Immigration," *The New Funk and Wagnalls Encyclopedia*, 25 vols. (New York: Unicorn, 1945–46), vol. 19, p. 6892. *The World Almanac and Book of Facts, 1992* (New York: World Almanac, 1992), p. 137.

20. See Paul Kennedy, "The American Prospect," *New York Review of Books*, March 4, 1993, p. 50.

21. *New York Times*, Feb. 8, 1997.

inhabitants, 5.2 million (7 per cent) are foreign immigrants; for France the figures are 3.6 (7 per cent) out of 56 million; for the United Kingdom, 1.8 (2 per cent) out of 57 million; for Switzerland, 1.1 (16.3 per cent) out of 6.8 million.[22] (Even insular, restrictive Japan is said to have a million or so legal and illegal alien residents.) And the economic and political implosion of the Soviet Union is already moving people in a way that no fin-de-siècle Continental System can stem.

At the same time, the communications revolution of our time has profoundly affected the subjective experience of migration. The Tamil bus-driver in Melbourne is a mere dozen sky-hours away from his *land van herkomst*. The Moroccan construction worker in Amsterdam can every night listen to Rabat's broadcasting services and has no difficulty in buying pirated cassettes of his country's favourite singers. The illegal alien, *Yakuza*-sponsored, Thai bartender in a Tokyo suburb shows his Thai comrades karaoke videotapes just made in Bangkok. The Filipina maid in Hong Kong phones her sister in Manila, and sends money in the twinkling of an electronic eye to her mother in Cebu. The successful Indian student in Vancouver can keep in daily e-mail touch with her former Delhi classmates. To say nothing of an ever-growing blizzard of faxes.

It is as if, were Mary Rowlandson alive today, she could see, in her small apartment bedroom, in perfect electronic safety on the screen beyond her toes, "truly" English fields and cattle. But of course the meaning would have changed completely. Not least because she can only see what the masters of the screen choose to let her see. Her eye can never gaze more widely than its frame. The "Englishness" of the fields comes not from within but from a narrating conglomerate voice outside her. More concretely, consider the well-known photograph of the lonely Peloponnesian *Gastarbeiter* sitting in his dingy room in, say, Frankfurt. The solitary decoration on his wall is a resplendent Lufthansa travel poster of the Parthenon, which invites him, in German, to take a "sun-drenched holiday" in Greece. He may well never have seen the Parthenon, but framed by Lufthansa the poster confirms for him and for any visitor a Greek identity that perhaps only Frankfurt has encouraged him to assume. At the same time, it reminds him that he is only a couple of flight hours from Greece, and that if he saves enough money, Lufthansa will be glad to assist him to have a fortnight's "sunny holiday" in his *Heimat*. He knows too, most likely, that he will then return to exile in Frankfurt. Or is it that, in the longer run, he will find himself in brief

---

22. See "In Europe's Upheaval, Doors Close to Foreigners," *New York Times*, Feb. 10, 1993. Note that these figures do not include an estimated 25 million political refugees around the world, mostly living in squalid, "temporary" dwellings outside their homelands.

annual exile in the Peloponnese? Or in both places? And what about his children?

Before turning to the political consequences of this broad sketch of post-1930s nomadism, two smaller but important related effects of postindustrial capitalism need briefly to be underscored. Consider the two most widely prevalent, quite modern official documents of personal identity: the birth certificate and the passport. Both were born in the nationalist nineteenth century and later became interlinked. It is true that in the Christianized regions of the world the registration of births long preceded the rise of capitalism. But these births were recorded locally and ecclesiastically in parish churches; their registration, foreshadowing imminent baptisms, signified the appearance of Christian souls in new corporeal forms. In the nineteenth century, however, registration was taken over by states that were increasingly assuming a national colouring. In industrially pre-eminent England, for example, the Registrar General's office was created only in 1837. Compulsory registration of all births, whether to be followed by baptisms or not, did not come until 1876. Identifying each baby's father and place of birth, the state's certificates created the founding documents for the infant's inclusion in or exclusion from citizenship (through jus sanguinis or jus soli). (He or she was no longer born in the parish of Egham but in the United Kingdom.) The passport, product of the vectoral convergence of migration and nationalism in an industrial age, was ready to confirm the baby's political identity as it passed into adulthood.

The nexus of birth certificate and passport was institutionalized in an era in which women had no legal rights to political participation and the patriarchal family was the largely unquestioned norm. But in our time all this has radically changed. When the League of Nations was founded—and female suffrage was coming into its own—the ratio of divorces to marriages in the United States was about one to eight; today it is virtually one to two. The percentage of American babies born to never-married mothers has increased spectacularly from 4.2 per cent in 1960 to 30.6 per cent in 1990.[23] The intranational as well as international nomadism of modern life has also contributed to making the nineteenth-century birth certificate a sort of counterfeit money. If, for example, we read that Mary Jones was born on October 25, 1970 in Duluth, to Robert Mason and Virginia Jones, or even Robert and Virginia Mason, we cannot nonchalantly infer that she was conceived in that same Duluth, was brought up there, or lives there now. We have no idea whether her grandparents are buried in Duluth, and, even if they were, we

---

23. Data drawn from Bureau of the Census figures cited in *The World Almanac and Book of Facts, 1992*, pp. 942, 944.

have few grounds for supposing that Mary will some day be buried alongside them. Is Virginia still a Mason? Or a Jones? Or something else again? What are the chances that Mary has much beyond periodic long-distance telephone contact with either Robert or Virginia? How far is she identifiable, also to herself, as a Duluthian, a Mason, or a Jones?

The counterfeit quality or, shall we say, the low market value of the birth certificate is perhaps confirmed by the relative rareness of its forgery. Conversely, the huge volume of passport forgeries and the high prices they command show that in our age, when everyone is supposed to belong to some one of the United Nations, these documents have high truth-claims. But they are also counterfeit in the sense that they are less attestations of citizenship, let alone of loyalty to a protective *Heimat* nation-state, than of claims to participation in labour markets. Portuguese and Bangladeshi passports, even when genuine, tell little about loyalties or habitus, but they reveal a great deal about the relative likelihood of their holders being permitted to seek jobs in Milan or Copenhagen. The segregated queues that all of us experience at airport immigration barricades mark economic status far more than any political attachments. In effect, they figure differential tariffs on human labour.

Let me now turn finally to the political realm. The processes explicated above may be unravelling the classical nineteenth-century nationalist project—which aimed for the fullest alignment of habitus, culture, attachment, and exclusive political participation—on at least two distinct but related political sites.

The first site is more or less congruent with the postindustrial cores. During the nineteenth and early part of the twentieth centuries the so-called countries of immigration—the Americas, primarily but also the antipodes—had a remarkable capacity to naturalize and nationalize their millions of immigrants. The names Galtieri, Eisenhauer, Fujimori, Van Buren, O'Higgins, and Trudeau tell the tale. But the birth certificate then had a primarily political significance, as we can see from the constitutional proviso that US presidents be born inside that nation's borders. One was, thus, an American or one was not. Furthermore, military participation in the service of a state other than the United States was subject to the legal sanction of loss of citizenship, not that this was always rigidly enforced. When did this regime begin to weaken? Perhaps in our epochal 1930s, when Americans were permitted to join the International Brigade in the Spanish Civil War? Or in the later 1940s when Americans were tacitly permitted to participate in the defence of the infant state of Israel? But these breaks in the established rules were, I think, permissible precisely because of a confidence that these extralegal affairs were minor matters, concerning unimportant people with rather low visibility. Besides, the Americanness of the Americans involved was never seriously in question. These conditions began to change, however, after the middle of the 1960s. Andreas Papandreou started life as a Greek citizen, became an American citizen, and then, when opportunity beckoned, became again a Greek citizen and prime minister of Greece. A certain protocol is still evident in his progress. But what are we to make of the 1993 Cambodian presidential candidacy of self-made Long Beach millionaire Kim Kethavy? In the solemn words of the *New York Times*, he "carries an American passport . . . The offices of his campaign headquarters bloom with American flags. (Under American immigration law, Mr. Kethavy would probably be forced to give up his United States citizenship in the unlikely event that he won.)"[24] Everything here is indicative: Mr. Kethavy's citizenship is in parentheses and the newspaper of record thinks that he will only "probably" be forced to give it up if he becomes Cambodia's president. Nothing suggests that the *Times* of the 1990s finds anything odd or discomforting in the behaviour of Mr. Kethavy— or of the American government. After all, American citizens Milan Panič and Mohammed Sacirbey have recently served as premier of Yugoslavia and Bosnian ambassador to the United Nations, while Rein Taagepera ran unsuccessfully for president of Estonia from a tenured professorship within the University of California at Irvine. Nor is this a uniquely American phenomenon; the Canadian citizen and computer-systems capitalist Stanislaw Tyminski ran against Lech Walesa for the presidency of Poland.

The other side of this coin is the recent emergence in the United States and other older nation-states of an ethnicity that appears as a bastard Smerdyakov to classical nationalism's Dmitri Karamazov. One emblem of the American variant is perhaps the espionage trial of Jonathan Pollard a few years back. In the age of classical nationalism, the very idea that there could be something praiseworthy in an American citizen's spying on America for another country would have seemed grotesque. But to the substantial number of Jewish-Americans who felt sympathetic to Pollard, the resentful spy was understood as representing a transnational ethnicity. What else could so subversively blur American and Israeli citizenship? Another emblem is the colossal non-black audience magnetized in 1977 by Alex Haley's mini-series *Roots*. (The final episode was watched in an astonishing 36 million households.) The purpose of the programme was to counter melting-pot ideology by underlining the continuous "Africanness" that Haley's ancestors maintained as it were despite their Americanization. There can be little doubt that the popularity of *Roots* owed much to this transposable theme, given the

---

24. "For the Cambodian Vote, a Fourth of July Flavor," *New York Times*, Feb. 17, 1993.

rush, especially during the 1980s, of thoroughly American youngsters to lobby for various ethnic-studies programmes at universities, and their eagerness to study languages that their immediate parents had so often been determined to abandon. Out of these and other impulses has emerged the ideological programme of multiculturalism, which implies that a simple nineteenth-century version of Americanism is no longer adequate or acceptable. (But what version is? For a long time participation in American elections has been declining, to the point where in the 1990 counting barely 36 per cent of eligible voters cast a ballot.)

The shift from, say, American through Armenian-*American* through *Armenian*-American is being accentuated both by the general revolution of transportation and communications discussed earlier, and by the recent disintegration of the Soviet Union and Yugoslavia. Cleveland, for example, contains more people of Slovene descent than does Ljubljana, and now that Slovenia has become an independent state, being Slovene in Cleveland, and in the United States, assumes a heightened significance. Such ethnicities typically share a strongly fictive character with *Roots*. We can easily be amused by the determinedly "Irish" Bostonian who knows no Irish literature, plays no Irish sports, pays no Irish taxes, serves in no Irish army, does not vote in Irish elections, and has only holiday conceptions of the Old Sow as she is today. It is less amusing, however, to reflect on the fact that the visible presence of gays and lesbians at St. Patrick's Day celebrations in Cork has done nothing to temper the passions surrounding sister celebrations in New York.[25]

In Europe comparable tendencies are at work and may even be accentuated within the European Community by economic integration and the free movement of labour. The National Front, Le Pen's movement, and the rise of right-wing extremism in Germany are all signs of the "ethnicization" process.[26] For the thrust of their propaganda is essentially to draw a sharp line between the political nation and a putative original *ethnos*. Even if a black in the United Kingdom was born there, went to schools and university there, pays taxes there, votes there, and will be buried there, for the National Front he or she can never be genuinely English. Similarly in Le Pen's imagination, France is today teeming with aliens, not immigrants still carrying Algerian

---

25. Last year the gay and lesbian float won first prize in Cork. But in New York the Ancient Order of the Hibernians continues to act as if gayness is simply incompatible with Irishness. In effect, the "real Ireland" has moved westward to a new transatlantic location.

26. The Lega Lombarda of the late 1980s, now the Lega Nord, while not strictly analogous to these movements, nonetheless shows that something close to ethnicization can threaten to break down even a supposed core nation. The Lega's attitudes to southern Italians are often rabidly contemptuous, as if the latter were of another, lesser breed.

passports, but "non-French" citizens of political France.[27] We could thus conceive of him looking out of the window of a railway carriage and seeing not fields, not even "French fields," but "dammit, French fields." In these movements racism is a very strong element, but I think the racism will prove in the longer run to be less important than ethnicization as Europeans circulate more massively around Europe.

The second type of political consequence of all the rapid changes I have been discussing concerns the migrants themselves. Not least as a result of the ethnicization of political life in the wealthy, postindustrial states, what one can call long-distance nationalism is visibly emerging. This type of politics, directed mainly towards the former Second and Third Worlds, pries open the classical nation-state project from a different direction. A striking illustration is the fateful recent destruction of the Babri mosque in Ayodhya, which plunged India into her biggest crisis since Partition. The dismantling, which was carefully planned and involved extensive rehearsal and training by retired military and police personnel, was officially sponsored by the Vishwa Hindu Parishad (World Hindu Council), which "raised huge sums of money from its supporters in North America and Britain."[28] Needless to say, the vast majority of such supporters are Indians living permanently overseas.[29] Many of the most uncompromising, fanatical adherents of an independent Khalistan do not live in the Punjab but have prosperous businesses in Melbourne and Chicago. The Tigers in Jaffna are stiffened in their violent struggles by Tamil communities in Toronto, London, and elsewhere, all linked on the computer by Tamilnet.[30] Consider the malign role of Croats not only in Germany but also in Australia and North America in financing and arming Franjo

---

27. Here there is an important change from the nineteenth century. Today it is possible to demand that such people be sent back to *"their own* nation-states," while a hundred years ago such providential homes did not yet exist.

28. Praful Bidwai, "Bringing Down the Temple: Democracy at Risk in India," *The Nation,* Jan. 23, 1993, p. 86.

29. The numbers of such people are very substantial. The official figure for South Asians outside South Asia is close to 8.7 million. The breakdown is as follows: Europe 1,482,034 (of which 1,260,000 are in the United Kingdom); Africa 1,389,722; Asia 1,862,654 (of which 1,170,000 are in Malaysia); Middle East 1,317,141, mostly in the Gulf states; Latin America and the Caribbean 957,330 (of which 730,350 are in Guyana and Trinidad); North America 728,500 (of which 500,000 are in the United States); and the Pacific 954,109 (of which 839,340 are in Fiji). Professor Myron Weiner kindly informs me that although this table counts South Asians abroad, the major areas of emigration have long been inside the present borders of India. He also believes the figures to be too conservative: for example, the recent US census shows the Indian population in America to be close to 900,000. Most likely, in his estimate, the true total for Indians living overseas is between eleven and twelve million. "Introduction: Themes in the Study of the South Asian Diaspora," in Colin Clarke, Ceri Peach, and Steven Vertovec, eds., *South Asians Overseas: Migration and Ethnicity* (Cambridge, Mass.: Harvard University Press, 1990), p. 2.

30. See the extensive, detailed coverage in *Asiaweek,* July 26, 1996.

Tudjman's breakaway state and pushing Germany and Austria into a fateful, premature recognition.[31] Not to be overlooked is the role of a wealthy global Armenian diaspora in finding the funds and weapons to assure Yerevan's military triumph over Baku.[32]

It would obviously be a mistake to assume that long-distance nationalism is necessarily extremist. There were substantial numbers of Filipinos outside the Philippines who contributed, not from *political* exile, to the struggle against Marcos; the Philippine economy today is heavily dependent on remittances sent in by such people from the Gulf, Italy, Saudi Arabia, England, California, Hong Kong, Japan, and Spain. Financial and other support for the democracy movement that culminated in the Tiananmen Square massacre also came from many Chinese not resident in China and often, indeed, citizens of other states.

Nonetheless, in general, today's long-distance nationalism strikes one as a probably menacing portent for the future. First of all, it is the product of capitalism's remorseless, accelerating transformation of all human societies. Second, it creates a serious politics that is at the same time radically unaccountable. The participant rarely pays taxes in the country in which he does his politics; he is not answerable to its judicial system; he probably does not cast even an absentee ballot in its elections because he is a citizen in a different place; he need not fear prison, torture, or death, nor need his immediate family. But, well and safely positioned in the First World, he can send money and guns, circulate propaganda, and build intercontinental computer information circuits, all of which can have incalculable consequences in the zones of their ultimate destinations. Third, his politics, unlike those of activists for global human rights or environmental causes, are neither intermittent nor serendipitous. They are deeply rooted in a consciousness that his exile is self-chosen and that the nationalism he claims on e-mail is also the ground on which an embattled ethnic identity is to be fashioned in the ethnicized nation-state that he remains determined to inhabit. That same metropole that marginalizes and stigmatizes him simultaneously enables him to play, in a flash, on the other side of the planet, national hero.

---

31. Emblematic is the figure of Canadian citizen Goyko Šušak. A successful Ottawa-based pizza-millionaire, he built over the years a huge right-wing network of "overseas" North American Croatians, used the ample funds he extracted from them to buy Franjo Tudjman his first election as Croatia's president, and obtained as his reward Croatia's Ministry of Defence (aka War). See the remarkable interview in the *New York Times,* Jan. 16, 1994. His excellent contacts in the Pentagon won him the services of the retired American generals who planned Croatia's blitzkrieg victories over the forces of Slobodan Milosevič.

32. See "Revenge of the Armenian Diaspora," *Financial Times,* Sept. 15, 1994.

PART II

SOUTHEAST ASIA: COUNTRY STUDIES

4

A Time of Darkness and a Time of Light

Just before his death in 1873, in the old royal capital of Surakarta, R.Ng. Ronggawarsita, the last of the great Javanese *pujangga* (court poets), wrote a despairing poem that he called *Serat Kala Tidha* (Poem of a Time of Darkness).[1] Something of the tone of this poem may be gleaned from the following lines:

> The lustre of the realm
> Is now vanished to the eye
> In ruins the teaching of good ways
> For there is no example left
> The heart of the learned poet
> So coiled about with care
> Seeing all the wretchedness
> That everything is darkened
> The world immersed in misery
>
> The King kingly perfection
> The Chief Minister chiefly in truth
> The *bupati* constant of heart
> The lower officials excellent
> Yet none can serve to stay
> The time of doom . . .

---

1. Radèn Ngabèhi Ronggawarsita, *Serat Kala Tida* ([Surakarta]: Persatuan, [1933]).

In this time of madness
To join the mad is unbearable
Anguish to the suffering heart
Yet not to join
Means losing all
Starvation at the end.[2]

Taken one by one, most of these lines are unremarkable variations on classical *topoi* in Javanese culture. Both Javanese folklore and court literature contain highly conventionalized descriptions of *jaman kalabendu*—times of flood, earthquake, and volcanic eruption in the natural order and famine, violence, and immorality in the social. Both traditions also present time-honoured images of golden ages—periods of cosmic order and social well-being, in which each person plays out his appointed role, hierarchies are maintained, and harmony prevails. The explanation for the primordial oscillations between such epochs lay, according to traditional Javanese thought,[3] in the success or failure of the ruler to concentrate around and in himself the immanent power of the universe, through ascesis, selfless devotion to duty, and the capacity to attract or absorb other power-full persons or objects. The more perfect the ruler, the more brilliant and happy the society.

If the lines I have cited are in themselves so unremarkable, what accounts for the strange and painful sensations they arouse? Simply their extraordinary *juxtaposition*. For stanzas 2 and 8 belong to the topos "time of darkness," while the first four lines of stanza 3 are a central part of the classical imagery of a "time of light." According to traditional Javanese logic, if "the king [were] kingly perfection, the Chief Minister chiefly in truth," then cosmos and society should *necessarily* be in order. But the next two lines show precisely the opposite. The single terrible word *parandéné* (yet) expresses Ronggawarsita's desperate, and quite untraditional, sense that the old conception of the world was no longer valid, the cosmic rhythm had come unsprung and Javanese Power was impotence. In their history the Javanese had gone through many "times of darkness," but always with the sure expectation

---

2. I have translated freely, and rather coarsely, from stanzas 2, 3, and 8. The Javanese text runs as follows: *Mangkya darajating praja / Kawuryan wus sunya ruri / Rurah pangrèhing ngukara / Karana tanpa palupi / Ponang para mengkawi / Kawileting tyas maladkung / Kungas kasudranira / Tidhem tandhaning dumadi / Ardayèng rat déning karoban rubéda / / Ratuné ratu utama / Patihé patih linuwih / Pra nayaka tyas raharja / Panekaré becik-becik / Parandéné tan dadi / Paliyasing kalabendu . . . / / Amenengi jaman édan / Éwuh ayahing pambudi / Mèlu édan nora tahan / Yèn tan mèlu anglakoni / Boya kaduman melik / Kaliren wekasanipun.* Here *bupati* refers to high-ranking court officials not of royal blood. My attention was first drawn to this poem by Tony Day.

3. A more extensive treatment of traditional Javanese conceptions and images of power is given in chapter 1 of my *Language and Power*.

that eventually a ruler would come to reconcentrate the Power and inaugurate a new "time of light." In 1873, however, the dying poet spoke his fear that now was a "time of darkness" that might never end.[4]

Thirty-five years later, on May 20, 1908, a small group of teenage Javanese students in the colonial capital of Batavia formed an organization that they called Budi Utomo. May 20 is now celebrated annually in Indonesia as the Day of National Awakening. Akira Nagazumi's fine study on the early years of this organization is fittingly entitled *The Dawn of Indonesian Nationalism*[5]—dawn marks the passage from darkness to light, from sleep to wakefulness. And if both Nagazumi and contemporary Indonesians speak of May 20, 1908 in these figurative terms, they are not being wilfully anachronistic. How many of the newspapers and periodicals from the early years of this century contain, in their very names, images of radiant light![6] Kartini's famous collected letters, *Door Duisternis tot Licht* (Through Darkness to Light), bear the same symbolic stamp.[7]

What are we to make of this metamorphosis of imagery? Some scholars have tended to read it as signifying the passage from tradition to modernity, as though they "who walked in darkness [had] seen a great light." Robert Van Niel, for example, writes that

in the atmosphere of the Westernized school . . . young Javanese found a life that differed from what they had known in their home environment. Not only was the

---

4. Ronggawarsita's words may be the sharpest and most explicit expression of the general crisis of the nineteenth-century Javanese spirit, as Dutch colonial rule steadily consolidated itself. But many other texts convey the same feeling in more oblique form. It is instructive to compare style and subject matter in a major pre-nineteenth-century text, such as the *Babad Tanah Jawi* and the strange but typically nineteenth-century poem *Suluk Gatholoco*. The *Babad Tanah Jawi* recounts the bloody events of precolonial Javanese history in plain and matter-of-fact language. In the *Suluk Gatholoco*, which deals mainly with an imaginary theological debate between some "Arabized" Javanese Muslims and a champion of "Javanese" Islam in the form of an ambulatory, philosophizing penis (*gatho* = penis, *ngloco* = masturbate), no violence occurs. But the language employed is unforgettable in its ornate ferocity.

5. Akira Nagazumi, *The Dawn of Indonesian Nationalism: The Early Years of Budi Utomo, 1908–1918* (Tokyo: Institute of Developing Economies, Occasional Papers Series no. 10, 1972).

6. About 25 per cent of the Indonesian newspapers for the period 1900–25 listed in Godfrey Raymond Nunn, *Indonesian Newspapers: An International Union List* (Taipei: Chinese Materials Research Aids Service Center, Occasional Series no. 14, 1971) include in their titles one or more of the following words: *matahari* (sun), *surya* (sun), *bintang* (star), *nyala* (flame), *suluh* (torch), *pelita* (lamp), *sinar* (ray), *cahaya* (radiance), *api* (fire), and *fajar* (dawn). Others contain such words as *muda* (young), *baru* (new), and *gugah* (awakened).

7. The title was actually given by Kartini's editor, Jacques Henry Abendanon, when he published her letters posthumously in 1911. But he was closely involved with, and sympathetic to, the "awakening" movement, and his choice of title fitted well with that milieu. See Hildred Geertz's introduction to Radèn Adjeng Kartini, *Letters of a Javanese Princess* (New York: Norton, 1964), especially pp. 15–16, 23.

difference one of physical environment, but what was far more important, one of mental environment: perhaps only slightly inaccurately generalized as the difference between a scientific-rational attitude and a mystical-animistic attitude.[8]

In this perspective, Budi Utomo represents simply the earliest Indonesian attempt to cope with the colonial condition in western (modern) ways. Even though Budi Utomo's very name was more Javanese than Indonesian; though its membership was restricted ethnically to what Clifford Geertz has called "Inner Indonesia" and socially to *priyayi* students and officials;[9] and though its formal aims did not encompass political independence;[10] yet its *structural* novelty seemed to mark a clear break with the past. As Van Niel puts it, "Budi Utomo appears on the Indonesian scene as an *organization* based upon a *free and conscious* united effort by *individuals*.[11] With its programmes, branches, subscriptions, reports, and congresses, Budi Utomo seemed to have no indigenous ancestry, but rather to be the wind-borne seed from which the Indonesian nationalist movement grew.[12]

If Indonesian writers have usually been unwilling to accept Van Niel's psychological and pedagogical dichotomies, they have developed dichotomies of their own, conceived in moral, political, and generational terms, as is evidenced by the pervasive pairing of *maju/kolot* (progressive/backward), *muda/tua* (young/old), and *sadar/masih bodoh* (aware/still ignorant).[13] In both perspectives Budi Utomo has come to seem the locus of a fundamental transformation of consciousness. Yet much about this transformation remains obscure. What follows below is a preliminary attempt to illumine that obscurity.

Budi Utomo was founded by students at the STOVIA[14] medical school in Batavia, led by a nineteen-year-old East Javanese boy called Soetomo, who

---

8. Robert Van Niel, *The Emergence of the Modern Indonesian Elite* (The Hague: van Hoeve, 1950), p. 173.

9. "Inner Indonesia" refers to the islands of Java, Bali, and Madura and their "Hinduized" populations. *Priyayi* refers to the traditional Javanese upper class of officials and literati. In fact, the founding members of Budi Utomo were exclusively ethnic Javanese. See Nagazumi, *Dawn*, p. 39.

10. For details on these aims, see ibid., pp. 157–60.

11. Van Niel, *Emergence*, p. 57. Emphasis added.

12. It is this organizational novelty, clearly derived from the West, that has encouraged some western scholars to interpret Indonesian (and Southeast Asian) nationalism as a western import and to date the beginnings of this nationalism to the formation of western-style organizations. (For example, the founding of the Young Men's Buddhist Association in Rangoon in 1906 is often taken to mark the onset of the Burmese nationalist movement.) Cf. Brian Harrison, *Southeast Asia, A Short History* (London: Macmillan, 1954), pp. 236–7.

13. For example, Lintong Mulia Sitorus, in his *Sedjarah Pergerakan Kebangsaan Indonesia* (Jakarta: Pustaka Rakjat, 1951), writes: "Till the end of the 19th century, the coloured peoples still slept soundly, while the whites were busily at work in every field." (p. 6).

14. *School tot Opleiding van Inlandsche Artsen*—School for the Training of Native Doctors.

eventually became one of the most prominent nationalist leaders of his generation. Van Niel may be exaggerating a little when he writes that "it is doubtful if any one man was of greater importance in shaping Indonesian life in the 1920s."[15] But as founder of the Surabaya-based Indonesian Study Club in 1924, of Partai Bangsa Indonesia (Party of the Indonesian Nation) in 1930, and of Parindra (Great Indonesia Party) in 1935, Soetomo was certainly a central figure in pre-independence Indonesian politics.[16] On his death in 1938 he was mourned by thousands as a devoted servant of his people.[17] A successful graduate of the most advanced western-style school in the Netherlands Indies, he could, in the first two decades of the century, be regarded as the epitome of all that was *maju, muda,* and *sadar.*[18] By chance, Soetomo was also the first prominent Indonesian to write something like an autobiography, the well-known *Kenang-Kenangan*—a title that can be translated as Memoirs, but is really better rendered as Memories. It seems reasonable, therefore, that the study of this "autobiography" may offer clues as to what it meant to be a member of the generation of the "awakened," and, more generally, of the way in which past, present, and future were conceived of and linked together in the mind of that generation's most enduring political personality.[19]

Before exploring *Kenang-Kenangan,* however, we may remind ourselves of the main facts of Soetomo's life. He was born in the village of Ngepèh, near Nganjuk, East Java, on July 30, 1888.[20] His maternal grandfather was a well-to-do *kepalang* (superior village headman) who had earlier served in the Binnenlandsch Bestuur (territorial native administration). His father was a very

---

15. Van Niel, *Emergence,* p. 224.

16. For details on these parties, see Jan Meinhard Pluvier, *Overzicht van de ontwikkeling der nationalistische beweging in Indonesië in der jaren 1930 tot 1942* (The Hague: van Hoeve, 1953).

17. "Fifty thousand people followed his bier; the image of this man of the people lived in the hearts of the masses who had so much to thank him for. *Soetomo* was indeed an extraordinary figure, one of the noblest leaders of the nationalist movement in its decades-old history." Daniel Marcellus Georg Koch, *Batig Slot: Figuren uit het oude Indië* (Amsterdam: De Brug/Djambatan, 1960), p. 145. The standard general account of Soetomo's life is Imam Supardi, *Dr. Soetomo— Riwajat Hidup dan Perdjuangannja* (Jakarta: Djambatan, 1951).

18. This is the judgement of Nagazumi, *Dawn,* p. 34. For details on the evolution of the STOVIA, and the character of its curriculum and student body, see Van Niel, *Emergence,* p. 16.

19. For some discussion of Indonesian autobiography, see Savitri Scherer, "Harmony and Dissonance: Early Nationalist Thought in Java" (M.A. thesis, Cornell University, 1975), pp. 188–9. For specific studies in Indonesian biography and autobiography, see Scherer's treatment of Soetomo, Tjipto Mangoenkoesoemo, and Ki Hadjar Dewantara; Taufik Abdullah, "Modernization in the Minangkabau World: West Sumatra in the Early Decades of the Twentieth Century," in Clare Holt, ed., *Culture and Politics in Indonesia* (Ithaca, NY: Cornell University Press, 1972), pp. 179–245; Rudolf Mrázek, "Tan Malaka: A Political Personality's Structure of Experience," *Indonesia,* 14 (Oct. 1972), pp. 1–48; and John D. Legge, *Sukarno: A Political Biography* (New York: Praeger, 1972).

20. He was thus an almost exact contemporary of Ho Chi Minh and Burma's first prime minister, Dr. Ba Maw.

able teacher and administrator who rose to the rank of *wedana*, then the highest bureaucratic rank normally open to Javanese not born to aristocratic *bupati* families.[21] To the age of six, Soetomo was brought up by his maternal grandparents. Then he was sent to a Dutch-language primary school (ELS) in Bangil. It is an indication of his privileged educational background that in 1895, probably the year he was enrolled, there were no more than 1,135 Indonesians enrolled in such primary schools throughout the Netherlands Indies.[22] In 1903, largely at his father's insistence, he entered the STOVIA. He was then fourteen. He graduated in 1911, at twenty-two, and subsequently, by the contractual terms of his initial enrolment, worked as a government doctor in various parts of Java and Sumatra. In 1917, while stationed in Blora, he met a widowed Dutch nurse and married her. Two years later he was given the opportunity to continue his medical studies in Holland, returning home only in 1923. He was by then prominent enough to be selected as a member of the Surabaya Municipal Council. But shortly thereafter he resigned from this position and formed the first and most famous of the political "study clubs" of the 1920s. From that time until his death in 1938, he was immersed in nationalist politics.[23]

Such is the skeletal outline of Soetomo's life, following in abbreviated form the fuller picture presented in Imam Supardi's quiet hagiography. In what ways does Soetomo's "autobiography" correspond to this silhouette? Scarcely at all. There is, for example, virtually no mention of his political successes or failures in the thirty years that followed the founding of Budi Utomo. We learn of his political activities only in passing—as, for instance, when he compassionately describes his wife having to cook constantly for the stream of student visitors to their house in Holland.[24] The very structure of the autobiography is rather strange and hardly follows what we imagine as the contours of Soetomo's historical life. The first 48 pages are devoted to his parents and grandparents, and the last 57 to his schoolfellows (and political comrades), his wife, and some family retainers. Only the central 30 pages deal substantively with his own life—and they close with his schooldays in Batavia.

In a notice to his readers, and in a brief preface, Soetomo gives some accounting of this shape:

> As mentioned in the introduction to his book, the purpose of the writer in writing this book of memories is the desire to accede to the requests of various people who would like to understand the story [*riwayat*] of my life. In this book I do not set

---

21. See Scherer, "Harmony," pp. 191–200, for further detail. Here *bupati* refers to Java's traditional provincial nobility.
22. Ibid., p. 30.
23. Supardi, *Dr. Soetomo*, pp. 2–8.
24. Radèn Soetomo, *Kenang-Kenangan* (Surabaya: n.p., 1934), pp. 118–19.

down the story of my life[25] in the plainest terms, because, as mentioned in the intro-duction, it is inappropriate for me to be the one to write my story. I [therefore] only depict various excerpts [*pungutan*] from the stories of various people who were con-nected with my life, so that, from the excerpts of the stories of these people, my story can be envisaged . . .[26] For a long time now, and from various quarters, I have received requests to write the history of my life (*biografie*). Above all from my own group there have been not a few requests of this type. In addition, several journal-ists have made the same request. But I rejected them all, for I am of the opinion that it is inappropriate for a man to make a history of the life of someone who has not yet returned to eternity [*belum pulang ke zaman yang baka*], in other words the picture of his life is not yet completed . . .[27]

So I have taken another way, whereby I can have the fullest opportunity to pay my respects to my forefathers and whoever else has helped me,[28] so that as a result my own *lelakon* can be thereby revealed.[29]

Mindful of the Javanese saying *kacang mangsa ninggal lanjaran*, which means that a man's descendants will never abandon his qualities, from my describing the qualities and character of my forefathers the reader will easily be able to under-stand my true character.[30]

The writer's hope is that . . . this book of memories . . . can be used as a means for comparing conditions in the former time [*zaman dahulu*] with the present [*masa sekarang*].[31]

Some of the more important themes of Memories are already laid out in these modest explanatory words, which deserve some comment before we proceed further with the text.

First of all, it is striking that, although western scholars have habitually referred to Memories as an autobiography, Soetomo himself never uses the word, or any Indonesian-language version of it: he notes that he had long

---

25. Although in modern Indonesian the terms *penghidupan* and *kehidupan* have rather dif-ferent meanings (perhaps "style of life" and "life"), Soetomo seems to use them interchangeably in this passage.

26. Ibid., inside of cover.

27. Ibid., p. 3. Soetomo adds the Dutch word *biografie* in parentheses, as if he were uncer-tain that his Indonesian readers would understand the phrase "history of my life."

28. Compare the words of another very Javanese Indonesian leader, Communist Party sec-retary-general Sudisman, in his defence speech before the Extraordinary Military Tribunal that sentenced him to death in 1967: "I am a Communist who was born in Java, and therefore it is my duty, in accordance with the custom of the Javanese, to take my leave by saying: First, *matur nuwun*, I thank all those who have helped me in the course of the struggle" (Sudisman, *Analysis of Responsibility*, trans. Benedict Anderson [Melbourne: The Works Cooperative, 1975], p. 24).

29. *Lelakon* is a Javanese term that is notoriously impossible to translate. It is something like a mixture of "destiny," "role," "life aim," and "moral responsibility."

30. Soetomo, *Kenang-Kenangan*, p. 4. The saying literally means: "How could the bean abandon the bean-pole?" The word *tabi'at*, translated here as "character," could also be rendered as "nature."

31. Ibid., p. 6.

rejected requests to write his *biography.* Yet Memories is not a biography in any ordinary sense. Even when he writes at length about his forefathers, we are not given their biographies, but simply excerpts or "pluckings" from their "stories." Soetomo makes no attempt to place these ancestral figures in a maturing personal or historical context. They loom up in episodes to which no clear time can be assigned, except, as we shall see, for the significant markers *zaman dahulu* and *masa sekarang.*

I think we will not begin to make sense of this method of writing if we are not clear about the nature and assumptions of modern western-style biography and autobiography. These literary forms are essentially about the interplay between "person" and "history." "History" is a global and linear framework for comprehending the evolution of man and society. "Person" is the individual subjectivity that experiences this "history" and takes part in it. The study of a man's life is therefore usually a study of his progress towards and absorption into his historical role. If parents and grandparents appear in such works, they serve to illuminate a social, economic, and psychological context out of which the "person" emerges—or a sort of starting line from which to judge his performance in the race to come. The fundamental movement of such texts is therefore *away* from ancestry towards the "individual." They are analogous to paintings built up on canvas and easel by the constant addition of small dabs of colour until an unexpected whole—the work of art—appears.

In Memories we find, I think, a method that is more analogous to that of classical sculpture—the discovery of essential form in the contingency of stone or other raw materials. The homely folk saying "kacang mangsa ninggal lanjaran" implies a very different sense of person and time from those typical in western biography or autobiography. For, as we shall see, here history appears not as the painter who gives a life its essential meaning but as contingency, the raw stone through which the search for an essential nature is pursued. Soetomo's pages about his parents are not meant to show the social and psychological environment out of which the nationalist leader goes to meet his destiny, but look rather to reveal the *lanjaran* towards which the *kacang* seeks its homeward-wending way. We are, in effect, being shown the character (nature) of his ancestry, *towards* which his life's movement tends. The quest is not for individual fulfilment or historical uniqueness, but for reunion and identification. It is in this sense, by showing the nature of his ancestors, that Soetomo can invite his readers, who know his historical role, to see what his nature really is.[32] In a

---

32. This is no less true of all the other personages who appear in Memories. There are a few occasions when some of them seem to change—for example, Soetomo's ambitious mother learns the hard way that official position does not always bring happiness. But Soetomo makes it clear that the real "she" has not changed at all. She has simply lost some illusions about the nature of the world. Ibid., p. 25.

context where historical time is so adventitious, chronology is necessarily of minor importance; this is why, I believe, Soetomo's own life and those of his forefathers appear to us in the pages of Memories so fragmented, episodic, and unanchored.[33]

In the second place, the generally melancholy tone of Memories is set from the start. Soon after the basic draft was written, his beloved wife died, and the last-minute addition that Soetomo devotes to her is marked by some spare, anguished language. He records also the deaths of the two other people whom he most admired: Goenawan Mangoenkoesoemo, a friend so close that Dr. Tjipto Mangoenkoesoemo, Goenawan's elder brother, referred to their relationship as that of *wayang* (puppet) and *dhalang* (puppeteer);[34] and his father—an event that, as he observes himself, was crucial to his sudden emergence as the leading spirit of Budi Utomo. But the tone of melancholy has deeper causes than these personal losses. It derives, I think, from what we have seen in the last quoted passage from Soetomo's preface, signalled there and throughout Memories by the repeated contrast between *zaman dahulu* and *masa sekarang*. There are pages where one seems to get a clear idea of the nature of the contrast between these "times," if not of the point of transition between them. Soetomo records asking villagers in Ngepèh what it was like in the *zaman dahulu*: "The villagers answered: 'Tuan, there was nothing to equal conditions in the *zaman* of Lurah Kadji [Soetomo's grandfather].' What was the difference? '*In that time,* the time of Lurah Kadji, people were absolutely forbidden [by Lurah Kadji] to rent their land to the [sugar] factories.'"[35] He describes his grandfather's education in the following terms:

He was the son of a rich man who used to be headman there. For that reason, *if one looks at his time*, he received an adequate education. He was sent from *pesantrèn* to *pesantrèn*,[36] wherever there were famous teachers. Because of his travels my grandfather had a rather broad perspective. According to what people say, it was only in the *pesantrèn* of Sepanjang (near Surabaya) that he got a broad and adequate

33. Nothing could be more striking in this regard than the fact that *Kenang-Kenangan* makes no mention of the three most "world-shaking" events experienced by Southeast Asians in the early years of the twentieth century: Asian Japan's stunning defeat of European Russia in 1905; the outbreak of World War I in 1914; and the Bolshevik Revolution in 1917. By contrast, almost all later Indonesian memoirs are tightly linked to the on-going march of world history. See, for example, Sutan Sjahrir, *Out of Exile,* trans. Charles Wolf, Jr. (New York: John Day, 1949); Cindy Adams, *Sukarno: An Autobiography as Told to Cindy Adams* (Indianapolis: Bobbs-Merrill, 1965); and Ali Sastroamidjojo, *Tonggak-tonggak di Perjalananku* (Jakarta: Kinta, 1974).

34. When Goenawan died, Tjipto is said to have remarked: "Now Soetomo has lost his *dhalang.*" Soetomo, *Kenang-Kenangan,* p. 95.

35. Ibid., p. 13. Emphasis added.

36. *Pesantrèn*—traditional Javanese Islamic school. Here, as elsewhere, Soetomo first gives the Javanese word and then translates it into Indonesian for his non-Javanese readers.

ilmu.[37] *At that time,* there was no *sekolahan* yet.[38] Aside from studying Koranic recitation, he also learned to read and write Javanese and Malay, and studied *ilmu falak* [astronomy], which explains the course of the stars and moon. He also studied *ilmu kebatinan*[39] and *ilmu kedotan* (the knowledge whereby one is not wounded if stabbed and if struck feels no pain)[40] . . . In the time of my grandfather, youngsters were very fond of *sport* [*sic*] and art (*kunst*). One was not a man if one could not ride a saddleless horse and did not dare to stand up on the horse's back. One was also not a man if one could not use bow and arrow and handle a lance. Dancing and *nembang* [classical Javanese singing] were a part of art which self-respecting youngsters had to know, while *rampok harimau* was a sport widely popular among the People.[41]

And here is Soetomo's description of his grandfather offering his guests refreshments: "If one looks *at the time,* it is not surprising that my grandfather gave his labourers genever [Dutch gin]. *At that time,* too, even though people were already beginning to be aware [*sadar*] and ashamed [*malu*], there were many occasions when my grandfather would offer his guests opium . . . In olden times [*zaman kuno*], smoking opium was regarded as a sign and instrument of high status and luxury."[42]

The ambiguity of these descriptions undermines any initial confidence that the two "times" correspond either to two historical periods or to "tradition" and "modernity."[43] At no point does Soetomo express either nostalgia or contempt for the education of his grandfather. All we get is the enigmatic "if one looks at the time." Genever was a Dutch import into Java, and probably opium too, at least on a large scale, but here both appear as emblems of the *zaman kuno*.[44] There is no clear indication of the relationship between

---

37. The semantics of this passage are significant. Soetomo always uses the highly respectful "deep" word *ilmu* (clearly a translation of the Javanese *ngèlmu*) for "traditional" Javanese and Islamic studies. The sense is always knowledge of what is "real" or ontologically true. So far as I have been able to discover he never uses this word for things learned in Dutch schools.

38. *Sekolahan,* an indigenization of the Dutch word for school, has no particular resonances. Soetomo's laconic reference here leaves one in doubt about his stance towards these westernized schools. One might imagine that the sentence should be understood to run parallel to "no one yet rented their land to the sugar factories."

39. *Ilmu kebatinan*—knowledge of the inward—is the highest form of traditional Javanese religious learning, commonly referred to by westerners as "Javanese mysticism."

40. Soetomo, *Kenang-Kenangan,* pp. 10–11.

41. Ibid., p. 12. *Rampok harimau* is an Indonesian translation of the Javanese *rampog macan,* a gladiatorial battle between a panther or tiger and a group of armed men.

42. Ibid., p. 17. Emphasis added. The word translated as "high status" is *kebangsaan,* which usually means "nationality" or "race." I suspect that it may be a misprint for *kebangsawanan* (noble rank).

43. Yet note that, from our historical perspective, the *zaman kuno* must roughly coincide with Ronggawarsita's Time of Darkness.

44. The phallic hero of the *Suluk Gatholoco* is described as a dedicated opium-user.

sadar and *malu* (this is one of the rare occasions when these words occur in Memories). Social evolution? Political development? Cultural enlightenment? Or the transformation Hildred Geertz describes from *durung Jawa* (not yet Javanese, unaware, not knowing shame) to *wis Jawa* (Javanese, aware, knowing shame), transposed from Javanese children to Javanese society as a whole?[45]

The ambiguous relationship of past and present is nowhere better expressed than in the vivid episode where Soetomo describes his discomfort at the kind of village justice his grandfather meted out. The old man would tie village offenders to the pillars of his *pendhapa* (a sort of wall-less front pavilion to the headman's house) for several days at a time. "When I was adult, I had already been influenced by the writings of Multatuli[46]—the foremost champion of seizing and protecting the rights of our people—and I asked my grandfather what power [*kekuasaan*] gave him the right to be so bold as to sentence villagers in this way."[47] Here one might expect a conventional contrast of traditional and modern, old and new. But the story proceeds in an unexpected way, for the grandfather explains that his punishments are actually *a reform*—previously, criminals were sent away to jails in towns. Since, in his view, they typically returned as hardened characters, he created a new, local system of justice that would keep them within the village community. Soetomo concludes with these words. "So, though I could not agree with his stance, I could understand the reasons why my grandfather established these rules. And therefore, although I was already influenced by the new current [*aliran baru*], my respect for him did not diminish in the least, *especially if one looks at his time*."[48]

Soetomo's reference here to being influenced by Multatuli and the rather obscure "new current" is one of the very rare instances where "new thinking" is mentioned in Memories. But one does not get a strong feeling that the implications are developmental or progressive at all. The adult Soetomo simply did not initially understand his grandfather's reforms. There is neither an endorsement of his grandfather's actions nor an insistence on the correctness of the "new current." One merely senses a certain asymmetrical separation in moral stance. Soetomo, standing on his own moral ground,

---

45. Hildred Geertz, *The Javanese Family: A Study of Kinship and Socialization* (Glencoe: The Free Press, 1961), p. 105.

46. The reference is to the famous colonial iconoclast Eduard Douwes Dekker (1820–87), who under the pen name Multatuli ("I have suffered much") published a largely autobiographical novel called *Max Havelaar* in 1859. A vitriolic attack on the injustices of nineteenth-century colonial administration and the cruelty and corruption of the co-opted Javanese ruling class, it created a sensation, and helped to arouse a movement for reform in the Indies.

47. Soetomo, *Kenang-Kenangan*, p. 13.

48. Ibid., p 14. Emphasis added.

has learned to understand and to retain respect for his grandfather. But the old man, calmly confident of his good judgement, does not reciprocate.[49]

Over and over again in Memories this picture of connection and separation occurs. The ancestors remain "achieved," self-contained figures, fully manifesting and representing their ancestral qualities. When they quarrel, as Soetomo's grandfather and father are described as doing, they quarrel in a wholly unironical and representational way.[50] The father objects to the views of his father-in-law on the proper career for his son, but on the matter-of-fact grounds that they are practically and morally wrong. The two men are separated by their quarrel but united in the solid way they fill up their skins. Soetomo, their descendant, is not only bound to their "qualities" and "character," but sees this "bondedness" in a strange, new, detached way. He does not say that his ancestors' views are "wrong," precisely because he sees them as bathed in "time." Soetomo's separation from his forefathers is located exactly at this conceptual level: that he perceives himself and them encased in different times. Yet the *connection* is at the level of that pluralized perception. Here are signs of a new "watching self," of a distancing between person and culture. It looks very much, too, as if Soetomo is embarking on the construction of an *idea of a tradition*. For what, in the end, is a tradition, so understood, but a way of making connections in separation, of acknowledging by not repeating? The distinction between *zaman dahulu* and *masa sekarang*, then, is probably less one of historical epochs than of altered states of consciousness.

At the same time, we shall not exhaust the meaning of the term *zaman dahulu* if we do not juxtapose it to other uses of the word *zaman*. For example, we find Soetomo writing that it would be better for others to write the story of his life "after I have escaped from this fleeting time [*zaman yang fana*]";[51] or that it is inappropriate for a man's history to be written before he returns to "eternal time [*zaman yang baka*]."[52] Repeatedly, he says that in this *zaman yang fana* "no happiness or suffering lasts for ever."[53] In another passage he uses the old image of the "turning world."[54] In these figures there is, of course, something quite traditionally Javanese, but it would be inadequate to stress this point alone. What is more significant is their new relation to the other uses of *zaman*. In traditional Javanese thought there was, as it were, a

---

49. Soetomo presents a vivid contrast to Multatuli. One of the things that most outraged the Dutchman was the personalized (i.e., arbitrary) "justice" meted out by powerful native officials.

50. See below, p. 94. The relevant passages in *Kenang-Kenangan* are at pp. 66–8.

51. Ibid., p. 4.

52. Ibid., p. 3.

53. Ibid., p. 7.

54. Ibid., p. 22.

natural consonance between the movement of a man's life and the movement of the cosmos. The turning wheel is an image of motion and stillness, departure and return. The form of universal time is one of creation and destruction, and again creation and destruction.[55] Man is born into this *zaman yang fana*, lives his life, and then, as Soetomo puts it, "returns" to the *zaman yang baka*. The circle is completed and another generation starts a new cycle. So, for traditional Javanese man, death was the point towards which life moved, and in some sense becoming Javanese was learning to live in rhythm with this movement.[56]

It is clear that Soetomo understood and accepted an idea of time that could be either fleeting or eternal, an idea in which, indeed, that distinction overrode all others. In this sense he was a traditional Javanese. But he was also a man who had been educated in a western-style medical school, of which Darwinism was the cosmological underpinning, and for which death was defeat.[57] In this mode of consciousness the cosmos no longer turned but moved on, up, ahead, and death was not "return" but the real end of a man. Soetomo was thus fully exposed to the fundamental disjunction of progressive western thought—history as species development and life as individual decay. Memories shows that he was not only influenced by the "new current" (with all the ironies sprung tight within the phrase) but saw it within two quite different conceptions of time—and thereby found a recording self within.

In the central part of Memories, the life of Soetomo moves to its intersection with what today is taken as national history—the founding of Budi Utomo. Soetomo begins his account of his own life with six years of great happiness spent at the home of his grandfather in Ngepèh. The section is characterized by two contrasting themes: the basic harmony of village life and Soetomo's own unpleasant and destructive behaviour in it. The harmony of village life is not conveyed in the way that many later Indonesian nationalist leaders would figure it, in statements *about* that harmony and its ideological and cultural basis. Rather, it emerges in a way that is both typically Javanese and strongly reminiscent of the writing of Indonesia's greatest author, Pramoedya Ananta Toer. Here is Soetomo's description of a major village occasion:

---

55. See my *Language and Power*, chapter 1, especially pp. 33–5.

56. I well remember how my former music teacher in Jakarta, one of the most distinguished classical musicians of his generation, gradually divested himself of all his possessions and family responsibilities as he saw his end approaching. Nothing more gently determined could be imagined.

57. On the impact of Darwinian conceptions in Java in the early twentieth century, see, for example, Bernhard Dahm, *History of Indonesia in the Twentieth Century* (New York: Praeger, 1971), p. 30; Nagazumi, *Dawn,* pp. 45, 53, 185 (n. 80).

When the time came for *sambatan*—a request for help in carrying out some project that required many hands—a very big reception took place in the *pendhapa* of my grandfather's house. Dozens were given food there, so that the big *pendhapa* was full of people. The kitchen too was full of people working and serving those who were eating. *Sambatan* was usually performed when people were working the rice-fields. During the *sambatan* the rice-fields were bustling with villagers full of joy. Dozens of people were ploughing or harrowing side by side. "Hèr, hèr, hèr" or "Giak, giak, giak," signal-words to oxen or water-buffalo, could constantly be heard here and there. Tembang and *uran-uran*,[58] sung by those at work, made the hearts of those who saw and heard them filled with joy.

It was not only humankind that was drawn to and could experience the atmosphere, from the influence of this joy and happiness. It was as though the oxen and water buffalo also shared this joy of heart, shared in the seductive sound of that melodious and exalted *tembang* and *uran-uran*. Slowly, with steady pace, step by step, the oxen and water-buffalo walked on, dragging ploughs and harrows and chewing their cud. Sometimes, goaded by the flies that settled on and crawled over their bodies, they swung their horned heads from left to right, fanning their tails as well. Hearing the crack of the whip—though pestered by the flies—the oxen and water-buffalo walked on, walked on, mindful of and fulfilling their duty. Seeing such a peaceful scene, who would not share the fresh coolness in his heart, when everything was so tranquil and pleasing to the heart? What more could be hoped or asked for on this earth? Perhaps because of this feeling, because of the peace and unity of nature and living creatures, farmers find it hard to change their nature, a nature that loves this calm and peace. When work ceased about 11 o'clock, in the *pendhapa* plates of rice, dishes and pitchers were laid out in rows, awaiting the arrival of those who were coming to eat. Clamorous was the sound of the people heading for the *pendhapa* . . . Very often I was seated in the lap of one of the people in the *pendhapa*, facing the various bamboo plates and wooden trays filled with betel and tobacco, with a joyful heart because I was listening to the jokes of those who were filling their bellies. One by one, after each had eaten his fill, they came to where I was, to accept their share—a roll of betel with its accompanying ingredients and with tobacco. Anyone who knew me or who was rather bold, with kindly face and much laughter, would play with me by caressing that part of my body which is not fit to be mentioned here. Who would not feel happy, who would not feel the desire to be at one, with the fullest love, with those farmers?[59]

My playmates were Sadimin and Tjengèk, who at that time were youngsters. They shared in looking after me by playing their flutes. Tjengèk was a young blind boy, but it was as though he was never sad, always gay and joking. Only the voice of his flute, when it was blown, made a sound that was terrifying and moved the heart, as though hoping for some hope that could never be attained.[60]

---

58. *Tembang*—classical Javanese songs; *uran-uran*—folk songs.
59. Soetomo, *Kenang-Kenangan*, pp. 15–16.
60. Ibid., p. 58. Compare Pramoedya Ananta Toer's beautiful story "Anak Haram," in his *Tjerita dari Blora* (Jakarta: Balai Pustaka, 1952), pp. 227–62.

The most striking thing about these descriptions is the way they are filled with sound, not words. Words may be alluded to, as in the case of Tjengèk's jokes, but we know nothing of their content. No need to give words, except those without signification,[61] for the sense of happiness (and of Tjengèk's anguish) comes from sheer sound. The image of harmony is conveyed precisely by the absence of any separation between sound and meaning. (The harmony is only "spoiled" by the adult Soetomo, who, by writing words, tries to catch what to be caught cannot be spoken.)

By contrast, Soetomo describes his childhood self in the most unflattering terms. He was very spoiled, could twist his grandparents around his little finger, enjoyed whining to them about his uncles and aunts and seeing the latter reduced to tears.[62] "I felt myself extremely naughty, acted like a king and treated the people connected with me . . . in a quite arbitrary way."[63] Later, when he went to school, he was "spendthrift, arrogant, and proud if I could deceive my parents by asking for extra money on the pretext of needing books or a jacket, but actually to treat my friends or anyone else, if I happened to be going for snacks."[64] He liked to fight, was lazy about his studies, and regularly used to cheat in his examinations.[65] He was jealous of his younger brother, who he felt was favoured by his parents. On one occasion he felt so mortified by this discrimination that he rode off into the woods and burst into tears of anger and self-pity.[66] He used to steal as well.[67] There is only one aspect of his childhood character that he admires in retrospect—his rage at injustice and willingness to fight it.[68] But generally we are given a clear picture of a person with the traits least approved of by Javanese, and least like his forefathers, who in different ways are described as serious, hardworking, far-sighted, responsible, and "deep" people. One need not doubt that some of this is true and that Soetomo was indeed a spoiled and troublesome child. What is interesting, however, is that he makes so much of his bad behaviour.[69] As will become apparent later, the point is certainly *not* that the

---

61. For example, *hèr* and *giak*, sounds used to turn the oxen to the right and left.
62. Soetomo, *Kenang-Kenangan*, p. 55.
63. Ibid., p. 56.
64. Ibid., p. 68.
65. Ibid., pp. 65, 68.
66. Ibid., p. 64.
67. Ibid., pp. 61–2.
68. Ibid., p. 65. For more on this, see below, p. 93.
69. The full point of this emphasis will be brought out below, at pp. 95–7. To all this there is a remarkable parallel in the autobiography of the Burmese leader U Nu, *Saturday's Son*, trans. U Law Yone (New Haven, Conn.: Yale University Press, 1975). In chapter 1, "Flaming Youth," Nu cheerfully describes himself as a youthful liar, cheat, thief, brothel-frequenter, and dabbler in cocaine and opium. In this case, however, I am convinced that a systematic correspondence with the structure of the Gautama Buddha's life is intended.

"person" Soetomo developed forward from naughty child to respected national leader.

As mentioned earlier, before being enrolled in the STOVIA Soetomo was sent to a Dutch-language elementary school in Bangil. While in Bangil, he stayed with a maternal uncle. He gives us two main memories from this time in his life. The first is what he learned from this uncle, who is introduced to the reader in a rather curious way. Soetomo writes:

> [He] was an individual who was very strange in his manner of eating and drinking, let alone of sleeping . . . [He] rarely ate like ordinary people, and he mainly slept in the middle of the floor, on a chair. So too, after I had been Islamized [*dise-lamkan*—circumcized], as a result of his teaching I was ashamed to eat to the point my belly felt full. At that time I usually ate just once a day, and took care not to feel full and satisfied. If one found oneself in the midst of eating something extremely tasty, went my uncle's teachings, one should stop and not continue eating. Also, every evening I had to step outside the house, at least twice a night, and he required me to study how to have power over [*berkuasa*] the course of my thoughts. They had to be given direction, just like the desires of my own heart. To this end, every night I had to gaze with a calm mind to the West, East, North, and South, while Heaven and Earth too were not to be neglected. At that time, I did not fully understand the purpose of all this. But if I did not carry out this kind of obligation, my thoughts seemed impure and confused; while the act of gazing ahead, behind, left and right, above and below would bring cool freshness to my heart.[70]

What is remarkable about this passage is not the behaviour of the uncle, which is quite normal for a Javanese *priyayi* steeped in the meditative practices of *kebatinan* culture. Rather, it is that Soetomo should describe it as strange—and then go on to show that it became second nature to him. I suspect that we are to understand the word "strange" in two ways: the strangeness of the uncle's behaviour as it appeared to the child Soetomo, who was still "not yet Javanese"; and the strangeness felt by the new "watching self" in recording the long-past experiences of the inner self (*batin*).

The second interesting aspect of Soetomo's years in Bangil is what he tells of his activities in the elite *sekolahan* of his primary school: "My teachers and Dutch schoolmates never humiliated me—*quite the opposite*. But if I heard insulting words addressed to other Javanese students, like *penthol*[71] or

---

70. Soetomo, *Kenang-Kenangan*, p. 65. It is hard to know how to translate the latter part of this quotation, since the Indonesian has no automatic indicator of tense. It may be that Soetomo is here referring simultaneously to past and present.

71. *Penthol*—coarse Javanese for "idiot" or "dummy." Even today one can hear this phrase on non-Javanese lips.

"Javanese"—my listening ears burned. And if there was any situation that was unjust [*tidak adil*] I also acted, so that quite often I fought with the children at that school. I never won, for the Dutch pupils were bigger and stronger than my friends, and they could easily beat me down."[72] The description is quite matter-of-fact. But it is the first time in Memories that Soetomo speaks of himself favourably, even if wryly. The reader has learned in earlier passages that one essential aspect of Soetomo's father's nature was precisely his concern for justice (*keadilan*).[73] One could say, then, that the young Soetomo is starting to grow closer to the ancestral qualities. But he also goes out of his way to show that he was not ill-treated by his Dutch teachers or fellow pupils; "quite the opposite." It is important to see this not as a boast of his social acceptability to the Dutch,[74] but as a way of showing that the struggle for justice must involve an absence of personal interest (*pamrih*).[75] For in the Javanese tradition one does not seek justice for oneself, but out of commitment to one's *darma* (duty). The story thus has a double significance: it shows both a growing (sociological) consciousness of the racial injustices of colonial society, from which an intensifying nationalist movement was to grow, and a "deep" Javanese in the process of formation.

Following his account of his clashes with Dutch schoolchildren, Soetomo describes his holidays back at Ngepèh. Returning to his grandfather's home was "living in freedom with respect to naughtiness and pleasure. There I was spoiled and praised till I felt myself a truly extraordinary child."[76] Yet the very next thing he records is his very ordinary fear of lightning and thunder. When storms came he would run and hide his head in his grandmother's lap. But then his grandfather would take him by the hand and say to him "sweetly and gently": *Lé, kowé aja wedi karo bledhèg. Kowé rak turunan Ki Ageng Séla, mengko bledhèg rak wedi dhéwé.* Soetomo translates this for his non-Javanese

---

72. Soetomo, *Kenang-Kenangan*, p. 65.

73. Among many vivid examples perhaps the most affecting is Soetomo's account of his father's "hypermodern" (*sic*) attitude towards women. He was so "progressive" in wanting to give his daughters a good Dutch education that his neighbours suspected that he had become a Christian! "Very often in the evening, after work, he would take his daughters on his lap, one by one, or would support them with slow, quiet singing of *tembang*. And very often he would let fall some words on the injustice [*ketidakadilan*] of our people towards women." Ibid., pp. 48–9.

74. Compare the smug, colonial way in which Abu Hanifah, a leader of the political generation after Soetomo's, describes how he was fully accepted by the Dutch, unlike his friends and classmates, because of his superior understanding of the Dutch language and western ways. Abu Hanifah, *Tales of a Revolution* (Sydney: Angus & Robertson, 1972), pp. 39–40.

75. On *pamrih* in Javanese thinking, see my *Language and Power*, pp. 51–3.

76. Soetomo, *Kenang-Kenangan*, p. 66. Note the interesting negative use of *kemerdékaan* (freedom), jewel word to a later generation of Indonesians, in this moral context.

readers thus: "Child,[77] do not fear the lightning. Are you not the descendant of Ki Ageng Séla? Surely the lightning will come to be afraid of you." Soetomo concludes: "And because of the conviction in his words, gradually I lost my fear of thunder and lightning, however terrible their voice."[78]

It is difficult not to see in this passage, coming directly after Soetomo's defeats at the hands of the Dutch children, a veiled allusion to the struggle of Indonesians generally against the Dutch, "however terrible their voice." But in addition, we may note that courage here comes from memory—memory of one's origins. One grows up by growing back.

Next, in a section entitled "Why I followed my father's wishes,"[79] Soetomo turns to the reasons he became a student in the STOVIA. Here he describes the bitter conflict between his father and grandfather on the subject of his future. His grandfather desperately wanted Soetomo to become a high official. He used to urge the boy to refuse if his father tried to send him to medical school. His father, overwhelmed by the frustrations and humiliations of native official life, would have none of it for his son. Soetomo gives us two reasons why he followed his father's wishes and, somewhat surprisingly, tells us at what age each reason took effect. At the age of eight, he was childishly impressed by the white uniforms of the STOVIA students, which seemed much grander than the black garments worn by government officials. The second reason "happened" when he was about thirteen:

> At that time my father was an Assistant Wedana in Glodok, and once it so happened that I was at home. Very early in the morning my father had to go to Magetan in a *bèndi*.[80] About 4 a.m., my mother was already seated before the charcoal fire, toasting bread for breakfast, and I and my little brother were already awake. We saw father coming out of his room, already dressed in his official clothes, standing before us and grumbling about the status [*derajat*] of anyone who worked as a *priyayi* of the Binnenlandsch Bestuur . . . Because my father went on and on grumbling, I asked him: "Father, why do you do this work then?" My question was immediately answered: "If I did not do this work, would all of you be

---

77. *Lé* is probably untranslatable. A short form of *konthlé* (his penis), it is the usual affectionate Javanese term of address to a small boy. Javanese folklore has it that when the lightning attempted to strike the magically powerful Ki Ageng Séla, the sage seized it and tied it firmly to a nearby tree. The sobbing lightning was only released when it promised never to strike a descendant of its captor. These descendants—the people of Java—would be identified by the leaves of the poison-tree worn on their hats. To this day, some Javanese villagers wear these leaves if they are out in the open in thundery weather.

78. Soetomo, *Kenang-Kenangan*, p. 66. Note again, what is impressive to Soetomo is the conviction *in* the words, i.e. the *sound* more than the meaning.

79. Ibid., pp. 66–8.

80. *Bèndi*—two-wheeled horse-drawn carriage. In parts of rural Java even today the *bèndi* is a status symbol.

able to eat bread and butter?"[81] The word *korban* and the meaning of this word I did not yet understand, but hearing it in my inmost self [*batin*] I revered my father deeply. "I have only one request to make of you," so my father continued, "I ask that none of my children grow up to be B[innenlandsch]. B[estuur]. *priyayi*."[82]

In this passage we still see Soetomo as a child who "does not yet understand" (*belum mengerti*)—a phrase, it may be noted, that he never uses for any western-style teaching that he later receives. But the narration here is really more remarkable than the event. For while we can be sure that "historically" Soetomo's father spoke to his son in Javanese, his words here are given in Indonesian.[83] And we observe that Soetomo is caught by the word *korban*—which does not occur in the sentences his father utters! In one sense, it is clear what has happened. In his memory Soetomo must be recalling his father's words in Javanese, among them, very probably, *ngurban*. *Ngurban* is one of the deep moral and emotional words of Javanese, meaning to do without in order to achieve some great goal, or to help someone in need. It precisely echoes the teachings of Soetomo's uncle in Bangil.[84] The child Soetomo was thus struck by a word he did not yet understand, of which he was not yet "aware," but the understanding of which would later allow him to "become Javanese." The strange thing here, however, is the interlingual slippage. For the Indonesian sentence gives little sense of the moral exchange alluded to—which indeed has meaning primarily in a Javanese context. If Soetomo earlier translated his grandfather's words into Indonesian, now, perhaps involuntarily, he reverses course, moving from Indonesian back to Javanese. This is perhaps why he is not explicit about the lesson he learned. It may be that Soetomo, understanding something of his father's sacrifice, agreed to go to medical school, rather than become a "B.B. *priyayi*," out of gratitude and respect. Or, possibly, intimations of the idea of *ngurban*—giving direction to thoughts and desires for some greater purpose—led him to will his entry into an institution that would keep him permanently out of the old Javanese official elite and the traditional status hierarchy.

The following section brings us to the STOVIA. The picture of the author as a dirty, naughty, lazy, and spendthrift character is further elaborated. He

---

81. It is curious that Soetomo makes no particular point of this European-style breakfast, which must have been something of a rarity in the Javanese world of Madiun at the turn of the century.

82. Soetomo, *Kenang-Kenangan*, pp. 67–8.

83. This is true of all Soetomo's quotations from his father, whereas his grandfather's words are always first given in Javanese and then translated into Indonesian.

84. See the account of how his grandfather won his higher-status wife by prolonged ascetic self-denial. Ibid., p. 11. Cf. also *Language and Power*, pp. 24–5.

takes nothing seriously, since if he is expelled his grandfather will be pleased and his parents will support him anyway.[85] We learn almost nothing of what happens in the westernized classroom, only of childish pranks. But the section closes with these significant words: "Even though I was still spendthrift, obstinate, and naughty, yet about one year before my father left for eternal time [*zaman yang baka*]—it was only then that I understood that I too could work without copying (*nurun*) and thereby came the awareness [*kesadaran*] that working by copying is work in degradation."[86]

At first sight, this seems quite straightforward: a lazy boy comes to see that cheating is bad and childish. Yet I think there is more involved. Soetomo's language, particularly the terms *nurun* and *kesadaran*, suggests complexities of two different kinds. He gives us a hint by first using the Indonesian word *meniru* (to imitate, copy) and then adding the Javanese-derived *nurun* in parentheses.[87] On the one hand, this seems a clear allusion to the whole issue of modernization as "imitation" of the West, which haunted Soetomo's generation of Indonesian leaders.[88] Soetomo's readers in the 1930s would certainly have seen the words "working by copying is work in degradation" in the context of the whole colonial experience. That *kesadaran*—the key word of early nationalist thought—is used in this small classroom episode suggests the larger meaning of the narration. On the other hand, we should remember the significance of the idea of *turun* in Javanese culture. Being a true *turunan* (descendant) means not abandoning the nature or qualities of one's forefathers. Imitation, in the sense of drawing close to this nature, is central to the genealogy of Javanese morals.[89] We have already seen that the most important parts of Soetomo's education so far have been the occasions when he learned to imitate, following his grandfather, his uncle, or his father. So the passage quoted above gives us a pregnant image of the contrary directions of his dual education, symbolized by the antagonistic Dutch and Javanese meanings of imitation. "Without copying" in the Dutch classroom means "copying" Dutch culture, in other words, absorbing its values seriously; this however, implies not imitating Javanese tradition, which extols imitation. But it also foreshadows

---

85. Soetomo, *Kenang-Kenangan*, p. 69.

86. Ibid.

87. This is one of the very rare cases in Memories where Soetomo first uses an Indonesian term and then "explains" it in Javanese, rather than the other way round. *Nurun*, in the sense of cheating by copying, seems to have entered the Indonesian language from Javanese quite recently. For instance, it is not found in this sense in Welfridus Joseph Sabarija Poerwadarminta's standard *Kamus Umum Bahasa Indonesia* (Jakarta: Perpustakaan Perguruan Kementerian P.P. dan K., 1954).

88. This view is supported, I think, by the placing of the passage in the text—immediately *before* Soetomo's "change of nature." See below, pp. 97–9.

89. Imitation was, and is, a central tool of traditional Javanese pedagogy, whether in dance schools or *pesantrèn*.

the nationalist solution—imitating one's forefathers by not imitating them. Being a good Javanese by becoming a good Indonesian.

We come finally to the moral centre of Soetomo's Memories, the section that he calls "Change of Nature" [*Perobahan Perangai*].[90] Its content is simple but surprising, and in effect, perhaps for extra emphasis, it is told twice over. Soetomo has been accustomed to copying the work of his more industrious classmates. Then one day a teacher asks the class a pair of questions—one on algebra and the other on physics. Seeing no one else prepared to answer, even the brightest, Soetomo raises his hand just for fun and discovers "to my own astonishment" that he somehow knows the correct answer. This sudden ability is put in an interesting context: "The Director of the school had established a new system in my class, insisting that mathematics be taught over, so that the pupils could continually make use of their intellects . . . The reader should understand that our class had hitherto been given lessons that could be followed with very little *intellect*, provided one's memory [*geheugen*] was sufficient."[91] In the narrative the change in pedagogy is tied to Soetomo's discovery: "'Hey,' I thought, 'in this case I too have a brain.'" In other words, once the Dutch lessons stop being rote learning and imitation, Soetomo comes to perceive his own quality and capacity.[92] "From that time on, I grew ashamed to copy [*nurun*] any more."[93] It is with this awareness of shame—as it were, "becoming Javanese," but in the setting of a western classroom—that Soetomo shows his nature as having changed, so that he now can write: "It was only about two years before my father left me that it appeared from the expression on his face that he had some hopes for me. This is understandable because at that time my nature began to change. From childhood up till then, my life had always depended on others."[94]

About that time the character of his relations with his father also began to change. He no longer wrote home only to ask for money, but exchanged letters with his father about the proper education for his younger brothers and sisters. "My father began to have some esteem for me, whereas I had *drawn close to his batin*. In this happy condition, full of good hope for the flourishing of my family, in a time [*zaman*] of glorious ideals, suddenly and

---

90. Soetomo, *Kenang-Kenangan*, pp. 69–73.

91. Ibid. p. 70. Note the use of Dutch terminology here—*intellect* and *geheugen*. It is suggestive of the wide divergence between western and Javanese ideas of the components of personhood. Compare the earlier references to *batin*, and the remarks on *budi* below, p. 103.

92. A further involution of the paradox of imitation.

93. Soetomo, *Kenang-Kenangan,* p. 71. But Soetomo adds that, because he understood so well the misery of those pupils regarded as "stupid," he began regularly to help them with their work and to allow them to copy from him (p. 72). It is as if cheating is legitimate provided it is done without *pamrih*.

94. Ibid., p 69.

quite unexpectedly, on July 28, 1907, came a telegram telling of my father's death."[95]

Considering Soetomo's earlier account of his emotional relationship with his father as none too close,[96] the description of his feelings on the morrow of his bereavement may seem rather odd.

> Who can feel for the trouble that then assailed me?[97] No one in this world but those in a situation like my own. Even at that time, let alone now, I could not describe the trouble and the darkness that were in my heart; and my closest friends, even though they shared my sorrow, could not console me. I thought of the lot of my mother, I thought of that of my little brothers and sisters with the death of my father. It was as though they had lost the umbrella that protected them, lost the staff on which they leaned, lost everything, every promise and foundation that they needed for their development. What had we done wrong? Was God just? . . . My father's death at that time contained this meaning for me: it was as though I had received a punishment, quite unexpectedly and of immeasurable severity, meaning the loss of dignity, humiliation, and the rest . . . I felt that people had changed their attitudes towards me and my family. The respectful words, the generosity, the sweetness of their talk, and the kindliness of some of our acquaintances appeared not to be genuine, but only an external veneer—and this was because of the influence of my father's death.[98]

The people who came to console the family often stole his father's belongings, gossiped about his debts, and speculated about how much property he had left his children. "So I felt troubled and anguished, I felt humiliated, I felt deprived of honour, I felt that I lived like someone stripped stark naked in public . . . At this time of great grief, when it seemed as if the sun no longer showed his rays, at this time it was only my grandfather and my uncle who eased my burden."[99] In school he completely changed his behaviour: he stopped being spendthrift, naughty, and lazy—to the point that a gulf opened between him and his friends. "And so my life changed. At night it was the stars and the moon that became my friends, to help me concentrate [*mengheningkan cipta*], so that I could succeed, as eldest son, in fulfilling my responsibilities . . .[100] My

---

95. Ibid., p. 74. Emphasis added.

96. "My relationship to and love for my parents, up till the day of my father's death, was not very close and intimate. I was not much at ease with my father and mother, so that to them I used high Javanese [*bahasa kromo*]. In addition I felt not so much love as simply respect (*eerbied*). At that time, my love was directed only to my grandfather and grandmother" (ibid., p. 63).

97. This sentence seems grammatically confused. Soetomo has *tiada merasai* (cannot feel) when the sense requires simply *merasai*.

98. Ibid., pp. 74–5.

99. Ibid., p. 75.

100. Ibid., p. 76. *Mengheningkan cipta* (Javanese, *ngeningaken cipta*) means the practice of meditation for the concentration of one's inner being. Here Soetomo applies the teachings of his uncle in Bangil.

thoughts and feelings became separated from their environment, seeking another course for their life, heading in another direction which would bring them an opportunity to flower."[101]

Soetomo now became the head of the stricken family and had to assume the responsibilities involved. What is interesting in his description of that time, however, is his new perception of exterior and interior (*lahir* and *batin*) and the separation he records himself experiencing from the world.[102] This separation prepares the way for a denouement that is not depicted as such in Memories but is prefigured in the passages cited above. For Soetomo now seeks to "meet" his father and to live up to the moral responsibilities of family and tradition.[103] But he will do this by "finding *another* direction."

Five months later, at the onset of the rains at the end of 1907, Dr. Wahidin Soedirohoesodo arrived in Batavia to rest from his long search for funds to help intelligent young Javanese pursue western education. During his stay, he came to speak to the STOVIA students. Here is how Soetomo describes that meeting, from which Budi Utomo was to be born a few months later:

> The meeting with Dr. Wahidin Soedirohoesodo, with his tranquil features, his wise manner and tone, and his conviction in explaining his ideals, left a deep impression on me. His melodious and *rustig* [Jav., *sarèn*] voice opened up my thoughts and spirit, and brought me new ideals and a new world that could, it seemed, console my wounded heart. Speaking with Dr. Wahidin, listening to his aims . . . removed all narrow feelings and goals limited to my own private needs. One became another person, one felt oneself in motion, trembling throughout one's flesh and bones, one's views became broad, one's feelings refined [*halus*], one's ideals beautiful . . . in short, one felt one's most high obligations in this world.[104]

---

101. Ibid., p. 78.

102. This is figured in the disjuncture depicted between the sounds of the neighbours' words and their meaning. Contrast this disjuncture with the deep correspondence shown in Soetomo's accounts of the *sambatan* in Ngepèh (above) and of his feelings about Dr. Wahidin (below).

103. There is probably a parallel here with one of the basic themes of the Javanese *wayang*: a young hero's separation from his father and long search to find him. The moment of maximum separation occurs when the devoted young man, alone in the forest except for a wise guru (Dr. Wahidin?), practises meditation to find the means for completing his quest. The depth of his concentration produces the *gara-gara*, or churning of the cosmos (formation of Budi Utomo?). The play's resolution usually comes when the long-lost father acknowledges the hero as truly his descendant (*turunan*). On this theme, see K.P.G.A.A. Mangkunagara VII, *On the Wayang Kulit (Purwa) and Its Symbolic and Mystical Elements*, trans. Claire Holt (Ithaca, NY: Cornell University, Southeast Asia Program Data Paper no. 27, 1957), pp. 11–16.

104. Soetomo, *Kenang-Kenangan*, pp. 80–81. In this passage, as so often, Soetomo turns from Dutch or Indonesian to Javanese to express the nuances of his feelings. Note that the very syntax of the closing sentence—the shift from "I" to "one" (my poor translation of *orang* here)—conveys the abandonment of egoism and *pamrih*—and perhaps a movement from Soetomo the individual to the whole audience of Javanese boys.

Here the autobiographical part of Memories comes to an end, with Soetomo just nineteen and Budi Utomo still unformed. The rest of the book records the services of Soetomo's friends, retainers, and, above all, his wife. From these pages one can infer something of his later life, but that is not the focus of the writing. From Soetomo's perspective, I think, what is essential has already been said.

Had his life, in his own eyes, had a linear trajectory, had it run in some sense parallel to the movement of the world, the political events of 1907–8 would have been a mere beginning. But I think that it should now be clear that the perceived movement of his life had another shape, not so much political, in our sense of the word, as moral. To specify this shape more clearly, it may be useful to turn to a term that Soetomo himself elsewhere employs— *lelakon*, appointed course in life, somewhere between *darma* and destiny. For the events of 1907–8—losing his father and finding Dr. Wahidin, leaving his family and finding his *guru*—reflect the passage of a Javanese man's life, from *kesenangan* (pleasure) to *kewajiban* (duty), from *kenakalan* (naughtiness) to *kemuliaan* (excellence), from imitation to setting an example.[105]

Nothing could be more striking, in this connection, than the strange link between the enormous, almost physiological surge of emotion, the giddy feeling of immensely expanding horizons that Soetomo records of his meeting with Dr. Wahidin, and the picture he gives of the doctor himself. Not only do we get a glimpse of a most traditional, if resolute, Javanese gentleman,[106] but we are brought back to a unified world where sight, sound, and meaning again coincide. "Calm," "melodious," "tranquil"—the expressions Soetomo uses for the sound and sight of Dr. Wahidin he had used earlier to describe the village life of Ngepèh, the circle of *zaman kuno*. "Not yet Javanese," he had then been a disruptive element. Now Javanese, he rejoins his forefathers.

Yet if he has found his *asal* (origins), we are not being treated to the simple

---

105. Compare the last two portions of Ronggawarsita's *Kala Tidha,* entitled *Sabda Tama* and *Sabda Jati.*

106. In a passage immediately antecedent (p. 80) Soetomo transmits a story that Wahidin told about himself. In a certain place where he hoped to call a meeting to raise scholarship funds, the Dutch Assistant Resident was antagonistic. Accordingly, the local *priyayi,* who secretly wished to attend, did not dare go. So Wahidin entered the Dutchman's office (here the syntax changes and Soetomo takes over the narration from Wahidin) and stood there quite still—until the Assistant Resident looked at him. Acting as though in awe, he prostrated himself below the Dutchman's table, offering the respectful *sembah* gesture and speaking in the humblest language: "Tuan Assistant Resident became *sabar* [got control of himself], and at that very moment his face became sweet and smiling. Tuan Assistant Resident said to him: 'Doctor, your purpose deserves the strongest support. It would be well if you spoke before a meeting, so that all my officials can hear you.' Thus by the aid of Tuan Assistant Resident, who had originally intended to block his purpose, [Dr. Wahidin] won extraordinary attention." The gentle irony of this episode, no less than the acceptance of submission to achieve a high aim, is characteristically Javanese.

story of a Javanese growing up. For the traditional Dr. Wahidin brings the young Soetomo "new ideals and a new world." What were these new ideals, this new world? The western science and rationalism of which Van Niel writes? In such matters Soetomo was already far better educated than the old doctor had ever been. With his years in the ELS and the STOVIA, with his excellent command of Dutch, Soetomo was much closer to the "new world" conceived by westerners than was his enlightener. I believe rather that Soetomo, and probably others in the STOVIA milieu, sensed in Wahidin an example of how to proceed into the colonial western world without imitation; at a deeper level, how to imitate one's forebears without imitating them, how not to abandon Javanese tradition when one no longer lived embedded in it, and how to match the watching self with the *batin*. Ronggawarsita had imaged the Time of Darkness with the harsh oxymoron of impotent kingly perfection. The *ratu utama*, sign for Glorious Java, was no longer believable. Wahidin, however, showed that it was possible, even essential, to detach adjective from noun. Once detached, the weight of its meaning shifted from what we might call political efficacy to ethical commitment: in a word, to a perfected moral faculty (*budi utama*). And this ethical commitment was a burden that anyone might assume—not excluding Javanese teenagers, especially one whose own name compounded *su* (excellent) with *utama* (perfected).[107]

But commitment to what? In the old Javanese tradition, kingly perfection meant commitment to kingly power. Concentrated power produced fertility, prosperity, and harmony in the community. Social well-being was a by-product of power's commitment to itself.[108] But once kingly power had proven impotent, the by-product could readily become the central goal.

If one looks at the ideas that Soetomo worked with all his life, one finds a vocabulary and an idiom of a very consistent kind. There is, for example, almost no utilization of political notions based in western sociology.[109] The Marxian categories central to the political language of Sukarno's entire generation, from its conservative to its radical members, are totally absent. Where Sukarno and his contemporaries talked of Indonesia Merdéka (Free Indonesia), Soetomo typically spoke of his ideal as Indonesia Mulia (Glorious, or Perfected Indonesia). *Merdéka*, liberation, implied, of course, much more radical and *political* aims. It is a word that is the peculiar glory of Indonesian, or "revolutionary Malay,"[110] but has few resonances in Javanese.

---

107. Koch, *Batig Slot*, writes: "The struggle for social betterment attracted him [Soetomo] more than politics. He radiated love for his country and his people" (p. 139).

108. See my *Language and Power*, chapter 1.

109. See Scherer, "Harmony," pp. 212–13. For a full discussion of Soetomo's political thinking, see also pp. 207–47.

110. See *Language and Power*, chapter 1.

Mulia is just the reverse. In the passage of Memories quoted above (p. 98) we can see what *mulia* naturally goes with, and it seems the very opposite of *kemerdékaan: kewajiban,* or obligation.

As Savitri Scherer has sensitively shown, Soetomo compared Indonesia Mulia to a *gamelan* orchestra in which each person plays the instrument allotted to him as best he can. From the intertwining of fulfilled musical obligations comes the glory (*kemuliaan*) of the gamelan sound.[111] Playing one's instrument is performing one's *lelakon,* living up to the responsibilities one has inherited or that have fallen to one's lot. Soetomo's idea of uplifting his society was to make it feasible for all the instruments to be played as perfectly as possible. Peasants and workers had to be fed, cared for, and educated to become good peasants and good workers, mindful of their obligations and capable of fulfilling them.[112] When in the 1930s—to the disgust of some of his younger nationalist colleagues—Soetomo appealed to the collaborationist aristocracy and *priyayi* for their support, he did so by way of urging them to "remember their origins," in other words, to accept the moral obligations of their tradition.[113]

We can perhaps then think of Soetomo's nationalist mission in terms of a musical simile, involving the systematic transposition of old melodies into new keys, different scales, and changed orchestrations. Memories offers some conspicuous examples of this. His uncle meditated in his Javanese home, Soetomo in the western STOVIA. His grandfather created a system of "useful justice" in Ngepèh, and Soetomo spent his life in search of a useful justice for the Indonesia being born.[114] His father tried to live with dignity in the chains of the colonial bureaucracy, Soetomo did so as an alien-trained doctor. His forefathers, as he described them, saw marriage as a cementing of solidarity

---

111. Compare the overwhelmingly *aural* depiction of the harmony pervading the *sambatan* in Ngepèh (above).

112. Scherer, "Harmony," pp. 218–39. This association of *gamelan* and politics is not merely an eccentricity of Soetomo's. I have heard from elderly court musicians in Surakarta that there is a special *gamelan* composition called "Dendha Séwu," traditionally played when the ruling dynasty was in grave trouble. The composition itself is not technically difficult, so that if the court's master-musicians could not play it perfectly, this was taken as a confirming omen of impending disaster.

113. Soetomo said of his party, Parindra, that it "makes the best effort to woo them [the upper *priyayi*] so that their dedication to the land and the people could be accelerated according to their own darma, that is, the darma of a true ksatrya according to their aristocratic blood." Taken from Soetomo's address to Parindra's opening congress, December 25, 1935, titled "Bekerdja dengan tiada mengenal buahnja," and cited in Scherer, "Harmony," p. 235.

114. In *Kenang-Kenangan,* p. 20, Soetomo notes that his grandfather, bitterly disappointed that the boy was not going to enter the native administration, requested that at the very least he keep a horse for riding, as a sign of *priyayi*-dom. "Quite unexpectedly, there came a time when I could fulfil my grandfather's longing. When as a doctor I had to care for the health of the people in the region of Mt. Lawu, I kept two horses which, every day, turn and turn about, bore me to the villagers." A nice image of transposition: rural doctor as the new *priyayi.* Soetomo also

in the Javanese world; and Soetomo, in his touching description of his Dutch wife, appears to have seen his own marriage in the same light.[115] But the central image of transposition is the organization that Soetomo made history by founding: Budi Utomo. For Budi Utomo is fully recognizable in both Javanese and Indonesian tonalities.[116] Situated across the two languages, it looked both forward and back, signifying committed endeavour—a later generation would say struggle[117]—to live up to something long there in the memory and imagination.

The images of light, dawn, and sun suffusing the publications of the Budi Utomo years are both specific to the course of Javanese and Indonesian history and larger symbols of revival and regeneration.[118] They are images

---

recalls (p. 42) that his father insisted on speaking in high Javanese to almost everyone and in this was among the first to spread "democratic ways." Supardi (*Dr. Soetomo*, pp. 36, 38) notes that Soetomo did exactly the same thing, and habitually addressed his driver, Pak Soemo, in *krama*. It is perhaps characteristic, nonetheless, that between *ngoko* (low, familiar Javanese) and *krama*, Soetomo and his father chose to "abolish" *ngoko* (as it were, levelling *up*). Nagazumi (*Dawn*, p. 193, n. 26) mentions the appearance of a movement, not long after the birth of Budi Utomo, called Jawa Dwipa (Dipo), which advocated the abolition of *krama* (as it were, levelling *down*). The roughly contemporaneous Saminist movement also resolutely refused to use *krama* to officialdom. See Harry J. Benda and Lance Castles, "The Samin Movement," *Bijdrage tot de taal-, land- en volkenkunde*, 125 (1969), p. 234.

115. "Here it is only fitting that I express my immeasurable gratitude to her. My wife was someone who truly loved her country. And so she understood and was aware, and constantly urged and prodded me to make my love for my land and people still deeper, and to give that love real expression. My wife was also someone who loved her people. And so she understood my obligation to my people, and constantly urged me to prove my love for my people. My wife stood, not above her people, but amongst them. And so her love was truly alive. As a true Dutchwoman, my wife loved freedom, justice, and equality; and so she could not endure a situation full of discrimination, and hated to see behaviour that could stain the good name of her nation. It was because of these feelings that she continually urged me to keep on fighting, to join the struggle to abolish this discrimination" (Soetomo, *Kenang-Kenangan*, pp. 127–8).

116. *Budi utama* is perfectly good, if stilted, Indonesian.

117. Compare Sudisman, *Analysis*: "We live in order to struggle, and we struggle in order to live. We live not just for the sake of life alone; we live to defend that life with courage till our hearts cease to beat. From the moment that a human being is born, from hls first whimper as a baby to his last breath, life is a struggle. Sometimes he will face a struggle that is very difficult, sometimes he will face a hard-fought battle. Not every such contest is crowned with victory. But the aim of life is to have the courage to enter this hard-fought battle and at the same time win the victory. This is the dream of everyone who struggles, not excluding the communists. This too is my dream of life. For without dreams, without ideals, life is barren and empty" (p. 24).

118. See Taufik Abdullah, "Modernization in the Minangkabau World," pp. 215–18. He speaks of one of the early modernizers in West Sumatra, Datuk Sutan Maharadja, the "father of Malay journalism," who from 1891 to 1913 was successively involved in newspapers entitled *Palita Ketjil* [Little Lamp], *Warta Berita* [News Report], *Tjaja Soematera* [Light of Sumatra], *Oetoesan Melajoe* [Malay Messenger], *Al-Moenir* [Enlightenment], and *Soeloeh Melajoe* [Malay Torch]. Compare the splendid discussion of comparable imagery in China during more or less the same period, in Maurice Meisner, *Li Ta-Chao and the Origins of Chinese Marxism* (Cambridge, Mass.: Harvard University Press, 1967), especially pp. 21–8.

conjured up at moments when men's lives appear to run in tandem with the world. When they appear under conditions in which progressive conceptions of time are influential, one would expect them to be linked to images of youth. This is clearly true of the early years of Budi Utomo. How close the nexus between life-moment and linear history was can be judged from the observation of Goenawan Mangoenkoesoemo, Soetomo's closest friend, that the aim of the boys in Budi Utomo was to "remain a motor in order to propel their seniors from behind."[119] The phrase not only employs a distinctly twentieth-century industrial metaphor but, in the Javanese context, sharply reverses the hoary pedagogic apophthegm *tut wuri andayani*—perfection comes when old people guide the young from behind.[120] It is a mordant, excited expression that belongs to youth.

We find nothing comparable in the Memories of Soetomo. Images of light and dawn are quite rare in it. The tone of the book is sombre and centres on death rather than birth. If we ask ourselves why this should be so, I think the answer is quite straightforward. By 1934, Soetomo, for all his political successes,[121] was no longer in the vanguard of the nationalist movement. As a man of his time, as well as a Javanese, he could see that the movement's progress and the trajectory of his own life were diverging. His wife had returned to the *zaman yang baka* and he was preparing in due course to follow her. It was time to think about bequests (*warisan*), and a *warisan* is really what Memories represents.

Ronggawarsita had lamented that there was "no example left." What he meant was that the old models no longer worked, and so could not be handed down. It was Soetomo's (and his generation's) quiet triumph to have reclaimed their ancestry and to have found thereby an example to bequeath to their posterity.

---

119. Cited in Nagazumi, *Dawn*, p. 42.

120. It became a central theme in the educational philosophy of the Taman Siswa school system created by Soetomo's famous contemporary Ki Hadjar Dewantara.

121. For example, Rukun Tani, the peasant organization he formed in East Java, had more than 20,000 members in 125 branches in 1933, making it easily the largest rural organization affiliated with the nationalist movement. See John Edward Ingleson, "The Secular and Non-Cooperating Nationalist Movement in Indonesia, 1923–1934" (Ph.D. thesis, Monash University, 1974), p. 419. On the successful growth of Parindra, see Susan Abeyasekere, "Relations between the Indonesian Cooperating Nationalists and the Dutch, 1935–1942" (Ph.D. thesis, Monash University, 1972), pp. 127–31.

5

Professional Dreams

Mark Twain put it characteristically: "A classic is something that everybody wants to have read and nobody wants to read." Few major works of the later era of traditional Javanese literature fit his words better than the *Serat Centhini.*[1] Ritually described as a masterpiece and, more interestingly (as we shall see), as an encyclopedia of Javanese culture, it has never been printed in its entirety. The only substantial published version, an eight-volume Romanized edition, appeared seventy-five years ago.[2] With a few notable

---

1. According to Behrend, ninety-eight variant manuscripts of this poem, in eight major recensions, can today be found in various public collections in Indonesia and The Netherlands. The oldest known version originates from a Cirebon manuscript of 1616. The fullest *Centhini,* a colossal work of almost a quarter of a million lines, was completed, he argues, in 1814. It is thought to have been prepared by a committee of poets in the entourage of the then crown prince of Surakarta, who later became Pakubuwana V. Tradition has it that the prince sent emissaries all over Java and Madura to gather every possible form of Javanese knowledge for inclusion in the final text. See Timothy E. Behrend, "The Serat Jatiswara: Structure and Change in a Javanese Poem, 1600–1930" (Ph.D. thesis, Australian National University, 1988), pp. 79–84.

2. *Serat Tjentini,* ed. R.Ng. Soeradipoera, R. Poerwasoewignja, and R. Wirawangsa (Batavia [Jakarta]: Ruygrok, 1912–15). Behrend believes that the initiative was taken by the scholar-bureaucrat Douwe Rinkes, then director of the Bataviaasch Genootschap van Kunsten en Wetenschappen (Batavian Society of Arts and Sciences), who had the text prepared in Leiden, then sent to Surakarta for checking by Soeradipoera and his aides, and finally printed in Batavia at the Society's expense. Behrend, "Serat Jatiswara," p. 89. The only other substantial Romanized version, appearing in four volumes sixty years later, covered barely half the material in the 1912–15 edition: viz., *Serat Centhini,* ed. Tardjan Hadidjaja (Yogyakarta: U.P. Indonesia, 1976–77).

exceptions, it has been neglected by both western and modern Javanese scholars.[3] Where not ignored, it has been mined primarily for the copious information it provides on Javanese artistic and religious traditions. But the text also marks an important milestone in the historical development of Javanese political culture.

If the *Serat Centhini* can be said to have a story, it amounts to the following: after the bloody sack in 1625 of the prosperous Islamic, East Javanese port kingdom of Giri by the armies of Sultan Agung of the Central Javanese kingdom of Mataram, the three children of the vanquished ruler (two male, one female) are forced to flee for their lives. Hunted by the spies of Mataram, they are separated: the elder son, Jayèngresmi (later known as Sèh Amongraga), escapes to the west, while the younger son and the daughter (Jayèngsari and Rancangkapti) try to elude their pursuers to the southeast. The text describes their adventurous wanderings in a vain search to be reunited. They are, however, linked by the odd figure of Cebolang, who first appears attached to the small retinue of Amongraga and ends up marrying Rancangkapti. Cebolang is described as the only child of a revered sage living on Mount Sokayasa, who, however, disowns the youth on account of his inveterate gambling, thieving, and adulteries. Forced to survive by his wits, Cebolang earns his bread as a wandering musician, dancer, and what for want of a better word I shall call conjuror.

The fact that its leading characters are fugitives or outcasts permanently on the move means that the *mise en scène* of the *Centhini* is very different from that usually associated with traditional Javanese literature. There are no episodes on battlefields or in royal courts and capitals. The ruler of Mataram is merely an ominous, gloomy presence off stage. For the most part, the text's settings are a series of villages and rural Islamic schools (*pesantrèn*), while the cast of characters, male and female, are *kyai* (traditional Islamic men of learning), *santri* (their students), headmen, traders, professional musicians, singers, dancers, prostitutes, and ordinary villagers. The settings, and the encounters that take place in them, provide opportunities for the hugely elaborate descriptions of many traditional aspects of Javanese rural life—folk

---

3. The most substantial mining of the *Centhini*'s vast resources is in Theodoor Gautier Thomas Pigeaud's encyclopedic work on the traditional performing arts of Java and Madura: *Javaansche Volksvertoningen* (Batavia: Volkslectuur, 1938). The eminent ethnomusicologist Jaap Kunst quoted many short passages dealing with music in his monumental *Music in Java: Its History, Its Theory and Its Technique* [3rd enlarged edn., ed. Ernst L. Heins] (The Hague: Nijhoff, 1973; originally published by Nijhoff in 1934 as *De Toonkunst van Java*). See also S. Soebardi, *The Book of Cabolèk: A Critical Edition with Introduction, Translation, and Notes: a Contribution to the Study of Javanese Mystical Tradition* (The Hague: Nijhoff, 1975; based on his 1967 Australian National University Ph.D. thesis).

arts, architecture, cooking, cultivations, ceremonies, fauna and flora, religion, medicine, sexual practices, and so forth—that have earned the *Centhini* its reputation as the encyclopedia of Old Java.

ENCYCLOPEDIC POLITICS

Ann Kumar has drawn explicit comparisons between the rural social orders prevailing in Java and France during the eighteenth century. She has thereby signally advanced the conscious incorporation of Old Java's history into the larger history of the modern world.[4] I believe it is possible to extrapolate from her comparisons to reflect on class relations other than those between lords and peasants. An interesting point of departure is suggested by a glance at two encyclopedias—our own *Centhini,* and that of Diderot, d'Alembert, and their associates—composed within half a century of one another.[5] While it is true that the *encyclopédistes* foreshadowed the rise to power of the French bourgeoisie, their immediate circle was of quite mixed social origins;[6] moreover, the specific, revolutionary character of their *Encyclopédie* has no exact parallel in the historical rise of other European bourgeoisies. For their project was to marshal a colossal, systematically organized compendium of all the multifarious knowledge accumulated by, and available to, the professional men of learning of their time. The animus behind it was hostility, not merely to reactionary *idées reçues* but also to the ecclesiastical and monarchical authorities behind them. Against the *general* (cultural and political) power of Church and Crown, Diderot and his associates mobilized a formidable coalition of *specific* virtuosities. In effect, the aim was to show that on almost any topic—from the nature of magnetism to the origins of language—the (mostly) commoner, lay cognoscenti "knew more" than their putative social and religious superiors. In this sense, the *Encyclopédie* can usefully be understood as a weapon in the struggle between a professional, secular clerisy and the whole structure of hegemony of the *ancien régime.*

---

4. Ann Kumar, "The Peasantry and the State on Java: Changes of Relationship, Seventeenth to Nineteenth Centuries," in James Austin Copland Mackie, ed., *Indonesia: Australian Perspectives* (Canberra: Australian National University, Research School of Pacific Studies, 1980), pp. 577–99. For this essay she drew on several of her own earlier monographic studies, and also on the fine research of Robert Elson, Onghokham, Theodoor Pigeaud, and Bertram Schrieke.

5. I take Behrend's 1814 dating of the full *Centhini* as reasonable, and 1777 as the date of publication of the final supplementary volume of the *Encyclopédie ou Dictionnaire Raisonné des Sciences, des Arts et des Métiers.*

6. Montesquieu and d'Alembert had aristocratic backgrounds, though the latter was illegitimate. Diderot, Voltaire, and Rousseau were of bourgeois or lower origins.

Now I think it can be argued that the *Centhini* reflects a parallel animus, albeit in a very different political, social, and cultural setting. One might begin the argument by noting three striking general features of this immense poem. The first is that it is thickly strewn with what look very much like entries in an odd sort of encyclopedia.[7] There are, for example, many passages, some several stanzas long, that consist purely of lists: of Javanese sweetmeats, edible freshwater fish, joists and tenons, theological terms, musical compositions, names of mountains, cloths, dances, and so forth. These passages have no syntax—they read like unalphabetized, poetic Yellow Pages. Furthermore, it is very hard to fit them to the traditional aesthetics of Javanese poetry, which was almost always meant to be sung. (An English parallel might be a song consisting, without irony, of the names of forty-five brands of breakfast cereal.) Hence, one gets the distinct feeling that such passages are actually meant less to be recited than to be read (consulted?). In other words, if the Javanese reader (not listener) wished to check all the different types of Javanese cookie or *gamelan* composition, he could go to the *Centhini* and look them up. And the sources of all this knowledge (*ngèlmu*) are not priests, or sages, or noblemen, but virtuoso professionals and compilers.

The second striking feature of the *Centhini* is the way in which the text treats such topics as supernatural entities and sacred objects attached to kings and courts. For they are handled in exactly the same matter-of-fact, encyclopedic way as fish, flora, or food. Canto 85, stanzas 4–5, for example, offers the reader a deadpan catalogue of a score of typical Javanese ghosts and goblins, organized neither alphabetically nor in order of scariness, but simply to fit the prosodic requirements of the metre Wirangrong.

Third is the noticeable absence of any depiction of *kasektèn* (magical power) being deployed by members of the ruling strata, or indeed by anyone else.[8] The significance of this absence becomes apparent if one compares the *Centhini* with the tales of the *wayang purwa* (traditional shadow-puppet plays), or with such royal chronicles as the *Babad Tanah Jawi*. In the *wayang* stories the aristocratic heroes make the heavens tremble and the seas boil when they meditate; the arrows they shoot in battle turn into thousands of serpents or demons. One hero may fly comfortably through the air; another may simultaneously impregnate a dozen heavenly nymphs; still another penetrates to the depths of the ocean and enters the ear of a deity who is a

---

7. The *Encyclopédie* already used the most easily accessed of taxonomic principles—alphabetic order—to order its entries. In the *Centhini* there is no ordering principle beyond the requirements of narrative and prosody. The only way to find an entry is to know the poem very well.

8. See my *Language and Power*, chapter 1, for a discussion of the Javanese idea of Power.

miniature version of himself. In the chronicles one finds balls of magical radiance descending on the heads of those destined to become kings, mysterious couplings—over successive generations of a dynasty—with Nyai Lara Kidul, the Power-full Goddess of the Southern Seas, and so on. It is hard not to see in the *Centhini*'s refusal of all these marvels a discreetly Gibbonian iconoclasm.

What might be the social basis for the peculiarities that I have briefly adumbrated? Is there anything to be learned from comparison with eighteenth-century France? Two points seem especially worth bearing in mind. First, Diderot and his *confrères* were, in their own view, skilled professionals, men and women devoted to the mastery and development of particular types of knowledge. Second, thanks to the rise of print-capitalism in Europe already from the end of the fifteenth century, the importance of writers within the broader group of professionals was very high.[9] (This is why Diderot and Voltaire exemplify mid-eighteenth-century Europe for us, rather than the professional musicians Mozart and Haydn and the professional painters Tiepolo and Fragonard.) By contrast, Java did not encounter print-capitalism until the late nineteenth century. This lateness did not mean that Old Java lacked a substantial professional stratum, but rather that, because print-capitalism did not arrive till the latter half of the nineteenth century, littérateurs had no special prestige or political position within this stratum.[10] Alongside (not above) them were ranged the architects who envisioned, planned, and supervised the construction of Java's myriad mosques, palaces, and fortifications; the puppet masters (*dhalang*) who over generations built the varied traditions of the shadow-play; the expert musicians who created the panoply of Javanese musical genres; the adepts of the many branches of Islamic learning; not to speak of dancers, actors, sculptors, smiths, painters, curers, astrologers, magicians, folk botanists, martial-arts teachers, burglars, and so on.[11] Such people were almost invariably commoners, but they were certainly not common people. Some were drawn into the service of royal courts and provincial lords, particularly if the exercise of their knowledge and skills required the backup of sizeable amounts of manpower and capital (for example, architects), which only such centres of political and economic power could provide. Others preferred the freedom of the road—joining Pigeaud's

---

9. See my *Imagined Communities: Reflections on the Origin and Spread of Nationalism* (London: Verso, 1983), chapter 3.

10. One notes that the bureaucratic rank-titles given to court poets and chroniclers were rarely higher than those bestowed by the rulers on senior dance masters and leaders of court *gamelan* ensembles.

11. There exist a number of interesting manuscripts that treat the science of housebreaking with encyclopedic thoroughness.

memorable swarm of *zwervers en trekkers*[12]—peddling their specialities on the broader social market (for example, actors and teachers of martial arts). Still others, such as kyai and *guru ngèlmu* (teachers of mystical lore), would settle in rural retreats, drawing to themselves acolytes and clients by word of respectful or astonished mouth.

There is no satisfactory way to estimate the size of this stratum of experts as a proportion of the Javanese population in the later eighteenth century.[13] But it was certainly much larger than the ruling class. How far different kinds of specialists recognized in one another members of a common stratum is also impossible to guess. What is clear is that, in different degrees, they recognized that they knew things and could do things that the rulers could not. (Born to rule, the Javanese aristocracy had no need to develop specialized knowledges, and assumed, like English gentlemen, an autocratic amateur status.) But because of the existing distribution of social prestige, economic resources, and political power the specialists were almost always forced to defer to, and often to depend for their livelihood on, such privileged amateurs. This general subordination did not mean that they were not proud of their virtuosities, merely that they were usually prevailed upon to conceal or cloak that pride. (I remember very well from the early 1960s when I visited the decrepit court of Surakarta, how the elderly court musicians sat poker-faced through a long speech about the nature of Javanese music delivered by a no less elderly prince; only after the prince was out of sight did discreetly mocking smiles

---

12. In his *Javaansche Volksvertoningen*, pp. 35–6, Pigeaud observes that travelling players "were unquestionably part of the large group of vagabonds and wanderers which must have been a key element in Java's social traffic in olden times." Other elements he mentions are pedlars, merchants, *santri*, and *satria lelana* (banished or masterless "knights") with their retinues, who were often "hard to distinguish from bandits."

13. But the remarkable statistics collected by Jaap Kunst in the early 1930s are suggestive (*Music in Java*, pp. 570–71). At that time the population of Java and Madura was just under 41 million. Yet he had counted 17,282 orchestral ensembles, including 12,477 "complete bronze gamelan" in either the *pélog* or *sléndro* tuning, and 6,362 *wayang* sets of various types, mostly *wayang purwa*. Assuming conservatively that a complete bronze *gamelan* requires 10 to 12 skilled players (including reserves and apprentices), we can estimate the number of skilled musicians at about $12 \times 12,000 = 144,000$. (I take it that the same players would handle smaller, non-full *gamelan* ensembles.) If we eliminate women (who in public rarely played *gamelan* instruments except for the *gendèr*) and children, this means a skill density of about 1 adolescent or adult male in 10. To be sure, most of these musicians were not wanderers but villagers who made their main livelihood from farming. Still, the depth of skill and talent is remarkable. Recognizing that most *wayang* sets were owned by *dhalang* and "played" only by members of his immediate family, we can estimate the skilled puppeteering population at about 15,000, or 1 in 120 adolescent or adult males. Again, only a minority would have earned their main livelihood from this skill.

To project these figures back to the early nineteenth century is obviously problematic. But I can think of no obvious reason why the proportions should have been lower, and given the rise of primary and secondary education after 1900, which began to take youths out of traditional apprenticeships, it could well have been a bit higher.

and sarcastic comments begin.) The only medium that by its very nature would have permitted a conscious, systematically ordered coalition of various, separate, professional mockeries—the mass-produced printed word—did not yet exist.[14]

One might therefore think about this half-veiled class antagonism as a struggle over the "means of production" . . . of knowledge. It was a struggle that pitted gifted commoners with their various particularistic skills and *ngèlmu* against a royalty-cum-aristocracy with its generalized claims to sacral authority and *kasektèn*.

SODOMY AND CONJURING

So far we have been dealing with broad and general suppositions. To try to make them plausible and vivid, we now turn to two topics that are almost never mentioned in contemporary discussions of "traditional Javanese culture" but that nonetheless are prominently featured in the *Centhini,* one of that culture's most touted classics. In contrasting ways they offer a peculiarly clear silhouette of the incipient class antagonism referred to above.

One of the characteristic *topoi* in the "anthropological" writings of nine-teenth- and twentieth-century colonial officials and missionaries is gloomily pleasurable reference to the natives' incorrigible addiction to pederasty and homosexual sodomy. Dayaks, Acehnese, Balinese, Buginese, Javanese, Batak, Minangkabau, or Chinese—however much these peoples might differ in other ways, they were all said to share a passionate addiction to such vices.[15] This *topos* served to demonstrate either the primitiveness or the degeneracy of the population concerned, and the urgent need for civilizing, Christianizing, and

---

14. I use "professional" here to refer both to level of skill and knowledge and to primary source of income and social status.

15. For example, the noted ethnologist George Alexander Wilken observed that "pederasty [is] a vice universal among the Dayaks" (*Verspreide Geschriften,* ed. Frederik Daniel Eduard van Ossenbruggen [The Hague: van Dorp, 1912], 3, p. 389); the celebrated Islamicist Christiaan Snouck Hurgronje wrote of "the general prevalence of immorality of the worst kind in Acheh," symbolized by the popular *seudati* shows, where the poetry sung was "paederastic in character" (*The Achehnese* [Leiden: Brill, 1906], 2, pp. 246 and 222). The sharp-tongued physician Julius Jacobs, after visiting Bali in the early 1880s, observed many dance performances by young boys dressed up like women, and commented: "One knows that they are boys, and it is sickening to see men from all strata of Balinese society proffering their *kèpèngs* (Chinese coins) to have the chance to dance with these children, sometimes in the queerest postures; one is still more revolted to discover that these children, sometimes after exercising for hours in a *perpendicular* position, are compelled, utterly exhausted though they may be, to carry out *horizontal* maneuvers with the highest bidders, after being fondled by this man and kissed by that" (*Eenigen tijd onder de Baliërs, eene reisbeschrijving, met aanteekeningen betreffende hygiène, land- en volkenkunde van de eilanden Bali en Lombok* [Batavia: Kolff, 1883], p. 14, emphasis in the original).

otherwise uplifting them. Pederasty and sodomy also served to draw a dras-
tic moral contrast between "abandoned" natives and good Dutchmen, who
naturally regarded such unnatural practices with practised horror. (Needless
to say, once Indonesia became an independent nation, the shoe went on the
other foot: the repulsive vices were unheard of in the archipelago until
depraved Dutchmen arrived on the scene.) One of the agreeable things about
the *Centhini* is that it shows, by the many examples it offers and its uncondi-
tionally Javanese technical vocabulary, that male homosexuality at least was
an unproblematic, everyday part of a highly varied traditional Javanese sexual
culture. (It includes, inter alia, detailed descriptions of sodomy, fellatio,
mutual masturbation, multiple-partner intercourse, and transvestitism.
Heterosexual sex is described in exactly analogous ways; the *Centhini* is quite
catholic—or should one say encyclopedic?—in its coverage.)

It is precisely the commonplaceness of male homosexual relations that
makes a particular episode of paired sodomies so instructive. The context of
the episode can be briefly described as follows: evicted from home by his
father for numerous offences, including many adulteries with married women,
Cebolang seeks his livelihood as the leader of a small troupe of travelling performers, the most important of whom is a somewhat effeminate young dancer
called Nurwitri. The group plays musics of all kinds (but specializes in an
Arabic-influenced ensemble called *terbangan*), puts on dances, and displays a
range of *sulapan* (which we might provisionally translate as "conjuring
tricks"). In the course of its journeys, the troupe arrives at the *kabupatèn*
(provincial administrative centre) of Daha and is immediately hired by the
local *adipati* (lord) to perform. No less than his many wives, officials, servants, and hangers-on, this lord is enraptured by the skill of the players,
particularly of Nurwitri, who dances exquisitely in female dress. After the
performance the young star is invited to sleep with the eager *adipati* who is
described as having "completely forgotten the love of women" (*supé langen-
ing wanita*).[16] Nurwitri is matter-of-factly complaisant about being
sodomized, pleases his patron greatly with his lovemaking, and is rewarded
on successive mornings-after with presents of money and expensive clothing.

Discussion assumed a calmer tone by the end of the colonial period: see, e.g., on the
Buginese and Makassarese, Hendrik Chabot, *Verwantschap, Stand en Sexe in Zuid-Celebes*
(Groningen-Jakarta: Wolters, 1950), pp. 152–8 ("Homosexualiteit"), and C. Nooteboom,
"Aantekeningen over de cultuur der Boeginezen en Makassaren," *Indonesië*, 2 (1948–49),
pp. 249–50. On Java and Madura, Pigeaud, *Javaansche Volksvertoningen*, pp. 299–304, 322–4;
and J.B.M. de Lyon, "Over de Waroks en Gemblaks van Ponorogo," *Koloniale Tijdschrift* (1941),
pp. 740–60.

16. *Serat Tjentini*, canto 2, stanza 17, through canto 4, stanza 30. The quotation is from
canto 4, stanza 29. Here, and in all subsequent quotations, I have modernized the spelling in the
source.

A few nights of revelry later, the *adipati*'s attention shifts to the more mascu-
line Cebolang, whom he orders to dance in female dress. As before, music and
dancing arouse the bigwig's sexual desire, and he has no difficulty in getting
Cebolang to sleep with him. Canto 4, stanzas 54–60, describe how, and with
what pleasure, the *adipati* sodomizes Cebolang. The troupe's leader is
described as "even better in bed than Nurwitri" (*lan Nurwitri kasornèki*) and
is rewarded proportionately in the aftermath.[17]

So far, so normal. The sexual relationship between the males appears
closely comparable to that between many males and females. A wealthy, powerful, high-ranking older male enjoys the "passive" favours of a sexually
attractive, low-ranking younger person, and rewards that person financially
or otherwise. Then something weird happens for which, so far as I know,
there is no parallel in any Indonesian literature. The *adipati* asks Cebolang
which partner in the act of sodomy gets the greater pleasure—the penetrator
or the penetrated. When Cebolang says "the penetrated, by far" (*mungguh
prabédaning rasa / asangat akèh kaoté / mirasa kang jinambu*), the older man
allows that he would like to judge for himself.[18] Whereupon Cebolang sodomizes the *adipati*. As it happens, things go very differently than Cebolang has
promised. Partly because of the size of Cebolang's penis, the *adipati* under-
goes an agonizing ordeal. His rectum is so torn that he cannot sit down the
next day. Cebolang has to apply a special poultice to the fissure in order to
relieve the pain. (This is the only example of painful sexual intercourse in the
Centhini, something that may indicate the poem's "politics.")

The most immediately remarkable thing about the second sodomy is that
the usual sexual declension is reversed: a young, attractive, low-ranking male
is described as dominating an older, less attractive, high-ranking male. But
more instructive insights emerge from a careful comparison with the first
sodomy.

In that first encounter one notices the following details[19]: the experienced
Cebolang has no trouble handling the *adipati*'s penis. He is described as
"supple and skilled in all his various movements" (*aluwes awasis ing satata
taténing pratingkah*). His "adeptness" (*baudira*) in passive sodomy far exceeds
that of his friend Nurwitri. He is in fact shown to be "actively passive." The
pair is said to be engaged in a "sweet battle" (*adu manis*). The constant use of
reflexive verb forms underscores the mutuality of their activity: "they writhed
and wrestled together, thrusting in opposite directions" (*dia-dinia dinaya-
daya / dinua-dua*). The *adipati*'s sex organ is "squeezed" (*sinerot*) by

---

17. Ibid., canto 4, stanzas 54–60. The quotation is from stanza 57.
18. Ibid., stanzas 74–84. The quotation is from stanza 76.
19. The following quotations are taken from ibid., stanzas 56–60.

Cebolang's practised sphincter. The younger man's "response" is "no less" (*tan wiwal dènya kiwul*) than his partner's. At one point he advises the older man, in the politest *krama*,[20] to "calm down" (*ingkang sarèh kéwala*)—as if to say "if you want to be good in bed, you have to pace yourself." He is described as "exhausted" (*lempé-lempé*), but his fatigue is that of an accomplished gymnast after a strenuous workout. (The *adipati* is described as scarcely less tired.) When at dawn Nurwitri walks in on the pair and slyly teases his companion, Cebolang responds with a cheerful grin and wink, and the insouciant claim that "it was the same for both of us" (*aran wong wus padha déné*). Finally, one observes that the author intends a certain complicity between Cebolang and Nurwitri at the expense of the *adipati*. Cebolang "gives [him] a secret sign" (*ngeblongken*) to indicate that they have succeeded in hoodwinking the aristocrat. While the latter laughs aloud in dull-witted satisfaction at what he regards as his sexual domination of the two young actors, the pair have shrewdly achieved their ends: money, favours, full access to the women's quarters of the *kabupatèn*, psychological mastery of their employer (he is now set up for Cebolang's role-reversal trap)—and sexual enjoyment to boot.

These details show clearly that (1) Cebolang is (deliberately) depicted as a virtuoso sexual professional (in the better sense of the word); (2) he is not lying when he claims that the penetrated partner may get more pleasure than the penetrator—the former simply has to have the right *ngèlmu* and experience; (3) he retains his masculinity throughout, responding to his partner as might a good boxer, wrestler, or dancer. True, his movements are so supple that the *adipati* experiences them as if they were a beautiful woman's, but Cebolang never psychologically "yields" to the older man.

The reverse sodomy represents a sharp contrast in almost every respect.[21] The *adipati* first yields up his social and political pre-eminence by permitting the young adventurer to address him in *ngoko*, the language level of intimacy and equality (*koko-kinoko kéwala*). Then he asks for knowledge, about which he concedes his ignorance, and in effect asks for instruction from an experienced teacher. The text goes out of its way to stress the impressive dimensions of Cebolang's penis (in implicit comparison with the undiscussed size of his partner's). The *adipati* is described as "yielding utterly" (*anjepluk*). More significantly, he is explicitly said to have "forgotten his manhood" (*supé priané*) and to "feel like a woman" (*lir dyah raosing kalbu*). Recall that when Cebolang was being sodomized, we were told that *in the eyes of his sodomizer* he seemed like, or better than, a woman. In contrast to Cebolang's practised acceptance of

---

20. *Krama* is the polite-respect level of the Javanese language.
21. The quotations in this paragraph are from *Serat Tjentini*, stanzas 74–84.

anal penetration, the older man proves incapable of bearing the initial pain. The "tears pour down his face, he whimpers for mercy" (*barebel kang waspa / andruwili sesambaté*). "Oh, stop . . . enough . . . please, no . . . take it out . . . ow . . . ow . . . please stop" (*lah uwis aja-aja / / wurungena baé adhuh uwis*). Indeed, he so loses control of himself that he involuntarily urinates (*kepoyuh*) on the mattress. Cebolang feels "touched" (*ngres tyasira*) and speeds up his thrusts to bring the ordeal to a quicker end. (Contrast this with Cebolang's suggestion that his partner slow down when himself being sodomized earlier on.) Finally, the *adipati* "collapses in utter exhaustion" (*ngalumpruk marlupa capé*), while the young man merely feels sorry (*sungkawa*) for him, and no mention is made of any fatigue. When he was the sodomizer the *adipati* was also worn out. Needless to say, Cebolang is also knowledgeable about the right kind of crushed-leaf poultice to heal the aristocrat's anus. And the scene ends with no cheerful jokes.

The paired sodomies, with each partner alternately taking the role of penetrator and penetrated, shows that Cebolang is the master of his master. He is a skilled professional in every aspect of sexual intercourse between males, without ever losing his control or manhood. Indeed, it is precisely because he retains these qualities that he is able, with evident sincerity, to insist that the pleasure obtained from being penetrated is greater than that derived from penetrating. He forces his lord first into linguistic equality, then into sexual submission. On the other hand, the *adipati* does not even gain the upper hand when he is the sodomizer. And when he is sodomized, he acts like a virgin, or beginning student.

At the same time we should remember that our paired sodomies take up only a dozen or so of the thousands of stanzas of which the *Centhini* is composed. We are not dealing with a sort of Javanese Lord Chatterley's Lover. The *adipati* experiences no sexual awakening and neither loves nor detests his young partner. Once his rectum has healed and he can again sit comfortably, life in the *kabupatèn* goes on as before. Cebolang is eventually evicted, but only because he is discovered to be making free with the *adipati*'s concubines. It is therefore difficult to believe that the double-sodomy episode is in any way a statement about sexuality qua sexuality, or for that matter about homosexuality. We may get a better idea of what it is really about if we take a brief, comparative look at conjuring.

As noted earlier, conjuring is a staple of the performance repertoire of many of the *Centhini*'s varied zwervers and trekkers. Cebolang is the first such figure to appear in the text, but his pyrotechnics, impressive as they are, will be topped by other adepts in due course. Regardless of who the particular "master" is, all the conjuring performances share certain generic features. They are always shows (*tontonan*)—in the sense that the conjuror and his associates are hired to display their talents, before audiences, and in the context of a larger set of festivities. They are always accompanied by music, often by specific kinds of dancing and dancers, and usually by ample incense-burning. The types of "turn" fall into roughly three categories: (1) Inanimate objects are, for a certain period, made to seem as if they have a life of their own. For example, a rice-pounder appears to thump up and down in its container, and a machete and sickle to hack and chop, without human agency.[22] (2) Various objects are temporarily transmogrified. For example, cones of cooked rice (*tumpeng*), or certain leaves, or young coconuts are covered with a *kurungan* (a hemispheric-shaped wicker cage); when the cage is removed they have turned, respectively, into bouquets of flowers, turtles, and snakes. On the cage being replaced, then removed once again, these objects have resumed their original, true forms.[23] (3) Horrifying events are made to occur, then reversed. This category is of such interest that it is worth offering details of three typical examples.

In the course of some festivities, Cebolang has one of his musicians bound hand and foot, then placed, along with a wheel, inside a *kurungan*.[24] While the other musicians play the composition Kinanthi Wiratruna, and incense smoke swirls up, Cebolang and his transvestite dancers circle the *kurungan* seven times. When it is removed, the bound musician is free and riding on a tiger's back. The spectators flee in terror, trampling on each other in the process. The *adipati* stays in place, but he does ask Cebolang whether "the tiger is real" (*apa nora anemeni ingkang sima*). On being assured that it is not, he bids the young conjuror to "terminate it at once" (*yèn mengkono nuli racuten dèn-ènggal*). Tiger and rider are returned to the cage. On its second removal, there are the bound musician and wheel, as before. In another display, the audience-hall where the spectators are sitting is suddenly invaded by huge stilts (*égrang*) of fire, which appear to rush after and do battle with one another.[25] It seems as if the whole building is going up in flames, and almost everyone is thrown into a panic. Then one of the experienced old men present tells the troupe that they have gone too far and must bring the act to an end. A flick of the sash of one of the transvestite dancers makes the blazing stilts immediately vanish. It turns out, however, that in the stampede to escape the illusory flames a small child has been trampled unconscious.[26] The conjurors are now bidden by the same old man to repair the damage. Two of them proceed to lay the child out on a mat and with a big, sharp knife cut his body in half. When the boy's mother, hysterical with grief, collapses over the corpse,

---

22. Ibid., canto 3, stanzas 19–23; canto 37, stanza 332.
23. Ibid., canto 3, stanzas 1–18.
24. Ibid., stanzas 39–48.
25. Ibid., canto 48, stanzas 28–33.
26. Ibid., stanzas 42–52.

the conjurors behead her. The horrified audience, believing that what they are seeing is quite real, terrifyingly so, conclude that Cebolang's men have been possessed by evil spirits. At this point the two bodies are enshrouded, while the transvestite dancers circle them, strewing flowers from the garlands that form part of their costumes. Immediately mother and son are restored to life and health. The third example has two of the younger players in Cebolang's troupe, Jamal and Jamil, performing a duel.[27] In the course of battle, Jamal's forehead is struck with a crowbar. When he collapses, covered in blood, his antagonist rushes up and smashes his head and body with heavy rocks. Again, the audience is frightened witless. Then, at the master conjuror's command, Jamal's corpse is wrapped in a long cloth and transvestite players dance and sing around it, accompanied by a small *angklung* ensemble and billowing clouds of incense.[28] A still-panting Jamal immediately sits up, very much alive and well. And, as always happens even when the most terrifying show has been put on, the audience in the end roars its applause. (Quite often, the combined effect of conjuring and its music is to arouse uncontrolled sexual desire; members of the audience grope one another's breasts and genitals and even engage in public intercourse.)

What are we to make of all the conjuring, especially conjuring of the third type? To put it another way, what kind of *ngèlmu* is being deployed? Is "conjuring" even the appropriate term for these *sulapan* turns?

That we are dealing with a distinct professional specialization can be confirmed from two directions. First of all, the *sulapan* are neither supernatural events nor cases of possession. If one thinks of the *wayang* repertoire, the chronicles, folk tales—or even whispered gossip in today's Jakarta—the exercise of true power (*kasektèn*) always has real effects in the world, and causes irreversible change. Kingdoms fall, princes and ogres are killed, bad village boys turn into permanent monkeys, bloody coups (successful and unsuccessful) actually occur. In contrast, *sulapan* has no prise on the world; everything always reverts to what it was before. Living people are quickly "killed" and as quickly resurrected. Leaves become turtles, then leaves once again. Nothing really changes. Each "turn" has the same lack of consequences as the dramatic sodomies we considered earlier.

But if *sulapan* and *kasektèn* are utterly different from one another, can the same be said of conjuring and possession? In one sense, they are obviously distinct. During Cebolang's show, the audience misunderstood what it was seeing; the horrible illusions created by the conjurors made it seem that they

---

27. Ibid., canto 37, stanzas 256–61.

28. An *angklung* is an instrument made of suspended bamboo tubes which tinkle against each other when struck by the player.

were really possessed. For possession, like *kasektèn*, does affect the world. On the other hand, a number of the turns performed by Cebolang's men are given specific names by the *Centhini*—*gabus, réog,* and *jaran képang,* for example—that even today refer to specific ritual performances involving trance possession. Yet if the external look of certain *sulapan* turns and certain forms of possession may resemble one another, their inner natures are understood as basically different. In *sulapan,* a commercial show, after all, everything is under immediate human control, whereas in possession human control yields, at least for the nonce, to that of the spirit world.

In the second place, the *sulapan* conspicuously involve a specific technology and technical vocabulary. The *Centhini* takes a great deal of trouble to tell the reader exactly what combinations of musical instruments, what compositions, what modes of dance, and what costumes are required for each show. The props are virtually unvarying—*kurungan,* incense, sashes of a certain type. Some of the turns have their own technical names. Perhaps most striking of all is the use of the word *racut,* which might be translated as "to terminate" (an act) or "to dispel" (a phantasm). It is also noticeable, from the examples I have cited, that there are always a few spectators (typically old men) who are not taken in. They may, like the *adipati,* be amused when the audience scatters in panic, but they make sure that things do not go too far. The players are then told to *racut* the apparitions back "into the bag." And how simple *racut* always is (almost like switching off an electric current), compared to the rituals and time usually needed to end possession!

Yet in spite of all that has been said about technique, we are not, in the *Centhini,* in the world of Kinsey or Houdini (though perhaps not far from that of Cagliostro). When Cebolang is being sodomized we are not told which anal muscles he uses to give the *adipati* such pleasure, or how he acquires his muscular control. Similarly, we are never taken back stage and let in on the actual methods by which *sulapan*'s effects are achieved. Sometimes the reader is left in doubt as to how far they are effects at all. For while Cebolang assures the *adipati* that his tiger is not real, the text also describes, deadpan, the bisected spectator boy and beheaded mother as dead. Perhaps we should replace the word *conjuror* by *magician.* For the latter blurs two ancient meanings: the virtuoso prestidigitator, who employs ingenious but ordinary means to create uncanny illusions; and the dabbler in the real uncanny, who nonetheless uses his powers pointlessly, for the gratification of an audience. Seen from this angle, the skills of Cebolang and his fellow magicians occupy a distinct site in the cultural landscape of late eighteenth-century Java. They are not the skills of a faker, but neither are they those of someone with the general, superordinate power of *kasektèn.*

A renewed comparison here with eighteenth-century France is valuable.

The decisive thing about Diderot's encyclopedia is that it was meant to inform. Its entries are lists with *explanations* about how the world works, and on what principles. Its purpose is to spread enlightenment, to the whole world so far as possible. But the *Centhini*'s lists explain nothing. They refer to knowledges, but these remain more or less esoteric. They can only be properly read by those who already have the necessary *ngèlmu*. Enlightenment of the ordinary Javanese, let alone the world, is the last thing the text has on its mind.

What then? Sodomy and magicianship may be sources of pleasure, but it would be difficult to argue that either is centrally important to the life of any society, even that of Old Java. I have stressed them here because they so conspicuously set off their master practitioners from other social strata. The sodomies separate the virtuosi from the Power-full, the magic tricks the same virtuosi from the populace: for the latter, the secrets of Cebolang's *ngèlmu* are as unfathomable as (maybe more unfathomable than) the *kasektèn* of their lords. The very uselessness, gratuitousness, of sodomy and conjuring helps also to discourage any easy hypostasizing of Old Java as a seamless web of interlocking functional roles or mutually reinforcing patron–client ties. (Other types of *ngèlmu*, such as puppetmastership or medicine, precisely because they appear useful and socially integrative, may cause the interpreter to let down his guard against *idées reçues*.) Their luxuriant secular display in the *Centhini,* alongside so many other knowledges, shows that something new is in the air, a visible, if probably not wholly self-conscious, claim to leadership of the Javanese—so to speak the supersession of *kasektèn* by a coalition of the *ngèlmu*. It is significant, too, that Cebolang, like other adepts in the *Centhini,* practises his *ngèlmu* in exchange for cash.[29] The Old Java of lord and peasant is on its way out.

PROFESSIONAL DREAMS

So far, so clear. Probably too clear. For I have treated the *Centhini* as if it were a mirror of society or a quasi-ethnological treatise, permitting us to infer

---

29. See Peter Brian Ramsay Carey, "Changing Javanese Perceptions of the Chinese Communities in Central Java, 1755–1825," *Indonesia*, 37 (April 1984), pp. 1–47, for a pithy, informed account of the economic and social changes experienced in Central Java during the six decades before the completion of the "full" *Centhini*. The United East India Company's 1740 annexation of Java's northern littoral and its military suppression, in the 1750s, of the endless wars of succession that had racked the island's interior since the 1670s had contradictory consequences. On the one hand, the restoration of peace permitted a quick rise in agricultural production and commerce; on the other hand, it facilitated the more systematic imposition of taxation. The era was marked by the rapid spread of tax farms, usually managed by Chinese, especially in respect to opium, market taxes, and rural tollgates. Increasingly payments had to be made in cash (typically lead Chinese or copper Company coins). To be able to pay in this form, peasants had to mortgage their crops or sell a larger portion on the market. Hence a significant monetization of the Javanese economy occurred by the turn of the century.

that its pages more or less directly transcribe the life of late eighteenth-century Java. Musicians of course really played their *gamelan, dhalang* surely puppeteered, and Islamic mystics definitely instructed youthful *santri*. But were there really Cebolangs who stylishly sodomized their aristocratic employers and made villagers flee in terror from the apparitions they conjured up? Who can be sure? Supposing, on the other hand, that the great poem reflects not so much reality as . . . professional dreams?

The gratuitousness of Cebolang's virtuosities can tempt one into regarding them as the last, superfluous, elements in a total inventory of "real" traditional life. But a wider overview of the *Centhini* shows us very quickly its dreamlike nature. The sexual life so vividly depicted in its pages already suggests something phantasmagoric. For while scores of couplings between men and women of all types and ages throng its pages, only once, and in casual passing, is mention made of pregnancy or childbirth. (This is why the text's homosexual and heterosexual episodes can seem so matter-of-factly similar. Its interest is in sexual virtuosity—including, by the way, female sexual prowess—not at all in demography or social realism.)

But there are still larger absences than that of procreation. We observed earlier on the way in which, with the exception of the *adipati*, the Javanese ruling class is peripheralized, if not eliminated, from the reader's field of vision. More striking still is the invisibility of foreigners. Sèh Amongraga flees his royal home in Giri in 1625, by which time the United East India Company had already established its imperial Asian headquarters in Batavia (1619), a mere 450 crow-miles west along Java's northern shore. By the time of the *Centhini*'s final compilation the Dutch had been in Java for two centuries—but only a few Dutch loan words trace their presence in the text. Nothing in its pages hints at the wars that raged between the 1670s and the 1750s, in which, for the first time in Java's history, it was ravaged not merely by Dutch and Javanese, but by Buginese *condottieri*, Madurese warlords, and Balinese mercenaries. There is not the slightest acknowledgement that, since 1740, Java's north-shore ports had all passed "legally" into Company hands; or that conquering Mataram had long since splintered into three small and feeble interior principalities, all of whose rulers were on the Company's payroll.[30] No wars, no plagues, no taxation, no corvée, no death.

---

30. On the feckless politics of late eighteenth- and early nineteenth-century Central Java, the best studies are Merle Calvin Ricklefs, *Jogjakarta under Sultan Mangkubumi, 1749–1792* (London: Oxford University Press, 1974); Ann Kumar, "Javanese Court Society and Politics in the Late Eighteenth Century: The Record of a Lady Soldier. Part I: The Religious, Social and Economic Life of the Court," *Indonesia*, 29 (April 1980), pp. 1–46; and Peter Brian Ramsay Carey, ed., *Babad Dipanegara: An Account of the Outbreak of the Java War (1825–1830)* (Kuala Lumpur: Art Printers, 1981).

On the contrary, for most of the *Centhini* Java manifests itself as a phantasmagoric utopia: a proliferation of prosperous, contented, tolerant, politically autonomous, sexually sophisticated rural communities through which professionals are free to roam. As they wander, they display their knowledge to the populace and to each other and are regarded with unrivalrous respect and even cheerful awe. There is no political intrigue, no fear, no kowtowing to noble ignoramuses, and no humiliating dependence on incompetent, venal rulers.[31]

It is just the character of this "perfect Java," benignly co-ordinated by its specialist virtuosi, that reveals the limits of the *Centhini*'s embryo radicalism. Cebolang may sexually master his master and make free with the latter's wives and concubines, but his mastery is that of the conjuror. As noted earlier, when the *adipati*'s rectum heals, life reverts to what it was before the pair climbed into bed. Nothing changes. The benignity of the professionals is the benignity of men who are masters of traditional knowledge. It contrasts powerfully with the agreeable malignity of the *philosophes,* whose knowledge was anything but traditional, was indeed implicitly or explicitly revolutionary. In Java, the perfect society is pre-*ancien régime*; in France, it will come with the *ancien régime*'s supersession.

The very poetics of the *Centhini* underscore its political stance, which, most of the time, wishes away the ruling class and foreign oppressors, rather than assaulting them. Its tone is invariably cool, sweet, smiling—never alienated, furious, or despairing. Its composers display, without false modesty, absolute control of all the stylistic forms, metrical varieties, and sophisticated rhetorical devices then available in Javanese literary culture. But this awesome control is never used ironically; it functions, almost always, to align form and content.

---

31. Nothing better reveals the Louis Seize character of Java's surviving dynasts—including the employers of the *Centhini*'s composers—than that they did nothing creative to exploit the disasters that overwhelmed the East India Company and the United Provinces after 1780, when the latter became involved in the wars among England, France, and the young United States. In 1795, French revolutionary armies occupied the Low Countries and established the Batavian Republic under its aegis, and London responded by, *inter alia*, seizing Ceylon from the Company. In 1798 the Company, already bankrupt for some years, was taken over by the Batavian Republic, which assumed its 143 million guilder debt. (See Clive Day, *The Policy and Administration of the Dutch in Java* [London: Macmillan, 1904], pp. 80–81.) In 1806, Napoléon made his younger brother Louis the first-ever king of the Lowlands, but in 1810 dismissed him for his "manie d'humanité" and peremptorily absorbed the realm into metropolitan France. London retorted by seizing, by 1811, all overseas Dutch possessions, including Java, which fell to Stamford Raffles's men in that year without a struggle. A brief, informative account of these developments can be found in Bernard Hubertus Maria Vlekke, *Nusantara: A History of Indonesia* (Brussels: Editions A. Manteau, 1961), chapter 11. The source for Napoléon's characteristic *mot* is Simon Schama's wonderful *Patriots and Liberators: Revolution in the Netherlands, 1780–1813* (New York: Knopf, 1977), p. 543.

THE *SULUK GATHOLOCO*

If the composition of the full *Centhini* was completed in 1814, as Behrend plausibly argues, then this may have been the last possible historical moment in which such a vast, sweet, and controlled Javanese masterpiece could appear. For in 1812 Stamford Raffles's men marched into Yogyakarta, deposed the sultan, and divided the territory into two micro-principalities, as the East India Company had done in neighbouring Surakarta in the 1750s. Moreover, in all four principalities he seized control of the rulers' financial lifeline, the tax farms, running them henceforth from Batavia.[32] In 1816, as a result of a complex deal emerging from the Congress of Vienna—whereby William of Orange was made the first monarch in his line (succeeding Louis Bonaparte) and was granted the Company's possessions in the Indies by way of compensation for permanent British seizure of Ceylon, the Cape, and other valuable territories—the Dutch took over again from Raffles. Economic and political conditions deteriorated rapidly in Central Java, leading to the outbreak of Prince Diponegoro's rebellion in 1825 and the ensuing five-year Java War, which brought devastation to much of the region. The high cost of the war, and the Netherlands' own near-bankruptcy (the result of the exactions of the Napoleonic era and Belgium's secession in 1830) led to the installation in that year of the brutally exploitative Cultivation System (*Cultuurstelsel*), which between 1831 and 1877 netted the Dutch treasury as much as 823 million guilders.[33] To ensure no further political trouble, Batavia parked on Central Java's mini-thrones a series of utterly pliable, mediocre, *fainéant* princelings. In this long process *kasektèn* and its putative bearers lost more and more credibility, to the point that in 1873 the last court poet of Surakarta, R. Ng. Ronggawarsita, wrote despairingly on his deathbed that there was "no example left."[34]

This background may help to explain the astonishing contrast between the *Centhini* and Javanese culture's next great phantasmagoria, the *Suluk Gatholoco*. Internal evidence makes it clear that this long poem was composed sometime between 1854 and 1873 (most likely in the 1860s)—probably by a single, anonymous author.[35] If the *Suluk Gatholoco* is a classic, it is

---

32. See Carey, "Changing Javanese Perceptions," sections 4, 5.

33. Far and away the best study of the political and economic aspects of the Cultivation System is Cornelis Fasseur, *Kultuurstelsel en Koloniale Baten, De Nederlandse Exploitatie van Java, 1840–1860* (Leiden: Universitaire Pers, 1975).

34. See chapter 4 above.

35. At canto 7, stanza 52, the poem mentions what it calls *rispis pérak*. *Rispis* is clearly a Javanization of *recepis*, a special scrip introduced by Governor-General Rochussen on February 4, 1846, in a desperate attempt to remedy the financial and currency chaos bequeathed by his predecessors. Convertible at a fixed rate with Holland's silver-based coinage, the *recepis* proved to

nonetheless one of the underground kind. When, in 1873, the eminent missionary-scholar Poensen brought a (heavily truncated) version of the poem to the light of printed day, he commented:

> From a literary point of view, the text has very little value . . . But if we look more carefully at its spirit, then the writer strikes us—with his conceptions of honour and virtue, and his sensible views on such things as what foods are permissible for human beings to eat—as very much a man of the world, wholly lacking in the deep religious strain that characterizes such works as the Wulang Rèh, the Sèh Tékawardi, etc., and thereby also lacking their cultivation and breeding. In fact, he often arouses our disgust, since he does not refrain from committing the most trivial things to paper, and in the grossest way goes into detail about matters which it is not decent to mention.[36]

This sketch of a sort of third-rate Javanese Pantagruel cut no ice with Snouck Hurgronje, grandest of colonial scholar-panjandrums, who denounced the poem as "the heretical dreams of an undoubtedly opium-besotted Javanese mystic!"[37] Not at all, opined the liberal scholar-bureaucrat Rinkes in 1909, the poem was "a serious satire against all that mystagogic rigmarole."[38] Not until 1951 did Philippus van Akkeren, forced by the arrival of Japanese imperialism and the subsequent national revolution of 1945–49 to abandon his missionary labours in East Java, publish the first full text of the *Suluk*, along with a translation, a full critical apparatus, and a thoughtful, anthropologizing thematic analysis.[39]

Only one version has ever been printed in Java—a limited Surabaya

---

be the first stable colonial currency in the Indies. By the Currency Law of 1854 it was formally replaced with a silver guilder, though it was not finally withdrawn from circulation until 1861. See "Muntwezen," in *Encyclopaedie van Nederlandsch-Indië* (The Hague/Leiden: Nijhoff/Brill, 1918), 2, pp. 793–811, esp. at pp. 803–4. *Rispis-pérak* (silver *rispis*) must refer to the silver coins replacing the paper *recepis* between 1854 and 1861. Hence, the *Suluk* cannot have been composed before the late 1850s, and, since a printed version of sorts (see n. 36, below) appeared in 1873, we can assume that it was probably completed in the 1860s. The poem was most likely composed in Kedhiri, East Java, well away from the royal courts, and by a member of the small group of literati not by then in Dutch employ.

36. Carel Poensen, "Een Javaansch geschrift," *Mededeelingen vanwege het Nederlandsche Zendelinggenootschap*, 17 (1873), p. 227. The good missionary here gets in a timely jab at Islam's dietary proscriptions.

37. Christiaan Snouck Hurgronje, "De betekenis van den Islâm voor zijne belijders in Oost-Indië," *Verspreide Geschriften* (Bonn and Leipzig: Schröder, 1924), 4, p. 15. This essay originally appeared in 1883.

38. Douwe Adolf Rinkes, *Abdoerraoef van Singkel* (Heerenveen: "Hepkema," 1909), p. 130.

39. Philippus van Akkeren, *Een gedrocht en toch de volmaakte mens: A Monster, Yet the Perfect Man* (The Hague: "Excelsior," 1951), p. 1. The citations in nn. 33–5 above I have taken from p. 1 of van Akkeren's text.

edition of 1889, which attracted little attention at the time.[40] But in 1918 the poem became the centre of a Java-wide controversy when an article in *Djawi Hiswara,* organ of the Surakarta branch of the Sarékat Islam (Islamic League—the most popular anticolonial movement of the time) cited passages from it, notably one in which the eponymous hero insists that his frequenting of opium dens is in faithful imitation of the Prophet Muhammad. A rancorous debate ensued in the by-then-lively Indonesian- and Javanese-language press, culminating in a huge protest demonstration in Surabaya organized by a hastily formed Army of the Most Reverend Prophet Muhammad. The army, alas, had no weapons, so was forced to content itself with appeals to the Governor-General to have the editor of *Djawi Hiswara* criminally prosecuted.[41] After that, the poem went permanently under ground—no Indonesian publisher has dared take the risk of being branded religious apostate, or, for reasons described below, pornographer.[42]

What was all the anger about? The plot of the 397-canto *Suluk* is both simple and strange. The first part, covering the meagre thirteen stanzas of cantos 1 and 2, introduces the reader to the hero, Gatholoco, described as the only son of King Suksma Wisésa of Jajar, and his inseparable retainer, Dermagandhul. Appalled by the boy's monstrous and repulsive appearance, the king bids him spend his first sixteen years in isolated meditation, accompanied only by Dermagandhul. Returning home after the sixteen years are up, the lad now has his head "clipped" by his father. But since this rite only makes him more hideous he is sent off for another four years of ascesis, hanging upside down, batlike, in a sacred banyan. This second meditation is rewarded with the gift of matchless skill in language. The king now gives him his adult name of Gatholoco and sends him off to see the world, warning him of a dangerous adversary, the female recluse Perjiwati, who is meditating in a mountain grotto.

The physical description of Gatholoco and Dermagandhul in canto 2,

---

40. According to Gerardus Willebrordus Joannes Drewes, "The Struggle between Javanese and Islam as illustrated by the Serat Dermagandul," *Bijdrage tot de taal-, land- en volkenkunde,* 122 (1966), pp. 309–65, at p. 314. Van Akkeren wrote that the one printed version he used for his study was a "second printing" of an edition issued by the well-known Javanophile Sino-Javanese publisher Tan Khoen Swie of Kedhiri. But he gave no date for this printing or for that of its antecedent.

41. For insulting Islam. The above account is taken from Drewes, "The Struggle," pp. 313–15.

42. For in the meantime the poem's explicit scatological and sexual language (Poensen's "in the grossest way") was becoming an embarrassment to the emerging western-educated Javanese middle class, which was determined to make "Javanism" Victorianly respectable in their own eyes and those of the Poensens.

stanzas 3–5, hints openly at what their names make explicit.[43] *Gatholoco* is a compound of *gatho* (penis) and *ngloco* (rub, masturbate); *Dermagandhul* combines *derma* (closely attached) and *gandhul* (hanging down) to denote testicles; while the root of *Perjiwati* is *parji* (female genitalia). In other words, the hero and his attendant are a walking, talking penis and scrotum, and at one level the poem can be taken as an allegory of a man's sexual development.[44]

The second part, covering the 191 stanzas of cantos 3 to 6, describes Gatholoco's activity on his travels. Between bouts of gambling and visits to opium dens, he engages in a long series of vitriolic debates with "orthodox" Islamic teachers (*guru santri*) on the true nature of divinity, man, the cosmos, Islam, and much else. In every case he triumphs by his wit and depth of *ngèlmu*. One after another, the *guru santri* concede defeat and flee his presence in profound humiliation.

The third part, covering the 193 stanzas of cantos 7 to 12, depicts Gatholoco's encounter with Perjiwati and her four female attendants. After solving a series of conundrums posed by the five women, he gains entry to Perjiwati's hitherto unpenetrated cave. Dermagandhul attempts to follow, but cannot squeeze in. The motifs of the first part are revived, in that the violent "battles" between Gatholoco and Perjiwati are thinly veiled descriptions of sexual intercourse. After nine months a male child is born, just as hideous as his father, but adored by both parents. The poem then ends with a brief meditation on the meaning of this birth and the nature of life.

The stance and nature of the *Suluk Gatholoco* are best understood in juxtaposition to the *Centhini*. First, one notices the contrast between the two heroes. Sèh Amongraga is a tolerant, gentle paragon of the virtuosi of Old Java.[45] He is handsome, polite, learned, adept in syncretic Javanese (Hindu)-Islamic mysticism, sexually energetic, and cultivated in the traditional arts. He

---

43. "Shaped unlike a normal man / His body shrivelled, shrunk / And scaly, dry his wrinkled skin / Without a nose at all / Or eyes, or ears; his pleasure but / To sleep and sleep, day in, day out, continuously / / Yet once aroused from his deep sleep / Unruly, not to be appeased . . . Ugly his body, like a sack / His slumber deep beyond compare / When sleeping he was like a corpse / He too had neither eyes nor ears / Merely a pair of lips / Nor thews, nor bones." The Javanese goes: *warnané tan kaprah janmi / wandané apan bungkik / kulité basisik iku / kelawan tanpa nétra / tanpa irung tanpa kuping / remenané anéndra sadina-dina / Yèn ngelilir lajeng monthah / tan kena dèn arih . . . Awon dedegé lir keba / lèmboné kepati-pati / yèn néndra anglir wong pejah / nora duwé mata kuping / amung ing lambé iki / nora duwé otot-balung.* The spelling in this and other quotations from the *Suluk* has been modernized. The doggerel translation is taken from my English version of the complete poem, published in *Indonesia*, 32 (Oct. 1981), pp. 108–50, and 33 (April 1982), pp. 31–88.

44. Taken this way, the first part of the poem describes the growth of a male organ/person from latency through the ordeal of circumcision (the "clipping") to mature potency and the prospect of initiation into intercourse.

45. Amongraga's title, Sèh, a Javanized version of *sheikh*, suggests how unselfconsciously in those days Islam and older Javanese traditions were harmoniously blended.

treats the mischievous Cebolang and his troupe with elder-brotherly amusement. Both are solid human beings. Gatholoco is something unique. Not
only does he fail to conform to any of the traditional models of Javanese hero
(elegant warrior-knight, ascetic sage-priest, Muslim saint, or righteous king),
but it is as if he were constructed in deliberate opposition to Amongraga. As
canto 2, stanzas 3 and 11, and canto 4, stanzas 1 to 5 reveal, he is a hideous,
stinking, foul-mouthed, opium-smoking, cantankerous, philosophical, ambulatory penis.

Second, the civilized encyclopedism of the *Centhini* has completely disappeared. Gatholoco and his creator have no interest whatsoever in lists and the
multifarious lores that they represent. There is now only one knowledge that
matters—the mystical knowledge of the Perfect Male—and Gatholoco
expounds and defends it with enraged fanaticism and scabrous, malignant
wit. His theological antagonists in the long second part of the poem represent
something wholly outside the *Centhini*'s dreaming: the oxymoron "false
knowledge." The easy syncretism of the previous century, which upheld a
flexible mélange of Sufi mysticism and pre-Islamic Hindu-Javanese tradition,
has gone up in smoke. It is as if the older culture has broken into violently
antagonistic halves: a Mecca-oriented Islamic orthodoxy and what van
Akkeren, with some justification, calls a Javanese (cultural) nationalism, back
against the wall, fangs bared.

Third, the depiction of sexual life, which is the focus of the poem's final
section, emphasizes, at length and in great detail, everything that the *Centhini*
passes over in silence: stink, heat, slime, blood, frustration, pregnancy, and
childbirth. Gatholoco has only one (and female) sexual partner, and he mates
with her in the most coarse, and even brutal, manner.[46] It is also quite clear
that this sexual activity has a single purpose: the procreative reproduction of
a new Gatholoco, Perfect Male in embryo, ready one day to replace his father
in Java's religious war. Nothing could be further from the playful, spendthrift
relationship between religion and sexuality of the *Centhini,* as exemplified by
the episode where Cebolang, after a sleepless night of fellatio and mutual
masturbation with two *santri* teenagers, nonchalantly rises to lead the
pesantrèn's early morning prayers.[47]

Finally, the phantasmagoric *mise en scène*. The *Centhini*'s elisions have
been drastically extended and perfect Java turned into an eerie moonscape. As
before, the Dutch are invisible (though the frequency of Dutch loan words

---

46. It should be noted, however, that Perjiwati is fully Gatholoco's equal in the sexual
combat. Indeed, Gatholoco is described as ultimately defeated by her (i.e. after intercourse the
penis slips limply out of the vagina).

47. *Serat Tjenṭini,* canto 37, stanzas 309–28.

has markedly increased). The kingdom of Jajar is mentioned only once, in the very first stanza, and its "mighty sovereign" disappears for good after the eleventh. Gone are all the actors, conjurors, musicians, artisans, tradesmen, puppeteers, and rowdy villagers who crowd the *Centhini*'s pages. Gatholoco and Dermagandhul pursue their wanderings utterly alone. Stage-lit in this way, Java appears as a surreal terrain on which the only landmarks are opium dens, grottoes, mountains, and *pesantrèn*. An imagined, not an idealized, landscape.

But none of this would, in itself, make the *Suluk Gatholoco* a candidate for "classic." What renders the poem exemplary is first hinted at when the reader learns, in canto 2, stanza 8, that, after four years of meditation upside down in a banyan tree, the young hero "gained the *wahyu* and the skill / To best his fellow-man in words / Unschooled in rhetoric, he knew / The varied arts of argument. Not studying to write / He knew all literary arts."[48] For it is exactly the *Suluk*'s angry, subversive exploitation of "all literary arts" that shows its author as among the desperate last of Old Java's literary professionals.

Take, for example, the opening lines: "The tale to be related here / Concerns a kingdom celebrated / Both far and wide, called Jajar, and / Its mighty sovereign, in war / Valiant, invincible / His royal appellation was / Mahraja Suksma Wisésa / / Great was the King's authority / Submissive were the outer lands."[49] The stanza, by itself, is a standard traditional opening to a narrative poem and should introduce a leisurely, expansive account of the beauties of the royal palace, the prosperity of the realm, and so on. But all this is eliminated, and within eighteen lines we are at the description of Gatholoco as a walking penis. There is an extraordinary insolence in this perfunctoriness (as if to say, "you know as well as I do that in Java today there are no celebrated kingdoms, invincible kings, or submissive outer lands").

Or take the way in which the author deploys, with easy mastery but for completely untraditional purposes, the evocative alliterations and punning assonances of the *Centhini*'s *haute style*. For example, in canto 5, stanzas 34–5, when his adversaries abuse him as a "tailless dog," Gatholoco turns the tables on them by exploiting the assonance between *asu* (dog) and *asal* (origin, source) to interpret the insult as a deeper truth: that he is in fact the

---

48. The Javanese is: *sinung wahyu bisa nyrékal / iya sesamaning urip / nora sangu ing wicara / sakèhing bicara bangkit / nora sinau nulis / sakèhing sastra pan putus.*

   Wahyu is a term usually employed for the mysterious radiance that descends on the head of one destined to be king. That it is used here to signify literary-rhetorical talent suggests the pass to which kingship had fallen in Java by the 1860s, and perhaps hints that Java's only hope lies with its independent literary intelligentsia.

49. The Javanese is: *Wonten carita winarni / anenggih ingkang negara / Jajar iku ing naminé / pan wonten ratu digjaya / agagah tur prakosa / jejulukira sang Prabu / Mahraja Suksma Wisésa / Tuhu ratu kinuwasa / kéringan mancanegari.*

Perfect Male.[50] Again, in canto 4, stanzas 32–3, the hero makes a witty theological retort by playing on the double meaning of *klèlèt* as both "opium-ball" and "turd."[51] It is hard to convey in English the peculiar, jarring poetry that erupts from the violent bonding of "turds" and "dogs" with the easy flow of traditional literary artifice: a polytonality quite new to Javanese literature. Yet the reader is always aware that this polytonality is deadly serious— neither an idle playing with styles nor a self-conscious satire on classical tradition. Dogs, truth, God, conundrums, opium, Muhammad, turds—none stands in privileged literary relation to the others. The poem's words remain "within the world," parts of its truth. No irony.

The *Suluk*'s polytonality does not end here. One must remember that the poem, like all Javanese poetry before this century, was composed to be sung, if not always aloud, at least under the breath. Its twelve cantos are distinguished from each other less by subject matter than by shifts between the seven musico-metrical forms in which they are variously composed: Asmarandana, Sinom, Mijil, Dhandhanggula, Gambuh, Kinanthi, and Pangkur. These musico-metric forms have had, at least since the start of the nineteenth century, accepted uses: they are felt, by their music, to arouse and reflect distinct moods and to be appropriate for distinct themes and topics.[52]

---

50. My English version is: "Spitefully Ngabdul Jabar said: / 'I'm uitterly fed up / Debating with a tailless dog!' / Ki Gatholoco said: / 'That name you gave me is correct / For all my ancestors, through every generation / / Each one of them was tailless, so / That truly none possessed a tail / Now "dog," interpreted, means "source" / While "tailless" indicates that I / Am truly human, with / No tail, unlike your ancestors / You on the other hand / Are who? With shaven, outplucked heads / Are you from Holland, China, Northwest India / / Or are you from Bengal?'" The Javanese is: *Ngabdul Jabar ngucap bengis / apegel ati mami / rembugan lan asu buntung / Gatholoco angucap / bener gonira ngarani / bapa biyung kaki buyut embah canggah / / ya padha buntung sedaya, tan duwé buntut sayekti / basa asu makna asal / buntung iku wis ngarani / ulun jinising jalmi / tan buntut kaya bapakmu / balik sira wong apa / dhasmu gundhul anjedhindhil / apa Landa apa Cina apa Koja / / apa sira wong Benggala.*

51. "And as for what I eat from day to day / I pick out everything that is most hot / And what is bitterest alone / For thus each turd I drop / Becomes another mountain high / And that is why their peaks / All belch forth smoke / The charred remains are what I eat / (What has become encrusted stone and rock) that is / The *klèlèt* I consume / / In truth, until I drop my burning turds / These mountain peaks have no reality / They'd disappear immediately / If I should once refrain / From dropping turds. Check for yourselves / My truthfulness from what / My anus spouts!" In Javanese: *Kang sun-pangan dhéwé saban ari / ingsun pilih ingkang luwih panas / sarta ingkang pait dhéwé / déné tetinjaningsun / kabèh iki pan dadya ardi / milanya kang prawata / kabèh metu kukus / tumusing geni sun-pangan / ingkang dadi padhas watu lawan curi / kalèlèt kang sun-pangan / / sadurungé ingsun ngising tai / gunung iku yekti durung ana / ing bésuk iku sirnané / lamun ingsun wus mantun / ngising tai kang metu silit / lah iyu nyatakena / kabèh sakandhaku.* "Turd" here refers to the dross left in an opium pipe after a smoke. "Dropping turds" has thus the esoteric meaning of going into a mystical opium trance.

52. Behrend, "The Serat Jatiswara," pp. 212–16. For a sophisticated and sensitive treatment of the relationship between Javanese song and poetry, see Martin F. Hatch, "Lagu, Laras, Layang: Rethinking Melody in Javanese Music" (Ph.D. thesis, Cornell University, 1980).

The author of the *Suluk* proceeds, systematically, to disrupt all these conventional associations. Thus, for example, Asmarandana, the metre in which Jajar and Suksma Wisésa's glory is abruptly polished off, is said variously to be "absorbed, sad, mournful, but sad or mournful in the sense of being lovelorn. Suitable for a tale concerned with the pain of love" and "[arousing] sadness."[53] Dhandhanggula, used for the esoteric discussion of turds and opium balls, is "flexible . . . if used for didactic purposes, very clear; if used for the fever of love, attractive," and "supple, pleasurable . . . good for ending a poem." Mijil, understood as "suitable for moral education, but also for a tale of love," is deployed for the first abusive altercation between Gatholoco and the *guru santri*. Most striking of all is the fact that canto 5, stanzas 58 and 59, where his adversaries call Gatholoco and his mother "pig's ass-holes" (*silité babi*), and the hero replies in kind, is composed in Sinom, whose character is, we are told, "friendly, clear" and "suitable for moral instruction."[54]

The effect, in each case, is savagely to rub the written words against the smooth grain of the mellifluous singing voice.[55] The peculiar power of the text comes precisely from the wound it slashes open between form and content. Professional skill of this kind makes one think of a solitary ballerina pirouetting on the rim of a precipice.

EPILOGUE

Not long after the composition of the *Suluk Gatholoco*, change began to accelerate in colonial Java, spurred above all by the deepening of industrialism in Europe (even in backward Holland) and the revolution in communications. In the early 1870s, the monopolistic Cultivation System was liquidated under pressure of liberal reformers and powerful business interests in the Netherlands. In over the rubble came hordes of planters, merchants, lawyers, physicians, and new-style civil servants. The opening of the Suez Canal hastened their passage, while the extension of telegraphic communication kept them in unprecedentedly close touch with the metropole. A local press began to appear in the 1860s, dominated at first by Dutchmen but soon with increasing Eurasian, Chinese, and native participation.[56] In the

---

53. Quoted from S. Padmosoekotjo, *Ngèngrèngan Kasusastran-Djawa* (Yogyakarta: Hien Hoo Sing, 1960), 1, pp. 22–3; and R. Hardjowirogo, *Paṭokaning Njekaraken* (Jakarta: Balai Pustaka, 1952), pp. 66–7. The other quotations in this paragraph are drawn from the same two texts.

54. For English and Javanese versions of this passage, see my *Language and Power*, p. 212.

55. A few years ago, as an experiment, I asked a young Javanese poet to "read aloud" this passage, blind, at an informal party. He tried twice, but on each occasion had to stop singing because he was laughing so hard.

56. See Ahmat B. Adam's fine study, *The Vernacular Press and the Emergence of Modern Indonesian Consciousness* (Ithaca, NY: Cornell University, Southeast Asia Program, Studies on Southeast Asia no. 17, 1995).

1880s came the railways, intended initially to haul exportable sugar from the vast plantations in the interior of Java, but soon carrying millions of Javanese passengers every year.[57] Alongside them appeared the beginnings of a state-sponsored, state-financed schooling system—for the first time in the by then almost three hundred years that Dutchmen had been meddling in the archipelago.[58]

Soon after 1900, signs of nascent nationalism were clearly visible, fostered by the new types of professionals produced by late colonial capitalism: editors and journalists, mechanics and accountants, school teachers and apothecaries, politicians and surveyors. As the new century wore on, people of this kind became culturally, sociologically, and economically positioned—thanks above all to print and print-capitalism—to undertake the *encyclopédistes'* co-ordination of professional knowledge against the *ancien régime* in Batavia. The dreams of these professionals, as articulated in the speeches and writings of Sukarno, Dr. Soetomo, Sjahrir, Semaun, and so many others, are familiar enough to us: "Perfect Indonesia"—some short or long way down the yellow brick road.[59] "Perfect Java" and "Perfect Male," however, are today obscure imaginings, all the more so in that the dream of "Perfect Indonesia," like all new forms of consciousness, brought with it its own amnesias. All the more reason, therefore, to take Twain's advice and return to the study of Old Java's ruined maps.

---

57. See Takashi Shiraishi, *An Age in Motion: Popular Radicalism in Java, 1912–1926* (Ithaca, NY: Cornell University Press, 1990), pp. 8–9.

58. See George McT. Kahin, *Nationalism and Revolution in Indonesia* (Ithaca, NY: Cornell University Press, 1952), pp. 31–2, for a succinct account of the halting progress of the colonial educational system.

59. Cf., in this regard, my *Language and Power*, p. 267.

Gravel in Jakarta's Shoes

Oldest among its European competitors, the Portuguese transcontinental empire lasted the longest, collapsed the fastest, and left the most bloodshed and ruin behind it. It owed its durability to Portugal's own backwardness and poverty—which ruled out the ambitious modernizing colonialisms of industrial America, France, England, and the Netherlands—and to its strategic position in Spain's armpit, at the mouth of the Mediterranean, which earned it for centuries the backing of London's naval might. It collapsed fastest because of the bizarre longevity of the Salazarist dictatorship, and its fanatical determination to fight three Vietnam wars simultaneously— Mozambique, Angola, and Guinea-Bissau, thousands of miles apart from one another—with a half-mercenary pre-professional army and no prospect of success. Within a year of the April 1974 coup in Lisbon, engineered by disillusioned officers, the empire was gone. The bloodshed and ruin, however, were only indirectly the responsibility of Lisbon. The atrocious twelve-year "civil war" endured by Mozambique was orchestrated and financed by South Africa. Pretoria and Washington bear most of the blame for the twenty-year conflict in Angola. But the holocaust in Portuguese East Timor, half a small island off the northern coast of Australia, was the doing of the Indonesian dictatorship of former general Suharto—with crucial support at the outset from the United States, and later, to lesser extents, from the governments of the big EEC states, Japan, and Australia.

No anticolonial guerrilla resistance had developed in this remote outpost of empire when the Salazarist dictatorship fell. Though the Portuguese had been there since the middle of the sixteenth century, a modern system of roads and transportation barely existed; the 600,000-odd indigenous, largely animist, population was overwhelmingly illiterate, and spoke two dozen or more local languages. The tiny literate elite, beneath a thin stratum of Portuguese clerics and officials, was substantially mestizo, descendants not only of Portuguese and local people, but also of African soldiers occasionally deployed on the island. There was no legislature, nor political parties, and only the shadow of a press. Needless to say, there was not the slightest suggestion of decolonization.

The Left-leaning officers who had taken power in Lisbon were fully occupied with the turbulent politics of Portugal itself, and with the problems of the African territories, in which there were substantial numbers of Portuguese settlers. East Timor was largely abandoned to its own devices. When General Costa Gomes, President of the Republic at this time, later declared that he had thought it would end up like Goa, and that the neighbouring Indonesians would peacefully absorb the territory, he was not being wholly insincere. Nehru had sent his troops into Goa in 1960, without a drop of blood being shed. But he was a humane man, and the freely elected leader of a democracy; he gave the Goanese their own autonomous state government, and encouraged their full participation in India's politics. In every respect, General Suharto was Nehru's polar opposite.

For a year or so after April 1974, the government in Jakarta did everything it could, short of an invasion, to gain control of East Timor. Leaders of the fledgling East Timorese parties were cajoled, bribed, and threatened, their rivalries exacerbated and manipulated. These machinations culminated in August 1975 in an Indonesian-backed coup by the UDT, the more conservative of the two substantial political parties. But the coup was quickly countered by its Left-leaning rival, Fretilin, and a brief civil war ensued in which several thousands lost their lives. The UDT leaders fled over the border into Indonesian West Timor, while Fretilin took control of the colony, and began to move towards formal independence, with wide popular support according to many foreign observers.

The only option now left to Indonesia's expansionists was an invasion, duly launched on Pearl Harbor Day, 1975, within hours of the departure of visiting President Ford and Secretary of State Kissinger. The assault was a bloody mess, with Indonesian troops firing on each other, and committing numberless atrocities in the East Timorese capital of Dili. The East Timorese troops, armed with high-quality NATO-issue weapons taken from the Portuguese garrison, gave a good account of themselves; and the Fretilin government held its ground and the bulk of the population—a source of mounting frustration in Jakarta.

Why did Suharto, his top generals, and his all-powerful intelligence apparatus take this course? The simplest answer is that they thought it would be easy. About six weeks before the invasion, two of the key military architects of policy on East Timor, Generals Ali Murtopo and "Benny" Murdani, visited my university, and laughingly assured uneasy questioners that "it would all be over in three weeks." Kissinger himself had advised Jakarta to "do it quickly." But there were other considerations. Indochina had "fallen" only a few months back, and generals who had come to power in Jakarta via the mass murder, in 1965–66, of hundreds of thousands of Indonesian communists (and others) would not tolerate an independent "left-wing" state on their borders. There was also the prospect of the vast undersea oilfields known to exist off East Timor's shores—especially attractive after the quadrupling of world oil prices in the autumn of 1973, and the extraordinary ten-billion-dollar bankruptcy, early in 1975, of Indonesia's state oil company Pertamina.

At the same time, the role of the United States was central, so central indeed that without it the invasion would probably not have happened. Some 90 per cent of the weapons used for the invasion came from the USA. Although their use outside Indonesia was expressly prohibited by a 1958 American-Indonesian agreement, Washington, well informed by the CIA of Jakarta's preparations for invasion, turned a blind eye to the violation. In 1977, when the desperate Indonesian army sought to acquire the OV-10 Bronco counter-insurgency airplanes needed for a massive aerial assault on Fretilin's mountain redoubts, the Carter administration secretly supplied them, while lying to Congress and the public that an embargo on military equipment was in place. At the United Nations, the US ambassador Patrick Moynihan did everything he could to line up support to block UN diplomatic intervention—he boasted in his memoirs of his success.

Two factors came to determine Washington's policy. First and foremost was the gratitude of its Vietnam-War-era establishment to Suharto for wiping out, in 1965–66, the largest (and legal) communist party in the world outside the socialist bloc (not a drop of American blood was shed) and for the economic policies he subsequently pursued which threw open resource-rich Indonesia to foreign investment and trade. Second were strategic calculations in an era when Soviet military (especially naval and air) power was at its apogee. Indonesia sprawled across the sea lanes between the Indian and Pacific oceans, and Suharto's secret offer to permit American nuclear submarines to pass through Indonesian waters, now including the deep channel along East Timor, without surfacing for Soviet satellite monitoring, was irresistible.

At the end of 1977, Jakarta was ready for a decisive breakthrough, using its Broncos in particular to destroy the fields and villages of the interior with bombs, napalm, and chemical defoliants. Tens of thousands of villagers were forced to flee into the Indonesian-held coastal plains, where they were herded into grim "resettlement" camps under Indonesian military control. Between

1977 and 1979 about one-third of the entire East Timorese population died as a result of famine, epidemics, and the brutal fighting. As Peter Carey points out, this death toll was proportionately much higher than in Pol Pot's contemporary Cambodia.[1] But the Indonesian regime had long closed off the island from the outside world, and the American ambassador in Jakarta colluded with the regime in keeping the tragedy from the Congress and the American public. In the meantime, virtually all the top leaders of the Fretilin government, including its capable military commander, Nicolau Lobato, had been killed or had surrendered.

By the beginning of the 1980s, most interested observers believed the struggle was all but over. Yet today East Timor is closer to real independence than at any time in the past two decades. The Dutch had dominated the East Indies from the early seventeenth to the early twentieth centuries without much difficulty, mostly because, between 1700 and 1900 the Netherlands was, like Portugal, a weak, poor, and small imperial power whose strategic location in Europe made it a useful subordinate for London. By 1900, however, the engines of Dutch capitalism were running well, and in The Hague the "new imperial thinking" had taken hold. This meant massive investment in communications infrastructure in the colony. It meant the institution, to be sure on a conservative scale, of modern education for the natives. It also meant the creation of a police state, capable of surveillance and repression in a way that would have been unimaginable in the late 1880s. Out of this explosive combination of development, education, and repression grew, quite suddenly, the Indonesian nationalism that only a few decades later ended Dutch rule.

Suharto and his generals were, alas, poorly informed about their own country's modern history, and so they proceeded in the 1980s to do exactly what the Dutch had done at the beginning of the century. Furthermore, like all "second imperialists," they were determined to show up the deficiencies of the aged colonialism they supplanted. So large sums were invested in East Timor's infrastructure, mainly but by no means entirely for military purposes. They established an elaborate hierarchy of schools, and eventually a university. The number of pupils enrolled was fifty times higher than in the Portuguese era; illiteracy was reduced from 90 per cent in 1972 to 42 per cent in 1990. It was hoped that this would help to instil the Indonesian language, the New Order state ideology, and loyalty to Jakarta. Under the aegis of the sinister Catholic intelligence czar, General Murdani, an apparatus of repression was created which, because it was shielded from the view not merely of the outside world, but of most Indonesians, soon stood above the law. Anything went: systematic torture, disappearances, termless

---

1. In Steve Cox and Peter Carey, *Generations of Resistance* (London: Cassell, 1995).

imprisonments, and so forth. The consequences during the 1980s were exactly those that emerged in the Dutch East Indies in the 1920s and 1930s.

By 1990, sleepy little Portuguese Dili's population had increased more than fivefold. A greatly expanded cohort of literate, educated East Timorese had developed for whom Jakarta's colonial-style economy offered only limited and subordinate employment. Fluent in Indonesian, as the young Indonesian nationalists seventy years earlier had become in Dutch, these youngsters now knew their rulers intimately, and through the Indonesian language had varying access to the Indonesian intelligentsia and the Indonesian press, and through both to the outside world. Moreover, they understood that they were being colonized, for all the Suharto regime's vaunted success in promoting assimilation. There was no more striking indication of this reality than the frequency with which Jakarta spoke of their "ingratitude" for all that Indonesia had done for them. Colonialists in trouble always speak of the natives' ingratitude, nationalists never. The holocaust of 1977–79 was in the childhood memories of young East Timorese, and they had direct experience of the systematic repressions of the 1980s. In these ways, Jakarta vastly deepened and widened East Timorese nationalism.

The Suharto regime unwittingly undermined its own aims by one other policy, the encouragement of Catholicization. In the wake of the massacres of 1965–66, justified partly as a crusade against communist atheism, the state had insisted that all Indonesians belong to some organized, recognized religion. Suspicious itself of militant Islam, it encouraged conversion by the East Timorese Catholic Church, which, in those days, it had every reason to trust. Catholic officers and civilians were a powerful presence in the country's security apparatus and the small Catholic minority had always been quietly reliant on the regime for protection against the Muslims. By the end of the decade East Timor was overwhelmingly Catholic, not least because the Church was the only institution offering some limited protection from the military. But here an unexpected hitch occurred. Under heavy external pressure—no state except oil-greedy Australia had recognized Indonesia's de jure absorption of East Timor—the Vatican decided to administer its East Timorese flock directly, rather than through the Indonesian episcopate. The rapidly expanding East Timorese Church was manned by indigenous clergy, who used the local lingua franca, Tetun, for their parish work and, where it was possible, Portuguese for communication with the outside world. As in an earlier Ireland, the priesthood thus became identified with the nationalism of a brutally colonized population. No one better represented this transformation than the seemingly timid young man, Carlos Ximenes Belo, named Bishop of Dili in 1983, who by the end of the decade had become a courageous, outspoken symbol of his countrymen's endurance.

At the very end of 1988, Suharto decided, after removing Murdani from his position as Commander-in-Chief, that things were going well in East Timor and that the moment had arrived for some controlled glasnost. The country was cautiously opened up to ordinary Indonesians and even to foreign visitors, and an able young Protestant general, Rudy Warouw, was sent out to pursue a "soft" policy. But the timing was unfortunate and the move in any case came far too late.

Internationally, the Cold War, which had made Suharto Washington's darling, was coming to an end. Portugal had entered the European Community, and its conscience-stricken leaders began using its veto to obstruct the Community's commercial relations with ASEAN, of which Indonesia was the largest member. In August 1990, Saddam Hussein invaded and "absorbed" the dubious Emirate of Kuwait, leading in February 1991 to a massive international military effort aimed, formally, at preventing him from doing exactly what Suharto had done in 1975—occupying and "integrating" a small neighbour. In Africa, Mengistu's Ethiopia was collapsing before the military prowess of Eritrean nationalists—a case once again with close similarities to East Timor. And ever since Amnesty International won the Nobel Peace Prize in 1976, the strength of the international human-rights movement had been increasing.

With the "opening" of East Timor, thousands of Indonesian carpetbaggers poured into the country to take advantage of the business opportunities that government policies and foreign donors were making available. This peaceable "second invasion" by private enterprise was widely interpreted by young East Timorese as a scheme hatched in Jakarta to reduce them to a demographic minority in their own land—so that if ever a referendum on its future were held, the Suharto regime would command a stable majority for integration. The appearance of outside visitors, most notably Pope John Paul in late 1989, gave the East Timorese the sense that they had not been forgotten by the outside world, and increasingly they found opportunities to communicate with it. For the first time they began to organize demonstrations for independence, which, though harshly repressed, showed clearly that the struggle's focus had moved from scattered armed groups in the mountains to the mass of urbanized youth.

The turning point came early on the morning of November 12, 1991, when a huge, peaceful procession of youngsters walked through Dili to the cemetery of the Santa Cruz Church to lay flowers on the grave of a young activist who had recently been killed by the Indonesian security forces. For reasons that are still unclear—few people believe that General Warouw gave the orders—two hundred or so heavily armed troops appeared and started shooting down the mourners trapped within the cemetery's high walls. At least two hundred and fifty were killed on the spot, many others were gravely injured, and over three hundred were subsequently disappeared. Massacres of this type had often occurred before, but this one was videotaped and photographed by two intrepid Englishmen, Max Stahl and Steve Cox, who managed to smuggle their films out of the country. Stahl's videotape, shown first on British television and then around the world, proved to have more immediate political impact than the mountains of written evidence accumulated by human rights organizations on the sixteen previous years of brutal Indonesian rule.

The international uproar was so great that Suharto was forced abruptly to dismiss General Warouw and his immediate superior, the dashing Commander of Military Region 9. (Thus began a process whereby East Timor ceased to be a fast track for military promotion and became a place shrewd officers tried to avoid.) When Xanana Gusmão, the poet and, after Lobato's death, legendary leader of the guerrilla underground, finally fell into the hands of the military late in 1992, his execution was out of the question. He was tried by the regime's complaisant judicial system, but in more or less open court, and was sentenced first to life, then to twenty years in prison. (In just this way, in late 1948, the Dutch found it impossible to execute Sukarno, the nationalist leader, and so incarcerated him. Sukarno quickly emerged to lead his country into a negotiated independence.)

Since the Santa Cruz massacre, though the repressions continue, East Timor has become for the first time an open political issue inside Indonesia. For by this time the state's near-monopoly on information was collapsing, thanks to CNN, and especially to the fax and e-mail revolution. The tone of official pronouncements was becoming steadily more defensive. Foreign Minister Ali Alatas told the Indonesian press that East Timor was "gravel in our shoes," and Suharto said that it was "a pimple on our face"—expressions they would never have used for any province which they genuinely felt to be Indonesian. For the first time the braver Indonesian journalists investigated for themselves what was happening on the spot. Some Jakarta dailies printed "short stories" which were thinly disguised accounts of the experiences of a devastated society. When the prominent environmentalist George Aditjondro of Java's Satyawacana University spoke out openly in favour of East Timorese independence, and defied a government ban on his attendance at an international conference on East Timor in Portugal, the regime harassed him, but did not dare to imprison him. Still more striking evidence of the East Timorization of Indonesian politics came late in 1994 with the spectacular, minutely planned invasion of the compound of the American Embassy in Jakarta by East Timorese students—just as Suharto was welcoming Clinton and other heads of state to the APEC summit conference. Within days, the Jakarta Metropolitan Region commander, the astute, ambitious General Hendro, was dismissed—the third general to fall to the Timorese in three years. And there was nothing for it but to permit the students safe-conduct into exile in Portugal.

The success of this *coup de théâtre* in Jakarta has had powerful reverberations in East Timor, where it is taken as yet another sign that History is now on the youngsters' side. One outcome has been the increasing frequency of violent incidents between East Timorese youth and the (mostly Muslim) carpetbaggers who dominate provincial markets, culminating in urban riots across most of the territory in October 1995. Hundreds, perhaps thousands, of the recent immigrants were forced to flee to their homes in Celebes and Java. The regime, having earlier announced that improved conditions had permitted the withdrawal of substantial troop units, felt compelled to send in new battalions, with the predictable consequences of massive arrests and brutalities, which represent nothing but the politics of the cul-de-sac. While a few hard-line Muslim intellectuals in Java have cynically taken up the cause of their fleeing co-religionists, demanding punishment of "disloyal Christians," Suharto cannot afford to play the Islamic card: too many of his political and military associates are Catholic or Protestant; so are many influential intellectuals and powerful Sino-Indonesian businessmen. He also knows that nothing would undermine his regime faster than the prairie-fire spread of interreligious violence out of East Timor across Indonesia's patchwork of ethnoreligious groupings.

All of this has resulted in a marked, if gradual, shift in American policy. The US voted against Indonesia at the last UN Human Rights convocation in Vienna; the State Department has blocked the sale of certain military aircraft. Clinton gently lectured Suharto at the G7 meeting in Tokyo and has visibly supported the reactivated Indonesian-Portuguese talks being held under Boutros-Ghali's aegis. In the meantime, longstanding bipartisan Congressional concern has subtly shifted from the human rights of the East Timorese towards their right to self-determination. In this shift, Suharto's age, and growing signs of popular unrest in Indonesia, as well as conflicts among the ruling elite, certainly play their role.

For Jakarta there is no way out. A return to the cruelties of the late 1970s is out of the question; while the "development" of the 1980s has led precisely to intensification of Timorese nationalism and Catholicism. Nothing shows the awareness of this impasse better than the recently published memoirs of General Murdani. This text is primarily a boastful catalogue of its author's political and military triumphs; but on East Timor it is wholly silent, except for an account of the botched invasion of 1975, which is blamed on unnamed supervisors. Probably the final breakthrough will have to wait until Suharto's political or physical demise, though he has shown in the past a capacity for realism and surprising demarches. No plausible successor will have the power or the capacity to resist for very long the ebb-tide of Indonesia's imperial venture.

7

Withdrawal Symptoms

... And in those days all men and beasts
Shall surely be in mortal danger
For when the Monarch shall betray
The Ten Virtues of the Throne
Calamity will strike, the omens
Sixteen monstrous apparitions:
Moon, stars, earth, sky shall lose their course
Misfortune shall spread everywhere
Pitch-black the thundercloud shall blaze
With Kali's fatal conflagration
Strange signs shall be observed throughout
The land, the Chao Phraya shall boil
Red as the heart's-blood of a bird
Madness shall seize the Earth's wide breast
Yellow the colour of the leadening sky
The forest spirits race to haunt
The city, while to the forest flee
The city spirits seeking refuge ...
The enamel tile shall rise and float
The light gourd sink down to the depths.

Prophetic Lament for Sri Ayutthaya (*c.* seventeenth century AD)

INTRODUCTION

In themselves, military coups are nothing new in modern Thai history. There
have been at least eight successful, and many more unsuccessful, coups since

the one that overthrew the absolute monarchy in 1932.[1] It is therefore not altogether surprising that some western journalists and academics have depicted the events of October 6, 1976 as typical of Thai politics, and even as a certain return to normalcy after three years of unsuitable flirtation with democracy.[2] In fact, however, October 6 marks a clear turning point in Thai history for at least two quite different reasons. First, most of the important leaders of the legal left-wing opposition of 1973–76, rather than languishing in jail or in exile like their historical predecessors, have joined the increasingly bold and successful maquis. Second, the coup was not a sudden intra-elite *coup de main*, but rather was the culmination of a two-year-long right-wing campaign of public intimidation, assault, and assassination best symbolized by the orchestrated mob violence of October 6 itself.[3]

Political murders by the ruling cliques have been a regular feature of modern Thai politics—whether under Marshal Phibunsongkhram's dictatorship in the late 1930s, under the Phibunsongkhram–Phao Siyanon–Sarit Thanarat triumvirate of the late 1940s and 1950s,[4] or the Sarit Thanarat–Thanom Kittikajon–Praphat Jarusathien regime of the 1960s and early 1970s.[5] But these murders, sometimes accompanied by torture, were typically "administrative" in character, carried out by the formal

---

1. See, for example, David Wilson, *Politics in Thailand* (Ithaca, NY: Cornell University Press, 1967), chapter IX; Fred W. Riggs, *Thailand: The Modernization of a Bureaucratic Polity* (Honolulu: East–West Center Press, 1966), Appendix B.

2. A liberal variant of this approach is to describe October 6 in Sisyphaean terms, as yet another in an endless series of frustrating failures to bring democratic government to Siam. For a nice example of this, see Frank C. Darling, "Thailand in 1976: Another Defeat for Constitutional Democracy," *Asian Survey*, 17: 2 (Feb. 1977), pp. 116–32.

3. *Far Eastern Economic Review*, April 16, 1976, in its account of the April 1976 elections, spoke of "a spate of shootings, bombings and other violent incidents aimed mainly at left-wing and reformist parties." *Prachachart Weekly Digest*, 20 (March 16, 1976) and 21 (March 23, 1976), lists the names of close to fifty victims of political assassination in the period 1974–76, all of them on the Left.

4. On the repression following the "rebellion" of Phraya Song Suradet in 1938, see Wilson, *Politics in Thailand*, p. 261. On March 3, 1949, four well-known MPs and former cabinet ministers were murdered by Phao's police while being moved from one prison to another. See Samut Surakkhaka, *26 Kānpattiwat Thai lae Ratthaprahān 2089–2507* (Twenty-six Thai Revolutions and Coups, 1546–1964) [Bangkok: Sue Kānphim, 1964], pp. 472–89. In December 1952, two prominent northeastern politicians, Thim Phuriphat and Tiang Sirikhan, disappeared. It was revealed later that they had been strangled by Phao's police. See Charles F. Keyes, *Isan: Regionalism in Northeastern Thailand* (Ithaca, NY: Cornell University Southeast Asia Program Data Paper no. 65, 1967), p. 34; and Thak Chaloemtiarana, "The Sarit Regime, 1957–1963: The Formative Years of Modern Thai Politics" (Ph.D. thesis, Cornell University, 1974), p. 118.

5. See, e.g., Thak, "The Sarit Regime," pp. 266–9, for accounts of the public executions of Suphachai Sisati on July 5, 1959; of Khrong Chandawong and Thongphan Sutthimat on May 31, 1961; and of Ruam Phromwong on April 24, 1962. Victims of the Thanom–Praphat era belonged to groups well beyond the circle of intellectuals and politicians. For example, an official inquiry in 1975 by the Ministry of the Interior, headed by the Ministry's own inspector-general, confirmed

instrumentalities of the state, very often in secret. The public knew little of what had occurred, and certainly did not participate in any significant way. What is striking about the brutalities of the 1974–76 period is their non-administrative, public, and even mob character. In August 1976, Bangkokians watched the hitherto inconceivable spectacle of the private home of Prime Minister Kukrit Pramote being sacked by a swarm of drunken policemen.[6] In February, Socialist Party Secretary-General Dr. Boonsanong Punyothayan had been waylaid and assassinated outside his suburban home by professional gunmen.[7] Hired hooligans increasingly displayed a quite untraditional style of violence, such as indiscriminate public bombings,[8] which sharply contrasted with the discreet, precise murders of an earlier era. Ten innocent persons died when a grenade was thrown into the midst of a New Force party election rally in Chainat on March 25, 1976.[9] And the gruesome lynchings of October 6 took place in the most public place in all Siam—Sanam Luang, the great downtown square before the royal palace.

What I propose to do in this article is to explore the reasons for this new level and style of violence, for they are symptomatic of the present social, cultural, and political crisis in Siam. My argument will be developed along two related lines, one dealing with class formation and the other with ideological upheaval.

---

student charges that in 1970–71 at least seventy people were summarily executed by the Communist Suppression Operations Command in Patthalung province. In the words of the report: "Communist suspects arrested by the soldiers were mostly executed. Previously, soldiers would have shot these suspects by the roadside [*sic!*]. But later they changed the style of killing and introduced the red oil drum massacre in order to eliminate all possible evidence. The sergeant would club the suspect until he fell unconscious, before dumping him in the oil drum and burning him alive." *Bangkok Post*, March 30, 1975. For indiscriminate napalming of minority Meo [Hmong] villages in the north, see Thomas A. Marks, "The Meo Hill Tribe Problem in Thailand," *Asian Survey*, 13: 10 (Oct. 1973), p. 932; and Ralph Thaxton, "Modernization and Peasant Resistance in Thailand," in Mark Selden, ed., *Remaking Asia* (New York: Pantheon, 1971), pp. 265–73, especially at p. 269.

6. These policemen, in civilian clothes, were escorted by police cars with flashing lights and motorcycle outriders. Aside from stealing brandy and cigarettes, they did an estimated $500,000 damage to Kukrit's palatial home. *New York Times*, Aug. 20, 1975. At precisely the same moment, Thammasat University, spiritual home of student radicalism, was assaulted and put partly to the torch by the right-wing hooligans of the Red Gaurs (on whom see below)—with complete impunity.

7. The murder took place on February 28. See *Far Eastern Economic Review*, March 12, 1976.

8. On February 15, 1976, the moderate New Force party's Bangkok headquarters were fire-bombed by right-wing hooligans. See *Far Eastern Economic Review*, Feb. 27, 1976. Though one of these hooligans got an arm blown off in the process, he was released by the police for "lack of evidence." On March 21, a bomb thrown into a mass of marchers in downtown Bangkok—they were demanding full removal of the American military presence—killed four people and wounded many others. See *Prachachart Weekly Digest*, 22 (March 30, 1976), p. 1.

9. *Far Eastern Economic Review*, April 9, 1976.

The class structure of Thai society has changed rapidly since the late 1950s. Above all, new bourgeois strata have emerged, rather small and frail to be sure, but in significant respects outside of and partially antagonistic to the old feudal-bureaucratic upper class. These new strata—which include both a middle and a petty bourgeoisie—were spawned by the great Vietnam War boom of the 1960s when Americans and American capital poured into the country on a completely unprecedented scale (rapidly followed by the Japanese). It is these strata that provide the social base for a quasi-popular right-wing movement clearly different from the aristocratic and bureaucratic rightism of an earlier age. This is by no means to suggest that old ruling cliques of generals, bankers, bureaucrats, and royalty do not continue to hold the keys of real political power; rather, that these cliques have found themselves new, and possibly menacing, "popular" allies.[10]

The ideological upheaval was also in large part due to the impact of American penetration, and manifested itself primarily in an intellectual revolution that exploded during the "democratic era" of 1973–76. Reacting to the intellectual nullity and crude manipulation of traditionalist symbols by the Sarit–Thanom–Praphat dictatorship, many young Thai came openly to question certain central elements of the old hegemonic culture. In response to this, there was an enormous increase in the self-conscious propagation and indoctrination of a militant ideology of Nation–Religion–King—as opposed to the *bien-pensant* "traditionalism" that reigned before. Rather than being seen generally as "naturally Thai," Nation–Religion–King became ever more explicitly the ideological clubs of highly specific social formations. The obvious audiences for this self-conscious rightist ideologizing were the new bourgeois strata; the propagandists were both fanatical elements in these strata themselves and some shrewd manipulators in the ruling cliques.

TROUBLES OF NEW CLASSES

In the 1950s and 1960s most western social scientists took the view that Siam was a "bureaucratic polity"—a political system completely dominated by a largely self-perpetuating, modernizing bureaucracy.[11] Below this bureaucracy there was only a pariah Chinese commercial class and an undifferentiated

---

10. This is perhaps the place to emphasize that the present essay, being centrally concerned with the emergence of *new* social formations and *new* cultural tendencies, deliberately pays little attention to these old ruling groups, or to such powerful bureaucratic institutions as the military and the Ministry of the Interior. The political roles of these groups and institutions have been extensively discussed in the literature on modern Thai politics.

11. The phrase was, I think, coined by Riggs. See p. 11 of his *Thailand*. But the basic idea was central to Wilson's *Politics in Thailand*, the single most influential study of that era.

peasantry, both with low political consciousness and virtually excluded from political participation. The relations between bureaucracy and peasantry were understood to be generally harmonious and unexploitative,[12] involving only the classical exchanges of taxes, labour, and deference for security, glory, and religious identity. Thanks largely to the shrewdness and foresight of the great nineteenth-century Chakkri dynasts, Siam, alone among the states of Southeast Asia, did not succumb to European or American imperialism and thereby escaped the evils of rack-renting, absentee landlordism, chronic peasant indebtedness, and rural proletarianization so typical of the colonized zones. The Siamese economy, by no means highly developed until the 1960s, was essentially in the hands of immigrant Chinese, who, by their alien and marginal status, could never play a dynamic, independent political role.[13] This picture of a peaceful, sturdy, and independent Siam was in important ways quite false. Western capital, western "advisers," and western cultural missionaries exercised decisive influence on Siamese history after the 1850s.[14] On the other hand, when compared to the changes brought about by the American and Japanese penetration in the Vietnam war era, the years before the 1960s appear relatively "golden." As late as 1960, Bangkok could still be described as the "Venice of the East," a somnolent old-style royal harbour-city dominated by canals, temples, and palaces. Fifteen years later, many of the canals had been filled in to form roads and many of the temples had fallen into decay. The whole centre of gravity of the capital had moved eastwards, away from the royal compounds and Chinese ghettoes by the Chao Phraya river to a new cosmopolitan zone dominated visually and politically by vast office buildings, banks, hotels, and shopping plazas. The city had expanded with cancerous speed, devouring the surrounding countryside and turning rice-paddies into speculative housing developments, instant suburbs, and huge new slums.[15]

---

12. Thadeus Flood, in his excellent article, "The Thai Left Wing in Historical Context," *Bulletin of Concerned Asian Scholars*, 7: 2 (April–June 1975), p. 55, quotes the following entertaining sentences from Wendell Blanchard *et al.*, *Thailand* (New Haven: Human Relations Area File, 1957), pp. 484–5: "It is doubtful whether [Thai peasants] could conceive of a social situation without distinction between superior and inferior position. Peasants and others of low social status have never viewed such a social system as particularly unreasonable or severe, and there is no history in Thailand of general social oppression."

13. See G. William Skinner's *Chinese Society in Thailand: An Analytic History* (Ithaca, NY: Cornell University Press, 1957); and his *Leadership and Power in the Chinese Community in Thailand* (Ithaca, NY: Cornell University Press, 1958). Cf. Donald Hindley, "Thailand: The Politics of Passivity," *Pacific Affairs*, 41: 3 (Fall 1968), pp. 366–7.

14. Frank C. Darling, *Thailand and the United States* (Washington, DC: Public Affairs Press, 1965), p. 29, noted that, at the time of the 1932 coup that overthrew the absolute monarchy, 95 per cent of the Thai economy was in the hands of foreigners and Chinese.

15. Over a quarter of a century the population of the metropolitan complex of Bangkok–Thonburi rose as follows:

This transformation, which on a smaller scale also occurred in certain provincial capitals, was generated by forces exogenous to Siamese society. It may be helpful to describe these forces in terms of three interrelated factors. The first and most important was undoubtedly America's unceremonious post-1945 extrusion of the European colonial powers from their pre-war economic, political, and military hegemony in Southeast Asia.[16] The second was Washington's decision to make Siam the pivot of its region-wide expansionism. Bangkok became the headquarters not only for SEATO, but also for a vast array of overt and clandestine American operations in neighbouring Laos, Cambodia, Burma, and Vietnam.[17] A third factor—important in a rather different way—was the technological revolution that made mass tourism a major industry in the Far East after World War II. (Hitherto tourism in this zone had been an upper-class luxury.) For this industry Bangkok was a natural nexus: it was not only geographically central to the region, but it was thoroughly safe under the protection of American arms and native dictatorships, and, above all, it offered an irresistible combination of modern luxury (international hotels, comfortable air-conditioned transportation, and up-to-date films) and exotic antiquities.[18] Elsewhere in Southeast Asia the colonial powers had typically constructed culturally mediocre, commercially oriented capital cities in coastal areas far removed

1947	781,662
1960	1,800,678
1970	2,913,706
1972	3,793,763

See Ivan Mudannayake, ed., *Thailand Yearbook, 1975–76* (Bangkok: Temple Publicity Services, 1975), p. E28.

16. Darling, *Thailand*, pp. 29, 61, 170–71. By 1949, US trade with Siam had increased by 2000 per cent over the immediate pre-war level. By the late 1950s the US was buying 90 per cent of Siam's rubber and most of its tin.

17. This line of analysis is developed more extensively in Thaxton, "Modernization," pp. 247–51.

18. Some indication of the scale of this tourism is suggested by the following figures:

	1965	*1966*	*1970*	*1971*	*1972*	*1973*	*1974*
Foreign visitors (in thousands)	225.0	469.0	628.7	638.7	820.8	1037.7	1107.4
United States	78.3	133.3	159.2	147.0	151.6	161.4	156.8
(R&R)	(15.0)	(70.7)	(44.3)	(26.6)	(7.7)	(4.4)	(3.5)
Japan	17.3	42.9	47.0	55.8	93.5	151.9	132.7
Foreign exchange earnings from tourism (in millions of *baht*)	506	1770	2175	2214	2718	3399	4292
(R&R)	(50)	(459)	(390)	(240)	(63)	(13)	(11)

Note: In gauging the significance of the figures for 1972–74, one must bear in mind the then high rate of inflation. *Source*: World Bank, "Thailand: Current Economic Prospects and Selected Development Issues," II (Statistical Appendix), Nov. 14, 1975, Table 8.7. Tourism was typically among the top eight foreign-exchange earning industries during these years.

from the old indigenous royal capitals. (Tourists had thus to make time-consuming pilgrimages from Jakarta to Surakarta, Rangoon to Mandalay-Ava, Saigon to Hué, and Phnom Penh to Angkor.)

If the American penetration of Siam was a general feature of the post-World War II era, there was nonetheless a marked difference in degree and pace after 1959, when the absolutist dictatorship of Sarit Thanarat was installed. His predecessor, Marshal Phibunsongkhram, was a relatively pol-ished product of St. Cyr and the pre-war European-dominated world. Sarit, on the other hand, was a provincial, a product of the Royal Military Academy, and a man who rose to power in the postwar era of American global hegemony. It was he who personally presided over the Americanization (in terms of organization, doctrines, training, weaponry, and so forth) of the Thai military, following his first visit to Washington in 1950.[19] Almost a decade of close ties with the Pentagon prior to his seizure of power meant that after 1959 he found it easy and natural to link Siam to the United States in an unprecedented intimacy.[20] In other ways, too, Sarit was a perfect dictator from Washington's point of view. He was willing and eager to make "devel-opment" part of his quest for legitimacy and to accept the advice of US-trained technocrats in drawing up and implementing developmental pro-grammes.[21] As unquestioned "strongman," he had far more power to act swiftly and decisively than his predecessor.[22] Most important of all, Sarit did everything in his power to attract foreign (and especially American) capital to

---

19. The best single source on Sarit is Thak, "The Sarit Regime." For his role in the Americanization of the Thai military, see especially pp. 120–22. But Darling, *Thailand*, is very useful on the American side of the Sarit–Washington relationship.

20. Sarit was especially supportive of US aggressiveness in Laos. Whereas Phibun had been born near Ayutthaya in central Thailand, and was "central Thai" in his basic orientation, Sarit was a northeasterner in many ways. His mother had come from Nongkhai on the Thai border with Laos, and he himself had spent part of his childhood there. Through her, he was closely related to Gen. Phoumi Nosavan, the Pentagon's perennial rightist-militarist candidate for strongman in Vientiane.

21. There had never been a national plan in the Phibun era. Siam's six-year First National Development Plan was developed under Sarit and formally inaugurated in 1961. On this plan, and the degree to which it abjectly followed the recommendations of the International Bank for Reconstruction and Development, see Pierre Fistié, *L'Évolution de la Thaïlande contemporaine* (Paris: Armand Colin, 1967), pp. 334–5. But cf. Thak, "The Sarit Regime," pp. 327–8, for an argument that Sarit did not allow himself to be wholly guided by international technocrats.

22. While Phibun had been a virtual dictator in the late 1930s and early 1940s, during his second long term as Prime Minister, 1948–1957, he was in a much weaker position. The coup group of 1947 had brought him back as a sort of figurehead who could serve to give some inter-national "class" to their regime. Phibun survived mainly because of US support and his own astute balancing of the increasingly antagonistic factions of Police General Phao and General Sarit. By the coups of 1958 and 1959, Sarit destroyed the power of the police, and made the army, which he controlled, the undisputed master of Thai political life.

Siam, believing it to be an essential means for consolidating his rule and that of his successors. Thus strikes were banned and unions forcibly dissolved. Branches of foreign corporations were not only permitted to remain largely foreign-owned, but could purchase land in Siam, were largely exempted from taxation, and were even allowed to bring technicians freely into the country, bypassing the existing immigration laws.[23] The *baht* was managed according to the most orthodox economic principles and remained a rock of stability until the end of the 1960s.

After five years in power Sarit succumbed to cirrhosis of the liver. But his heirs, Thanom and Praphat, continued the basic thrust of his policies. The onset of their rule virtually coincided with Lyndon Johnson's escalation of the Vietnam War, and they were quick to seize the opportunities thereby presented. Washington was encouraged to treat Siam as a sort of gigantic immobile aircraft carrier: in the peak year 1968, there were almost 50,000 US servicemen on Thai soil, and the Americans had been allowed to build and operate at least eight major bases as well as dozens of minor installations.[24] Not only were the Thai rulers amply rewarded in terms of military aid, but this huge American presence generated a rapid economic expansion, above all in the construction and service sectors.[25] A massive war-related boom developed, which built on, but far outstripped, the "pre-war" prosperity of the early Sarit years. It was the Thanom–Praphat regime that presided over the proliferation of hotels, restaurants, cinemas, supermarkets, nightclubs, and

---

23. For a summary of Thai enticements to foreign investors, see Fistié, *L'Evolution*, p. 337.

24. According to the *New York Times*, April 14, 1968, there were then 46,000 troops in Thailand, as well as 5,000 troops a month on R&R from Vietnam. The *Nation*, Oct. 2, 1967, listed 46,000 troops, 7,000 personnel in economic and propaganda activities, and 8 airbases.

25. Part of this transformation is shown by comparing employment in various sectors between 1960 and 1970:

	1960	*1970*	*Change*
Agriculture	11,300,000	13,200,000	(+ 17%)
Mining	30,000	87,000	(+ 290%)
Manufacturing	470,000	683,000	(+ 45%)
Construction	69,000	182,000	(+ 64%)
Commerce	779,000	876,000	(+ 13%)
Transport, storage, communications	166,000	268,000	(+ 62%)
Services	654,000	1,184,000	(+ 81%)

Rounded figures computed from Table 1.2 in World Bank, "Thailand," II (Nov. 14, 1975). In the years 1960 to 1965 Gross National Income increased annually by 7.5 per cent, Gross Domestic Investment by 14.4 per cent. See Annex I of the "Report and Recommendation of the President of the International Bank for Reconstruction and Development to the Executive Directors of the World Bank on a proposed loan to the Industrial Finance Corporation of Thailand," Sept. 1, 1976. Clark Neher, "Stability and Instability in Contemporary Thailand," *Asian Survey*, 15: 12 (Dec. 1975), pp. 1100–101, gives an average 8.6 per cent annual increase in GNP between 1959 and 1969.

massage parlours generated by the torrential inflow of white businessmen, soldiers, and tourists.

If the boom itself was basically fuelled by American (and Japanese) investment and spending, the mode of Thai participation in its benefits was influenced significantly by regime policies. Of these, one of the most decisive was Sarit's early decree eliminating the existing 50-*rai* (*c.* 20-acre) limit on permissible landholding.[26] This decree laid the legal foundations for large-scale land speculation which continued to accelerate so long as the boom itself lasted. Nor was the speculative wave confined to Bangkok. As the Americans built and paved great strategic highways to the borders of Laos and Cambodia (the "Friendship" Highway, *inter alia*),[27] metropolitan and provincial speculators followed in their train, buying up wayside land very cheaply from subsistence farmers who had little understanding of land-as-speculative-commodity.[28] Land speculation is an economic activity in which legal skills, "inside information," "pull," and access to cheap bank loans are peculiarly important. It is not surprising, therefore, that the main beneficiaries of the real estate boom were not merely the traditional Sino-Thai commercial class, but high and middle-level bureaucrats (military and civilian) and provincial notables with good political connections. The zones hardest hit tended to be those closest to Bangkok, the funnel through which capital poured so fast. The situation in central Thailand is illustrative: whereas in the Phibunsongkhram era, scholars agree, tenancy was not a serious problem, by the latter 1960s, USAID reports indicated that less than 30 per cent of the farms were still owner-operated.[29]

---

26. See, e.g., Fistié, *L'Évolution*, p. 353; Robert J. Muscat, *Development Strategy in Thailand: A Study of Economic Growth* (New York: Praeger, 1966), p. 138.

27. See Thak, "The Sarit Regime," Appendix IV, for details and a sketch map.

28. Vivid evidence to this effect is provided by Howard Kaufman in his *Bangkhuad: A Community Study in Thailand* (Rutland, Vt. and Tokyo: Tuttle, 1976), pp. 219–20. Revisiting Bangkhuad, which he had studied in 1954 when it was still a small rural community on the fringes of Bangkok, he found seventeen years later that: whereas in 1954 a *rai* (1 *rai* = *c.* 0.4 acres) was valued at 3,000 *baht* (approximately $150), by 1971 it had gone up to 250,000 *baht* (approximately $12,500). In addition, the most valuable land was no longer the most fertile, but the land closest to the developing road system. Thak, "The Sarit Regime," pp. 337–8, notes that many peasants with land along the major highways were simply extruded without compensation by powerful officials and their accomplices.

29. See Anonymous, "The U.S. Military and Economic Invasion of Thailand," *Pacific Research*, I: 1 (Aug. 3, 1969), pp. 4–5, citing Department of Commerce, OBR 66-60, Sept. 1966, p. 6. Neher, "Stability," p. 1110, speaks of tenancy and indebtedness having "jumped precipitously." Takeshi Motooka, in his *Agricultural Development in Thailand* (Kyoto: Kyoto University, Center for Southeast Asian Studies, 1971), pp. 221 ff., observes that: (1) According to the Thai government's 1963 agricultural survey, over 60.8 per cent of the farmed land in the Central Plain was operated by full- or part-tenants. (2) From his own local study in a district of Pathum Thani province (very close to Bangkok), 90 per cent of the operating farmers were tenants. On the other hand, the

The general "dynamization" of the Thai economy as a result of the factors mentioned above served to create or expand at least four social formations that are significant for our purposes here—in the sense that their survival largely depended on the continuation of the boom. In those rural areas where the process of commercialization had spread most rapidly, strategically positioned notables, rice-mill owners, traders, headmen, and so forth, acquired sudden new wealth, a good deal of which was reinvested in land. As rural landlordism rose, so there was a complementary exodus of the young and the dispossessed to the booming urban centres.[30] In the towns, and especially in Bangkok, the flow of migrants generated two sorts of politically volatile social groups: first, a large mass of unemployed, or underemployed, youthful drifters, with few substantial prospects either in the city or back home in their villages; second, a considerable number who were able to better themselves by finding niches in a broad array of burgeoning service-type occupations. This petty-bourgeois army included barbers, pimps, manicurists, dry-cleaners, chauffeurs, tailors, masseuses, tour guides, motorcycle repairmen, bartenders, receptionists, tellers, and small shop owners. To a considerable degree this new petty bourgeoisie served and was dependent on the prosperity of a fourth group. This segment, mainly of previous urban origin, was a largely new middle bourgeoisie, in certain respects as closely tied to foreign capital as to the Thai state apparatus.

Tables 7.1 and 7.2 may serve to suggest the nature of these changes in the Thai class structure and, in very rough terms, both the absolute sizes of the middle and petty bourgeoisies and their relative share of the population as a whole. The extraordinary increase in category B, and the sizeable increases in categories A, F, and I (largely middle/upper and petty-bourgeois occupations), clearly reveal the nature of the boom's sociological impact over a decade.[31] Data drawn from the 1970 census, in which the above broad

---

thesis of rapidly increasing tenancy has recently been strongly attacked by Laurence Stifel in his "Patterns of Land Ownership in Central Thailand during the Twentieth Century," *Journal of the Siam Society*, 64: 1 (Jan. 1976), pp. 237–74. For some comparative material on growing land-lordism, indebtedness, and land-title manipulation in the northern province of Chiengrai, see Michael Moerman, *Agricultural Change and Peasant Choice in a Thai Village* (Berkeley: University of California Press, 1968), chapter V.

30. This flow, however, was extensive even before the onset of the boom. Mudannayake, ed., *Thailand Yearbook, 1975–76*, p. E30, notes that in 1960 no less than one-quarter of Bangkok's population had been born elsewhere.

31. A striking example of such "non-bureaucratic" *nouveaux riches* produced by this era was Mr. Thawit ('Dewitt') Klinprathum, head of the large Social Justice Party in 1974–76. The son of a poor government official, with not much more than a secondary-school education, he started work at $10 a month as a bookkeeper. He later did stints as pedicab driver, shipping clerk, bus operator, and so forth. As his official biography records, "While working on subcontracts from the Express and Transportation Organization (ETO—a state-owned corporation intimately

categories are broken down into great detail, allow one to make the very rough calculation (see Table 7.2) that by 1970 the middle and upper bourgeoisie formed about 3.5 per cent of the working population (divided perhaps into 3.0 per cent and 0.5 per cent), and the petty bourgeoisie about 7.5 per cent.[32]

It is always useful to remember that social groupings become social classes in so far as they consolidate themselves through the *family*—a key institution for linking power, wealth, and status in one generation and transmitting them to the next. An important sign of class formation in Siam during the Sarit–Thanom–Praphat era was a massive expansion of education at all levels, partly at the "modernizing" behest of American advisers and Thai technocrats, but also in bureaucratic response to the demands of the new upwardly aspirant social groups—and the families within them. In 1961, there were 15,000 students enrolled in a total of five universities; by 1972, there were 100,000 enrolled in seventeen.[33] From 1964 to 1969, the numbers enrolled in government secondary schools rose from 159,136 to 216,621; in private secondary schools from 151,728 to 228,495; and in government vocational schools from 44,642 to 81,665.[34] "Traditionally" (for our purposes here from the 1880s until World War II), education had been sharply

---

tied to JUSMAG) unloading and transporting equipment, he realized the need for trailers. With the money he had saved and credit from the bank, he purchased two trailers to deliver heavy machinery and equipment . . . He started carrying equipment for the Joint U.S. Military Advisory Group (JUSMAG) and Accelerated Rural Development (ARD). Mr. Dewitt chose the right time to buy his trailers because mechanization was becoming necessary for economic development. With no other local companies possessing trailers and cranes, his company, Trailer Transport Company, secured a contract for transporting military equipment . . . His godown expanded and his trailers and trucks numbered in the hundreds *as the transportation network in the country expanded.*" *Bangkok Post*, Dec. 24, 1974 (special advertisement paid for by the Social Justice Party). Emphasis added. By 1974, "Dewitt" was a multimillionaire with an eight-storey office building to himself.

32. The figures in the two right-hand columns are likely to be too low. Category E, in particular, must include numbers of rural merchants and businessmen, though there is no way of telling even roughly how many.

33. Neher, "Stability," p. 1101; Frank C. Darling, "Student Protest and Political Change in Thailand," *Pacific Affairs*, 47: 1 (Spring 1974), p. 6. To understand class formation in a capitalist society like Thailand's, it is important to study the "non-productive" elements (schoolchildren, students, etc.). To build and to perpetuate their positions/wealth, the new bourgeois and pettybourgeois groups steer their children into the educational institutions. One only knows when a *class* has really come to exist (rather than a suddenly rising elite) when one sees "privileged kids"—and two generations of power. Aristocracies can consolidate themselves by intermarriage; bourgeoisies cannot, at least not to the same degree. Education tends to replace marriage.

34. See Darling, "Student Protest," p. 6. These figures should be understood in the context of the budgetary statistics cited by Thak, "The Sarit Regime," pp. 437–8, which show the expenditures on the ministries of Education, Defence, and the Interior as percentages of the total budget over the years 1953–73. For brevity's sake I will give only his computations for the years 1958–73.

Table 7.1 Economically active population aged 11 and over classified by occupation

Occupational group	1960	1970	% increase
Total	13,836,984	16,850,136	21.7
A Professional, technical & related workers	173,960	284,104	63.3
B Administrative, executive & managerial workers	26,191	246,591	941.5
C Clerical workers	154,303	190,238	23.3
D Sales workers	735,457	833,607	13.3
E Farmers, fishermen, hunters, loggers, & related workers	11,332,489	13,217,416	16.6
F Miners, quarrymen, & related workers	26,255	42,605	62.2
G Workers in transport & communications	144,610	225,204	55.7
H Craftsmen, product-process workers & labourers not elsewhere classified	806,205	1,109,943	37.7
I Service, sport & recreation workers	273,375	471,999	72.7
J Unclassifiable	99,259	30,560	−59.2
K New entrants to the workforce	64,880	197,869	305.0

Source: Adapted from National Economic and Development Board, National Statistical Office and Institute of Population Studies, Chulalongkorn University, "The Population of Thailand [1974]," in Mudannayake, ed., *Thailand Yearbook, 1975–76*, p. E41.

Table 7.2 Economically active population aged 11 and over classified by occupation and class (1970)

Occupational group	Total	State employed	State employed (%)	Middle & upper bourgeoisie (est.)	Petty bourgeoisie (est.)
A	284,104	198,792	70.4	250,000	35,000
B	246,591	212,752	86.3	230,000	15,000
C	190,238	108,632	57.1	negl.	190,000
D	833,607	1,492	.2	negl.	600,000
E	13,217,416	10,169	.1	negl.	?
F	42,605	568	1.3	negl.	negl.
G	225,204	24,759	11.0	negl.	100,000
H	1,109,943	106,292	9.6	negl.	150,000
I	471,999	114,528	24.3	70,000	160,000
J	30,560	–	–	–	–
K	197,869	–	–	?	?
Total	16,850,136	777,984	4.7	550,000	1,250,000

Source: Adapted from Department of Labour, Ministry of the Interior, *Yearbook of Labour Statistics 1972–1973* [using 1970 census figures], cited in Mudannayake, ed., *Thailand Yearbook, 1975–76*, pp. E41–68.

bifurcated. A tiny upper class received a gentlemanly western-style education, while the bulk of the population either went uneducated, attended government primary schools, or received instruction in Buddhist temples.[35] Neither level of education generated nationally significant social mobility; rather, each helped to conserve its constituents in their existing social and economic positions. Western-style higher education gave polish to those already born to rule. State primary education was so elementary that it seems to have had few vectoral consequences: its existence was more a gesture by Thai governments concerned to show a modern face to the outside world than a response to peasant demand. Buddhist education was essentially ethically and cosmologically oriented, rather than geared to providing career-related skills (though for a small group of commoners success in the Sangha's tiered examination system could lead to very steep social mobility).[36]

Accordingly, the real significance of the educational expansion of the 1960s was that it took place mainly at the secondary and tertiary levels.[37] For the first time, sizeable numbers of Thai began to desire and to have some access to career-oriented educations for their children, educations which, past history suggested, were the badges of, or the avenues to, elevated social status— above all entry into the secure upper reaches of the state bureaucracy.[38] It is

	1958	1959	1960	1961	1962	1963	1964	1965
Education	4.6	18.4	17.3	15.4	14.9	15.6	15.4	15.3
Defence	10.2	19.6	17.8	16.6	16.9	15.6	15.4	15.5
Interior	7.0	16.3	15.1	15.0	13.9	14.3	15.5	16.9

	1966	1967	1968	1969	1970	1971	1972	1973
Education	14.3	13.2	5.8	5.5	5.9	6.2	6.0	6.7
Defence	15.0	13.6	15.3	15.7	17.0	17.9	18.2	18.2
Interior	17.1	15.6	20.7	21.3	20.7	21.5	22.1	23.5

When one remembers that the costs of primary education came out of the Interior Ministry's budgets, the scale of expenditures on secondary and tertiary education (represented by the Education Ministry's budgets) is rather startling.

35. Kaufman, *Bangkhuad*, p. 220, notes that in this community, very close to Bangkok, only 6 per cent of the teenage cohort was attending any form of secondary school in 1954.

36. See, e.g., David K. Wyatt, *The Politics of Reform in Thailand: Education in the Reign of King Chulalongkorn* (New Haven, Conn.: Yale University Press, 1969), chapter 1; and his earlier "The Buddhist Monkhood as an Avenue of Social Mobility in Traditional Thai Society," *Sinlapakorn*, 10 (1966), pp. 41–52.

37. Cf. above, p. 149. Kaufman, *Bangkhuad*, p. 220, comments that by 1971 60 per cent of the community's teenage cohort was enrolled in secondary schools.

38. Ibid., pp. 229–31, has some excellent material on this topic. Hans Dieter-Evers, "The Formation of a Social Class Structure: Urbanization, Bureaucratization, and Social Mobility in Thailand," in Clark D. Neher, *Modern Thai Politics* (Cambridge, Mass.: Schenkman, 1976), pp. 201–5, indicates that this tendency had been in the making from the period of the 1932 coup on. From the sample of higher civil servants he studied, 26 per cent of those who entered government service before 1933 had foreign university degrees, while the figure was 93 per cent for those entering after World War II.

in this light that one must understand the *political* meaning of the proliferation of universities under Sarit and his heirs: as a kind of symbolic
confirmation that the boom was not fortune but progress, and that its blessings would be transmitted to the next generation within the family. It was
possible to *imagine* within the confines of a single household a successful
dry-cleaner father and an embryonic cabinet secretary son.[39] So the university boom served to consolidate the economic boom sociologically and to
confirm it culturally.[40]

Yet, in spite of the rapid expansion in numbers, size, and enrolments of
Thai universities, many aspiring families could not get their children into
them: hence, in part, the no less rapid expansion of technical, vocational,
commercial, and other colleges as second bests. And in the context of all this
stratificatory turmoil, one must understand, I think, a significant shift in the
semantics of the word "student" itself. In an earlier time, "student" had been
almost synonymous with "member of the national elite"—a being on an
almost stratospheric plane above the mass of his countrymen. But by the
late 1960s and early 1970s, social mobility had created conditions where "student" might still have elevated connotations, but could also signify something
like "the neighbour's kid who got into Thammasat when mine didn't." It
became possible to envy and resent students in a way that would have seemed
incongruous a generation earlier.

39. The degree of mobility imagined possible is what needs underlining here, i.e. the change
in public consciousness. Real mobility was, unsurprisingly, less spectacular, as Kraft's sample
survey indicates:

Occupations of Parents of University Students (c. 1968)

Parents' occupation	No. enrolled	% enrolled
Proprietors & self-employed	4,508	53.72
Government officials	2,020	25.12
Employees	657	8.19
Agriculturalists	580	7.31
Others	437	5.31
Unknown	29	.35
Total population of study	8,231	100.00

Source: Richard Kraft, *Education in Thailand: Student Background and University Admission*
(Bangkok: Educational Planning Office, Ministry of Education, 1968), cited in Mudannayke, ed.,
Thailand Yearbook, 1975–76, p. 117. Kraft estimated that the children of government officials
had a 268 times better chance of being admitted to a university (and those of manufacturers and
industrialists a 36 times better chance) than children of farm families.

40. True to the general shift in world power from Europe to the US after World War II, the
acme of the Thai educational pyramid came to be university schooling in California, Indiana,
and New York, rather than London or Paris. Harvey H. Smith *et al.*, *Area Handbook for
Thailand* (Washington, DC: Government Printing Office, 1968), p. 175, for example, state that in
1966 of 4,000 Thai youngsters studying abroad, 1,700 were doing so in the US. (There is good
reason to believe that both figures are unrealistically low.) As late as 1955, the total number of
Thai studying abroad had been only 1,969 (Evers, "Formation," p. 202).

But even for parents who were successful in getting their children into a university, the idea of the "student" came to have ambiguous resonances. The paradox of mobility is that movement upwards is also movement away. Poorly educated fathers, regarding university education in essentially instrumental terms, often found themselves appalled by quite unpredicted changes in the manners, goals, and morals of their student offspring, as these came to be influenced, in universities and teacher-training colleges, by the iconoclastic ideas seeping in from the United States and China.[41] One must imagine the concern and anger of middle-bourgeois or petty-bourgeois parents when their sons began coming home with "messy" long hair, impertinent talk, casual morals, and subversive ideas: how would they ever make successful officials?

About 1971 or 1972, the feeling began to spread that the golden days were fading. The Americans were withdrawing their troops from Indochina, and the long-standing spectre of communist consolidations on Siam's border began to assume a threatening reality. The bureaucracy, ultimate target of many social hopes, had expanded to saturation point, and increasingly university degrees no longer guaranteed what they had been assumed to guarantee—secure and high-status employment.[42] After a long period of price stability, double-digit inflation suddenly struck the Thai economy.[43] A certain uneasiness and dissatisfaction developed among the beneficiaries of the great boom as it seemed to draw to its close. Exclusion from political participation had been tolerable so long as the dictatorship "produced" in the economic, security, and educational sectors, but became much less so as problems accumulated. In addition, neither Thanom nor Praphat had the frightening personal presence of Sarit.[44]

---

41. See, e.g., Thanet Aphornsuwan, "Khwām khlụanwai khong nak sụksā Thai nai yukh rāek (The Thai Student Movement in the Early Period)," in Witthayakorn Chiengkun *et al.*, *Khabuankān nak sụksā Thai adīt thụng patchuban* (The Thai Student Movement from the Past to the Present) (Bangkok: Samnakphim Prachan Siao, 1974), p. 28; and Sawai Thongplai, "Some Adults' Ideas about Some Youngsters," *Prachachart Weekly Digest*, 22 (March 30, 1976), pp. 15–18.

42. Neher, "Stability," p. 1101; Darling, "Student Protest," pp. 8–9.

43. Compare the following figures on the Bangkok consumer price index (1962 = 100): 1964, 102.9; 1965, 103.8; 1966, 107.7; 1967, 112.0; 1968, 114.4; 1969, 116.8; 1970, 117.7; 1971, 120.1; 1972, 124.9; 1973, 139.5; 1974, 172.0; Jan./Aug. 1975, 176.4. Figures adapted from World Bank, "Thailand" (1975), II, Table 9.1 Neher, "Stability," p. 1100, gives an inflation rate of 15 per cent for 1972 and 24 per cent for 1974.

44. It is significant that, when the twin dictators finally held national elections in 1969, the civilian opposition Democrat party, in some ways a mirror of the new bourgeois strata, swept every seat in Bangkok. This sweep should be seen as a portent for middle-class participation in the events of October 14, 1973. On the Democrat sweep, see J.L.S. Girling, "Thailand's New Course," *Pacific Affairs*, 42: 3 (Fall 1969), especially at p. 357.

In this context the snowballing mass demonstrations that brought down Thanom and Praphat in October 1973—the month the world oil crisis began—are of extraordinary interest.[45] There is no doubt that the new bourgeois strata contributed decisively to the huge crowds that came out in support of students' and intellectuals' demands for a constitution and respect for civil liberties. Indeed, it can be argued that these strata ensured the *success* of the demonstrations—had the crowds been composed of slum-dwellers rather than generally well-dressed urbanites, the dictators might have won fuller support for repression.

At the same time, the participation of these bourgeois strata must be understood more as a product of their immediate history than as a portent of their future political role. It is clear, in fact, that they completely lacked political experience and so had no real idea of what the consequences of ending the dictatorship would be. The regime was simultaneously blamed both for failing to exact fuller American commitments to Siam and for excessive subservience to Washington. (The obverse side was an irritable, mystified, anti-American nationalism expressed in the combination of such sentiments as "Why have you let us down in Indochina?" and "Look how you've corrupted our girls!") The open corruption of Praphat, the dynastic marriage of Narong, Thanom's son, to Praphat's daughter, and his nepotistic, meteoric rise to power, all offended bourgeois sensibilities. It was also important that, for their own reasons, the monarch and certain senior generals supported the demonstrators, if only indirectly. Finally, one must remember that the student demands were essentially legalistic (constitutional) and symbolic. No one imagined that something dangerous or undesirable could come out of them. True enough, the students had destroyed a number of police stations in the last days of the demonstrations, but had they not kept traffic flowing smoothly and thereafter cleaned up the mess in the streets in a thoroughly responsible manner? With the corrupt and incompetent dictators gone, prosperity, peace, and progress would be restored under the benevolent supervision of the king with his enlightened entourage of senior justices, respected professors, and capable bankers.

None of these expectations came close to realization. The global oil crisis had broken out almost simultaneously with the October 1973 demonstrations. The disorder that resulted in the world capitalist economy began to make itself felt in Siam by early 1974. In the spring of 1975, the American position in Indochina collapsed with stunning speed. Siam was now no longer

---

45. The important thing to note here is the size of the final demonstrations against the Thanom–Praphat regime. Neher, "Stability," p. 1103, gives a figure of 500,000—a mass demonstration without parallel in earlier Thai history.

the safe pivot of America's Southeast Asian empire, but close to its fragile outer perimeter. It seemed conceivable that henceforth Singapore would play Bangkok's role, while the Thai capital itself would take Vientiane's. As a direct consequence of these events beyond its borders, Siam found its economy lagging badly.[46] The injury seemed compounded by the post-October 1973 liberal governments' public commitment to civil rights and liberties, above all the rights of farmers and workers to organize, demonstrate, and strike. The Sanya Thammasak (October 1973–February 1975) government made real, if timid, efforts to respond directly to worker demands.[47] It is true that, to some extent, especially insecure new enterprises were vulnerable to the squeeze between declining profits and rising wage claims.[48] Under the dictatorship, workers had had to accept miserable pay while the middle classes prospered; now their turn had come. Yet the growing anger of the bourgeois strata as a whole had more complex roots. In the first place, the development of unions in itself threatened to undermine the patron–client "familial" style of employer–employee relations that had largely prevailed hitherto.[49] (It would be a mistake to underestimate the psychic profit that socially aspiring bourgeois elements derive from the opportunity to play quasi-feudal roles vis-à-vis their subordinates.) Second, many of the strikes occurred in sectors such as transportation, where it was particularly easy for bourgeois groups to interpret personal inconvenience as an affront to the public interest. Third, and perhaps most important of all, influential sections of the Thai press, under the control

---

46. Gross Domestic Investment, which had grown at an annual rate of 14.4 per cent in 1960–65, and 13.5 per cent in 1965–70, dropped to 5.1 per cent in 1970–75. The balance of payments situation deteriorated rapidly from 1973 on.

Year	Net balance of payments in US $ millions
1973	−50
1974	−90
1975	−618
1976 (est.)	−745

Source: Annex I of "Report and Recommendation of the President of the International Bank for Reconstruction and Development," Sept. 1, 1976.

47. Strikes and unionizing had been virtually outlawed by Sarit, both to crush left-wing opposition and to encourage foreign investment. Neher, "Stability," p. 1100 notes that "Over 2,000 labor strikes were carried out in 1973, almost all of them *after* [my emphasis] the October 1973 uprising, and some 1,500 strikes were counted in the first six months of 1974. In contrast, during the three-year period between 1969 and 1972 a total of only 100 strikes occurred." The Sanya government raised the 60 c. minimum wage, first to $1.00 and later (October 1974) to $1.25 a day. *Indochina Chronicle*, May–June 1975.

48. The profit margins of some poorly managed Thai concerns certainly depended directly on the extremely cheap labour the dictatorship guaranteed.

49. In 1966, only 5 per cent of 30,672 manufacturing enterprises registered with the government employed more than fifty persons. Smith *et al.*, *Area Handbook*, p. 360.

of large business interests, constantly hammered on the theme that such strikes were antinational, in the sense that they scared away the foreign investors on whom the "national economy" so depended. It was thus only too easy to blame the general economic deterioration on worker irresponsibility.

Finally, in still another sphere the chickens of the dictatorship came home to roost during the liberal era: rapidly growing unemployment among high school, vocational school, and even university graduates.[50] In effect, the educational boom, with its promise of rising status and security, went into a slump. Under the circumstances, it is scarcely surprising that the image of the student as unemployed (unemployable?) layabout at home and restless trouble-making agitator in shop or plant became the prime focus of a whole complex of resentments and frustrations among the new bourgeois strata.[51]

We are to visualize then a very insecure, suddenly created bourgeois strata—Bangkok's immense traffic problems are partly the result of a flood of *first-generation* car owners and drivers[52]—faced by straitened economic circumstances and the menace of worse troubles still to come; not merely worried by the ending of the long boom but haunted by the fear that the boom was part of a single historical parabola, that the golden days of Sarit would never return, and that their ascent from backstreet dust would end where it had begun. Furthermore, we must understand that this bourgeoisie, with little experience in politics and unsophisticated ideas about government, but precisely *therefore* a strong consciousness of "not being to blame for the mess," was peculiarly liable to evince paranoiac responses to their

---

50. "Strangely enough, vocational school graduates have a difficult time finding jobs. In the rural areas, only 25 percent are able to find jobs and in the greater Bangkok area the situation is not much better, with only about 50 percent able to find employment." Mudannayake, ed., *Thailand Yearbook, 1975–76*, p. 110.

51. Highly significant is the fact that in the 1973–76 period perhaps the most militant of all labour unions was the Hostel and Hotel Workers' Union, led by the well-known activist Therdphum Chaidee. (By 1976, there were at least fifty first-class hotels alone in Siam, employing more than 30,000 workers. *Bangkok Post*, May 22, 1975.) No one sees more bitterly than a badly paid waiter or chambermaid how luxuriously some of their fellow countrymen really live. It is revealing that the main targets of union militancy were not foreign-owned or Chinese hotels (which were usually quite willing to recognize the union and deal with it in a reasonable way), but those owned by Thai (old and new rich), who insisted on treating their employees in patronal style. The most violent strike of 1975 erupted at the downtown luxury Dusit Thani hotel, when the Thai management hired Red Gaur gunmen as strike-breakers. See the account given in the *Bangkok Post*, May 30, 1975, which also quotes Prime Minister Kukrit Pramote's strong criticism of what he called a "private army."

52. Chaktip Nitibhon, "Urban Development and Industrial Estates in Thailand," in Prateep Sondysuvan, ed., *Financial, Trade and Economic Development in Thailand* (Bangkok: Sompong Press, 1975), p. 249, notes that between 1967 and 1971 the number of vehicles registered in Bangkok rose by 15 per cent (road surfaces increased by 1 per cent). In 1973, with over 320,000 vehicles registered, Siam's capital contained more than half of the national total.

predicament. (Depending on the circumstances, one could imagine this para-noia being vented on corruption, students, communists, foreigners, or Chinese.) In the event, in 1975–76, for reasons to be discussed below, the rad-icalized students—bourgeois successes who seemed to spit on that success—came to be the main target of this panicked anger. Such, I think, is the explanation of why many of the same people who sincerely supported the mass demonstrations of October 1973 welcomed the return to dictatorship three years later.

Yet they were not the immediate perpetrators of the brutalities on October 6. It remains therefore to attempt to identify the culprits and to situate them within the broad sociological framework sketched out so far. Undoubtedly the most notorious men of violence, not only on October 6, 1976, but during the preceding two years, were the Krathing Daeng (Red Gaurs). These hooligans have been given (I think somewhat mistakenly) a quasi-sociological respectabil-ity by journalists and academics who have identified them simply as vocational-school students. Since vocational more than university students bore the brunt of the police repression of October 1973, so the argument goes, it is plausible to interpret Red Gaur attacks on university students as express-ing the honest resentment of long-suffering low-status vocational students against high-status, arrogant, and cowardly "college kids."[53] The Red Gaur–vocational student identification was probably strengthened in many people's minds by a series of spectacularly violent (but mainly apolitical) clashes between adolescents from rival vocational schools in late 1974 and 1975.[54]

---

53. See, e.g., Somporn Sangchai, "Thailand: Rising of the Rightist Phoenix [*sic*]," in *Southeast Asian Affairs 1976* (Singapore: Institute of Southeast Asian Studies, 1976), pp. 361–2.

54. "Police said about 300 students from Uthane Thawai Construction School, armed with bombs, clubs, guns and other weapons, marched [yesterday] to Pathumwan Engineering School in front of the National Stadium where they engaged in a point blank-range fight with 300 Pathumwan students." (*The Nation*, June 17, 1975.) Some earlier and subsequent confrontations include the following: (1) On October 29, 1974, a small boy was killed and fourteen people injured by a bomb thrown during a clash between students from the Dusit Construction, Nonthaburi Engineering and Bangsorn Engineering schools. (*Bangkok Post*, Dec. 9. 1975.) (2) On December 26, one student was killed and several injured in a fight conducted with bombs and rifles between boys from the Bangsorn Engineering and Northern Bangkok Engineering schools. (*The Nation*, Dec. 27, 1974.) (3) Three students suffered severe knife and gunshot wounds after a brawl between gangs from the Dusit Construction and Archivasilpa schools on December 27, 1974. (*Bangkok Post*, Dec. 28, 1974.) A further bottle-bomb, rifle, and grenade battle between Bangsorn and Northern Bangkok, on January 22, 1975, led to the death of a *Bangkok Post* cam-eraman. (*Bangkok Post*, Jan. 23 and 24, 1975.) (4) On June 12, two students died in a series of bottle- and plastic-bomb mêlées between boys from the Rama VI Engineering, Bangsorn Engineering, Uthane Thawai Construction, Nonthaburi Engineering, Pathumwan Engineering, and other vocational schools. (*The Nation*, June 13, 1975.) (5) On June 18, after a quarrel between Archivasilpa students and bus and construction workers, the students fire-bombed some buses, causing serious injuries. (*The Nation*, June 19, 1975.) Of these schools, only Rama VI had a somewhat political (left-wing) reputation.

Since these boys used guns and bombs against each other, and these were the favoured weapons of the Red Gaurs, it was easy to jump to the conclusion that the latter politically represented the former.

A more complex picture of the Red Gaurs is suggested by the following passage from an article in the conservative *Bangkok Post*:

> Another interesting man is Doui, who is appointed as the leader of a mobile unit [of the Red Gaurs], a force which could shift rapidly from place to place. Long-haired in hippy style and with a big scar on his face, Doui said he had 50 men under his control. Most of these are mercenaries, he said, who live in Loei Province as a security unit for road construction in the area.
>
> I was a former soldier, but later I became a mercenary. I liked the uniform, but I disliked there being too many disciplines and regulations in the army. I like the freedom to follow my own style, wearing long hair or whatever dress I wish.[55]

Well-informed sources in Bangkok confirm that many of the key Red Gaur cadres were ex-mercenaries and men discharged from the army for disciplinary infractions, while their followings were mainly composed of unemployed vocational-school graduates, high-school dropouts, unemployed street-corner boys, slum toughs, and so forth.[56] Hired by various cliques within the ISOC (Internal Security Operations Command) and other agencies specializing in police and intelligence work,[57] the Red Gaurs were not recruited primarily on the basis of ideological commitment, but rather by promises of high pay, abundant free liquor and brothel privileges, and the lure of public notoriety. It is striking how these rewards mirror the privileges anticipated for successful students on their entry into government service (money, prestige, expenses-paid visits to nightclubs and massage parlours)—anticipated at least

---

55. *Bangkok Post*, June 1, 1975. Emphasis added.

56. Personal communications. Compare note 50 above for unemployment rates among vocational school graduates.

57. Two of the better-known leaders of the Red Gaur clusters are directly connected to ISOC. They are Praphan Wongkham, identified as "a 27-year-old employee of the Internal Security Operations Command;" and Suebsai Hatsadin, son of Special Colonel Sudsai Hatsadin, formerly in charge of ISOC's Hill Tribes Division. *Bangkok Post*, June 1, 1975; and Norman Peagam, "Rumblings from the Right," *Far Eastern Economic Review*, July 25, 1975. It is known that other Red Gaur groups were controlled by General Withoon Yasawat, former leader of the CIA-hired Thai mercenary forces in Laos, and General Chatchai Choonhawan, brother-in-law of the late Police General Phao, top figure in the Chat Thai party, and Foreign Minister in the Kukrit Pramote government (March 1975–April 1976). It should be noted that ISOC had also heavily infiltrated the section of the Education Ministry in charge of vocational education, and was the clandestine paymaster and manipulator of the NVSCT (National Vocational Student Center of Thailand), a small, aggressively right-wing antagonist of the large NSCT (National Student Center of Thailand), vanguard of left-wing student activism during the liberal era.

in the aspiring petty-bourgeois milieux from which the Red Gaurs emerged.[58] In other words, there is a sociological underpinning to the political role played by these hooligans. Children of a new and vulnerable petty bourgeoisie, caught in a time of widespread unemployment,[59] unsuccessful in obtaining jobs in government offices and scornful of jobs in factories, they were easy targets for anti-(unsuccessful) student and anti-worker propaganda.

A second group, no less involved in the right-wing violence of 1974–76,[60] but with a somewhat more respectable public image, was the Village Scouts. Founded in 1971 under the joint aegis of the Border Patrol Police (BPP) and the Ministry of the Interior, it was evidently then conceived as a paramilitary, anticommunist rural security organization.[61] In the liberal period, however, it developed a significant urban component, and played an important mobilizing role for various right-wing forces. If, prior to October 1973, it had been the arena for discreet competition between Praphat, military strongman and Minister of the Interior, and the royal family, very influential in the BPP, the Village Scouts became, after the fall of the dictators, ever more openly a means for building up an activist constituency for royalist politics. Even under the dictatorship, the palace had worked hard to bind to itself the beneficiaries of the boom by a variety of public-relations techniques.[62] This experience proved very useful when the Scouts expanded after October 1973.

---

58. While the bulk of the Red Gaurs were probably petty bourgeois in origin (working-class Thai were much less likely to get their children as far as high school or vocational school), it is possible, even likely, that some were recruited from the migrant unemployed population alluded to on p. 148 above.

59. Prime Minister Thanin Kraiwichian, in a radio broadcast on October 17, 1976, observed that: "Another group of people facing poverty are the seasonal workers, laborers, *new graduates* and other unemployed people. The unemployed now number over 1 million." FBIS (Foreign Broadcast Information Service) Daily Report, October 18, 1976. Emphasis added.

60. They played an important role in intimidating liberal and left-wing elements during the 1976 election campaign; in expelling student activists trying to organize peasant and tenants' unions in the villages; in demanding the resignation of the Seni Pramote government's three "progressive" ministers (Surin Masdit, Chuen Leekphai, and Damrong Latthaphiphat) on the eve of the October 6, 1976, coup; and in the violence of October 6 itself. See, e.g., Sarika Krirkchai, "Do Not Corrupt the Village Scouts," in *Prachachart Weekly Digest*, 23 (April 6, 1976), pp. 14–15.

61. Much of the information on the Village Scouts contained in the following sentences is drawn from the illuminating, detailed article by Natee Pisalchai, "Village Scouts," in *Thai Information Resource* (Australia), no. 1 (May 1977), pp. 34–7.

62. Thak, "The Sarit Regime," pp. 414–25, offers instructive material on three such techniques. First, the king stepped up both the absolute number of weddings at which he officiated and the relative number involving bourgeois, as opposed to royal, aristocratic, or military partners. Second, by the deft distribution of official decorations the monarch was able to levy very large sums of money from the new bourgeois strata in the form of donations for charitable (and, after 1966, anticommunist) organizations and campaigns. (However, contributions were also elicited even from poor pedicab drivers, essentially for "populist" image-making purposes.) Third, the ruler increased his personal contacts with circles outside officialdom to a very pronounced degree.

Scout leadership was drawn heavily from the well-to-do and the middle-aged, provincial officials, rural notables, and urban nouveaux riches.[63] Such people were not only ideologically amenable to assuming such roles, but had the private economic resources to enable the organization to develop rapidly and, to a considerable degree, independently of the state bureaucracy.[64] "Training programmes," co-ordinated by BPP headquarters, were essentially political in character: lectures by right-wing monks, parades, oath-swearings, salutes, beauty and dance contests, visits to military installations, royal donation ceremonies, and "sing-songs."[65] From a right-wing perspective, the beauty of the Village Scouts was that the organization worked by the following reciprocal motion: for the palace, it provided continuous public evidence of militant political support, outside the Bangkok upper class, among the "establishments" of provincial capitals, small towns, and even some villages. (The word "Village" in its title gave a reassuring, if deceptive, picture of rustic communities organizationally engaged—as it were, a concrete manifestation of the natural ties between Nation and King.) For the Scouts' leaders, on the other hand, royal patronage made it easy to legitimize private, localized repression of protesting peasants and student activists as essential for the preservation of Nation–Religion–King.

Beyond the Red Gaurs and the Village Scouts, there were other agents of

| | Frequency of the king's contacts with non-official groups | | | |
Year	Private sector function	Citizen group audience	Meeting with students	Meeting with subjects
1956	17	1	–	–
1961	35	45	3	–
1966	71	116	9	5
1971	121	191	10	31

Table adapted from "The Sarit Regime," p. 422. As Thak rightly observed, all this activity "clearly indicates that the throne was developing links with the rising (private) middle-class sector."

63. Natee notes that of his 496 fellow applicants for admission to the Scouts branch in Nakhon Pathom in September 1976, 70 per cent were between the ages of 35 and 42, 2–5 per cent were young people, and most of the rest in their sixties and seventies. He adds that "most of the people who joined the program were reasonably well-off." See "Village Scouts," pp. 34–5. Indeed, this would have had to have been so, for the trainees were required to buy expensive badges and coloured group photographs; contribute 40–50 *baht* daily for food; make religious donations; and pay for the elaborate costumes used for the beauty and dance competitions. (Ibid., p. 36.)

64. While the provincial governor was usually the local chairman of the Scouts, financing was deliberately left up to prestige- and status-conscious local notables. (Ibid., pp. 34–5.)

65. For a good description, see ibid, pp. 34 and 37. Natee's group was taken to visit the Naresuan paratroop training camp near the royal resort town of Hua Hin. (These paratroops worked closely with the Village Scouts in the violence of October 6.) Some idea of the style of instruction given to the trainees may be gleaned from the songs they were required to learn. These included: "Wake up, Thai!," "Ode to the Queen Mother," "Ode to the King," "They Are Like Our Father and Mother," "Punctuality," and "Any Work!" Themes of plays put on included scenes of communists being tormented in hell.

right-wing violence, less well organized and directed, but no less products of the great boom and its anxious aftermath. Typically, these men came from marginal and/or recently developed sectors of the security bureaucracy: up-country policemen and counter-insurgency personnel who saw budgets, staff, and promotion chances decline as a result of world depression and US strategic withdrawal; officials assigned to the career dead-end of service in the south (whether for lack of good connections or for poor performance elsewhere); and superannuated guards at US bases.[66] Such people found the experience of the liberal years frustrating and alarming on almost every front. Accustomed to exacting cowed deference, to exercising often arbitrary local authority, above all to enjoying virtual immunity to law and criticism,[67] they were deeply enraged by the irreverent and muckraking journalism permitted after October 1973. As salaried men, they were hurt by the inflation, and by a certain decline in opportunities for moonlighting and extortion. Given the chance to enter government service by the great bureaucratic expansion of the 1960s, they now had to face the same prospect as non-official segments of the new middle and petty bourgeoisie: stagnation, if not decline. Small wonder that out of frustration and resentment came nostalgia for the heyday of the dictatorship and fury at its insolent opponents.

IDEOLOGICAL UPHEAVAL

One way of getting a sense of the dimensions of the cultural crisis that developed out of the economic and social changes sketched above is to begin with one striking contrast between Siam and its regional neighbours. Thanks in part to their colonized pasts, most Southeast Asian countries have inherited a political vocabulary and rhetoric which is essentially radical-populist, if not left-wing, in character. It is very hard to find anywhere, except perhaps in the Philippines, a calm, self-confident conservative ideology: indeed, since the nineteenth century, conservative culture has been in epistemological shock and on the political defensive, its nationalist credentials deeply suspect. In

---

66. In June 1975, a rather spectacular strike of 2,000 "security guards" at various US bases took place. The guards not only demanded government guarantees for their future livelihood, but accused the Supreme Command of embezzling over 8,000,000,000 *baht* (= $400,000,000) of their US-supplied severance pay—charges that Supreme Command Chief of Staff General Kriangsak Chomanan hastily denied. *The Nation*, June 19 and 21, 1975. The NSCT strongly supported the guards' demands, and, curiously enough, developed close working relations with some of them.

67. One must imagine the shock experienced in such circles when, on January 22, 1975, the official residence of the governor of Nakhǫn Si Thammarat, Khlai Chitphithak, was burned to the ground by an angry crowd of about 3,000 people. The governor, widely suspected of corruption and incompetence in the handling of relief supplies for the victims of recent severe flooding, had to flee secretly to Bangkok. *Bangkok Post*, Jan. 23 and 24, 1975.

Siam, mainly because the country escaped direct colonial control, the situation has been, until recently, almost exactly the reverse.[68] The heroes in Thai children's schoolbooks have not been journalists, union leaders, teachers, and politicians who spent years in colonial jails, but above all the "great kings" of the ruling house. In fact, until 1973, it would be hard to imagine a single Thai children's hero who had ever been inside a prison. The prevailing rhetoric had typically been conservative, conformist, and royalist. It was the Left that was always on the defensive, anxious to defend its nationalist credentials against charges of being "Chinese," "Vietnamese," "un-Thai," and "antimonarchy" (this last a clear sign of a successful identification of royal and nationalist symbols). It would even be fair to say that until the repressions of October 6, the taboo on criticism of monarchy as an institution or the monarch as a person was accepted even by those firmly on the Left.[69]

To be sure, the capable monarchs of the nineteenth century, above all Rama IV and Rama V, did, in some sense, "save" Siam from conquest and colonization by adroit concessions to, and manoeuvres between, the European imperialist powers. But one must not forget the other side of this coin: that the "saving" of Siam made these rulers simultaneously the most powerful and the most dependent sovereigns in Thai history. For if, in the course of the nineteenth century, the Europeans threatened Siam, they also completely eliminated the menace of her traditional foes—the Burmese, Khmers, Vietnamese, and Malays. Thai armies did not fight a serious engagement with *anyone* for almost one hundred years (roughly 1840–1940).[70] The old enemies were too weak, the new ones too strong. This externally generated and maintained security enabled the rulers to concentrate, in a quite unprecedented way, on the consolidation of their domestic power. To a very considerable degree, however, even this consolidation was only made possible by royal reliance on European advisers, technology, capital, and weaponry.[71]

---

68. I say this in spite of the material assembled in Flood's fine "Thai Left Wing." Flood ably shows the real element of continuity on the Thai Left, but also, possibly inadvertently, how oppressed and marginal it was until quite recently.

69. This applies no less to the Communist Party of Thailand in the maquis than to left-wing elements attempting to participate in parliamentary-style politics. It is true that in the 1930s the monarchy went through a difficult time, to the point that Rama VII went into self-imposed exile in England. But there seems to have been no real question of getting rid of the monarchy as such, merely of bringing it into conformity with internationally-respectable standards of constitutionality.

70. It was only in 1894 that a modern-style Ministry of Defence was set up.

71. The *facts* of this reliance are a commonplace of modern Siamese historiography. They are traditionally *interpreted*, however, in good *bien-pensant* fashion, as signs of the "modernity" and "progressiveness" of the rulers. For a very instructive picture of how Siam's northeast (Isan) was subjugated by Bangkok in the reigns of Rama V, VI, and VII, see Keyes, *Isan*, chapter III ("The Consolidation of Thai [sic] Control"). He stresses the importance of external peace, extension of rail, road, telegraph, and telephone systems, and "modern" state-controlled education.

In a pattern prophetic of the "absolutism" of Sarit, the dynasty was able to exploit externally created security and externally generated resources to maximize internal control. The Thai "absolute monarchy" came closest to realization precisely when Siam was most completely at the mercy of the Europeans.[72]

In 1932, the immensely expanded "western-style" civil and military bureaucracy, earlier instrument of royal aggrandizement, turned on its master. The leaders of the 1932 coup decisively put an end to the monarchy's direct, practical political power without, however, attempting any serious or permanent undermining of its cultural centrality and "nationalist" prestige. "Thailand," as Phibunsongkhram would eventually name Siam, remained defined as a (constitutional) *monarchy*. When Rama VII, deeply involved in the political crises of the late 1920s and early 1930s, abdicated in 1935, the coup leaders immediately offered the throne to a grandson of the legendary national saviour Rama V (Chulalongkorn)—then, fortunately, still a minor.[73] The fact that this lad remained at school in Switzerland throughout World War II merely preserved the monarchy from any contamination from Phibunsongkhram's collaboration with Japanese militarism.

Yet there is a sense in which the Phibunsongkhram era of the late 1930s and early 1940s did mark a real cultural-ideological change in Siam. For the dictator worked hard to legitimize his power by nationalistic propagandizing. To a considerable degree he was able to make the bureaucracy, and above all its military sector, where his effective power lay, appear the public custodian of the nation's interests. Much more clearly than hitherto, nation and monarchy became intellectually separable ideas, with the *state* (essentially the armed forces) as representative of the one and guardian of the other.[74] In important ways this development helped to enshrine the monarchy as a sort of precious palladium of the nation.[75]

---

72. The effect of European imperialism on the Thai monarchy was important in two other ways. First, it changed the effective principle of succession from political capacity and seniority to quasi-primogeniture. It is unlikely that Rama VI or VII would have come to the throne under pre-imperialist conditions, as they lacked much real politico-military competence. Second, it put an end to the possibility of a new dynasty. Realization of this must have begun about the turn of the century. Able, ruthless figures like Phibun and Sarit, in many ways very similar types to Rama I, could no longer start new royal lines. In Phibun's expansionist and irredentist policies of the late 1930s and early 1940s, however, one can see clear dynastic lineaments. He was, as it were, restoring Greater Siam (bits of Burma, Cambodia, Laos, and Malaya), as kings Taksin and Rama I had done before him.

73. See Wilson, *Politics in Thailand*, p. 18.

74. There are curious parallels here—which may not entirely have escaped Phibunsongkhram's attention—to the shogun's relationship to the emperor in Tokugawa Japan.

75. Among the important prizes at stake in the power struggles of traditional Laos and Siam were certain highly venerated, magically charged objects (Buddha images in particular),

In spite of all this, Phibunsongkhram's deep involvement in the 1932 coup and the suppression of Prince Bǫwǫradet's royalist counter-coup of 1934, earned him the lasting hostility of the royal family. During his second tenure of office (1948–57), therefore, he was unable to exploit the symbolic resources of the monarchy as he might by then have wished.[76] Perhaps *faute de mieux*, he turned to the symbols of democracy for help when, by 1956, he felt his power ebbing away.[77]

It was Marshal Sarit who brought out the full "shogunal" potential of Phibunsongkhram's early militarism, and thereby significantly changed the whole ideological atmosphere of Thai politics. Sarit was a home-grown product of the Royal Military Academy; he was too young to have played any important role in the 1932 coup and its aftermath; and, unlike Phibun, he had never even pretended to an interest in constitutionalist or democratic conceptions. There was thus no serious obstacle to a rapid rapprochement with the palace. Shortly after seizing power, Sarit began a systematic campaign to "restore" the monarchy, and, in giving it new lustre, to fortify his own position. In Phibun's time the king and queen had scarcely ventured outside the national capital. Now they were sent on long world tours to hobnob with other heads of state, especially European monarchs; reciprocal visits by assorted European royalty were encouraged—and so forth.[78] Royal

---

referred to by many western historians of Siam as palladia. After 1932, one detects a developing interest in control of the monarch-as-sacred-object. The tendency was probably facilitated by the domestic circumstances of the royal family. In the late 1930s and early 1940s Rama VIII was a minor, and mostly at school overseas. (In effect, there was then almost no *bodily* royal presence in Siam.) Shortly after World War II he returned home, but almost immediately died of a gunshot wound under circumstances that are still mysterious. He was succeeded by his younger brother, the present king, who was then still a minor and thus incapable of playing an independent political role.

Palladium-ization achieved a certain spectacular climax in 1971, when Marshal Thanom appeared on television after organizing a coup against his own government, and solemnly opened before the viewers a purported letter of approval from the palladium, brought in on a gold tray.

76. He did, however, make efforts to clothe himself with Buddhist legitimacy, especially at nervous moments. In 1956, for example, when his regime was nearing its end, he had 1,239 temples restored at government expense. (In 1955 the number had been only 413, and a puny 164 in 1954.) See Thak, "The Sarit Regime," p. 128. He also spent a great deal of money on the 25th Centennial of the Buddhist Era celebrations (1957), and attempted to keep the monarchy from sharing in the resulting glory. In return, the palace pointedly disassociated itself from the proceedings. Ibid., pp. 129–30.

77. For a description of Phibunsongkhram's "restoration of democracy," which culminated in the rigged elections of 1957, see Wilson, *Politics in Thailand*, pp. 29–31. It is one of the oddest ironies of modern Thai political history that the famous Democracy Monument in downtown Bangkok, the central visual symbol of the October 14, 1973 demonstrations and student activism thereafter, was constructed by Siam's most durable dictator.

78. This side of Sarit's manipulation of traditional symbols is analysed in Thak, "The Sarit Regime," pp. 397–402. In late 1959 and early 1960, the king and queen left the country for the first

ceremonies not performed since the days of the absolute monarchy were now revived.[79] The king and queen not only were brought into much more frequent contact with the Thai population, but also were sent out to help "integrate" the tribal minorities by kindly donations. One could almost say that under Sarit a strange displacement of traditional roles occurred: the field marshal playing the part of the ruler (punisher of crimes,[80] collector of taxes, deployer of armies, and political power-boss in general), and the ruler that of the Buddhist hierarchy (consecrator of authority and epitome of disinterested virtue). We need not be surprised, therefore, that in some ways the monarchy became more "sacred" as the dictatorship entrenched itself.

Not content with utilizing the monarchy, Sarit also exploited Buddhism. In 1962, he eliminated the existing decentralized, rather democratic Sangha organization and replaced it with a despotic centralized system under the control of the Supreme Patriarchate, an office he filled with pliable characters.[81] At his instigation, two popular, liberally minded senior monks were stripped of their ecclesiastical ranks and prosecuted on fabricated charges (in the one case of communist sympathies, in the other, of sodomy).[82] Finally, important

---

time to visit Saigon, Jakarta, and Rangoon. Between June 1960 and January 1961, they visited the US, England, West Germany, Portugal, Spain, Switzerland, Denmark, Norway, Sweden, Italy, Belgium, France, Luxembourg, and the Netherlands (note that half of these countries are monarchies of sorts). Before Sarit's death at the end of 1963, further visits had taken place to Malaysia, Pakistan, Australia, New Zealand, Japan, and the Philippines. International "recognition" of the Thai monarchy followed with visits by royalty from Malaysia and the United Kingdom.

79. Ibid, pp. 410–25, for excellent details. Thak also notes the organized and direct participation of the royal family in anticommunist and counter-insurgency propaganda campaigns.

80. Sarit's willingness to take personal responsibility for executions and other regime violence accords well with the style of pre-nineteenth century Thai monarchs.

81. See Mahāmakuta Educational Council, ed., *Acts on the Administration of the Buddhist Order of Sangha* (Bangkok: The Buddhist University, 1963) for full texts of the 1962 regulations and the regime (dating back to 1941) they replaced. The 1941 system was tripartite, with authority divided between legislative, executive, and judicial branches. The 1962 system created a single administrative–judicial hierarchy. As Yoneo Ishii rightly says, the new rules completely eliminated "the idea of democracy which had been the spirit of the previous law." (See his "Church and State in Thailand," *Asian Survey*, 8: 10 [Oct. 1968], p. 869.) They also permitted, I believe for the first time, the arrest of monks by the lay authorities (police) without consultation with the Sangha authorities.

82. On this case, see Somporn, "Rightist Phoenix," p. 384; and S.J. Tambiah, *World Conqueror and World Renouncer* (Cambridge: Cambridge University Press, 1976), pp. 257–60. Though the two men, Phra Phimonladham and Phra Sasanasophon, were completely exonerated by the courts, the Sangha hierarchs were too timid, venal, or jealous to restore them to their former positions. After October 1973, a quiet campaign for their rehabilitation was begun, initially to little effect. Then on January 12, 1975, in an action unprecedented in modern Thai history, a number of young monks began a hunger strike at Wat Mahāthat in Bangkok, refusing to take food till the Supreme Patriarch agreed to reopen the case (*The Nation*, Jan. 13. 1975). The strike caused a sensation, and, on January 17, the Supreme Patriarch surrendered, promising rehabilitation within the month. (*Bangkok Post*, Jan. 18, 1975.) On January 30, a specially appointed Sangha committee finally cleared the two men. (*Bangkok Post*, Feb. 23, 1976.)

segments of the Sangha were mobilized for "integrationist" (vis-à-vis non-Buddhist hill tribes) and counter-insurgency programmes, particularly in the disturbed north and northeast.[83] More than ever before, Buddhist symbols and institutions were cynically manipulated to generate regime legitimacy.[84] It was in the Sarit era that the triolet Nation–Religion–King was transformed from placid motto to fighting political slogan, and was increasingly understood as such.[85]

It would be a mistake to suppose from the above, however, that the prestige of the monarchy and the Sangha was affected by the dictatorship and the great boom in the same way. As we have seen, there is good reason to believe that the monarchy, for one, improved its position. The "royal revival" had coincided with the start of the boom, and for many newly prosperous Thai the coincidence hardly seemed fortuitous. In a reciprocal motion, development confirmed the legitimacy of the throne, and the throne gave moral lustre to development. On the other hand, it seems clear that the powerful secularizing influence of capitalism was simultaneously eroding the authority of Buddhism, particularly in aristocratic and upper-bourgeois circles. Boys from these strata were less and less inclined to enter the monkhood even for a nominal period, let alone commit themselves to a lifetime of religious devotion. Even more than hitherto, the committed younger monks tended to come from lower-class and rural backgrounds. The consequence, predictably enough, was sharpening politico-religious conflict within the Sangha itself.[86] Growing numbers of young monks, especially those from the impoverished

---

The Supreme Patriarch who connived with Sarit in the original frameup, Somdet Phra Ariyawongsakhatayan, died a gruesome death in a traffic accident on December 18, 1971. Many Thai regarded his end as karmic retribution for abuse of power.

83. See Charles F. Keyes, "Buddhism and National Integration in Thailand," *Journal of Asian Studies*, 30: 3 (May 1971), pp. 551–67, especially pp. 559–65; also Ishii, "Church and State," pp. 864–71.

84. When the Buddhism-promoting Sarit died, it came out that he had accumulated a $140 million fortune by corrupt practices and maintained perhaps as many as 80 mistresses. See Thak, "The Sarit Regime," pp. 427–30, who also cites much of the contemporary Thai literature on the scandal.

85. This is naively illustrated by the section "Education and Society," in Smith *et al.*, *Area Handbook*, pp. 175–7.

86. See Chatcharintr Chaiyawat's article, "Protests divide the monkhood," in the *Bangkok Post*, Feb. 23, 1975, for some useful material on this. Cf. Kaufman, *Bangkhuad*, pp. 224–6, for comparable data in a local community setting. Sarcastic comment on misconduct by high-ranking monks began to be heard publicly around 1971. See, e.g., Phra Maha Sathienpong Punnawanno, "Phra Song Thai nai Rǫb 25 Pï" (The Thai Sangha Over 25 Years), in *Sangkhomsat Parithat* (Social Science Review), 9: 6 (Dec. 1971), p. 28. For this citation I am indebted to an unpublished paper, "The Buddhist Monkhood in Thai Politics" by Mr. Somboon Suksamran. During the series of protests and demonstrations that led to the overthrow of Thanom and Praphat, monks were increasingly in attendance as sympathetic observers.

northeast, moved towards social activism[87] and a left-wing interpretation of religious doctrine.[88] Others, such as the notorious Kitti Wuttho, openly linked Buddhism to an ultra-rightist ideology.[89] In all these ways, then, the Sangha was brought directly into the midst of the political fray.

So far we have considered only the transformation of elements in the hegemonic cultural tradition. But, as Flood has helped to show, change was also occurring among the tradition's opponents. Students and intellectuals in particular were profoundly affected by the Vietnam War. The courage and stamina with which the Vietnamese resisted the American juggernaut aroused increasing admiration. Many bright students who had gone to study in Europe and the United States in the latter 1960s were influenced by, and participated in, the antiwar movement. In China, the Cultural Revolution was in full spate, and internationally the prestige of Mao Tse-tung's anti-bureaucratic ideas was at its zenith. In Siam itself, the huge American presence was generating serious social problems—rampant prostitution,

---

87. On November 19, 1974, a group of 100 monks, with arms linked, actually formed the front line for a massive demonstration by peasants who had come to Bangkok eleven days earlier to press demands for land reform. Somboon Suksamran, "The Buddhist Monkhood," p. 6. Predictably, this move aroused a rabid reaction in the "moderate" and right-wing press, which straightfacedly insisted that the Sangha had always been above politics and should remain so. On December 8, the "radical" monk Phra Maha Jad Khongsuk announced the formation of a Federation of Thai Buddhists to promote democratization of the Sangha and orientation of Buddhist education towards social service. *Prachathipatai*, Dec. 9, 1974; see also *Bangkok Post*, Dec. 10–12, 1974. The hunger strike referred to in n. 82 above, which occurred in January 1975, was organized by a group called Yuwasong (Young Monks), which had learned a good deal about political organization from the NSCT since 1974.

88. See, e.g., Phra Maha Jad Khongsuk's speech to the Seminar on "Is Thailand a Genuinely Buddhist Country?," published in *Phā Tat Phutsasanā* (Operating on Buddhism) (Bangkok: Pharbsuwan Press, 1974), pp. 48–9, cited in Somboon Suksamran, "The Buddhist Monkhood," p. 22.

89. The best account of Kitti Wuttho's career and political ideas is in Charles F. Keyes, "Political Crisis and Militant Buddhism in Contemporary Thailand," in Bordwell Smith, ed., *Religion and Legitimation of Power in Thailand, Burma, and Laos* (Chambersburg, Pa.: Wilson, 1977). This essay includes a fine analysis of Kitti Wuttho's famous 1976 speech, "Killing Communists Is Not Demeritorious." Keyes quotes the speech as follows: "[Killing communists is not killing persons] because whoever destroys the nation, the religion, or the monarchy, such bestial types are not complete persons. Thus, we must intend not to kill people but to kill the Devil (Māra); this is the duty of all Thai . . . It is just like when we kill a fish to make a stew to place in the alms bowl for a monk. There is certainly demerit in killing the fish, but we place it in the alms bowl of a monk and gain much greater merit." Keyes's translation is of Kitti Wuttho's *Khā Khōmmūnit mai bāp* (Bangkok: Abhidhamma Foundation of Wat Mahādhātu, 1976). In spite of the vociferous protests of the liberal press, the NSCT, and others at the "anti-Buddhist" nature of this speech and Kitti Wuttho's membership in the secretive ultra-right-wing organization Nawaphon (for which, see below at n. 94), the Sangha hierarchy refused to administer even a mild reprimand, though earlier they had arranged to have Jad Khongsuk and others (temporarily) expelled from their monasteries for "political activities unbecoming a monk."

fatherless mixed-blood babies, drug addiction, pollution, and sleazy commercialization of many aspects of Thai life. By the early 1970s an increasingly
strong anti-American (and anti-Japanese) nationalism was making itself felt,
symbolized by the bitter title of an influential book published in 1971: *White
Peril*.[90] In 1972, students successfully organized a boycott of Japanese commodities in Bangkok.[91]

Yet the censorship that the dictatorship imposed (to be sure, weaker under
Thanom than under Sarit) concealed from almost everyone the real extent of
the intellectual ferment going on. After October 14, 1973, censorship disappeared overnight, and, to general astonishment, a steadily swelling torrent of
critical poetry, songs, plays, essays, novels, and books flooded first the capital and later the provinces. Many of these works had been written or
composed under the dictatorship but had never seen the light of day.[92] Others
were produced by the radicalizing effects of the October days themselves,
and the rapid increase in political consciousness among students in the free
atmosphere of the liberal era.

The cultural and ideological consequences of October 1973 took two dia-
metrically opposite forms. On the Left, an almost giddy sense of exhilaration,
iconoclasm, and creativity was born. For a time it seemed that one could say,
sing, or do almost anything. On the Right, the illusion rapidly took root that
the newly established liberal regime was the *cause* of the sudden epidemic of
subversive ideas. Democracy was quickly blamed for the consequences of the
dictatorship and its complicity with American and Japanese capitalism.

Predictably, the issue came to be joined on the ideological tools self-
consciously forged to buttress Sarit's autocracy: Nation–Religion–King. Of
these, religion was the least important and did not at first generate much heat.
But on the national issue, the Left quickly went onto the offensive, making its
case more or less along the following lines: just as Phibunsongkhram had collaborated with the Japanese, so Sarit and his heirs had betrayed the country
to the Americans. Never before in Thai history had almost 50,000 foreign
troops been stationed on Thai soil. The economy had been allowed to fall
overwhelmingly into foreign hands. For all the talk of national identity, the

---

90. See Thanet, "Khwām khlụanwai," p. 30.

91. See Neher, "Stability," p. 1101.

92. Of crucial importance were the varied works of the brilliant Marxist historian, poet, linguist, essayist, and social critic Jit Phumisak, killed by agents of the dictatorship at the early age
of thirty-six. Most of his works had either been suppressed shortly after publication or existed
only in manuscript form prior to 1974. Indeed even the mention of Jit's name was publicly
taboo under the Thanom–Praphat regime. In 1974–75, however, his *Chomnā Sakdinā Thai nai
Patchuban* (The Face of Thai Feudalism Today) had gone through three editions and become the
bible of a whole generation of radicalized youth.

dictators had complacently permitted the corruption of Thai society and culture. So slavishly had the old regime aped the Americans' anticommunism and paranoia about Chinese expansionism that it was left ludicrously paralysed by the Machiavellian Nixon–Kissinger approach to Peking. All in all, the policies of the Right had proven not only venal and opportunistic, but shortsighted and ultimately bankrupt.

Of even greater significance in the long run were clear signs of a Copernican shift of perspective on the core element of conservative Thai ideology: the historical centrality and nationalist legitimacy of the monarchy. The popularity of Jit Phumisak's *Chomnā Sakdinā Thai* is symptomatic here because this closely argued book, dealing exclusively with pre-nineteenth-century (and thus pre-European-imperialist) Siam, interpreted the whole course of Thai history in terms of *fundamental conflicts* between oppressive rulers and struggling ruled. But Jit's book was only one element in a broad array of scholarly and journalistic writing appearing after 1973 which explored the Thai past in categories that implicitly denied or marginalized the traditional royalist-nationalist mythology. It is useful to try to visualize the everyday social feedback from such cultural-ideological developments. One must imagine Thai students discussing in their parents' presence a Siamese nineteenth century not in terms of the great King Rama V, but of the commercialization of agriculture, the growth of compradore communities, foreign penetration, bureaucratic aggrandizement, and so forth. Simply to use a vocabulary of social processes and economic forces was to refuse centrality to Thai monarchs as heroes in or embodiments of national history. Indeed, in some ways this *bypassing of traditional historical categories*, doubtless often perpetrated with naive insouciance or calm contempt by the young, may have seemed more menacing than any direct denial of royal prestige and authority.[93] (One should never underestimate the power of intergenerational hostility to exacerbate ideological antagonisms.[94])

---

93. Symptomatic are the following enraged remarks delivered by the Thanin regime's Public Relations Office on November 6, 1976: "Our culture, upheld by our ancestors and customs [*sic*], was neglected, considered obsolete and regarded as a dinosaur or other extinct creature. Some had no respect for their parents, and students disregarded their teachers. They espoused a foreign ideology without realizing that such action is dangerous to our culture and did not listen to the advice of those who have much knowledge of that ideology. National security was frequently threatened over the past 3 years. Anyone who expressed concern for the national security was mocked and regarded as a wasted product of the bureaucratic society by those who labeled themselves as progressive-minded . . ." FBIS Daily Report, Nov. 8. 1976.

94. It is interesting that an important component of the ultra-rightist organization Nawaphon, founded in 1974 (of which Prime Minister Thanin is reputed to be a member), was (and is) middle-aged and elderly university professors. Many of these men, with M.A. degrees

It should now be possible to understand more clearly why, not long after liberal democratic government was installed and censorship abolished, prosecutions for *lèse majesté* began to be inaugurated.[95] It was not just that the ruling cliques were angered by the hostile rhetoric of radicalized students. Rather a whole concatenation of crises in Thai society began to crystallize around the symbol of the monarchy. The end of the long economic boom, the unexpected frustrations generated by rapid educational expansion, intergenerational estrangement,[96] and the alarm caused by the American strategic withdrawal and the discrediting of the military leadership—these linked crises were experienced most acutely of all by the insecure new bourgeois strata. For these strata the monarchy was both a talisman and a moral alibi. The historical depth and solidity of the institution appeared as a kind of charm against disorder and disintegration. And whatever the venality of their lives or their actual economic and cultural dependence on foreigners, members of these strata felt their nationalist self-esteem morally guaranteed by their loyalty to the throne, the epitome of the national heritage. Thus any assault, however indirect, on the legitimacy of the throne was necessarily sensed as a menace to that alibi.

The malaise of 1974, which generated the first of the *lèse majesté* trials, was then immeasurably deepened by events in Indochina. In the space of a few weeks in the spring of 1975, Vientiane, Phnom Penh, and Saigon were all conquered by communist forces. In the short run, the main effect was a panicked capital outflow. In the slightly longer run came a crucial change in the practical, as opposed to the symbolic, role of the throne. For there can be little doubt that the abolition of the Laotian monarchy in December (the end of the Khmer monarchy at right-wing hands five years earlier had actually been

---

from second-rate foreign universities and long records of toadying to the dictatorship, were outraged by the openly critical, even contemptuous way they were regarded by younger men (often with Ph.D. degrees from good universities, and influenced by the idealism of the antiwar movement). In a number of important cases, senior university officials were deposed for corruption, scandalous laziness and incompetence, and spying on students for the state bureaucracy. On Nawaphon, see, e.g., Keyes, "Political Crisis," pp. 8–12.

95. The first case was that of left-wing student activist Praderm Damrongcharoen, accused of slyly attacking the king in a poem written for an obscure student magazine. Praderm was fortunate to be acquitted finally at the end of February 1975 (see *The Nation*, March 1, 1975, for details). The second was that of the journalist Seni Sungnat, charged with insulting the queen by criticizing one of her speeches in the pages of the rabidly rightist *Dao Sayam*. Seni was sentenced to two years in prison on February 4, 1976. (See *Prachachart Weekly Digest*, 15 [Feb. 10, 1976], p. 36.) The punishment of a right-wing journalist is a clear indication that the *lèse majesté* prosecutions were not simply cynical conservative manoeuvres against the Left, but stemmed from genuine cultural-ideological panic.

96. Kaufman, *Bangkhuad*, pp. 229–31, is good on this conflict in a local community setting.

applauded)[97] raised the alarming spectre that Rama IX might prove the last of his line. The king took an increasingly back-to-the-wall conservative anti-communist line in his public statements. The royal shift was noted duly by a whole gamut of right-wing groupings, which were thereby encouraged to go violently on the offensive.

Thanks to the entrenched position of right-wing elements in the mass media—especially radio and television[98]—this offensive, initiated in the fall of 1975, went into high gear in the spring of 1976, particularly during the campaign for the April parliamentary elections. The head of the Chat Thai party, General Pramarn Adireksan, for example, used his ministerial powers over state-controlled media to launch openly the slogan "Right Kill Left!'—something he would not have dared to do a year earlier.[99] Radio stations controlled by rightists, and especially the extremist Armored Division Radio, commissioned and played incessantly such violent songs as "Nak Phaendin" (Heavy on the Earth) and "Rok Phaendin" (Scum of the Earth). Kitti Wuttho's dictum that Buddhism endorsed the killing of communists was given wide and constant publicity. Nor, of course, was the violence merely verbal. As mentioned earlier, the spring and summer of 1976 witnessed a whole series of physical outrages.

The essential point is that the pivot on which this whole right-wing offensive turned was the monarchy, increasingly identified with and under the influence of the enemies of the liberal regime. It was therefore characteristic that the flash-point for the overthrow of the regime on October 6, 1976, should have been a fabricated case of *lèse majesté*. Some days earlier, on September 24, two workers at Nakhon Pathom, putting up posters protesting former dictator Thanom's re-entry into Siam under the cloak of monkhood,

---

97. The Thanom–Praphat government immediately reopened diplomatic relations with Phnom Penh, and in the summer of 1970 came very close to sending Thai troops into Cambodia in support of the Lon Nol regime and the US-South Vietnamese "incursions." Even in the early 1950s, when the Khmer monarch Norodom Sihanouk had come to Bangkok in the course of his "Royal Crusade" for Cambodian independence, the Phibunsongkhram government treated him with scarcely veiled contempt. See Roger M. Smith, *Cambodia's Foreign Policy* (Ithaca, NY: Cornell University Press, 1965), p. 48. Nonetheless, political change in Cambodia was not left wholly unexploited over the border. Kitti Wuttho, for example, justified his anticommunist militancy in part on the grounds of alleged communist massacres of Khmer monks during the final stages of the Cambodian civil war.

98. At that time, the military alone owned more than half the radio stations in the country and all but one of the TV stations in Bangkok, according to the National Anti-Fascism Front of Thailand, "Three Years of Thai Democracy," in *Thailand Information Resource*, No. 1 (May 1977), p. 3.

99. Pramarn, a well-known partner of Japanese big business, is a brother-in-law of the late, unlamented Police General Phao Siyanon, whose brutalities in the late 1940s and early 1950s have been briefly detailed above.

were beaten to death by some local policemen and their corpses hanged.[100] Two days before the coup, a radical student troupe staged a dramatic re-enactment of the murder in the Bo-Tree courtyard of Thammasat University as part of a nationwide campaign for Thanom's expulsion.[101] The rabid right-wing newspaper *Dao Sayam* touched up photographs of the performance in such a way as to suggest that one of the actors "strangled" had been made up to look like the crown prince.[102] In a co-ordinated manoeuvre, the Armored Division Radio broadcast the slander, urged the citizenry to buy copies of *Dao Sayam*, and demanded retribution for this "cruel attack" on the royal family.[103] From this stemmed the lynch-mobs that paved the way for the military takeover.

It is perhaps worth stressing that this type of frame-up and co-ordinated media campaign is quite new in Thai politics. When Sarit framed Phra Phimonladham and Phra Sasanasophon, or when Phao murdered opposition parliamentarians, they committed their crimes administratively, behind closed doors. The mass media of the 1960s had always warned that the *government* would deal severely with communists and subversives. In 1976, however, the frame-up was staged out in the open, and the *public* was invited to exact vengeance for subversion.

The reason for this is that the old ruling cliques, weakened by developments at home and abroad, have been seeking new domestic allies, and have found them in the bewildered, buffeted, and angry middle and petty bourgeoisie created under the old dictatorship. The crudity with which such formulations as Nation–Religion–King are being elaborated and deployed is symptomatic both of a growing general awareness that they are no longer

---

100. Natee, "Village Scouts," p. 35, claims that several hours before these murders took place the Village Scout training camp at Nakhon Pathom had staged a mock killing and hanging of the corpses of "bad students." He also avers that some of the real-life murderers had come from this camp.

101. The Bo-Tree courtyard had become a national symbol of resistance to dictatorship, for it was from this courtyard that the demonstrations started which overthrew Thanom and Praphat in October 1973.

102. It is worth noting that *Dao Sayam*, founded by a typical nouveau-riche figure, ran a regular Village Scout activities column. Wealthy donors and activists could see their names given good publicity and even intermingled with those of royalty, aristocrats, and important government officials. The newspaper was thus the logical place to launch a swift, violent Village Scout mobilization campaign.

103. The eminence grise of the Armored Division Radio, Col. Utharn Sanidwong na Ayutthaya, is a relative of the queen—and thus of the crown prince. See *Far Eastern Economic Review*, Feb. 11, 1977. His key role in the fabrications of October 5–6 is an indication of the complicity of the palace in the overthrow of the parliamentary constitutional regime. Another effective hate-monger was Dr. Uthit Naksawat, Cornell University graduate and President of the Chomrom Witthayu Seri (Independent Radio Group of Thailand).

genuinely hegemonic, and of the real fear and hatred generated by the cultural revolution of the 1970s.[104]

The consequences of October 6 point therefore in two different but related directions. On the one hand, the coup has obviously accelerated the secular demystification of Thai politics. Direct and open attacks on the monarchy loom imminently.[105] Sizeable groups, both liberal and radical, have come to understand that they have no place in the Bangkok order, and so, in unprecedented numbers, have left for exile or the maquis. On the other hand, the political conceptions and symbols of the once hegemonic Right have become self-conscious slogans with an increasingly *specific* social constituency. In the 1950s and 1960s, it was possible for many Thai conservatives to view the Thai Left quite sincerely as a kind of alien minority ("really" Vietnamese, Chinese, or whatever), and the anticommunist struggle as a loftily national crusade. Today, such ideas have become less and less plausible even to the Right. The events of October 6 have served to speed up the process whereby the Right gradually concedes, almost without being aware of it, that it is engaged in *civil* war. In the long run, this change is likely to prove decisive, for modern history shows very clearly that, with the exception of Lenin's Bolshevik party, no revolutionary movement succeeds unless it has won or been conceded the nationalist accolade.[106]

---

104. It is a bizarre, but characteristic, sign of the almost cosmological panic involved that the Thanin regime should have banned the teaching of *all* (i.e. even right-wing) forms of political theory in Thai schools. See *New York Times*, Oct. 21, 1976; and *Far Eastern Economic Review*, Nov. 5, 1976.

105. This is clear from recent broadcasts over the maquis radio and from clandestine leaflets circulating in Bangkok. Interestingly enough, there are indications that certain dissatisfied right-wing groups are becoming increasingly critical, if not of the monarchy as an institution, at least of the present incumbent and his consort.

106. In the analysis presented in this essay, I have deliberately focused on the *new* elements in the Thai political constellation. I certainly do not mean to suggest that the new bourgeois strata are more than a secondary element in the Bangkok power structure; they are probably even an *unreliable* secondary element from the point of view of the ruling cliques. It is instructive that, after the October 6 coup, the junta returned as far as possible to the old "administrative" style of repression. The Red Gaurs were silenced or packed off to combat zones in the north, northeast, and south (where they reportedly suffered severe casualties). Nawaphon was encouraged to crawl back into the woodwork. Col. Utharn has been removed from control of the Armored Division Radio. The generals currently on top—"moderates" all—would probably like to run the regime in the Sarit–Thanom–Praphat style. But one suspects that this may no longer prove feasible. The new bourgeois strata are there, the new provincial landlords are there—and these erstwhile allies cannot be safely ignored or discarded. Nor, probably, can the problems of these strata be solved by the generals. The boom is unlikely ever to return with its old élan; the ideological seamlessness of the past cannot be restored; unemployment swells; the bureaucracy grows ever more congested and expensive; the university paradox is seemingly insoluble. The new right-wing groups have experienced participation and it is improbable that they can be totally excluded from it again. The genie has been let out of the bottle and it will be very difficult for the junta or its successors to put it back again for good.

8

Murder and Progress in Modern Siam

In 1983, one of the biggest box-office hits in Siam was a remarkable film entitled *Mue Puen*. English-language advertisements translated this title as "The Gunman," but an alternative, probably better, translation would be "The Gunmen." For the director invited his audiences to contemplate the contrast between two hired assassins—hero and villain—one working for private enterprise, the other for the state. In an early flashback, the two men are shown as comrades in the "secret" mercenary army hired by the CIA to fight in Laos in the late 1960s; there they learn to become crack shots with high-powered automatic rifles. In one savage firefight, however, the hero is seriously wounded and then abandoned to the enemy's tender mercies by his cowardly comrade. The story proper of the film is set in contemporary Bangkok, and depicts the subsequent careers of the two protagonists. The hero, one leg badly damaged, officially supports himself by working as a barber; but we are soon shown that he is secretly a highly paid professional killer. His paymasters are wealthy businessmen—and so are his victims.

The villain, on the other hand, has become the head of a high-publicity SWAT team of the Bangkok metropolitan police. He specializes in luring criminals into traps where he shoots them down with icy, pinpoint accuracy. He is known to the mass media as *Mue Dam* (Black Hand) because he ostentatiously puts a black glove on his gun hand when preparing to kill for his employer, the state. In another society he would be the natural boss of a death squad.

The killers are distinguished morally by what we are shown of their circumstances and motivations. The hero has been abandoned by his wife, and is left to care for his critically ill child all on his own. Murder is his only means of raising the money needed for expensive surgery for the little tyke. The villain kills to compensate for the memory of his earlier cowardice, to gain media attention, and to impress an alcoholic wife, with whom his sexual relations are distinctly sadistic. He thus exploits his position as state-licensed killer to gratify a range of unpleasant private desires. But lest the audience think that the villain is a pathological aberration, the director makes sure to provide him with a young police henchman who takes an even grimmer pleasure in assassination-for-the-state.

It is hard to imagine a film of this sort being made, let alone screened, anywhere else in Southeast Asia. Nor, I think, would it have been possible in Siam except in the 1980s. It is particularly interesting that the Thai police insisted successfully on only two changes in the original print before the film's public release. The hero's main paymaster could not be shown to be a moonlighting senior police officer; and the masked motorcycle gangsters gunned down by Black Hand could not be shown to be young women. On the other hand, there is also something curious about the film's popularity with the public. One can readily understand why young audiences would enjoy the rare filmic spectacle of villainous police. But a hero (even one played by top box-office star Soraphong) who kills "innocent people" for money? The answer, I suspect, is "yes," provided the victims are clearly middle-aged, male, and very rich (in other words, big capitalists). Provided, too, that there is some resonance between what is seen on the screen and the contemporary realities of Thai society.

This reality, or rather the part of it with which I am here concerned, is that in the 1980s political killing in Siam has assumed a completely unprecedented character, one which is, oddly enough, probably a positive omen for the future. For it seems tied to the eclipse of a long-standing tradition of military–bureaucratic dictatorship and its supersession by a stable, bourgeois parliamentary political system. To get a sharper focus on the relationship between "The Gunmen" and the rapidly changing structures of Thai politics, it may be useful to sketch out antecedent patterns of political murder in Siam.

EARLY PATTERNS

The modern era of Siam's history is conventionally said to have begun in 1855. In that year, Sir John Bowring, representative of Queen Victoria and coiner of the immortal axiom "Free Trade is Jesus Christ and Jesus Christ is Free Trade," imposed his commercial divinity by means of a treaty which compelled the Thai state to abolish all substantial barriers to imperialist economic penetration.[1] Prior to 1855, the pattern of political killing was exactly what one would expect in a society where political participation was confined, most of the time, to a very small, largely endogamous, "feudal" upper class. The victims were typically members of this class—princes, noblemen, courtiers, and high officials—and so, on the whole, were their assassins. If commoner bodyguards or soldiers participated, it was rarely on their own behalf, rather they acted at the behest of their patrons. Political murder was an intrafamily affair, pitting fathers against sons, uncles against nephews, half-brothers against half-brothers. Most killings took place in the royal capital itself, which was the only real arena of political competition. The state was still so archaic and so personalized in the ruler himself that there was no sharp conceptual line between execution and murder, between "state" and "private" killing.

Between 1855 and 1932 this pattern of intra-upper-class murder went into suspension, most likely because of fear of European intervention in the political sense, and thanks to European intervention in the economic. Political leaders in Bangkok could see that in neighbouring Southeast Asian states, where ruling circles permitted themselves too much fratricidal carnage, European imperialists found easy pretexts for marching in to establish law'n'order or to restore a "rightful," compliant claimant to the local throne. On the other hand, the rapidly expanding free-trade economy of the last half of the nineteenth century lessened the ferocity of intra-elite competition by enlarging the available pie. (The contrast between Siam's experience and the blood-drenched final decades of the Burmese monarchy, deprived by two Anglo-Burmese wars of more than half its territorial revenue base, is instructive.) These conditions remained sufficiently stable so that even when the old nobility faced political and economic challenges from the "new men" of the modern-style bureaucracy created by Rama V (r. 1868–1910), the conflicts were handled without bloodshed.

Something rather like the pre-1855 pattern only began to emerge after 1932, when the would-be absolutist monarchy was overthrown in a bloodless coup plotted by military and civilian commoner civil servants, who called themselves the Citizens Group.[2] During the later 1930s, serious assassination attempts were directed against the two paramount military leaders of the Citizens Group, Generals Phahon Phonphayuhasena and Plaek Phibunsongkhram, by members of their own circle; and violent retribution (by "legal" execution) was exacted by a still significantly personal state. By

---

1. The quotation is drawn from Charles R. Boxer, *The Dutch Seaborne Empire, 1600–1800* (London: Hutchinson, 1965), p. 249.

2. The fullest English-language account is in Thawatt Mokarapong, *History of the Thai Revolution: A Study in Political Behaviour* (Bangkok: Chalermnit, 1972).

then, there was no real fear that such killings would precipitate external intervention, as the imperial powers were abandoning even their longstanding
extraterritorial rights. At the same time, the inauguration of a constitutional
monarchy—and the twentieth-century impossibility of starting a new (say,
Phibunsongkhram) dynasty—meant in principle a much wider circle of par-
ticipants in the struggle for political and economic dominance. The pattern
became still clearer in the late 1940s and early 1950s when violent conflict
within the residual elements of the 1932 Citizens Group, their followers, and
some potential successors, erupted. We may take as characteristic of this
period the assassinations, on March 3, 1949, of four former cabinet ministers,
all of them civilians hailing from the impoverished northeast, by the ferocious
asawin ("knights") of Police General Phao Sriyanon.[3] The four victims moved
in the same social milieu as Phao; they were killed in the capital; and for nothing to do with class, or even regional, conflict in the wider sense. As in the
pre-1855 era, it is almost beside the point to ask whether the murders were
committed by the state or by private individuals. Certainly no form of legal
process was involved; but even if it had been, we know from the executions of
perfectly innocent people in the so-called regicide trials of the period, that
legal mechanisms were easily used for private murders.[4] Yet it is also true that
the clumsy moves made by Phao and Phibunsongkhram to cover up these
murders indicate their awareness of a widened political public in the post-
World War II world.

STATE KILLINGS

As with so much else in modern Thai history, political killing assumed a new
character under the despotic regime of Field Marshal Sarit Thanarat,
installed by coup d'état in October 1958.[5] During his time, the range of

---

3. See Thak Chaloemtiarana, *Thailand: The Politics of Despotic Paternalism* (Bangkok:
Social Science Association of Thailand, 1989), p. 48, for details.

4. On June 9, 1946, the 21-year-old king Rama VIII was found shot dead in his bed. The circumstances of his death have never been cleared up. But the Thai military, temporarily sidelined
after 1945 because of Allied anger at Phibunsongkhram's wartime alliance with Tokyo, seized on
the affair to accuse the civilian government of complicity in the king's alleged murder, and eventually, in late 1947, to overthrow it. The staging of the show trials was managed by General Phao.
The fullest account of the king's death (with a substantial exploration of alternative explanations)
and the trials is in Rayne Kruger, *The Devil's Discus* (London: Cassell, 1964). This book remains
banned in Siam.

5. The fullest account of the Sarit regime is in Thak Chaloemtiarana's *Thailand.* "Bronze-
throat" Sarit died of cirrhosis of the liver in 1963, but his regime survived until October 1973
under the control of his two chief lieutenants, Field Marshal Thanom Kittikajon and General
Praphat Jarusathien.

victims of political murder expanded outwards and downwards, while the killers became, more unambiguously than before, the state-qua-state and its employees. Illustrations of the change are afforded by the executions in 1958 of five "notorious" arsonists, in 1961 of two left-wing ex-members of parliament, and in 1962 of an alleged leading communist.[6] For the victims were completely outside Sarit's elite circle (he had probably never met any of them); all were accused of endangering *state* security; and the executions were performed in public by acknowledged agents of the state.[7] The real reason for these murders was simply the desire to build up Sarit's image as absolute strongman for a now national audience of newspaper-readers and radio-listeners, and, potentially, voters.[8] In other words, these killings were done in a spirit of public relations, mass-media-style.

The appearance of a mass-media audience for which political murders needed to be staged also meant that certain other political killings had to be kept secret from that audience. A good example of this paradox is the case of the Red Drum (*Tang Daeng*) slayings in Patthalung province in 1971–72.[9] These murders, designed to terrorize a *local* peasant population suspected of communist sympathies, were not acceptable to a *national* audience which even the military regime of Sarit's successors felt somewhat constrained to respect. Similarly, in the immediate aftermath of the fall of the military regime in October 1973 (see below), student activists were able to expose the locally public, nationally secret Ban Na Sai affair to undermine severely the state security apparatus's legitimacy.[10] A conspicuous gap was opening up between the state as law and the state as apparatus.

---

6. See ibid., pp. 193–5, 203–4.

7. The executions of the "arsonists" were carried out on Bangkok's vast downtown Pramane Square, in front of the Grand Palace, with the victims lined up against the wall of the imposing Mahathat Buddhist temple.

8. On coming to power Sarit abolished the existing constitution, closed down parliament, liquidated political parties and trade unions, arrested hundreds of intellectuals, politicians, and journalists, and established severe censorship. After his death, the iron grip was somewhat relaxed, a provisional constitution eventually created, and (heavily manipulated) elections held.

9. The victims, some dead, most still alive, were incinerated by the security forces in gasoline-filled, used oil drums. See Norman Peagam, "Probing the 'Red Drum' Atrocities," *Far Eastern Economic Review*, March 14, 1975.

10. The village of Ban Na Sai, suspected of communist sympathies, was burned to the ground, and many of the villagers summarily executed. See Marian Mallet, "Causes and Consequences of the October '76 Coup," in Andrew Turton, Jonathan Fast, and Malcolm Caldwell, eds., *Thailand: Roots of Conflict* (Nottingham: Spokesman, 1976), pp. 80–103, at p. 82; and David Morell and Chai-anan Samudavanija, *Political Conflict in Thailand*, Cambridge, Mass.: Oelgeschlager, Gunn & Hain, 1981), pp. 169–72.

ARMED STRUGGLE

The other big change in the era of Sarit, Thanom, and Praphat was the emergence of two very important new types of participant in Thai politics. The first of these was the Communist Party of Thailand (CPT), which after 1965 waged an increasingly successful armed struggle in the state's territorial peripheries.[11] The CPT leaders did not belong to the old capital-city political elite, nor did they attempt to participate directly in capital-city politics. They took very good care to remain out of the reach of the state's executioners. And they carried on their struggle in remote rural areas which traditionally had had next to no political importance, but which now, in an age of territorially defined nation-states, had become accepted by the state as a significant political arena. Because the CPT was successful, in many rural communities, in mobilizing lowland peasants and upland minorities—in effect, getting them to participate in a national struggle for power—these people began to join the ranks of potential victims of political murder. In the early years of the state's counter-insurgency campaigns, violence (including murder) against the rural population remained largely the prerogative of the central state apparatus itself. But as the conflicts deepened and widened, with arms of the CPT attacking not merely official emissaries of the state but also its local private supporters, so a significant "private enterprise" sector emerged alongside the "state sector" in the murder field. In the northeast, the north, and the south, vigilante groups, village toughs, moonlighting security personnel, and so on, started to step up their activities. The unprecedented availability of firearms—thanks to American aid to the Thai military and police, as well as to the American "secret war" in Laos—substantially intensified the level of violence in rural politics.[12] Of particular interest were the sizeable numbers of rural and small-town Thai who were enrolled in paramilitary security units while the American money lasted, but demobilized when this money ran out.[13] Demobilization meant that they were no longer in the employ of the state; but they took back to private life militarized attitudes and terroristic skills which, as we shall see, began to acquire real commercial value in the 1970s. The final point to note in this context is that the CIA's secret army was

---

11. See Morell and Chai-anan, *Political Conflict*, pp. 80–81, and Patrice de Beer, "History and Policy of the Communist Party of Thailand," in Turton, Fast, and Caldwell, eds., *Thailand*, pp. 143–94.

12. See Andrew Turton, "Limits of Ideological Domination and the Formation of Social Consciousness," in Andrew Turton and Shigeharu Tanabe, eds., *History and Peasant Consciousness in Southeast Asia* (Osaka: National Museum of Ethnology, Senri Ethnological Studies no. 13, 1984), pp. 19–73.

13. See chapter 7 above, especially p. 161.

a *mercenary* army, fully understood as such by its recruits. In this way, one could say that the profession of a hired gunman—a profession rather new to Siam—derived directly from America's prosecution of its Indochina war, and was thus political from the start.

THE NEW BOURGEOISIE

The second new participant in Thai politics can be broadly described as an extra-bureaucratic bourgeoisie. Its origins lay in the Sino-Thai merchant and trading communities of Bangkok, Chonburi, Paknam, and a few towns of the prosperous south.[14] In the 1940s and 1950s their numbers were still fairly small, their wealth limited, and their political influence negligible (not least because in many cases the process of assimilation was not yet complete). But by the early 1960s a generation of fully assimilated Sino-Thai was reaching high-school and college age, just at the point when the great Vietnam War boom got under way. They arrived in time to take advantage of the huge growth of tertiary education in the 1960s, and of the massive expansion and diversification of employment that the boom engendered.[15]

Never in its history had Siam been so deluged with external economic resources—the result not merely of American capital investment in military bases and strategic infrastructural development, but also of direct American aid to the Thai regime, and substantial Japanese and American private investment in a low-wage, union-free society. There were three especially notable consequences of the deluge. First, it was by no means wholly concentrated in the metropolitan region but had a major impact, direct and indirect, on many parts of the northeast, north, and south. Second, it encouraged a stratum of businessmen to emerge who were far less sharply counterposed to the modern bureaucrat than had been the case with the older Sino-Thai merchants. Among its leaders were the proprietors and managers of good hotels, shopping plazas, automobile franchises, insurance companies, and, of course, banks.[16] These were people who dressed like bureaucrats, lived in the new suburban housing complexes alongside bureaucrats, and dined, partied, shopped, and travelled in the same places as bureaucrats. Increasingly, from the 1960s on, they came out of a single common institution—the university. Third, it

---

14. The standard works are two books by G. William Skinner, *Chinese Society in Thailand: An Analytical History*, and *Leadership and Power in the Chinese Community of Thailand* (Ithaca, NY: Cornell University Press, 1957 and 1958).

15. See chapter 7 above, for a detailed discussion of class formation in this period.

16. See Suthy Prasartset, *Thai Business Leaders: Men and Careers in a Developing Economy* (Tokyo: Institute of Developing Economies, 1982).

meshed nicely with the meteoric rise of the Sino-Thai banking system, and indeed was probably the major factor in its rise. These Sino-Thai banks were not elbowed aside by Japanese and American giants. Surely advantaged by the difficulties foreigners faced in mastering the Thai and Chinese languages, to say nothing of their formidable orthographies, the banks moved briskly to develop the domestic capital market. They quickly discovered that, in the age of the boom, there were substantial profits to be made by elaborating their provincial operations. In the early 1960s, far the most imposing edifice in most provincial capitals was the governor's office, symbol of the old bureaucratic domination of Thai social and political life. A decade later, many of these Thai-Edwardian buildings had been completely overshadowed by spectacular glass-concrete-marble structures housing local branches of the great Bangkok banks.

EMERGENT PARLIAMENTARY DEMOCRACY

One needs therefore to look at the rise of the extra-bureaucratic bourgeoisie from two angles. The first, and most familiar, highlights the emergence of a very large number of educated youths (a portion of whom made the National Student Center of Thailand [NSCT] the briefly formidable political force it was in the early 1970s). Already in the late 1960s they could no longer be absorbed into the bureaucracy as earlier university cohorts had been. But they were aware that they were in institutions that had traditionally prepared the new generation of the ruling class for its tasks: thus they felt that they had a natural right to participate politically. In so far as many of them were now coming from the provinces, they expected to exercise that right not merely in Bangkok but wherever in their careers they ended up. Hence, for the first time in Thai history, the real possibility of significant non-bureaucratic mini-intelligentsias in the regions arose. A second, less familiar, angle focuses on the strengthening (on the basis of bank credit and the general, rapid commercialization of provincial life) of small-town entrepreneurs—some independent, some operating as agents of metropolitan giants. In most provincial towns people of this type quickly developed incomes, then life styles and status pretensions, that were competitive with those of locally stationed state officials. Furthermore, since they were not subject to the officials' routine transfer to other locales, they put down strong local roots, social as well as commercial. For these roots to engender local power, it was necessary only that the unity and authority of the central state apparatus, standing behind local officialdom, be substantially compromised.

The historic "break" came with the popular movement of 1973, which culminated, on October 14, in the collapse of the Thanom–Praphat regime.[17] It is true that the duumvirate would not have fallen without high-level factional interventions by the king and by army Commander General Krit Sivara. But the fact that Krit removed his seniors, not by a coup d'état, but by abetting the activism of students and intellectuals, joined by the popular masses in Bangkok (including segments of the middle and lower-middle classes), signalled his own recognition that the traditional form of "legitimate politics" was no longer viable. The country had changed too much. Events between 1973 and 1977 showed that even though reactionary groups remained powerful, this recognition was becoming widespread even within the state apparatus, which was thus incapable of acting with its earlier unity of purpose.

What was emerging was that characteristic bourgeois political system we know as parliamentary democracy—the style of regime with which all ambitious, prosperous, and self-confident bourgeoisies feel most comfortable, precisely because it maximizes their power and minimizes that of their competitors. If one thinks of 1973 as Siam's 1789, then one can view the entire subsequent period (up to the present) within a single optic—that of the struggle of the bourgeoisie to develop and sustain its new political power (institutionalized in parliamentary forms) against threats from both Left and Right, the popular sector, and the state apparatus. The patterns of political killing over these sixteen years provide good evidence that this optic is a useful one.

PERIOD OF CONSOLIDATION

The period might plausibly be divided into two: 1973–78 and 1978–89. In the first period, one of great instability and uncertainty, the bourgeoisie, feeling its way, was in an openly contradictory position. On the one hand, it needed the support of the popular sector, ideally channelled mainly through electoral mechanisms, to strengthen its legitimacy and power against military and civilian officialdom: in this struggle, "democracy" was a domestically powerful and internationally respectable weapon. On the other hand, it also felt the need for the support of the repressive arm of the state apparatus to contain "popular excesses" in the urban areas, to fight the rising CPT in the countryside, and, given the rapid decline of the American position in Indochina, to defend the nation-state from its new communist-ruled neighbours to the east.[18] In the

---

17. For a good, brief account, see Morell and Chai-anan, *Political Conflict*, pp. 146–50.

18. Given Siam's massive complicity in the American war effort, the Thai bourgeoisie had good grounds for fearing revenge.

second period, the main problem for the bourgeoisie has been fending off the efforts by opportunist and ultra-rightist elements in the security bureaucracy who have sought to regain their old dominance by exploiting the "external threat" and resorting to sham-populist, "anticapitalist" public rhetoric.

In the bourgeoisie's successful struggle, the importance of the press should not be underestimated; above all that of the popular newspaper *Thai Rath* which, with its huge nationwide readership, represents another kind of imagined national community, alongside those conjured up by parliamentary institutions or the Nation–Religion–King shibboleth of the old regime. Most of this press has been, if not explicitly antagonistic to military–bureaucratic pretensions (let alone coups), at least sceptical and suspicious. After all, successful newspapers are large business enterprises, which succeed because they voice, at least to some extent, their readers' aspirations. Correspondingly, the role of the press in this period can be viewed as that of an ally of the new bourgeois political ascendancy. However, of still greater interest is that in this second period the bourgeoisie has become so confident of its power, and so certain of the value of the parliamentary system for the protection of its own interests, that it has proved willing to permit violent internal competition among its own ranks. We have had the extraordinary spectacle, in the 1980s, of MPs being assassinated, not by communists or military dictators, but by other MPs or would-be MPs.

Before turning to look more closely at the contrasting patterns of political killing in the two periods, we may remind ourselves again of the reasons why the parliamentary system is so attractive to new middle classes of the current Thai type. In the first place, in the face of domineering civilian and military bureaucracies, it opens up channels to political power in both vertical and horizontal dimensions. To be elected to parliament one does not need to have a university degree, or to have entered in early youth the low rungs of an institutional hierarchy. Femaleness is no longer a fatal political disadvantage. Hence a huge, at least theoretical, increase in vertical social and political mobility for the less educated and non-male. At the same time, in a territorially based electoral system, provinciality is no special handicap, and may even be an advantage. One can be based in Nakhon Sawan and still be a cabinet minister; indeed, it may be that *only* by being solidly based in Nakhon Sawan can one obtain a cabinet seat. Parliament thus gives provincial elites the opportunity to short-circuit the Ministry of the Interior's powerful, territorially based hierarchy, and to make themselves felt, on their own terms, in the metropolitan home base of the bureaucracy itself—Krung Thep Maha Nakhon, aka Bangkok. Put in more general terms, electorally based parliamentary systems, more than any other type of regime, serve to reduce the power gap between the provinces and the metropolis: this, of course, is why they are so attractive to provincial notables.[19] Second, reduction in the power of the bureaucracy tends to weaken the regime of bureaucracy-controlled and protected monopolies, which always works to subordinate the bourgeoisie to the state apparatus. While such monopolies of course benefit particular businessmen or business cliques, they are against the general interest of the class. Third, electoral politics favour bourgeois interests in more narrow, technical ways. Money is crucial for sustained electoral success, and money is precisely the resource with which the bourgeoisie is most amply endowed.[20] On the other hand, the prestige of electoral politics, if it can be solidly entrenched, serves to delegitimize extra-parliamentary political activity—especially strikes, demonstrations, and popular movements, which the bourgeoisie is less likely to be able to control and may, on occasion, profoundly fear. Finally, it is evident that in countries like Siam, where "feudal" residues remain strong, especially in rural areas, the position of MP may offer possibilities of becoming far more powerful at the local level than is usually the case in industrial societies. It is thus no accident that the consolidation of the parliamentary system in Siam has coincided with the visible rise of so-called *chao phaw*—mafioso-like politician–capitalists who, by the use of violence, political connections, and control of local markets and rackets, become feared provincial bosses.

LOCAL AND NATIONAL KILLINGS

We may now return to political killings. In the period from late 1974 to the coup of October 6, 1976, the typical victims were middle-class student activists associated with the NSCT, leaders of peasant organizations, trade unionists, and left-wing, muckraking journalists.[21] The murders seem to fall

---

19. See the exceptionally detailed, well-informed article by Anek Laothamatas, "Business and Politics in Thailand: New Patterns of Influence," in *Asian Survey*, 28: 4 (April 1988), pp. 451–70. Anek notes that in 1979 only four provinces had local chambers of commerce, but by 1987 all seventy-two provinces had established them. Furthermore, interprovincial alliances of these chambers of commerce have fought with increasing success to expand their influence vis-à-vis the metropolis (both the metropolitan bureaucracy and the capital city big bourgeoisie) using parliamentary channels.

20. Anek has some striking figures to illustrate this point. In the three cabinets of the 1963–73 period, under military dictators Sarit, Thanom, and Praphat, there were precisely two businessmen—less than 4 per cent of the total. In the election-based cabinets of 1975–76 there were thirty-five—roughly 40 per cent. In the aftermath of the October 6, 1976 coup (1976–early 1980) the proportion dropped to 13 per cent. Under the restored election-based parliamentary system of the 1980s (1980–86), it shot up again to almost 44 per cent. Ibid., p. 455.

21. For a solid discussion, with detailed statistics, of these killings, see Morell and Chaianan, *Political Conflict*, pp. 225–53.

into two broad groups. (1) Local killings—typically of peasant leaders, trade unionists, and journalists who were felt to threaten the power or profits of provincial notables, including landowners, businessmen, and corrupt village headmen. Most of these killings were private-enterprise murders, with the gunmen (*mue puen*) hired by these local notables from the Vietnam-era pool of professional assassins, former security guards, moonlighting policemen, and petty gangsters.[22] (2) National killings—a conspicuous example is the ambush assassination, in Bangkok, of Socialist Party leader Dr. Boonsanong Punyothayan on February 28, 1976. But the periodic assassinations of prominent student leaders, and, above all, the massacre that took place at Thammasat University, in Bangkok, on October 6, 1976 itself, form the general category. These victims threatened no particular private interests. Rather they were regarded as enemies of the *state,* or were cynically depicted as such for Machiavellian reasons (e.g. to create the atmosphere in which the state apparatus could plausibly reverse the parliamentary tide). Hence the killers were more or less direct agents of this apparatus.[23] The massacre of students at Thammasat University on October 6 is especially useful for showing the difference between category 1 and category 2 murders. For the victims were, many of them, the privileged children of the bourgeoisie itself (one has only to look at the Sino-Thai faces of the students inside Thammasat's gates, any day of the working week, and the Thai-Thai faces of the vendors outside, to sense this). There is very little reason to think that the Thai bourgeoisie wished for these killings—which were replicated nowhere outside the capital city.

The "national" killings, performed by agents of the state, were thus anti middle class, and intended to return the political order to what it had been before October 14, 1973. The "local" killings, performed by private mercenaries, were pro middle class, and intended to intimidate members of the subaltern classes and their self-appointed tribunes.

THE COLLAPSE OF RURAL INSURGENCY

It has been plausibly argued that Siam, Thai parliamentary democracy, and/or the Thai middle class benefited from an extraordinary stroke of luck

---

22. Most of the killings were carried out in small towns and villages. Their highly uneven geographical distribution (most were in the north) underscores the absence of the central state-qua-state in the violence.

23. Most notoriously the so-called Red Gaurs, many of them ex-mercenaries from the CIA's "secret army" in Laos, who operated at the behest of the dominant clique in the ISOC (Internal Security Operations Command) of the armed forces; but also the Village Scouts, right-wing vigilante groups under the aegis of the palace. See chapter 7 above, pp. 157–60, and the sources there cited; and Morell and Chai-anan, *Political Conflict*, pp. 241–6.

in the collapse of the CPT's rural insurgency as a result of the triangular Cambodia–Vietnam–China war that opened in December 1978. It is true that the party was gravely damaged by its leadership's decision to remain wholly loyal to Peking's positions. It thereby lost its secure retreats in Laos and Cambodia, its opportunities for training cadres in Vietnam, and even its powerful radiotransmitter in Yunnan. (Prime Minister [General] Kriangsak Chomanan was shrewd enough to see the advantages of cementing close ties with "Little Bottle" (Teng Hsiao-p'ing) and his henchmen.)[24] But it can also be argued that the damage was especially severe because the party was already struggling with the problem of what to do with the hundreds of middle-class youthful activists who fled to its jungle protection in the wake of the bloody October 6, 1976 coup. From a much younger generation, from comfortable homes, well-read and articulate, and with some real experience in national-level legal politics, these activists found it hard automatically to accept many CPT positions; the party's obtuse response to the crisis of 1978–79 made it almost impossible. Prime Minister Kriangsak was shrewd enough to offer a general amnesty, enabling the activists to come safely home. It is significant that the CPT made little effort to stop them, even though the spectacle of "massive defections" compounded the severe political damage it had already suffered. All in all, there can be no doubt that the CPT's decline, caused not by the Thai military's battlefield successes, but by international political developments and its own internal haemorrhage, redounded principally to the benefit of the new Thai bourgeoisie. After 1978–79, it faced no serious threats from the Left, or from below. By then it was also no longer much alarmed by the presence of Vietnamese troops on the country's eastern border, though the military tried hard to make it so. The bourgeoisie recognized the real limits of Vietnam's power and Siam's advantages in having the US–China–Japan axis ranged firmly behind it.

But the Cambodia–Vietnam–China fighting erupted well *after* the fall of the post-October 6, 1976 right-wing regime of Thanin Kraiwichian, and it is his rise and fall that are really instructive for understanding the changing dynamic of Thai politics in the bourgeois era.

---

24. In the immediate aftermath of the October 6, 1976 coup, an awkward compromise between the palace and the coup leaders produced an ultra-rightist, but civilian, government headed by Supreme Court justice Thanin Kraiwichian. Almost exactly one year later, this government was bloodlessly overthrown by General Kriangsak, an unusually skilful military politician. It was Kriangsak's policy to persuade Peking to stop supporting the CPT in exchange for Siam's co-operation in supporting the Khmer Rouge against the invading Vietnamese forces. The deal was publicly sealed when "Little Bottle" popped up in Bangkok as a distinguished guest at the ordination ceremonies of the Crown Prince. (In Siam, it is customary for most young males to enter the Buddhist monkhood for a short period.)

THE THANIN REGIME

Thanin himself, a Sino-Thai jurist of eccentric and extremist views,[25] had no political base of his own, and represented no substantial group or institution. His appointment as Prime Minister reflected the conflict between the palace and the generals. The royal family, panicked by the recent abolition of the Laotian monarchy to which it was related, wanted a strong anticommunist, but also a civilian (since it never fully trusted the military). The generals, even more interested in power than in anticommunism, wanted the installation of one of their own. The palace initially prevailed, but not for very long. Ridiculous in its rhetoric, so that it soon became popularly referred to as the Clam Cabinet,[26] the Thanin government quickly alienated almost everyone by its incompetence and ideological extremism. But its leaders took their historic mission—anticommunism but *also* civilian supremacy and the rule of (right-wing) law—sufficiently seriously that they did something absolutely unprecedented in modern Thai politics: have a top-ranking general sentenced to death *and* executed. To be sure, General Chalard Hiransiri, leader of an attempted coup in March 1977, had managed to kill palace favourite, General Arun Dewathasin, in the course of his brief bid for power, but it is most unlikely that he would have been executed if a true military junta had been in control.[27] Chalard's fate was certainly one factor that helps to explain why General Kriangsak's successful, bloodless coup the following October was advertised from the start as a blow for "moderation" and as foreshadowing the restoration of at least quasi-parliamentary government. The audience for the advertisement was not merely the United States and Western Europe ("international public opinion"), but also, above all, the Thai bourgeoisie.[28] Kriangsak himself was the first Thai coup leader who took pains to act as kindly, home-loving bourgeois in public. For example, in a splendid *coup de théâtre* he had himself photographed by the press cooking noodles at his home for the Bangkok 18 (eighteen students imprisoned since October 6, 1976 on the grave charge of *lèse majesté*). The point in all this is that even before the Indochina imbroglio and the collapse of the CPT, the rise and fall of the Thanin regime attests to the continuing consolidation of bourgeois power in Thai politics.

---

25. He had published some dotty books on rape, brainwashing, and the communist menace.

26. In an early speech Thanin foolishly compared his government to a tender mollusc needing the protection of the hard, thick shell provided by the military, the palace, and the proliferating right-wing vigilante groups.

27. This does not exclude the possibility that some generals were content to see the choleric Chalard sped to join his Maker.

28. The military itself was becoming increasingly aware that in a vastly changed Thai society dreams of a new Sarit-style army despotism were obsolete.

MPs AND THE GUNMEN

Finally, we may turn to the very recent past and to the subject matter of "The Gunmen." Any reader of the Thai press after 1978 will have been struck by the sudden conspicuousness of stories about *chao phaw* and *phu mi itthiphon* ("men of influence"), and also by the new dangerousness of provincial political life. While there have been few cases as spectacular as the assassination of "Sia" Jaew,[29] the celebrated *chao phaw* of Chonburi, who was ambushed military-style by men driving armoured cars and firing submachine-guns, the killing of MPs by "unknown gunmen" has become commonplace. Next to MPs, nouveau riche tycoons, big speculators and/or smugglers and judges (local bosses or potential bosses) have been frequent victims. These people appear to have taken the place of peasant leaders and student activists—who are now almost never the objects of attack. There is, however, good reason to think that the killers are more or less the same people, at least the same kind of people, as the murderers of 1974–76: *mue puen,* guns for hire. Their paymasters seem almost invariably to be the victims' fellow-bourgeois political and business rivals. (The highly uneven territorial distribution of the deaths indicates little or no involvement by the state-qua-state.)

What all these killings suggest is that in the 1980s the institution of MP has achieved solid market value. In other words, not only does being an MP offer substantial opportunities for gaining wealth and power, *but it promises comfortably to do so for the duration.* It may thus be worth one's while to murder one's parliamentary competition—something inconceivable in the 1950s and 1960s, when parliament's power and longevity were very cheaply regarded.

What we are now seeing in Siam is a consolidation of the economic and political circuits created during its "American period." An almost uninterrupted thirty-year boom has given the country the most advanced, productive capitalist economy in Southeast Asia (outside the municipality of Singapore). The great Bangkok banks have been funnelling once undreamed-of credit to the provinces, funds which are as available for politics and gangsterism as for productive entrepreneurial activities. Competition between the banks, at all levels, means that each has a strong interest in developing political agents and allies. As the financial bankers of many MPs, the banks can exert direct, independent political influence in a way that would be very difficult under a centralized, authoritarian military regime. Furthermore, as the representatives of a national electorate, the parliamentarians as a group veil bank power

---

29. "Sia" is a Thaified version of the Teochiu (Chinese) word for "tycoon." Earlier used only for Sino-Thai (with an ambiguous mixture of contempt and awe), more recently it has been increasingly applied, with less contempt and more awe, to rising Thai-Thai tycoons.

(and the power of big industrial and commercial conglomerates) with a new aura of legitimacy. This is a real and valuable asset. It can thus provisionally be concluded that most of the echelons of the bourgeoisie—from the multi-millionaire bankers of Bangkok to the ambitious small entrepreneurs of the provincial towns—have decided that the parliamentary system is the system that suits them best; and that they now have the confidence to believe that they can maintain this system against all enemies. These enemies still exist—in the military and in the civilian bureaucracy in particular. But they seem in secular decline. For all officialdom's grumblings about "dark influence"—self-serving propaganda meant to suggest that "benign influence" is a monopoly of the bureaucracy—it has been gradually accommodating itself to the new system.[30]

It is in this context that the assassinations of MPs by professional gunmen can be read as a historic portent. Parliamentary democracy has little trouble gaining the support of liberal intelligentsias. But they are not sufficient to sustain it. Substantial numbers of ruthless, rich, energetic, and competitive people from all over the country must also be willing to invest in the system. That in Siam such people are prepared to kill one another to become MPs indicates something really new is now in place.

The film *Mue Puen* reflects this situation. It refuses to side with state murder over private enterprise murder—and the state is not in a position forcibly to change its mind. It reassures its audiences that the new bourgeois world is profoundly stable. After all, if capitalists are being murdered, their killers are neither communists, student radicals, nor agents of a police state: merely employees of fellow capitalists. And there is surely this wholly intended subtext for the defeated Left among the viewing masses: at least *some* capitalists are being killed, and by a maimed victim of American imperialism and the unjust social system to boot. A sort of dream revenge for October 6, 1976.

POSTSCRIPT

In the course of finishing this essay, I received from a Thai student of mine, recently returned to America, a description of a recent assassination so

---

30. This is true even of the military. Both coup attempts since Kriangsak's *coup de main* in October 1977 have been fiascos. Their leaders, a group of ambitious colonels loosely referred to as the Young Turks, have never managed to unite the military behind their schemes. It is symptomatic, however, that the "platform" of the Young Turks claims a mission to save the country not so much from communism as from greedy mega-capitalists. The gap between these idealists' salaries and the sums required to purchase their palatial suburban homes suggests another reason for their lack of political plausibility.

exemplary, and so rich in detail, that I cannot resist including it here in somewhat edited form.

At the beginning of April 1990 Mr. Phiphat Rotwanitchakorn (known as "Sia Huad"), a prominent *chao phaw* in Chonburi district southeast of Bangkok, was spectacularly ambushed and slain, along with his driver and his bodyguard (a captain in the local police). He had known for some time that he was targeted for assassination, and almost never left his big, heavily guarded mansion. But on "Cheng Meng" Day, when Sino-Thai families pay homage to their ancestors, he had been summoned by a close friend and prominent Bangkok banker of the multimillionaire Tejaphaiboon family to attend the rites at the Tejaphaiboons' private cemetery in Chonburi.[31] He felt he had to go because this friend had earlier given him a billion-*baht* ($40,000,000) line of credit enabling him to outbid a rival *chao phaw,* Kamnan (Commune Head) Poh, for control of a gigantic trade-centre building project in downtown Chonburi. Afraid for his life, "Sia Huad" called in his brother and several professional gunmen to follow him in another car. He even switched cars on returning from the cemetery, in the hope of eluding his enemies. But the assassins, in three cars, first smashed into and thus blocked his brother's car. Then they pursued him in a wild shooting spree for about five minutes, by which time his car had halted and all three men inside were dead. To make sure of this, however, a limping gunman (not Soraphong?) climbed out of his vehicle, pulling on a mask, and took a close look at the corpses, surrounded by a growing crowd of curious spectators.

"Sia Huad" had begun his career as a small-time enforcer for a local *chao phaw.* When his boss was murdered, he set up his own gang and found a new patron in a local political leader. His youngest sister subsequently married the son of a well-known Chonburi MP, who became a cabinet minister, and "Sia Huad" himself worked for this man as a "vote collector" at election time. As his wealth and power grew, so did the number of his enemies. He specialized in land speculation, ordering his gang to use the most ruthless methods to force small peasants owning land in areas scheduled for commercial and industrial development to sell to him dirt-cheap. He was also involved in a successful plot to overthrow a local mayor (also a political boss) and install his own henchmen in the municipal government. The arrogant way in which he and his gang treated the local police earned him many enemies in uniform.

---

31. The Sino-Thai Tejaphaiboons own the giant Bangkok Metropolitan Bank. Two of the younger-generation Tejaphaiboons, including one who was former chairman of the board of the Mekhong distillery conglomerate, ran successfully for parliament in 1986—the first time that the family had thought it worth putting its sons into electoral politics. Mr. Phiphat's friend is known as the "eighth Sia"—meaning that all his seven elder brothers are also big tycoons.

So when the powerful Kamnan Poh, angered over being outbid on the trade-centre building project, gave the green light, a lot of people who wanted "Sia Huad" dead pooled a million *baht* ($40,000) and plenty of guns in a united front against him.

About a month after the slayings, the police made several arrests in the case, including some of the dead man's *chao phaw* rivals, some politicians and gunmen, and, most important, four members of the Special Operations Police—allegedly the actual triggermen.[32]

Though no newspaper or magazine dares to say so, it is widely rumoured that the mastermind of the assassination was Kamnan Poh. But who dares touch him now? Just one week after the killings, Kamnan Poh celebrated his victory in the first mayoral election of the newly established Saensuk district (close to the tourist resort of Phattaya) by throwing a party for ten thousand people, including several cabinet ministers from the Social Action Party, other prominent MPs, popular singers, and movie stars. This was a much bigger and splashier affair than the party given by Prime Minister Chatchai Choonhawan when he became Prime Minister! In response to reporters' questions about the death of "Sia Huad," Kamnan Poh replied: "In Chonburi, bad guys must die." But probably not as spectacularly as "Sia Huad." These days, being killed by gunmen is becoming a class privilege of the bourgeoisie. After all, who will pay gunmen a million *baht* to slay a poor man?

---

32. This organization is not under the control of the national police department, but is a special paramilitary unit under the supervision of the armed forces. It was originally created as part of the anti-CPT counter-insurgency campaign.

9

Cacique Democracy in the Philippines

On March 9, 1987, President Corazón Aquino told a most instructive public lie. In a vigorous address to the Filipino-Chinese Federated Chambers of Commerce, she described her sudden appearance before them as a "homecoming," since her great-grandfather had been a poor immigrant from southeast China's Fukien province.[1] Doubtless her desperate need—given the Philippines' near-bankrupt economy and $28 billion external debt[2]—to inspire feelings of solidarity and confidence among a powerful segment of Manila's business class made some embroidery understandable. But the truth is that the President, born Corazón Cojuangco, is a member of one of the wealthiest and most powerful dynasties within the Filipino oligarchy. Her grandfather, putative son of the penniless immigrant, was Don Melecio Cojuangco, born in Malolos, Central Luzon, in 1871. A graduate of the Dominicans' Colegio de San Juan de Letran and the Escuela Normal, and a prominent *agricultor* (i.e. *hacendado*) in the province of Tarlac, he was, in 1907, at the age of thirty-six, elected to the Philippine Assembly, the quasi-legislature established by the American imperialists in that year.[3] One of his sons (Corazón's uncle) became Governor of Tarlac in 1941, another (her

---

1. *Philippine Star Week*, March 8–14, 1987.

2. In July 1987 she estimated that debt payments would consume 40 per cent of government revenues, and 27 per cent of all export earnings for the following six years. The economic growth rate in 1986 was 0.13 per cent. *Philippine Daily Inquirer*, July 28, 1987.

3. *Philippine Daily Inquirer*, Feb. 12, 1987; and information kindly supplied by Philippine historian Michael Cullinane. He ran as a candidate of the Progresistas, the most openly American-collaborationist of the parties of that era. The above article implausibly suggests that Melecio's grandfather, a certain "Martin" Cojuangco, was the real immigrant founder of the dynasty.

father, Don José) its most prominent Congressman. In 1867, one of his grandsons (her cousin), Eduardo "Danding" Cojuangco, became Governor of Tarlac with Ferdinand Marcos's backing, and went on to count among the most notorious of the Marcos cronies. Another grandson (her younger brother), José "Peping" Cojuangco, was in those days one of Tarlac's Congressmen, and is today again a Congressman—and one of the half-dozen most powerful politicians in the country. Her marriage to Benigno Aquino, Jr., at various periods Governor of Tarlac and Senator, linked her to another key dynasty of Central Luzon. Benigno Aquino, Sr., had been a Senator in the late American era and won lasting notoriety for his active collaboration with the Japanese Occupation regime. At the present time, one of her brothers-in-law, Agapito "Butz" Aquino, is a Senator, and another, Paul, the head of Lakas ng Bansa (one of the three main "parties" in her electoral coalition); an uncle-in-law, Herminio Aquino, is a Congressman, as are Emigdio "Ding" Tanjuatco (cousin) and Teresita Aquino-Oreta (sister-in-law).[4] A maternal uncle, Francisco "Komong" Sumulong, is majority floor-leader of the House of Representatives. Nor was Corazón herself, on becoming President, quite the simple housewife of her election broadsheets. For thirteen years she had served as treasurer of the Cojuangco family holding company, which controls a vast financial, agricultural, and urban real-estate empire.[5]

Yet there is a core of truth in President Aquino's claims of March 9, 1987 and this core offers a useful guide to understanding the peculiarities of modern Philippine politics. The "-co" suffix to her maiden name is shared by a significant number of other dynasties within the national oligarchy: Cuenco, Tanjuatco, Tiangco, Chioco, etc. It originates from the Hokkienese *k'o*, a term of respect for older males; and it shows that her family originated among the Chinese mestizos who bloomed economically under the Spanish colonial regime and consolidated their wealth with political power under the Americans.[6] It is the dominance of this group which decisively marks off the Philippines from Spanish America (mestizos frequently in power, but not Chinese mestizos) and the rest of Southeast Asia (Chinese mestizos, indeed any mestizos, removed from political power, with the ambiguous exception of Siam). How did this happen?

---

4. Emigdio is Secretary-General of the Lakas ng Bansa. José "Peping" Cojuangco is Chairman of another main coalition component, the PDP–Laban.

5. *Time*, Jan. 5, 1987.

6. On this stratum the locus classicus remains Edgar Wickberg, *The Chinese in Philippine Life, 1850–1898* (New Haven, Conn.: Yale University Press, 1965).

SPANISH COLONIALISM, THE CHURCH AND THE MESTIZO ELITE

By the time the Spanish arrived to conquer, in the 1560s, the empire of Felipe II had reached its peak, and the islands, named after him, were the last major imperial acquisition. Iberian energies were absorbed in Europe and the Americas. The few Spaniards who did travel on to the Philippines found little on the spot to satiate their avarice. The one substantial source of rapid wealth lay not in mines but in commerce with Imperial China. Manila quickly became the entrepôt for the "galleon trade," by which Chinese silks and porcelains were exchanged for Mexican silver, to be resold, at colossal profit, across the Pacific and eventually in Europe. It was not a business that required much acumen or industry; one needed merely to be in Manila, to have the right political connections, and to work out relationships with the Chinese traders and artisans who flocked to the entrepôt.[7]

The absence of mines, and, until much later, of hacienda-based commercial agriculture, meant not only a concentration of the Spanish in the Manila area, but the lack of any sustained interest in massive exploitation of the indigenous (or imported) populations as a labour force. At the same time, the fact that the pre-Hispanic Philippines (in contrast to Burma, Siam, Cambodia, Vietnam, or Java) lacked any states with substantial military or bureaucratic power meant that relatively little force was required for the initial conquest and for its subsequent consolidation. Small garrisons, scattered here and there, generally sufficed.[8] Hence, *in the provinces*, to a degree unparalleled anywhere in the Americas except Paraguay, Spanish power in the Philippines was mediated through the Church.

The ardently Counter-Reformation clerics were fortunate in finding the great bulk of the indigenous population to be "animists." Buddhism and Hinduism had not reached so far. And though Islam was sweeping in from what today is Indonesia, it had consolidated itself only in parts of Mindanao

---

7. On the galleon trade, see William L. Schurz, *The Manila Galleon*, reprint edn. (New York: Dutton, 1959). Furthermore, responding to pressure from enlightened clerics and officials appalled by the savage extortions of the settlers in the Americas, Madrid attempted to make amends in the Philippines by (fitfully) barring the residence of private Spaniards in the provinces.

8. There is a sizeable literature on the Spanish Philippines, but see especially, James L. Phelan, *The Hispanization of the Philippines: Spanish Aims and Filipino Responses, 1565–1700* (Madison: University of Wisconsin Press, 1959); Nicholas P. Cushner, *Spain in the Philippines: From Conquest to Revolution* (Quezon City: Ateneo de Manila University Press, 1971); Renato Constantino, *The Philippines: A Past Revisited* (Quezon City: Tala, 1975), Parts 1 and 2; and the many impressive essays in Alfred W. McCoy and Ed. C. de Jesus, eds., *Philippine Social History: Global Trade and Local Transformations* (Quezon City: Ateneo de Manila University Press, 1982).

and adjacent southern islands. There it could be contained, if never subdued.[9] Meanwhile a vast proselytization was launched which has resulted in the contemporary Philippines being 90 per cent Christian.[10] (Only in twentieth-century Korea has Christianization in Asia been comparably successful.) The most noteworthy feature of this campaign was that it was conducted, most arduously, not through the medium of Spanish, but through the dozens of local languages. Till the very end of the Spanish regime no more than 5 per cent of the local population had any facility with the colonial language. Spanish never became a pervasive lingua franca, as it did in the Americas, with the result that, certainly in 1900, and to a lesser extent even today, the peasants and fishermen in different parts of the archipelago could not communicate with one another: only their rulers had a common archipelago-wide speech.

Two other features of clerical dominion had lasting consequences for the evolution of Philippine social structure. On the one hand, the quarrelling Orders, parcelled out among the various islands by Felipe II in the sixteenth century, pioneered commercial agriculture in the later eighteenth century, at the prodding of Carlos III's last, enlightened governor, José Basco y Vargas (1777–87). It was they who built what, in effect, were the first great haciendas. But these "conglomerates" remained institutional, rather than family (dynastic) property. The friars might liberally father children on local women, but they could not marry the women, or bequeath property to the progeny. In due course, the conquering Americans would dispossess the friars of their lands, as the eighteenth-century Bourbons had dispossessed the Jesuits; and these

---

9. Drawing on their experiences in the Iberian peninsula, the Spaniards termed these Southeast Asian Muslims "Moors" (*"Moros"*). The name has, after four centuries, stuck. Those Muslims today seeking independence from the Philippines are loosely united in what they call the Moro National Liberation Front. The ghost of Felipe II must be amused.

The best historical-anthropological sources on the "Moros" are: P.G. Gowing, *Muslim-Filipinos—Heritage and Horizon* (Quezon City: New Day, 1979); Cesar Adib Majul, *Muslims in the Philippines* (Quezon City: University of the Philippines Press, 1973), and his *The Contemporary Muslim Movement in the Philippines* (Berkeley: Mizan, 1985); and T.J.S. George, *Revolt in Mindanao: The Rise of Islam in Philippine Politics* (Oxford: Oxford University Press, 1980). Important monographs on two of the major ethno-linguistic groups within the Moro People are Thomas Kiefer, *The Tausug: Violence and Law in a Philippine Muslim Society* (New York: Holt, Rinehart & Winston, 1972); and Reynaldo Clemeña Ileto, *Magindanao, 1860–1888: The Career of Dato Uto of Buayan* (Ithaca, NY: Cornell University, Southeast Asia Program Data Paper no. 32, 1971).

10. The standard work is Horacio de la Costa, *The Jesuits in the Philippines, 1581–1768* (Cambridge, Mass.: Harvard University Press, 1961). But see also Gerald H. Anderson, ed., *Studies in Philippine Church History* (Ithaca, NY: Cornell University Press, 1969); and the brilliantly iconoclastic text of Vicente L. Rafael, *Contracting Colonialism: Translation and Christian Conversion in Tagalog Society under Early Spanish Rule* (Ithaca, NY: Cornell University Press, 1988).

lands would fall like ripe mangoes into the hands of the likes of President Aquino's immediate ancestors.[11] The Philippines thus never had a substantial *criollo hacendado* class.

On the other hand, the Church, at least in its early days, had serious dreams of Christianizing the Celestial Empire. From the start it set eagerly to converting those whom the Spanish generally referred to as *sangleys*.[12] Usually unlucky with the itinerant fathers, they were spectacularly successful with the children fathered on local mothers. Spanish colonial law helped by assigning these children a distinct juridical status as mestizos (in due course the word meant, typically, not the offspring of Spaniards and "natives," but of Chinese and local women). Christianized through their mothers, organized in their own guilds (*gremios*), compelled to avoid political transvestitism by wearing a distinctive costume and coiffure, these children, and their in-marrying further descendants, came to form a distinct stratum of colonial society. In some cases, perhaps only the "-co" suffix to their names betrayed distant celestial origins.

They might, however, have remained a marginal and stigmatized group, had it not been for the services of British imperialism. When Madrid joined in the Seven Years War, London responded, *inter alia*, by occupying Manila in 1762 and holding it for the next two years. The local *sangleys*, frequent victims of Iberian extortion and contempt, rallied to the invaders, who, when they retired, insouciantly left these humble allies to the vengeful mercies of their erstwhile oppressors. Most were then expelled from the Philippines, and further immigration was legally barred for almost a century. Into the vacuum created by the expulsions came the mestizos, who took over much of local trade, and began, following the friars' example, to move into small-scale latifundism.[13]

But they were, world-historically, several generations behind their ladino confrères in the Americas. Among them there were still no great rural magnates, no lawyers, few priests or prominent exporting merchants; above all there was no intelligentsia. The Church, characteristically reactionary,

---

11. In the provincial environs of Manila alone, the clerics had accumulated, by the end of the nineteenth century, over 500,000 acres of land. The basic text on these developments is Dennis Morrow Roth, *The Friar Estates of the Philippines* (Albuquerque: University of New Mexico Press, 1977).

12. From the Hokkienese *sengli*, meaning "trader." It is a lesson for our nationalistic age that neither the Spaniards nor the Hokkienese could yet imagine "Chinese." In this regard, they lagged far behind Amsterdam's United East India Company, the giant transnational of the seventeenth century, which devoted intense penal, juridical, and "sumptuary" effort to forcing targeted groups under its power to realize that they were, after all, *Chinese*.

13. The account in this and the following paragraphs is summarized from Wickberg, *The Chinese in Philippine Life*.

controlled printing and what miserable travesty of educational institutions existed. Hence the great nationalist upheaval that rocked the Americas between 1810 and 1840 had no counterpart in the archipelago until the 1880s.

The nineteenth century, nonetheless, was kind to the mestizos. One might have expected Spaniards to flock there after the loss of the Americas. But the last galleon had sailed in 1811. Spain itself was racked with ceaseless conflict. And Cuba was so much closer, so infinitely richer. New people arrived, but the ones who mattered were not Spaniards but Anglo-Saxons (British and Americans) and, once again, *sangleys*, by now of course "Chinese." In 1834 Manila was fully opened to international trade, and Cebu City and other smaller ports followed in due course; the ban on Chinese immigration was abolished. Chinese discipline, austerity, and energy quickly drove the mestizos out of interisland trade and small-scale urban business. On the other hand, the internationalization of the economy after 1834 offered the mestizos— now a quarter of a million strong in a four-million population—new opportunities in the countryside, in combination with British and American trading houses. These businesses saw the possibilities in full-scale commercialization of Philippine agriculture, and thus provided the necessary capital and commercial outlets to permit the mestizos to become, for the first time, real *hacendados*.

Nothing better illustrates this interplay between Anglo-Saxons, mestizos, and Chinese than the modern history of the island of Negros, today the "sugar island" par excellence of the Philippines. Almost uninhabited when British interests set up the first sugar mill there in 1857, the island's population had increased almost tenfold by the end of the century, and 274 steam mills were in operation.[14] If the British supplied capital, transoceanic transport, and markets, it was mestizos from Panay and Cebu, threatened by the Chinese influx into the port cities of Cebu City and Iloilo, who managed the transfer of the peasant labour needed to grow and process cane. In no time at all, these frontier capitalists turned themselves, on the Spanish model, into "feudal" *hacendados* in the nouveau riche grand style. Thus, in the summer of 1987, when talk of land reform was in the Manila air, Congresswoman Hortensia Starke, one of the great sugar-planters of Western Negros, could tell the newspapers: "Your land is like your most beautiful dress, the one

---

14. See David Steinberg, "Tradition and Response," in John Bresnan, ed., *The Marcos Era and Beyond* (Princeton: Princeton University Press, 1986), p. 44. This text also contains important essays by Wilfredo Arce and Ricardo Abad on "The Social Situation," and by Bernardo Villegas on "The Economic Crisis."

that gives you good luck. If someone takes it from you, he only wants to destabilize you, to undress you."[15]

THE GROWTH OF NATIONAL SENTIMENT

The next step was to get educated. A serious education was not easy to acquire in the colony, where the Church was violently opposed to any inroads of liberalism from Madrid and controlled most local schools. But the mestizos' growing wealth, the internationalization of the economy, and the steamship combined to make it possible for a number of young mestizo males to study in Europe. Quickly termed *ilustrados* (enlightened ones), they created during the 1880s the colony's first real intelligentsia, and began a cultural assault on benighted clericalism and, later, on Spanish political domination.[16] No less significant was the fact that, going to the same schools, reading the same books, writing for the same journals, and marrying each other's sisters and cousins, they inaugurated the self-conscious consolidation of a pan-Philippine (except for the Moro areas) mestizo stratum, where their elders had formed dispersed clusters of provincial caciques. It was these people who, at the very end of the century, began calling themselves "Filipinos," a term which up till then had designated only Spanish creoles.[17]

Wealthy and educated they might now be, but they had no political power. Late nineteenth-century Spain was too feeble economically and too divided politically to cope intelligently with rising mestizo demands. Repression was the order of the day, culminating in the execution in 1896 of the brilliant mestizo polymath José Rizal, whose two great, banned novels, *Noli Me Tangere* and *El Filibusterismo*, mercilessly satirized, in Spanish, clerical reaction, secular misrule, and the frequent opportunism and greed of his own class.[18]

Yet, not unsurprisingly, the inevitable insurrection did not originate with the *ilustrados*. In 1892, Andrés Bonifacio, an impoverished autodidact from

---

15. *The Manila Chronicle*, July 19, 1987. She went on: "To give up the land is to go against everything you have been taught as a child. It is like changing your religion." Another Dragon Lady, coconut *hacendada* Congresswoman Maria Clara Lobregat, wailed: "The land has been there for years and years, and you develop some attachment to it. It's like you have a house with many rooms and you are asked to share the rooms with others."

16. See especially Horacio de la Costa, *The Background of Nationalism and Other Essays* (Manila: Solidaridad, 1965); John N. Schumacher, *The Propaganda Movement: 1880–1895* (Manila: Solidaridad, 1973); Cesar Adib Majul, *Political and Constitutional Ideas of the Philippine Revolution* (Manila: University of the Philippines Press, 1967); and Renato Constantino, *Insight and Foresight* (Quezon City: Foundation for Nationalist Studies, 1977).

17. "These people" included, at the non-Europe-educated edge, Don Melecio Cojuangco.

18. Several English-language translations of these novels exist, the most recent by Soledad Lacson-Locsin (Honolulu: University of Hawaii Press, 1997 and 1998).

the Manila artisanate, formed a secret revolutionary society with the mellifluous Tagalog name of Kataastaasang Kagalanggalang na Katipunan ng
mga Anak ng Bayan (The Highest and Most Respectable Society of the Sons
of the People—Katipunan for short), after the Masonic model.[19] The
Katipunan's title already implied its reach and limitations. The use of
Tagalog, rather than a Spanish understood only by a tiny elite, showed
Bonifacio's intention of appealing to, and mobilizing, the *indio* masses. On the
other hand, in those days Tagalog was spoken only by the masses of Central
and Southern Luzon, and was incomprehensible in Mindanao, the Visayas,
and even Ilocano-speaking northwestern Luzon.[20] In August 1896, Bonifacio
launched an ill-prepared insurrection in Manila, which was quickly suppressed, but the movement spread rapidly in the surrounding provinces, where
leadership was increasingiy taken over by youthful mestizos.[21] Preoccupied by
the revolutionary movement that had broken out in Cuba in February 1895,
the Spanish fairly quickly give up the struggle. In 1899, a Republic of the
Philippines was proclaimed under the leadership of "General" Emilio
Aguinaldo, a youthful *caudillo* from the province of Cavite (who had had
Bonifacio judicially murdered in 1897).[22]

It was, however, a fragile Republic, with more than a few similarities to
Bolívar's abortive Gran Colombía. It had no purchase on the Muslim southwest; parts of the Visayas seemed likely to go their own independent way; and
even in Luzon mestizo leadership was contested by a variety of religious
visionaries and peasant populists carrying on the tradition of Bonifacio's

---

19. The standard nationalist texts on the Katipunan and the revolution it initiated are:
Teodoro A. Agoncillo's *The Revolt of the Masses: The Story of Bonifacio and the Katipunan*
(Quezon City: University of the Philippines, 1956); and *Malolos: The Crisis of the Republic*
(Quezon City: University of the Philippines, 1960). Agoncillo's theses are undermined by
Reynaldo Clemeña Ileto's masterly *Pasyón and Revolution: Popular Movements in the Philippines,
1840–1910* (Quezon City: Ateneo de Manila University Press, 1979), which is unquestionably the
most profound and searching book on late nineteenth-century Philippine history. See also T.M.
Kalaw, *The Philippine Revolution* (Kawilihan, Mandaluyong, Rizal: Jorge B. Vargas Filipiniana
Foundation, 1969).

20. As late as 1960, fifteen years after American-style independence, and thirty years after
it had been decided to promote Tagalog as an official, national lingua franca, less than 45 per
cent of the population understood the language—marginally more than the 40 per cent claiming
to understand English. See the 1960 census data cited in Onofre D. Corpuz, *The Philippines*
(Englewood Cliffs, NJ: Prentice-Hall, 1965), p. 77.

21. See Milagros C. Guerrero, "The Provincial and Municipal Elites of Luzon during the
Revolution, 1898–1902," in McCoy and de Jesus, eds., *Philippine Social History*, pp. 155–90; and
Nick Joaquín, *The Aquinos of Tarlac, An Essay on History as Three Generations*, unexpurgated
version (Manila: Solar, 1986), Part One.

22. Teodoro A. Agoncillo, *The Writings and Trial of Andrés Bonifacio* (Manila: Manila
Bonifacio Centennial Commission, 1963), contains most of the relevant documents in Tagalog
and in English translation.

radicalism.[23] Moreover, the mestizo generals themselves (who included the grandfathers of both Ferdinand Marcos and Benigno Aquino, Jr.) began to follow the pattern of their American forebears, by setting themselves up as independent *caudillos.* Had it not been for William McKinley, one might almost say, the Philippines in the early twentieth century could have fractured into three weak, *caudillo*-ridden states with the internal politics of nineteenth-century Venezuela or Ecuador.

But the McKinley Administration, egged on by William Randolph Hearst, went to war with Spain in April 1898, claiming sympathy with Filipino (and Cuban) revolutionaries. A week later Admiral Dewey destroyed the Spanish fleet in Manila Bay; and by the Treaty of Paris signed in December, the Philippines was sold to the Americans. From that point, "pacification" replaced "sympathy." By 1901 Aguinaldo had surrendered, with most other caciques following suit, though peasant resistance continued in some areas until 1910.

US COLONIZATION AND THE NATIONAL OLIGARCHY

The American colonization changed everything.[24] In the first place, it ensured the political unification of the archipelago by smashing, often with great

---

23. See Ileto's often heart-rending account in *Pasyón and Revolution.*

24. The contrasting fates of the contemporary anticolonial movements in Cuba and the Philippines are instructive. In Cuba, American imperialism, claiming to side with the revolutionaries, ousted the Spaniards, established its own military rule for four years, and then installed a quasi-independent Republic, which, however, came under its full economic control. The island had far less strategic than pecuniary value. With the Philippines it was largely the other way round. Washington's strategists, giddy at their navy's first imperial circumnavigation of the globe, saw in the superb harbour of Manila Bay a perfect trans-Pacific "coaling-station" and jumping-off point for the penetration of China and the outflanking of Japan. These "bases" could only be secured—not least from rival imperialist powers— by political means, i.e. colonization. Ever since, American relations with the Philippines have ultimately centred on military considerations. A succinct account of the thinking behind the American intervention can be found in William J. Pomeroy, *American Neocolonialism: Its Emergence in the Philippines and Asia* (New York: New World, 1970), chapters 1–2. In 1897, Captain Alfred Mahan had been appointed to McKinley's Naval Advisory Board, from which he peddled his imperial sea-power theories to substantial effect.

There is a vast literature on the American era. The classical text is Joseph Ralston Hayden, *The Philippines—A Study in National Development* (New York: Macmillan, 1942). Peter W. Stanley's penetrating and highly entertaining *A Nation in the Making: The Philippines and the United States, 1899–1921* (Cambridge, Mass.: Harvard University Press, 1974) and the later volume he edited, *Reappraising an Empire: New Perspectives on Philippine–American History* (Cambridge, Mass.: Harvard University Press, 1984), are the best modern guides. See also Norman G. Owen, ed., *Compadre Colonialism: Studies on the Philippines under American Rule* (Ann Arbor: University of Michigan, Papers on South and Southeast Asia no. 3, 1971); and Theodore Friend's unintentionally revealing *Between Two Empires: The Ordeal of the Philippines, 1926–1946* (New Haven: Yale University Press, 1965). A useful recent text is Daniel B. Schirmer and Stephen R. Shalom, *The Philippines Reader: A History of Colonialism, Dictatorship and Resistance* (Boston: Southend, 1987), chapters 1–2.

brutality, all opposition.[25] Even the Muslim areas, which Spain had never wholly subdued, were fully subjected to Manila, thereby probably losing their last chance at sovereign independence. Secondly, it vastly improved the economic position of the mestizos. The American regime decided to expropriate much (about 400,000 acres) of the rich agricultural land hitherto held by the Orders, and to put it up for public auction. The mestizos, well-off *hacendados* even in late Spanish times, were the group with the money and the interest to take advantage of this opportunity, and most of the former ecclesiastical property fell into their hands. Still more important, after 1909, by the terms of the Payne–Aldrich Act, the Philippines were enclosed within the American tariff wall, so that their agricultural exports had easy, untaxed access to the world's largest national market—where, in addition, prices, especially for sugar, were often well above world norms.

But it was above all the political innovations of the Americans that created a solid, visible "national oligarchy." The key institutional change was the stage-by-stage creation of a Congress-style bicameral legislature, based, in the lower house at least, on single-district, winner-take-all elections.[26] The new representational system proved perfectly adapted to the ambitions and social geography of the mestizo nouveaux riches. Their economic base lay in hacienda agriculture, not in the capital city. And their provincial fiefdoms were also protected by the country's immense linguistic diversity. They might all speak the elite, "national" language (Spanish, later American), but they also spoke variously Tagalog, Ilocano, Pampango, Cebuano, Ilongo, and a dozen other tongues. In this way competition in any given electoral district was effectively limited, in a pretelevision age, to a handful of rival local caciques. But Congress, which thus offered them guaranteed access to national-level political power, also brought them together in the capital on a

---

25. See Leon Wolff, *Little Brown Brother* (London: Longman, 1960); and Russell Roth, *Muddy Glory: America's "Indian Wars" in the Philippines, 1899–1935* (West Hanover, Mass.: Christopher, 1981). The newly baptized "Filipinos" put up a stout resistance. The repression cost at least 5,000 American lives and 600 million still-golden dollars. Probably the high price, and the "Indian-hunter" mentality of the troops dispatched, accounts for the savagery of the Americans. The killed to wounded ratio among Filipinos was 5 to 1. At least 20,000 died in action, and a further 200,000 from war-related famine and pestilence. General "Jake" Smith, assigned to pacify recalcitrant Samar, told his men: "I want no prisoners. I wish you to kill and burn; the more you burn and kill the better it will please me." Samar was to be turned into "a howling wilderness." To the Fairfield, Maine, *Journal*, Sergeant Howard McFarlane of the 43rd Infantry wrote: "On Thursday, March 29, [1900] eighteen of my company killed seventy-five nigger bolomen and ten of the nigger gunners . . . When we find one that is not dead, we have bayonets." Wolff, *Little Brown Brother*, pp. 360 and 305.

26. But with a highly restricted, property-based franchise. Even on the eve of World War II, only about 14 per cent of the potential electorate was permitted to vote.

regular basis. There, more than at any previous time, they got to know one another well in a civilized "ring" sternly refereed by the Americans. They might dislike one another, but they went to the same receptions, attended the same churches, lived in the same residential areas, shopped in the same fashionable streets, had affairs with each other's wives, and arranged marriages between each other's children. They were for the first time forming a self-conscious *ruling* class.[27]

The timing of American colonization also had a profound formative influence on the emerging oligarchy and its style of rule. The America of 1900–1930 was the America of Woodrow Wilson's lamented "congressional government." The metropole had no powerful centralized professional bureaucracy; office was still heavily a matter of political patronage; corrupt urban machines and venal court-house rural cliques were still pervasive; and the authority of presidents, except in time of war, was still restricted. Hence, unlike all the other modern colonial regimes in twentieth-century Southeast Asia, which operated through huge, autocratic, white-run bureaucracies, the American authorities in Manila, once assured of the mestizos' self-interested loyalty to the motherland, created only a minimal civil service, and quickly turned over most of its component positions to the natives. In 1903, Filipinos held just under half of the 5,500 or so positions in this civil service. By the end of the "Filipinizing" governor-generalship of (Democrat) Francis Harrison in 1921, the proportion had risen to 90 per cent (out of a mere 14,000 jobs); and by the mid-1930s Americans held only 1 per cent of civilian bureaucratic posts, most of them in the educational field.[28] (American power depended on military dominance and the tariff.) As in the United States, civil servants frequently owed their employment to legislator patrons, and up to the end of the American era the civilian machinery of state remained weak and divided.

The new oligarchs quickly understood how the Congressional system could serve to increase their power. As early as Harrison's time, the Americans acquiesced in the plundering of the Central Bank of the

---

27. One gets a nice close-up feel for this change in Joaquín's *The Aquinos of Tarlac*, pp. 155–98.

28. See Teodoro A. Agoncillo, *A Short History of the Philippines* (New York: Mentor, 1969), p. 169; and David Wurfel, "The Philippines," in George McT. Kahin, ed., *Governments and Politics of Southeast Asia*, second edn. (Ithaca, NY: Cornell University Press, 1964), pp. 679–777, at pp. 689–90.

Next door, in the Dutch East Indies, the colonial state of the 1930s had about 250,000 officials on its payroll, 90 per cent of them "natives." See my "Old State, New Society: Indonesia's New Order in Comparative Historical Perspective," *Journal of Asian Studies*, 42 (May 1983), p. 480.

Philippines. House Speaker Sergio Osmeña, Sr., and his friends helped themselves to huge, virtually free loans for financing the construction of sugar centrals, and cheerfully ignored the subsequent bankrupting of the bank of issue. In a more general sense, Congressional control of the purse, and of senior judicial appointments, taught the oligarchy that the "rule of law," provided it made and managed this law, was the firmest *general* guarantee of its property and political hegemony. (As we shall see, it was Marcos's suspension of the "rule of law" that aroused the alarm and hostility of significant portions of the oligarchy in the 1970s and early 1980s.)

One final feature of the American political system is worth emphasizing: the huge proliferation of provincial and local elective offices—in the absence of an autocratic territorial bureaucracy. From very early on mestizo caciques understood that these offices, in the right hands, could consolidate their local political fiefdoms. Not unexpectedly, the right hands were those of family and friends. Brothers, uncles, and cousins for the senior posts, sons and nephews for the junior ones.[29] Here is the origin of the "political dynasties"—among them the Aquinos and Cojuangcos—which make Filipino politics so spectacularly different from those of any other country in Southeast Asia.

Those were palmy days. But after 1930 the clouds began to gather. As the Depression struck the United States, Washington came under increasing pressure from trade unions and farm organizations (who opposed the influx of Filipino labour and agricultural products) to impose independence on the colony. Though the caciques could not decently say so in public, independence was the last thing they desired, precisely because it threatened the source of their huge wealth: access to the American market. Besides, they had now switched from Spanish to English, and their children were going to school in Manhattan and Boston. And they lacked the monarchical residues which, suitably transformed, underpinned the imagined "national traditions" of Khmer, Burmese, and Indonesians: the mestizos had no Angkor, Pagan, or Borobudur at their service. It was thus with real reluctance that in 1935 they accepted Commonwealth status. The one evident plus was the initiation of a Filipino chief executive. The urbane, rascally mestizo, Manuel Quezon, became Commonwealth president.[30]

---

29. Such policies did not always guarantee harmony. Members of these cacique dynasties frequently quarrelled and competed with each other in local elections. But it can safely be said that an oligarchy is truly in place when rulers and opposition leaders, ins and outs, both come from the same families.

30. See Friend, *Between Two Empires*, chapters 3–11, for an exhaustive account. The role of President Aquino's father-in-law is recounted in chatty detail in Joaquín's *The Aquinos of Tarlac*, chapters 3–5.

THE JAPANESE OCCUPATION AND AFTER

Six years later, in December 1941, the armies of Imperial Japan struck south. In a matter of weeks most of the Americans were sent packing, including General Douglas MacArthur, who carted President Quezon and Vice-President Osmeña along with him.[31] The rest of the oligarchy (one or two celebrated exceptions aside) bustled to collaborate with the invaders. Among the most prominent of these collaborators were Corazón Aquino's father-in-law (who became Speaker of the Occupation Assembly and Director-General of the pro-Japanese "mass organization" Kalibapi) and the father of her Vice-President (Don José Laurel, Sr., who in 1943 became President of the puppet republic then inaugurated by Tokyo).[32]

But collaboration could do nothing to save the hacienda-based export economy. Japan would permit no exports to America, and American bombers and warships ensured, after 1942, that few crops would reach Japan. The treasured "rule of law" began to break down as anti-Japanese guerrilla bands, sometimes led by the small socialist and communist parties, expanded in the remoter rural areas, as inflation soared, and as Japanese exactions increased. Former tenants and landless labourers were emboldened to squat on hacienda lands and grow, not sugar, but crops needed for their everyday survival. Many refused now to pay the old brutal rents, and had the insolence to threaten the bailiffs who demanded them. Above all in the Central Luzon of the Cojuangcos and Aquinos, where rural poverty and exploitation were most acute, such peasants joined hands with the guerrillas in forming the Hukbalahap armies which harassed the Japanese and assassinated such collaborators as they could reach.[33] Unsurprisingly, many of the oligarchs

---

31. MacArthur had longstanding Philippine connections. His father, General Arthur MacArthur, had been second-in-command of the original American expeditionary force, and replaced his odious superior, General Elwell Otis, in May 1900. He stayed in power till July 4, 1901, when "civilian rule" replaced that of the soldiers. The MacArthur family also had substantial business investments in the archipelago.

32. For some amusing glimpses of these stately ruffians at work, see chapter 5 of Renato and Letizia Constantino, *The Philippines: The Continuing Past* (Quezon City: Foundation for Nationalist Studies, 1978). The standard text on the occupation remains David Joel Steinberg, *Philippine Collaboration in World War II* (Ann Arbor: University of Michigan Press, 1967). But see also Hernando J. Abaya, *Betrayal in the Philippines* (New York: A.A. Wyn, 1946); and Alfred McCoy's essay in the volume he edited entitled *Southeast Asia under Japanese Occupation* (New Haven: Yale University, Southeast Asia Studies, Monograph Series no. 22, 1980).

33. The classic text on the peasant resistance during the Japanese occupation, and its relationships with socialist and communist cadres, is Benedict J. Kerkvliet, *The Huk Rebellion* (Berkeley: University of California Press, 1977). See also Eduardo Lachica, *The Huks: Philippine*

abandoned their haciendas to their unlucky bailiffs and retreated to Manila, where they turned their experienced hands to war-profiteering.[34]

One might have expected the returning Americans to punish the oligarchs for their collaboration with the enemy. Senior officials in Washington indeed made noises to this effect. But the on-the-spot Liberator was, of course MacArthur, who had close personal and business ties with the pre-war oligarchy, and who, like Lyautey in Morocco, enjoyed playing lordly proconsul to native houseboys.[35] Quezon having meanwhile met his incautious Maker, MacArthur in 1946 arranged the election of his old mestizo friend (and prominent collaborator) Manuel Roxas as first president of the now sovereign Republic of the Philippines.[36]

Roxas had only two years in power before he joined Quezon, but they were exceptionally productive years. An amnesty was arranged for all "political prisoners" (mainly fellow oligarchs held on charges of collaboration). In 1947, an agreement was signed permitting the United States to retain control of its twenty-three (large and small) land, sea, and air bases for a further ninety-nine years (this was what, as in 1900, most mattered to Washington).[37] And the Constitution of 1935 was so amended as to give American citizens "parity" access to the resources of the newly sovereign Republic (in return for which the oligarchy was granted continuing access, for a defined period, to the protected American market.)[38] There was an additional bonus in this move, since it guaranteed activation for the Philippines of the Tydings Rehabilitation Act, which offered $620 million to those Americans and Filipinos who could demonstrate that they had lost a minimum of $500 as a

---

Agrarian Society in Revolt (New York: Praeger, 1971); and "Documents—The Peasant War in the Philippines," *Philippine Social Sciences and Humanities Review*, 23: 2–4 (June–Dec. 1958), pp. 375–436. (The documents, originally composed in 1946, offer valuable data on land concentration, peasant landlessness, tenancy rates, and exploitation of sharecroppers.) Note, in addition, the remarkable special issue of *Solidarity*, No. 102 (1985), devoted mainly to retrospective discussion of the Huk rebellion.

34. See Resil B. Mojares, *The Man Who Would be President: Serging Osmeña and Philippine Politics* (Cebu: Maria Cacao, 1986), for example. This excellent text shows how while father Sergio Osmeña, Sr., was serving in Washington as vice-president in exile, son Sergio, Jr., was making money hand over fist supplying the Japanese occupation regime in Manila.

35. See William Manchester's edifying *American Caesar: Douglas MacArthur, 1880–1964* (Boston: Little, Brown, 1978).

36. Quezon died in the United States in 1944, and was succeeded, ad interim, by his vice-president Sergio Osmeña, Sr. MacArthur had no time for Osmeña, whom he regarded as old, tired, and too Spanish in personal style.

37. Wurfel, "The Philippines," p. 761.

38. Stuck with the Constitution's quorum requirements for amendments, Roxas found no way to achieve the necessary change except by disqualifying, on charges of terrorism and electoral fraud, those opposition Congressmen representing areas dominated by the Hukbalahap. See Kerkvliet, *The Huk Rebellion*, pp. 150–51.

result of the war.[39] (Since the average annual per capita income of Filipinos was then a quarter of this sum, the major Filipino beneficiaries of Senator Tydings's generosity were the caciques.)

The next aim was to restore fully the pre-war agrarian and political order. For three basic reasons this goal proved difficult to achieve. First was the price of independence itself: removal of the American ringmaster for domestic political competition, severe weakening of the state's capacity for centralized deployment of violence,[40] a fisc no longer externally guaranteed, and a war-ravaged and near-bankrupt economy. Second was the appearance, in Central Luzon at least, of an emboldened peasantry backed by armed Hukbalahap forces, which, denied access to constitutional participation by Roxas's manoeuvres, had little reason to make accommodations. Third was a rapid expansion of the suffrage that UN membership, in those innocent days, made it impossible to deny.

THE HEYDAY OF CACIQUE DEMOCRACY

Hence it was that in the last year of Roxas's life the Philippines saw the first conspicuous appearance of the country's now notorious "private armies." Drawn from lumpen elements in both Manila and the countryside, these armed gangs, financed by their *hacendado* masters, terrorized illegal squatters, peasant unions, and left-wing political leaders, with the aim of restoring uncontested cacique rule.[41] The term "warlord" entered the contemporary Filipino political vocabulary. Unsurprisingly, the new warlords found that their private armies were also highly functional for a now unrefereed electoral politics. The presidential elections of 1949, won by Roxas's vice-presidential successor Elpidio Quirino,[42] were not merely corrupt in the pre-war style, but also extremely bloody and fraudulent: not so much because of central

---

39. See Friend, *Between Two Empires*, pp. 258–60.

40. The Philippine Army was still small, and "second army" in character. In other words, it belonged to that array of mercenary forces, racially segmented, poorly armed and trained, and deployed for "internal security" purposes, that we find throughout the late colonial world. (After independence, some of their former NCOs—such as Idi Amin, Sangoulé Lamizana, Suharto, Jean-Baptiste Bokassa—became colonels and generals in an unhappy truce.) The contrast is with the "first armies" of the industrial world, including that of the Soviet Union, which were self-armed, officered by military-academy graduates, technologically sophisticated, amply financed, and capable of substantial external aggression.

41. More than anything else it was the ravages of the private armies that precipitated the open Hukbalahap insurrection against the state in 1948. See Kerkvliet, *The Huk Rebellion*, chapter 5, for a fine account.

42. His defeated opponent was none other than fellow-oligarch Don José Laurel, Sr., president of the wartime puppet republic.

management, as because of the discrepancy between state power and cacique ambitions under conditions of popular suffrage and acute class antagonism.[43] (Characteristic of the time was what Nick Joaquín, the country's best-known writer, called the "bloody fiefdom" of the Lacson dynasty in the sugar-planter paradise of Western Negros. Manila was virtually impotent vis-à-vis Governor Rafael Lacson's murderous "special police" and "civilian guards."[44])

This was not what the Americans had bargained for. Besides, China had just been "lost," Vietnam seemed likely to go the same way, and major communist insurrections had broken out in neighbouring Malaya and Burma. Colonel Edward Lansdale was dispatched to restore order through the agency of Quirino's Secretary of Defence, Ramon Magsaysay, one of the few prominent politicians of the era who did not have cacique origins. Thanks to a mere million dollars in military and other aid, the physical isolation of the Philippines, the restricted Luzon base of the Hukbalahap, and the errors of the Huk leaders themselves,[45] Lansdale prevailed. By 1954, the Huk rebellion had been crushed; thousands of impoverished Luzon peasants transmigrated to "empty" Mindanao[46] (where they soon came into violent conflict with the local Muslims); and Magsaysay manoeuvred into the presidency.[47]

The period 1954–72 can be regarded as the full heyday of cacique

---

43. It is probably a general rule that *private* armies appear only under such conditions. The reappearance of these armies in President Aquino's presidency indicates the weakness of the state's army and a general social polarization.

44. Proximate ancestors of today's so-called "vigilantes." See *The Aquinos of Tarlac*, pp. 221 ff.

45. Characteristically, even the Communist Party of the Philippines was vulnerable to caciquism. Among its top leaders in the late 1940s were Casto Alejandrino, scion of a large landowning family, and the brothers Lava, intellectuals of landowning origins (an uncle had been a colonel in Aguinaldo's Revolutionary Army). They eventually quarrelled violently with the Hukbalahap Supremo, Luis Taruc, who came from a family of tenant-farmers (both his grandfathers had been sergeants in the Katipunan Army). No real surprise that the well-born stood to the militant Left of the commoner. This information comes from the extraordinary, recent joint interview conducted by *Solidarity* editor F. Sionil José, with Casto Alejandrino, Jesus Lava, Luis Taruc, and Fred Saulo, and printed in the above-cited 1985 issue of *Solidarity*.

46. See the valuable, if ingenuous, text by former CIA officer Alvin Scaff, *The Philippine Answer to Communism* (Stanford: Stanford University Press, 1955), chapters 3–6 especially.

47. Declassified documents cited in Raymond Bonner's *Waltzing with a Dictator: The Marcoses and the Making of American Policy* (New York: Times, 1987), give a nice picture of the Lansdale–Magsaysay relationship. During the 1953 election campaign Lansdale insisted that all Magsaysay's speeches be written by a CIA operative masquerading as a *Christian Science Monitor* correspondent. When he discovered that the candidate had had the impudence on one occasion to use a Filipino speech-writer, the enraged Quiet American walked into Magsaysay's office and knocked him out (pp. 39–40).

democracy in the Philippines.[48] The oligarchy faced no serious domestic challenges. Access to the American market was declining as postindependence
tariff barriers slowly rose, but this setback was compensated for by full access
to the state's financial instrumentalities. Under the guise of promoting economic independence and import-substitution industrialization, exchange
rates were manipulated, monopolistic licences parcelled out, huge, cheap,
often unrepaid bank loans passed around, and the national budget frittered
away in pork-barrel legislation.[49] Some of the more enterprising dynasties
diversified into urban real estate, hotels, utilities, insurance, the mass media,
and so forth. The press, owned by rival cacique families, was famously free.[50]
The reconsolidated, but decentralized, power of the oligarchy is nicely
demonstrated by the fact that this press exposed every possible form of corruption and abuse of power (except for those of each paper's own
proprietors), but, in the words of historian and political scientist Onofre
Corpuz: "Nobody in the Philippines has ever heard of a successful prosecution for graft."[51] It was in these golden times that Corazón Aquino's father,
Don José Cojuangco, acquired 7,000 hectares of the 10,300-hectare Hacienda
Luisita in Tarlac, and turned its management over to his energetic son-in-law
Benigno "Ninoy" Aquino, Jr.[52]

But cacique democracy contained within itself the seeds of its own decay,
and these began visibly sprouting towards the end of the 1960s.
Uncontrolled and parasitic plundering of state and private resources tilted
the Philippines on its long plunge from being the most "advanced" capitalist society in Southeast Asia in the 1950s to being the most depressed and

---

48. It was the time when Ferdinand Marcos and Corazón's husband, Benigno "Ninoy"
Aquino, Jr., came to national prominence.

49. See Frank H. Golay, *The Philippines: Public Policy and National Economic Development*
(Ithaca, NY: Cornell University Press, 1961). See also the Villegas chapter in Bresnan, ed., *The
Marcos Era*, especially pp. 150–55. This well-intentioned economist puts it modestly thus: "If one
were to look for a political explanation of this flawed economic policy, he could find it in the
imperfections of a fledgling democracy in which power was still concentrated in the hands of the
former landed gentry who turned into manufacturing entrepreneurs during the fifties and sixties.
The Philippine legislature, through which tariff, fiscal, and monetary reforms had to pass, was
dominated by groups that represented the very industrial sector that had been pampered by over-
protection."

50. The internationally celebrated symbol of this freedom was the muck-raking *Philippines
Free Press*. It is less well known that the Locsin family which ran it was violently opposed to any
unionization of its staff, and used brazenly brutal methods to thwart it.

51. *The Philippines*, p. 86.

52. See Joaquín, *The Aquinos of Tarlac*, pp. 273–86, for a sly account. Luisita is certainly the
most famous hacienda in the Philippines today, and still, pending land reform, in the hands of
the Cojuangcos. Don José acquired it from a French-financed, Spanish-managed company,
which became discouraged by persistent "labour unrest." In the mid-1950s, its sugar central ser-
viced 1,000 sugar-planters and its annual production was valued at 18 million pesos.

indigent in the 1980s. By the end of the golden era, 5 per cent of the country's income-earners received, probably, about 50 per cent of total income. At the same time, over 70 per cent of state revenues came from regressive sales and excise taxes, and a mere 27.5 per cent from income taxes—largely paid by foreign corporations.[53] Combined with a characteristically tropical Catholic birthrate of over 3 per cent (which since 1850 had increased the islands' population eightfold), the result was a massive pauperization of the unprivileged.[54]

FERDINAND MARCOS: THE SUPREME CACIQUE

Cacique democracy in the independent Philippines also led to secular changes in the operation of the political system. The oligarchs more and more followed Chairman Mao's advice to walk on two legs. Manila was where the President resided and where Congress met, where pork-barrel funds were dealt out, where licences and loans were secured, where educational institutions proliferated, and where imported entertainments flourished. The dynasties began leaving their haciendas in the hands of sons-in-law and bailiffs and moving into palatial new residential complexes on the outskirts of the old capital. Forbes Park was the first, and still the most celebrated, of these *beaux quartiers*, which remain sociologically unique in Southeast Asia. Elsewhere in the region luxurious houses are jumbled together with the dwellings of the poor.[55] But the golden ghetto of Forbes Park was policed, as a complex, by armed security guards; access even to its streets required the production of identification papers.

This partial move to Manila combined with demographic increase and the postwar expansion of the suffrage to monetarize political life. It was less and less possible to win elections, even provincial elections, on a forelock-tugging basis. The costs of campaigning increased exponentially in the 1960s, not least because the period saw the renewed growth of the private armies. In contrast to the late 1940s, these armed groups were now deployed mainly in

---

53. Cf. Corpuz, *The Philippines*, pp. 77 and 105.

54. The Marcos era did not initiate this process, merely accelerated it. Today 70 per cent of the population lives below the World Bank's lordly poverty line. A recent article in the *Philippine Inquirer* (Jan. 17, 1988) offers instructive comparative demographic data on Bangkok and Manila. Bangkok has 25 births per thousand population, and suffers 17.2 postnatal deaths among every 1,000 babies born alive; the figures given for Manila are 63.9 and 69.5 respectively.

55. I remember that in the Jakarta of the late 1960s naked slum children played football in the mud thirty yards from the house of a Supreme Court judge. Some of Bangkok's wealthiest families' homes are still located a stone's throw from stinking, cess-pool-infested squatter clusters. But the tendencies are in Manila's direction as new, segregated suburbs develop.

intraoligarchy competition.[56] Corazón Aquino's husband was conforming to general practice in the late 1960s when he campaigned for a senatorial seat in a black Mercedes ringed with Armalite-toting bodyguards.[57] With splendid, grumbling insouciance, Senator Sergio "Serging" Osmeña, Jr., on losing the 1969 presidential race to Ferdinand Marcos, complained: "We were outgunned, outgooned, and outgold."[58] By then, at 40 per 100,000 head of population, the Philippines had one of the highest murder rates in the world.

So the stakes slowly grew, and American-era inhibitions slackened. The crux was the presidency, which always had the potentiality of dislocating cacique democracy. We noted earlier that the stability of the system, and the solidarity of the oligarchy, depended on the Congress, which offered roughly equal room at the top for all the competing provincial dynasties. The one-man office of president was not, however, divisible, and came to seem, in the era of independence, a unique prize. The shrewder, older oligarchs had foreseen possible trouble and had borrowed from the United States the legal provision that no president could serve for more than two terms—so that the office could sedately circulate within the charmed circle. But it was only a matter of time before someone would break the rules and try to set himself up as Supreme Cacique for Life. The spread of military juntas and one-party dictatorial regimes throughout the Third World in the 1960s made a break of this kind seem more normal: indeed it could even be justified opportunistically as a sign of liberation from "western" ideological shackles.

The final destabilizing factor was education. As noted earlier, in Spanish times educational facilities were extremely limited, and the only "national" language available was Spanish, to which, however, no more than 5 per cent of the indigenous population had access. Secular, twentieth-century American imperialism was a different sort of beast. Immensely confident of Anglo-

---

56. The best structural accounts of the system's entropy remain Thomas Nowak and Kay Snyder, "Clientelist Politics in the Philippines: Integration or Instability?" *American Political Science Review*, 68 (Sept. 1974), pp. 1147–70; and their "Economic Concentration and Political Change in the Philippines," in Benedict J. Kerkvliet, ed., *Political Change in the Philippines: Studies of Local Politics Preceding Martial Law* (Honolulu: University of Hawaii Press, 1974), pp. 153–241.

57. *New York Times*, Aug. 9, 1967. The same account describes Cojuangco financing of Aquino's political career, and the heavily guarded family compound (six California-style ranch houses grouped around a colossal swimming-pool)—a useful antidote to the current martyrology surrounding the assassinated senator.

58. *New York Times*, Nov. 16, 1969. Marcos spent other people's money so lavishly in this campaign that inflation increased 18 per cent, the blackmarket value of the peso fell 50 per cent, and he had to ask for a $100 million prepayment of military-base rent from Washington. Ibid., Dec. 6, 1969. It surely helped his case that he had contributed $1,000,000 to Nixon's 1968 election campaign (according to Rafael Salas, his executive secretary from 1966 to 1969, as cited in Bonner, *Waltzing with a Dictator*, p. 141).

Saxon world hegemony and the place of English as the language of capitalism and modernity, the colonial regime effortlessly extruded Spanish[59] and so expanded an English-language school system that by 1940 the Philippines had the highest literacy rate in Southeast Asia.[60] After independence, the oligarchy, like other Third World oligarchies, found that the simplest way of establishing its nationalist credentials was to expand cheap schooling. By the early 1960s university degrees were no longer a ruling class near-monopoly.

The huge expansion of English-language education produced three distinct, politically significant, new social groups. Smallest was a radical intelligentsia, largely of bourgeois and petty-bourgeois urban origins, and typically graduates of the University of the Philippines. Among them was Nur Misuari, who in the later 1960s formed the Moro National Liberation Front in the Muslim southwest. Still better known was José Maria Sison, who broke away from the decrepit post-Huk communist party to form his own, and, borrowing from the Great Helmsman, founded the New People's Army which is today a nationwide presence and the major antagonist of the oligarchy.[61] (The spread of English, and, later, of "street Tagalog," in nationalist response to American hegemony, has made possible an archipelago-wide *popular* communication—below the oligarchy—that was inconceivable in the era of Bonifacio or the Hukbalahap.)

Next largest in size was a *bien-pensant* prototechnocracy, which also included graduates from American universities. Drawn from much the same social strata as the radical intelligentsia, it was enraged less by the injustices of cacique democracy than by its dilettantism, venality, and technological backwardness. This group also deeply resented its own powerlessness. When Marcos eventually declared martial law in 1972 and proclaimed his New Democracy, it flocked to his standard, believing its historic moment had come. It stayed loyal to him till the early 1980s, and long remained crucial to

---

59. Virtually no Filipinos today speak Spanish, but a certain sham-aristocratic aura still surrounds the *idea* of Iberian culture. Older members of the oligarchy prefer to be addressed as Don and Doña. Ideologically the hacienda remains un-Americanized. And children are still overwhelmingly baptized with Spanish names, even if later they acquire American or local nicknames (Juan "Johnny" Enrile, Benigno "Ninoy" Aquino).

60. According to Wurfel, *The Philippines*, pp. 691–2, by the early 1920s the funds spent on education had reached nearly half of annual government expenditures at all levels. Between 1903 and 1939 literacy rates doubled, from 20 to 49 per cent. By the latter date nearly 27 per cent of the population could speak English, a percentage larger than for any single local tongue, including Tagalog.

61. The NPA's top leadership was originally composed largely of University of the Philippines graduates. The same is true today, if to a lesser extent. This leadership appears still to think in English, to judge from the fact that many key party documents have no Tagalog versions.

his credibility with Washington planners, the World Bank and the IMF, and foreign modernizers all and sundry.

Largest of all—if not that large—was a wider urban bourgeois and petty-bourgeois constituency: middle-level civil servants, doctors, nurses, teachers, businessmen, shopkeepers, and so on. In its political and moral outlook it can perhaps be compared with the Progressives (definitely not the Populists) of the United States in the period 1890–1920. In the 1960s it made its political debut in campaigns for honesty in government, urban renewal, crackdowns on machine and warlord politics, and the legal emancipation of municipalities and the new suburbs. As might be expected, this group was both anti-oligarchy and anti-popular in orientation. Had it not been English-educated, and had not President Kennedy secured a major change in the American immigration laws, it might have played a major role in Philippine politics in the 1970s and 1980s. But these factors offered it enticing alternatives, such that, by the mid-1980s, well over a million Filipinos (mainly from this stratum) had emigrated across the Pacific, most of them for good.[62] This bourgeois haemorrhage in the short run weakened a significant political competitor for the oligarchy, but in the longer run cost it an important political ally—one reason why the Aquino government has so little room for manoeuvre.

The Marcos regime, which began to entrench itself long before the declaration of martial law in 1972, was an instructively complex hybrid.[63] From

62. "Before the revolution," so to speak, by comparison with the migration, "after the revolution," of comparable strata from Cuba, China, and Vietnam. There are instructive contrasts with other parts of Southeast Asia. The Suharto regime in Indonesia is far bloodier and more efficiently repressive than that of Marcos, but emigration has been small. Holland has a low absorptive capacity, and after 1945 Indonesians had abandoned Dutch for "Indonesian"— neither of them world languages. Burma (till 1963) and Malaysia were English-educated, but since the late 1950s the regime in London has been increasingly hostile to colonial immigration.

63. There is no satisfactory overall study of the Marcos regime, *as a regime*. But there are any number of useful texts on its leading personalities and its policies. Bonner's book is not always accurate, but it is good, and extremely funny, on the Marcoses' relationships with assorted American presidents and proconsuls. Otherwise, see: Gary Hawes, *The Philippine State and the Marcos Regime: The Politics of Export* (Ithaca, NY: Cornell University Press, 1987); David A. Rosenberg, ed., *Marcos and Martial Law in the Philippines* (Ithaca, NY: Cornell University Press, 1979); Alfred W. McCoy, *Priests on Trial* (Victoria: Penguin, 1984); R.J. May and Francisco Nemenzo, eds., *The Philippines After Marcos* (New York: St. Martin's, 1985); Walden Bello *et al.*, *Development Debacle: The World Bank in the Philippines* (San Francisco: Institute for Food Development Policy, 1982); Walden Bello and Severina Rivera, eds., *The Logistics of Repression: The Role of U.S. Assistance in Consolidating the Martial Law Regime in the Philippines* (Washington, DC: Friends of the Filipino People, 1977); Filemon Rodriguez, *The Marcos Regime: Rape of the Nation* (New York: Vintage, 1985); Stephen R. Shalom, *The U.S. and the Philippines: A Study of Neocolonialism* (Philadelphia: Institute for the Study of Human Issues, 1981); Robert B. Stauffer, "The Political Economy of a Coup: Transnational Linkages and Philippine Political Response," *Journal of Peace Research*, 11:3 (1974), pp. 161–77; Carolina G. Hernandez, "The Role of the Military in Contemporary Philippine Society," *Diliman Review* (Jan.–Feb. 1984), pp. 16–24; and the volume edited by Bresnan, cited above.

one point of view, Don Ferdinand can be seen as the Master Cacique or Master Warlord, in that he pushed the destructive logic of the old order to its natural conclusion. In place of dozens of privatized "security guards," a single privatized National Constabulary; in place of personal armies, a personal Army; instead of pliable local judges, a client Supreme Court; instead of a myriad pocket and rotten boroughs, a pocket or rotten country, managed by cronies, hitmen, and flunkies.

But from another viewpoint, he was an original; partly because he was highly intelligent, partly because, like his grotesque wife, he came from the lower fringes of the oligarchy. In any case, he was the first elite Filipino politician who saw the possibilities of reversing the traditional flow of power. All his predecessors had lived out the genealogy of mestizo supremacy—from private wealth to state power, from provincial bossism to national hegemony. But almost from the beginning of his presidency in 1965, Marcos had moved mentally out of the nineteenth century, and understood that in our time wealth serves power, and that the key card is the state. Manila's Louis Napoléon.

MARCOS SETTLES IN

He started with the army, which until then had been politically insignificant.[64] The size of the armed forces was rapidly increased, the amplitude of its budget multiplied, and its key posts allotted to officers from the Ilocano-speaking northwestern Luzon from which Marcos himself originated. The final decision to declare martial law, for which plans had been prepared months in advance, was taken in concert with the military high command—Corazón's cousin Eduardo "Danding" Cojuangco and Defence Secretary Juan "Johnny" Ponce Enrile being the only civilian co-conspirators.[65] The civil service followed, particularly that ambitious sector identified earlier as candidate-technocrats. The state would save the country from what Marcos identified as its prime enemies—the communists and the oligarchy.

Marcos exploited state, rather than hacienda, power in two other

---

64. Following American constitutional practice, all military appointments at the rank of colonel or above had to be approved by Congress. Ambitious officers, aware of how bread is buttered, cosied up to powerful Congressional politicians, who exploited their position to build personal cliques within the military by determining the territorial positioning of favoured clients. Come election time, it was always handy to have the local commandant in one's pocket. The most substantial study of the Philippine military remains Carolina G. Hernandez, "The Extent of Civilian Control of the Military in the Philippines, 1946–1976" (Ph.D. thesis, State University of New York at Buffalo, 1979). It is especially interesting on Marcos's manipulation of budgets, promotions, and educational ideology to secure the installation of the dictatorship.

65. Bonner's account, based on declassified American documents, is the most detailed. *Waltzing with a Dictator*, chapters 5–6.

instructive ways. The first was to deal with the Americans, the second with his fellow oligarchs.

He understood, more clearly than anyone else—including the Filipino Left—that for Washington the Philippines were like Cyprus for London. The huge bases at Subic and Clark Field had nothing to do with the defence of the Philippines as such, and everything to do with maintaining American imperial power along the Pacific Rim. It followed that Manila should treat them as luxury properties, for the leasing of which ever more exorbitant rentals could be charged.[66] So too the Philippine army. Raymond Bonner's book, *Waltzing with a Dictator*, amply documents how Marcos, at considerable personal profit, rented a (non-combattant) army engineering battalion to Lyndon Johnson, who in 1965 was busy hiring Asian mercenaries to bolster the "international crusade" image desired for the American intervention in Vietnam. Next to the South Koreans, he got, mercenary for mercenary, the best price in Asia. (In this effort he had considerable help from his egregious wife, who splashed her way into high-level Washington circles in a way that no Dragon Lady had done since the shimmering days of Madame Chiang Kai-shek.[67]) But he also had the imaginative insolence to try to do to the Americans what they had so long been accustomed to doing to the Filipinos. According to Bonner, Marcos contributed a million dollars to each of Richard Nixon's presidential election campaigns—with, of course, "state money"—thereby joining that select group of Third World tyrants (Chiang Kai-shek, Pak Chung Hee, Reza Pahlavi, Rafael Trujillo, and Anastasio Somoza) who played an active role in the politics of the metropole.[68]

As far as the oligarchy was concerned, Marcos went straight for its jugular—the "rule of law." From the very earliest days, Marcos used his plenary martial-law powers to advise all oligarchs who dreamt of opposing or supplanting him that property was not power, since at a stroke of the martial pen it ceased to be property.[69] The Lopez dynasty (based in Iloilo) was abruptly deprived of its mass-media empire and its control of Manila's main supplier

---

66. Subic and Clark Field are the two bases that get the most publicity, but the base-complex as a whole includes, at one extreme, the ultra-secret San Miguel electronic eavesdropping facility, and at the other, the ultra-open Fort John Hay pleasure-dome. The latter, situated just outside the popular mountain resort of Baguio, technically belongs to the American Air Force, but in practice to Manila's rich. It is composed of almost nothing but swimming-pools, golf courses, tennis courts, bowling-alleys, movie halls, diners, dance clubs, and so on. Anyone can enjoy these amenities if they can pay in dollars. I recently visited the "base," and in the course of several hours' perambulations met not a single American, military or civilian, but saw hundreds of prosperous Filipinos amusing themselves.

67. Ibid., chapter 3.

68. Ibid., pp. 140–41.

69. The best account is Hawes, *The Philippine State*.

of electricity.[70] The 500-hectare Hacienda Osmeña was put up for "land-reform" somewhat later on.[71] There was no recourse, since the judiciary was fully cowed and the legislature packed with allies and hangers-on. But Marcos had no interest in upsetting the established social order. Those oligarchs who bent with the wind and eschewed politics for the pursuit of gain were mostly left undisturbed. The notorious "cronies" were, sociologically, a mixed bag, including not only relatives of Ferdinand and Imelda, but favoured oligarchs and quite a few "new men."

At its outset, the martial-law regime had a substantial, if restricted, social base. Its anticommunist, "reformist," "modernizing," and "law and order" rhetoric attracted the support of frustrated would-be technocrats, much of the underempowered urban middle class, and even sectors of the peasantry and urban poor. Shortly after winning absolute power he announced that the state had seized no less than 500,000 guns from private hands, raising hopes of a less visibly dangerous public life.[72] A limited land reform succeeded in creating, in the old Huk stamping-grounds of Central Luzon, a new stratum of peasant owners.[73] But as time passed, and the greed and violence of the regime became ever more evident, much of this support dried up. By the later 1970s the technocrats were a spent force, and the urban middle class became increasingly aware of the decay of Manila, the devastation of the university system, the abject and ridiculous character of the monopolized mass media, and the country's economic decline.

The real beneficiaries of the regime—aside from the Marcos mafia itself[74]—were two military forces: the National Army and the New People's

---

70. More precisely, Marcos seized Meralco, the holding company of a giant Lopez conglomerate that controlled the Manila Electric Company, the nation's second largest bank, plus oil pipelines, an oil refinery, and a major construction business.

71. See Resil B. Mojares, "The Dream Lives On and On: Three Generations of the Osmeñas, 1906–1990," in Alfred W. McCoy, ed., *An Anarchy of Families: State and Family in the Philippines* (Madison: University of Wisconsin, Center for Southeast Asian Studies, 1993), pp. 312–46, at p. 316.

72. See Lena Garner Noble, "Politics in the Marcos Era," in Bresnan, ed., *Crisis in the Philippines.* p. 85. While quite successful in the northern and central parts of the country, the arms sweep was a catastrophic failure in the Muslim south. It is clear that the large-scale insurrection of the Moro National Liberation Front launched shortly after the proclamation of Martial Law was precipitated by the fear that a disarmed Muslim population would be wholly at the mercy of Manila and the Christian majority.

73. See David Wurfel, *Philippine Agrarian Policy Today: Implementation and Political Impact* (Singapore: Institute of Southeast Asian Studies, Occasional Paper No. 46, 1977); and Ernesto M. Valencia, "Philippine Land Reform from 1972 to 1980: Scope, Process and Reality," in Temario Rivera *et al.*, eds., *Feudalism and Capitalism in the Philippines* (Quezon City: Foundation for Nationalist Studies, 1982). For a recent array of perspectives, see the issue of *Solidarity* (106–107 [1986]) devoted wholly to the problems of agrarian reform.

74. The word is used advisedly. The one Hollywood blockbuster banned under Marcos was *The Godfather*. A crumb under the rhinoceros's hide.

Army. Martial law in itself gave the former unprecedented power. But Marcos also used favoured officers to manage properties confiscated from his enemies, public corporations, townships, and so forth. The upper-echelon officers came to live in a style to which only the oligarchy had hitherto been accustomed.[75] Military intelligence became the regime's beady eyes and hidden ears. Legal restraints on military abuses simply disappeared. And there was only one master now to determine postings and promotions. To be sure, the Old Cacique packed the leadership with pliant placemen from his Ilocano-speaking homeland, but there was still plenty to go round.

On the other hand, the dictatorship encouraged a rapid growth, and slower geographic spread, of the communist guerrilla forces. No less significant than their expanding rural support was their organized reach into urban areas. One of the most striking features of the last years of the regime was the gradual adoption of a nationalist-Marxist vocabulary by notable sections of the bourgeois intelligentsia, the lower echelons of the Church hierarchy, and the middle class more generally.[76] Only the militant Left appeared to offer some way out.

The story of the unravelling of the regime following the brazen assassination of Benigno Aquino, Jr., at Manila's airport on August 21, 1983 is too well known to need detailing here. More important is an understanding of the regime that has replaced it.

RIDING THE "PEOPLE POWER REVOLUTION"

The initial coalition behind the dead man's widow was wide and (variably) deep: she was then above all Corazón Aquino rather than Corazón

---

75. The officers' Forbes Park, an exclusive new residential area amusingly entitled "Corinthian Gardens," was the one part of Manila to which, during a recent visit to the metropolis, I was unable to obtain even taxi access.

76. The nationalism was important. It made generally popular the Left's depiction of Marcos as the *tuta* (running dog) of the Americans. Privately, of course, the Left's leadership was well aware that Marcos was actually the *least* docile of the country's presidents. This evaluation is confirmed by Bonner's book, which shows that Ferdinand was vastly more astute than his opposite numbers in Washington. He had Carter's vain mini-Kissinger, Assistant Secretary of State for East Asian and Pacific Affairs Richard Holbrooke, in his pocket and charged half a billion dollars for a new five-year bases agreement in 1971. Reagan, an old friend from the 1960s, bundled his fatuous Vice-President off to Manila to inform Marcos that "we love your adherence to democratic principle and to the democratic process." CIA Director Casey, in an earlier incarnation as chairman of the Export–Import Bank, had pushed through the bank's largest-ever foreign loan ($644,000,000) to finance a splashy nuclear power project in Central Luzon. (The project remains uncompleted though the interest on the loan accounts for about 10 per cent of the Philippines' annual debt payments.) Marcos got $80 million under the table from contractor Westinghouse, which simultaneously raised its estimates 400 per cent. See *Waltzing with a Dictator*, pp. 307–9, and 265.

Cojuangco. It was based on a huge groundswell of revulsion against the Old Cacique and his *manileña* Miss Piggy. It included, from the Right, ambitious middle-ranking and junior officers of the National Army, frustrated finally by the old regime's visible decay and the ethnic nepotism of its *premier danseur*; the ever-hopeful technocracy and the non-crony segments of Manila's business community; almost all factions of the Church; the middle class; the non-NPA sectors of the intelligentsia; sundry self-described "cause-oriented groups" which regarded themselves as the vanguard of a newly legal Left; and the oligarchs.

The coalition was far too diverse and incoherent to last very long. Two years after the "People Power Revolution," it has become far narrower and, as it were, more densely packed. First to go were its right and left wings. For the cowboy activists of the Reform the Armed Forces Movement (RAM), who had played a pivotal role in February 1986 by betraying Marcos, the only genuinely tolerable successor to the old regime was a military junta, or a military-dominated government under their leadership. But this course had no serious domestic support, and was, for a Washington basking in Port au Prince television glory, in any case out of the question. Besides, cold-eyed realists in the Reagan administration perfectly understood that the Philippine military was far too factionalized, incompetent, corrupt, vainglorious, and ill-trained to be given any blank cheques.[77] A series of risible brouhahas, culminating in the Gregorio ("Gringo") Honasan *coup de force* of August 28, 1987, only confirmed the soundness of this judgement. On the Left, the situation was more complex. Far the most powerful component within it was the NPA, which had greatly benefited from the martial-law regime, and had now to decide how to respond to the new constellation of forces. The issue of whether frontally to oppose the Aquino regime, or try substantially to alter its internal equilibrium, was seriously debated in 1986–87. For a complex of reasons, too intricate to detain us here, and the wisdom of which is yet to be determined, the die was cast, early in 1987, for confrontation.[78] The immediate consequence was the collapse of the legal Left, and the manifest enfeeblement of the "cause-oriented groups," which, by the time of the Honasan comedy, had lost almost everything but their causes. Out of these developments emerged the real, unbalanced, and uneasy partners of the

---

77. See Francisco Nemenzo's fine article, "A Season of Coups: Military Intervention in Philippine Politics," *Diliman Review*, 34: 5–6 (1986), pp. 1, 16–25.

78. The core judgement was certainly based on estimates of Washington's long-term goals amply justified by the course of events in Central and South America. A valuable introduction to the polymorphous culture of the Philippine Left is Randolph G. David, ed., *Marxism in the Philippines* (Quezon City: University of the Philippines, Third World Studies Center, 1984).

contemporary Aquino coalition: the oligarchy, the urban middle class, and the Church.

During the new regime's first year, when the elan of the "People Power Revolution" remained quite strong, the coalition's junior partners were optimistic. The restoration of an open-market press, greatly expanded freedom for assembly and organization, and the crumbling of the crony monopolies and monopsonies, filled the various sectors of the middle class with giddy exhilaration. They could be fully themselves once again. Business confidence would be restored and the Philippines re-routed onto the path of progress. Good Americans were on their side. Honest technocratic expertise would at last be properly appreciated and rewarded. The intelligentsia (or at least major parts of it) now felt free to detach itself from the radical Left; it had a new home on television and radio, and in the press.

Furthermore, President Aquino's inner circle included not only Cardinal Sin but a number of idealistic human-rights lawyers and Left-liberal journalists and academics. And Corazón herself, perhaps taking a leaf out of the Book of Modern Kings, made every effort to appear in public *en bonne bourgeoise*. Tita ("Auntie"), as she was now called, was a brave, pious, unpretentious housewife who wanted only what was best for her nephews and nieces. The treasurer of Don José Cojuangco's holding company and the co-heiress of Hacienda Luisita remained mostly invisible. There was a touching confidence that the country's problems were on their way to sensible solution. She had opened talks with the NPA and with the Muslim insurrectionaries. A major land reform—which would not affect the middle class, but which promised to undermine the NPA's expanding rural base—would be enacted. The Americans would provide substantial sums in support of restored constitutional democracy. And People Power would, through free and honest elections, create a progressive legislative partner for the President, giving the middle class its long-dreamed-of chance to lead the country. In substantial measure the ecclesiastical leadership shared these hopes, trusting that the new situation would permit the Church to become once again ideologically united and organizationally disciplined.[79] The catchword of the era was "democratic space," which is perhaps most aptly translated as "middle-class

---

79. On Church politics, see Dennis Shoesmith's chapter in May and Nemenzo, ed., *The Philippines After Marcos*; and two texts by Robert Youngblood, "Church Opposition to Martial Law in the Philippines," *Asian Survey*, 18 (May 1978), pp. 505–20; and "Structural Imperialism: An Analysis of the Catholic Bishops' Conference of the Philippines," *Comparative Political Studies*, 13 (April 1982), pp. 29–56. See also *Touching Ground, Taking Root: Theological and Political Reflections on the Philippine Struggle* (Quezon City: Socio-Pastoral Institute, 1986), by Edicio de la Torre, who is among the most socially committed and thoughtful of contemporary Filipino clerics.

room for manoeuvre between the military, the oligarchy, and the communists."

The second year of the new regime dashed most of these illusions. The talks with Muslim and communist leaders broke down for essentially the same reason: the Aquino regime found itself in no position to make any attractive concessions. Haunted by nationalist dreams, even those Muslim leaders who seemed prepared to accept "autonomy," rather than independence, still demanded a Muslim autonomous zone remembered from the American colonial era. Yet ever since the Lansdale–Magsaysay regime had begun transmigrating potential and actual Hukbalahap peasant supporters to "empty" lands in Mindanao, the island had been rapidly "Christianized," by spontaneous migrants, land speculators, logging and mining conglomerates, large-scale commercial agribusinesses, and so on. Even had it wished—which it did not—to accede to Muslim dreams, this would have required the Aquino government either forcibly to relocate these tens, if not hundreds, of thousands of "Christians" (but where to?) or to leave them to the political mercies of justifiably angry Muslims. It lived by its own American-era dreams—a United Philippines—and besides, the army, which had suffered far more severe casualties fighting the Muslims than combatting the communists, would not have stood for "weakness." With the NPA the same was true. There was nothing President Aquino could offer the communists which they did not already have or which the army would be likely to permit.[80]

Nor were the Americans much help. The Reagan administration was preoccupied with its own survival, and a dozen "more important" foreign policy tar-babies. Its own financial recklessness meant that it had now very little to offer the Philippines even in military aid (which remained a pittance, more or less what it wished to give the Nicaraguan *contras*). Talk of a "Marshall Plan" for the Philippines vanished with the noise of escaping steam. And the overseas middle class stayed put. Its members might periodically return home with armfuls of presents for the relatives, but they had decided that the future

---

80. Her one important success was the "coming over" of Comrade/Father Conrado Balweg, a militant and charismatic (ex-)priest, who in the Marcos era had formed his own guerrilla force among the oppressed highland minorities of the Luzon Cordillera. The NPA, which had long featured him in its publicity as a popular hero and an example of Party–Church co-operation, while privately criticizing his womanizing and periodic "disobedience," now denounced him as an opportunist and counter-revolutionary. The army continued to distrust and dislike him, not least because the condition of his "coming over," Aquino's promise to establish a genuinely "autonomous" Cordillera region, appeared to pave the way for sellouts in the Muslim southwest.

It is instructive that a very successful commercial film on Balweg appeared in 1987. The real Balweg is an extremely complex figure, but in the movie he appears as a surrogate for the Manilan liberal middle class, fighting heroically against both army barbarity and communist treachery—of course, for the People.

of the bourgeoisie in the Philippines was too uncertain to be worth any substantial investments.[81] In the first year of the regime there had been much bold talk of liquidating the American bases, but by the second it was already clear that they would stay put: the Aquino government felt it could not afford seriously to antagonize Washington, and besides, it could not contemplate the loss in income and jobs that closure would imply. (In the 1980s, the US military was still the second largest employer—after the Filipino state—in the country.) The one important service the Americans did provide was explicit political support in the face of the various buffo coup attempts that anticlimaxed in the "Gringo" ringer of August 1987.

The pivotal issue for the regime coalition was, however, the "restoration of democracy," signalled by the May 11, 1987 elections for a reanimated Senate and House of the Representatives, and the January 18, 1988 elections for provincial governors, mayors and other local power-holders. The middle-class hope was that these elections would not only set the provisional Aquino government on a firm constitutional base, but would forcefully demonstrate to the army and the communists where the popular will lay. Moreover, it would translate People's Power into sufficient institutional power to carry out the domestic reforms deemed essential to the future leadership prospects of the middle class.

THE CACIQUES CLAIM THEIR OWN

It was now and here that the senior partners in the ruling coalition finally made themselves felt. During the first year the oligarchy had had its uneasy moments. Corazón herself might be sound enough, but some of her closest advisers were not; the mass media, for the moment still dominated ideologically by middle-class urban reformists, kept up a constant drumfire in favour of a land reform that hopefully would destroy the basis of NPA rural power. Even the World Bank, along with senior Japanese and American officials, were arguing the same logic. And, pending the elections, the President held plenary powers. Who could be sure that in a moment of frailty she might not do something fatal?

The alarm was real, if probably ill-founded. COLOR (Council of Landowners for Orderly Reform—500 magnate members) was hastily established;

---

81. Nor were they really encouraged to return. There were few jobs for them in the Philippines, and their remittances did much to ease the foreign exchange crisis faced by the government. The same was true of the huge wave of non-middle-class Filipino migrants to Saudi Arabia and the Gulf in the late 1970s and early 1980s. It is likely that the Philippines is now among the largest net exporters of national personnel in the world.

it sent Corazón resolutions signed with (happily, its own) blood, threatening civil disobedience in the event of serious land reform. A Movement for an Independent (Sugar) Negros appeared, claiming to be ready to offer armed resistance to impending Manilan injustice.[82] Lawyers were said, by the press, to be "going crazy," reclassifying agricultural lands as "commercial-industrial," signing off surplus plots to infant relatives, fraudulently antedating mortgages, etc.[83]

What was needed in 1986, as in 1916 and 1946, was cacique democracy. If elections could be promptly and freely held, the oligarchy could hope to return to its pre-1972 control of "the rule of law," and put everyone—the middle class, the military, their tenants, and the "rabble'—in their respective places.

On May 11, 1987, national-level elections were held for 24 senatorial, and 200 congressional seats. The outcome turned out to be eminently satisfactory. To quote a well-informed Filipino study: "Out of 200 House Representatives, 130 belong to the so-called 'traditional political families,' while another 39 are relatives of these families. *Only 31 Congressmen have no electoral record prior to 1971* and are not related to these old dominant families . . . Of the 24 elected senators, there are a few non-traditional figures but the cast is largely made up of *members of prominent pre-1972 political families.*"[84] Newly elected Senator John Osmeña—grandson of Commonwealth Vice-president Sergio Osmeña, Sr., and nephew of defeated 1969 presidential candidate Sergio Osmeña, Jr.— told the press: "One member of the family who does not do good is one too many, but ten members in the family doing good are not even enough."[85]

The results were widely interpreted as a triumph for Corazón Aquino in so far as 23 of the 24 victorious senatorial candidates ran as her supporters and as members of various nominal parties in her electoral coalition.[86] Something

---

82. *Philippine Daily Inquirer*, July 23, 1987.

83. *Manila Chronicle*, July 23, 1987. One particularly panic-stricken cacique family was reported to have set up forty separate dummy corporations to retain its landholdings.

84. A survey conducted by the Institute of Popular Democracy, quoted in the *Philippine Daily Inquirer* of Jan. 24, 1988. (Italics added to emphasize the "comeback" nature of the new legislature.) I owe this reference and the one that follows to Mojares, "The Dream," p. 312.

85. "Sonny move vs. Barcenas explained," *Sun Star Daily*, Oct. 29, 1987. The Osmeñas had gone through difficult times under martial law. Sergio ("Serging") Osmeña, Jr., had been severely wounded in the notorious Plaza Miranda affair in 1971 (the grenading of an—oligarchic, but anti-Marcos—Liberal Party election rally in downtown Manila; Marcos declared it the work of the NPA, but it was widely believed that the killers were military men or convicts in Marcos's own pay). After the declaration of martial law he exiled himself to California, where he died in 1984. There John, after initially applauding Ferdinand's declaration, eventually wended his way, returning only after the Aquino assassination.

86 Vice-President Salvador "Doy" Laurel's United Nationalist Democratic Organization (Unido); José "Peping" Cojuangco's Philippine Democratic Party–Laban (PDP–Laban); Paul Aquino's Lakas ng Bansa (Strength of the Nation); and Senator Jovito Salonga's Liberal Party. Only the Liberals date back to the pre-martial law era.

comparable occurred in the Lower House.[87] But probably the outcome is better designated as a triumph for Corazón Cojuangco. The study quoted above notes that: "Of the 169 Representatives who belong to the dominant families or are related to them, 102 are identified with the pre-1986 anti-Marcos forces, while 67 are from pro-Marcos *parties or families.*" A shake in the kaleidoscope of oligarchic power.

Not that the shrewder caciques failed to recognize certain new realities, including the genuine popular appeal of the President herself. (A significant number of Marcos collaborators swung over to her bandwagon.) When Congress finally opened in the late summer of 1987, it proclaimed itself committed to land reform, and appointed "outsiders" to the chairmanships of the Senate and House committees in charge of agrarian affairs. But within days the chairman of the House Committee on Agrarian Reform, Representative Bonifacio Gillego, an ex-military-intelligence official converted to "social democracy," was bemoaning the fact that 17 of the 21 members of his committee were landlords—including presidential brother José Cojuangco, presidential uncle-in-law Herminio Aquino, and the virago of Negros, Hortensia Starke.[88]

A fuller revival of the *ancien régime* came with the provincial and local elections which opened on January 18, 1988, and which found 150,000 candidates competing, *à l'américaine*, for close to 16,500 positions—an average of nine aspirants per plum.[89] These elections were of such an exemplary character that they deserve comment in their own right. In some places they represented happy reconsolidations. On the island of Cebu, for example, Emilio "Lito" Osmeña, brother of Senator John, won the island's governorship, while his cousin Tomas ("Tommy"), son of Sergio "Serging" Osmeña, Jr., defeated a candidate from the rival mestizo Cuen-*co* dynasty to become Mayor of Cebu City.[90] A little to the north, in the fiefdom of the Duranos, the 82-year-old Ramon Durano, Sr., ran successfully for Mayor of Danao City, with the backing of one violent son, Jesus "Don" Durano, against the opposition of another. The night after the election, losing candidate Thaddeus "Deo" Durano, waylaid by intrafamily assassins, ended up in a critical

---

87. The pro-government coalition won 150 out of 200 seats. The Left, running under the umbrella organization alliance of New Politics, secured a mere two.

88. *Manila Chronicle*, July 25, 1987.

89. *Manila Bulletin,* Jan. 18, 1988.

90. The Osmeña triumph represents the optimum outcome for a dynasty: it has a member in the national legislature, controls the provincial government, and runs the largest local commercial centre. Note that Tomas's defeated rival, José "Boy" Cuenco, is a younger brother of Senate President pro tem Antonino "Tony" Cuenco, and grandson of former Senate President, the late Mariano Cuenco.

condition in a Cebu City emergency ward.[91] The old warlord, who for the duration of martial law was a key Marcos henchman on Cebu, this time ran on the ticket of the PDP–Laban, the machine of President Aquino's brother José Cojuangco—who successfully recruited many other Marcos caciques under his sister's banner. Similar victories occurred in Olongapo—downtown from the Subic naval base—where Richard Gordon, husband of Congresswoman Katharine Gordon, became Mayor; in Western Negros, where Congressman José Carlos Lacson was now joined by governor-elect Daniel Lacson, Jr.; and so on . . .

Not that the old dynasties had things entirely their own way by any means. In some areas close to metropolitan Manila, middle-class reformists mobilized popular elements as well as "minor" dynasties to break up old fiefdoms. The Laurel machine in Batangas collapsed, to the embarrassment of the ineptly scheming Vice-President, Salvador "Doy" Laurel. The Rizal empire of Corazón's uncle, Congressman Francisco "Komong" Sumulong, was decimated. In Pampanga, out went the Nepomucenos, Lazatins, and Lingads. In the Iloilo fiefdom of the Lopezes, Olive Lopez-Padilla, daughter of one-time Vice-President Fernando Lopez and sister of Congressman Albertito Lopez, ran for governor on the wonderful vulgarian-*hacendado* slogan of "Bring Iloilo back to the Lopezes," but was nonetheless soundly thrashed.[92] In Mindanao's Cagayan de Oro, the Fortich dynasty, described by the *Manila Bulletin* as having run the place "since the beginning of the century," was humiliated.[93] No less interesting were certain military participations. In the Cagayan valley of northeastern Luzon, ex-Lieutenant-Colonel Rodolfo Aguinaldo, a key member of the Honasan rebel group, out-intimidated the local caciques (Dupayas and Tuzons) to seize the governorship. In Marcos's old base in Northern Ilocos, the vice-governorship was won, from military prison, by ex-Colonel Rolando Abadilla—once the dreaded chief of the Metropolitan Command Intelligence Security Group under Marcos, a thug widely suspected of helping to mastermind the assassination of Corazón's husband, and a major participant in the abortive coups of January and April 1987.[94]

---

91. *Philippine Daily Inquirer*, Jan. 22, 1988, and *Philippine Star*, Jan. 23, 1988.

92. *Philippine Star*, Jan. 22, 1988, and *Philippine Daily Inquirer*, Jan. 21, 1988. She meant, of course, "back" from Ferdinand and Imelda.

93. *Manila Bulletin*, Jan. 21, 1988.

94. See *Philippine Daily Inquirer*, Jan. 22, 1988, for an account of Abadilla's past, and *Manila Times*, Jan. 19, 1988, for a description of the torturer being flown, at state expense, from his Manila cell to a polling booth in Ilocos Norte. Corazón's advisers may have been pleased to see Aguinaldo "join the system"—and a long way from Manila. Even the case of Abadilla (whom army leaders insisted would not be allowed to assume office) may have served the purpose of demonstrating how free the balloting really was.

Even the NPA was indirectly drawn in. It was widely, and credibly, reported that in many areas where it had politicomilitary ascendancy, the movement charged candidates substantial fees for permission to campaign unmolested, and, here and there, lent unofficial support to sympathetic local aspirants.[95] Not that the civil war seriously let up. A day or two after the polls closed, Hortensia Starke's Hacienda Bino was burned to the ground, and the Hacienda La Purisima of Enrique Rojas, a top official of the National Federation of Sugar Planters, barely escaped the same fate.[96]

POLITICS IN A WELL-RUN CASINO

These variable outcomes need to be viewed in a larger framework for their implications to be well understood. The key facts to be borne in mind are these: no less than 81 per cent of the country's 27,600,000 eligible voters voted.[97] One or other elective post was available for every 1,400 voters. The average number of contestants per post was roughly nine. In most places the contests were "serious" in a rather new way—forty-one candidates were assassinated by rivals (*not* the NPA) in the course of the brief campaign.[98] In different ways, and to different extents, almost all political leaderships, from Right to Left, participated and could imagine that they had, up to a certain point, benefited. Everywhere, local patronage machines were replacing the centralized Marcos-era appointive *apparat*.

In any well-run casino, the tables are managed in the statistical favour of the house. To keep drawing customers, the owners must provide them with periodic, even spectacular, successes. A win is a splendid confirmation of the player's skill and heaven's favour. A loss demonstrates his/her misfortune or

---

95. The army leaked a purported NPA circular warning that "all candidates wishing to campaign in guerrilla zones have to get a safe-conduct pass from us for their own safety. The CPP–NPA will not answer for those without it." A guerrilla leader in Quezon Province, interviewed by Agence France Presse, confirmed NPA taxation of candidates, affirming that the money would be used to "advance the revolution." It is said that such "election passes" were sold for between 10,000 and 30,000 pesos ($500–$1,500) apiece. The army claimed that about 10 per cent of all candidates (say, 15,000 people) were paying for such passes. See *Philippine Daily Inquirer*, Jan. 18, 1988.

96. *Malaya*, Jan. 21, 1988.

97. *Manila Bulletin*, Jan. 21, 1988.

98. The government claimed that the elections were quite exceptionally peaceful: only 124 deaths all told, compared to 204 deaths in the May 11, 1987 congressional elections, 296 in the 1986 presidential elections, 178 in the 1981 presidential elections, 411 in the 1980 local elections, and 534 in the 1971 (pre martial law) congressional campaign. *Malaya*, Jan. 19, 1988. But as the *Philippine Daily Globe*, Jan. 20, 1988, rightly pointed out, in both the 1986 and 1981 campaigns only four *candidates* had been murdered—the huge bulk of the victims being "small fry." What was new about January 1988 was that a full third of the dead were actual contenders.

ineptitude. Either way, it's back to the tables as soon as possible. So with the blackjack of cacique democracy. Each local triumph for reform promises a rentier future; each loss signals miscalculations or ill-luck. At the end of the week or the year, however, the dealer is always in the black.

The truth is that American electoralism remains powerfully attractive, even when, perhaps especially when, married to Spanish caciquism in a geographically fragmented, ethnolinguistically divided, and economically bankrupt polity. It disperses power horizontally, while concentrating it vertically; and the former draws a partial veil over the latter. "Anyone" can get elected: look at the high, uncoerced turnout; look at the number of competing candidates (you too can run); look at the execrable colonels (better they campaign in the provinces than plot in the capital); look at the (probably temporary) fall of the Laurels and the Nepomucenos; look at the NPA's electoral levies, which, from a certain angle, can be aligned with the election-time exactions of the warlords.[99] Precisely because the competition is violently real, it is easy to be persuaded to cheer for, as it were, Arsenal or Chelsea, without reflecting too hard on the fact that both are in the First Division, and that one is watching the match from the outer stands, not playing in it.

But, of course, by no means everyone enjoys spectator sports. Shortly after the January 18 elections a curious reporter went to interview employees at the Cojuangcos's Hacienda Luisita, who had just voted massively for Arsenal. What difference had it made to their lives that Tita Cory had become President? "We used to get rice and sugar free, now we must pay. We used to get free water from the pumps in our yards. Now we must pay for pumped-in water because molasses from the sugar mill has seeped into our wells." Daily wages? They had been raised by 2.50 pesos ($0.12) for field hands, and 8 pesos ($0.40) for mill-workers. Level of employment? Usually from two to four days a week, in good times. One elderly man spoke of trying to survive by busing to additional work in the neighbouring province of Pampanga: transportation costs took 23 pesos from the daily wage of 40 pesos, leaving him a net of 17 pesos ($0.85). It still made sense to go. The reporter was told

---

99. In the summer of 1987 the liberal part of the Manila press was every day reporting with alarm on the growth of a nationwide, co-ordinated system of extremist anticommunist vigilante groups, financed by the oligarchy, the CIA, and the gonzo American ex-General Singlaub. In January 1988, during the election campaign, this broad fascist front virtually disappeared from print. Needless to say, the groups had not themselves disbanded. It had become apparent that by then most had abandoned Singlaubian mufti and gone back to duty as local gangs of thugs, recruited each to promote the local power, especially in elections, of particular, contentious local dynasties. There is no question but that these gangs are instruments of class oppression and frequently co-operate closely with local military and police personnel. They play an important part in the on-going civil war. But their very dispersion and localism show how confident the caciques are, and how little they feel the need to crawl together under the apron of the military.

that a worker, who had been quoted in an international magazine as saying that on the hacienda horses ate better than the hands, had been "summoned" by management. He had had to retract the slander. But one of the interviewees concluded: "Of course it is true. The horses get Australian grain and eggs, while we hardly have the meat."[100] All those interviewed either refused to give their names, or asked not to be identified.

---

100. *Philippine Daily Inquirer*, Jan. 23, 1988. The end of the final sentence is clearly garbled, and probably should read "anything to eat," or "any meat."

10

The First Filipino

Few countries give the observer a deeper feeling of historical vertigo than the Philippines. Seen from Asia, the armed uprising against Spanish rule of 1896, which triumphed temporarily with the establishment of an independent republic in 1898, makes it the visionary forerunner of all the other anticolonial movements in the region. Seen from Latin America, it is, with Cuba, the last of the Spanish imperial possessions to have thrown off the yoke, seventy-five years after the rest. Profoundly marked, after three and a half centuries of Spanish rule, by Counter-Reformation Catholicism, it was the only colony in the Empire where the Spanish language never became widely understood. But it was also the only colony in Asia to have had a university in the nineteenth century. In the 1890s barely 3 per cent of the population knew "Castilian," but it was Spanish-readers and -writers who managed to turn movements of resistance to colonial rule from hopeless peasant uprisings into a revolution. Today, thanks to American imperialism, and the Philippines' new self-identification as "Asian," almost no one other than a few scholars understands the language in which the revolutionary heroes communicated among themselves and with the outside world—to say nothing of the written archive of pre-twentieth-century Philippine history. A virtual lobotomy has been performed.

The central figure in the revolutionary generation was José Rizal, poet, novelist, ophthalmologist, historian, doctor, polemical essayist, moralist, and political dreamer. He was born in 1861 into a well-to-do family of mixed Chinese, Japanese, Spanish, and Tagalog descent: five years after Freud, four years after Conrad, one year after Chekhov; the same year as Tagore, three years before Max Weber, five before Sun Yat-sen, eight before Gandhi, and nine before Lenin. Thirty-five years later he was arrested on false charges of inciting Andrés Bonifacio's uprising of August 1896, and executed by a firing squad composed of native soldiers led by Spanish officers. The execution was carried out in what is now the beautiful Luneta Park, which fronts the shore line of Manila Bay. (On the other side of the Spanish world, José Marti, the hero of Cuban nationalism, had died in action the previous year.) At the time of Rizal's death, Lenin had just been sentenced to exile in Siberia, Sun Yat-sen had begun organizing for Chinese nationalism outside China, and Gandhi was conducting his early experiments in anticolonial resistance in South Africa.

Rizal had the best education then available in the colony, provided exclusively by the religious Orders, notably the Dominicans and Jesuits. It was an education that he later satirized mercilessly, but it gave him a command of Latin (and some Hebrew), a solid knowledge of classical antiquity, and an introduction to western philosophy and even to medical science. It is again vertiginous to compare what benighted Spain offered with what the enlightened, advanced imperial powers provided in the same Southeast Asian region: no real universities in French Indochina, the Dutch East Indies, or British Malaya and Singapore till after World War II. From very early on, Rizal exhibited remarkable literary abilities. At the age of nineteen he entered an open literary competition, and won first prize, defeating Spanish rivals writing in their native tongue.

He was growing up at a time when modern politics had begun to arrive in the colony. More than any other imperial power, nineteenth-century Spain was wracked by deep internal conflicts, not merely the endless Carlist wars over the succession, but also between secular liberalism and the old aristocratic-clerical order. The brief liberal triumph in the Glorious Revolution of 1868, which drove the licentious Isabella II from Madrid, had immediate repercussions for the remote Pacific colony. The revolutionaries promptly announced that the benefits of their victory would be extended to the colonies. The renewed ban on the Jesuits and the closure of monastic institutions seemed to promise the end of the reactionary power of the Orders overseas. In 1869, the first "liberal" Captain-General, Carlos María de la Torre, arrived in Manila, it is said to popular cries of "Viva la Libertad!" (How unimaginable is a scene of this kind in British India or French Algeria.) During his two-year rule, de la Torre enraged the old-guard colonial elite, not merely by instituting moves to give equal legal rights to natives, mestizos, and peninsulars, but also by going walkabout in Manila in everyday clothes and without armed guards. The collapse of the Glorious Revolution brought about a ferocious reaction in Manila, however, culminating in 1872 in the public garrotting of three secular (i.e. non-Order) priests (one creole, two mestizo), framed for masterminding a brief mutiny in the arsenal of Cavite.

The Rizal family was an immediate victim of the reaction. In 1871, when José was ten years old, his mother was accused of poisoning a neighbour, forced to walk twenty miles to prison, and held there for over two years before being released. His elder brother Paciano, a favourite pupil of Father Burgos, the leader of the garrotted priests, narrowly escaped arrest and was forced to discontinue his education. Under these circumstances, in 1882, with his brother's support, José left quietly for the relative freedom of Spain to continue his medical studies.

He spent the next five years in Europe, studying on and off, but also travelling widely—to Bismarck's Germany and Gladstone's England, as well as Austro-Hungary, Italy, and France—and picking up French, German, and English with the ease of an obsessive and gifted polyglot. Europe affected him decisively, in two related ways. Most immediately, he came quickly to understand the backwardness of Spain itself, something which his liberal Spanish friends frequently bemoaned. This put him in a position generally not available to colonial Indians and Vietnamese, or, after the Americans arrived in Manila, to his younger countrymen: that of being able to ridicule the metropolis from the same high ground from which, for generations, the metropolis had ridiculed the natives. More profoundly, he encountered what he later described as "el demonio de las comparaciones," a memorable phrase that could be translated as "the spectre of comparisons." What he meant by this was a new, restless double-consciousness which made it impossible ever after to experience Berlin without at once thinking of Manila, or Manila without thinking of Berlin. Here indeed is the origin of nationalism, which lives by making comparisons.

It was this spectre that, after some frustrating years writing for *La Solidaridad*, the organ of the small group of committed "natives" fighting in the metropole for political reform, led him to write *Noli Me Tangere*, the first of the two great novels for which Rizal will always be remembered. He finished it in Berlin just before midnight on February 21, 1887—eight months after Gladstone's first Home Rule Bill was defeated, and eight years before *Almayer's Folly* was published. He was twenty-six.

The two most astonishing features of *Noli Me Tangere* are its scale and its style. Its characters come from every stratum of late colonial society, from the liberal-minded peninsular Captain-General down through the racial tiers of colonial society—creoles, mestizos, *chinos* ("pure" Chinese) to the illiterate *indio* masses. Its pages are crowded with Dominicans, shady lawyers, abused acolytes, corrupt policemen, Jesuits, small-town caciques, mestiza school-girls, ignorant peninsular carpetbaggers, hired thugs, despairing intellectuals, social-climbing *dévotes,* dishonest journalists, actresses, nuns, gravediggers, artisans, gamblers, peasants, market-women, and so on. (Rizal never fails to give even his most sinister villains their moments of tenderness and anguish.) Yet the geographical space of the novel is strictly confined to the immediate environs of the colonial capital, Manila. The Spain from which so many of the characters have at one time or another arrived is always off stage. This restriction made it clear to Rizal's first readers that "The Philippines" was a society in itself, even though those who lived in it had as yet no common name. That he was the first to imagine this social whole explains why he is remembered today as the First Filipino.

The novel's style is still more astonishing, for it combines two radically distinct and at first glance uncombinable genres: melodrama and satire. For all its picaresque digressions, the plot is pure opera. The novel opens with the wealthy, handsome, and naively idealistic mestizo, Don Crisóstomo Ibarra, returning from a long educational sojourn in Europe with plans to modernize his home town and his *patria*, and to marry his childhood sweetheart Maria Clara, the beautiful mestiza daughter of the wealthy *indio* cacique, Don Santiago de los Santos. At first he is welcomed with respect and enthusiasm, but the clouds soon gather. He discovers that his father has died in prison, framed by the brutal Franciscan friar Padre Damaso, and that his body has been thrown into the sea. Later he will learn that Damaso is the real father of his bride-to-be. Meanwhile, the young parish priest Padre Salvi secretly lusts after Maria Clara, and has covered up the murder of one of his young acolytes. Gradually, Ibarra also learns of the sinister origins of his own line in a cruel, carpetbagging Basque, who, after ruining many local peasants, hanged himself. He makes friends with Don Tasio, the local freethinking *philosophe,* with liberal-minded local caciques, even with the Captain-General himself, as well as with the mysterious *indio* rebel Elias. (The dialogues between the two men on whether political reform is possible in the Philippines or a revolutionary upheaval inevitable continue to this day to be a part of Philippine progressive discourse and historiography.) Meanwhile, the friars and their various local allies scheme to abort Ibarra's marriage and his plans for establishing a modern school in his home town. Finally, Padre Salvi, learning of a planned rebel attack on his town, frames Ibarra as its instigator and financier. The young man is imprisoned in a wave of antisubversive arrests, torture, and executions, but escapes with Elias's help, and ends as an outlaw. Maria Clara, to avoid being forced into a loveless marriage with an insipid peninsular, chooses to become a nun, and compels her real father, whom she confronts with his adultery, to help her take her vows. She disappears into a convent where, however, Padre Salvi has managed to get himself appointed as spiritual adviser, so that "nameless horrors" lie in wait for the unfortunate girl.

So far, so Puccini, one might say. Yet this melodramatic plot is interspersed not only with brilliant sketches of colonial provincial society, but with the novelist's own unquenchable laughter at the expense of his own inventions— so that *Tosca* changes into Goya's *Caprichos*. Consider the famous opening of the novel:

> Towards the end of October, Don Santiago de los Santos, popularly known as Capitán Tiago, was hosting a dinner which, in spite of its having been announced only that afternoon, against his wont, was already the theme of all conversation in Binondo, in the neighbouring districts, and even in Intramuros. Capitán Tiago was reputed to be a most generous man, and it was known that his home, like his country, never closed its door to anything, as long as it was not business, or any new or bold idea.
>
> Like an electric jolt the news circulated around the world of social parasites: the pests or dregs which God in His infinite goodness created and so fondly [*cariñosa-mente*] breeds in Manila. Some went in search of shoe polish for their boots, others for buttons and cravats, but all were preoccupied with the manner in which to greet with familiarity the master of the house, and thus pretend that they were old friends, or to make excuses, if the need arose, for not having been able to come much earlier.
>
> This dinner was being given in a house on Anloague Street, and since we can no longer recall its number, we will try to describe it in such a way as to make it still recognizable—that is, if earthquakes have not ruined it. We do not believe that its owner would have had it pulled down, this task being ordinarily taken care of by God, or Nature, with whom our government also has many projects under contract.[1]

Or consider the opening of the novel's final chapter ("Epilogue"), which comes immediately after the story has reached its grim, gothic conclusion:

> Many of our characters being still alive, and having lost sight of the others, a true epilogue is not possible. For the good of the public we would gladly kill [*mataríamos con gusto*] all our personages starting with Padre Salvi and finishing with Doña Victorina, but that is not possible . . . let them live: the country, and not we, will in the end have to feed them.

This kind of authorial play with readers, characters, and reality—which reminds one of Machado de Assis's sardonic *Memorias póstumas de Bras Cubas* published five years earlier—is quite uncharacteristic of most serious nineteenth-century novels, and gives *Noli Me Tangere* a special appeal. It is what has always doomed nationalist attempts to put the book on stage or

---

1. *Noli Me Tangere* (Manila: Instituto Nacional de Historia, 1978). The translation is my own.

screen. It was surely this same laughter that earned Rizal the implacable enemies who brought him to his early death.

It is impossible to read *Noli Me Tangere* today in the way a patriotic young
Manileño of 1897 would have read it: as a political hand-grenade. We all
have the spectre of comparisons crouched on our shoulders. It was only the
second novel ever written by a putative Filipino, the first being minor, experimental trash. So what about other great colonial novels by the colonized?
There is nothing in the Americas, nothing in the rest of Southeast Asia, nothing in Africa till three-quarters of a century later. What about the comparison
with metropolitan Spain? It has been said that Rizal borrowed heavily from
Galdós, in particular from his 1876 anti-clerical novel *Doña Perfecta*. But
Rizal's novel is so superior in scale and depth that this "borrowing" is very
doubtful. In his voluminous correspondence Rizal never mentions Galdós—
whose opinions on colonial questions were wholly *bien-pensant*. The one
Spanish writer for whom he had a passionate admiration was not a novelist
at all, but the brilliant satirical journalist José Mariano de la Larra, who had
committed suicide in 1837, at the attractive age of twenty-eight.

And Tagore, Rizal's exact contemporary? Here one sees a profound contrast. Tagore was the inheritor of a vast and ancient Bengali literary tradition,
and most of his novels were written in Bengali for the huge Bengali population of the Raj. The mother tongue of Rizal was Tagalog, a minority language
spoken by perhaps two million people in the multilingual Philippine archipelago, with no tradition of prose writing, and readable by perhaps only a few
thousand. He tells us why he wrote in Spanish, a language understood by only
3 per cent of his countrymen, when he invokes "tú, que me lees, amigo o enemigo"—"you who read me, friend or enemy." He wrote as much for the
enemy as the friend, something that did not happen with the Raj until the
work, a century later, of Salman Rushdie.

Rizal could not know it, but there were to be huge costs involved in choos-
ing to write in Spanish. Five years after his martyrdom, a greedy and
barbarous American imperialism destroyed the independent Republic of the
Philippines, and reduced the inhabitants once again to the status of colonial
subjects. American was introduced as the new language of truth and international status, and promoted through an expanding school system. By the eve
of World War II, it had (narrowly) become the most widely understood language in the archipelago. Spanish gradually disappeared, so that by the time
a quasi-independence was bestowed in 1946, it had become unreadable. Not
merely the novels, essays, poetry, and political articles of Rizal himself, but
the writings of the whole nation-imagining generation of the 1880s and 1990s
had become inaccessible. Today, most of the work of the brilliant anticolonial
propagandist Marcelo del Pilar, of the Revolution's architect Apolinario

Mabini, and of the Republic's tragically assassinated general of genius Antonio Luna remain sepulchred in Spanish.

Hence the eerie situation which obliges Filipinos to read the work of the most revered hero of the nation in translation—into local vernaculars, and into American. Hence also a politics of translation. Translations of *Noli Me Tangere* into most of the major languages of the Philippines were bound to fail, not merely because of the absurdity of the many Spanish characters "speaking" in Tagalog, Cebuano, or Ilocano, but because the *enemigo* readers automatically disappear, and the satirical descriptions of mestizos and *indios* speaking bad Spanish, and Spanish colonials slipping into bad Tagalog, become untranslatable. The most important American translation, done by the alcoholic anti-American diplomat Leon María Guerrero in the 1960s—still the prescribed text for high schools and universities—is no less fatally flawed by systematic bowdlerization in the name of official nationalism. Sex, anticlericalism, and any perceived relevance to the contemporary nation are all relentlessly excised, with the aim of turning Rizal into a boring, long-dead national saint.

Which brings us to the present translation, more or less timed for the centenary of Rizal's execution. A few years ago, Doreen Fernandez, one of the Philippines' most distinguished scholars, deeply disturbed by the corruption of Rizal's texts, went in search of a compatriot linguistically capable of making a reliable translation. She eventually found one in Soledad Lacson-Locsin, an elderly upper-class woman born early enough in this century for Rizal's Spanish—by no means the same as 1880s Madrid Spanish—to be second nature to her. The old lady completed new translations of both *Noli Me Tangere* and its even more savage 1891 sequel *El Filibusterismo* just before she died.

In most respects, it is a huge advance over previous translations, handsomely laid out and with enough footnotes to be helpful without being pettifogging. But the barbarous American influence is still there, to say nothing of the basic transformation of consciousness that created, for the first time, within a year or so of Rizal's execution, a national idea of "the" Filipino.

In Rizal's novels the Spanish words *filipina* and *filipino* still mean what they had traditionally meant—i.e. creoles, people of "pure" Spanish descent who were born in the Philippines. This stratum was, in accordance with traditional imperial practice, wedged in between *peninsulares* (Spain-born Spaniards) and mestizos, *chinos*, and *indios*. The novels breathe nationalism of the classical sort, but this nationalism has to do with love of *patria*, not with race: "Filipino" in the twentieth-century ethnoracial sense never appears. But by 1898, when Apolinario Mabini began to write—two years

after Rizal's execution—the old meaning had vanished. Hence the fundamental difficulty of the present translation is that *filipino/filipina* almost
always appear in the anachronistic form of Filipino/Filipina: for example, "el
bello sexo está representado por españolas peninsulares y filipinas" ("the
fair sex being represented by peninsular and creole Spanish women") is rendered absurdly as "the fair sex being represented by Spanish peninsular ladies
and Filipinas."

The other problem is a flattening of the political and linguistic complexity
of the original, no doubt because Mrs. Lacson-Locsin was born just too late
to have had an elite Spanish-era schooling. When Rizal had the racist
Franciscan friar Padre Damaso say contemptuously, "cualquier bata de la
escuela lo sabe," he mockingly inserted the Tagalog *bata* in place of the
Spanish *muchacho* to show how years in the colony had unconsciously cre-
olized the friar's language. This effect disappears when Mrs. Lacson-Locsin
translates the words as "any schoolchild knows that." Rizal quotes three
lines of the much loved nineteenth-century Tagalog poet Francisco Balagtas
in the original, without translating it into Spanish, to create the necessary
intercultural jarring, but quoting the poem in the same language as the text
surrounding it erases the effect. The ironical chapter heading "Tasio el loco ó
el filósofo" shrinks to "Tasio," and one would not suspect that the chapter
heading "A Good Day is Foretold by the Morning" was originally in Italian.
The translator also has difficulties with Rizal's frequent, sardonic use of
untranslated Latin.

There are a few prophets who are honoured in their own country, and José
Rizal is among them. But the condition of this honour has for decades been
his unavailability. Mrs. Lacson-Locsin has changed this by giving the great
man back his sad and seditious laughter. And it is badly needed—if one
thinks of all those "social parasites: the pests or dregs which God in His infinite goodness created and *tan cariñosamente* breeds in Manila."

11

Hard to Imagine

In the difficult late 1950s, the domestic controllers of the Philippine state began preparations for an elaborate centennial celebration of the birth of Dr. José Rizal on June 19, 1861. Not only was Rizal the greatest national martyr—having been executed by the collapsing Spanish colonial regime in 1896—but he was also a highly gifted poet, historian, scientist, journalist, linguist, satirist, political activist, and, above all, novelist. It had long been generally agreed that his two novels, *Noli Me Tangere* (published in Berlin in 1887) and *El Filibusterismo* (published in Ghent in 1891), are the *chefs d'oeuvre* of Philippine literature, and had a central role in the "awakening" of Filipino nationalism. Unluckily, the "First Filipino" had composed these works in Spanish, the lingua franca and language of cultivation of the late Spanish-colonial period. Still more unfortunately, the American colonial regime of 1899–1942 had by the end wiped out—not wholly intentionally— the local use of Spanish except in a few rich mestizo and creole families, instilling in its place American. Thanks to the spread of public education under Washington's auspices, American ended up (slightly) more widely understood than any of the Philippines' indigenous vernaculars.[1] One result of these developments was that, by the 1950s, Rizal's two novels had become inaccessible in their original form. English translations did exist, but these had been composed, some even by foreigners, in the colonial era.[2] It therefore

---

1. According to the last colonial era census (1939), 26.5 per cent of the sixteen million population of the Philippines could speak English, 25.4 per cent Tagalog, and 2.6 per cent Spanish (Andrew B. Gonzales, *Language and Nationalism: The Philippine Experience So Far* [Quezon City: Ateneo de Manila Press, 1980], p. 62).

2. The best and best-known of these are the versions of Charles E. Derbyshire and Jorge Bocobo.

seemed only appropriate, in the era of independence, to sponsor, as the climax of the centennial celebrations, a prize competition for the best new translation.

The competition was, however, not merely an occasion for national remembrance. In the middle 1950s, against most expectations, the Hero had become the centre of a bitter political controversy. In reprisal for what they regarded as bigoted intervention in the nation's electoral processes by certain senior members of the ultra-conservative Catholic hierarchy, a group of senators and congressmen sponsored a bill making the reading of Rizal's two novels required for all students, whether in state or private schools. The Church was put in a difficult spot. The chief villains of both novels are clerics: brutal Franciscans, lascivious Dominicans, power-hungry Jesuits. Both texts contain brilliant pages mercilessly satirizing the benighted medievalism of nineteenth-century Church thinking and pastoral practice. While the Hierarchy was quite happy to commemorate Rizal as a national hero, indeed claimed that he had recanted all his Masonic and deist views on the eve of his execution, it was strongly opposed to parish-school students reading much of what the great man had written. Various political comedies ensued, the outcome of which was a tactical victory and a strategic defeat for the Church. Students were not required to read *these* two particular texts; others, less inflammatory, might be substituted. But the Hierarchy was put, as its adversaries intended, in the embarrassing position of appearing to censor the First Filipino.

Among those stimulated by the competition to undertake a new translation was Leon Ma. Guerrero (1915–82), at that time the Philippine Ambassador to the Court of St. James.[3] I will have more to say about Guerrero later. It is enough to note here that his fluent translations were very successful, and quickly supplanted all older versions in high-school and university libraries. As Doreen Fernandez noted, they have become "the only translation[s] anybody reads now."[4] It is safe to say that virtually all today's young and middle-aged Filipinos who have actually read the novels in American have read them in Guerrero's version.

When I first read these translations, perhaps twenty years ago, I knew no Spanish, and since they read so easily and smoothly it never occurred to

---

3. According to his own later account, Guerrero decided only at the last minute not to enter his translations in the competition. He was frank enough to say that the reason was money. The prize was worth only 10,000 *pesos*, and he would have had to surrender the copyright. He sold instalment rights in the Philippines to the *Manila Times*, and the foreign rights to Longmans, the well-known London publishing company. See Edilberto N. Alegre and Doreen G. Fernandez, *The Writer and his Milieu: An Oral History of the First Generation Writers in English* (Manila: De La Salle University Press, 1984), pp. 79–80, 85.

4. Ibid., p. 75.

me—nor to anyone I knew—that there was anything peculiar about them. But five years ago, having opted to do research on Philippine nationalism, I recognized that I needed to learn to read Spanish, and decided to teach myself by reading the *Noli* and the *Fili* in the original, with Guerrero's translations as cribs. This delicious, painful, line-by-line reading quickly brought home to me that Guerrero's version was systematically distorted in the most interesting ways. Since he himself was a man of sophistication and excellent education, and was also completely fluent in Spanish, it seemed highly unlikely that such systematic distortions could be attributed either to haste or to incompetence. What then? The suggestion I wish to make in the pages that follow is that they were caused mainly by a fundamental change in nationalist consciousness between the 1890s and the 1950s, and also by the halting rise in Manila, after independence, of "official nationalism."[5]

In trying to understand Guerrero's *Noli,* it is essential to bear in mind certain strange features of his Introduction.[6] He began by describing his translation as an "attempt" to make the novel "palatable to a new generation of English-speaking Filipinos, and give it, beyond them, a wider audience among other English-speaking peoples [*sic*] on the centenary of Rizal's birth." Previous translations, he continued, were all unsatisfactory.

> When prepared by those whose native language is English, they lack a feeling or understanding of the Filipino *milieu*. When essayed by Filipinos, they suffer from, it seems to me, an exaggerated reverence for the original text which makes for tortured constructions. Both kinds are usually encumbered with numerous explanatory footnotes which are irritating and discouraging, although no doubt they are helpful to foreigners and even for many contemporary Filipinos who no longer have any idea of the customs of their forefathers.

In his own new version, he averred, he had tried to give "the reader 'the ease of original composition,' the *Noli* as Rizal might have written it if he had been writing in English for the present generation of Filipinos." Finally, he observed that,

> Rizal's style is often unlikely to appeal to the modern era; Spanish, moreover, is a language that can afford to be more florid and sentimental than modern English.

---

5. For an explication of this term, originally coined by Hugh Seton-Watson, see my *Imagined Communities: Reflections on the Origin and Spread of Nationalism*, rev. edn. (London: Verso, 1991), chapter 6.

6. José Rizal, *The Lost Eden (Noli Me Tangere)*, trans. Leon Ma. Guerrero (Bloomington: Indiana University Press, 1961). All quotations in the following paragraph come from the translator's introduction (pp. ix–xviii). Subsequent quotations from this translation are indicated by page number only.

I have therefore allowed myself the further liberty of paraphrasing certain passages that might otherwise have provoked a sophisticated snigger, particularly the love-scene on Maria Clara's balcony which has been the delight of generations of Filipino sentimentalists.

There is something painful about these introductory comments. The national hero's novel is to be made "palatable" to a younger generation of Filipinos (high-school and college students?), "who no longer have any idea of the customs of their forefathers"—seventy years back. It will be rendered as if Rizal were writing in the 1950s for Guerrero's contemporaries. It will be paraphrased to prevent sophisticated sniggers, even if this means disappointing generations of Filipino sentimentalists. Since it is unlikely that Guerrero thought high-school students much given to sophisticated sniggering, one might surmise that the sniggerers he had in mind were foreigners, especially American and English readers. Bowdlerization and modernization—about which Guerrero is quite frank—are, one is told, the necessary nationalist means for keeping Rizal alive for Filipino youth, and preserving his Filipino glory from Anglo-Saxon mirth. So far, so clear. Yet what Guerrero actually did with the *Noli* seems—at first sight—to have almost no connection with these stated purposes.

One could summarize the key elements of Guerrero's translation strategy—which is quite consistently employed over the hundreds of pages comprising the *Noli*[7]—under the following (somewhat arbitrarily titled) seven rubrics.

DEMODERNIZATION

It is characteristic of Rizal's bravura style that although the story of the *Noli* is set in the (recent) past, and thus the dominant tense is the past, there are frequent glissando modulations into the present. Yet, every such present was systematically turned by Guerrero into the past. For example, on the wonderful opening page, Rizal maliciously writes: "Cual una sacudida eléctrica corrió la noticia en el mundo de los parásitos, moscas ó colados que Dios crió en su infinita bondad, y tan cariñosamente multiplica en Manila" (Rizal 1978, p. 1). One might ploddingly render this passage as: "Like an electric shock the news [of Don Santiago de los Santos's party] ran through the world of parasites, spongers, and gatecrashers whom God *created* in his infinite goodness, and so affectionately *multiplies* in Manila." Guerrero, however, rendered the final phrases as: "whom God, in his infinite wisdom, had created and so fondly *multiplied* in Manila" (p. 1; here and subsequently emphasis

---

7. Exactly the same strategy is pursued in his version of the *Fili,* but for convenience I will confine my analysis here to the *Noli.*

added). Another simple example is a passage where Rizal bitterly satirizes the way that the rich townsfolk of "San Diego" abuse the poor, while piously paying for indulgences and masses for the departed souls from whom they have inherited their properties. "A fé que la Justicia divina no parece tan exigente como la humana" (p. 73). This means: "In truth, divine Justice *seems* less demanding than that of humanity." Guerrero, however, wrote: "They *found* it easier to satisfy divine than human justice" (p. 79).

In every instance the effect of Guerrero's alterations is not at all to "update" Rizal's novel, but rather to push it deep into an antique past. It is as if he wished to reassure himself that God no longer fondly multiplies parasites and spongers in Manila, and has finally become no less demanding of justice than is humanity.

EXCLUSION OF THE READER

Throughout the novel Rizal regularly turns and speaks to the reader. As if author and reader were ghosts or angels, they penetrate invisibly, at the author's gleeful invitation, into monkish cells, ladies' boudoirs, and the Governor-General's palace, to eavesdrop together on what is there transpiring. This technique sets time aside and sucks the reader deep into the narrative, engaging her emotions, teasing her curiosity, and offering her malicious voyeuristic pleasures (in an odd way, the technique anticipates that of the cinema). A simple example is the transition between a scene where Father Damaso pushes Don Santiago into the latter's study for a secret confabulation, and the following scene which features some lively scheming between two Dominicans. Rizal writes (p. 45): "Cpn. Tiago se puso inquieto, perdió el uso de la palabra, pero obedeció y siguió detras del colosal sacerdote, que cerró detras de sí la puerta. Mientras conferencian en secreto, averigüemos que se ha hecho de Fr. Sibyla." Or: "Capitan Tiago became uneasy, and lost his tongue, but obeyed and followed after the colossal priest, who locked the door behind him. While they are conferring in secret, let us find out what has happened to Fr. Sibyla." Guerrero's version goes: "He made Capitan Tiago so uneasy he was unable to reply, and obediently followed the burly priest who closed the door behind them. Meantime, in another part of the city the scholarly Dominican, Father Sibyla, had left his parish house . . ." (p. 48).

A more complex instance is provided in the opening chapter where Rizal writes:

Pues no hay porteros ni criados que pidan ó pregunten por el billete de invitacion, subiremos, oh tú que me lees, amigo ó enemigo, si es que te atraen á tí los acordes de la orquesta, la luz ó el significatívo clin-clan de la vajilla y de los cubiertos, y quieres ver cómo son las reuniones allá en la Perla del Oriente. Con gusto y por comodidad mía te ahorraría á tí de la descripcion de la casa, pero esto es tan importante, pues nosotros los mortales en general somos como las tortugas: valemos y nos clasifican por nuestros conchas; por esto y otras cualidades más como tortugas son tambien los mortales de Filipinas. (p. 2)

This is roughly:

Since there are no porters or servants requesting or asking to see invitation cards, let us proceed upstairs, O reader mine, be you enemy or friend, if you are drawn to the strains of the orchestra, the light(s), or the suggestive clinking of dishes and trays, and if you wish to see how parties are given in the Pearl of the Orient. With pleasure, and were it merely for my convenience, I would spare you a description of the house. Yet it is so very important, since we mortals are in general like turtles; we have value and are classified according to our shells. In this, and indeed in other respects, mortals in the Philippines *are* also like turtles.

Guerrero astonishingly rendered this splendour as:

No porter or footman would have asked the visitor for his invitation card, he would have gone up freely, attracted by the strains of orchestra music and the suggestive tinkle of silver and china, and perhaps, if a foreigner, curious about the kind of dinner parties that were given in what was called the Pearl of the Orient. Men are like turtles; they are classified and valued according to their shells. In this, and indeed in other respects, the inhabitants of the Philippines *at that time* were turtles. (p. 2)

At a stroke Rizal's wittily insinuating voice is muffled, a silent wall is set up between author and reader, and, once again, everything urgent and contemporary in the text is dusted away into History. It is surely not simply that Guerrero probably felt uncomfortable with the prospect that even in an independent Philippines the inhabitants might still be classified and valued by their shells. For the, original text makes its readership marvellously problematic: *amigo ó enemigo?* Who are these *enemigos?* Surely not other Filipinos? Surely not Spaniards? After all, the *Noli* was written to inspire the nationalism of Filipino youth, and for the Filipino People! What on earth would Spanish readers be doing "inside it"?[8]

---

8. Rizal certainly expected copies of his novels to fall into the hands of the colonial regime and the hated friars, and doubtless enjoyed the prospect of their squirming at his biting barbs.

EXCISION OF TAGALOG

Rizal's Spanish text is bejewelled with Tagalog words and expressions. Sometimes they are deployed for sheer comic effect, sometimes to deepen the reader's sense of the conflicts between peninsular Spaniards, creoles, mestizos, and *indios*. But most often they simply reflect, as did the Anglo-Indian that developed in Victorian times, the casual penetration of the imperial vernacular by local languages. For example, the brutal peninsular Franciscan, Father Damaso, may say: "Cualquier bata de la escuela lo sabe!" (p. 16). *Bata* is the Tagalog word for a child of either sex, but here clearly means "boy." Guerrero (p. 19) translated this as: "Any schoolboy knows as much!" as if Rizal had written *muchacho* rather than *bata*. In other places, Tagalog words such as *salakot* (a type of local straw hat), *timsim* (a type of kerosene lamp), *paragos* (a Tagalog sled), or *sinigang* (a kind of local food), far from being kept in their original form—where they would be immediately familiar to young Filipino readers of the early 1960s—were rendered, as if from the Spanish, as "native straw hat," "crude lamp," "native sled," and "native dish."[9] Similarly, the Tagalog exclamations *naku!*, *aba!*, and *susmariosep!*—with which almost all the characters lace their Spanish conversations—were summarily eliminated.[10] This translation stance is especially strange in that one can hardly imagine even the most Americanized Filipinos of the early 1960s speaking to each other of "native hats" and "native dishes." Furthermore, most inhabitants of Manila were by then quite familiar with some form or other of "Taglish," in which there is constant interchange and fusion between Tagalog and English—so that the mestizo language of the original *Noli* would surely have seemed agreeably "contemporary."[11] Once again, its elimination in the translation serves to distance rather than familiarize the national hero.

BOWDLERIZATION

It is plain that Guerrero bowdlerized many passages which made him uncomfortable—passages alluding to political or religious matters as well as swear words and references to bodily functions. A nice example of the first is a sly passage where Rizal discusses the superstitious veneration of Capitan Tiago for certain religious images:

---

9. Pp. 32, 44, 47, 80.

10. Compare, e.g., *Noli*, pp. 148, 219, and 352, with *The Lost Eden*, pp. 167, 250, and 405.

11. In 1981 Guerrero recalled that: "I learned Tagalog only when I started working in the *Free Press*. Really, my Tagalog is completely fractured. It isn't bad now, but still, it used to be horrible!" Alegre and Fernandez, *The Writer and his Milieu*, pp. 85, 86.

> No había él visto por sus proprios ojitos á los Cristos todos en el sermon de las Siete Palabras mover y doblar la cabeza á compás y tres veces, provocando el llanto y los gritos de todas las mujeres y almas sensibles destinadas al cielo? Más? Nosotros mismos hemos visto al predicador enseñar al público, en el momento del descenso de la cruz, un pañuelo manchado de sangre, é íbamos ya á llorar piadosamente, cuando, para desgracia de nuestra alma, nos aseguró un sacristan que aquello era broma . . . era la sangre de una gallina, asada y comida *incontinenti* apesar de ser Viernes santo . . . y el sacristan estaba grueso. (p. 28)

This means roughly:

> Had he not seen with his own piggy eyes, during the sermon on [Jesus's] Seven Last Words, all the images of Christ thrice moving and bending their heads in unison, provoking to tears and shrieks all the women and sensitive souls destined for Heaven? We have ourselves observed a preacher displaying to the public, at the moment of the Descent from the Cross, a blood-stained handkerchief; then, just as we too were about to burst into pious tears, a sacristan assured us—to our spiritual misfortune—that it was just a joke: it was the blood of a hen, roasted and devoured instanter, despite its being Good Friday . . . and the sacristan was fat.

Guerrero offers simply: "Had he not seen with his own little eyes the images of Christ, during the Good Friday sermons on the Seven Last Words, thrice raising and hanging their heads in unison, moving to tears and pious exclamations all the women in church and indeed all sensitive souls destined for salvation?" (p. 32). It seems that it is one thing for the Chinese mestizo's credulity to be ridiculed, but quite another to permit the First Filipino, in his own sarcastic voice, to mock the priesthood's cynical manipulations of popular Filipino piety—and that piety itself. Hence the elision of Rizal's hilariously wicked second sentence.

Rizal frequently has his rougher characters swear, using the typographical convention "p—" This "p—" may signal the mestizo expression *putangina,* in which are combined the Spanish *puta* (whore) and the Tagalog *inay* (mother), i.e. "your mother is a whore!" (This curse word one hears dozens of times every day on Manila's streets, and it is certainly one that "every schoolboy knows.") Another, perhaps more likely, referent is *puñeta* —a phrase sufficiently coarse to ensure exclusion from the Royal Academy of Madrid's standard Spanish dictionary—which we could render as "jack off!" In every case, however, Guerrero either erased "p—" completely, or rendered it as "dammit," or, more bravely, "damn you."[12] If one wanders about Manila, the most common single graffito one sees is: *Bawal umihi dito,* or "No pissing

---

12. Compare *Noli*, pp. 217, 218, 220, and 294, with *The Lost Eden*, pp. 247–9 and 337.

here!" Like men in the Mediterranean countries, males in the Philippines are accustomed to relieving themselves whenever and almost wherever the urge strikes them. In general urination is treated absolutely matter-of-factly by both men and women. It is therefore curious that where Rizal has his characters urinate, these passages were deleted by his translator. More remarkable, however, is Guerrero's treatment of a famous passage in which Rizal describes the dilapidated condition of the old cemetery of "San Diego." He writes sardonically of the bones and skulls that: "Allí esperarán probablemente, no la resurreccion de los muertos, sino la llegada de los animales, que con sus líquidos les calienten y laven aquellas frias desnudeces" (p. 56). Or: "Most likely they awaited there, not the resurrection of the dead, but the arrival of the animals, which with their liquids would warm them, and bathe those chilly nakednesses." Guerrero, evidently shrinking from this bitterness, offers us: "There they awaited, not the resurrection of the dead, but the attentions of some animal to warm and wash their coldness and their bareness" (p. 61). From this, the young reader might easily imagine not a jet of boar's piss, but the gentle touch of a fawn's tongue.

DELOCALIZATION

Almost all the scenes in the *Noli* are set either in "San Diego" (present-day Calamba, and Rizal's home town) or in Manila. The Manila chapters are replete with references to, and descriptions of, streets, churches, neighbourhoods, cafés, esplanades, theatres, and so forth. Some of these have, of course, disappeared over the course of the last century, and others have changed their names and the purposes for which they are used. But the great bulk remain fully recognizable to anyone who has lived in Manila for any length of time. The density of these places and placenames are among the elements that give the reader the most vivid sense of being drawn deep inside the novel—in much the same way that Dickens used the detailed urban geography of London to bring to life the world of Bill Sikes and Fagin, Daniel Quilp and Little Nell. It is therefore odd that Guerrero eliminated as much as 80 per cent of these still-recognizable placenames. It would be quite easy, using the original Spanish text, to follow Rizal's heroes and villains as they move around the metropolis, but almost impossible if one employs Guerrero's American version. Furthermore, Rizal on occasion brings on stage the well-known music-hall and operetta "stars" of his day: Chananay, Yeyeng, Marianito, Carvajal, and so on. These figures function as might Woody Allen, Pavarotti, and Madonna in a sophisticated novel about contemporary New York. They do not need explaining since every 1880s reader would automatically know who they were. Guerrero eliminated all these stars, representing them in anonymous collectivity as "the most renowned performers from Manila."[13] What is puzzling is that Guerrero was certainly widely enough read to know that references to now forgotten show-biz celebrities in the novels of Balzac, Tolstoy, and Proust in no way impede—but rather accentuate—the immediacy and verisimilitude of the worlds they present their readers. And while young Filipinos of the 1950s would certainly not know "who" Yeyeng was, they would recognize her name as Tagalog and thus see her as a Filipina; if Carvajal is a Spanish name, it is nonetheless borne by a contemporary mestizo mini movie star. One would have thought that keeping Rizal's names would have served to bring the milieu of the 1880s closer to modern readers rather than estranging them from it.

DE-EUROPEANIZATION

Rizal was an unusually cultivated man, made familiar through his Jesuit schooling with Latin and the world of antiquity. He knew Spanish, English, French, and German, as well as a smattering of Italian and Hebrew.[14] He also read widely in European literature. It is not surprising, therefore, to find the *Noli* filled with untranslated classical tags (often used for wonderfully satirical purposes), as well as references to, and quotations from, famous European masters. Guerrero's approach to all these references was to eliminate them or to naturalize them, as far as possible. Sometimes the effect is bizarre. For example, in a conspiratorial discussion between two Dominican friars, Rizal has the older one say: "Temo que no estemos empezando á bajar: Quos vult perdere Jupiter dementat prius" (p. 47). Or: "I fear lest we may be beginning to decline. Whom Jupiter wishes to destroy he first makes mad." Rizal does not translate the Latin because he assumes his readers will understand his tag. He is also having fun at the Dominican's expense by having the divines refer, with comic mislearning, to the Roman superdivinity, although the Church Fathers had long ago converted Euripides' mysterious Greek *daimon* into a Christian *Deus.* Guerrero eliminated both the Latin and the barb, and translated it as: "Whom God would destroy, He first makes mad" (p. 50). The result is the erasure of Rizal's civilized laughter.

In another striking passage Rizal writes that Father Damaso's sinister appearance "os acordareis de uno de aquellos tres monjes de que habla Heine en sus 'Dioses en el destierro', que por el Equinoccio de Setiembre, allá en Tyrol pasaban á media noche en barco un lago, y cada vez depositaban en la

---

13. Compare *Noli*, pp. 145, 224, and 226, with *The Lost Eden*, pp. 164, 257, and 259.

14. Chapter 7 ("Idilio en una azotea") has an untranslated Hebrew subtitle; chapter 53's Italian title is "Il Buon Di Si Conosce da Mattina;" chapter 57 is simply headed "Vae Victis!"

mano del pobre barquero una moneda de plata, como el hielo fria, que le dejaba lleno de espanto" (p. 4).[15] Or, roughly: "would make you think of one of those three monks of whom Heine speaks in his *Gods in Exile,* who, at the September equinox, yonder in the Tyrol, at midnight would cross a lake in a boat, and each time deposit in the hand of the poor boatman a silver coin, cold as ice, which left him full of dread." Guerrero made this: "recalled one of those three monks in the German story who would cross a Tyrolean lake at midnight, and each time place in the hand of the terror-stricken boatman a silver coin, cold as ice" (p. 5). Where Rizal's sarcastic use of "la palanca del mundo" (p. 91) makes a clear reference to Archimedes' celebrated lever, Guerrero bleached the erudite malice out to: "I realised that the sight of daily floggings killed the sense of pity, and stifled that of personal dignity, *which moves the world*" (p. 99). (The reader might well read "moves" here to mean "stirs the heart.") Where Rizal calls his chief villainess "Medusa" (pp. 262–3), Guerrero simply used her name, Doña Consolacion (pp. 299–300). Champollion (p. 217) became "the most eminent Egyptologist" (p. 247). The wise old man Tasio, whom Rizal (p. 62) describes as a "filósofo"—i.e. as a *philosophe,* Philippine representative of Diderot's Enlightenment rationalism and scepticism—became Guerrero's contextless "scholar" (p. 67). Vanished are Chloe, Actaeon, Snow White, Leonidas, Pluto, Argus, Ariadne, Minos, Bacchus, Astarte Genetrix, and "the Diana of Ephesus with her numerous breasts," as well as many others.[16]

There is a curious irony in all this, since Guerrero, as we shall see, prided himself on his anti-American nationalism. For the effect of his de-Europeanized translation is not to Filipinize Rizal, but rather to Americanize him.

ANACHRONISM

The most striking examples of anachronism all, in different ways, relate to the changing "official" social-political classification systems operating in the Philippines in the 1880s and 1950s. One gets a feel for this from quite small details from the start. For example, Rizal (p. 27) laughingly says of a kitschy image of St. Michael in a rich man's home that the archangel "embraza un escudo griego y blande en la diestra un kris joloano," or "holds a Greek shield on his arm and brandishes in his right hand a Jolonese kris."

---

15. The reference is to one of Heine's last, most profound set of poems, *Die Götter in Exil.*

16. Compare *Noli,* pp. 38 (Chloe), 49 (Astarte and the Diana of Ephesus), 126 (Actaeon), 168 (Sigismund and Dornröschen [Snow White]), 189 (Leonidas and Pluto), 298 (Argus), 351 (Ariadne, Minos, and Bacchus), with *The Lost Eden,* pp. 41, 52, 137, 191, 214, 341, and 404.

Guerrero's version is: "carried a Greek shield on one arm and with the other wielded a Malay *kris*" (p. 31). Aside from the characteristic distancing shift of tenses, the obvious metamorphosis is of "Jolonese kris" into "Malay *kris*." Rizal saw no need to italicize "kris," a word (and a short sword) known to everyone in the archipelago, then and now. The Muslim town of Jolo was then, and still is, among the best manufacturers of these fine traditional weapons. Guerrero's italicization makes the kris stick out as some kind of "foreign" word/object needing to be explained to young Filipinos. "Malay," is odder. Read one way it could refer to the peoples of Malaya/Malaysia and Indonesia, who indeed also manufacture krises; such a reading would accentuate the foreignness of the weapon—as if to suggest that by the 1960s Filipinos would know nothing of such weapons. But the word could also, more plausibly, be read "racially," to mean something like "Malayo-Polynesian," the population type that supposedly includes Filipinos, Chams, Malays, and Indonesians. If so, the "Malay" would here serve to erase the fact that the Muslims of the Philippines were/are a religious minority beleaguered by a 90 per cent Christian majority, and thereby emphasize that the kris was "essentially Filipino."

The problems accumulate if we look at the way in which Rizal uses ethnic, racial, and political terminologies. On the whole, he sticks to the later Spanish-colonial classifications: *peninsulares* (Spaniards born in Spain), *criollos* (Spaniards born in the Philippines or Latin America), mestizos (persons of mixed descent, Spanish-native, Spanish-Chinese, Chinese-native, and other complications), *sangleyes* and *chinos* (Chinese born outside the Philippines), and *indios* or *naturales* ("Indians" or indigenes of the Philippine islands). But sometimes he also uses the terms *mestizo* and *criollo* inconsistently, so that they appear to overlap or even correspond. This inconsistency was characteristic of the 1880s and 1890s when political, cultural, and social changes were making problematic the older hierarchy. Not less important to bear in mind is the fact that the word *filipino* was then just beginning a momentous transformation. For most people in the country—which everyone called *Filipinas* or *Las Filipinas*—up to the end of the nineteenth century, the word was principally a synonym of criollo, or pure-blooded Spaniard born in the archipelago, and it was always spelled, Spanish-style, with a small "f." But it was also, almost imperceptibly, starting to be claimed by upwardly mobile Spanish and Chinese mestizos, in periodic alliance with the traditional *filipino* creoles in political opposition to the *peninsulares* controlling the colonial army, administration, and ecclesiastical high command. After 1900—i.e. after Rizal's death and the success of the anti-Spanish revolutionary movement of 1896–98—it quickly acquired a primarily political meaning, referring to all the "sons and daughters of the country," no matter what their racial origins.

And it went upper case. But in Rizal's novels it is never used in this twentieth-century sense.

Guerrero's handling of these terms is exceptionally instructive. In the first place, *filipina* (Rizal for some reason seldom used the male form of the adjective or noun), meaning *mestiza* or *criolla* is typically rendered as *Filipina*, meaning a female national of the Philippines. Creoles virtually disappear, while *mestizo* is most commonly rendered, Anglo-Saxon racist style, as "half-breed." For example, of the Chinese-mestizo Don Santiago de los Santos Rizal slyly writes (p. 29) "si se criticaba á los mestizos sangleyes ó españoles, criticaba él tambien, acaso porque se creyese ya ibero puro." ("If people criticized the Chinese or Spanish mestizos, he would criticize them himself, perhaps because he already believed himself to be pure Iberian.") Guerrero wrote (p. 33): "If he heard criticism of the Chinese and Spanish half-breeds, he added his own, perhaps because he already considered himself of pure Spanish blood." When the stupid, ambitious Doña Victorina thinks about appointing an administrator for her family's financial affairs, Rizal (p. 239) says that she "pensó en un administrador peninsular, no confiando en los filipinos." Aside from anything else, the context makes it quite plain that Rizal means "she thought of an administrator from the Peninsula, having no confidence in the creoles." But Guerrero modernized, nationalized, and nonsensicalized the sentence as: "he would have to be a Spaniard from Spain; she had no confidence in Filipinos" (p. 273). Where Rizal (p. 325) has "pregunta una criolla" ("a creole girl enquired"), Guerrero offered: "a half-breed girl interrupted" (p. 373). Most striking of all, perhaps, is the contrast between Rizal's (p. 329) description of the guest list for Maria Clara's wedding as "únicamente españoles y chinos; el bello sexo está representado por españolas peninsulares y filipinas" ("consisted solely of Spaniards and Chinese; the fair sex was represented by peninsular and Philippine [creole] Spaniards") and Guerrero's "exclusively Spaniards and Chinese, the women only local Spaniards and Spaniards from the Peninsula" (p. 379). For this is the one place where the translator does *not* dystranslate *filipinas*. One can see, nonetheless, a characteristic mind set at work. In Rizal's sentence *filipinas* appears as an adjective qualifying *españolas*, so that "Filipina Spaniards" would be an intolerably *visible* dystranslation. Furthermore, it would seem strange to young Filipinos of the 1960s to read of a very exclusive wedding to which Filipinas (but not Filipinos) were invited. Guerrero's ingenious solution is to give a correct translation but at the same time to make sure that nothing betrays the presence in Rizal's original of . . . *filipinas!*

Before attempting to decipher the meaning of Guerrero's strategy of translation, it is necessary to say something about the man himself. He was born in

1915, sixteen years after the United States assumed sovereignty over the Philippines from Spain. He died in 1982, thirty-six years after the inauguration of the (Second) Republic of the Philippines. He came from the large middle-class, mestizo, Guerrero family of Manila, one of the few genuinely to earn the title of *ilustrado* by its production, over three generations, of reasonably distinguished intellectuals and professional men.[17]

His grandfather, Leon Ma. Guerrero I (1853–1935), known as the "Father of Philippine Botany," was a notable scientist, educator, journalist, and patriotic-conservative politician. Professor of botany at the University of Santo Tomás, he became politically active after Emilio Aguinaldo's proclamation of the revolutionary Republic in the summer of 1898. He wrote for Aguinaldo's newspaper *La República Filipina*, was a member of the revolutionary legislature, served in Aguinaldo's second cabinet, and helped lead the Philippine delegation in peace negotiations with the Schurman Commission. When the Americans set up the first colonial legislature in 1907, he served one term as a Nacionalista Party member for the second district in Bulacan. Subsequently, he went back to academic life, and was elected the first president of the Liceo de Manila. One of his sons, Cesar Ma. Guerrero (1885–1961), became a prominent ecclesiastic, serving as Bishop of Lingayen (1929–37), and later of San Fernando (1948–57). His reputation was damaged, however, by his alleged collaboration with the Japanese occupation forces in 1942–45, for which he was later charged with treason (the case was eventually dropped thanks to lobbying by the Hierarchy). The other son, Dr. Alfredo Ma. Guerrero, a wealthy and popular doctor, was our translator's father.

The collateral branch of the family was just as prominent. Leon Ma. Guerrero I's elder brother, Lorenzo (1835–1904), was a well-known professional artist, and the teacher of the Philippines' most famous painters, Juan Luna and Resurrección Hidalgo. One of his sons, Fernando Ma. Guerrero (1873–1929), the "Poet of the Revolution," is still remembered for his patriotic verses. During the revolution he served as a young staff-writer for General Antonio Luna's *La Independencia*, and later became the fiery editor of such nationalist papers as *El Renacimiento, La Vanguardia, El Patria,* and *La Opinión*. He also served in the first American-era legislature. Another son, Dr. Manuel Severino Guerrero (1877–1919), taught medicine at the University of Santo Tomás, worked for *La República Filipina* and *La Opinión,* and published a lively collection of short stories under the title of *Prosa*

---

17. The biographical materials in the following paragraphs are drawn from W.M. Guerrero, *The Guerreros of Ermita* (Quezon City: New Day, 1988), chapters 3–4, 16–21, 24–5, especially 24; Carlos Quirino's faintly sly introduction to Guerrero's prize-winning biography of Rizal, *The First Filipino* (1963), pp. xv–xix; and a biographical press release, series C, no. 52, issued by the Philippine Department of Foreign Affairs on May 9, 1966.

Literaria. One of Fernando's sons, Wilfrido, still alive, became a notable play-wright, director, and professor at the University of the Philippines. One of Manuel's daughters, Evangelina, was a Spanish-language author who won the 1935 Zobel Prize for her *Kaleidoscopio Espiritual.* All the Guerreros down past our translator's generation still spoke Spanish at home; but in the sphere of public life there was a sharp break between the first two generations, who wrote primarily in Spanish, and that of Leon Ma. and his second cousin Wilfrido, who published almost wholly in American.[18]

A young colonial very much aware of his *ilustrado* lineage, Guerrero seemed destined for a brilliant career. He won his B.A. (summa cum laude) at the Jesuits' Ateneo de Manila in 1935, and his L1. B. (summa cum laude) at the University of the Philippines in 1939. In 1940, at the age of twenty-five, he was already teaching law at the Ateneo and working in the office of the Solicitor-General. Among his first tasks was preparing a brief for the Philippine Supreme Court urging rejection of the appeal of the young Ferdinand Marcos against a conviction for murder (perhaps because the Chief Justice, José Laurel, Sr., had himself fought off such a charge of murder when a young man, Marcos won his appeal). During this period Guerrero became a protégé of Claro Recto, wealthy lawyer, Nacionalista politician, and Hispanophile littérateur. This association was to determine much of his later career. Although he fought alongside the Americans in Bataan and Corregidor, he is said by Carlos Quirino to have become disenchanted by America's failure to protect his country. Accordingly, he resumed under Japanese auspices a nightly radio political commentary which he had made popular in the American period—using the alias "Ignacio Javier" (i.e. a com-bination of the Jesuit heroes St. Ignatius of Loyola and St. Francis Xavier). When Recto became the Foreign Minister of José Laurel's wartime Republic in 1943, the young Guerrero joined the diplomatic corps and from 1943 to 1945 served as First Secretary of the new Philippine embassy in Tokyo. While both Laurel and Recto were (rather briefly) imprisoned by the Americans for wartime collaboration—like Guerrero's ecclesiastical uncle Cesar Ma.—the young commentator–diplomat was too small a fish for retribution. After a short period under a cloud, he bounced back as legal counsel to the Senate in 1947, and later joined Recto's prosperous law firm. By 1954, at the age of thirty-nine, he was Undersecretary of Foreign Affairs under the wily Carlos Romulo. He was a great "1950s success" and there seemed no reason why he should not continue to rise higher. Then things began to go awry.

---

18. Asked by Doreen Fernandez what he considered his primary language, Guerrero replied: "English. of course." DF: "No longer Spanish?" LMG: "I'm very funiliar with Spanish, but it's not like English." Alegre and Fernandez, *The Writer and his Milieu*, p. 86.

Uncleared speeches that he made on the theme of "Asia for the Asians" irritated Romulo and the American Embassy, and worried those who detected in them certain echoes of wartime Japanese propaganda themes. The tone of the speeches seemed to align his views tightly with those of Senator Recto, who was then, for his own reasons, advancing a neutralist and implicitly anti-American foreign-policy position, at a time when the Senator and President Magsaysay had become bitter enemies. Guerrero was then packed off to be Ambassador to London, where he served from 1954 to 1962.

Worse was to follow. In October 1959, at a diplomatic lunch in New York, which he attended as a member of the Philippine delegation to the United Nations, he got into a noisy quarrel with Walter Robertson, a member of the American delegation who had been Foster Dulles's powerful and reactionary Assistant Secretary of State for Far Eastern Affairs. Guerrero is said to have been angered by Robertson's sneering references to Recto, and patronizing enumeration of America's altruistic policies towards the Philippines. Robertson concluded by saying that: "You are very rude . . . you know, you are the first Filipino who has ever spoken to me like this." To which Guerrero is said to have replied: "The trouble is that you are not used to Filipinos talking back to Americans."[19] Washington then made it clear it would not welcome Guerrero in any central diplomatic functions. He became Chairman of the International Sugar Council in 1960, and sank to becoming Ambassador to Spain in 1962. In the meantime his patron, Senator Recto, had died at the end of 1960. When the pro-American and American-backed Marcos took power, Guerrero eventually tagged along, to the point of publishing a defence of the martial-law regime in 1975. Entitled originally *Today Began Yesterday*, it did neither his reputation nor his career much good. He became an alcoholic and died a disappointed man in 1982.[20]

The circumstances under which Guerrero undertook his translation of Rizal were thus quite important. His introduction to *The Lost Eden* was dated "Rizal Day [December 30], 1959," a bare three months after the Robertson brouhaha; that to the *Fili*, "Mayday of the Centenary of Rizal's Birth, 1961," a few months after Recto's death. It seems plausible that,

---

19. See the account given in *The Manila Times,* Oct. 2, 1959.

20. It was an expanded version of a text "commissioned" by Marcos's Foreign Minister Romulo to rebut an anti-martial-law text published in the *New York Times* by the exiled politician Raúl Manglapus. In his interview with Doreen Fernandez, done shortly before his death, Guerrero was painfully self-denigrating about much of his life in public. Commercially very successful as translator, biographer, journalist, and essayist, he said, "I wouldn't call myself a writer," and virtually accused himself of becoming a hack by penning "stupid formula stories" and making "my living as a ghost writer [for Recto among others]" (Alegre and Fernandez, *The Writer and his Milieu,* pp. 71–3).

realizing he had little hope of playing any further role in high-level politics, he was turning, as others in his family had done before him, to the construction of a reputation as a nationalist intellectual and litterateur. Indeed, he quickly followed up these translations with a prize-winning English-language biography of Rizal (completed, he claimed later, in one month!)—and a collection of Spanish-language articles and speeches, entitled *El Sí y el No*, which won the Zobel literary prize in 1963.

That so much of this energy was devoted to Rizal, and that its achievements were so strange, is the difficult problem to be considered in the final section of this essay.

Two general lines of investigation suggest themselves, to be followed up at different levels, but by no means necessarily in conflict with each other. Both invite us, from contrasting perspectives, to think about the passing of political time.

The first is the near-universal passage from the era in which nationalism was primarily a popular insurrectionary movement, outside of and against a state, to an era in which it is partially transformed into a legitimating instrumentality of a new-old state. In the final decade of his short life—thirty-five years—Rizal was the central figure in the imagining and mobilization of a popular Philippine nationalism against two states: the autocratic, clerical-colonial state based in Manila, and the fissiparous, half liberal-republican, half clerical-monarchical imperial state based in Madrid. This task involved a strenuous campaign both of deconstruction and construction. The colonial state and its reactionary ecclesiastical allies had to be unmasked, while a Philippines profoundly distinct from Mother Spain had to be conjured up. For both purposes, in different ways, the novel as literary genre (which Rizal virtually pioneered in the Philippines) was perfectly adapted.[21] For it permitted the imagining of "Las Filipinas" as a bounded sociological reality[22] encompassing dozens of social types, at every social level, engaged in daily, "simultaneous" interaction with one another. But it also allowed the reader to see, in unmatched polemical detail, the congeries of exploitation, brutality, hypocrisy, cowardice, fanaticism, stupidity, ignorance, and corruption which made colonial domination possible. In other words, it was ideally suited for Rizal's remarkable satirical gifts. It is in this context that we can observe how essential to his purposes were some of the *Noli*'s rhetorical mannerisms and devices which Guerrero precisely did his best to erase. The novel was, perhaps

---

21. The theme here is elaborated in chapter 2 of my *Imagined Communities*.
22. Reading the novel, we are aware of Spain, Hong Kong, Germany, and America, but always "off stage."

necessarily, set in the (recent) past, but the author was eager to assure readers that God continued affectionately to multiply spongers and gatecrashers
in Manila. Under the colonial autocracy the ordinary reader would have no
chance to observe directly the secret machinations of Dominicans or
governors-general; but the author could take the same reader—*amigo ó
enemigo*—by the hand and let him invisibly eavesdrop on these shady doings.
Everyone knew that under the façade of statesmanlike *pronunciamentos* and
pious sermons, the rulers, and their wives, mistresses, and concubines swore
obscenely, urinated, mixed Tagalog expressions with their often ungrammat-
ical Spanish, got their Latin wrong—and lived on exactly this street, sent
people to that prison, enjoyed a tacky vaudeville show in this theatre, and
plotted in that friary. It was Rizal's prime strategy to show all of this with the
most convincing and immediate social realism at his command: hence *puñeta,
susmariosep,* Yeyeng, Pasay, *salakot,* Jolo, and so forth. Everything here is a
call to arms.

But in the independent Philippines of the 1950s, how much of all this was
really bearable? The country had been economically, physically, and morally
devastated between 1942 and 1945 as American and Japanese masters fought
over it. From 1948 to 1953 it had experienced its first great insurrectionary
movement since the turn of the century. Its real freedom was enchained by
American military bases and the American-imposed Parity agreement. But it
was ruled by children of the revolutionary mestizo elite of the 1890s, who had
gained enormously in wealth and power under the American colonial system,
who had collaborated with the Japanese occupation regime, and who now
intended firmly to be full masters in their own house.

For this postindependence establishment, with its precarious domestic and
international prestige, Rizal—Lolo [Grandfather] Rizal—appeared as both
amigo and *enemigo.* Of mixed Spanish–Chinese–*indio* descent, and of comfortable circumstances, he was one of them. His heroism and self-sacrifice
were utterly exemplary. He was the one Filipino after whom streets were
named in Spain and Germany, and whose writings were translated into Hindi,
French, Indonesian, English, and Russian. His statues dotted the plazas of a
hundred Philippine small towns. He was the centre of a widespread popular
mystical cult among the peasants. Thus he acted as a general guarantor of the
truth of Philippine nationalism—in a certain sense, even as its alibi.

But he was also an *enemigo,* not least because, unlike Joan of Arc or
William Tell, he was himself a nationalist and he wrote and wrote and wrote.
Much of what he penned was inevitably, by the 1950s, upsetting if not sub-
versive—also for his nationalist translator. Rizal had denounced the
oppression of women: Claro Recto had singlehandedly prevented the
Philippines from following the United States in granting female suffrage after

World War I. Rizal had satirized collaborating mestizo *hacendados*: Leon Ma. was President of the International Sugar Federation, and the Filipino legislature was dominated by collaborating sugar barons. Rizal mercilessly ridiculed the Catholic hierarchy: but in the 1950s the Filipino Cardinal Rufino Santos was very much the spiritual child of the reactionary Spanish clerisy of the colonial era; and Leon Ma.'s uncle, Bishop Cesar, could easily have wandered into the pages of the *Noli* or the *Fili*. Perhaps these considerations encouraged the translator to undertake some bowdlerization, and, by de-modernization, exclusion of the reader, and delocalization, to distance Rizal's Philippines as much as possible from the Philippines of his own time.

But beside these narrow considerations, others were probably deeper and more important. The very fact of independence made possible, even necessary, from a certain perspective, the appearance in the archipelago of official nationalism. This is the form of nationalism which surfaces as an emanation and armature of the state. It manifests itself, not merely in official ceremonies of commemoration, but in a systematic programme, directed primarily, if not exclusively, through the state's school system, to create and disseminate an official nationalist history, an official nationalist pantheon of heroes, and an official nationalist culture, through the ranks of its younger, incipient citizens—naturally, in the state's own interests. These interests are first and foremost in instilling faith in, reverence for, and obedience to its very self.

One can see that a socially radical, iconoclastic, satirical, earthy, moralizing Rizal was not readily adaptable to this programme. From the point of view of official nationalism, heroes should be revered, not admired; seen, not heard—nor read. No surprise that the official Rizal is the silent waxwork martyr of the museum in Intramuros, the statue that holds (closed) copies of the *Noli* and the *Fili* in his hands, and the elegiac poet of *Mi Último Adiós*.[23] If Rizal is exemplary in this respect, he is not at all unique. The crippled revolutionary statesman Apolinario Mabini has a museum in his honour and is invoked officially as the "Sublime Paralytic," but his lucid, acerbic Spanish writings remain mostly untranslated into English or Tagalog. Statues abound in honour of Antonio Luna, the most creative general of the Revolutionary Republic, but they do not say that he was assassinated at the orders of the Republic's President, Emilio Aguinaldo; nor are his splendid letters and other writings available to the contemporary citizen. The "Great Plebeian," Andrés Bonifacio, is commemorated by a remarkable monument in a seedy part of north Manila, but the great man's words, inscribed around the base, are in the secret code he devised to elude the Spanish-colonial security services—and

---

23. This is why Ambeth Ocampo's wonderfully funny and down-to-earth book about Rizal (*Rizal without the Overcoat* [Manila: Anvil, 1990]) is so refreshing and important.

are unreadable by the ordinary public.[24] The effect, always, is to say that "then was then, now is now." No connection, only examples.

For much of his adult life Leon Ma. Guerrero was a loyal and intelligent servant of the Philippine state. It is hard not to suspect that in his translations of Rizal the demands of this state did not serve, consciously or unconsciously, as his strategic compass.

Yet I do not believe that we have solved the problems posed by Guerrero's translations if we attribute them simply to the bad conscience of the postin-dependence elite or the requirements of official nationalism. For these explanations cannot cope adequately with de-Europeanization, de-Tagalogization, and, above all, anachronism.

At this point we have to turn to American imperialism and its conse-quences. From the point of view of this essay at least, the most important of these consequences were the substitution of American for Spanish as the lingua franca of the archipelago, and a fundamental reshaping of Filipinos' conception of themselves. I will be trying to argue, from here on, that these transformations literally made Rizal's *Filipinas* virtually unimaginable.

We noted above that according to the census of 1939 (forty years after the installation of American colonialism) less than 3 per cent of the popu-lation claimed competence in Spanish, while over 26 per cent professed ability in "English." Both figures are of interest and need their own expli-cations. While it is true that a number of powerful colonial officials despised Spanish (and Spanish culture), it cannot be said that it was general American imperial policy to eliminate the language: after all, Puerto Rico, essentially an American colony, remains basically a Spanish-speaking soci-ety. The fact is that even at the very end of the Spanish period only 5 per cent of the population of the Philippines was Spanish-fluent.[25] Yet given that the elite of Rizal's generation used Spanish comfortably as its lingua franca, we can scarcely doubt that, if the First Republic had been permitted

---

24. Does one also detect here a sort of "beatification," whereby the argumentative revolu-tionary leaders are adroitly turned into silent *santos*?

25. This surprising aberration from the general pattern within the Spanish empire has its only parallel in Paraguay, where Guaraní remains a living national tongue alongside Spanish. The explanation is that in both zones, for peculiar historical reasons, preponderant political power was held for a long time by ecclesiastics who wished to convert the natives as well as to exploit them. Unlike most other Spaniards, these clerics made it their business to learn the local languages in order to transmit God's truth to their flocks in tongues that they understood. (The secular power, rather weak in itself, also recognized that the costs of spreading Spanish through a modern school system would substantially outweigh the income derived from two relatively resource-poor colonies.) But on account of the antiquity of Spanish colonialism in the Philippines, and the pervasive presence of the clerics, Iberian influence on the local languages was extensive. Some linguists estimate that as much as a quarter of the root words in the major regional languages of the Philippines derive from Spanish.

to survive, its educational institutions would have rapidly spread Spanish as the national language. The speedy triumph of American came about because the colonial regime established the first modern state school-system (classroom enrolments expanded 500 per cent in the first generation after 1899), and at the same time made competence in English necessary for access to proliferating bureaucratic jobs and most professional careers. Hence the language became, for tens of thousands of ambitious, upwardly mobile Filipinos, the gateway to social, political, and economic advancement.[26] The Catholic schools moved in the same direction, albeit more slowly.[27] At the same time, while American thus replaced Spanish as the language of power in the colony, it bore a quite different relationship with local vernaculars, especially Tagalog. Over the centuries of Iberian dominion, many terms and phrases from these vernaculars seeped into Spanish, which in any case was not "policed" by a standardized school system. This fact accounts for the casual proliferation of Tagalogisms throughout the *Noli,* even in the mouths of Spaniards. The Americans, however, were too new, too powerful, and too fleeting in their presence to have any truck with Tagalog, and their schools reinforced this stance.[28] Hence the widespread myth in the Philippines that American teachers systematically punished any schoolchildren found using their mother tongues in the classroom.[29] (Was this perhaps the reason that the American-educated Guerrero expunged Tagalog from his translation of the *Noli*?)

Beyond language change, however, was the wider impact of an imperial rule that in almost every way was a total contrast with the regime that had preceded it. Early twentieth-century America was immense, wealthy, highly industrialized, secular, republican, philistine, and, within definite limits,

---

26. The statistics are revealing. In 1903, Filipinos held less than half the 5,500 or so positions in the colonial civil service. By 1921, they held 90 per cent of 14,000 such jobs. By the mid-1930s the percentage had risen to 99 per cent. See Teodoro A. Agoncillo, *A Short History of the Philippines* (New York: Mentor, 1969), p. 169; and David Wurfel, "The Philippines," in G. McT. Kahin, ed., *Governments and Politics of Southeast Asia* (Ithaca, NY: Cornell University Press, 1964), pp. 689–90.

27. The decisive turn came in 1921, when the Vatican, under American pressure, moved the Spanish Jesuits in the Philippines to India, and turned the Philippines over to the New York–Maryland Province. See Martin Noone, *The Life and Times of Michael O'Doherty, Archbishop of Manila* (Quezon City: R.P. Garcia, 1988), pp. 146 ff. Hence, by the time Guerrero attended the Jesuits' famous Ateneo de Manila University in the early 1930s, it was an American, no longer a Spanish, institution, as it had been when Rizal studied there half a century earlier.

28. This attitude persisted after independence. American scholars of Indonesia and Siam were busy learning Indonesian and Thai in the 1950s, but their colleagues working on the Philippines did not generally apply themselves to Tagalog until the 1970s.

29. A myth because as early as 1927 some 99 per cent of public-school teachers were Filipino! See David Wurfel, *Filipino Politics: Development and Decay* (Ithaca, NY: Cornell University Press, 1988), p. 9.

democratically governed.[30] Spain was small, poor, agrarian, confessional, semi-monarchical, classically cultivated, and minimally democratic. Under the American regime the once powerful Catholic church was reduced to the political margin. After the passage of the Payne–Aldrich tariff Act in 1909, the Philippines passed behind the high walls of American protectionism, producing for the first time a vastly wealthy *hacendado* oligarchy. Outlying regions, especially Mindanao, were incorporated into a newly integrated capitalist economy. Albeit on a highly restricted suffrage base, an elected Filipino national leadership was created. A new American-style educational system was installed which turned out lawyers and engineers, rather than theologians and classicists.[31] And American rule coincided with the advent of commercial radio and film, which had an enormous general impact on at least urban Philippine society. Bearing all the above in mind, we can perhaps better understand why Guerrero de-Europeanized his *Noli,* and why he could speak of so many young Filipinos who "no longer have any idea of the customs of their forefathers." Along with Actaeon and Chloe, Champollion and the *philosophes,* a whole world had vanished—and not only for young Filipinos. In the imperial metropole itself residues of classical culture had largely disappeared. In this respect 1950s Washington and Manila were not far apart.

Last, and most important, was a fundamental change in the imagining of the Philippines and of Philippine society that started in the 1880s but reached its full fruition only two generations later. One might formulate the change simply by saying that Rizal was a patriot, while Guerrero was a nationalist.[32]

It is very striking, for example, that the beautiful poem Rizal composed shortly before his execution was addressed not to his fellow Filipinos and Filipinas, but to his *patria adorada.* Indeed the only people mentioned in it are his immediate family, and the *dulce extranjera,* his wretched "Irish" wife Josephine. Perhaps one should not be surprised at this form of dedication. Rizal had been to America, Spain, Italy, France, Germany, Britain, Belgium, and Hong Kong, but never to Ilocos, Bicol, or the Visayas. He owed his

---

30. It does no harm to remind ourselves that women were only allowed to vote after 1918, and that millions of blacks were disfranchised up to the 1960s.

31. Guerrero's reminiscences of his schooldays are enlightening. "Literature in the AB course at the time was the tops— in the Ateneo. It was supposed to be the elite course . . [Yet] I don't think we studied even one of Shakespeare's plays in detail . . . We didn't even read what you might call the last century's literature— even less (the more modern). We didn't even make the acquaintance of people like Hemingway, Faulkner, not even Edna Ferber, Willa Cather . . . A complete cultural desert!" Alegre and Fenandez, *The Writer and his Milieu,* pp. 72–3.

32. My thinking along these lines has been greatly stimulated by David Brading's massive, wonderful *The First America: The Spanish Monarchy, Creole Patriots and the Liberal State, 1492–1867* (Cambridge: Cambridge University Press, 1991).

limited acquaintance with Mindanao to the Spanish authorities who exiled him to Dapitan. (In this respect he was absolutely typical of the *ilustrados* of his time.) Nonetheless, he knew very well what *Las Filipinas* was, and its features were found in maps, atlases, newspapers, and books.[33] Las Filipinas had been around for 350 years.[34] It was there in the imagining to be loved—as a place, a *Heimat*. But in his time, as we have observed earlier, there was as yet no general name for the varied inhabitants: *filipinos* were still mainly Spanish creoles. He did, of course, speak of the *pueblo*, the "people," but its lineaments remain obscure, not least because he used it very often for the local inhabitants of Calamba, or Manila. The real lines he drew were those characteristic of what Brading calls "creole patriotism"—political, moral, and affectional lines—between lovers of the *patria adorada* and of justice, and their enemies and oppressors. He thus saw nothing strange in dedicating the *Fili* to the memories of the creoles José Burgos and Jacinto Zamora, and the Chinese mestizo Mariano Gómez, the three patriotic secular priests publicly garrotted by the colonial regime in 1872. He found it quite ordinary to make both the hero and heroine of the *Noli* mestizo.[35] Throughout the two novels there are patriotic and oppressive members of each traditional stratum of colonial society—*criollos*, mestizos, *indios*, and even *peninsulares*.[36]

As we remarked earlier, it was among the achievements of Rizal and the revolutionaries of his generation to imagine, gradually, a new historical person: the Filipino. Into this Filipino disappeared, for most political purposes at least, the *indio*, the mestizo, and the *criollo*. The *peninsulares* went back to Spain after 1899, or, if they remained, were destined to become "Filipino citizens," again a new imagining. As time passed, as nationalism spread, as the suffrage expanded, and as a second independence was achieved, "Filipinos" increasingly took the place of *Las Filipinas* as the objects of rhetorical and genuine attachment. Guerrero was a striking product of this immense subterranean shift. His introduction to the *Noli* concerned itself with Filipinos and did not even mention the Philippines.[37] Moreover, these Filipinos were for the most part now conceived as an ethnoracial unity. So deeply rooted was this conception, not merely in Guerrero but in most

---

33. For general considerations on this point, see "Census, Map, Museum," chapter 10 of my *Imagined Communities*.

34. The name is said to have been coined in 1527–29 by Alvaro de Saavedra, a member of Magellan's circumnavigationary expedition.

35. Indeed Maria Clara is the product of an adulterous relationship between the peninsular Father Damaso and Doña Pia Alba, the presumably mestiza wife of Capitán Tiago.

36. See, for example, the liberal peninsular student Sandoval in the *Fili*.

37. Was there in this reticence a foreshadowing of President Macapagal's formal 1962 claim to Sabah, certainly no ancient part of Las Filipinas?

educated Filipinos of his time, that Rizal's way of viewing the world around him had become virtually incomprehensible. It is in this transformation of social classifications, I suspect, that we may find the solution to the puzzle of anachronism in Guerrero's translation of the *Noli*. For young Filipinos would at once see, in any straight translation from the Spanish, that they do not exist within the novel's pages. *Filipinas,* of course, appear, but they are exactly what Filipinas today are not: "pure-blood" Spanish creoles. This, along with the influence of Anglo-Saxon racism, may help to account for Guerrero's strange translation of *mestizo* (a colonial social and legal category) by "half-breed," despite the fact that both Rizal and he himself were, by these terms, also "half-breeds." But was a "half-breed" First Filipino thinkable in the 1950s?

Nor, most likely, should we forget a different transformation that began in a small way in the 1930s and has reached flood tide today: the permanent movement of innumerable inhabitants of *Las Filipinas* far beyond the old archipelago's borders: first to Hawaii and Alaska; later, after reform of the American immigration laws under the Kennedy administration, to California and the rest of continental America; finally under Marcos and Aquino, to Europe, South America, the Middle East, Hong Kong, Japan, Singapore— wherever hope can be found. For this mass emigration has created hundreds of thousands of people who come from the Philippines but are no longer among its citizenry, no longer figures in the landscape of the Heimat. But they are profoundly attached to an "identity" which Guerrero would have understood completely and which to Lolo José would have seemed quite extraordinary.

Yet it would probably be rash to say that the transformation is complete. This is one reason, most likely, that the writing of Philippine history remains so parcellized and fragmented. In a standard history text sponsored by the Department of Education, Culture, and Sports, the Filipino child is taught that he "has 40 per cent Malay blood in his veins, 30 per cent Indonesian, 10 per cent Negrito, 10 per cent Chinese, 5 per cent Hindu, 2 per cent Arab, and 3 per cent European and American."[38] Furthermore, all Filipinos come from somewhere else: "The Aetas or Negritos were the first to come to the Philippines."[39] Conversely, Onofre Corpuz, former Secretary of Education and President of the University of the Philippines, finds the originary Filipino in "Tabon Man," whose fragmentary tools, found in a remote cave on

---

38. See Niels Mulder, "Philippine Textbooks and the National Self-Image," *Philippine Studies*, 38: 1 (1990), pp. 84–102, at p. 88, citing N. Carmona-Potenciano and T.T. Battad, *Our Country and its People*, vol. 1 (Manila: Bookmark, 1987), pp. 3–5.

39. Ibid., pp. 84–102.

Palawan, are said to date to at least 60,000 BC.[40] The hispanophile man of letters Nick Joaquín wrote that, "Before 1521 we could have been anything and everything *not* Filipino; after 1565 we can be nothing *but* Filipino,"[41] thanks to the technical and cultural revolution produced by the Spanish conquest. While for some eminent Catholic historians, the true course of Philippine history has its providential origins in the birth of Christianity half a world away.[42]

A speculative final comment may be warranted. In his study of the long evolution of Spanish-American thought, David Brading shows the reader very clearly how contrary impulses were always at work, and that these contrarieties grew more severe as local patriotisms in the Americas developed and were transformed. For hundreds of years, creoles and mestizos struggled to find ways to claim Moctezuma and his seducer Hernán Cortés, Atahualpa and his executioner Francisco Pizarro, as their joint-forefathers. Today, after almost two centuries of nationalism, there is, I am told, only one statue of Cortés in the whole of Mexico, and it is discreetly hidden away in a quiet part of Ciudad México. But the language in which Aztec and Maya ancestors are now publicly extolled is that of the invisible conquistador. This kind of double erasure—of Cortés the ancestor and, say, Maya, the language—strikes one as a likely trait of the nationalism of elites who are profoundly aware of their hybrid histories and cultures. Nationalism in our time dreams of purities, and finds it hard to linger *cariñosamente* over the oxymoron "pure mix." Maybe this is, in the end, the reason why the *creole–mestizo* world of Rizal's novels became, so soon, so hard to imagine—and impossible to translate.

POSTSCRIPT

In the interview with Doreen Fernandez cited earlier, Guerrero mentioned with special pride (p. 76) his success in rendering the celebrated scene where the not-yet-sinister, still young Doña Consolacion and her husband argue over how to pronounce "Filipinas." It is worth examining the curious nature of his achievement.

The Spanish original reads as follows:

---

40. See Corpuz's *The Roots of the Filipino Nation* (Quezon City: Aklahi Foundation, 1989), pp. ix, 2.

41. *Culture and History* (Mandaluyong: Solar, 1988), p. 14.

42. See, for example, John N. Schumacher, S.J., *Revolutionary Clergy: The Filipino Clergy and the Nationalist Movement, 1850–1903* (Quezon City: Ateneo de Manila Press, 1981); and Horatio de la Costa, S.J., *The Jesuits in the Philippines, 1581–1768* (Cambridge, Mass.: Harvard University Press, 1961).

—Una de las bellas cualidades de esta señora era el procurar ignorar el tagalo, ó al menos aparentar no saberlo, hablándolo lo peor posible: así se daría aires de una verdadera *orofea*, como ellos solía decir. Y hacía bien! porque si martizaba el tagalo, el castellano no salía mejor librado ni en cuanto se refería á la gramática, ni á la pronunciación. Y sin embargo su marido, las sillas y los zapatos, cada cual había puesto de su parte cuanto podía para enseñarla! Una de las palabras que costaron más trabajo aun que à Champollion los geroglíficos, era la palabra *Filipinas*.

Cuéntase que al día siguiente de su boda, hablando con su marido, que entonces era cabo, había dicho *Pilipinas*; el cabo creyó deber suyo corregirla y le dijo dándole un coscorron: "Dí Felipinas, mujer! no seas bruta. No sabes que se llama así á tu p— país por venir de Felipe?" La mujer, que soñaba en su luna de miel, quiso obedecer y dijo *Felepinas*. Al cabo le pareció que ya se acercaba, aumentó los coscorrones y la increpó . . . "Pero, mujer, no puedes pronunciar: Felipe? No lo olvides, sabe que el Rey Don Felipe . . . quinto . . . Dí Felipe, y añadele *nas* que en latin significa islas de indios, y tienes el nombre de tu rep— país!" La Consolación, lavandera entonces, palpándose el chichon ó los chichones, repitió empezando á perder la paciencia. "Fe . . . lipe, Felipe . . . nas, Felipenas, así *ba*?"

El cabo se quedó viendo visiones. Por qué resultó *Felipenas* en vez de *Filipinas*? Una de dos: ó se dice *Felipenas* ó hay de decir *Felipi*? Aquel día tuvo por prudente callarse; dejó á su mujer y fue á consultar cuidadosamente los impresos. Aquí su admiración llegó al colmo; restrégose los ojos: A ver . . . despacio! —*Filipinas* decían todos los impresos bien deletreados: ni él ni su mujer tenían razon.

"Cómo?" murmuraba, "puede mentir la Historia? No dice este libro que Alonso Saavedra había dado este nombre al país en obsequio al infante D. Felipe? Cómo se corrompió este nombre? Si será un indio el tal Alonso Saavedra . . .?"

A literal translation might be:

One of the charming qualities of this lady was attempting not to know Tagalog, or at least pretending not to know it, speaking it as badly as possible: thus she could give herself the airs of a true *orofea* [European], as she was wont to say. Just as well! For if she tortured Tagalog, Castilian fared no better either in grammar or pronunciation. And yet her husband, chairs, and boots had each done their best to teach her! One word which cost her more trouble than hieroglyphics had cost Champollion, was the word *Filipinas*. The story goes that on the day after her wedding, while talking with her husband who was then a corporal, she had said *Pilipinas*. The corporal, believing it his duty to correct her, gave her a cuff and said: "Say Felipinas, woman! Don't be an idiot. Don't you know that's what they call your f—g country, from Felipe?" The woman, then in her honeymoon dreams, wanted to obey and so said *Felepinas*. The corporal felt she was getting closer, so he stepped up his cuffing and scolded her thus: "But woman, can't you pronounce Felipe? Don't forget it, you know that King, Don Felipe the . . . Fifth . . . Say Felipe, then add on *nas*, which is Latin for 'islands of the indios,' and then you'll have the name of your f—g country!"

La Consolación, in those days a washerwoman, gingerly felt her bruise or bruises, and repeated the word, trying not to lose her patience. "Fe . . . lipe,

Felipe . . . nas, Felipenas, that it *ba*?" The corporal found himself seeing visions. How could it turn out to be *Felipenas* instead of *Filipinas*? One of the two: either it was *Felipenas* or one had to say *Felipi*?

That day he found it prudent to keep quiet. Leaving his wife, he went off to consult, very anxiously, the books. Here his astonishment reached its peak; he rubbed his eyes. Let's see . . . slowly now . . . All the well-printed books said *Filipinas*: so neither he nor his wife was right.

"How's this?" he murmured. "Can History lie? Doesn't this book say that Alonso Saavedra gave the country this name in honour of Prince D. Felipe? How did the name get corrupted? Could it be that this Alonso Saavedra was an indio?"

Guerrero's version, on the other hand, goes like this:

Indeed, one of this lady's lovable qualities was to try to unlearn her Tagalog, or at least to pretend she did not understand it, speaking it as badly as possible, thus giving herself the air of a true "Yorofean," as she put it. It was just as well; if her Tagalog was deliberately tortured, her Spanish was no better, either grammatically or in pronunciation, for all that her husband, with the aid of his boots and a handy chair or two, had done his best to teach her. One of the words she had the most trouble with, even more than hieroglyphics had given the most eminent Egyptologists, was *Philippines*.

It is said that the day after her wedding, conversing with her husband, who was then a corporal, she had pronounced it: *Pehleefens*. The corporal thought it his duty to correct her and admonished her with a cuff: "Say *Feeleepines,* girl! Don't be so stupid. Don't you even know your goddam country is named after King Philip?" His wife, who was still wrapped in honeymoon dreams, did her best to obey him and made it: *Feeleefeens*.

The corporal thought she was getting closer, gave her a few more cuffs, and upbraided her: "Can't you even say Philip, woman? Don't forget King Philip the . . . fifth . . . Anyway, say Philip, add *pines*, which in Latin means nigger islands, and you have the name of your goddam country!"

Doña Consolacion, who was then a laundress, gingerly felt with her fingers the effects of her husband's cuffings, and repeated, almost at the end of her patience: "Peeleep—Peeleep . . . pines—*Peeleepines*, is that it?"

"Not *Peeleep*, with a *p*!" roared the corporal. "*Feeleep*, with an *f*!"

"Why? How do you spell *Peeleep*? With a *p* or an *f*?"

The corporal thought it the better part of wisdom to change the subject that day, and meantime to consult a dictionary. Here his wonder reached its highest pitch. He rubbed his eyes. Let's see . . . slowly now . . . but there was no doubt about it. P–h–i–l–i–p–p–i–n–e–s; he and his wife were both wrong: it was neither *p* nor *f*, but *ph*.

How now, he muttered to himself. Could the dictionary be wrong? Or was this dictionary written by some stupid native?

Rizal's laughter in this passage is aimed at the brutishness, ignorance, and stupidity of La Consolación's *peninsular* (Spanish-Spanish) husband. He gets even the Spanish name for the colony wrong, as well as the name of the man who is said to have coined this name in the sixteenth century: Alvaro de Saavedra. He thinks the naming was in honour of Philip V (1683–1746), founder of the eighteenth-century Borbón dynasty, whom Rizal could be sure his readers knew as a feckless Spanish ruler who ended his days in imbecility. But as a minor motif, Rizal quietly shows up La Consolación's pathetic "European" pretensions by having her blurt out the Tagalog interrogative particle *ba*. All of this fun is erased in Guerrero's version.

A second, minor target is the *Spanish* language, since Las Filipinas is not a form which can be "logically" derived from Felipe, no matter how "logically" the corporal and his young wife try to make it so. But in Guerrero's version the target has become *Filipino* difficulties in distinguishing between *p* and *f*.

What is most instructive of all, however, is Guerrero's omission of the final paragraph. There is, in this way, no lying History. Quite deliberately, Alonso/Alvaro de Saavedra, who gave the Philippines the name it still bears 450 years later—as well as the Spanish ruler thereby honoured (Prince D. Felipe, later to become Braudel's Habsburg antihero Felipe II)—have been, as we say these days, "disappeared." Hernán Cortés?

PART III

SOUTHEAST ASIA: COMPARATIVE STUDIES

Elections in Southeast Asia

GENERAL CONSIDERATIONS

"National"-level elections, that is, those designed to produce a legislative body with a status and jurisdiction formally nearly equal to that of the pre-existing executive, are a quite recent innovation in Southeast Asia.[1] For the three countries under discussion in this essay, the relevant dates are 1907 for the Philippines, 1918 for the Netherlands East Indies (now Indonesia), and 1933 for Siam (now Thailand). In each case, the innovation came on the heels of, and was a clear response to, political crisis: in the Philippines to the anti-Spanish revolution of 1896–98, and a brutal, costly American "pacification" of the insurrectionary movement; in the Netherlands East Indies to a brief post-World War I revolutionary upsurge in the Netherlands itself, as well as the spectacular expansion of the Sarékat Islam on Java; and in Siam to the overthrow of the absolutist monarchy via the coup of June 24, 1932.

This pattern followed closely the one that can be observed in the historical evolution of the electoral mechanism in the areas from which it was imported to Southeast Asia, that is, Western Europe and the United States: in other words, the development of national-level legislatures and the expansion of the suffrage followed a certain democratization of political life rather than brought it into being. In the United States, we have only to think of the women's-suffrage and civil-rights movements, with their elaborate repertoires

---

1. In the colonized territories, there was, of course, no question of the colonial executive being elected or substantially answerable to the new legislatures. In uncolonized Siam, the monarch, after 1932, was supposed to be merely the head of state. Accountability only began to develop, hesitantly, as the executive branches were nationalized.

of extra-electoral political activities, culminating in the passage of the Nineteenth Amendment in 1920 and the Civil Rights Act of 1965. In Europe, we remember the agitations that led to the summoning of the Estates-General and the Duma, as well as the political emancipation of Catholics in the early nineteenth-century United Kingdom.

These precedents demonstrate rather clearly the Janus-face of electoralism. On the positive side, the right to vote in elections, even when they were scarcely free or competitive, was understood as the most signal emblem of full citizenhood in the modern age: it conveyed legal *status* and entitlement. Hence the irresistible push towards adult suffrage in polities moving towards self-definition as nation-states. (How important this aspect of things is can be seen from the reaction one could expect to a law that would deprive people of the vote if they did not exercise it over, say, a ten-year period.) The second key positive side of electoralism was the promise it held out, to the socially disadvantaged above all, of the enactment, in brief, decisive historical moments, of laws enforceable on every relevant site of struggle within the state's geographical stretch. Legislation would do at a sweep what a myriad of strikes, demonstrations, absenteeisms, featherbeddings, sit-ins, marches, assassinations, and prayer meetings could not, precisely because the latter were inevitably local or regional, episodic, and without legal force. If one thinks of the series of laws passed between 1850 and 1950 in the United Kingdom forbidding child labour, protecting female workers, guaranteeing minimum wages, developing social security, legalizing trade unions and certain kinds of strikes—laws which had their parallels in most of Western Europe—the attraction of electoral politics is completely understandable. Furthermore, not only were such laws in place, but also, because they emerged from the electoral process rather than as boons granted by a paternalistic executive, they were understood as largely irreversible.

At the same time, confidence in the electoral process in Western Europe was also based on the general assumption that laws, once enacted by legislatures, would be nationally enforced and with reasonable impartiality. This assumption in turn derived from the pre-existence of powerful, centralized bureaucracies, inherited from the age of absolutism and to varying degrees modernized as civil services in the aftermath of the French Revolution. (The United States formed a striking exception to the pattern, with consequences for the Philippines to be discussed in that section.)

For the other side of the coin, one has only to remind oneself that the Civil Rights Act 1965 was designed not merely to enfranchise millions of southern blacks, but also to put an end to or to make obsolete, sit-ins, freedom marches, riots, and so forth. "After all, now you have the vote," the Congress appeared to be saying. But normal voting is in many ways a peculiar activity. On a particular day, determined either by law or by government decision, between hours regulated by the same, at places settled on usually by local authorities, one joins a queue of people whom one does not typically know, to have a turn to enter a solitary space, where one pulls levers or marks pieces of paper, and then leaves the site with the same calm discretion with which one enters it—without questions being asked. It is almost the only political act imaginable in perfect solitude, and it is completely symbolic: it is thus almost the polar opposite of all other forms of personal political participation. In so far as it has general meaning, it acquires this meaning only by mathematical aggregation. From this perspective, one can readily conclude that, under normal circumstances, the logic of electoralism is in the direction of domestication: distancing, punctuating, isolating. If one asks in whose interests this domestication occurs, one comes immediately to the question of "representation."

It is, of course, notorious that the socio-economic and gender profiles of elected legislatures differ enormously from those of their electorates: for example, legislators are almost invariably much richer and much better educated, as well as far more likely to be male, than their constituents. The reasons for this wide discrepancy are well known and need not detain us here. The point to be underscored is rather that one effect of electoralism is in the direction of confining active and regular political participation to specialists—professional politicians—who not only have a strong interest in their institutionalized oligopoly, but who are largely drawn from particular social strata, most often the middle and upper-middle classes. If one therefore considers that electoral systems open to those groups which accept its terms are as characteristic of bourgeois political dominance as absolutist monarchies are characteristic of aristocratic hegemony, then one is probably well positioned to reflect comparatively on electoralism in modern Southeast Asia.

SIAM

Elections were inaugurated in Siam in the wake of the overthrow of the absolutist monarchy in a bloodless coup organized by a small conspiratorial group of military and civilian commoners. Most of these commoners were government officials, and the prime animus for the conspiracy was the near-monopoly of top bureaucratic positions, especially in the armed services, by mediocre members of the royal family and related aristocratic lineages.[2] But the coup group's formal claims to legitimacy rested on both its nationalism and its inauguration of constitutional democracy.

---

2. See Benjamin A. Batson, *The End of the Absolute Monarchy in Siam* (Singapore: Oxford University Press, 1984); and Thawatt Mokarapong, *History of the Thai Revolution* (Bangkok: Thai Watana Panich, 1972).

At the same time, the economic and social structure of Siam in the 1930s made the second of these claims largely nugatory. The country's good fortune in not being directly colonized, and the conservative policies pursued by Rama V (r. 1868–1910), which together helped to shelter much of the Thai agricultural population from the direct impact of capitalism, meant that what non-bureaucratic bourgeoisie existed in the 1930s was substantially of immigrant Chinese origins, like the still very small working class. Furthermore, literacy was then little advanced. It was only in the 1920s that a law on compulsory primary education was promulgated; and it was so casually enforced that in only one-fifth of the country's provinces had more than half the population completed primary schooling even by the end of the 1950s.[3] In effect the social basis for serious electoralism did not yet exist. Hence, the suffrage was restricted, and a large proportion of the early legislators were appointed. Under these circumstances it is not surprising that the army, the most powerful arm of the state, quickly became dominant, and the rule in Thai politics up until the 1970s was military dictatorship, more or less thinly disguised.

This situation did not begin to change until the era of Marshal Sarit Thanarat's dictatorship (1958–63) and the onset of the Vietnam War. At the prodding of the World Bank, the Thai government dismantled many inefficient state corporations and opened the country far more extensively than hitherto to foreign capital. Bangkok's close relationship with Washington meant a huge infusion of funds for—aside from expanding and equipping the armed forces and the police—infrastructural and communications development. At the same time, an enormous increase in institutions of higher education quintupled the student population within one decade. As a result, a new non-governmental middle class was created, which encompassed both the assimilated children of the old Chinese bourgeoisie as well as ethnic Thai, while the working class essentially became Thai rather than Chinese. By the early 1970s Japanese capital investment was overtaking American, and an extraordinary economic boom began that continued with only minor interruptions up to 1997.[4]

While the social and economic bases for bourgeois democracy were thus quietly being established, the political structure began to show signs of unravelling in the later 1960s. The iron-fisted Sarit had drunk himself to death in 1963, and his two lieutenants, Marshals Thanom Kittikajon and Praphat

---

3. Harvey H. Smith *et al, Area Handbook for Thailand* (Washington, DC: U.S. Government Printing Office, 1968), p. 161.

4. The processes sketched out in this paragraph are elaborated on and documented in "Withdrawal Symptoms," chapter 7 above.

Jarusathien, did not have his decisive ruthlessness. Increasingly close ties with the United States as the Vietnam War deepened led to the stationing of almost 50,000 American military personnel on Thai soil by 1968. Their presence—inevitably bringing with it ostentatious prostitutions, births of Amerasian children, the spread of modernized drug trafficking—aroused a growing nationalist reaction. The American presence also provoked Peking and Hanoi to encourage a hitherto rather tame Communist Party of Thailand to begin a rural guerrilla movement with which the Thai military found it increasingly difficult to deal. Thai youngsters sent to the United States for advanced study came substantially under the influence of the anti Vietnam War movement, with its bitter criticism of Washington's mercenary, authoritarian satellite regimes in East and Southeast Asia.

In the palmy days of the late 1950s Sarit found it quite easy to abolish both the existing constitution and the legislature, and not to make even the pretence of holding elections. But in the late 1960s, with the demise of this *esprit fort,* the Thanom–Praphat government responded to growing internal and external pressures by writing itself a conservative constitution and by re-establishing elections. It was a sign of the times that while the dictators patched together an election machine that, backed by the territorial military, the police, and the Ministry of the Interior, won them a large majority in the rural areas, they were overwhelmingly defeated in Bangkok, the capital of the new Thai and Sino-Thai bourgeoisie, as well as of the bulk of the working class. When rivalries among military and bureaucratic cliques threatened the cohesion of the dictators' parliamentary majority, they responded in November 1971 by a seriocomic "self-coup" against their own creations—immediately after Kissinger's secret visit to Peking, and on the eve of Nixon's official visit there to rub noses with Chairman Mao. That Washington could deal so with so-called Red China—whose menace Thai military leaders had for a generation insisted on to the public—and moreover without notifying its "close ally" Siam, demoralized the regime and encouraged those who detested it. In the autumn of 1973 demands for a constitution and for elections, initiated by a small group of liberal students and university lecturers, quite suddenly snowballed into an extraordinary uprising which brought 500,000 persons out on the streets of Bangkok—militant political participation on a scale without even close precedents in Thai history.[5]

While most student leaders insisted that the aims of the demonstrations

---

5. The best sources for the activities described in this and the following three paragraphs are David Morell and Chai-anan Samudavanija, *Political Conflict in Thailand: Reform, Reaction, Revolution* (Cambridge, Mass.: Oelgeschlager, Gunn & Hain, 1981); and John L.S. Girling, *Thailand: Society and Politics* (Ithaca, NY: Cornell University Press, 1981).

that brought about the dictatorship's abrupt collapse and the ignominious flight of Thanom and Praphat were the restoration of constitutionalism and electoral democracy, there is no reason to suppose that these were the primary aims of most of the protesters. Under the interim regime of Professor Sanya, which lasted from mid-October 1973 to February 1975, the country experienced more, and more various, political participation than in any period before or since: press censorship virtually disappeared, to the delight of bourgeois editors, newsmen, and readerships; genuine trade unions were rapidly formed, pressing a host of demands by means of strikes and marches; peasant leagues were created to urge land reforms of various kinds; high-school children demanded the expulsion of hated principals; all kinds of people insisted on the removal of the American military presence, and so on.

The elections finally held at the beginning of 1975 were certainly the most competitive that Siam has ever experienced and produced a parliament in which for the first time three moderately left-wing parties won a significant minority of seats. Probably as important, if not more so in the longer run, was the fact that there was no government party managing the elections from within the Supreme Command and the Ministry of the Interior. Hence there emerged a proliferation of conservative and centrist parties, coalitions among which formed the bases of the two politician-led cabinets holding power before the bloody events of October 6, 1976. These conditions permitted a very new horizontal dispersion of power outside Bangkok, just as the "Great Boom" was producing a new class of provincial entrepreneurs in many parts of the country. For these people, bourgeois electoral democracy offered substantial benefits. A parliamentary seat opened direct access to governmental decision-making outside the centralized bureaucratic structures before which these people had earlier always had to appear as clients. One did not have to be well educated, or well connected in the capital, or male in gender, to gain a seat: one simply had to have strong local roots and plenty of money. (The vast expansion into the provinces of powerful Bangkok banks in this period also opened up important new credit opportunities.) By playing one's cards right, one could parlay all this into a cabinet position (something unimaginable before) and then use that cabinet position to enlarge one's financial resources and build up further one's provincial power-base.[6]

The parliamentary regime of 1975–76 was not without its successes, which included negotiating the withdrawal of American military personnel and creating a large fund for rural development (a response to the new influence of provincial legislators), but it failed in its central pacificatory function. Strikes

---

6. The argument in this and the following paragraphs is drawn from "Murder and Progress in Modern Siam," chapter 8 above.

and demonstrations continued and gradually became more violent because the cabinets were neither able to enact serious labour or land-reform legislation nor to suppress the agitations. In the spring of 1975 the *ancien régimes* in Indochina abruptly collapsed, panicking the monarchy, the military, and the new bourgeoisie. Out of this came the right-wing extraparliamentary mobilizations of 1976 and a rising number of assassinations by hired professional gunmen of student activists, left-wing politicians, and labour and farm leaders.

The political polarization climaxed in the bloody events of October 6, 1976, which drove most of the legal Left underground, or into the jungle arms of the Communist Party (CPT), or into exile abroad. The dictatorial regime installed after October 6, was, however, very unlike those of 1958–73. The fragile outcome of complex bargaining between the military factions, the royal family, and right-wing professional politicians, it was headed by an extremist civilian judge who so angered the military that they deposed him within a year. For the first time in Thai history, an army coup was presented to the public as a blow for moderation and accommodation, as well as for the restoration by stages of a parliamentary regime.

At this juncture, the government of Siam had a remarkable stroke of luck. The Vietnamese invasion of Cambodia in December 1978, and the subsequent Sino-Vietnamese war, encouraged Peking to ally itself with Bangkok in support of Pol Pot. Bangkok's price was the withdrawal of Chinese Communist Party support for the CPT (which, furthermore, by supporting Peking's anti-Hanoi policy, immediately lost its safe bases in Vietnam-dominated Laos and Cambodia). A hopelessly divided Thai Left became demoralized and collapsed, and General Kriangsak Chomanan's government was shrewd enough to offer a general amnesty and to abide strictly by its terms. Hence by 1980, the crisis atmosphere of the later 1970s had fully dissipated. There was no longer a Left to fear, and Bangkok had solid support in Washington, Peking, and Tokyo.

It was now the moment for a relieved Thai bourgeoisie to resume its struggle for political hegemony, primarily through sustained pressure for the restoration of regular elections and a parliamentary-controlled national executive. Elections were held quite regularly during the 1980s, producing parliaments with no representation of the Left and heavily dominated by provincial entrepreneurs.[7] While General Prem Tinsulanonda was Prime Minister for much of the decade, his cabinets were always based on coalitions

---

7. The best overall account of Thai politics in the 1980s is James Soren Ockey, "Business Leaders, Gangsters, and the Middle Class: Societal Groups and Civilian Rule in Thailand" (Ph.D. thesis, Cornell University, 1992).

of political parties. How solidly this new electoral system was coming to be entrenched is best demonstrated by three political novelties: (1) powerful generals became eager to stand for election and serve in parliament (Kriangsak himself, Athit Kamlangaek, Chaowalit Yongjaiyut, and others); (2) a new style of political assassination appeared, targeting not students, trade unionists, and farmer-association leaders, but parliamentarians and would-be parliamentarians. These murders were typically carried out by gunmen hired by other parliamentarians and would-be parliamentarians—proving that in the 1980s the market value of futures in parliamentary seats had soared astronomically; (3) the huge uprising of May 1991 against the regime of General Suchinda Kraprayoon was led by cellular-telephone-wielding capitalists and parliamentary politicians (including former senior military officers)—but not student activists or trade unionists.[8] Their aim was quite clear: the full restoration of an electorally based parliamentary regime, which they know suits their interests best, and which they can be confident of dominating. They are also fairly sure that in the present constellation of international and national forces, elections can finally fulfil their pacificatory promise.

At the same time, because the full emergence of bourgeois electoralism came historically well after the development (from the end of the last century) of a centralized bureaucracy, capable, more or less, of executing national policy, there is the possibility of the other side of Janus coming to the fore: that is, that meaningful legislation in the sphere of labour, social welfare, land law, and so forth, could some day be administratively implemented into irreversible social gains. In this sense, electoral democracy holds out some genuine prospects in the longer run.

THE PHILIPPINES

National-level elections were introduced in the Philippines by its American conquerors in 1907. The immediate background for this innovation was Asia's first modern revolution, the successful insurrectionary movement launched in 1896 against Spanish rule, which began in the environs of Manila and later spread through much of Luzon and tangentially into parts of the Visayas. While the movement was led largely by small-town notables and

---

8. In February 1991, ambitious leaders of Academy Class 5 of the Thai military exploited anger within the armed forces at various policies of the civilian Chatchai Choonhawan government to stage a successful coup. Coup leader Suchinda installed a well-respected businessman and former diplomat as Prime Minister promising not to assume this role himself. When he broke this promise in the spring of 1992, a bloody political crisis began which led to his fall and disgrace towards the end of May. Civilian government was then restored and confirmed by elections in the fall of 1992.

provincial gentry, it also involved widespread participation of the popular classes, and by women and adolescents, as well as by adult males. Hence the Americans' counter-revolutionary intervention required a ruthless military campaign which may have cost up to a quarter of a million Filipino lives. But colonial policy-makers recognized from the start that stable colonial rule required the creation of a class of Filipino political leaders with a strong interest in collaboration with the conquerors and in the demobilization of the mass of the population.[9] They quickly decided that the first necessary step was the creation of a national legislature representing at least those areas of the colony where the revolutionary Republic of 1898 had drawn a following. (The Muslim far south was initially excluded.)

Naturally enough, the form of electoralism introduced was modelled, even if parodically, on America's own. It is useful to recall that, in the first decade of the twentieth century, the United States had arguably the most corrupt form of electoralism among all the industrial powers. Not only were women excluded from the vote, but so were millions of adult non-white males. Poll taxes and gerrymandering were widespread, to the benefit of court-house cliques and urban machines. Violence, in the South and the West, was far more a part of electoral politics than in advanced Western Europe. Furthermore, the United States of that era was quite peculiar in the general absence of a national-level professional bureaucracy, such as had emerged in Britain, Sweden, Germany, or France.

Out of this background came the strange malignities of colonial-era electoralism (which in significant ways recall V.O. Key's classic study of politics in the American South during much the same era).[10] First of all, linguistic, property, and literacy qualifications were set so high in the Philippines that as late as the eve of World War II only about 14 per cent of the adult population of the colony was entitled to vote. This mechanism effectively confined legitimate participation to the small stratum that commanded English or Spanish, and/or had substantial property. Second, the American system of single-member districts with legal residence in those districts required of candidates, took on a peculiarly oligarchic hue from its linkage with the colony's ethno-linguistic heterogeneity. (Spanish had never become a lingua franca there, as it had in Latin America, and English was only just beginning to make inroads.) Hence cacique politicians could hunker down behind walls not only

---

9. See especially the splendid essays by Ruby Paredes, Michael Cullinane, and Alfred McCoy, in Ruby B. Paredes, ed., *Philippine Colonial Democracy* (Quezon City: Ateneo de Manila Press, 1989); Peter Stanley's shrewd A *Nation in the Making: The Philippines and the United States, 1899–1921* (Cambridge, Mass.: Harvard University Press, 1974); and Glenn A. May, *Social Engineering in the Philippines* (Westport, Conn.: Greenwood Press, 1980).

10. V.O. Key, Jr., *Southern Politics in State and Nation* (New York: Vintage, 1949).

of local money–power and patron–client relations, but also of language. (One recalls colonial master-politician Manuel Quezon's frustration at having to have his public speeches translated only 100 miles north of Manila.[11]) This system had one further stabilizing advantage, which reminds us indirectly of Thai electoralism in the 1980s. It dispersed power across the archipelago, while assuring the provincial caciques of more or less equal representation in Manila. A final malignity was the development of this decentralized system of oligarchy in tandem with the failure to create a professional central bureaucracy. Pre-Hatch Act American practice,[12] translated to the Philippines, produced a quickly Filipinized state machinery, subordinate to congressional oligarchs, both more corrupt and less unitary than anywhere else in colonial Southeast Asia.

But political mechanisms in themselves were not enough to stabilize the colonial regime. The real cement to the emerging system was free economic access to the highest-tariff state of the advanced industrial world. The key crop was sugar, which could be sold in the United States at prices well above those on the world market, and which could be produced by a serflike, miserably exploited workforce at very small cost. Hence the rapid rise, in the American era, of hugely wealthy provincial sugar magnates. Other caciques profited by Washington's selling off of 400,000 acres of rich agricultural land confiscated from Spanish friars. Furthermore, their control of the colonial legislature enabled them to plunder the state treasury via such institutions as a quickly bankrupted Central Bank of the Philippines. Thus, thirty-five years of colonial elections to a national-level legislature failed to produce a single significant piece of legislation for the benefit of the Filipino population as a whole. All this made the American stabilization project exceptionally successful. Backward Malaya aside, the Philippines was the one important colony in Southeast Asia which, in the 1930s, had no serious nationalist movement.

During and immediately after World War II the Philippines plunged into a new participatory crisis. Under the Japanese occupation, the American market for Philippine hacienda agriculture collapsed, electoral mechanisms

---

11. See Andrew B. Gonzalez, *Language and Nationalism: The Philippine Experience Thus Far* (Quezon City: Ateneo de Manila University Press, 1980), p. 58, with documentary citations.

12. The Hatch Act of 1939 was an unprecedently far-reaching law designed to establish a coherent merit-based national civil service by protecting it from being abused by powerful and unscrupulous politicians. To see how far American practice was from northern European, and how close to Filipino, one might note that provisions of the Act prohibited threatening, intimidating, or coercing voters in national elections; forbade the current practices of promising and withholding certain kinds of employment and unemployment relief as a reward or punishment for political activity; and outlawed interference with the nomination and election of candidates to federal office by administrative servants of the United States.

were frozen, and a variety of armed guerrilla groups came into being, the most powerful of which (in Luzon) was led by a mix of communist and socialist activists. Furthermore, the independence which the American Congress, for its own reasons, had insisted on promising for 1946, could no longer be avoided. In the new world of the United Nations, a state becoming independent in 1946 could not bar women from voting, and the exclusionary suffrage of the colonial years was no longer respectable or tolerable.

The resolution of this crisis had two fundamental features, in both of which electoralism was a central element. First, the cacique oligarchy saw no other way to restore its old position except in close collaboration with the United States. On the one hand, this meant the activation of the Tydings Act on war-damage compensation, which was made contingent on passage of the so-called parity amendment.[13] Passage of this amendment to the Philippine constitution required a three-fourths vote in a Congress that, as a result of elections under unsettled postindependence conditions, for the first time contained representatives of the wartime insurgent Left (the only time that the Left in the Philippines has had significant congressional representation). President Manuel Roxas therefore arranged the unseating of these representatives on trumped-up charges of electoral fraud, thereby starting the polarization process which led to the Hukbalahap insurrection of 1948–54. This move was followed by utilization of the Constabulary and various private armies to restore order on haciendas largely abandoned by their owners during the Japanese period. The violent crushing of the Huks, with substantial American help, ended in the political incapacitation of the popular sector for a generation.[14]

Second was the adaptation of electoralism to conditions of independence in a state without a coherent bureaucracy, or a serious professionalized military,[15] and with control of police and privately armed goons fragmented between provincial oligarchs. The huge disruption of the war, a steady increase in the population along with growing urbanization, as well as normalization of the suffrage, meant that old-style cacique power was no longer

---

13. On all this, see "Cacique Democracy," chapter 9 above, at pp. 205–6.

14. The classic account of the rise and fall of the Hukbalahap is Benedict J. Kerkvliet, *The Huk Rebellion* (Berkeley: University of California Press, 1977).

15. In 1947, Washington arranged for a continuation for a further ninety-nine years of its twenty-three land, sea, and air bases in the Philippines. Manila was effectively told that the United States would handle its defence for the indefinite future and that the Philippines had no need of real armed forces. Even today, almost half a century after independence, the Philippines' military is worse trained, more poorly equipped, and more disorganized than the military of any other major country in Southeast Asia. Furthermore, imposition of the American practice of having all senior military promotions and appointments subject to congressional approval encourages factionalism and political favour-seeking among the officer corps.

sufficient in itself. Sustaining the system of oligarchic control required far greater use of money and guns than had been true before the war, leading to further pillaging of the state's finances. On the other hand, an extension of American electoral practice turned out to have unexpected advantages; there was an astonishing proliferation of electoral offices at every level of government, to the point that by the mid-1980s one elective post was available for every 1,400 voters—something completely unimaginable in contemporary Siam. This development made possible, not any real democratization, but the channelling of electoral participation into a complex network of patronage-based local machines. The joke went that everyone in the Philippines was connected to *someone* who held *some* electoral office or another.

The peculiarity of this very expensive and malignant system was that it was designed to secure cacique hegemony and was not in any way the expression of new political power accruing to the rather small urban bourgeoisie that started to expand in the 1950s. In the early 1960s the latter did make some efforts to reform the electoral system along lines reminiscent of the Progressive Movement in the United States half a century earlier. But these efforts came to little, and meantime, changes in American immigration laws encouraged more and more urban, middle-class Filipinos to pack their bags for California. When a new generation of activists emerged in the later 1960s, it devoted itself mostly to extraparliamentary politics, culminating in the formation, and later rapid expansion, of the armed, illegal, insurrectionary CPP–NPA (Communist Party of the Philippines—New People's Army). In the meantime, the enormous costs (in money and violence) of cacique democracy led to ever greater looting of the state and hence to the institution of the Marcos dictatorship in 1972.[16]

There is here an instructive comparison with the Sarit–Thanom–Praphat dictatorship in Siam a decade earlier. That these three military men were, like Marcos, thieves, is indubitable. But they were thieves on a far smaller scale, and the money they stole remained in-country. Their power was based on the long-established hierarchy of a national army (something the Philippines has never had, for the reasons already mentioned) and a centralized bureaucracy. Hence they did not in the least feel threatened by the expansion of a successful Sino-Thai entrepreneurial class (from whom most made their private fortunes, rather than from the state). Marcos, on the other hand, to the end of his days, remained a cacique, a politician who built his power—"by hand" as it were—on patronage and a military and police establishment that he

---

16. See the elegant, data-backed analysis in Thomas Nowak and Kay Snyder, "Clientelist Politics in the Philippines: Integration or Instability?" *American Political Science Review,* 68 (Sept. 1974), pp. 1147–70.

treated as his private security forces. Hence the paradox that the regime of civilian Marcos was far more brutal and murderous than that of the Thai field-marshals; and that through his system of crony-monopolies, "business-man" Marcos ruined the Philippine economy just as the Thai military regime was presiding over the onset of a great boom.

Marcos's cacique dictatorship was finally brought down in 1986 by a rather bizarre convergence of forces. The first and foremost factor, ironically, was the illegal CPP–NPA that operated entirely outside any electoral process but built a huge nationwide network of participatory political organizations down to the *barrio* level. The rapid growth of the CPP–NPA so alarmed the United States that it finally turned against Marcos and eventually hauled him into golden imprisonment in Hawaii.[17] Most direct, of course, was electoral-ism itself. Bastard political son of Quezon that he was, Marcos was incapable of Sarit's absolutism. Hence, in the end, he went down in electoral flames.[18] By then he had alienated the non-crony big entrepreneurs, the Catholic Church, the fragmented residual middle class, the intelligentsia, many younger military officers, substantial parts of the popular sector, and, above all, many still powerful caciques who longed for a restoration of the old hor-izontal dispersion of oligarchic power. The irony is that Marcos may actually have won (in technical terms) the elections of 1986, by the usual brutish methods, but that this victory, precisely because it was electoral, ended his reign. The response was a military mutiny followed immediately by a massive popular uprising in Manila in which tens of thousands of fed-up citizens suddenly participated: People Power.

As in Bangkok after October 14, 1973, Philippine politics was for a brief time more open and participatory than it had been since the end of the nine-teenth century. But the interregnum did not lead to a renewed polarization of political life, or to a successful October 6, 1976-style right-wing military coup (though not for want of trying). The army was too weak, too divided, and too incompetent. There was no powerful civil bureaucracy to lend its support. The feeble Filipino bourgeoisie had been haemorrhaging for years through emigration and a downward-spiralling economy. The CPP–NPA, wracked with internal problems, failed to take any decisive steps: and, besides, the 1986 of Teng Hsiao-p'ing and Mikhail Gorbachov was not the 1976 of the Gang of

---

17. See the very entertaining, detailed account in Raymond Bonner, *Waltzing with a Dictator* (New York: Times Books, 1987), especially the last three chapters.

18. It will be recalled that late in 1985 he decided to prove his domestic legitimacy to the United States by calling for a snap presidential election. He assumed that the "guns, goons, and gold" methods by which he had been winning elections for three decades would do the trick again. But now the Americans had turned against him, and, as Bonner shows (ibid.), the CIA went into action on behalf of Corazón Aquino.

Four, Leonid Brezhnev, and the triumphs in Indochina. World communism was by then in rapid, irreversible decline. Hence the ultimate beneficiaries of 1986 were the caciques, who, under the leadership of Corazón Aquino and her brother Peping Cojuangco, largely restored the old electorally based, pacificatory congressional system of the pre-Marcos era.[19] Nothing is more striking than the contrast between the restorationism of Philippine electoralism in the post-1986 years, and the transformatory character of Thai electoralism in the same period. Nor is it easy to imagine in the future an evolution of the system such that broad electoral participation would produce positive legislation seriously enforceable on a nationwide basis.

INDONESIA

During the last two decades of conservative Dutch colonial rule a national-level legislature of sorts did exist—the so-called Volksraad, or People's Council. Like the Philippine Congress it was established by the colonial regime with cautious co-optation in mind. But its electoral basis was even scantier; it included substantial representation of Dutch officials and planters; many of its members were appointees; and it had no real power at all. Hence the popular nationalist and Islamic movements largely ignored it, and it never effectively fulfilled even the narrow purpose for which it was established. The version of the Volksraad established by the Japanese occupation authorities had even less power and was entirely appointive, but it did include a considerable number of leaders of the popular movement in Dutch times.[20]

In the last year of the Pacific War, the Americans were already fighting their way back through the Philippines, so that when the Japanese Empire collapsed in mid-August 1945, there was no vacuum of power. Such was not the case in the Indies, where the Dutch, themselves only liberated from Nazi occupation in the late winter of 1945, were for a long time in no position to reimpose themselves by military means. The result was the spontaneous outbreak of what everyone in Indonesia at the time speedily named "The Revolution."

But it was a revolution of a special kind. It was, for example, neither planned nor led by a single disciplined party; its legal armed forces were only one segment of a mass of *badan perjuangan* (paramilitary organizations) of various political persuasions and varying levels of military training and

---

19. For a more detailed discussion of the Bourbon character of the Aquino regime, see chapter 9 above.

20. The Japanese divided the Indies into three separate terrains: Sumatra under the 25th Army, Java under the 16th Army, and the "Great East" under the Navy. Each terrain had its own distinct quasi-Volksraad.

equipment. It was so highly decentralized that a weak national leadership had no means to prevent the social-revolutionary movements that wiped out the hated collaborator ruling classes in, for example, Aceh and East Sumatra, in 1945–46. The sufferings endured by much of the population during the Great Depression, and especially the Japanese occupation, shattered the prestige of the once all-powerful colonial bureaucracy, which by the 1930s was manned 90 per cent by "natives." The experience of fighting what by 1948–49 was effectively a guerrilla war against the Dutch further politicized the population in the contested areas of Western Indonesia, and invited a still wider popular participation. No country-wide elections were held during the revolutionary years, but President Sukarno and Vice-President Hatta were wisely careful enough to appoint to the revolutionary parliament, the so-called Komité Nasional Indonesia Pusat (Central Indonesian National Committee), representatives of all the major political groups and *badan perjuangan,* not least because of the absence of a single powerful party, a united military, and a cohesive, authoritative bureaucracy. The Republic, to survive, required this participation.[21]

If one inspects the political photographs of the period—which include cabinet ministers in shorts and sandals—one is struck by how little the KNIP members were distinct in dress and housing from the ordinary townspeople around them. The contrast with congressional opulence in the Philippines is at first startling, until one recalls that in the colonial period the Dutch and Indonesian Chinese had completely dominated economic life; there was no substantial group of native or mestizo agrarian magnates, and an independent indigenous bourgeoisie was in its delicate infancy. Hence in the revolutionary period, leadership was in the hands of youthful former political activists and military men who were not at all sharply distinguished from one another in social origins or economic resources. (Ex-political prisoner Sutan Sjahrir became Prime Minister at age thirty-six; former private-high-school teacher Sudirman became supreme commander at thirty.)

The final political settlement (1949) with the Dutch left the vast archipelagic country sovereign but flat on its back in terms of its finances, material infrastructure, and modern-sector economy. It had neither an air force nor a navy, and the eastern part of the nation had been largely cut off from the western since 1942. Even had important politicians or colonels been so inclined, a dictatorial, authoritarian political system was out of the question for these practical reasons. Moreover, the agreement with The Hague had

---

21. See George McT. Kahin's classic *Nationalism and Revolution in Indonesia* (Ithaca, NY: Cornell University Press, 1952); and for a more detailed discussion of the early stages of the revolution, my *Java in a Time of Revolution* (Ithaca, NY: Cornell University Press, 1972).

stipulated that members of various local puppet mini-parliaments set up by the colonial authorities after 1946 in areas they controlled militarily would merge with the KNIP into a larger independent parliament. Because many of these members believed that they might not be returned if free elections were held, passage of the necessary legislation was repeatedly delayed, and the elections—the only free national-level elections Indonesia has ever had—did not take place until 1955.

In the meantime, the participatory traditions of the nationalist movement and of the revolution, combined with the difficulties of demobilizing the huge, disorganized congeries of armed groups, and various disappointments with the immediate fruits of the independence agreement (such as Dutch retention of West Irian, the immunity of Dutch corporate capital from nationalization, and so on), led in some provinces to armed rebellions and in others to militant extraparliamentary political activities.

The elections were thus quite consciously set up to channel and contain these forces and dissatisfactions. It could indeed be argued that they ended up being the most open and participatory elections held anywhere in Southeast Asia since World War II: full adult suffrage, a competitive press, very little violence or gerrymandering, remarkably little emphasis on money, and so on. Dozens of parties participated, though the final tally was dominated by the Big Four (Masyumi, the Nahdlatul Ulama, the Indonesian Nationalist Party, and the Partai Komunis Indonesia), each supported by millions of voters.[22] Of particular importance was the success of the PKI—the only Southeast Asian communist party both eager to participate electorally and permitted by the system to do so. (It gained almost the same percentage of the popular vote as did Fidel Ramos in narrowly winning the 1992 Philippine presidential elections.)

Yet this electoral success was to have ironic outcomes. The Communists, like the others of the Big Four, had discovered quite quickly that in vast, backward, heavily illiterate rural Indonesia, where the bulk of the voters resided, the most efficient way to do well electorally was to attract to its ranks village headmen and other local notables. Once attached, these people could often be counted on to bring in their villagers' votes, without the Party itself having to make substantial and expensive efforts lower down. (After all, voting is a very simple act usually involving very little personal cost.) But since village headmen typically owned or controlled the most land in the villages, recruiting them required electoral programmes which did not

---

22. The key study of Indonesian electoral democracy is Herbert Feith's *The Decline of Constitutional Democracy in Indonesia* (Ithaca, NY: Cornell University Press, 1962); an excellent detailed study of the 1955 elections is the same author's *The Indonesian Elections of 1955* (Ithaca, NY: Cornell Modern Indonesia Project, 1957).

threaten their interests. Furthermore, the Party's success in these elections, and the provincial elections in Java that followed in 1957, began to give Party members a personal stake in electoral offices at all levels. Hence it is not surprising that quite early on Donald Hindley was speaking of the "domestication" of the PKI, a domestication in which electoralism played a central role.[23] The same logic pushed the Party's leaders to disband leftover communist guerrilla bands in Central Java, and to control leaders of trade unions and farmers' organizations whose militancy threatened the accommodations on which parliamentary success depended. On the other hand, the Party's electoral successes deeply alarmed its competitors, as well as the army leadership. In part, out of this fear came the end of electoral politics with the Declaration of Martial Law in 1957, the big regional rebellions of 1958 (also the banning of the Masyumi for its involvement), and the institution of Guided Democracy by Sukarno and the army leaders in 1959.[24]

Although for his own reasons Sukarno co-operated with the military in destroying the parliamentary regime, he was not eager to become the military's prisoner. Recognizing the importance of a political counterweight to his generals, he succeeded in protecting and encouraging the (now) Big Three to continue building their political bases in return for their solid backing of his personal authority and especially of his foreign policy: *but without elections.* The largely unanticipated consequence of intense party competition without elections was the extraordinary mass politicization and mobilization of the Guided Democracy era, particularly after Sukarno revoked martial law in May 1963. Within each of the Big Three, influence and activity tended to shift away from party parliamentarians (though Sukarno's appointive Gotong-Royong parliament continued to meet throughout), towards their mass affiliates—unions, youth and women's groups, peasant organizations, intellectuals' associations, and so on—who carried the burden of the round-the-clock struggle for Sukarno's favour and for the organized popular support that guaranteed that favour.

This mass mobilization was accompanied and exacerbated by the collapse of the economy and the rise of hyperinflation, especially after 1963, as a consequence mainly of the rash nationalization of Dutch corporations in 1957, and their takeover and mismanagement by the military thereafter, to say

---

23. Donald Hindley, "President Sukarno and the Communists: The Politics of Domestication," *American Political Science Review*, 56 (Dec. 1962), pp. 915–26.

24. The classic text on all this is Daniel S. Lev, *The Transition to Guided Democracy: Indonesian Politics, 1957–1959* (Ithaca, NY: Cornell Modern Indonesia Project, 1966). For his most recent evaluation, see the trenchant remarks in his "On the Fall of the Parliamentary System," in David Bourchier and John Legge, eds., *Democracy in Indonesia, 1950s and 1990s* (Clayton, Victoria: Monash University, Centre of Southeast Asian Studies, 1994), pp. 38–42.

nothing of the hostility with which the capitalist powers regarded Sukarno's active foreign policy and alleged coddling of the communists. Hence a growing political hysteria prepared the way, after the so-called coup of October 1, 1965, for the vast army-steered pogrom against the Left, in which half a million people were murdered and hundreds of thousands imprisoned under brutal conditions for many years.

There is no need here to spend any time on the series of elections held regularly since 1971 by Suharto's New Order military regime. They are carefully managed to produce externally plausible two-thirds majorities for Golkar, the government's electoral machine, and a passive parliament without any genuine representative character. One of the more effective propaganda devices used by the regime to justify its highly authoritarian and centralized character has been that the former political system encouraged intense social conflict and unstable, fractured government. But it is important to observe the elisions here involved between the electoral regime of the 1950s and the non-electoral Guided Democracy system of the early 1960s. There is not much evidence that the electoral regime created, in itself, intense social conflict, but the evidence abounds that an electionless Guided Democracy did so. Nor was liberal democracy brought down by the communists or even the parties as a whole; the cabinets of the period were less unstable in themselves than they were destabilized by the military and military factions, as well as (to a lesser extent) Sukarno—who between them controlled the regime of Guided Democracy.[25]

At the same time, the peculiar experience of Guided Democracy allows us to think about the faces of electoralism in an unexpected way. The intense, competitive political mobilizations it encouraged were precisely the consequence of no elections. No mechanisms existed for temporary, punctuated adjudications of who were winners and losers, and thus ultimately the struggle for power and influence could only be decided by violently coercive means. Seen from this angle, the pacificatory aspect of electoralism appears in a warmer light—for one could then pose the question of whether free elections in 1964 might not have prevented the bloodbath of 1965–66.

Because of the economic successes of the New Order regime, to which oil and massive foreign aid and investment have been essential, Indonesia's social structure has substantially changed over the past twenty-five years. For the first time a substantial Indonesian bourgeoisie has been created, alongside the Sino-Indonesian one inherited from the colonial era—even if it is still

---

25. For lively, up-to-date discussions of this whole question, see especially the essays by Ruth McVey, Herbert Feith, Jamie Mackie, Daniel Lev, Adnan Buyung Nasution, Greg Fealy, and Anton Lucas, in ibid.

politically weak and very much concentrated in the capital and a few other large cities. Should one thus cast Suharto as Indonesia's Sarit? Should one thus expect in the longer run a middle-class struggle for a demilitarized, genuinely electoral regime, now that any political threat from the Left has long since been violently eliminated? This prospect is by no means implausible, but the obvious incomparabilities should be noted. Sarit presided over a small country, largely homogeneous in ethnic and religious terms, which did not suffer the ravages of colonial capitalism, Japanese military occupation, a bitter revolutionary struggle for independence, or mass murder. While he and his immediate clique dominated the state, the military as such did not form a ruling caste, not least because they had available to them a centralized, reasonably professional civilian bureaucratic apparatus inherited from absolutism, whose authority had never been fatally undermined, as Indonesia's had been, by collaboration, inflation, and revolution. The survival of the monarchy meant that there was no possibility, even under his dictatorship, of a Sukarno- or Suharto-style monopolistic leadership-for-life. The high rate of assimilation of immigrant Chinese into Thai society and the absence of a characteristic colonial racialized economic hierarchy also meant that when the Thai bourgeoisie began to feel its oats it was not structurally divided along racial/religious lines as in Indonesia.

Suharto dominates a highly centralized state apparatus, which is largely his own creation over the past quarter of a century. But it is far more deeply penetrated by the military than Sarit's bureaucracy ever was. It has little self-confidence and no tradition of autonomy. It is not fundamentally based in law, as is the Thai civil service. (It is useful to compare the prestige that the judiciary enjoys in Siam with the general contempt felt for its opposite number in Indonesia.) In this sense, the future of the Indonesian state apparatus in the post-Suharto era is highly uncertain. It seems much less likely than the Thai civil service to evolve into the sort of structure that made the promises of electoralism in Western Europe attractive.

CONCLUSION

It is at least superficially ironic that uncolonized Siam, which began to have elections well after they had been instituted in the American Philippines and the Dutch Indies, has today the nearest approximation to Western-style bourgeois democracy. But only superficially. The sunny face of Janus offers the expectation that elections will have real policy outcomes satisfactory to substantial sections of the voting population. This means the necessity of a coherent civil bureaucracy capable of enforcing electorally generated policies: that is, a strong state. There are good historical reasons for thinking that it is hard to build such a state *after* the spread of mass electoralism. Siam was probably fortunate therefore to have electoralism begin half a century after the initiation of a modern-style bureaucracy by a Thai monarch. Colonial states were, for all their absolutist pretensions, typically weak because of external domination from distant metropolises and because of their rigidly racial internal hierarchies. For reasons already described, the Philippines has had an exceptionally weak state in modern times, while electoralism was instituted very early in this century. In Indonesia the huge native component of the late colonial apparatus was always vulnerable to the accusation of treason, and it came close to disappearing in the early revolution. In that sense, too, electoralism preceded the creation of a genuinely powerful and national civil apparatus, and part of the price has been the effective nullification of any serious form of popular representation for the past quarter of a century. Under conditions where elections have no visible positive policy outcomes for substantial social groups, one should not be surprised to find that they are meaningful only when, under rare favourable historical circumstances, their tallies can be read as a fundamental repudiation of the rulers. The most striking examples in modern Southeast Asia come not from the three countries here under analysis, but from Burma: the overwhelming rejectionist returns of the elections of 1960 and 1990.

The shadow face of Janus is pacification, and the tendency towards the delegitimation of a vast range of popular participatory practices. This is one reason why in our times dictatorial regimes like those of the People's Action Party in Singapore, and of the New Order in Indonesia, think it useful to stage elections regularly. One can thus easily understand the ambivalence of the radical Left towards electoralism in general and to the subnational electoral successes of the mainstream Italian and Indian Marxist parties in particular. For these successes come at the price of the leaderships' assimilation into the political class, and the marginalization of that popular participation that has always been central to the radical project.

Radicalism after Communism

One might think that "after communism" is an uncomplicated idea, experience, or sociopolitical condition, but in the two countries of Southeast Asia which I intend to discuss—namely, colonized, Muslim Indonesia, and uncolonized, Buddhist Thailand—"after communism" has markedly different meanings, which therefore in turn affect the imaginary of contemporary radicalism. To set the stage, therefore, it is necessary to say something about the trajectory of communism in each of the two countries.

The Netherlands East Indies was the first Asian "country" outside the Soviet Union to have a communist party at all. The PKI (Communist Party of Indonesia) was founded on May 23, 1920. In the relatively liberal climate of the immediate post-World War I era, it developed rapidly, especially among estate labourers, dockers, and railway personnel. As there were then no universities in the colony, and very few natives had gone to Holland for tertiary education, its leaders were a mix of Indonesian autodidacts and junior high-school graduates, along with a sprinkling of Dutch radicals, whom, however, the colonial regime quickly jailed or extruded. Although the young Party leaders frequently quarrelled with various Muslim political notables, the Party had no difficulty in cultivating a following among the Muslim masses, and it was in two of the most Muslim provinces of the colony that the Party's millenarian call for an uprising in 1926–27 was most courageously, if disastrously, answered. The Dutch crushed the insurrection without much difficulty, executing some leaders, and banishing or imprisoning many others. For the remainder of the colonial period the Party did not seriously exist. It did not start to rebuild itself until after the outbreak of what Indonesians remember as their "Revolution of 1945," when, between the collapse of the Japanese occupation regime, and the delayed return of the Dutch, an infant

Republic of Indonesia was born. During the bitter struggle that ensued till late 1949, when The Hague finally conceded the transfer of sovereignty, freed, returning, and newborn communists played a significant but never a dominating political role.

Already, however, a difference in generations was visible. Many of the older generation were quite fluent in Dutch—some had even served in the anti-Nazi underground in Holland itself; they had travelled abroad, or been exiled there, and self-consciously saw themselves as part of a world revolutionary movement; many had European friends and sometimes wives and lovers; they worked closely with progressive local Chinese; and they were by experience "activists," above and below ground, trade-unionists, propagandists, strike organizers, and occasionally "terrorists." They had no experience of parliamentary, legal politics. The second generation came to adulthood during the bloody Japanese occupation; their Dutch was usually minimal, they had never been abroad, and they had no foreign friends; they were not fond of Chinese (so that when they took control of the Party in 1951 they excluded Chinese from open Party membership); they were ardent nationalists, and also Party men and women first and foremost, because they entered politics under the infant Republic which governed itself as best it could by a regime of parliamentary institutions and political parties with their various affiliates.

About halfway through the Revolution, the Cold War set in with a vengeance, and increasingly polarized the internal politics of the Republic. The outcome was a brief but very bloody civil war on Java in the autumn of 1948 in which the Left, branded by a Muslim-dominated government as the traitorous agent of Moscow, was ruthlessly crushed. Many older leaders were executed or murdered, and more would have been had not the Dutch in December made a last, large military effort to suppress the Republic. A good number of second-generation communists escaped from jail and joined the short guerrilla struggle if only in a marginal capacity. When the fighting ended and a liberal-democratic Republic covering all of Indonesia was formed in the last days of 1949, this generation emerged to take over and rebuild the Party's membership and reputation.

In this endeavour they were astonishingly successful, for reasons that are too complex to go into here. Suffice it to say that already in the 1955 general elections, the only free elections Indonesia has ever had, the Party emerged as one of the Big Four, with millions of voters behind it and a large parliamentary fraction to represent it at the centre of governance. One of the key conditions of the Party's electoral success was its extreme caution on domestic issues, and its strong nationalist stance externally, which enabled it to work out effective alliances with other political parties, and to begin to live down the "treason" of 1948. While in practice the Party's electoral successes committed it to peaceful, legal parliamentary politics, more or less like those of Togliatti's PCI, it could not bring itself publicly to say so; hence when in 1959 the Left-leaning President Sukarno and the generally right-wing army leaders co-operated to replace constitutional democracy with the authoritarian, populist-nationalist system of Guided Democracy, in which no elections would ever be held, the Party leaders felt they had no alternative but to go along.

Under Guided Democracy, which lasted from 1959 to 1965, the Party's mass affiliates—of youth, women, peasants, estate workers, and so on—continued to grow rapidly, because these were better adapted than the parliamentary Party itself to conditions of non-electoral competitive politics. By 1965, the PKI's leaders claimed a "family" of twenty million partisans, and the dubious honour of being the largest such communist family in the world outside the Socialist bloc. But this success was matched by the development of comparable Muslim and so-called secular-nationalist (bourgeois) families, leading to increasing polarization, especially as hyper-inflation set in and the economy spun downwards. The Party clung to its legality, and in any case had no guns.

It could do little in the more advanced sectors of the nationalized economy since these were controlled by the deeply hostile military. The Party leaders tried to compensate for this weakness with vociferous support for Sukarno's anti-western foreign policy and a kulturkampf against "liberal" intellectuals which was never forgiven them.

The end started on October 1, 1965, when a small group of military officers, nominally headed by an obscure lieutenant-colonel in the Presidential Guard, assassinated six top generals, and seized parts of the capital city for a few hours. The "coup," if it was such, was quickly suppressed by the commander of the Army's Strategic Reserve, General Suharto, who proceeded to manipulate the horror aroused by the midnight murders to launch an extermination campaign against the Party, which he accused of masterminding the coup attempt. Between mid-October 1965 and late January 1966, the PKI was physically destroyed. At least half a million people, perhaps as many as a million, were killed either by the army itself, or by the Muslim and secular-nationalist vigilante groups it armed and protected. Hundreds of thousands of other people thought to be associated with the Party were imprisoned and tortured. Virtually the entire Party leadership was executed, mostly without even the flimsiest legal formalities.

In March 1966, as Suharto effectively supplanted Sukarno as head of state, the Party was declared illegal, along with anything that even smelled of Marxism. It has never been reborn, not merely because of the brutal efficiency of the dictatorship's intelligence apparatus, but also because the Party leaders were profoundly discredited in the eyes of their followers. How could the leaders have permitted the catastrophe to happen, leaving twenty million supporters defenceless against their enemies? Worse still, a large number of militants, hoping to save their own lives, turned, in Suharto's gulag, into informers on their own people, and sometimes even torturers and executioners.

Notice the timing: 1966, just as Mao's Cultural Revolution was in full swing, Lyndon Johnson's United States was becoming engulfed in the Vietnam War, and the new Brezhnev leadership in Moscow was showing every sign of confidence and vigour. Perhaps the apogee of world-communist success.

A CONTRASTING HISTORY

The story of communism in Thailand is shorter, and also very different. Uncolonized Thailand was much more slowly assaulted by capitalism than was the Netherlands Indies, and this capitalism was not dominated by giant plantation agribusiness. It was the policy of the long-reigning, highly intelligent Rama v (Chulalongkorn, r. 1868–1910) to leave indigenous Thai society as undisturbed as convenient; the brunt of capitalist modernization was therefore borne largely by young male immigrants imported from the coastal parts of southeastern China. Most of those who did not manage to return home to China married Thai women, producing towards the end of his reign the first substantial generation of what the Thai call *lūk jin*, or Sino-Thai. A minority of these Sino-Thai moved up socio-economically to become the core of the country's nascent bourgeoisie, concentrated heavily in the royal capital of Bangkok, and in the smaller towns that grew up along the railway lines which the king started to build for strategic-political purposes. The rest formed the country's real working class, and continued to do so until after World War II.

It was among such immigrants and their children, as well as among Vietnamese fleeing French colonialism in Indochina, that communism in Thailand got its start—well after the absolute monarchy had been overthrown in the bloodless coup of 1932, and just before the Pacific War broke out. Thus the Communist Party of Thailand (CPT) was only formed in 1941, a generation later than in the Netherlands Indies, was based on still largely alien minorities rather than on "natives," was urban rather than semi-urban / semi-rural, and was oriented north towards China rather than west towards Europe and the USSR. In the brief period of liberal civilian rule after World War II, its influence began to spread among the small Thai intelligentsia, and it even managed to elect one solitary MP to parliament before the Thai military seized full powers in 1947. At the strong urging of the United States, which was inclined to regard Thailand as a fortress in its struggle against Asian Communism, the CPT was declared illegal, and remained so ever afterwards. No contrast could be more striking with the contemporary PKI. At the same time, the Party was small enough, and the military-dominated Thai establishment secure enough, that arrested communists were usually well-treated in prison, and torture and execution a distinct rarity.

This situation changed quite rapidly in the 1960s as the Vietnam War deepened and the American presence in Thailand massively expanded. The Asian communist states, especially China and Vietnam, saw every reason to support the CPT, and their influence was decisive in persuading the underground Party to move into the rural peripheries of the country and commence a guerrilla struggle. In 1966: just as the PKI was being destroyed in Indonesia. As the Vietnam War dragged on, the CPT steadily expanded its bases, while depending substantially on Peking and Hanoi for funds, weapons, training, and ideological guidance. The fact that the Party's leadership was overwhelmingly Sino-Thai or even "Chinese" made these links especially strong. On the other hand, the American presence—there were 48,000 US military personnel in Thailand in 1968, to say nothing of vast American expenditures on infrastructure, and on the Thai military and police—initiated changes in Thai society far more rapid than it had ever previously experienced. A huge economic boom got under way, which rapidly expanded the middle class in which, however, Sino-Thai remained predominant. Concomitantly, public education, especially at the university level, expanded spectacularly, perhaps by 500 per cent in less than a decade.

In October 1973, small university-based protests against the dictatorship suddenly and rapidly swelled into huge popular demonstrations in the capital, and, thanks to internal divisions in the military itself, as well as the intervention of the young monarch Rama IX, the dictatorship abruptly collapsed. Between October 1973 and October 1976, Thailand had the most open, democratic political system it has experienced, before and since. Pent-up dissatisfactions—with oppressive land laws, with corruption, with bans on strikes, with American domination—burst into the open, and a quite rapid political polarization commenced, pushing especially student activists to the Left, and many others, fearful of the way the Vietnam War was going, to the Right. It was in this period that the CPT speedily re-expanded its underground influence into the urban areas and into the intelligentsia in a way that had been impossible for a generation. In 1975, a wave of assassinations of leaders of student, worker, and farmer organizations prepared the way for the extremely brutal reimposition of military dictatorship on October 6, 1976. The repression was especially severe at the traditionally progressive

Thammasat University in downtown Bangkok, where students were publicly shot, hanged, and beaten to death. The immediate result was a massive flight of liberal and leftist youngsters into the maquis, where the CPT initially welcomed and protected them.

With the fall/liberation of Indochina in the spring of 1975, the abolition of the Laotian monarchy (which panicked the conservative Thai royal family), and a vast increase in the CPT's potential leadership cadres, the CIA station chief in Bangkok was gloomily predicting in early 1977 that Thailand would be the next domino to fall to communism. He could not have been more spectacularly mistaken. Instead, within three years, the CPT had lost virtually everything, and ceased to play any significant role in Thai politics—fifteen years after that fate had overtaken the PKI. Why?

The crucial factor was the outbreak of the three-cornered war between China, Vietnam, and Cambodia which opened at the end of 1978. The ageing Sino-Thai leadership of the CPT decided to throw in its lot with Teng Hsiao-p'ing, whereupon the Vietnamese, highly influential in Laos and now masters of Cambodia, ceased all co-operation and blocked off all border sanctuaries. The Macchiavelli of Peking then proceeded to Bangkok, and arranged an alliance against Vietnam with the Thai military leaders in exchange for the cessation of virtually all help to the CPT, including the powerful and effective Voice of the People of Thailand radio station in Yunnan. These proved devastating blows to the Party. Internal dissension broke out in its ranks, typically ranging the young, university-educated refugees of 1976 against their elders. In the meantime, a new intelligent military leadership had decided to offer a complete amnesty to all those in the maquis who surrendered—and it kept its promises. By the end of 1979 a massive haemorrhage had begun, which, in tandem with its international isolation, destroyed the Party's prestige and political possibilities. 1980, shall we say? just as Ronald Reagan was successfully campaigning for the presidency, in part on the basis of his programme for countering a never more powerful "Evil Empire" centred in Moscow.

There are two points to underscore in all of this. First, that "after communism" in both Indonesia and Thailand began long before the implosion of Stalin's empire, indeed long before anyone could imagine this implosion happening. Second, that the residues of communism in the two countries were utterly different.

People who had been with the Left in Indonesia before October 1, 1965 were rarely university-educated, and the Marxism they knew theoretically was 1950s Marxism-Leninism in its simpler Stalinist and early Maoist forms. They were overwhelmingly indigenous Indonesians rather than members of the Sino-Indonesian minority. Their political experience had been in parliamentary and para-parliamentary legal politics. They were nationalists determined to live down their enemies' accusations of "treason" in 1948. And their lives "after communism," if they had lives at all, had meant torture, lengthy imprisonment without trial under often barbarous conditions, destruction of marriages and families, as well as continuous social ostracism, intensive military surveillance, and unemployment on their release.

In Thailand, a substantial number of the most capable recruits to communism, especially after 1975–76, were students at the best of Thailand's universities. While some of their Marxism came from Cultural Revolution China and Vietnam, they were also, as children of the 1960s, exposed to the New Left Marxism of northern Europe and the United States, as well as Gramsci, Althusser, and the Frankfurt school. They were often devoted to Joan Baez and Bob Dylan who, however, came too late on the international scene for any legal PKI cadres to think of enjoying them. A substantial number were second- or third-generation Sino-Thai, products of an assimilated middle class which had grown so vastly from the late 1950s. As often happens with the children and grandchildren of immigrants, they were determined to demonstrate their patriotic Thai-ness—a major reason for their revolt against the CPT leadership's subservience to Peking—but this was somewhat self-conscious. They had only the briefest and most tangential experience of parliamentary politics and had been formed by extra-parliamentary activism and by life in the maquis. But their lives "after communism" were in most cases gently normal (though there were significant numbers who took to drugs or committed suicide). They returned home to join the family business, or went back to their universities, or studied abroad, mostly in Europe, America, and Australia, or decided to participate in parliamentary politics that began to take real roots in Thailand in the 1980s once the CPT was destroyed. Nothing was seriously held against them, not least because they were the children of a well-educated, now very successful bourgeoisie.

FOOTPRINTS IN THE MIRE

If one looks at "radicalism after communism" in the two countries, these contrasts have to be borne centrally in mind. Yet, in a strange way, there are also partly hidden connective threads linking them together, and these are nationalism, history, and print.

Indonesia first. The best-known and probably the most important radical in Indonesia today is the brilliant autodidact-writer Pramoedya Ananta Toer (or "Pram" as he is generally known), whose novels and stories have been translated into dozens of languages, and who is Southeast Asia's likeliest candidate for a Nobel prize when the region's turn of the Oslovian wheel comes round. Pram's political record is quite unique. Born in 1926, he was first imprisoned by the Dutch in 1948–49 as a nationalist revolutionary, then by the Sukarno regime in 1959–60 for publicly defending the Chinese minority, and finally by the Suharto dictatorship in 1966–78 for his vocal leadership of the Left intelligentsia from the late 1950s until 1965. Today, nearly thirty years after the Indonesian holocaust, his works are all prohibited, and students who circulate them clandestinely have incurred long prison sentences. By far the most influential of his writings is the tetralogy which he initiated in the mid-1970s in the remote penal colony of Buru, by oral recitation to his fellow prisoners. The tetralogy is loosely based on the life of a hitherto little-known pioneer nationalist called Tirtoadisuryo, a young man of aristocratic Javanese birth, who founded the first nationalist newspaper in the first decade of this century, helped promote the first radical movement of opposition to Dutch colonial rule, and ended his days in imprisonment and obscurity.

The titles of the novels already reveal something of their character: *Earth of Mankind, Child of All Nations, Footprints in the Mire, The Glass House.*[1] The first two announce something without precedent in Indonesian literature (and on which the PKI of the pre-1965 era would certainly have frowned): that "this earth" of Indonesia is for all those who love it, not merely its passport-carrying citizens, and that the heroic originator of Indonesian nationalism was the heir of emancipatory nationalists in every country. The third title summons up the image of all those who have left nothing behind them in their struggles—1910s, 1940s, 1960s, 1990s—except "footprints in the mire;" while the fourth allegorizes, after the manner of Foucault's Benthamite Panopticon, the contemporary police state in the Dutch colonial regime's ambition to put everything in the colony under surveillance.

The young radical hero of the novels is not only shown to us learning about the world from the French, Dutch, Japanese, and other Java-dwelling foreigners he encounters, and from the novel newspapers which, at the turn of the century, were bringing the whole planet into the cities of the colony, but he is destined to be married successively to the most outsider of outsider women: a pitiful Eurasian beauty, a Chinese immigrant fleeing the brutality of a dying Ch'ing dynasty, and a fierce Muslim from the most remote (from Java) eastern fringes of the sprawling archipelagic colony. Still more striking is the fact that the figure who dominates all four novels is not the young hero, but his first mother-in-law, sold off, after her initial menstruation, by her

---

1. The original novels, all published by Hasta Mitra in Jakarta, were *Bumi Manusia* (1979), *Anak Semua Bangsa* (1980), *Jejak Langkah* (1985), and *Rumah Kaca* (1988). The current English versions are those published by William Morrow in New York, under the titles *This Earth of Mankind* (1991), *Child of All Nations* (1993), *Footsteps* (1994), and *House of Glass* (1996).

servile Javanese parents to a drunken, licentious Dutch plantation-owner, but who fully masters her later destiny, against all odds taking on the colonial secret police itself. (In a brilliant, unexpected move, Pram has the narrator of the fourth novel be the senior native intelligence-officer assigned by the Dutch to watch the hero and hound him to his end.)

Set in the period 1896–1916, i.e. "before communism," the novels nonetheless are radically oriented to Indonesia "after communism." The traces of an older Marxism are perfectly clear in the many episodes of oppression by plantation-owners, vice-lords, colonial officials, native aristocrats, and secret police; and resistance by peasants, small traders, journalists, women, and minorities. But the we (radical Indonesians) versus them (white colonialists and their Chinese pariah-entrepreneur collaborators) axis, which had been more or less *de rigueur* from the 1940s on, on the Indonesian Right as well as Left, is gone. The more sinister figures are most often future Indonesians, and the heroes and heroines are not only a mixed-nationality batch, but of many types of culture and political persuasion. Perhaps we should not be too surprised at all of this. At the end of the 1970s, when the manuscripts were finished, Pram was fully aware of the roles played by Congressman Donald Fraser of Minneapolis, and of Amnesty International, in securing his release after twelve terrible years in prison, and of the contrasting indifference of the "actually existing" communist regimes to his condition. Prison had shown how wide could be the gap between communist credentials and moral courage. At the same time, he was writing between the lines against a brutal dictatorship which claims legitimacy among its own citizens on the grounds of the total unsuitability of "western democracy" as well as "Marxism in all its forms" for an Indonesian nation whose origins are said to lie solely and exclusively in a pristine, thousand-year-old, 200 per cent native past.

A second style of Indonesian radicalism can be presented more briefly. Pipit Rochijat Kartawidjaja, now in his early forties, is more than a generation younger than Pram. He lives a precarious existence in Berlin, since his passport has long been taken away from him on the grounds of his seditious and insolent writings, but he refuses to renounce his citizenship and seek asylum. He survives partly because he has built up close personal ties with activists among the German Greens and Social Democrats. In 1965 his father was the pious Muslim manager of a nationalized sugar plantation, who came under strong attack by the communist plantation-worker union. As a kid in junior high-school, he was naturally drawn by family loyalty into the ranks of a local anticommunist youth group, which, when the time came, joined in the *matanza*. Among the butchers were some of Pipit's classmate friends. The memories of what he had witnessed haunted him, but he found no way to think or act coherently about them till he went to Germany to study electrical engineering. There he married the daughter of a second-rank PKI intellectual who happened to be out of Indonesia when the massacres were under way—but his relations with his father-in-law are fairly chilly. Since the early 1980s he has become famous among Indonesian would-be radicals for three things. First, a flow of brilliantly satirical articles directed against the dictatorship in Jakarta, of which the most striking feature is their surreal jumbling of regime officialese, street slang, ironical Marxist vocabulary, scatology, and touches of pure poetry. The aim is always to demystify both the regime and its autocratic developmental language. Second, a series of reworkings of, or new imaginations of, those ancient Hindu-Javanese legends that underpin both Javanese tradition and Javanese Tradition. Here Krishna and Arjuna may equally talk as public information officers, transvestite prostitutes, university professors, or religious charlatans. His rule is "Anything may be said." Third is a justly famous and unique account of his high-school brush with mass murder—on the side of the murderers. He is determined both that the massacres never be forgotten, and that they never become the basis for further massacres one day. He broods on the mindless identifications that brought him and his comrades to the abattoir. This means shattering any easy walls between "us" and "them."

I can only try to give the flavour of this extraordinary text, entitled "Am I PKI or Non-PKI?"[2] by quoting two short passages. First, of the perhaps communist corpses floating down the Brantas river through his home town, he wrote: "Usually the corpses were no longer recognizable as human. Headless. Stomachs torn open. The smell was unimaginable. To make sure they didn't sink, the carcasses were deliberately tied to, or impaled upon, bamboo stakes. And the departure of the corpses from the Kediri region down the Brantas achieved its golden age when bodies were stacked together on rafts over which the PKI banner grandly flew." Second, of unemployment at the local whorehouses, he recalled: "Once the purge of Communist elements got under way, clients stopped coming for sexual satisfaction. The reason: most clients—and prostitutes—were too frightened, for, hanging up in front of the whorehouses, there were a lot of male Communist genitals—like bananas hung out for sale." This is a language utterly repellent both to the old communists who survived the horror, and to the regime and political groups that carried it out, because it makes unanswerable the question: am I executioner or not-executioner? But Pipit is not speaking to them, but to a young Indonesia which, if it begins to think radically as surely it will some day, will also have to confront the meaning of "communism" and "not-communism" in the world-epoch, not the Indonesian time, of "after communism."

---

2. It was first translated into English and published in *Indonesia*, 40 (Oct. 1985), pp. 37–56.

A NEW SUBJECTIVITY

In contemporary Thailand it is not a question of exorcising ghosts, but rather, perhaps, of summoning them. The end of the CPT came with, as it were, a gentle whimper rather than a terrifying bang. And while its fall preceded the collapse of the USSR, the dates were close enough that those reflecting seriously on the one very soon had to reflect upon the other. Radically minded thinkers in Thailand were, in the 1980s and early 1990s, living freely and usually comfortably in a buoyant, crassly rich, thoroughly corrupt, bourgeois semi-democracy, unlike their Indonesian comrades terrorized by a merciless military regime. Most of them ended up with respectable positions in the universities, in the mass media, and in the Thai parliament. For them the questions were, characteristically, such as these: Had the CPT gone up in smoke because, as its conservative enemies had claimed all along, it had never been authentically Thai? Had their own attachments to it been the product of naive youthful illusions? Had they completely misunderstood their country's culture and history? Was there nothing left to do but anticipate Fukuyama's dicta, and tag along in the interminable train of Adam Smith and Thomas Jefferson?

One should not be surprised that the most significant radical thinkers were academics, rather than exiled or forbidden imaginers of alternative histories; and that they spent a lot of energy thinking about why they had been politically defeated, and where lay the strength of their successful adversaries. This thinking, nonetheless, was almost always historically focused, if in significantly different ways. Let me briefly discuss just three important texts written in the last decade by Marxist activists of the 1970s, two of them Sino-Thai.

First is that of Seksan Prasertkul, pre-eminent student activist in the heady days of October 1973, further radicalized in 1973–75, trained briefly in Vietnam and Laos, and vigorous participant in the armed guerrilla struggle after 1976. Like many of his generation, Seksan had concluded by the middle 1980s that not only had the CPT leadership been crippled by a "Chineseness" that led it to an absurd and catastrophic identification with "Little Bottle" and his Peking associates; much more importantly, it had, almost without thinking, conceded Thai nationalism to a reactionary Buddhist monkhood, right-wing military leaders, and, above all, the monarchy with its powerful hold on Tradition and the popular imagination. Most fundamental in his view was a construction of Siam's history by which it had been saved from imperialism, and set on the road to modernity, by a selfless and far-sighted sequence of monarchs, beginning with the Rama IV we know from Yul Brynner's fanciful impersonations. On the basis of careful and extensive archival research, he produced a "Marxist" thesis which nonetheless turned both traditional left- and right-wing historiographies upside down.[3] He was, for example, able to show that it was precisely the typically despised and marginalized "Chinese" and "Sino-Thai" bourgeoisie of the late nineteenth and early twentieth centuries that, far from being a gaggle of compradores, had most vigorously defended the autonomy of the Thai economy from British imperialism, whereas the monarchy and aristocracy had caved in to, and then closely collaborated with, that imperialism. He also convincingly argued that the prime impetus towards liberalization and modernization was in fact British Free Trade imperialism which had unilaterally, and insouciantly, destroyed the complex of mercantilist monopolies on which the old royal order had been based; at the same time, however, it had thereby taken away from the local bourgeoisie the ground for undertaking its historic political task of destroying the *ancien régime*. Hence the survival of much of the old social order into contemporary Thailand, and a profoundly false, mystified account of Thai history. Among the CPT's greatest failings, he argued, had been its contempt for serious historical study, its lazy adoption of Stalinist and Maoist vulgar-Marxism, and hence its long-run inability to create a hegemonic presence.

Second is Thongchai Winichakul, nationally famous as one of the "Bangkok 18" activists tried and convicted after the bloody coup of 1976 on charges of *lèse majesté*. Thongchai, a Sino-Thai, was sufficiently younger than Seksan that he came intellectually to maturity in what we may look back on as the age of Foucault. His radical assault on the contemporary *ancien régime* therefore came from another direction. By a brilliant microstudy of the maps produced in Bangkok during the nineteenth century, and the institutions and discourses that enveloped them, he was able to show conclusively that the eternal "Thailand" or "Siam" of the hegemonic conservative culture was an invention of the 1870s.[4] Prior to that moment of Foucauldian "break," created by the European imperialists' introduction of Mercatorian mapping, the institution of mathematically-based surveying, and the imagining of continuous, invisible borders, dynastic realms had been defined by their centres, and rulers thought of their subjects as infinitely variable, and variously exploitable, assemblies of corvée labourers, footsoldiers, and taxpayers of whom the last question asked was their "nationality." This was among the reasons that the armed forces of "Thai" rulers had been so full of Chinese seamen, Malay navigators, and Vietnamese archers. Thongchai went further to show how, after the 1870s, the new royal mapping service began, in the

---

3. See Seksan Prasertkul, "The Transformation of the Thai State and Economic Change" (Ph.D. thesis, Cornell University, 1989).

4. See his *Siam Mapped: A History of the Geo-Body of a Nation* (Honolulu: University of Hawaii Press, 1994).

European manner, to create wholly imaginary historical maps that pushed what he sarcastically called the "Geobody of Thailand" back into the mists of the legendary past. Needless to say, the implications of an argument that, far from continuously, bravely, and patriotically defending Thailand from ancient times, the ruling class had actually invented it a little more than a century ago (and invented it in a style that powerfully supported its hegemony) were decidedly subversive. But Thongchai also saw his aim as the opening of a huge space for many kinds of alternative historical narrative, decentred, localized, egalitarian, and popular. In this way, the road would be cleared for future counter-hegemonic left-wing appropriations of historical subjectivity.

Last is Kasian Tejapira, Sino-Thai, youngest of the three, too young to participate in the *émeute* of October 1973, but a committed underground Marxist in the later 1970s. Unlike the other two, he began his studies more or less as world communism was self-destructing. Perhaps this is the reason why his research, influenced substantially by Walter Benjamin, aimed at a half-ironical recuperation of Thai Marxism in its 1940s and 1950s youthful exuberance. He is the first Thai intellectual to think carefully about the historical relation of the adjective (Thai) to the noun (Marxism), and to recognize that it had always been an illusion to imagine that Marxism moved frictionlessly from culture to culture and language to language. He was also the first to think of Marxism as a certain type of cultural commodity in a capitalist society for which in different eras there was a traceably various "demand" and "supply."[5] His work is of enormous sophistication and impossible here to summarize, but one can get some of its thrust from the following quotation from its opening page:

> To English-reading audiences in the present post-Communist world of the final decade of the 20th century . . . [a text] on the now defunct doctrine of Marxism-Communism in its reincarnation in a remote and reposeful Third World capitalist country almost half a century ago must seem superfluous; even the [text's] "right to exist" appears dubious. After all, during the past decade, the theory, practice and organization of Marxism-Communism had already proven bankrupt and utterly collapsed in Thailand, like most of its counterparts in other countries round the world. So why bother to read, let alone write, such a lengthy and tedious obituary for this political corpse? My answer is that, though dead, the Spectre of Communism is still haunting us; that having had such a long and stormy engagement with the living, the dead did not depart without leaving deep imprints on the cultural soul of its intimate interlocutors; and that, as such, only through the writing, reading and understanding of a communist ghost story can the living become fully aware of their own subconscious cultural selves.

---

5. See Kasian Tejapira, "Commodifying Marxism: The Formation of Modern Thai Radical Culture, 1927–1958" (Ph.D. thesis, Cornell University, 1992).

Sauve Qui Peut

On March 11, 1998, precisely thirty-two years after he directed a *coup de force* which removed Sukarno, "Father of the Nation," from power, Indonesia's President Suharto spoke the following pregnant words as he was sworn in, with a unanimous vote of the puppet People's Consultative Assembly, to a seventh five-year term of office: "We will never enjoy again an economic growth such as we have experienced for more than a quarter of a century."[1] This is the language of the mill towns of New England, the coal-and-steel belts of Pennsylvania and Belgium, the ghost towns of Australia and the American West—those places where capitalism has been and gone, leaving behind scarred landscapes and ruined social edifices. It is a language that nudges the observer to ask two related questions about the "Asian crisis" which are rarely raised in the flood of contemporary newspaper and magazine analyses of its proximate causes. The first is: what made the World Bank's "Asian miracle" of the past two decades possible? The second: is Suharto's prognosis correct, not merely for Indonesia, but also for the other advanced countries of Southeast Asia?[2]

Anyone who predicted in 1950 that within a generation "miracles" would occur in the region would have been regarded as an idle dreamer. Indonesia, devastated by ten years of military occupation, war, and revolution, had a literacy rate of not more than 10 per cent. Even a decade later, the income accruing to the Indonesian state was not much bigger than that of a large

---

1. *Bangkok Post,* March 12, 1998, p. 5.
2. For most of the period to be discussed Burma and the states of Indochina had war-torn socialist or pseudo-socialist economies. Capitalist Brunei and Singapore will largely be ignored, since the one is essentially an oil sheikhdom, the other a municipality.

American university. The Philippine economy, weak even in colonial times, had been trampled to rubble by warring Japanese and American armed forces. The country had no national language binding it together beyond an American English commanded (perhaps) by a quarter of the population. Siam was a sleepy, rice-exporting country which even in 1960 had no nation-wide, effective system of primary education. Malaya's tin-and-rubber colonial economy was prostrate, and the colony was a battlefield where imperial British armed forces fought against a powerful, audacious, communist insur-rection. And then?

It can plausibly be argued that there were four basic conditions-of-possi-bility for the "miracle," and that these conditions existed only in the long strip of coastal capitalist states stretching down from South Korea to the eastern edge of the Indian Ocean.

The first was the peculiar arc of the Cold War in the region. Nowhere in the world was the Cold War "hotter" in the third-quarter of this century, and perhaps nowhere did it cool down more rapidly and dramatically, thanks to the Peking–Washington rapprochement of the middle 1970s. The only two big wars the Americans fought were in this zone: on the Korean peninsula they were forced to accept a costly stand-off, while in Indochina they suffered a bitter and humiliating defeat. In every important country of Southeast Asia, with the exception of Indonesia, there were major, sustained communist insurrections, and Indonesia itself, by the early 1960s, permitted the legal existence of the largest communist party in the world outside the socialist bloc. In all these states, except Malaysia, which was still a colony for the seri-ous duration of the local communist rebellion, the Americans intervened politically, economically, militarily, and culturally, on a massive scale. The notorious domino theory was invented specifically for Southeast Asia. To shore up the line of teetering dominoes Washington made every effort to create loyal, capitalistically prosperous, authoritarian, and anticommunist regimes—typically, but not invariably, military-dominated.[3] Many were tied to the United States in security arrangements, and in some the Americans had a broad variety of military installations. Its disasters only encouraged

---

3. In the 1950s, Kuomintang armies fleeing into Burma after Mao's triumph were abetted by the CIA in taking control of substantial areas in the poppy-growing northeast of the country. Siam became an American ally as early as 1948, was a founding member of SEATO, and even-tually hosted tens of thousands of American servicemen and warplanes at the height of the Vietnam War. Ngo Dinh Diem's South Vietnam was an American creation; Norodom Sihanouk's neutralist regime in Cambodia was toppled in 1970 with American connivance. The various shaky right-wing regimes in Laos were paid for on and off by Washington. The Dulles brothers armed and supplied the big regional rebellion of 1957–58 in Sukarno's Indonesia. The Philippines was not only a founding member of SEATO, but was the site of many of the most important American military bases in the Western Pacific region.

Washington to put more muscle and money behind its remaining political cards. No world region received more "aid" in various forms than did this tropical antipode.

On the other hand, the Washington–Peking coalition against Moscow, consolidated after the "fall" of Indochina, meant that from the late 1970s till the collapse of the Soviet Union those countries of Southeast Asia who so wished could continue to profit from Washington's Cold War largesse without facing any severe internal or external difficulties (the Philippines was a partial exception, as we shall see). Nothing quite like this whole process occurred anywhere else in the world.

The second condition-of-possibility was the accident of the region's geographical propinquity to Japan. Coming late to the imperialist game at the very end of the nineteenth century, Tokyo faced Tsardom on its northern periphery, and Europeans entrenched in Southeast Asia and dominant in China, while the Americans were pushing fast across the Pacific—Alaska, Hawaii, Midway, Wake, Guam, the Philippines. Beginning with the acquisition of Taiwan in 1895 and the rape of Korea in 1910, Japanese ruling elites sought by economic, political, and military means to create for their country, in East and Southeast Asia, a zone of hegemony equivalent to that of the United States in the western hemisphere. The end results were the onset of the Sino-Japanese war in 1937, the outbreak of the Pacific War at the end of 1941, the conquest of most of Southeast Asia in 1942, and atomic collapse in August 1945. In the period of postwar recovery, the old ambitions did not disappear, but took an essentially economic form. Assured of its political and military dominance over Japan, and eager to build the Japanese economy as a cornerstone of capitalist strength in Asia, Washington put no real obstacles in Tokyo's way. But in those early postwar years Mao's China was closed to Japanese capital, and South Koreans' bitter memories of Japanese colonialism made them scarcely more welcoming. Southeast Asia was the only real possibility available, not least because the European powers had now lost their colonial fortresses there. Beginning in the 1950s, through a series of war reparations agreements whereby Southeast Asian countries were substantially funded for purchasing Japanese manufactures, Tokyo's economic presence rapidly increased: first in Siam, which had been an ally in World War II, later in other new nation-states which had had less pleasant experiences under Japanese military rule. By the early 1970s Japan had become the single most important external investor in the region, both as extractor of natural resources (timber, oil, and so on), and in industrial and infrastructural development. All of this meant that Southeast Asia was the only region in the world in which the two most powerful capitalist national economies were deeply and on the whole co-operatively committed for four decades. Later, as they came on stream as major exporters of capital, South Korea and Taiwan followed the leading goose, reinforcing the already huge inflows of capital and technology from America and Japan.[4]

The third condition-of-possibility was, ironically enough, the successful communist revolution in China. The Maoist project of building a mighty, autarchic, socialist economy outside the global capitalist order, kept China from playing a significant economic role in, or in competition with, Southeast Asia until the middle 1980s.[5] Only then, under the regime of "Little Bottle" did the former Middle Kingdom—with its vast internal market, and its unlimited pool of desperately poor peasants and workers under the iron control of the CCP, start attracting huge investments from America, Japan, the EC, Taiwan, and even South Korea. In the 1990s, therefore, China was finally in a position to out-compete Southeast Asia in manufacturing exports, a situation which seems certain to continue indefinitely. Seen retrospectively, the Southeast Asian miracle was thus in part the product of an extraordinary forty-year sequestration from the global market of the greatest power in Asia.

The last condition was indirectly connected to the third. Over the melancholy century of decline between the Opium War and the onset of the Sino-Japanese War, millions of young, mostly male, mostly illiterate people left the coastal districts of Fukien and Kwantung for the labour-hungry European colonies in Southeast Asia, as well as Siam.[6] Up till the turn of the century most of these people, speaking such (on the whole) mutually unintelligible languages as Hokkien, Cantonese, Hakka, Hainanese, and Teochiu, scarcely regarded themselves as Chinese. They identified themselves by clan, home village or district, and by language group. Where circumstances were favourable, especially in Buddhist Siam and the Catholic Philippines, intermarriage with, and assimilation to, the local population were common, producing over time a distinct mestizo social stratum. In less favourable circumstances, as in (Muslim) Malaya and the Netherlands East Indies, they tended to be ghettoized by colonial policy-making. After 1900, however, this situation began to change. Migrant communities became more rooted and stable as women started to arrive from Kwangtung and Fukien; as schools started to be set up

---

4. It is emblematic that Toyota arranged for the production of a *soi-disant* national car for Malaysia in the 1980s, while Hyundai got round to trying—fortunately without success—to do the same for Indonesia only in the middle 1990s.

5. The self-imposed isolation was reinforced for a long time by an American-orchestrated trade embargo.

6. The flow slowed down during the Depression of the 1930s, when the colonial powers tightened immigration controls. It largely came to an end in the era of postwar independence, except for a small but important group of rich businessmen who fled with their wealth as the CPP took control of China: most went to the United States, Taiwan, Hong Kong, and Singapore, but some ended up in Bangkok, Manila, and Jakarta.

to teach children all-Chinese writing, as well as spoken Mandarin; and as Chinese nationalism proper made its various novel inroads. While most immigrants long remained poor—till World War II, for example, they formed the bulk of the true working class in Siam and Malaya—a significant number, through habits of hard work and the freedom created by uprooting, were working their way up the occupational ladder—petty trade, entrepreneurship, the professions, even the bureaucracy. Particularly in the Netherlands Indies, such people came to form a visible middle tier between the colonial administrative apparatus and the peasant bulk of the indigenous population.

In the same period, however, native nationalisms began to emerge in Southeast Asia, first in the Philippines and last in Cambodia, Laos, Malaya, and Singapore. The immigrants and their descendants often found themselves, for the first time, caught between increasingly racist colonial regimes (who despised, exploited, but also protected them) and nativist nationalists (who despised them as aliens and colonial collaborators, but envied their economic successes). The precariousness of their situation was accentuated by the collapse of European imperialism and the postwar independence of the former colonies. Colonial subjecthood could be worn lightly, but modern citizenship of a nation-state could not.[7] Choices had to be made, few easy; and the difficulties were compounded by the appearance of rival Chinas centred in Peking and Taipei, each eager to attract loyalty but neither able, or even much inclined, to intervene protectively on their behalf. At the same time, however, the end of colonialism opened up opportunities for economic advancement undreamed of before the Pacific War.

The general sociological trend after independence (though there were wide variations from country to country) was for upwardly mobile "natives" to secure for themselves an impregnable position in the political realm—especially in rapidly expanding state bureaucracies, and above all in the military and police. This tendency has been particularly evident in Indonesia and Malaysia; but even in Siam, which has had a large number of "Chinese" politicians, it is rare to find a senior military or police officer who claims such ancestry.[8] Furthermore, open or veiled policies of discrimination against "Chinese" in state universities were felt to limit their possibilities in public service and even in some professions. The effect of all this was to encourage people of Chinese ancestry to concentrate their energies and ambitions in the

7. In Indonesia today, it is telling that the only people referred to as "citizens" (WNI—Warga Negara Indonesia) are the "Chinese." Everyone else is a son/daughter of the soil.

8. In the middle 1970s, the speaker of the Thai parliament was the shrewd lawyer and businessman Prasit Kanjanawat. Newspaper cartoons regularly made fun—but without malice—of his heavy "Chinese" accent. Such a situation is, I think, inconceivable in any of the former colonies.

private commercial sector—legal and otherwise. The extreme case of such tendencies has been Suharto's Indonesia. Between March 1966 and March 1998, not a single person of known Chinese descent ever became a cabinet minister, senior civil servant, general, admiral, or air marshal; even among parliamentarians there have been very few. At the same time, the estimated 5 per cent of the population said to be Chinese controls 70–80 per cent of the domestic economy, and almost all the biggest crony capitalists around Suharto have come precisely from this group. Such a "racial" division of labour has encouraged massive rent-seeking on the part of state officials, limited the growth of a vigorous "native" entrepreneurial class, and made a marginalized Chinese minority the real domestic motor of the "miracle."

What portion of these conditions-of-possibility will survive into the early part of the next century? The peculiar American investment in Cold War Southeast Asia—which made possible the tyrannies of the Thai generals in the period 1948–77, the Marcos regime in the Philippines, and Suharto's endless Neues Ordnung—is no more. The American bases in the Philippines are gone, and the country now matters very little to its former colonial master. Siam is no longer seen as a bulwark against anything. Even huge Indonesia, with its 200 million people, is now understood more as a worry than an ally. The anti-western vociferations of Malaysia's durable Prime Minister Mahathir barely earn him a shrug in Washington.

Japan has enduring geopolitical interests in the region, but it is likely that the country's "historic moment," symbolized by the Plaza Accord of 1985, and the anti-Japanese scare that swept America in the 1980s, has passed. During the present decade, Tokyo has struggled, mostly unsuccessfully, to emerge with vigour from the burst bubble of the late 1980s. The country's inability to provide much help in overcoming the Crash in Southeast Asia is evidence of this weakness. On the other hand, although China's political future is full of uncertainties, the chances are high that it will soon resume its historically central role in eastern and southeastern Asia. It has resources which vastly outmatch those of any country in Southeast Asia, and it will for a long time be a domineering competitor on the world market. Thus perhaps only the overseas Chinese will remain an enduring miracle ingredient, even though this ingredient has its dubious and fragile aspects.

But if most of the conditions-of-possibility of the "miracle" have passed or will be passing soon, that does not necessarily mean that the countries concerned did not use the period of extraordinary growth to create the basis for long-term, and more self-sustaining, development. After all, both Germany and Japan, after suffering military defeat, economic ruin, and enemy occupation, bounced back within a long generation to become major economic powers. A closer comparison is offered by strongly nationalist South Korea, which used the growth possibilities of American-backed Cold War tyranny and its own historic fears of its mighty neighbours, to create an industrial society producing world-class manufacturing products: there are good grounds for thinking that the country will recover quickly from the Crash and soon resume much of its earlier role in the global economy. The central question therefore to be asked of Southeast Asia is how far the resources and assets accruing to it in the era of the "miracle" were used to prepare for the day when its conditions-of-possibility would substantially diminish.

There are three obvious sites for investigating, even if in a superficial, summary fashion, this question: the development of a skilled, well-educated workforce capable of moving each country up the value-added ladder; the uses of domestic savings and investment; and care of national environments and natural resources. Of these, which are, of course, closely interconnected, the most important for the future is the first.

One might consider uncolonized Siam, which, until just before the Crash, was trumpeted by the World Bank as an example that all forward-looking "Third World" countries might emulate for its very high rates of growth over three decades. At the end of the 1980s, a mere 28 per cent of its high-school-age population was actually in a high-school of any kind.[9] It is reliably estimated that in the year 2000, 70 per cent of the country's labour force will have primary education or less.[10] Tertiary educational institutions produce no more than half the engineers that Siam needs. Thai vocational schools are more famous for the savage brawls between their student bodies than for the advanced industrial skills that they instil. The quality of its universities, still overwhelmingly state-owned, is "uneven," to put it kindly, not least because professors and lecturers are wretchedly paid, and so spend much of their time moonlighting or speculating off campus. Finally, there has been a phenomenon which is also visible everywhere else in capitalist Southeast Asia: the decision of many upper-class and middle-class parents to side-step the national educational system as far as possible, sending their children to local "international" high schools and on to colleges in, depending on income levels, the United States, Ukania, Canada, and Australia. Some of these youngsters never return home, and those who do rarely wish to position themselves in the home country's educational system.

---

9. Gerald Tan, *ASEAN: Economic Development and Co-operation* (Singapore: Times Academic Press, 1996), p. 111.

10. Jomo K. Sundaram *et al.*, *Southeast Asia's Misunderstood Miracle: Industrial Policy and Economic Development in Thailand, Malaysia and Indonesia* (Boulder, Col.: Westview Press, 1997), p. 83. This book, which went to press just before the Crash, is beautifully researched and offers a prescient warning of the fragility of the "miracle."

Compared to Malaysia, the Philippines has three times the percentage of college-age youngsters in school (38 per cent versus 7 per cent),[11] but most of them are in miserable diploma mills which teach them next to nothing. Neither country has an effective industrially oriented system of "vocational" education. Both countries have experienced substantial young brain-drains, not least because of the marketable legacy of English-language colonialism. In Malaysia, bright young "Chinese," facing educational and other discrimination, have been leaving in visible quantities. Marcos's immiseration of the Philippines started a mass emigration of "native" Filipinos, many of them with local college degrees, to work all over the world as maids, nurses, bartenders, whores, chauffeurs, and so on. (Their remittances home are the largest single contribution to the Philippines' foreign exchange earnings.) Indonesia is still worse off. The problems of education have been accentuated by authoritarian regimes, which have usually regarded students as a dangerously volatile group, and which have used the educational system more to instil political loyalty rather than to stimulate inventive young minds.[12]

One key reason for the shortcomings of educational policy was that for many years the main investors in industrial development came from outside the region, especially from the United States, Germany, Japan, Korea, and Taiwan. All were looking for low-wage, submissive and non-unionized workers, and the latter three for offshore platforms offering low-tariff access to the American and European markets. Such investors rarely had the interest or the resources to engage in vocational training outside the immediate needs of their businesses. Furthermore, the manufacturing plants they developed had very weak back-linkages into the domestic economy and society, tending rather to operate as enclaves. In effect, rich foreigners and poor natives did much of the real work of export-developmental growth. But this situation's continuation was always dependent on the low-wage, low-skill status of the workforce; any marked improvements encouraged the investors to move to still poorer countries such as Vietnam. Yet as long as GNP figures continued to rise, few of the governments of the region thought seriously and structurally about the future until just before the Crash.

Precisely because export-oriented economic growth was so heavily engined by external investment, domestic investors, especially those with good

---

11. These figures are from Tan, *ASEAN,* pp. 101 and 104. The Philippine figure seems improbably high.

12. My highly intelligent younger Indonesian foster son, educated in the best high school his provincial home town could offer, had, on arrival in America at the age of 17, no basic geographical knowledge whatever, no knowledge of elementary world history, and only the most distorted understanding of his own country's history. On a more general level, there has been a strong tendency for state scholarships for study abroad to be allocated on the basis not of intellectual merit but of family connections, ethnic backgrounds, and political loyalty.

political connections, concentrated their activities in protected sectors of the economy: banking, real estate, construction, and natural resource exploitation. When the Crash came, Indonesia had over two hundred banks, most of them shady and politically connected, and virtually all wildly in debt. Metropolitan Bangkok had an estimated 700,000 unoccupied housing and office units. The Malaysian government ordered the construction of the tallest building in the world, only to find that its spaces were largely unrentable. The Suharto regime invested billions of dollars in an aeroplane-manufacturing industry, whose products, lacking FAA safety approval, still have almost no customers. And so on, white elephant after white elephant. The very length of the miracle encouraged not merely the ruling elites, but also the new middle classes to use their high levels of saving to plunge into every kind of speculative, unproductive, and rent-seeking endeavour.

These perhaps "natural" inclinations were encouraged after the middle 1980s by the very large gap between Japan's artificially low interest rates and those prevailing in the region. It was only too easy for Southeast Asian financiers to borrow cheaply and on an almost unlimited basis in East Asia, and then lend out profitably to all and sundry in their domestic markets. American pressures for "liberalization" under conditions where overvalued local currencies were pegged to the dollar, and the World Bank's insistent promotion of local stock exchanges, further accentuated these speculative tendencies.

Of the capitalist countries of Southeast Asia, only Indonesia and Malaysia proved to be endowed with substantial mineral resources. All, however, started in the 1950s with extensive, rich, and varied forests as well as well-stocked coastal waters. Today, the Philippines has become one of the most environmentally damaged countries in the world. Siam's forests are close to gone (a government ban on domestic logging, still feebly enforced, was only promulgated in the last decade), and unscrupulous Thai loggers have stretched their tentacles into impoverished neighbouring Burma and Laos. The great fires of the past year which have devastated hundreds of thousands of hectares of forest in Borneo and Sumatra—and poisoned the air for millions of people living in Malaysia, Indonesia, and southern Thailand—are the consequences of the greed of conglomerates connected to the Suharto family, which, to create vast plantations, have found it simpler to burn people, fauna, and the jungle itself out of the way.[13] High-tech, highly placed Japanese,

---

13. The primary villain, Mohammad "Bob" Hassan (aka The Kian Seng), at least nominally a Muslim, is of "Chinese" origins, and made his billions initially by logging and later by cornering, through a crony cartel, a dominant part (78 per cent in the early 1990s) part of the world's international trade in plywood. In the new cabinet announced after Suharto's reselection as president he was put in charge of trade, the first "Chinese" minister in thirty-two years.

Korean, and other fishing corporations have severely depleted the marine environment at the expense of poor local populations. For most of the "miracle" period Indonesia and Malaysia had the advantage of huge oil and/or natural gas deposits, as well as the prices for petroleum that at various points OPEC was able to impose. But these deposits are finite, and will never again be available on the scale of the 1970s and 1980s. Northern Pennsylvania?

It would probably be wrong to be too pessimistic; but it is difficult, especially if one thinks of the comparison with South Korea, not to conclude that "miracle years" were used by Southeast Asian leaders in a largely short-sighted, profligate, and even antipatriotic manner.

It remains to consider comparatively the political trajectories of the four main countries of miraculous Southeast Asia, in order to assess the likely consequences of the Crash in each. The spectrum runs from the Philippines at one end, through Malaysia and Siam, to Indonesia at the other.

For most of the "miracle" years, the Philippines was seen as the sad exception: the one capitalist nation-state—and the one former American colony at that—which sank into poverty while the others roared ahead. But during the Crash its currency has survived better than the Thai *baht*, the Malaysian *ringgit*, and, of course, the Indonesian *rupiah*; and the country is even in the process of extricating itself from, rather than falling into, the IMF's clutches. How has this been possible?

The answer lies in the character of the Marcos regime and the reasons for, and timing of, its collapse in February 1986. Except for the fact that he was a civilian politician, Marcos was a typical tyrant of the "hot" Cold War era in Southeast Asia. He was first elected president in 1965, as Lyndon Johnson began sending large-scale American forces to Vietnam. American bases in the Philippines, especially the naval base at Subic Bay, and the huge air base at Clark Field, were central to the prosecution of the war. Marcos charged high rents for these facilities, hired out Filipino troops for service in Vietnam, kept a happy silence on the storage of nuclear weapons on Philippine soil, and vociferously supported the American war effort. In turn, and perhaps also because of large personal contributions to the finances of Nixon's last two presidential campaigns, Washington turned a calm blind eye to the installation of his kleptocratic dictatorship in 1972, towards the end of his legal tenure as president. Between 1972 and 1986 the Marcoses and their cronies, relying fully on continued American support, systematically pillaged the not very strong Philippine economy, in the process both precipitating a debilitating separatist rebellion in the Muslim south, and stimulating a Maoist insurrection that spread in due course to almost all parts of the country. By the beginning of the 1980s, however, the "hot" phase of the Cold War in Southeast Asia was over, and cooler heads in the Reagan White House recognized that the Marcos dictatorship had to go: it was ruining the country politically and economically with no benefits for the United States.[14] Thus the CIA participated actively in the popular mobilization against the regime, and it was American military aircraft that finally whisked the hated couple from their palace to gilded imprisonment in Hawaii. Corazón Aquino, whose husband had been assassinated by Marcos henchmen on his return from American exile in 1983, took over the presidency, and immediately restored much of the pre-Marcos system of cacique democracy. When ultra-right-wing militarists attempted to overthrow her government, Washington intervened decisively against them (most particularly in December 1989).

In 1986, then, at the height of the "miracle," the Philippines was effectively bankrupt; but at the same time, and just for that reason, it escaped from the Cold War system. On the one hand, Aquino was forced to accept an IMF regimen of deregulation, liberalization, and austerity (which continued under her successor Fidel Ramos)—but she was with justice able to blame everything on her odious predecessor. On the other hand, for a complex of reasons, including the eruption of Mount Pinatubo which buried Clark Field in volcanic ash, the Americans started phasing out their military installations in the country, a process that ended in 1991.[15] With the fall of Marcos, the communist insurrection lost momentum, broke up into factions, and gradually disintegrated. A settlement of sorts was finally reached with the main groups of Muslim rebels. The current oligarchic, but competitive, political regime seems quite stable, and there are no strong reasons for thinking that the Philippines will not chug along at the modest pace it has assumed over the 1990s. In sum, the Philippines has suffered least from the Crash because it went bankrupt a decade earlier, never experienced the "bubble," and has had a "normalized" semi-democratic, semi-oligarchic, post-Cold War, civilian-run political system since the middle 1980s.

In comparison, Malaysia and Siam have been harder hit. Malaysia was in significant ways an anomaly in the "hot" Cold War era. The country was only created in 1963, when Whitehall arranged a hasty amalgam of Malaya, Singapore, and the Bornean regions of Sarawak and Sabah, from which

---

14. Between 1970 and 1987 manufacturing's share of total employment actually declined—from 12 to 10 per cent. Between 1980 and 1985, the country registered negative growth of 2.3 per cent in industry, 1.8 per cent in manufacturing, and 6.9 per cent in construction. Tan, *ASEAN*, p. 75.

15. One could add that the end of the overwhelming American presence—always more military than economic—opens the way for more direct engagement with the country's wealthier neighbours, especially off-shore Taiwan.

Singapore broke off in 1965.[16] Peninsular Malaya itself had only been granted its independence (in 1957) *after* the colonial state had smashed the powerful local communist movement. Malaysia inherited (and later improved on) the colonial regime's draconian antisubversion laws and steely security bureaucracy, but not the insurrection itself. Partly for this reason, and partly because of London's insistence (at least through Harold Wilson's premiership) on keeping its own presence in Southeast Asia, Washington intervened less in Malaysia than in any other part of the region. The country has had a permanent authoritarian government throughout its existence, but the basis of its permanence has nothing to do with the Cold War, and everything to do with a collective determination of the Malay ethnic group (52 per cent) to monopolize real political power in the face of the large "Chinese" (35 per cent) and the smaller (10 per cent) "Indian" minorities. This has meant that all the prime ministers have had to be Malays and civilians, and none has been removed from office by overt violence.[17] At the same time, the Malay leaders have been intelligent enough to permit controlled, and subordinate, political participation by the Chinese and Indians. The government has always been formally an Alliance of three ethnically distinct parties, and there have always been minority cabinet ministers. Massive preferential treatment for Malay entrepreneurs, usually in protected sectors, and under state patronage, has never been pushed to the point of completely alienating the prosperous and energetic minority business classes. The result has been an unusual political stability that has encouraged extensive foreign investment over the years. Substantial revenues from petroleum and natural gas have also provided a steadying basis for government finances. Although the speculative fever and the *goût* for strutting megaprojects struck Malaysia in the 1990s, and corruption increased rapidly, the country has been partly protected from serious disruption by two odd factors. The first is its peculiar competitive-symbiotic relationship with wealthy Singapore, situated a short causeway across from

---

16. London was careful to except Shell's Brunei, a tiny 5,780-square-kilometre combination of two enclaves entirely surrounded (on land) by Sarawak. Singapore's durable dictator, Lee Kwan-yew, agreed to the original merger because he believed he needed help against the left-wing Singaporean opposition. By 1964 he had destroyed this opposition, and began to fancy himself as a big-time player in Kuala Lumpur; at that point, the Malay political elite more or less politely kicked him out.

17. In the May 1969 elections, the ruling Alliance did sufficiently poorly, especially in the metropolitan state of Selangor, that politically engineered mob violence broke out against the Chinese in Kuala Lumpur. Close to two hundred people were murdered, martial law was declared, and the country was put under the dictatorship of a National Operations Council for almost two years. The Prime Minister, Tunku Abdul Rahman, lost all real power and had to resign in 1970. Ever since, fear of a repetition of May 1969 has been a powerful constraint on the ambitions of the Chinese.

Johore. The overwhelmingly "Chinese" municipal state, controlled for forty years now by the Lee Kwan-yew despotism, has always been nervous of its position sandwiched between two Islamic, Malay-speaking nations with modern histories of anti-Chinese violence. It has therefore had every reason to be helpful to Kuala Lumpur, and its wealth has put it in a position to do so—at least up to a point. The second is, curiously enough, the Malay leadership's own small-town provinciality, its felt need publicly to stress Malay/Islamic values, and one might even say its inferiority complex vis-à-vis Big Brother Indonesia.[18]

The major difficulties for Malaysia in the longer future should be the backwardness of its educational system, and a rentier mentality among many Malays who have for a generation been the privileged beneficiaries of government largesse in a pattern that reminds one of places like Kuwait.[19] In the short term, it remains to be seen whether the permanent government responds to the economic crisis by tightening its authoritarian controls, or by permitting more democratic participation and real public accountability.[20]

Siam by contrast was a front-line state for the Americans virtually from the start of the "hot" phase of the Cold War in Southeast Asia. As early as 1932, a military-civilian clique had overthrown the absolutist monarchical regime; from the late 1930s on, the military portion, led by Marshal Phibunsongkhram, became ascendant and brought Siam into the Pacific War as an ally of the Japanese. Momentarily discredited by Japan's defeat, the military resumed power by coup d'état in 1947, and immediately allied itself with Washington. It was characteristic of the time that the former legendary chief of the OSS (the CIA's ancestor), "Wild Bill" Donovan, was sent by Eisenhower to be Ambassador in Bangkok. American domination increased

---

18. The stability of the electorally based regime depends on these leaders' cultivation of the Malays' ambitions and pietistic sensibilities. Although Indonesia and Malaysia share a common language (with differences comparable to those between English and American), ethnic Malays are a tiny minority (concentrated on the eastern littoral of Sumatra) in the former, and *bahasa* is a second language for the vast majority. Indonesia's proud history of revolutionary struggle against European colonialism has encouraged a certain benign contempt for the peninsular "younger brothers" who have no record of this kind. Indonesia's precolonial monuments are much grander than Malaysia's, its contemporary culture is more cosmopolitan, and its modern artists, writers, and public intellectuals have been far more impressive.

19. Malaysia's small population is an important factor. At (currently) about twenty million, it is 33 per cent the size of Siam, 28 per cent of the Philippines, and 10 per cent of Indonesia. Labour shortages, partly induced by rentierism, encouraged over the past decade huge influxes of legal and illegal *Gastarbeiters* from Bangladesh and Indonesia. Many of these people are to be sent home as unemployment rises among the citizenry. It remains to be seen how willing the citizenry will be to return to menial occupations.

20. It seems likely that the elderly, blustering Mahathir has not long to go. His probable successor, Anwar Ibrahim, a generation younger, and currently Finance Minister, has made some public remarks on the Crash which are notable for their sensible and self-critical tone.

further under the regime of strongman Sarit Thanarat and his lieutenants (1958–73). At the height of the Vietnam War, almost 50,000 American ser- vicemen were stationed on Thai soil, and the country was covered with a grid of military bases from which the land, air, and sea assault on Indochina was waged. At the same time very large sums of money were poured into Siam by the United States for military-infrastructural, rural-development, and edu- cational purposes, and in the late 1960s the Japanese were also becoming a powerful investment presence.

The resultant social changes had (by the mid-1970s) produced a large new middle class, as well as (after 1965) a growing communist insurgency. These developments, combined with a growing reaction against the American alliance, precipitated the unexpected and unprecedented mass mobilization of October 1973 in Bangkok, which, with King Rama IX's discreet help, drove the dictators from power. A liberal constitution was promulgated and the fairest elections Siam has ever experienced were held. By March 1976 the American military presence had been removed, and cordial relations opened with Peking. In the same year, however, the communist triumphs in Indochina engendered a violent domestic polarization culminating in the bloody coup of October 6, 1976 after which thousands of idealistic and rad- icalized students fled to the communist maquis.

There seemed then every likelihood of the consolidation of an extreme right-wing military-dominated regime. But, as we have seen, the Cold War in Asia was by then cooling down very quickly. In October 1977, the extremists were overthrown by another coup led by the intelligent General Kriangsak Chomanan, who offered amnesties to the students in the maquis, and made a point of cultivating good relations with both Peking and Hanoi.[21] Kriangsak's flexible policies were fortuitously furthered by the triangular China–Cambodia–Vietnam war of 1978–79, in which the Peking-loyal Communist Party of Thailand lost its secure rear in Indochina, as well as its newly recruited and strongly nationalist student adherents. By 1980, the party had been reduced to insignificance, along with any other visible Left.

At the beginning of the 1980s, therefore, backed now by China, Japan, and the United States, Siam had essentially passed out of its Cold War phase. Though a general served as prime minister for most of the decade, his cabi- nets were coalitions of loose-knit conservative political parties. The economic "miracle" provided the resources for vote-buying on an unprecedented scale, and the political power of big business and provincial notables steadily

---

21. Teng Hsiao-p'ing made a successful visit to Bangkok, where he hobnobbed with the gen- erals, and attended the ordination of the Crown Prince as a (temporary) monk. A success not easily explained to a resistance that regarded the rulers in Bangkok as feudalists, compradores, and fascist American puppets.

increased at the expense of the military and the bureaucracy. The army briefly seized power once again in 1991—not on traditional "red scare" grounds but on those of the corruption of civilian politicians—but were driven out in the huge middle-class mobilization of "Bloody May" 1992.[22]

One valuable outcome of this episode was a movement for fundamental constitutional reform—to decrease the centralized power of a corrupt bureaucracy, curb vote-buying, strengthen party discipline, and increase accountability. The collapse of the *baht* in July 1997 discredited those groups who most energetically resisted the reforms. The new constitution, which in most respects is progressive, has recently been promulgated. The Crash itself caused no political upheaval, nor even major demonstrations, merely the fall of one corrupt civilian cabinet and its replacement by another, marginally more honest. Furthermore, thanks to the long and successful integration of the "Chinese" into almost all strata of society, there has been, so far, no racist scapegoating. The Thai political elite has sustained itself successfully for a century and half by bending with the international winds, and it has made little fuss about accommodating the demands of the IMF—for which it expects, probably rightly, that it will be rewarded as unemployment rises and prices steepen. For reasons outlined earlier, it seems unlikely that the miracle will ever return for Siam, but there are good reasons to believe that the country's post-Cold War political order is flexible enough, and rooted enough, to ensure a modest recovery in the not too distant future.

Indonesia, however, is a completely different story. The Indonesian economy effectively collapsed in 1964–65, as a result of hyperinflation, corrupt military management of the huge nationalized sector, and the autarchist policies of Sukarno. The collapse was a key factor in creating the psychological atmosphere in which a vast pogrom against the legal, unarmed Communist Party of Indonesia and its allies took place between October 1965 and January 1966—costing at least half a million lives, and the incarceration, without trial but often with torture, of hundreds of thousands of others for many years.[23] The removal of the radical-populist President Sukarno, a bugaboo for Washington, followed soon afterwards. The ghastly destruction of the

---

22. Typical of the new era was the first *pronunciamento* of the "National Peace-Keeping Council"—that the Bangkok stock exchange would open as usual the following day. Another sign of the times was that during the *émeute* of May 1992, resisters could watch themselves perform on CNN, and could outflank military control of communications through their mobile telephones. A touch of the antique, however, was visible in the final TV tableau of the NPKC leader, General Suchinda Kraprayoon, and the then leader of the popular movement, former General Chamlong Simuang, prostrating themselves at the feet of the monarch.

23. As late as 1978 there were still tens of thousands, including the country's great writer Pramoedya Ananta Toer, in Indonesia's gulag. Executions of communist leaders who had been on death row for more than two decades continued into the late 1980s.

largest communist party outside the socialist state bloc, at a time when American forces were sinking into the Indochina quagmire and the military power of the Soviet Union appeared to be rapidly growing, earned the director of the massacres, General Suharto, the immediate support of the United States. In the spring of 1966, Indonesia's first "hot" Cold War regime was installed in the wake of the terror.

In its early years, the dictatorship was fully compliant with American wishes, and was amply rewarded for so being. A team of neoclassical, American-trained economists took charge of the economy, ending hyperinflation, privatizing or returning to their original foreign owners many of the nationalized corporations, and encouraging foreign investment in the extraction of the country's abundant natural resources as well as manufacturing. A secret agreement was worked out permitting American nuclear submarines to pass through Indonesian waters without surfacing for the tracking eyes of Soviet satellites. In return, Washington organized the Intergovernmental Group for Indonesia (IGGI), a huge consortium composed of the United States, Japan, and the leading European capitalist countries, to provide, over the next quarter of a century vast and steady infusions to the country's "development" budget. These policies, whose effect was greatly enhanced for newly oil-rich Indonesia by the OPEC price-hikes of 1973, were two key foundations for the consolidation of Suharto's power and for the Indonesian miracle of the 1970s, 1980s, and early 1990s. So great was Washington's satisfaction that after December 1975, when Suharto decided to invade and occupy the small former Portuguese colony of East Timor, the Ford and Carter governments ignored the fact that this invasion, 90 per cent accomplished with American weapons, grossly violated the 1958 bilateral arms agreements between the two countries. Furthermore, they defended Jakarta in international fora, and secretly supplied the lethal Vietnam War OV-10 attack gunships so effective in damaging the East Timorese resistance and East Timor's rural environment and society. (More than 200,000 East Timorese, or one-third of the population, died unnaturally between 1975 and 1979.)

Over time, the Suharto regime gradually changed its internal character in ways that were to have serious long-term consequences. In the early years, he was *primus inter pares* among the ruling clique of generals, his power basically that of the military, and his authority based on fear and the salutary effects of American-arranged economic stabilization. In those days, the famously rich were senior military officers, most notoriously General Ibnu Sutowo, long-time head of the state oil corporation Pertamina, who managed to drive it to bankruptcy in 1975 at the height of the OPEC successes. In the longer run, however, Suharto shunted aside his comrades-in-arms and built the personal dictatorship which Jakarta's wags today call "our Titanic." The means were basically two.

On the one hand, he perfected an electoral system and a state party based in the huge bureaucracy that ensured him complete control over the legislature and the People's Consultative Assembly (which chooses the president and sets broad outlines for state policy). He was shrewd enough to create and finance two nominal opposition parties, one for devout Muslims and another for Christians and others afraid of such Muslims.[24] These mechanisms and the limitless funds he had available from foreign and domestic sources made possible an endless series of staged "free elections," and his own permanent reappointment, without opposition, as president.[25]

On the other hand, he started to use Indonesia's much disliked Chinese minority to ensure his personal control of the country's domestic wealth. In the early days of the regime, Suharto had broken off diplomatic ties with "Red China," closed down Chinese schools and newspapers, forced Chinese to change their names to ones sounding Muslim or Javanese, and legalized *tjina/cina* (basically "Chink") as the official term for these people.[26] He came later, it seems, to a realization that political-cultural repression and ghettoization of the Chinese could serve other purposes. On the one hand, Chinese were completely removed from formal political power, in a way that had never previously occurred.[27] At the same time, the "Chinese minority" was encouraged to concentrate on business, and a small elite among them was elevated to super-tycoon status under his personal protection. In this *divide et impera* system, one could say that the Chinese had economic but not political power, while the indigenous Indonesians (among whom a rival or successor to Suharto might arise) would have political positions, but no concentrated independent sources of wealth.

The "palace tycoons" were also the agents for building the Suharto extended family's fabulous riches, which dwarf the booty of the Marcoses in

---

24. This scheme had the dual advantage of structurally preventing a single opposition from emerging, and of blunting external criticism of the dictatorship.

25. Another Jakarta joke thus emerged: Sukarno gave himself the title President-for-life, while Suharto will keep himself President as long as he lives.

26. One of the more astute moves of the regime was to change the country's spelling system, ostensibly to adjust to that of Malaysia, but in reality to mark off orthographically Suharto's reign from everything that had gone before it.

27. During the anticolonial revolution (1945–49), the period of semi-liberal democracy (1949–59), and Sukarno's authoritarian-populist Guided Democracy (1959–65), Chinese were almost always represented in the cabinet, and had their places in almost all political party leaderships. The striking exception was the Communist Party after 1951, when its then leader, a mestizo Chinese called Tan Ling Djie, was purged by capable young "indigenous" upstarts. Up till the end, in 1965, the party's central committee had no Chinese members.

their heyday.[28] Their super-tycoon status depended on the recartelization and remonopolization, through political means, of key sectors of the economy, particularly banking, imports, and exploitation of natural resources. The "royal children" and other relatives of Suharto were given large shareholdings in the tycoons' companies, limitless credit from tycoon-owned banks, and spin-off monopolies over particular exports (e.g. cloves) and imports (e.g. plastics).[29] The example set at the top spread downwards during the "miracle" years, so that Indonesia was regularly listed alongside Nigeria and China as one of the three most corrupt countries in the world; hence a nation that had been at the same level of development with South Korea in 1960, had been completely surpassed by it three decades later.

The passing of time was bound also to have its social and political consequences. Suharto has been head of state longer than any non-monarchical leader in the world except Fidel Castro, and, at the margins, Togo's Gnassingbe Eyadema.[30] For years he could rely on memories of the *matanza* of 1965–66 to keep the Indonesian public politically quiescent. But today one would have to be in one's mid-forties to have such memories, and the majority of Indonesians are much younger than this. The regime still raises the spectre of "latent" or "recrudescent" communism to justify its repression, but this frozen Cold War rhetoric convinces no one. The generals who now lead the military were moustache-less cadets when the great massacres took place, and are a full generation younger than their president.[31] At the start of the 1990s, a new, much larger generation of factory-workers, many of them women, had come into existence and with increasing boldness mined, through strikes and other forms of resistance, the regime's corporate control of labour. The early gratitude of the new middle class, born out of the miracle, has been turning into frustration and resentment at the greed and oppressiveness of the last Cold War regime in capitalist Asia—not least because they have

---

28. The figure commonly quoted is about $30 billion. See, e.g., *New York Times*, Jan. 16, 1998.

29. Typical of the *arriviste* mentality of the Suharto children was the grinning acquisition by the youngest son, Tommy, of the Lamborghini de luxe racing-car manufacturing company. This type of splashy "investment" would be inconceivable in next-door Malaysia.

30. Formally speaking, at least. Singapore's Lee Kwan-yew, at 74, two years younger than Suharto, became Prime Minister in 1959, only relinquishing this office in 1990. But he remains head of the state party, as well as "Senior Minister," and still decides everything that matters in the municipality. Burma's General Ne Win, now aged 87 and formally retired from politics since 1988, after twenty-six years in power, is said still to have the ultimate say on politically vital policy questions. Curiously enough, in September 1997, after almost ten years out of public view, he emerged, like Rumpelstiltskin, for a brief visit to Crash-stricken Suharto. What did they talk about? Perhaps their common salad days as military youngsters trained by Hirohito's imperial armies? (One notes in passing that Malaysia's Mahathir is 72 years old, and the Philippines' Fidel Ramos 70.)

31. For them the formative combat experience has been in East Timor.

watched the happy decompressions that have taken place everywhere else.

What the catastrophic collapse of the Indonesian *rupiah*, a collapse far more severe than that suffered by any other bloated regional currency, means is that everyone, Indonesians and foreigners alike, is aware that for the second time in Indonesia's modern history economic crisis is inseparably linked to political crisis. It is characteristic of the situation that despite a bankrupt economy, "Father of Development" Suharto's political machine has secured his unanimous reselection as President and that of his dotty, German-trained aeronautical-engineer protégé Habibie as Vice-President.[32] His pushy daughter "Tutut" has been made Minister of Social Affairs, and his favourite Chinese tycoon Minister of Trade, while his son-in-law is commander of the army's elite Strategic Command.[33] Years of repression and manipulation of the two parties and dozens of social organizations, seem to have crippled their capacity for the kinds of purposeful social movements that freed South Korea, the Philippines, and Siam from their Cold War political systems. The result has been that the population has so far responded to the pain of the Crash mainly by rioting against, and looting the property of, those Chinese it can get its hands on—typically in provincial towns. The effect of such riots is only to cripple the economy further.

Suharto is perfectly aware that he is now regarded as a major problem, no longer as a useful ally, in all the metropoles of the world. He knows that Clinton, still a student at the time of the great massacres, would like him gone. But he will hang on as his Titanic goes down. He is too old, too provincial, and too proud to pack his bags.[34] The New Order was built by him and for him, and without him it cannot survive. But with him it is also doomed. Yet no one has any clear idea of what is possible after him, and this uncertainty, which increases by the day, only deepens the general fear of a permanently damaged national future, and the likelihood of spreading violence and disorder. Somewhere up there, or down there, Sukarno must be rubbing his spectral hands.

---

32. One can get an idea of the mind of Habibie from the following anecdote. Appointed some years ago by his mentor to head a state-sponsored Association of Islamic Intellectuals, he astonished a meeting of pious candidate-members in New York by informing them that the Prophet Mohammad was merely a "television set" for the transmission of Allah's satellite broadcasts.

33. This was the post from which Suharto overthrew Sukarno in 1966.

34. In the late 1930s he graduated from a private Muslim high school in Central Java before joining the mercenary colonial military (Royal Netherlands Indies Army) where he rose to be a sergeant. When the Japanese took over, he shifted to their police, and later to the auxiliary native army they formed in anticipation of an Allied assault. When the anticolonial revolution broke out in the autumn of 1945 he enrolled as a junior officer in the national army. In the mid-1950s he rose to be military commander in Central Java before being dismissed for corruption. But he made a successful comeback in 1961 as the first head of the Army's Strategic Command. He was one of the very few top military men of his generation who never went abroad for training. Not a man who could imagine a happy final retreat to Florida, Hawaii, or the Riviera.

15

Majorities and Minorities

It is easy to forget that minorities came into existence in tandem with majorities—and, in Southeast Asia, very recently. No indigenous language of the region has a traditional word for either concept. They were born of the political and cultural revolution brought about by the maturing of the colonial state and by the rise against it of popular nationalism. The former fundamentally changed the structures and aims of governance, the latter its legitimacy.

Unlike all its predecessors in Southeast Asia, the late colonial state imagined itself cartographically and juridically as a sovereign power within precisely marked geographic borders which, in turn, were ratified externally by international law. Hence its obsession with treaties, conventions, extraterritorialities, and boundary commissions. The other side of this subjection to international law—of which no better example exists than the solemn partitions of an Antarctica in which no people live—was an internal absolutism, a right of state, which stretched far deeper and wider than any earlier Southeast Asian domain. (Not for nothing did John Furnivall, greatest of Southeast Asian comparativists, speak of the "fashioning of Leviathan.") Moreover, this right of state, which had its origins in seventeenth- and eighteenth-century European monarchical absolutism, was backed in late nineteenth-century colonial Southeast Asia by an elaborate and sophisticated bureaucracy, invincible military might, and the eternally restless dynamism of industrial capitalism.

Just as the colonial state borrowed much from its monarchical European ancestors, so the nationalism of the twentieth century borrowed much from its antagonist, in the name of precisely the same doctrines that had swept Europe and the Americas earlier on. The People, newly conceived as a political entity in opposition to the colonial rulers, were to inherit their summary rights and, at the same time, to subject themselves, by the crucial mechanism of recognition, to the modalities of a now updated international law. The paradox expressed itself perfectly in each sovereign nation's rush to join the United Nations and its covenants, protocol, affiliated organizations and language.

At the same time, the formal abstraction "colonial state in Southeast Asia" conceals an enormous variety of structures, capacities, and aims. The earliest European conquerors, the Portuguese, had already been marginalized by the Dutch in the seventeenth century, and thereafter hung on only in a remote cartographic half of little Timor. To this day, Portugal, like Ireland, remains a sort of Third World country in Europe. Spain, an imperial power in decline since the seventeenth century, was swept out of Southeast Asia before the end of the nineteenth century; its archaic pre-industrial domination of the Philippines left residues quite unlike those of other colonial powers. At the other extreme, the great industrial powers—Britain, France, the United States, and Japan—arrived in force only in the nineteenth and twentieth centuries, but more than made up for their tardiness by the massive, rapid changes they instituted. Little Holland fell somewhere in between.

In addition, as is well known, there was little or no match between the European colonial states and the political entities that had existed previously in the region. The names are sufficiently revealing: the Philippines, named after the sixteenth-century Spanish monarch Felipe II, contained no substantial states except for a few, new Muslim sultanates, which continued to plague the Spanish to the end; the pseudoclassical compounds "Indonesia" and "Indochina" are modern inventions and map terrains covering, partly or fully, an extraordinary array of traditional kingdoms and principalities; Malaysia, whose -ia ending betrays its modernity, arose out of the last large British imperial garage sale. Even those colonies, such as Burma and Vietnam, that seem closest to direct descent from powerful, centralized pre-European states, in fact are quite remote from them. For most of its life, vast British Burma was a peripheral component of British India, and could have ended up as an eastern Kashmir. It would not have taken much for two major Vietnamese-speaking states to emerge in Indochina, as did two Malay-speaking states in the archipelago to the south. In the same way, Siam, though lucky to escape colonization, found itself inheriting whatever mix of territories the competing European powers left as residual buffers between themselves.

Given these circumstances, the Southeast Asian nationalist movements of the twentieth century faced formidable difficulties in their struggles against

Leviathan which should not be forgotten now that their leaders are mostly dead. Every advantage but one lay with the adversary—money, arms, scientific knowledge, external backing, and so forth. The rulers' only critical weakness was that by their own racist doing they were extremely visible minorities, perhaps the first minorities in Southeast Asian history. The key point is that they were *self-proclaimed* (white) minorities who, by the turn of the century, were arriving from metropoles where majority rule had become the politically legitimate norm and, furthermore, a norm that was spreading rapidly into Asia through newspapers and classrooms. Thus, even in their own eyes, they were unavoidably becoming illegitimate. It is this more than anything else that explains why few twentieth-century colonies around the world have been defended with full imperial conviction and to the death.

From the viewpoint of the nationalists, many of whom were quite aware of this weakness—especially those who had spent some time in Europe itself—the central problem was to create a political majority, a large WE. The character, timing, and depth of this struggle did more than anything else to determine the policies of the post-World War II nation-states towards the new minorities within their colonialism-derived boundaries.

We should note from the start that the Europeans were quite naturally the first to think in these majority–minority terms. They were the first rulers of Southeast Asia who carried out censuses in which the fundamental classificatory grid was not taxpayer or conscript, but ethnic group.[1] Many such ethnic groups in fact "disappeared" from successive censuses as European imaginings changed, but certainly almost all existed first and foremost in the minds of the Europeans. Precisely for this reason, the Europeans sought quite early to build "majority coalitions" around themselves, against groups they feared could seriously compete with them in majority terms.

To be valuable as coalition partners a certain size, power, modernity, and cohesion were required. Christianized groups are the best early examples precisely because they date back to before the era of ethnicity. Colonialists in the seventeenth and eighteenth centuries typically classified subject populations according to religion, not ethnicity, because enemies were conceived religiously. As the colonial rulers became less and less seriously Christian themselves, so groups once thought of as Christian were reclassified as ethnic. Good examples are the Moluccans in the Netherlands East Indies and the Karens in British Burma.

Today large numbers of those one might classify ethnologically as Moluccans and Karens are not Christian at all, but they are largely invisible.

---

1. For more detail, see my "Recensement et Politique en Asie du Sud-Est," *Genèses*, 26 (April 1997), pp. 55–76.

The important groups have been those that were Christianized and then educated, favoured, and employed in the colonial armies and police forces against other similarly conceived ethnic groups: especially the hypothetically majority Burmans and Javanese. By the twentieth century it was their Moluccan-ness and their Karen-ness, rather than their Christianity, that was emphasized, in accordance with the general secularization of political categories. Christianity could also be deployed within the potential majority—as in Vietnam—or to create a supra-ethnic majority—as in the Philippines, where Moro Muslim southerners remained useful bogeymen to the end of Spanish rule. In every case, Christianity was offered a place, albeit subordinate, within the ruling coalition.

A second fateful coalition-building strategy was the creation of the "Chinese minority." Here the exemplary early case is provided by the Dutch in Indonesia. We know from comparing United East India Company (VOC) and indigenous records of the sixteenth and early seventeenth centuries that powerful persons whom local courts regarded simply as aristocratic officials were denounced by the VOC as "really Chinese." The Company quickly developed a separate jurisprudence for these "Chinese" (who were clearly unaware of being such, being unable to read Chinese characters and speaking mutually unintelligible mainland languages if they spoke any non-indigenous language at all). Growing Company power meant increasing segregation of the Chinese in terms of legal status, required costuming and barbering, residence, possibility of travel, and so on. By the nineteenth century these policies had produced in Java a non-Chinese-speaking ethnic Chinese minority that increasingly was detached from any native coalition and hitched to Batavia's wagon. Spanish policy in the Philippines used different means to achieve comparable ends. The ease of Chinese assimilation into Siam's ruling class, including the royal family, up until the twentieth century, shows clearly how unnatural colonial ethnic politics actually were. The intimate ties between wealthy Chinese and Malay rulers in pre-colonial nineteenth-century Malaya are a further case in point.

The last designated ethnicities recruited for colonialism's majority game were those which had merely symbolic, quasi-juridical importance. Collectively, we can think of them as hill tribes, slash-and-burn swidden agriculturalists, "stone-age populations," and so on. Typically, these were groups, real or census, that were numerically small, geographically remote and without valuable economic resources.

In the nineteenth and most of the twentieth centuries they were generally ignored, since they were not worth the cost of administering seriously. We can think of the Orang Asli in Malaya, the Papuans in the Netherlands Indies, and the mountain tribes in Luzon. In cases where they were mobilized by the whites, it was characteristically at the last minute, to resist the majority nationalists. West Irian, cartographic half of New Guinea, is an exemplary case. The local populations, thin on the ground, scattered into hundreds of small communities speaking mutually unintelligible languages, were formally incorporated into the Netherlands Indies only in the twentieth century, and were then benignly neglected until the Indonesian nationalist revolution was on the eve of success. Thereafter, on the grounds that they were collectively part of a new non-Indonesian ethnic group (Melanesian, Papuan, Irianese, whatever), they were enlisted in the Dutch coalition. Members of the Dutch East Indies they could be, but not of Indonesia.

Between 1950 and 1963, the Dutch made frantic efforts, with some success, to create an Irianese ethnic—eventually nationalist—group. The irony is that the medium of their success was the Indonesian language! In less extreme and bizarre forms, one finds similar tactics deployed by the British on behalf of peripheral ethnicities in Burma and by the French of their Indochinese montagnards. The Dutch were also not unique in their attempts to exploit these peripheries after national independence. The Americans made cynical use of the montagnards against the Vietnamese communist forces, and of the Christian Moluccans against the Sukarno regime; international oil companies supplied ethnic rebellions in postindependence Burma, and Libyan and Malaysian Machiavellis assisted their Muslim brothers in the southern Philippines—as long as it suited their various books.

And, of course, there was class. In most parts of Southeast Asia the white minority attempted to create allies, with variable success, among the upper, comfortable classes of potential majorities, by turning them into either landlords or bureaucrats. Not that they could always be trusted. In the Philippines, some of the most energetic early nationalists were members of the wealthy Chinese-mestizo landlord class. On the other hand, in Malaya the old aristocracy, such as it was, came over almost wholesale.

It remains only to note that colonial ethnic politics also took, in its dying days, an important, specific institutional cast. When legislative institutions reluctantly began to be formed within the carapace of the absolutist colonial state, the white minorities frequently not only overrepresented themselves, but also created safe ethnic seats, rigging the electoral systems in various ways to achieve the required results. The argument was always that even though these ethnic groups were often small and scattered, as ethnic groups they needed peculiar, guaranteed representation. Phantom coalition-building occurred primarily because the representatives of these recognized ethnic groups were almost never genuinely elected. Rather they were designated by the colonial regime itself, usually from the most privileged, conservative, and collaborationist elements within each group.

In the long run, colonial ethnic politics could not be sustained on a census-juridical basis alone, but required its own culture. And this culture always had a slippery basis. Almost everywhere, the new census classifications were sustained by a politicomoral geography. Potentially majority populations— Burmans, Vietnamese, Javanese—were categorized as unmanly, treacherous, aggressive, degenerate, and feudal. The coalition partners—the minorities— were categorized as honest, brave, truthful, sincere, and loyal. Endlessly reiterated, these stereotypes ultimately had their effect. The minorities quite often not only came to regard the new majorities as degenerate, unmanly, or treacherous but, more seriously, to regard themselves as honest, brave, truthful, and, alas, loyal. Thus phantom characterizings of new-found ethnicities quickly developed profound roots in rapidly changing political circumstances.

Just how slippery the categories actually were can be seen if one considers the specific cartographic stretch of the colonies. Had Burma been thoroughly incorporated into India, as it might easily have been, the Burmans would have become a minority coalition partner like the Pathans or Baluchis, and doubt-less would also have ended up as honest, brave, and loyal. Had the Khmers not been incorporated into Indochine, one can be confident they would not have been pitied as passive, simple lotus-eaters, but denigrated as proto-Pol Pots. In Malaya, the Malays played Karen and Khmer to the British; in Sarawak they played Burmans and Vietnamese to the Brooke White Rajahs.

Once again the Chinese are exemplary. Although it was not until the 1890s that some Southeast Asian Chinese realized what the Europeans had insisted upon since the seventeenth century—that they were, *après tout*, Chinese— their situations in post-independence Southeast Asia were foreshadowed by their colonial destinies. Segregated, occupationally specialized, accustomed to playing junior partner in ruling coalitions, they attempted frantically to adjust themselves to nationalist regimes with, where possible, the larger support of any available external power (the Chinese People's Republic, Taiwan, the United States, Japan, the United Kingdom, and so forth) in their everyday roles as intermediaries for international capital.

It is essential to bear in mind the conditions of the colonial era when we turn to look comparatively at the rise of nationalism, since it was the colonial experience that profoundly shaped nationalism. Distinct cases are provided by the two Malay-speaking nations of the region, Indonesia and Malaysia. In the first case, one has to remember that the Netherlands East Indies was the only important colony in the world administered largely through an Asian language (the Dutch had too little confidence in the prestige of their own language and were too stingy to provide the investments in education needed to make Dutch an archipelago-wide administrative language). Administrative Malay could thus turn into *bahasa Indonesia* in the 1920s without much ado, and already with a colony-wide constituency. The vast and archipelagic character of the colony, in which by the 1870s even the millions of Javanese had become a demographic minority, combined with the exceptionally conservative character of colonial policy, indicated to nationalists early on that the widest possible coalition had to be built. They were deeply divided ideologically—Muslims, secular nationalists, and communists—but they repeatedly tried to find a modus vivendi and recruited as widely as possible, making no distinction among ethnic groups. Young Chinese intellectuals and politicians also participated, as one stripe or another of nationalist—not primarily as Chinese. Energetic recruitment efforts were made even among the favoured Christian Moluccans, although without much success. If the nationalist movement had a non-white enemy, it was the collaborationist aristocracies that formed a key subordinate element in the Dutch majority. The colony was far more divided by class than any other conflict. The experience of the anti-colonial revolution simply deepened these tendencies. It is striking that in the only free elections held in Indonesia (1955), all budding ethnic parties did poorly and all four major ideological parties recruited among all ethnic groups. When postindependence ethnic antagonisms increased, some of them exploited by the United States, the armed insurrections that resulted were in all cases but one—the secessionist Republic of the (Christian) South Moluccas—aimed at improving the position of the ethnic group *within* Indonesia. In every case the government had genuinely national leaders from these ethnic groups on its side. Today, the basic character of Indonesian politics remains class conflict, with ethnic politics playing a minor role. One can see this aspect quite clearly by looking at the two most obvious exceptions, state policy vis-à-vis West Irian and the former Portuguese colony of East Timor. Indonesians of *all ethnic groups* consider Irian part of the motherland and Irianese as fellow Indonesians. Aware of their double identities as members of ethnic groups and of the nation, they see no reason why the Irianese cannot comfortably be the same. In the 1960s there was a genuine popular campaign for the liberation of fellow Indonesians in Irian from Dutch colonial control; when sovereignty was transferred in 1963, many idealistic people from all parts of the archipelago volunteered to serve the local populations. Even today, immigrants into West Irian come from many different regions, especially Sulawesi and the Moluccas. But with the military's rise to power after 1965—a military that for largely accidental reasons is now dominated by Javanese, but considers itself Indonesian—the inevitable conflicts between Irianese elites (encouraged by the Dutch to think of themselves as leaders of an incipient Papuan nation) and the regime in Jakarta, have been cast increasingly in ethnic perspective. The discovery of valuable mineral resources on the island has further encouraged a regime which at bottom represents class interests, to treat West Irian as it treats every other region with sources of size-able gain. In the same way, the Suharto regime's invasion of East Timor in 1975, and its brutal occupation since that date, had—and I believe still has—no substantial ethnic motivation. The regime believed that the leftist independence regime of Fretilin posed a threat to its power, and was determined to extinguish it at whatever cost to the local population. True, Suharto's regime may have been even more callous than it might otherwise have been precisely because it did *not* believe the East Timorese were Indonesians.

Malaysia presents a strongly contrasting case in which ethnicity completely dominates political life. The need for a massive labour force to work the sparsely inhabited peninsula's booming tin mines and rubber plantations led the British colonial authorities to import hundreds of thousands of Chinese (from southeast China) and Indians (from the Presidency of Madras) in the period 1870–1930. So great was the inflow that by the end of the pre-war period the immigrants outnumbered the indigenous populations of the peninsula and Singapore. The colonial regime thus attempted to build its twentieth-century administration by recruiting not merely the indigenous Malay upper class, but the Malay minority as a whole. Malay nationalism, such as it was, thus appeared two generations after Indonesian nationalism; it was aimed far more against the local Chinese than the whites; and the Malay language manifested itself as an ethnic rather than a supra-ethnic means of political communication. At all stages, the British worked closely with their local partners, quickly creating juridical and political administrative hierarchies based on ethnicity. Virtually everything the postindependence governments of Malaysia have done follows directly in the line of colonial British policy. The great success of the British came in the immediate postwar period, when it was confronted with an armed insurrection of the Malayan Communist Party. For reasons of social structure—the contingent ethnic composition of the plantation and mining labour force—this party recruited heavily among Chinese, but it did not consider itself an ethnic party and made serious attempts to enlist Malay peasants and the "tribal" Orang Asli of the mountainous interior. Seizing on this opportunity, the British branded the insurrectionaries as above all ethnics, and in fighting them played ethnic politics to the limit, most significantly disfranchising a large part of the Chinese community and enhancing the position of the conservative, collaborationist Malay leadership. Since a late, comfortably negotiated independence in 1957, politics have remained institutionally segmented along ethnic lines; every serious attempt to break this pattern has been ruthlessly repressed.

But the outcomes have not, in fact, been as bad as one might have expected. Political killing in Malaysia has been far lower, even in proportion to population, than in Indonesia. The Chinese near-majority has been too big, too economically important, and too well connected internationally to be seriously assaulted. Malay majority politics have led Malay political leaders to insist that the indigenous, non-Malay peoples of eastern Malaysia (Dayaks, Kadazans, etc.) are actually Malays, and to encourage the Malay-ization of the Orang Asli, not so much to oppress or suppress these people as to recruit them into the fancied Malay ethnic majority. It is certainly true that this poses threats to the identity of these recruits, but the intent at least is locally benign, and should be exploitable by these groups's more intelligent leaders.

With regard to the Chinese, the situation is more complex. It is a paradox of the extreme form of ethnic politics practised in Malaysia that the Chinese are essential to its maintenance—and not only for economic reasons. Strong class conflicts already are apparent within the Malay community, as the Malay elite has enriched itself at everyone's expense during the past two decades. Without the Chinese threat, these conflicts would certainly become the key fissure in Malaysian politics; thus, in a backhanded way, the Chinese are essential for the continuance of the present power structure. Nonetheless, continuing present political arrangement also strengthens the security appa-ratus of the state in a narrowly Malay manner; it also delays the arrival of a genuine civil society on the peninsula.

Between these polar cases lie Burma (on the Indonesian side) and the Philippines (on the Malaysian side). As in Malaysia, the British in Burma practised an unusually complex and ruthless form of ethnic politics. The colonial legislature included designated minority representatives chosen from restricted (mainly Indian and Chinese) electorates. Large parts of Burma were sealed off as so-called Scheduled Areas ruled directly and authoritatively by Rangoon, quite outside the legislative system. In these areas, inhabited by peoples the British decided were Chins, Kachins, or Shans, coalition-building was achieved through recruiting loyal, traditional leaders—almost invariably among the most conservative, privileged sectors. In so far as the internal security system was manned by local personnel, these people were heavily recruited from census minorities, especially Karens (read Christian Karens). The colonial army was organized along ethnic lines as well.

As in Indonesia, the nationalist movement, originating in the urban cen-tres, faced formidable difficulties in mobilizing a political majority, but it did so energetically as far as it could. It is very striking that in the colonial period there were no ethnic anticolonial parties or organizations. The final organi-zational form of this opposition, the Anti-Fascist People's Freedom League, included people from every major minority group, including Indians and Chinese. Similarly, in the post-1945 era, the major opposition also recruited from all major ethnic groups. As in Indonesia, there was—with inevitable equivocations— an attempt to create bipartite identities; one could perfectly well be Arakanese, Mon, or Burman, as well as being Burmese, just as one could be Minangkabau, Balinese, or Javanese, as well as being Indonesian. In so far as there were indigenous targets of this nationalism, they included the fringe members of the British coalition, Burman bureaucrats, Christian Karen police officers, and Shan aristocrats.

But Burma differed from Indonesia in two central respects. On the one hand there was a real demographic majority, ethnically conceived: the Burmans in census terms outnumbered the combined total of all other ethnic groups and the Burmese language could not be as unambiguously supra-ethnic as *bahasa Indonesia* was fortunate to be. On the other hand, Burma had the ill-luck not to be a free-floating archipelago. It bordered on India and East Pakistan (later Bangladesh), China, and Thailand, sharing minorities with each of these adjoining states. In different ways, and for different reasons, each of these neighbours participated in Burmese politics by offering sanctuary, funds, arms, or political support to contestants within the Burmese political arena.

It is also important to remember that the postwar independent Burmese state was extremely weak. Within a year of the assassination in 1947 of the Burmese nationalist hero Aung San by a rival Burman politician, the state was reduced to defending the capital city itself. It is striking that the opposition was not primarily ethnic at all, but came from two multi-ethnic communist parties, and from Christian Karen military personnel who temporarily received clandestine British military support and feared for their futures once the British were gone. All of these groups wanted power at the centre, not separation from it. Although these insurrectionaries were joined in the 1950s by other armed groups, including some with ethnic labels, drug-based warlords, and residual Kuomintang military refugees from the Chinese People's Republic, the impetus remained. Both the government and its enemies were in search of multi-ethnic coalitions. Only the elected U Nu government of 1960 made the clearly exclusionary mistake of attempting to make Buddhism the state religion, an error reversed by the Ne Win military regime after 1962.

As in Indonesia, the deeper lines of conflict in Burma remained those of class. It is often said that the radical programme of nationalization launched in 1962 was aimed at the Indian and Chinese minorities; but in fact the assault was against the postcolonial middle class in general, including various Burman groups. The military regime sought to build a strong class base among peasants and workers across ethnic lines, and found itself up against many of those British-sponsored ethnic elites once sheltered within the

Scheduled Areas. Unsurprisingly, these elites attempted to defend their positions by defining themselves as the champions of ethnic identity against Burman domination.

To Burma, the Philippines forms a notable contrast. The country contains far more ethnolinguistic groups than Burma, but ethnicity as such has played only a minor role in its politics. To explain this situation two factors need to be kept in mind. First, more than three centuries of Catholic colonialism and evangelism produced a population by World War II that was 90 per cent Christian—a huge majority by any definition. Second, for reasons too complex to be explored here, colonial rule generated a powerful Chinese-mestizo latifundist upper class, intermarried across ethnolinguistic lines and with common interests in dominating the country's political and economic life. Indeed the Philippines is the only place in Southeast Asia where such a powerful, consolidated landed upper class exists. And precisely because of its power and ability to claim a huge majority base in Filipino Catholicism, it found it easy to acquire political independence from the Americans less than fifty years after the latter had seized the colony from the Spanish and the anti-Spanish revolutionaries. The same factors made the upper class indifferent to any need to build a strong coalition with the Muslim minorities in the south. Indeed it is striking that these people were mishandled, not as ethnicities, but as religious deviants. Unsurprisingly, this produced in the end one of the few genuinely secessionist movements of modern Southeast Asian history.

What may we conclude from the above? First and foremost, the politics of ethnicity have their roots in modern times, not ancient history, and their shape has been largely determined by colonial policy. (It is no accident that uncolonized Siam has the least violently ethnicized politics in the region.) Second, ethnicity is intricately tied to the deeper forces of religion and class. From this perspective it may be useful to think about minorities as being roughly divisible into three types, with correspondingly different problems and futures.

Of the so-called alien minorities, the most prominent example is Chinese. Now overwhelmingly concentrated in urban centres and the more advanced sectors of the local economies, their futures are inextricably tied to capitalism and capitalist society's class structures. In the Catholic Philippines and Buddhist Siam they have made the necessary cultural adaptations to form a completely integrated element of those societies' upper and middle classes. Thanks to British and Dutch colonial policies, this integration is much less complete in Indonesia and Malaysia, but in both countries the Chinese are absolutely essential to the functioning of the existing political-economic order and continue to hold economic power quite disproportionate to their numbers. The most important difference between the two is that in Indonesia demographic factors preclude the Chinese making ethnic claims as such, whereas the same factors in Malaysia encourage majoritarian hopes. It is only in this one major country of Southeast Asia that Chinese identity is a central political issue. Unsurprisingly the countries where the Chinese have fared worst have been the socialist states of Indochina and Burma, less because of their ethnicity than because of their class position.

The classification of coalition-worthy indigenous minorities refers to ethnolinguistic groups of sufficient demographic size and political and economic sophistication to be substantial players in national-level coalition politics. These very characteristics, however, usually mean that each group is internally divided according to class and, sometimes, religion. They invariably also mean that a group's culture bears little relationship to what it was a century ago, and that its identity is a modern one, no matter how it is ideologized. Whether we are thinking of Kachins, Ilocanos, or Minangkabau, they have actively participated in national-level politics for a long time and in diverse coalitions, and have representatives in most ideological camps and social strata. It is difficult to imagine any form of national regime from which they would be excluded. Different regimes would only effect the types of strata by which their ethnicities would be articulated. At the same time, one should also expect that the degree of their prominence would vary over time, and according to the number of possible players in the national system. The greater the number (Indonesia) of players, the wider the possibilities for flexible coalition politics; the fewer (Malaysia, Burma), the greater the likelihood of asymmetric rigidities. All these groups are accustomed to a certain degree of bilingualism, since they have participated substantially in the modern educational system and modern politics. Their futures do not seem too dark; they are needed— politically, ideologically, educationally, and often economically.

Outside this category fall all those groups which, because they are small in numbers, geographically remote from the political centre, marginal to the national economy, and lacking in western education, are insignificant to any conceivable majority. Typically, they have played no role in colonial nationalist politics and thus have no easy claims on postindependence nationalist regimes. Most commonly, the degree of their internal stratification is low, as is their occupational diversity. Few of their members can be found in the national universities or in the officer corps of national armies. National communist parties have in some cases cultivated them, but this has often opened them to heavy repression. It is thus difficult for them to have a foot, let alone an important foot, in every camp.

In most cases their humble wish is simply to be left alone, or to make quiet, slow adaptations to the outside world. But this outside world—not merely the nation-state, but more importantly the great engines of planetary power—will not leave them be. They may sit on valuable mineral or forest resources coveted by the outside; their subsistence agriculture may be regarded as ecologically destructive by international bureaucrats and national planners; demographic pressures may push lowlanders up into their mountain retreats; and they may be unlucky enough to live on sensitive borders between rival nations or rival world blocs. Their very isolation leaves them unacquainted with the ceremonies of private property, the techniques of coalition politics, and even the organizational methods required for modern self-defence. The irony is that typically they are *not* ethnic groups; to survive they may have to learn to think and act as such (much as the ethnic group American Indian or Native American has had to be imagined recently to defend a heterogeneity of groups otherwise threatened with extinction). Yet the costs of going ethnic, that is, participating in ethnic majority politics and economics within the nation-state, are not to be underestimated. Often it means becoming Christian (in Siam or Indonesia) or Muslim (in Malaysia). Almost always it means the end of the kind of cultural autonomy and self-contained integrity they once enjoyed. Nothing better illustrates this bitter paradox than the appearance of Irianese and East Timorese ethnic, and potentially national, identities in the last two decades. These identities are American Indian in that they occlude and submerge non-ethnic local identities in the very process of attempting to defend them. Such identities may, under ill-starred circumstances, invite conscious oppression rather than malign neglect, but they also open the way to developing a necessary political and economic bargaining power. Perhaps this is, at the end of the twentieth century, the only way out.

PART IV

WHAT IS LEFT?

16

El Malhadado País

PART ONE

In the future, the aborigines shall not be called Indians and natives; they are children and citizens of Peru and they shall be known as Peruvians.

José de San Martín

Vine a Firenze para olvidarme por un tiempo del Perú y de los Peruanos y he aquí que el malhadado país me salió al encuentro esta mañana de la manera más inesperada.

Mario Vargas Llosa

There is no document of civilisation which is not at the same time a document of barbarism.

Walter Benjamin

For a fair part of the past two hundred years, narrating the nation seemed, in principle, a straightforward matter. Armies of historians, good and bad, helped by folklorists, sociologists, statisticians, literary critics, archaeologists, and, of course, The State, produced a vast arsenal of work to help existing or future citizens imagine the biography, and the future, of their political communities. There could be every conceivable difference in method, approach, data base, and political viewpoint, but these "historians" typically understood their texts as "documents of civilisation," or stories of progress, however meandering, because the nation was always, and without much question, regarded as historically factual and as morally good. There are all kinds of political and other reasons that allow us to be confident that the flow of such work will continue indefinitely, since nation-states require it, and, in the broad public arena, the legitimacy of the nation-state is still generally accepted, even insisted upon.

Nonetheless, the writing job, at least, is getting harder. More and more the work is done by journeyman teams and committees. More and more a clear "narrative line" is blurred by *longue durée* statistical analyses, interventions from Weltgeschichte, feminist theory, tertiary Marxism, identity politics, and so on. Today it is a rare historian of real calibre who would undertake seriously, on his or her own, the task of narrating the nation: not least because such people typically have reflected on Benjamin's bitter aphorism. The truth is that team-produced national histories as published at the twilight end of our century do not arouse a great deal of enthusiasm, and even appear to elicit a certain disquiet.

But, in any case, historians understand very well that they are fated to be superseded, by their younger successors and by the flow of historical time itself. Their best hope of remembrance lies in the possibility of quietly edging their way from the moving bivouacs of History to the settled retreats of Literature, following in the steps of Thucydides, Tacitus, Gibbon, Michelet, and Burckhardt. In these canonized retreats, however, they rub casual elbows with, among others, the better novelists. If they have done their work in the age of nationalism, which is still with us, they find that they are up against formidable competition.

In *Imagined Communities*, I argued that the historical appearance of the novel-as-popular-commodity and the rise of nation-ness were intimately related. Both nation and novel were spawned by the simultaneity made possible by clock-derived, man-made "homogeneous, empty time," and thereafter, of Society understood as a bounded intrahistorical entity. All this opened the way for human beings to imagine large, cross-generation, sharply delimited communities, composed of people mostly unknown to one another; and to understand these communities as gliding endlessly towards a limitless future. The novelty of the novel as a literary form lay in its capacity to represent synchronically this bounded, intrahistorical society-with-a-future. (National history would supplement this synchronicity with a diachronic form of narrative.)

This line of argument today does not seem to me entirely mistaken, but it led to the unstated assumption that the deep original affinity between nation-ness and the novel meant that they would always be adequate for one another: that the nation would continue to serve as the natural if unspoken frame of the novel, and that the novel would always be capable of representing, at different levels, the reality and the truth of the nation. It is an assumption rather easy to make for the nineteenth and early twentieth centuries. Balzac's *La Comédie Humaine* (which is really, if the expression can be excused, La Comédie Française), the huge oeuvre of Zola, and even that of Proust provide us with incomparable accounts of the France of their times; the same can be said of Melville and Twain in America, Dickens, Eliot, and Lawrence in England, Mann and Musil in Germany and Austria, Tolstoy, Turgenev, Dostoyevsky, and Goncharov in Russia, Tanizaki in Japan.[1] This capability is still quite visible in some recently decolonized parts of Asia and Africa.

In the second half of this century, however, the affinities have become visibly strained. The older, rather unified world of the novel has been breaking down through a vast process of niche-marketing: the gothic novel, the crime novel, the spy novel, the pornographic novel, the science-fiction novel, the "airport" novel, and the strictly historical novel, each with its own formal conventions and audiences, which are by no means necessarily the fellow nationals of the author. At the other end of the spectrum, a crucial aspect of the innovations of early modernism was the attempt to transcend or disrupt "homogenous, empty time." From the point of view of the nation, things were also changing rapidly. In 1945, the number of (self-conceived) stateless nations was certainly larger than the number of those which had such states. Today, this is no longer the case. Nations with states—nation-states—have less and less need of the novel. The best sign of this is the ubiquity of two institutions that were virtually unknown a century ago: ministries of information and ministries of culture. Representation of the nation is more and more under their supervision, and the job of the visual and aural media, handled by specialized state functionaries, advertisers, and the like. More and more the great novels of the past, to get a hearing, must endure the anachronizing indignities of being screened by Hollywood, mini-serialized by the BBC,[2] or force-fed to teenagers through a standardized statewide curriculum.

Beyond all the above, for reasons discussed elsewhere in this book, our century's hard times have made some at least of the utopian elements of nineteenth-century nationalism, for which universal progress was the foundation, decreasingly plausible; and this has had its effects on the highest-calibre novelists. This does not mean that other originary utopian elements do not strongly survive, but they are faced with aporiae with which the great novelists of the last century did not feel compelled to contend.

After several readings of Doris Sommer's *Foundational Fictions*, it

---

1. "Their times" should be understood fairly loosely. For example, *War and Peace,* published in the later 1860s, is set in a Russia just predating Tolstoy's birth in 1828—the time of his father.

2. The anachronizing works in two directions. On the one hand, one observes an obsession with the correct "period" costuming and decor, which relentlessly underscore the "Regency-ness" of Austen's novels, something that rarely occurs to the laughing reader. ("These books are great *historical* novels"!) On the other hand, there is the modernizing banalization that necessarily comes from the deployment of well-known actors and actresses simulating Mr. Woodhouse and his beguiling daughter. ("How brilliant X or Y is in this or that role.") In both directions, the effect is to remove as many traces as possible of relevance or bite.

occurred to me that the best place to go and look at the question of how the late-century writer might still attempt to figure the nation was Latin America.[3] The western hemisphere contained a large number of the oldest nation-states in the world, almost all of them the products of revolutionary struggles against imperial centres in Europe. But the United States and Haiti, oldest of all—the one risen to world hegemony, the other sunk in desperate abjection—were too sui generis for ready-to-hand comparisons within the region. The rest (Brazil aside), however, shared a dominant language and religion, and also had similar histories of great domestic violence. The region had produced some of the most outstanding writers of this century, but one would be hard put to it to name one nation-state within it whose contemporary situation is cause for solid optimism.

Doris Sommer has taken advantage of all the above, especially the unbeatable opportunities for comparison offered by the many Spanish-using nation-states of Latin America, to consider the fate of the nation–novel relationship over more than a century. Her interpretation is a complex one, to which, though my debt to it is great, I cannot do justice here. One part of the argument begins with the observation that the region was unusual in that the novel only came into its own there after formal statehood had been achieved.[4] It was thus primarily associated, in the days of its youth, with the era in which serious attempts were made to create order and progress after the ruinous years of the revolutionary wars and their *caudillo*-ridden aftermaths. She reads the canonical "classics" of the nineteenth century as a variety of endeavours—some more successful than others—to attract citizen–readers to the project of national consolidation. The primary means for achieving this end was the emotional engagement of such readers in the romantic tribulations and happinesses of couples who were characteristically figured to represent the sharpest conflicts in postcolonial society: conflicts between regions, physical environments, economies, classes, races. In such novels, eroticism was nationalized, and nationalism itself eroticized. Obstacles to the happiness of the lovers were understood as obstacles to the nation's well-being, and the achievement, or at least the promise, of their happiness taken as a foreshadowing of the nation's utopian future.[5] The last part of Sommer's

---

3. *Foundational Fictions* (Berkeley: University of California Press, 1992).

4. If Jean Franco is right, the first real Latin American novel, José Joaquín Fernández de Lizardi's *El Periquillo Sarniento*, only appeared in 1816. See her *An Introduction to Spanish-American Literature* (Cambridge: Cambridge University Press, 1969), p. 34.

5. One of the most illuminating of Sommer's additional theses is that the theme of conjugality as utopian portent tended to produce in these novels a type of hero and heroine which largely disappeared in this century. The heroes are strikingly feminized and eroticized, while the heroines are public-spirited, independent, and "activist."

argument was that the possibility of continuing to produce good novels in this nation-building vein grew less and less over time as the "promise of unification and development" faded. The rise of "magic realist" pessimism, in the longer *durée*, was a response not only to the collapse of the "naive optimism" of nineteenth-century nationalism, but also to the perceived failure of twentieth-century Latin American marxist movements to create a new form for national progress. Yet "magic realism" turned out not to be the only possibility, and perhaps not even the most instructive.

When, a few years ago, on first reading Mario Vargas Llosa's remarkable novel *El Hablador*, I felt immediately that I had run once again into the spectre of comparisons; for it brought immediately to my mind's eye the Buru Quartet of Indonesia's master Pramoedya Ananta Toer, and at a longer, complementary, run, the great Spanish novels of the Philippine national hero José Rizal (these were the incendiary pre-independence novels that Latin America never experienced). For the Buru Quartet, originally presented orally to fellow prisoners in the Indonesian Devil's Island of Buru during the interminable 1970s, was also a remarkable, deadly serious attempt to write the nation "in the time of cholera," and it was also written against/after "magic realism."[6] (This chapter is not the place to speak of Pramoedya in detail. But a few descriptive sentences are needed to bridge the space/time between "Southeast Asia" and "Latin America.") The first three volumes, narrated in the first person, have many of the appurtenances of the classical European *Bildungsroman,* and have affinities with the kind of national novels which Doris Sommer studied.[7] They show the reader how a privileged, highly educated, young Javanese man, in the early 1900s, gradually develops a national consciousness and conscience, thanks to a wide variety of foreign and indigenous teachers; and how this experience leads him to originate the nationalist movement. With the fourth volume, readers are in for a surprise. It turns out that everything they have read so far comes from the files of the colonial secret police, in particular of a

---

6. Aside from Pramoedya, Indonesia has produced two genuinely distinguished fictionists since independence, and both can be said to have strong affinities with "magic realism." The Christian Batak Iwan Simatupang, who died prematurely, had already produced his astonishing *Merahnya Merah* (The Redness of Red) in 1959, within a decade of his country's independence. The Balinese Putu Wijaya, whose writing career spans Suharto's New Order, has produced a huge volume of novels, short stories, and other fictions, also in a "magic realist" vein, of which the most Asturias-like is the horrifying *Nyali* (Guts).

7. With a local inflection of course. As I noted in *Imagined Communities* (London: Verso, 1991), the hero marries successively a neurasthenic Eurasian beauty, a radical Chinese clandestine immigrant, and a weapon-wielding Muslim princess from the eastern extremity of the Netherlands Indies. Rizal's *Noli Me Tangere,* curiously enough, is not so far away. Formally, the plot is driven by the mestizo hero Ibarra's ill-fated love for his mestiza childhood friend Maria Clara. But the national energy comes from his relationship with his revolutionary *indio* double, Elias, who lays down his life for him at the end.

high-ranking but publicly invisible native. This native, who narrates *The Glass House,* and whose mission it is to hound the hero to an early death and then to political oblivion, is shown as fascinated, obsessed by his victim. So fascinated and obsessed, indeed, that he openly suggests here and there that he has tampered with the documents in the files, which can therefore no longer be confidently assigned an uncontaminated truth.[8] Finally, Pramoedya's national readers (the novels are banned, but circulate semi-clandestinely) know that at no time in the colonial period was any native permitted to become a top-level officer of the secret police. The promotion came only fifty years later. The file-keeper and filer-contaminator of *The Glass House,* who is also the ultimate narrator, is a dystopic prolepsis. But he narrates, and the scope of what he narrates is nothing other than the nation.

It is, I think, necessary to make this half-digression, before turning to the detailed account of, and reflections on, *El Hablador* that take up the remainder of this chapter. They offer a view of a late-century, Latin American/Spanish/Peruvian nationalist masterpiece seen telescopically from, so to speak, Southeast Asia. It scarcely needs to be said that my command of Spanish is limited (what there is comes from Rizal), and my knowledge of Latin America and Peru still scantier. What does need to be underlined is that what follows is about *El Hablador,* not about Mario Vargas Llosa's oeuvre in general, nor about his life, though the novel contains plenty of clearly autobiographical elements.

Two last parenthetical sentences: Peru's sixteen million or so people live in a country that is four times the size of Italy. It was to the children and citizens of Peru that San Martín issued his celebrated liberatory/exterminationist promise.

PART TWO

The novel opens with the narrator (we might call him "MVLl," but I will refer to him hereafter as N.) in Florence where he has come to forget, for a while, his "unfortunate/damned" country, Peru, and his fellow Peruvians.[9] But his eye is caught by a side-street window display which includes three or four photographs that "suddenly brought back to me the savour of the Peruvian

---

8. This theme, as well as many others, is brilliantly analysed in Pheng Cheah, "Spectral Nationality: The Idea of Freedom in Modern Philosophy and the Experience of Freedom in Postcoloniality" (Ph.D. thesis, Cornell University, 1998).

9. In what follows, I will be referring to the 1991 edition of *El Hablador* (Barcelona: Biblioteca de Bolsillo, 1991) although the book first appeared in 1987. The translations of quotations are my own, though I have been helped by Helen Lane's published English version—*The Storyteller* (London: Faber & Faber, 1991).

jungle. The wide rivers, the corpulent trees, the fragile canoes, the frail huts on pilings, and the clumps of men and women, half-naked and daubed with paint, contemplating me unblinkingly from the glossy prints" (p. 7). These photographs, taken "without demagoguery or aestheticism" (p. 8) by a since deceased Italian, are of the Machiguenga, a remote tribe in Peruvian Amazonia, who had "until a few years ago lived virtually isolated from civilization, scattered about in units of one or two families. Only in our day had they begun to group together in those places documented by the photographs, but many still remained in the jungle" (p. 8). In two of the photographs, N. recognizes the new settlements of Nueva Luz and Nuevo Mundo that he had visited three years earlier as the guest of a controversial American Protestant missionary organization, the Summer Institute of Linguistics. The photograph that fascinates him, however, shows a twilit circle of mesmerized Machiguenga in the midst of which stands a man, largely in deep shadow, who is speaking and gesticulating. He realizes at once that this man is a figure whose role is, so to speak, translated into Spanish, that of *hablador*: storyteller, chatterbox, speaker, parroter, fictionist? (We shall consider this question at a later point.)

In the second chapter, N. takes us back to the early 1950s, when, as a freshman at the University of San Marcos, he became friends with Saúl Zuratas, who bore the nickname Mascarita (Mask-Face) thanks to a huge purple birthmark that covered the right side of his face. We learn that he was the son of Don Salomón, a Polish Jew who emigrated to Peru in the 1930s. Having cohabited with a barely literate Catholic *criolla* for some time, he married her on Saúl's birth. Don Salomón then converted to Catholicism for the sake of his family, but was "never accepted." After his wife's early death from cancer, the father moved with his son to Lima. Don Salomón then reverted to Judaism, and would take his extremely bored little boy to the city's synagogue. The two men, devoted to each other, lived in the father's little shop along with *un lorito hablador,* a talking parrot named Gregor Samsa (p. 12). We learn in passing that Saúl revered Kafka above all writers, and knew *La Metamorfosis* by heart.

After a holiday visit to a relative living on the fringes of Peruvian Amazonia, Saúl became increasingly interested in the lives of its small indigenous tribes threatened with extinction by the advance of missionaries, rubber-tappers, miners, loggers, and the national state: in particular, it turns out, in the surviving Machiguenga. He devoted himself initially to anthropology, having no interest in the *marxisant* politics of most of his university contemporaries (including N.). Much of this second chapter describes the discussions between N. and Saúl about the latter's jungle experiences. Saúl would say: "What's being done in the Amazon is a crime . . . Put yourself in their place, if only for a moment. Where do they have to go? They've been driven out of their lands for centuries, each time pushed farther into the interior, farther and farther. The extraordinary thing is that, despite so many disasters, they haven't disappeared . . . isn't that something to take your hat off to?" (p. 22). N. remembers: "Occasionally . . . I would provoke him. What did he suggest, when all was said and done? That, in order not to change the way of life and the beliefs of a handful of tribes still living, many of them, in the Stone Age, the rest of Peru abstain from exploiting Amazonia? Should sixteen million Peruvians renounce the natural resources of three-quarters of their country so that seventy or eighty thousand Amazonian indigenes could calmly continue to shoot at each other with bows and arrows, shrink heads, and worship boa-constrictors? . . . No, Mascarita, the country had to be developed. Hadn't Marx said that progress would come dripping blood? Sad though it was, it had to be accepted. We had no alternative. If the price to be paid for development and industrialization for the sixteen million Peruvians meant that those few thousand naked indigenes would have to cut their hair, wash off their tattoos, and turn into mestizos—or, to use the word most loathed by the ethnologist, become acculturated—well, there was no help for it" (pp. 23–4). Did Saúl regard his Indians as somehow superior? "Superior? No. I've never said so or believed it, little brother . . . Inferior perhaps, if the question is posed in terms of infant mortality, the status of women, polygamy or monogamy, artisanry and industry. Don't imagine that I idealize them. Not in the least . . . There are many things that would shock you very much, *mi viejo*, I don't deny that" (pp. 26–7). Saúl went on to mention that some of the tribes kill infants born with defects, because they know they will not be able to survive. " 'I wouldn't have passed the test, *compadre*. They'd have liquidated me . . . They say the Spartans did the same thing, right? That little monsters, Gregor Samsas, were hurled down from the top of Mount Taygetus, right?' he said, laughing" (p. 27). " 'But they're tolerant of those who have had accidents and survive . . . We've no right to kill them off' " (p. 28). He asked N. whether he really wanted to turn them into ' "zombies and caricatures of men like those semi-acculturated indigenes of the streets of Lima" ' (p. 28).

As time passed, it became clear that although Saúl completed a B.A. in anthropology to please his father, he had become convinced that anthropology was immoral, and had no intention of becoming an academic. The two college friends gradually drifted apart in their last years together at San Marcos.

Chapter 3 begins as follows (to feel its force, one should contemplate it first in the original Spanish).

Después, los hombres de la tierra echaron a andar, derecho hacia el sol que caía. Antes, permanecían quietos ellos también. El sol, su ojo del cielo, estaba fijo.

Desvelado, siempre abierto, mirándonos, entibiaba el mundo. Su luz, aunqué fuertísima, Tasurinchi la podía resistir. No había daño, no había viento, no había lluvia. Las mujeres parían niños puros. Si Tasurinchi quería comer, hundía la mano en el río y sacaba, coleteando, un sábalo; o, disparando la flecha sin apuntar, daba unos pasos por el monte y pronto se tropezaba con una pavita, una pérdiz o un trompetero flechados. Nunca faltaba qué comer. No había guerra. Los ríos desbordaban de peces y los bosques de animales. Los machcos no existían. Los hombres de la tierra eran fuertes, sabios, serenos y unidos. Estaban quietos y sin rabia. Antes que después. (p. 30)

[After, the men of the earth started walking, straight towards the sun that was falling. Before, they stayed in the same place, not moving. The sun, their eye of the sky, was fixed in place. Wide awake, always open, looking at us, warming the world. Its light was very strong, but Tasurinchi could withstand it. There was no injury, there was no wind, there was no rain. The women bore pure children. If Tasurinchi wanted to eat, he dipped his hand into the river and pulled out, flicking its tail, a shad; or he let fly an arrow without aiming, took a few steps through the forest, and soon stumbled on a little wild turkey, a partridge, or a trumpet-bird brought down by his arrow. There was never any lack of food. There was no war. The rivers teemed with fish, and the forest with animals. The Mashcos didn't exist. The men of the earth were strong, wise, calm, and united. They were peaceable and without anger. Before after.]

The rest of this long chapter proceeds anonymously in this manner, and in the process the reader begins, as it were, to enter into the cosmology, the history, the terrors, and the everyday lives, of the Machiguenga. At fitful intervals, images of the penetration of their world by the dark external force of "unfortunate/damned Peru" appear: for example, there are references to the terrible time of the "tree-bleeding" (which the reader can read as the brief rubber boom of 1900–18), and to the "white fathers," who are evidently missionaries. But who is speaking this chapter? Only towards the end are we told what kind of person it must be:

Apenas asomaba su ojo del sol en el cielo se ponían bajo techo, diciéndose unos a otros: "Es hora de descansar", "Es hora de prender las fagotas". "Es hora de sentarse a escuchar al que habla". Así lo hacían: descansaban con el sol o se reunían a oír al hablador hasta que empezaba a oscurecer. (p. 62)

[Once the eye of the sun appeared in the sky, they placed themselves under one roof, saying one to the other, "It is time to rest." "It is time to light the faggots." "It is time to sit down to pay heed to the one who speaks." So that was what they did. They rested with the sun, or they gathered to listen to the *hablador* till it started to get dark.]

With chapter 4, N. has us again in hand. He relates that in mid-1958, on the eve of leaving for study in Spain, a friend of his offered him a seat on a small plane going to Amazonia in the service of the Summer Institute of Linguistics missionaries. He recalls the controversy around this Institute, regarded by many as an agent of Yankee, Protestant, and English-language imperialism.[10] The trip made an overwhelming impression on N., overwhelming in memory even in Florence, a quarter of a century later. "This, too, was Peru, and only then did I achieve a full awareness of it: a world as yet untamed" (p. 71). The exploitation of the indigenes appalled him, but "was there the slightest chance that a Peruvian government, of whatever political persuasion, would concede the tribe's extraterritorial rights in the jungle? Obviously not. That being the case, why not change the Viracochas (Machiguenga for, shall we say provisionally, "Peruvians"?) so that they'd treat the indigenes differently?" (p. 76). A pivotal meeting then occurred with the Schneils, a sympathetic young American missionary couple, who gave him a horrifying account of "the depths of prostration and pessimism to which . . . the broken Machiguenga had been reduced" (p. 80). Mr. Schneil described their endless flight, from the Incas, from the conquistadors, from the Catholic missionaries, from capitalism in all its forms. They had no caciques, no organization beyond the nuclear family. They had no permanent personal names. Their counting went only to four, after which they used "many." Suicides were frequent. It had taken him a whole year to make contact at all, and he had done so in the end only because he decided to go naked to seek them out. N. remembers admiring the Schneils' willingness to live virtually as the Machiguenga, despite their backup of hydroplanes, radios, modern medicines, and Bibles.

It was towards the end of the conversation that the subject of the *habladores* came up. The Schneils said they had never met one. The Machiguenga usually evaded questions on the subject, but when they did mention them, it was always with the greatest respect. They were neither

---

10. In her fine article on *El Hablador,* Doris Sommer quotes extensively from David Stoll, *Fishers of Men or Founders of Empire? The Wycliffe Bible Translators in Latin America* (London: Zed Press, 1982), to discuss the extra-*El Hablador* reality of this organization. Founded in the early anticommunist American 1950s by Peter Townsend, former friend and biographer of Lázaro Cárdenas, it received substantial support from USAID and the CIA for its missionary work through the underdeveloped world, but especially in Latin America. By the mid-1970s, it was a more or less official arm of the governments of Mexico, Guatemala, Honduras, Panama, Surinam, Colombia, Ecuador, Peru, Bolivia, and Brazil. "No other transnational organisation surpassed Wycliffe's influence among Indians. None matched its command of Indian languages and loyalties, its logistical system and official connections." It was not long, however, before "each government faced the same, disquieting, phenomenon: increasingly visible, militant Indian organising, a trend to which, like a number of other brokers, SIL had contributed in largely unintended ways. Promotion of literacy, the trade language and inter-group contacts helped members of scattered communities identify themselves as ethnic wholes." Between 1976 and 1981 SIL was pushed out of Brazil, Mexico, Panama, Ecuador, and Peru. See Sommer's "About-Face: The Talker Turns," *Boundary 2,* 23: 1 (Spring 1996), pp. 91–133, at pp. 101–2.

medicine men nor shamans. How to translate the Machiguenga word? The Schneils discussed it hesitantly, before opting for *hablador*. The name "defined them. They spoke. Their mouths were the connecting chain-links of this society that the fight for survival had forced to split up and scatter to the four winds. Thanks to the *habladores,* fathers had news of their sons, brothers of their sisters, and thanks to them they were all kept informed of the deaths, births, and other happenings in the tribe" (pp. 90–91). Finally, said Mr. Schneil: "And something more besides . . . I have a feeling that the *hablador* not only brings news but also speaks of the past. He is probably also the memory of the community, fulfilling a function similar to that of the jongleurs and troubadors of the Middle Ages" (p. 91).

On his return to Lima, N. had what proved to be his last meeting and discussion with Saúl Zuratas. N. explained to Saúl how moved he was by the very idea of the *hablador*. "They're tangible proof that storytelling can be something more than mere entertainment . . . Something primordial, something on which the very existence of a people may depend" (p. 92).

Saúl surprised N. by his brusque lack of interest in the *habladores*. "I know now he was lying . . . when he said he'd never heard a word about any such storytellers" (p. 93). Instead, the usually cheerful, good-humoured, and kind-hearted Saúl launched into a violent tirade against the Institute. "They're the worst of all, those evangelizing linguists of yours. They worm their way into the tribes to destroy them from within, just like chiggers. Into their spirit, their beliefs, their subconscious, the roots of their very way of being. The others steal their vital space and exploit them or push them farther into the interior. At worst, they kill them physically. Your linguists are more refined. They want to kill them in another way. Translating the Bible into Machiguenga! Imagine that! Their aim is to wipe their culture, their gods, their institutions, off the map and corrupt even their dreams. Just as they did to the redskins and the others back in their own country" (pp. 93–4). "The only way to respect them is not to go near them. Not touch them. Our culture is too strong, too aggressive. It devours everything it touches" (p. 97). In Amazonia it was perhaps still not too late. "The great trauma that turned the Incas into a people of sleepwalkers and vassals still hasn't happened there" (p. 98).

N. records that during his subsequent graduate student years in Spain and Paris (roughly 1958–63) he received no answer to the letters he sent to Saúl, asking for help in some historical research on the *habladores* of the Machiguenga. He consulted retired Dominicans in Madrid, and studied old travellers' accounts, without making much headway. In 1963, Saúl's anthropology professor passed through Paris and told him that Don Salomón had decided he wanted to die in Israel, and so emigrated with his son, who never finished his thesis. But N. was sceptical: "I didn't think it would have been so easy for Saúl to make the Alyah. Because he was viscerally a part of Peru, too torn and infuriated by Peruvian matters—one of them at least—to cast everything aside overnight, the way one changes a shirt" (p. 105).

In chapter 5, which is a kind of extension of chapter 3, we are, so to speak, back with the anonymous Machiguenga *hablador*. But with a difference, for now the narration turns to a surprising account of the origin of the institution. It began with Pachakamue, younger brother of the first woman, who had the power by giving names to create and transform human beings and animals without even intending to do so. He caused so much chaos that the first woman's husband, Yagontoro, killed him, and cut out his tongue and buried it, thinking thereby the world could be at peace.

> Pero, a poco de estar andado, se sintió pesado. Y por qué, además, tan torpe? Asustado, notó que sus pies eran patas; sus manos, antenas; sus brazos, alas. En vez de hombre que anda, era ya carachupa, como su nombre indica. Debajo del bosque, atragantándose de tierra, a través de los dos virotes, la lengua de Pachakamue habría dicho: "Yagontoro." Y Yagontoro se había vuelto, pues, yagontoro. (p. 130)

> [But he hadn't walked far when he felt sluggish. And why was it such slow going? Terrified, he observed that his legs were insect legs; his hands, palps; his arms, wings. Instead of being a man who walks, he was now a carachupa, just as his name is. Beneath the forest, choking on earth, through the two darts piercing it, Pachakamue's tongue had said: "Yagontoro." And Yagontoro had become, then, a yagontoro.]

It is perhaps only at this jungled, mestizo recapitulation of *Die Metamorphose* that the reader becomes sure that the *hablador* must be Saúl Zuratas.

In chapter 6, N. jumps twenty-five years forward to 1981, when, helping to create a television programme called "The Tower of Babel," he learned that the Summer Institute of Linguistics was about the leave Peru. So he decided to do a programme on the Machiguenga for the occasion. "The subject had never been far" from his mind. Meantime, a great deal of good anthropology had finally been done on them—N. mentions the names of some "real" American, Peruvian, and other investigators[11]—but strangely enough, none

---

11. Mention is made specifically of France-Marie Casevitz-Renard (French), Johnson Allen (North American), Gerhard Baer (Swiss), Fr. Joaquín Barriales (Spanish), and Camino Díez Canseco and Victor J. Guevara (Peruvian). Casevitz-Renard started publishing on the Matsigenkas (i.e. Machiguengas) in 1972 with her article "Les Matsiguenga," *Journal de la Société des Américanistes*, 61 (1972), pp. 215–53; Allen Johnson (not Johnson Allen) in 1975, with his

of these authors mentioned the *habladores*. All reference to them seemed to have broken off around the 1950s. Had they died out? Yet the Dominicans of the 1930s and 1940s had mentioned them quite often.

Returning to Amazonia, N. found the Schneils preparing to leave, happy with the results of their long labours. Half the probably 5,000 living Machiguenga were now settled in permanent villages, with schools and agricultural co-operatives. Now, for the first time in their long history they had caciques—because now they "needed authorities" (p. 157). They had, N. reflected, "the Bible, bilingual schools, an evangelical leader, private property, the value of money, trade doubtless Western clothes." But was it right? Or were the Machiguenga, "from the free and sovereign 'savages' they had been, beginning to turn into 'zombies,' . . . as Mascarita had put it?" (p. 157).

"They were no longer that handful of indomitable, tragic beings, that society broken up into tiny families, fleeing, always fleeing [*huyendo, huyendo siempre*] from the whites, from the mestizos, from the mountain people, and from other tribes, awaiting and stoically accepting their inevitable extinction as individuals and as a community, yet never giving up their language, their gods, their customs. An irrepressible melancholy came over me at the thought that this society scattered in the depths of the vast, humid forests, for whom a few peripatetic tellers of tales served as circulating sap, was going to disappear" (p. 158).

But N. observed that even the assimilated Machiguenga either denied the existence of *habladores* or fell silent when the topic was brought up. The Schneils told him that after living with the Machiguenga for a quarter of a century, they still knew almost nothing about these storytellers. "It is something very secret, very private" (p. 169). Mr. Schneil described two half-encounters, the first perhaps in 1971. He'd been unable to make sense of what the *hablador* had spoken, and had fallen into exhausted sleep as the hours of storytelling rolled by. The second *hablador* was very strange: perhaps an albino, with a huge purple birthmark on his face, who was extremely hostile, keeping his back always to the young missionary as he told his tales. Again, Schneil had fallen into exhausted, uncomprehending sleep. N. comments that it was then that he realized that the Machiguenga were not hiding the *hablador* as an abstract institution, they were hiding him because he had asked them to.

"Time Allocation in a Machiguenga Community," *Ethnology*, 14 (1975), pp. 301–10; Gerhard Baer in 1976 with, *inter alia*, "Was Mythen Aussagen: Das Beispiel der Matsigenka, Ost-Peru," *Paideuma*, 22 (1976), pp. 189–98, followed in 1984 by *Die Religion der Matsigenka Ost-Peru* (Basel: Wepf); for Father Barriales, I have found only *Matsigenka* (S.A. Victoria: Heraclio Fournier, 1977); articles by Camino Díez Canseco appear from 1977, in "Trueque, Correrías e Intercambio entre los Quechuas Andinos y los Piros y Machiguengas de la Montaña Peruana," *Amazonia Peruana*, 1: 2 (1977), pp. 123–40. (Here, perhaps for the first time, one finds an academic journal devoted specifically to Peruvian Amazonia.) For Guevara I have found nothing so far.

Back in the national capital, N. uncovered the fact that Don Salomón had never gone to Israel, but had died in Lima and been buried there, on October 23, 1960. No one seemed to know what had happened to his son. "But I do, I thought to myself. I know everything" (p. 182).

With chapter 7, the reader is back for the last time with the *hablador*. The hallucinatory narrative is, in the same breath, increasingly personal. The *hablador* briefly appears as "Gregor-Tasurinchi" who finds himself turned into a machucoy cicada. He describes how, seemingly by accident—without the aid of ayahuasca potions or the *seripigari* (shamans)—he had become a *hablador*. He had long been an *eschuchador* (heeder, hearer), and eventually found people referring to him behind his back as a storyteller. The core of this chapter, however, is a long section recounting the history of the Jews, and their god, "Tasurinchi-jehová," which opens this way:

> El pueblo que anda es ahora el mío. Antes, yo andaba con otro pueblo y creía que era el mío. No había nacido aún. Nací de verdad desde que ando como machiguenga. Eso otro pueblo se quedó allá, atrás. Tenía su historia, también. Era pequeño y vivía muy lejos de aquí, en un lugar que había sido suyo ya no lo era, sino de otros. (p. 207)

> [The people who walk are now my people. Before, I walked with another people and I believed that they were mine. I had not yet been born. I was truly born when I walked as a Machiguenga. That other people stayed there, behind. It had its own story, too. It was a small people, and it lived far from here in a place that was once its own, and was no longer, but others'.]

There follows the story of the birth among this people of a boy who grew up to say he was the breath of Tasurinchi, the son of Tasurinchi, Tasurinchi himself, all three at once. He changed a few catfish and a little cassava into a whole lot of each. People thought he was a *hablador,* and many abandoned that people's customs and taboos. The *seripigari* got worried that the people would disappear. So they killed the man, and after that many disasters happened to the people. But they didn't disappear. The people of Tasurinchi-jehová was not warlike and never won wars. It was scattered throughout all the forests of the world. It survived by travelling, escaping, walking. Greater peoples, stronger peoples, disappeared, and nobody remembers them. It survived because it was faithful to its customs and its prohibitions. "People would like everyone to be the same, would like others to forget their own customs, to kill their *seripigaris,* to violate their own taboos, and imitate theirs" (p. 211). So remaining true to one's obligations, that is the right thing to do, "as I have learned from you." "Do we want to disappear without a trace? No, again" (p. 211).

The narration ends with a story about the *hablador* finding a mother parrot trying to kill one of her chicks because it was born deformed, with a twisted leg and its claws just stumps. He drove the mother off and kept the little parrot as a companion.

> Duerme aquí, dentro de mi cushma. Como no puedo llamarlo padre, ni pariente, ni Tasurinchi, lo llamo con una palabra que inventé para él. Un ruido de loros, pues. A ver, imítenlo. Despertémoslo, llamémoslo. Él lo aprendió y lo repite muy bien: Mas-ca-r-ita, Mas-ca-ri-ta, Mas-ca-ri-ta. . . . (p. 224)

> [He sleeps here, inside my cushma. As I can't call him father, or kinsman, or Tasurinchi, I call him by a name I invented for him. A parrot noise, then. Let's see, try to copy it. Let's wake him up, let's call him. He's learned it and repeats it very well. Mas-ca-ri-ta, Mas-ca-ri-ta, Mas-ca-ri-ta. . . .]

The concluding chapter brings the reader back to N. in Florence. He wonders whether the Machiguenga have survived the drug plague, the Sendero Luminoso, and the brutal military repressions that all entered Amazonia in the 1980s. "And does my ex-friend, the ex-Jew, ex-white man, and ex-Westerner, Saúl Zuratas, walk with them?" he reflects (p. 230). In the 1960s, other idealistic Peruvian youngsters had gone off in all directions, but Saúl had done it differently, by deliberately erasing all trace of his departure and intentions. "He had decided, irrevocably, to change his skin, his name, his habits, his tradition, his god . . . He had left Lima with the intention of never coming back, of being another person forever after" (p. 232). N. suspects that as a Jew he identified with small, itinerant, persecuted peoples. His birthmark also made him marginal among marginals in Peruvian society. But the real mystery lies not here but in his further transformation into a *hablador*. "Converting himself into a *hablador* was adding the impossible to what was merely improbable" (p. 233).

> For speaking the way a *hablador* speaks means to have reached the point of feeling and living the very heart of that culture; of submerging oneself in its mysteries; of penetrating the marrow of its history and mythology, giving body to its ancestral taboos, images, desires, and terrors. It means being, in the most profound way possible, a rooted Machiguenga . . . That my friend Saúl renounced all that he was and might have become, in order to roam through the Amazonian jungle for now more than twenty years, perpetuating, against wind and tide—and, above all, against the very notions of modernity and progress—the tradition of that invisible line of wandering tellers of tales [*contadores de historias*] is something that memory now and again brings back to me, and, as on that day when I first learned of it, in the starlit darkness of the village of Nueva Luz, it opens my heart with more force than love or fear has ever done. (p. 234)

N. closes the story he has told by describing himself looking out at the casual night-time chaos of tourist Florence. It will be useless to leave his room. For "wherever I might flee, trying to find refuge from the heat, the mosquitoes, the exaltation of my spirit, I would go on hearing, close by, ceaseless, crepitating, immemorial, that Machiguenga *hablador"* (p. 235).

PART THREE

And the "historical" Machiguengas, or, as they are known in less hispanized form, the Matsigenka?[12] Their ancestry is believed to go back thousands of years. They were intermittently subjected only to the most powerful of the Incas, and because of their isolation in the trans-Andean Amazonian jungle, they were virtually unknown in the era of Spanish imperialism. Even the contemporary name, Matsigenka, which literally means "human beings," only became normal among outsiders about seventy-five years ago. One of the earliest, albeit anonymous, texts about them, dated 1865, says that "No trace can be found among them of any communal bonds. Each family lives isolated or occasionally together with some others, and a headman is elected only during wartime."[13] The end of their isolation began in the 1860s when outsiders, many from Brazil and Bolivia, came in search of cinchona bark, source for the quinine then in huge demand as a febrifuge by British and French imperialists in (Southeast) Asia and Africa. In the last two decades of the nineteenth century the Peruvian state became increasingly concerned with firmly establishing and defending its porous eastern frontiers, and began financing explorers, among the most notorious of whom was Werner Herzog's Fermín Fitzcarrald.

But the tornado of modernity hit the Matsigenka only in the first two decades of this century, when—till outmatched by the colonial production in Southeast Asia and Africa—Peru experienced a meteoric boom in rubber. The sudden demand for labour for massive rubber-tapping in Amazonia

---

12. Having no pretensions to any knowledge of these people, I have relied, in what follows, on: (1) Dan Rosengren, *In the Eyes of the Beholder: Leadership and the Social Construction of Power and Dominance among the Matsigenka of the Peruvian Amazon* (Göteborg: Göteborgs Etnografiska Museum, 1987), vol. 37 of *Etnologiska Studier*; (2) Beverly Yvonne Bennett, "Illness and Order: Cultural Transformation among the Machiguenga and Huachipairi" (Ph.D. thesis, Cornell University, 1991); and (3) the entry for Matsigenka in the *Encyclopedia of World Cultures* (New York; G.K. Hall, 1994), vol. 7 (South America), pp. 230–32. I have also consulted, more briefly, the following texts of Dominican missionaries: P. Fr. Vicente de Cenitagoya, *Los Machiguengas* (Lima: Sanmarti y Cia, 1943); P. Andrés Ferrero, *Los Machiguengas: Tribu selvática del sur-oriente peruano* (Salamanca: "Calatrava" Libreros, 1966); and the *Matsigenka* of Father Joaquín Barriales cited above. The story of Pachakamue and Yagontoro given in *El Hablador*'s chapter 5 is drawn from pp. 185–9 of Cenitagoya's work.

13. Cited in Rosengren, *In the Eyes*, p. 3.

created the dreaded institution of the *correría,* which amounted to slave raids, on a vast scale. The peaceful, hardworking Matsigenka became among the favoured targets. Missionaries later estimated that perhaps 60 per cent of their population perished—in a region where "the only law in force was Law Calibre 44 [the Winchester rifle]"[14]—under the regime of slave labour accompanied by torture, murder, burning of homes, kidnapping of women and children, and the spread of hitherto unknown diseases.[15] It was in this period that the Amazonian indigenes came to be generally regarded by Peruvians either as tools for national development, or as obstacles that ought to be exterminated. About 1900, the Dominicans started serious missionary work, and at least some Matsigenka fled to them for protection. The end of the rubber boom, however, did not mean the end of slavelike exploitation—after rubber came sugar haciendas, then mining, and finally logging. (Slavery is said to have persisted, semi-clandestinely, well into the 1960s.)

The 1960s were marked by two important changes for the Matsigenka. On the one hand, the Summer Institute of Linguistics, said then to be "the largest Protestant missionary organisation in the world,"[16] moved in, and, other activities aside, opened the way for the proliferation of modern anthropological work on the Matsigenka in the 1970s and 1980s.[17] On the other hand, the first presidency of Fernando Belaúnde Terry (1964–68) assigned Amazonia the status of Peru's last frontier, the opening of which would save the

---

14. Ibid., p. 31.

15. The fate of the Matsigenka went largely unnoticed. But farther north along the upper Peruvian reaches of the Putumayo river, the same rubber-boom savagery against local indigenes erupted into one of the earliest great international scandals concerning the fate of "tribal minorities." The exemplary—so to speak—figure was the confused Irish patriot Roger Casement. Already world-famous for his exposure of the savagery of Léopold II's regime in the not-yet-Belgian Congo, he added to his reputation as defender of threatened minorities by his 1912 report on what his immediate predecessor, the American adventurer–traveller W.E. Hardenburg, had called "The Devil's Paradise." Casement had been the British consul in Rio de Janeiro from 1909 to 1913. Following up on Hardenburg's reports, and looking for a point of entry, he had discovered that the villain-in-chief was Juan Araña, a Peruvian entrepreneur, who, capital-short but politically "solid" in Lima, had incorporated himself anew with Ukanian backers into the "Peruvian Amazonian Company." He had also learned that Araña had employed significant numbers of (Ukanian) black Barbadians as foremen, torturers, and executioners. It was on the basis of City responsibility for the horrors of the Putumayo that Casement won a continuing hearing, and, in 1911, a weird knighthood from George "Windsor" the Fifth for his services to English respectability. He was relieved of this dubious honour five years later, when he was put on trial for treason to Ukania in the aftermath of the Easter Uprising of 1916. He was executed on August 3, 1916. On all of this, see W.H. Hardenburg, *The Putumayo: The Devil's Paradise* (London: T. Fisher Unwin, 1912); Roger Sawyer, *Casement: The Flawed Hero* (London: Routledge & Kegan Paul, 1984), chapters 7–9; and Brian Inglis, *Roger Casement* (London: Hodder & Stoughton, 1973), Part III.

16. The quotation is from Bennett, "Illness and Order," p. 113.

17. A comparison of the extensive bibliographies attached to the texts of Rosengren and Bennett shows a sudden and rapid increase in the number of "scientific" publications after the early 1970s.

malhadado país from poverty and overpopulation. For the first time the state itself actively promoted neolatifundista colonization. Following the overthrow of Belaúnde, the radical military regime of Juan Velasco Alvorado tried in part to reverse this policy by creating what were effectively "reservations" for the Amazonian indigenes, in which land would not be alienable. But on returning to power in 1980 Belaúnde resumed the policies of intensive capitalist development, by which the Matsigenka were to be acculturated, schooled (up to a point), hispanized, and made into a settled labour force.

By the later 1980s, their numbers were variously estimated to be between five and twelve thousand. Perhaps half were already corralled in seven settlements under the general name of Comunidades Nativas, with a sort of embryo political organization imposed from above, and without popular credence.[18] Traditional subsistence had become more and more difficult as capitalist colonization drastically reduced game and fish, and made swidden gardens harder and harder to find. The traditional healer shamans, or *seripigari,* were steadily disappearing.[19] Even so, the extreme variation in population estimates suggests that some part of the Matsigenka are still "huyendo, huyendo siempre" in search of livelihood, peace, and autonomy.

It remains only to add one thing that is decisive for our present purposes. *El Hablador*'s account of the modern history of the Machiguenga/Matsigenka is largely exact, and its description of their traditional cosmology, "social order," customs, and way of life, corresponds well with the published academic work: save for one striking thing. As N. casually notes, in not a single one of these professional accounts is there any mention of the institution of *hablador.*[20]

PART FOUR

What does Vargas Llosa intend by *hablador*? The word's ordinary connotations are "talker," "chatterbox," "bullshitter," and "gossip"—someone not at all to be taken seriously. The novel reminds us of this lightness in its description of Saúl Zuratas's *lorito hablador*—a little "talking" parrot that does not understand what it is saying. Doris Sommer notes that the usual serious words for a storyteller or narrator are *narrador, cuentista,* and *cuentero. Hablador* thus appears to be a deliberate quasi-neologism, and is matched by

---

18. See Rosengren's illuminating account, *In the Eyes,* pp. 176–85.

19. This is the conclusion of Bennett, "Illness and Order," p. 155.

20. I have not been able to consult all these accounts, but the work of Rosengren and Bennett is so thorough, and their bibliographies so extensive, that it seems inconceivable that they would have ignored the *hablador* if he had cropped up in any of their professional colleagues' work. Furthermore, though N. claims that the Dominicans frequently mentioned the *habladores* in their writings, they never appear in the three Dominican-authored texts mentioned in n. 12 above.

the displacement of the usual word *oyentes* (listeners, audience) by the rarer term *escuchadores* (hearers, heeders, perhaps).[21]

There can be little doubt that what the author has in mind is the figure of the *Erzähler*, whom Walter Benjamin so famously counterposed to the novelist and the journalist (Vargas Llosa's two primary avocations).[22] It is worth reminding ourselves of the lineaments of this figure. "Familiar though his name may be to us, the *Erzähler* in his living immediacy is by no means a contemporary presence. He has already become something remote from us and something that is getting ever more distant . . . the art of storytelling is coming to an end."[23] "Experience which is passed on mouth to mouth is the source from which all *Erzähler* have drawn."[24] Benjamin describes such people as coming, in the European Middle Ages, from two groups, itinerants such as seamen who bring tales from their experiences far away, and rooted residents, such as tillers of the land, who know all the local traditions and legends. "All this," he continues, "points to the nature of every real story. It contains, openly or covertly, something useful . . . In every case, the *Erzähler* is a man who has counsel for his listener/heeder. But if today 'having counsel' is beginning to have an old-fashioned ring, this is because the communicability of experience is declining. In consequence we have no counsel for ourselves or for others." This process "has quite gradually removed *Erzählung* from the realm of living speech and at the same time is making it possible to see a new beauty in what is vanishing."[25]

Of the novel, Benjamin writes that its key feature is its dependence on the book and the invention of printing. "What differentiates the novel from all other forms of prose literature—the fairy tale, the legend, even the novella—is that it neither comes from oral tradition nor goes into it . . . The *Erzähler* takes what he tells from experience—his own or that reported by others. And he in turn makes it the experience of those who are listening to his tale. The novelist has isolated himself. The birthplace of the novel is the individual in his solitude, who is no longer able to express in an exemplary manner his weightiest concerns, is himself uncounselled, and cannot counsel others. To write a novel

---

21. Sommer, "About-Face," p. 113. My reflections on *El Hablador* differ from hers, but I have learned enormously from her work.

22. At the risk of reader-irritation, I shall, as often as possible, fend off the pushy banality of the English "story-teller."

23. See "Der Erzähler: Betrachtungen zum Werk Nikolai Lesskows," in Walter Benjamin, *Illuminationen* (Frankfurt-am-Main: Suhrkamp, 1961), pp. 409–56, at p. 409. (The translated quotations that follow are my own modifications of those given in Walter Benjamin, *Illuminations*, trans. Harry Zohn [New York: Schocken, 1969], pp. 83–109.) This vanishing parallels that of the Machiguenga.

24. Ibid., p. 410.

25. Ibid., p. 412. It is instructive that Zohn translated *Hörer* as "readers," and *fühlbar macht* as "making it possible to see."

is to carry the incommensurable to extremes in the representation of human life. In the midst of life's fullness, and through the representation of this fullness, the novel gives evidence of the profound perplexity of the living."[26] (We shall see soon enough how appropriate this description is of *El Hablador*.)

Of journalism, Benjamin says: "Every morning brings us news of the globe, and yet we are poor in noteworthy stories. This is because no event comes to us any longer without being shot through with explanation. In other words, by now almost nothing that happens benefits storytelling; almost everything benefits information." Furthermore, "The value of information does not survive the moment in which it was new. It lives only in that moment it has to surrender to it completely and explain itself to it without losing any time. The *Erzählung* is different. It does not expend itself. It preserves its concentrated power and is capable of releasing it even after a long time."[27]

There is one other element in Benjamin's account of the *Erzähler*, and that is the central importance of death. "Just as a sequence of images is set in motion inside a man as his life comes to an end—consisting of the views of his own person by which he has encountered himself without being aware of it—so, suddenly in his expressions and looks the unforgettable emerges and imparts to everything that concerned him that authority which even the poorest wretch in dying possesses for the living around him. This authority is at the very source of the story. Death is the sanction of everything that the *Erzähler* can tell. He has borrowed his authority from death."[28] We might bear in mind that it is exactly this authority which is unavailable to the novelist or the journalist.

Benjamin's reflections allow us to see more clearly the central strangeness of *El Hablador*—that it is a novel about "stories" and also about a narrator "in love with" an *Erzähler*, as well as a novelist in love with the idea of the *Erzähler*. That Saúl Zuratas, has, shall we say, the capacity to become an *Erzähler*, is indicated early on when N. informs us that Mascarita "revered" Kafka and knew *La Metamorfosis* by heart. (Benjamin's essay turned on Nikolai Leskov's incomparable tales, but it could just as well have pivoted on the Master of Prague.) Yet this capacity could only become (imagined) reality when "my ex-friend, the ex-Jew, the ex-white man and ex-Westerner . . . decided, irrevocably, to change his skin, his name, his habits, his tradition, his god." Becoming a *hablador* meant, in words that are not far from Benjamin's, to "have reached the point of feeling and living the very heart of that culture; of submerging oneself in its mysteries; of penetrating to the marrow of its history and mythology, giving body to its ancestral taboos, images, desires, and terrors. It means being, in the most profound way possible, a rooted

26. Ibid., pp. 413–14.
27. Ibid., pp. 415–16.
28. Ibid., pp. 420–21.

Machiguenga." But there is more to it than that. Saúl is shown not merely to have become rooted, in the manner of the medieval tiller of the soil (or, supposing such existed, a traditional Machiguenga *hablador*), but to bring to the Machiguenga tales from afar, weaving them into the idiom and experience of his enraptured audience. These tales are drawn at first from Kafka, of course, but subsequently from the long inward history of the Jews and their suffering at the hands of the eternal following of that first "ex-Jew," Jesus Christ. Moreover, at every point, he is, as Benjamin observed of the *Erzähler*, the "righteous man" who brings with his tales good counsel.

That Saúl "borrows his authority from death" is underlined when N. notes that "an irrepressible melancholy came over me at the thought that this society scattered in the depths of the vast, humid forests, for whom a few peripatetic tellers of tales served as circulating sap, was going to disappear." It is as if the *hablador's* voice enunciates the last words of a community in its death throes, which thereby commands "heeders" in a way no novelist can hope to equal. At the same time, the authority also comes from Saúl's irrevocable disappearance from "Peru," and N.'s throat-catching awareness that he has long ago already heard his old friend's last words.

It is at this point that the question of the possibility, and impossibility, of a novel about the *Erzähler/Hablador* becomes unavoidable. There is that moment in N.'s last conversation with Saúl where the former describes why he is so moved by the idea of the *habladores*. "They're palpable proof that the telling of stories [here it is *contar historias*] can be something more than mere entertainment . . . Something primordial, something on which the very existence of a *pueblo* [people] substantially depends." He is moved because this is exactly what seems out of the novel's reach, no matter how canonical a country's literary inspectors may wish it to be. It silently jostles elbows with thousands upon thousands of other novels in the vast and ever increasing market of print where authors and readers almost never encounter one another except in the imagination. Moreover, the novelist's *pueblo* is, in the first instance, the imagined community of the nation, which is not in the least primordial, and whose everyday circulating sap is not the novel but the newspaper, radio, the electronic media, and other purveyors of "information." Hence it is an anguish for something unattainable that "opens" the "heart with more force than love or fear has ever done."[29]

---

29. "Actually, there is no story for which the question 'what happened next?' would not be legitimate. The novelist, on the other hand, cannot hope to take the smallest step beyond that limit at which he invites the reader to a premonitory realization of the meaning of life by writing 'Finis.'" "What draws the reader to the novel is the hope of warming his shivering life with a death that he reads about." Ibid., pp. 427–8. It seems impossible to render the malignant word-order of the original: "Das was den Leser zum Roman zieht, ist die Hoffnung, sein fröstelndes Leben an einem Tod von dem er liest, zu wärmen."

It is likely that *this* anguish for *this* unattainability had its origins in the Americas—though as the nation-state has extended its reach around the world such anguish no longer has a regional home. For the Americas produced the first nation-states, and the condition for that possibility was their status as overseas European colonies of emigration, which conjoined, with extraordinary violence, over vast areas, white immigrants, a huge variety of indigenes who, where not exterminated, were reduced to conditions of abjection, and, in many instances, vast numbers of Africa-originating slaves—to say nothing of their mixed progeny. These were societies for which there was no historical precedent, yet which were also controlled for centuries by invisible metropoles thousands of ocean miles away. Leskov's stories, like those of Gogol, can still, indirectly, communicate to us the tales of the *Erzähler* they encountered or heard word of, because they all came from, not the vast Tsarist Empire as such, but from the old, and still huge, Russian-speaking population within it (besides, the Empire was not understood as a nation). They had no need of the ventriloquist's artifices. But the European conquerors of the Americas were not traditional peasants; and over the centuries they imposed their habits, religions, economic life, and languages with such successful cruelty, and created such steep racial hierarchies on the bases of this success, that the hemisphere found it impossible to generate the kind of intimately eerie Leskovian story that might begin: It was Vera Petrovna who told me the story about the four horses found frozen upright in the middle of the Volga during the bitter winter of 1834.[30] (The seamless English of such sentences does not in any way deeply misrepresent a kind of seamlessness in the original Russian.)

In the Americas, however, Spanish, English, and Portuguese have always been incapable of such seamlessness because of their visible, contaminated origins in conquest, and because the tales of the indigenous communities, where these survived, had to emerge, in print, through dubious processes of translation. Everywhere the hand of the enemy left its imprint, no matter if that enemy took the form of anthropologist, missionary, parish priest, bureaucrat, litterateur, or mestizo broker.[31] No one is more aware of this

---

30. "Magic realism" stands to Leskov and Gogol as the ventriloquist stands to the grandmother, about whom there rarely hangs the aura of the virtuoso.

31. In colonial Southeast Asia, the early translations were published by missionaries and bored officials with amateur antiquarian and ethnological interests. Later the professional ethnologists and even some writers played a hand. Eventually, in the time of postcoloniality, there arrived the national anthropologist, the national literary man, or woman, and sometimes a combination of both. In the collection of Thai short stories of the 1960s and 1970s that I helped translate in *In the Mirror: Literature and Politics in Siam in the American Era* (Bangkok: Duang Kamon, 1985), there are two, more than sympathetic, stories about "national minorities." One,

condition than the novelist, *non-hablador,* Mario Vargas Llosa. Hence the need for a novelist's ingenuity. Put it this way: if one could imagine that the fleeing Machiguengas had real *habladores,* one could also imagine the open or surreptitious tape-recording of their tales. But these tapes, transcribed, would be unintelligible to the Peruvian Spanish-reading public which is the writer's first audience. As it were, authenticity yes, readability no. This is why, in the first place, the novel needs the bilingual Peruvian, or ex-Peruvian, intermediary who is Saúl Zuratas. But this intermediary is by no means enough. The novelist has set himself a much more arduous task. This task can be described as inventing a persuasive voice for the *hablador* which is as remote as possible from that of any self-imagining Peruvian, yet which at the same time radically undermines its own authenticity: the delicate features of inspired pastiche.

The main technical means for accomplishing this formidable mission are two. The first and most obvious is that the tales of the *hablador* are given, *without any claim to the status of translation,* in Spanish. The second, and much the more important, is the un-Leskovian absence of any "Vera Petrovna." When the *hablador* speaks, his tales come out of nowhere. There is no point in the novel at which N. claims to "report" what the *hablador* has said.[32] Indeed, the very structure of the novel is arranged to rule out such a possibility. For the last time N. saw Saúl was two decades earlier, in Lima, before the latter is made to become a *hablador:* and, of course, the two young men spoke in student-inflected Spanish. These devices proclaim/confess a certain necessary-to-the-novel fraudulence. At exactly the same time, however, every gift at the writer's disposal is deployed to summon up, over many pages, an overwhelming facsimile of the Machiguenga (*huyendo, huyendo siempre*) for the Peruvians from whom they flee. The impossible pair of intentions come brilliantly, momentarily, together in the novel's last sentence where

---

about a tragedy in a remote, impoverished shore-line village of Sea People, is written as an allegory of the violent national politics of contemporary Bangkok. The other, a semi-idyll put in the mouth of a young Hmong man, innocently has this lad refer to his own people as "Meo," which is the contemptuous terminology of Bangkok officialdom. In the 1990s, a very gifted young Javanese writer, anguished at the fate of the East Timorese under the heels of the conquistadors of Jakarta, published a series of tales about them from his personal acquaintance. Given the "American" conditions prevailing in occupied East Timor, the youngster, so to speak a nephew of the conquerors, wisely opted for a Javanese form of magic realism. See Seno Gumira Adjidarma, *Saksi Mata* [Testimony of the Eyes] (Yogyakarta: Bentang, 1994). The book has been translated into English with the normalizing title *Eyewitness* (New York: Harper Collins International, 1995).

32. As we have observed earlier, of the named characters only Mr. Schneil is said to have actually listened (twice) to a *hablador,* but on both occasions he found unintelligible what was recounted. He cannot pass on—as good counsel—what only his ears have received.

N. says that "dondequiera que me refugie tratando de aplacar el calor, los mosquitos, la exaltación de mi espíritu, seguiré oyendo, cercano, sin pausas, crepitante, inmemorial, a ese hablador machiguenga." The words are carefully chosen. N. is taking insignificant and Italian refuge from heat and mosquitoes, not *huyendo* the spectre of extinction; he is a cool, detached *oyente*, not a mesmerized *escuchador*; and the *hablador*, Saúl , is not exactly a Machiguenga (to say nothing of being a creation of Mario Vargas Llosa). Yet what N. says he hears is close by, crepitating, and immemorial. The inaccessible sound of the *Erzähler*.

It remains for us to consider the novelist's wider intentions and ambitions. Fortunately or unfortunately, in this case he has spoken about them seemingly without ambiguity. In an interview in October 1993, Doris Sommer asked him whether his decision to make Saúl Zuratas a Jew was because he was interested in the parallels between the historical fates of the Machiguenga— and other near-exterminated minorities—and the Jews. His reply evidently surprised her. "It was, instead, the polar extremes of their difference, he said. They revive the kinds of social and geographic differences whose co-ordination was the heroic project of nineteenth century nationalist consolidation, a project inherited from colonial times. Together, Indians and Jews represented Peru at its limits, like the geo-historical limits of dusty Piura in the north and the steamy jungles on the south side of the Andes that *La casa verde* barely braces together. Primitive and poor Amazonian Indians and generally rich cosmopolitan Jews were at opposite ends of the country's population, he explained. And the novel was an effort to talk about Peru in the most inclusive and capacious way possible—from a focus on its demographic extremities."[33]

That *El Hablador is* a nationalist novel is beyond doubt, but the interesting question is how its nationalism is "performed," as the current argot has it, especially in the light of that "heroic project of nineteenth century consolidation," of which Vargas Llosa spoke.

One might start the inquiry by looking at the pair of Sommerian "lovers," whose intertwined fates invite (Peruvian) readers into the erotics of nationhood: Saúl and N. Saúl is anything but a rich cosmopolitan Jew. Don Salomón is a lower middle-class immigrant, and his son, born to a non-

---

33. This explanation corresponds so closely to the theses of Doris Sommer's pathbreaking book—which Vargas Llosa surely had read—that the possibility of an element of collegial courtesy, or leg-pulling, cannot be ruled out. The explanation also, however, fits the words of Benjamin quoted earlier: "To write a novel is to carry the incommensurable to extremes in the representation of human life." At the same time: where does one have to stand to allow oneself to see the Machiguengas as Peruvians, as one of Peru's "demographic extremities"? (*La casa verde* is, of course, an earlier work by Mario Vargas Llosa.)

Jewish mother, is, from some points of view, not really a Jew at all. He is a non-believer, has never been outside the country, and shows no interest in anything not Peruvian (except the *Erzähler* Kafka). In the end, he is said by N. to have become ex-everything—*except ex-Peruvian*. In the debates he carried on with N. in their student days he was scarcely a cosmopolitan "generic" human-rights activist. He could speak of the living descendants of the Incas as "sleepwalkers" and "zombies" whose disintegration had proceeded so far that only assimilation now made any sense, and he defended the Machiguenga in a tone that could plausibly be called micronationalist, or indigenist. One might then initially imagine that he will become, in the course of the novel, an activist for the rights of indigenous peoples, helping them to organize politically, forging local, national, and international alliances along the way, thus integrating and acculturating themselves in the non-Machiguenga world. But, of course, no such expectations are fulfilled.

N.'s fascinated love for the future *hablador* is not in the least requited—his letters to Saúl after 1958 are never answered. Saúl's passion is exclusively for a little people fleeing as far from Lima as is humanly possible, and the condition of this love's fulfilment is the abandonment of Peru. Nothing here, at first sight, resembles the integrationist loves in the canonical novels of the heroic nineteenth-century nationalist project. At the same time, it is precisely because Saúl starts as a Peruvian, and because the Machiguenga live inside the space of Peru, not in Brazil or Colombia—i.e. that they are "Peruvian" and "children of Peru" in the line of San Martín's utopian formulation—that he is destined to fall in love with them. N.'s initial reason for doubting Saúl's emigration to Israel seems on the mark: "He was viscerally part of Peru, too torn and enraged by Peruvian affairs—at least one of them—to cast away everything overnight, the way one changes a shirt."

And N.? Here, if anywhere, is the rich (no financial worries anyway) and cosmopolitan figure, who studies in Madrid and Paris, has warm feelings for the "Yankee" missionaries of the Summer Institute of Linguistics, and tries to "forget" his "unfortunate/damned" country in the home town of Dante Alighieri. Yet he is also the obvious heir to the conquistadors and to the second Liberator. Here he is in 1958: "We travelled in a small hydroplane, and, in some places, in indigenous canoes, along narrow river channels submerged under a vegetation so intricately tangled that in full daylight it seemed like night. The force and the solitude of Nature—the immensely tall trees, the mirror-smooth lagoons, the immutable rivers—brought to mind a newly created world, innocent of mankind, a vegetable and animal paradise. When we reached the tribes, by contrast, we found ourselves face to face with prehistory, the elemental, primeval existence of our distant ancestors: hunters, gatherers, archers, wanderers, irrational people (*los irracionales*), magicians, and animists.

This, too, was Peru [*también, eso era la Perú*], and only then did I become fully aware of it: a world *todavía sin domar* [as yet untamed?/to be tamed?]."[34] In the course of his student-day discussions with Saúl, N. also takes up (albeit partly as devil's advocate), the standard liberal nationalist arguments for an ineluctable, hopefully benevolent, assimilation of "prehistory" into "history," in the name of the heroic project called Peru.[35] Progress has its own "force and solitude," and the best that a good Peruvian can manage is with sincerity and goodwill to do everything possible to dull the shock of acculturation and to work against the zombifications of the past. In this way, it turns out, at an oblique angle to Vargas Llosa's interview, that the social and geographical extremes of "Peru" are represented not by rich cosmopolitan Jews and primitive indigenes, but by metropolitan liberal nationalist intellectuals and those who stoically flee them to the exterminating end of the road.

The long time-stretch of the novel, from the early 1950s to the end of the 1980s, shows us less the imagined evolution/conversion of Saúl, than that of his unwanted lover. Till it becomes, for him, and for the novelist, "possible to sense a new beauty in what is vanishing." But this beauty depends upon vanishing, not zombification. Saúl is part of this vanishing. Mascarita will have no son or daughters, his maimed little parrot likewise—in the line of Gregor Samsa and his creator.[36]

Why then is Saúl created also a Jew/ex-Jew, in addition to what he deeply is: *mascarita, peruano, hablador*? No doubt Vargas Llosa partly meant what he said when he observed that it was the contrast between Jews and Machiguenga, not the parallels between them, that was on his mind when he composed *El Hablador*. But the contrast is actually not the one he went on to specify. The extinction of the Jews is less imaginable today than it has been for centuries. Rich, vociferous Israel is the most powerful state in the Middle East, and the world-hegemonic United States, as well as Europe, provide unconditional guarantees of its survival. (This unconditionality has its modern origins in the near-extermination of European Jewry in the 1940s by the European agents of European Adolf Hitler.) For the Machiguenga, however, like hundreds of other small "tribal minorities" around the world, there are no guarantees, and quiet extinction is absolutely on the cards.

---

34. *El Hablador,* p. 71.

35. It seems that the "extremes" are not merely geographical or socio-economic, they are also stretched to two ends of human history.

36. Vargas Llosa has described his half-horrified fascination with those human beings who are willing to sacrifice everything for an idea. This is perhaps normal for those who have no personal inclinations along these lines. What is extraordinary is his creative ability to conjure up such people in certain of his novels. A wonderful example is the doomed, ineffective, timidly homosexual underground Marxist, Alejandro Mayta, hero of *Historia de Mayta* (1984).

It seems likely that the Jewish motif, which at certain points in the novel has the feeling of being dragged in, serves apotropaic purposes. At the end of our bitter century, the perhaps 3,500 years of Jewish history have become available as a general trope for triumphant "cultural survival against all odds." It is this "good counsel" that only a contemporary Jew can provide, not just to the Machiguenga, so to speak, but to Vargas Llosa's national and international readers. No such possibilities are open, in the time of Fujimori, to a merely *peruano* Mask-Face *hablador*. One realizes at this juncture the contradictory importance to the author of the rebus "ex-Jew." In it, "Jew" stands as a figure for "hope against all odds"; "ex-" does not cancel "Jew" but makes room alongside it for local despair: Saúl Zuratas, doomed Redeemer.

Finally, we are to understand that it is as the mixed descendant of a local *criolla* and an immigrant Polish Jew, anchored to Peru through his mother, freed from it through his father, that Saúl is positioned to be the imagined intermediary, the common mesmerizer of both N. and the Machiguenga, who otherwise, in this novel, have no point of contact. We are living in a time in which ventriloquizing persecuted and oppressed minorities has become (and not only ethically) intolerable. *Mascarita* is the author's alibi in the court of cultural claims.

At precisely this juncture we can discern the profoundest difference between late twentieth-century *El Hablador* and those nineteenth-century canonical novels about which Doris Sommer has written so persuasively. Most of the latter were written early on the parabolic arc of nationalism's unfinished history, when it was only too possible to think, to borrow from Simone Weil, that by walking on one was walking up. There was as yet no conception that every document of civilization is at the same time a document of barbarism. *El Hablador,* however, considers the truth of Benjamin's paradox, taking all its terms together. One could say that it "performs" the impossibility of transcending it, as well as of escaping from it. This is, perhaps, the only way in our time that the national novel, the narrative of the nation, can properly be written, and rewritten, and rewritten.

At the beginning of the novel N. speaks of Peru—from which he is unsuccessfully trying to escape—as his *malhadado país. Malhadado* can be read not merely as "unfortunate," but also as "ill-fated," "accursed," and even "damned." In the juxtaposition of this adjective with the word for "country," "home," "nation," one feels the timbre of tragedy as well as the semantics of shame. One will have to learn to become accustomed to this.

The Goodness of Nations

One can see immediately where nationalism and religion part company if one tries to transform "My Country, Right or Wrong" into "My Religion, Right or Wrong." The latter is an inconceivable oxymoron. How could Islam for Muslims, Christianity for Christians, or Hinduism for Hindus possibly be Wrong?

Yet this contrast should not be taken wholly at face value. For if nations can, at least hypothetically, be Wrong, this wrongness is temporal, and is always set against a transcendent Right or Good. The question then is—and one poses it at a tangent to the eternal Goodness of religions—what are the sources of this Rightness, given that the nation, no matter how grandly conceived, is intrahistorical: it has no place reserved for it in Heaven or Hell. Below, I will try to sketch what are three interlinked locations of guaranteed national Goodness.

THE UNBORN

Nothing better illustrates the first of these three locations than one strange passage in Max Weber's well-known inaugural lecture on the occasion of taking up a post at the University of Freiburg in 1895.[1] The bulk of this address is a jeremiad on the existing state of his new country—Germany. Looking wearily about him, Weber saw the ruling class of Junkers as finished.

---

1. The original text can be found in Wolfgang J. Mommsen and Rita Aldenhoff, eds., *Max Weber: Landarbeiterfrage, Nationalstaat und Volkswirtschaftspolitik, Schriften und Reden, 1892–1899* (Tübingen: J.C.B. Mohr, 1993), vol. 2, pp. 545–74. A serviceable, but not always nuanced, English translation is printed in Keith Tribe, ed., *Reading Weber* (London and New York: Routledge, 1989), pp. 188–220.

"Sie haben ihre Arbeit geleistet und liegen heute im ökonomische Todeskampf." [They have done their work, and are today in the throes of an economic death-struggle.] From the German bourgeoisie as a whole nothing good could be expected. "Nur allzu offenkundig sehnt ein Teil des Grossbürgertums nach dem Erscheinen eines neuen Cäsar, der sie schirme— nach unten gegen aufsteigende Volksklassen—nach oben gegen sozialpolitische Anwandlungen, deren ihnen die deutsche Dynastien verdächtig sind." [One section of the haute bourgeoisie yearns only too shamelessly for the rise of a new Caesar, who will protect them—from below against the rising popular classes, from above against the sociopolitical impulses they suspect the German dynasties of harbouring.] Another section "ist längst versunken in jene politische Spiessbürgerei, aus welcher die breiten Schichten des Kleinbürgertums noch niemals erwacht sind" [is sunk in that political philistinism from which broad strata of the petite bourgeoisie have never awakened]. The proletariat he believed to be wholly immature: "weil es für eine grosse Nation nichts vernichtenderes giebt, als die Leitung durch ein *politisch* unerzogenes *Spiessbürgertum*, und weil das deutsche Proletariat diesen Charakter noch nicht verloren hat, *deshalb* sind wir seine politischen Gegner." [Since nothing is more destructive to a great nation than to be led by a *politically* uneducated *philistinism*, and since the German proletariat has yet to lose this philistine character, we are *therefore* its political adversary.][2] One might easily conclude from this analysis that the German nation—with the exception of the learned young professor himself—was All Wrong. But Weber also struck an altogether different, and at first sight very odd note. The passage is worth quoting in full:[3]

> Und—um ein etwas phantastisches Bild zu brauchen—vermöchten wir nach Jahrtausenden dem Grab zu entsteigen, so wären es die fernen Spuren unsres eignen Wesens, nach denen wir im Antlitz des Zukunftsgeschlechts forschen würden. Auch unsre höchsten und letzten irdischen Ideale sind wandelbar und vergänglich. Wir können sie der Zukunft nicht aufzwingen wollen. Aber wir können wollen, dass sie in unserer Art die Art ihrer eignen Ahnen erkennt. Wir, mit unsrer Arbeit und unsrem Wesen, wollen die Vorfahren des Zukunftsgeschlechts sein.

> [If—to use a somewhat fantastical image—we could rise from the grave thousands of years from now, we would seek the distant traces of our own being in the physiognomy of the race of the future. Even our highest, our ultimate, terrestrial ideals are mutable and transitory. We cannot hope to impose them on the future. But we can wish that the future recognizes in our nature the nature of its own ancestors. We wish, by our labour and our being, to become the forefathers of the race of the future.]

---

2. The emphases are Weber's.

3. This crucial passage occurs on p. 559 of the German edition.

In this passage, with its millenarian timbre, one can recognize something that echoes the religious impulse. The sober comparative sociologist of religions deliriously imagines a vast host of Germans, thousands of years in the future, proudly imagining . . . Weber! Moreover, these unborn Germans appear to impose obligations on the imaginer of 1895, who is already imagining himself as dead. It is up to him and his late-century German audience to rise to the expectations of the future. It is no less striking that, after thousands of years, nothing sociological or political remains of these future Germans. They are neither Junkers, bourgeois, nor proletarians. They long for no Caesars, and they are not even committed to "our highest and ultimate terrestrial ideals." The tense here is, so to speak, the Future Perfect. It is precisely the unbornness of these millions of future Germans that guarantees their Goodness.

It would be imprudent to dismiss Weber's words as a giddy moment of lunacy in an intellectual career of stately conservative sobriety. Less weirdly and poetically phrased, the same rhetorical trope is in use every day in every national polity. It is, after all, in the name of the Unborn that we are asked to work hard, pay our taxes, and make other substantial sacrifices—in order to preserve heritages, reduce national debts, protect environments, defend frontiers, and, if needs must, give our lives for our unborn descendants to not one of whom can we give a guaranteed personal name. And if we are Americans, we do not think of these Unborn as future replicas of the oil billionaires, welfare cheats, absentee fathers, Middle American philistines, racist fanatics, and inner-city gangsters who currently and variously haunt our imaginations. They have no social lineaments at all, except for their Americanness; and it is exactly this monochrome purity that guarantees their Goodness, and that allows them to impose on us obligations that we might resent accepting from a large number of Americans actually alive in say, for Weber's sake, 1995.

One could look at this Weberesque vision from another angle. The moral sentiment that underlies the great sociologist's apostrophe is clearly shame at the Germany of 1895. If one asks in the face of whom this shame is felt, the answer seems clear: it is the face of the Zukunftsgeschlecht. The shame is the obverse side of the millenarian hope that the race of the future will recognize "in our nature the nature of its own ancestors." There is nothing peculiarly German in this stance. One recalls, for example, all those Americans, who, without being draft-age males, strenuously opposed Washington's ignoble and brutal adventure in Indochina in a language of "it makes me ashamed of my country."[4] This kind of political shame, which we feel only in the presence

---

4. There is something very agreeable in this language; it makes one feel like propagating the slogan Long Live Shame!

of the Good and the Innocent, lowers our eyes before those who will come after us.

THE DEAD

On East Rock, a spectacular escarpment towering over the ruined New England town of New Haven there is a huge—and not at all ridiculous—monument to local representatives of the National Dead. The four faces on its pedestal are inscribed with the names of men and boys who died in four very different old wars: the heroic War of Independence against George III's England; the unheroic skirmishes against the same foe in 1812; the louche imperialist adventure against Mexico in 1848; and the traumatic Civil War of 1861–65. It is remarkable that the monument treats all these dead as absolutely equivalent; it makes not the slightest difference whether they met their ends on a glorious or a shameful battlefield. The sacrifice of their lives is thus radically separated from historical Right or Wrong. This separation is elegantly achieved by positioning them all as sacrificial victims. National Death has, so to speak, paid their bills and cleared their moral books. The National Dead are never killers. One has only to imagine the New Haven reaction to the academic busybody who, after years of careful research, proposed to the citizenry that after each name inscribed on the monument there be added the names or numbers of the enemies its bearer slew. After all, American Purple Hearts, like British Victoria Crosses, are usually awarded, not for killing, but for dying. One is invited to weep at the Vietnam War Memorial for the almost 60,000 Americans who died in Indochina, not for the three million and more men, women, and children in whose destruction each had his or her own small share.

The ethnographer of nationalism also observes the inscriptional style in which the New Haven monuments record the National Dead—a style which visits to national cemeteries and monuments in other countries show to be completely normal. The recording of actual personal names might seem, at first sight, to preserve a certain vestigial individuality for each of the fallen. But it does not take more than a minute to perceive the connection with Weber's millenarian moment. For the names are stripped of all substantive sociological significance, except in so far as one might cautiously infer, in some cases, some Irish, Italian, or Scottish ancestry. No class, no religion, no age, and no politics. (Translated into German, no Junkers, no bourgeoisie, no proletariat.) No priorities either: hence the usual telephone-book alphabetic sequences. The dead have become "pure American," and it is in this purity that Goodness lies secured.

There must still be a few denizens of New Haven who know that this or that name memorializes one of their genealogical forefathers. But, given the years that have passed since 1865, when the newest of the dead went to heaven, their descendants can have no personal memory of them. And the vast majority of visitors to the monument see the individual names as interchangeable signs for what they now have in common. Today's pilgrims to East Rock are put in the position of Weber's future Germans; they are invited to try to recognize in their own natures the nature of their (collective) ancestors.

In this way, we can observe how the national dead and the national unborn, in their uncountable billions, mirror each other, and provide the best sureties of the ineradicable Goodness of the nation. It is exactly their combined ghostliness that makes them past-perfect, future-perfect American.

THE LIVING

One should now ask whether the living can also help secure the Rightness of the country. Two fine recent essays dealing with the United States and with India suggest the possibilities.

In her "The Theory of Infantile Citizenship," Lauren Berlant begins by recounting a telling episode in the young remembered life of the distinguished and radical Black writer Audré Lorde.[5] In 1947, Lorde later recalled, her parents took her and her sister Phyllis on the national pilgrimage to Washington, DC. They were careful not to tell the children that the reason for the trip was that, as a young Black girl, Phyllis was barred from joining her graduating high-school classmates in a school-organized trip to the national capital. In Washington, the family nonetheless found themselves treated as not-quite Americans. They could order icecream in a restaurant but they were forbidden to eat it on the premises. At that moment, Lorde remembers, she felt physically nauseated, not least because she had recently written an innocently patriotic poem on the Heroes of Bataan.[6] But Berlant writes that, at that very same moment, the little Black girl decided she would "write to the President, to give the nation another chance not to destroy her desire for it."

Another chance, another chance—one of the clamant basic idioms of American culture. Yet was not Weber also, out of psychic nausea, writing to give Germany another chance not to destroy his desire for it? And do not most of us want, against the odds, to give our nations another chance?

---

5. Berlant's essay is most readily found in Geoff Eley and Ronald Gregor Suny, eds., *Becoming National: A Reader* (New York and Oxford: Oxford University Press, 1996), pp. 495–508.

6. When the imperial Japanese armies overran the American colony of the Philippines in early 1942, the last major American-Filipino military holdout was the fortress of Bataan. It surrendered in April 1942, after the senior American military man in the colony, General Douglas MacArthur, had unceremoniously fled to Australia.

Berlant continues her essay in a lighter vein with an analysis of an episode in Matt Groening's hugely popular satirical television series *The Simpsons*. The episode is titled *Mr. Lisa Goes to Washington* in an obvious parody of the beloved, naive pre-World War II patriotic film *Mr. Smith Goes to Washington*. The story of this episode begins with little Lisa Simpson being selected to go to Washington for a children's contest for the best composition on the theme of "Why I Love America." She descends on the national capital with her Spiessbürger father Homer, her ditzy mother Marge, and her cynical and bratty brother Bart. But her wide-eyed belief in the goodness of Washington and America is shattered when she happens to observe her crooked Congressman accepting a bribe from a developer with designs on her beloved local nature park. Lisa tears up her original composition, writes a new one on the theme of "Washington Stinks," and promptly loses what Berlant calls the "national jingoism contest." But then—abracadabra—a fairy godmother in the form of the FBI appears out of the blue to arrest the Congressman, who promptly becomes a born-again Christian. Whereupon Mr. Lisa concludes that after all "the system really works," and America really is "A-OK."

Groening assumes that his tickled audience is confident that the system barely works and that America is very far from A-OK. So why does he need to show a patriot at all, especially one who is a deluded little female blockhead? Probably because, he, too, wishes to be seen as giving America another chance. Mr. Lisa guarantees his good intentions.[7]

Nonetheless, Lisa Simpson's capacity to guarantee the nation's goodness runs on a timer. We can imagine one fateful day, a dozen years down the road, when she may, in the morning, become a citizen voter for the first time, and, in the afternoon, drop in on her abortionist. She is, after all, a replaceable part. She stands in, provisionally, for the generic national child, who is not merely sexually innocent, but is also still untainted by the quotidian squalors of adult political participation. This national child is, in America, American. But the same child shows up in every national imaginary, each with its own slight local inflection. A sort of vanguard of the imminent Unborn.

A more equivocal living guarantee of the Goodness of the nation is suggested by an illuminating essay in which Joseph Alter surveys the recent rise of a militant "male celibacy" movement in Northern India.[8] The spokesmen

---

7. Could Mr. Lisa be replaced by an adult male these days? It is perhaps telling that her nearest competitor is Forest Gump, whose sweet A-OK patriotism depends on mental retardedness.

8. Joseph S. Alter, "Celibacy, Sexuality, and the Transformation of Gender into Nationalism in North India," a paper presented to a conference on "Dimensions of Ethnic and Cultural Nationalism in Asia," sponsored by the University of Wisconsin and Marquette University's Center for International Studies in February 1993. See also his *The Wrestler's Body: Identity and Ideology in North India* (Berkeley: University of California Press, 1992), especially chapters 5–6, 8, and 10.

of this movement offer a stentorian denunciation of the moral and physical decadence of the nation's Hindu (male) youth, which has succumbed, if not to Spiessbürgerei, at least to hedonism, masturbation, irreligion, idleness, cynicism, narcissism, and concupiscence. This decay is attributed to the corruption of the country's political class, to consumer capitalism, and to the remorseless irruption of "Hollywood" and Western amorality. The actual locus of the decay lies literally in the youthful male body. According to a bio-metaphysics with ancient roots in Hinduism, semen is not merely a substance necessary for procreation, but is also the deep life-principle of its bearer. It is not to be wasted in masturbation, nocturnal emissions, or even intercourse, but rather cherished and preserved for moral, spiritual, and physical health. This is why a revival of celibacy is proclaimed as the necessary basis for the recuperation, along every dimension, of Hindu manhood.

It is impossible to overlook the parallels with a somewhat earlier Europe. The work of George Mosse and many others has demonstrated how deeply late nineteenth-century European politicians, moralists, scientists, and religious leaders were obsessed with fears of national degeneration, fears which often found their focus in their respective nations' male youth.[9] The roster of cancers then was not so different from that of Alter's contemporary Northern India: hedonism, masturbation, androgyny, irreligion, neurasthenia, perversion, materialism, sometimes even (western) capitalism. Baden-Powell's Boy Scouts and the German *Wandervogel* movement were among an array of turn-of-the-century attempts to transform an earlier generation's more naive emphases on Young Italy, Young Ireland, and the like. Virtually all of these later movements proclaimed the need for sexual self-control, strict physical and sometimes dietary regimens, as well as male brotherhood; and all drew, as the Hindu celibacy advocates do, on old local traditions of male asceticism.[10] And if one is tempted to think the "seminal" theory of male health bequeathed by Hinduism a little exotic, it is salutary to reflect on how central "health," read in the local idiom, has become to America's queasy and ultimately political self-representation. The obsession with (male) viewer sports comes partly from the endless spectacle of athletic young male bodies which can be enjoyed as synecdoches of national virility and non-decay. Conversely,

---

9. George L. Mosse, *Nationalism and Sexuality: Middle-Class Morality and Sexual Norms in Modern Europe* (Madison: University of Wisconsin Press, 1985). See also Andrew Parker, Mary Russo, Doris Sommer, and Patricia Yaeger, eds., *Nationalisms and Sexualities* (New York and London: Routledge, 1992), especially the chapters by Eve Kosofsky Sedgwick and Seth Koven.

10. Some of these prescriptions have emerged in our own fin-de-siècle age of anxiety. Nothing is odder than the way in which the antique word *celibacy* has recently been brought down from America's psychic attic, dusted off and burnished, and then uneasily displayed in the national drawing-room.

all that the American Medical Association's statistics reveal of national morbidity—cancer, heart disease, Alzheimer's, AIDS—is, so far as possible, kept out of human-form public view.[11]

A second striking aspect of Northern India's celibacy movement is that the young acolytes are steeling themselves, not so much for their own personal salvation, but above all—and this is absolutely not traditional—for Mother India. It is She who serves as the magnet around which a disorderly myriad of young Hindu males form themselves into a beautifully ordered field of force (in every sense). It is She, who, metaphorically speaking, makes them all face in the same direction, towards Her, looking neither right nor left, nor over their shoulders: close to Her but never joined or merged.[12] In the "normal" nuclear family, the one woman whom the young males are forbidden to think of sexually, and to whom all are bound to render unrivalrous, unconditional, and grateful loyalty is Mother (they cannot hope to supplant her one happy day, which will be Father's unhappy destiny). Writ large as Motherland—Mother India, Mother Italy, Mother Argentina—she is entitled to command the same ascetic and bowed-head devotion. We are all aware of the tropes in which national citizenries understand their relationships with one another: they are Antigone's brothers and sisters, not husbands and wives, parents and children, boyfriends and girlfriends, let alone girlfriends and girlfriends.[13] From citizen fraternity everything sexual is removed. We stand gazing, not at one another's bodies, or into one another's eyes, but Up Ahead.

This manner of imagining shows us the last source of Goodness in the nation: the possibility of fraternity framed by a sort of political incest taboo.[14] During the Gulf War, it is reported, a number of American pilots scrawled, on bombs or fuselages, the pregnant words "Saddam, Bend Over." Unremarkable perhaps, until one realizes how inconceivable it would be, even

---

11. The mass TV audience will never see Ronald Reagan ravaged by Alzheimer's, Franklin Roosevelt's matchstick polio legs, or the Marlboro Man undergoing chemotherapy.

12. In South India, "Mother Tamil" has been commanding a rival ascetic devotion—to the point of occasional self-immolations. See the remarkable account in Sumathi Ramaswamy, *Passions of the Tongue: Language Devotion in Tamil India, 1891–1970* (Berkeley: University of California Press, 1997), especially p. 1, and chapter 3 ("Feminizing Language, Tamil as Goddess, Mother, Maiden").

13. To see this, one has only to recognize how impossible it is for Helmut Kohl, Fernando Henrique Cardoso, or Hosni Mubarak to address, on television, their respective nationals as "My Children."

14. The shadow of Northern India looms over Washington. The American institution that best represents ascetic, dedicated celibate fraternity is, of course, the military, of which the traditional rules (with some unemphasized exceptions) kept everyone's eyes Up Ahead. Gay and lesbian soldiers raise the anxious possibility of eyes turned sideways or down. Female soldiers present the eternal possibility of public Brothers and Sisters turning into private Lovers. We are more than 2,500 years away from Epaminondas.

for the most rabid American Clinton-hater, to sport a bumper-sticker reading, "Bill, Bend Over." Political rape, even imaginary, is excluded from the ascetic imaginary of national citizenship.

There is something of value in all of this—strange as it may seem. It is the same value one can detect in Mr. Lisa, in the replaceable dead of the Mexican adventure, in the fantasies of young Professor Weber, in political shame, and in the future perfect. Each in a different but related way shows why, no matter what crimes a nation's government commits and its passing citizenry endorses, My Country is ultimately Good. In these straitened millennial times, can such Goodness be profitably discarded?

Index